Looking at Art

Chief Contributing Editor
DAVID PIPER

Contributors

Christopher Cornford
Peter Owen

Senior Editorial Consultant

Bernard S. Myers

Editors
Jack Tresidder
Paul Holberton
Art Editor
Michael McGuinness
Editorial Assistant
Margaret Ramsay

LOOKING AT ART
was edited and designed by
Mitchell Beazley International Limited,
Mill House, 87–89 Shaftesbury Avenue, London W1V 7AD
© Mitchell Beazley Publishers 1984

Published in the United States by Random House, Inc.,
New York, and simultaneously in Canada by
Random House of Canada Limited, Toronto.

Library of Congress Cataloging in Publication Data
Main entry under title:
Looking at art.
 Rev. and enl. ed. of 1st volume of: The Random House
library of painting and sculpture. © 1981.
 Includes index.
 1. Painting—Appreciation. I. Piper, David.
II. Random House library of painting and sculpture.
ND1143.L66 1984 750′.1′1 84–42634
ISBN 0-394-54047-6 (Trade edition)
ISBN 0-394-34447-2 (College edition)

Material in this book was first published in
The Random House Library of Painting and Sculpture.
© Mitchell Beazley Publishers 1981

Printed in the Netherlands
by Koninklijke Smeets Offset b.v., Weert

Looking at Art

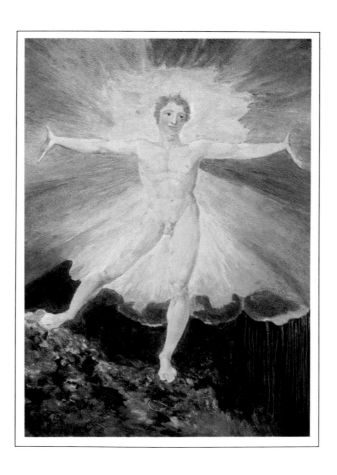

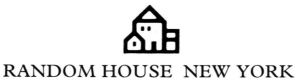

RANDOM HOUSE NEW YORK

Contents

Illustrations

The locations of works of art are not given in the captions to individual illustrations but can be found, together with the dimensions and medium, in the list of illustrations that precedes the index to this book. These lists are headed, as are the captions themselves, by the name of the artist or, if this is unknown, by the place of origin or original location of the work. This may be different from the present location; thus "*The Virgin of Vladimir*" appears under the heading CONSTANTINOPLE, where it was made, though it is kept in the Tretyakov Gallery, Moscow.

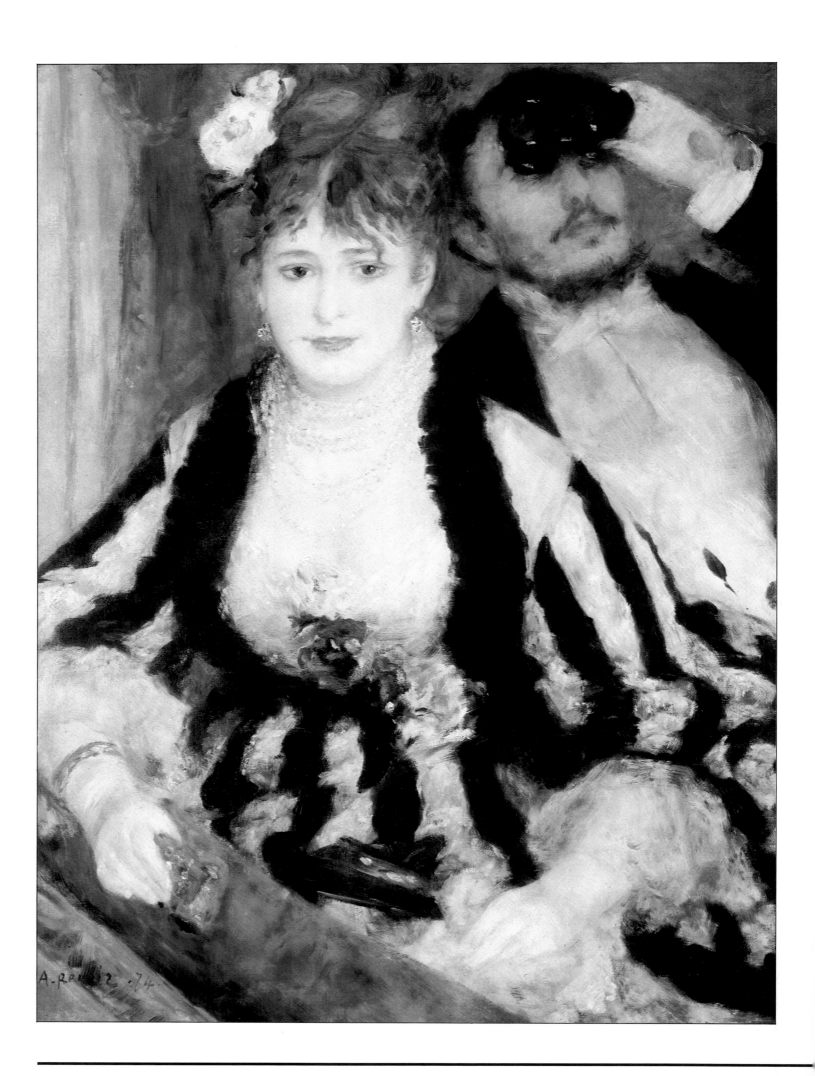

INTRODUCTION

by David Piper

THE WOMAN IN RENOIR'S PAINTING, looking negligently out at us, is herself a spectator, half-dreamy perhaps in the heady murmur rising like incense from a theatre audience below. As she surveys the scene, waiting for the lights to go down and the lights on the stage to come up and illusion to begin, she is watched no doubt in turn by many inquisitive eyes in the audience, taking bearings, noting unexpected alliances, generating gossip. So her companion, too, surveys the auditorium with his opera-glasses in search of recognized faces, of friends, of desirable unknowns perhaps as possible conquests – though what more he could want than the enchanting creature at his side, it is hard to imagine.

It may well be familiar to you, this painting. It is one of the best-known and most popular of Renoir's works, reproduced in countless books whether on Renoir himself, or on Impressionism, or on the general history of painting in the West. In part, its almost instantaneous appeal depends simply on the woman's beauty. Then, too, the painting breathes of leisure, of pleasure. Through it we participate in a world of well-being – the splendour of physical youth, the nonchalance of wealth. It seems to pervade almost all the senses; at least I sense in it the excited buzz of the expectant audience below, the warm fragrance wafted from their expensive persons; I almost feel the padded plush of the rim of the box on which her hand, holding the glasses, rests. But the real impact of the picture is most directly on the sense of sight. The dominants in the composition are black and white, but everywhere kindled and broken by the shifting lights, whites flushing with the subtlest pinks. The image is fused on to the canvas with a succulence of touch and texture in the oil-paint characteristic of certain French painters (Renoir very much amongst them) which seems to translate into matter the very essence of colour, almost a visual equivalent of *haute cuisine*.

It all seems so easy, so happy, no less relaxed in execution than in subject. But most people, when it was first shown, did not find it so at all. Renoir signed and dated this canvas 1874, and in that year it was shown in an exhibition in Paris which was at first notorious and derided, though it has now long become famous as marking a decisive turning-point in the history of Western art. A group of young painters, rejected by or spurning the official exhibitions of the art establishment, opened a show at the former studio of the famous photographer Nadar. Among the paintings shown was Monet's *Impression: sunrise*, from the title of which the Impressionist movement took its name, though it was applied derogatively by a hostile critic. Virtually all the artists involved were assailed with ridicule, nor was Renoir himself spared. The critic of *Figaro* wrote: "Try to explain to M. Renoir that a woman's torso is not a mass of flesh decomposing in the green or purplish

RENOIR: *The theatre box* (La loge), 1874

blemishes that indicate that a corpse is in full putrefaction. . . ."

Thus for many, used to the polished finish of Salon work, even Renoir's painting was incoherent and unintelligible, an insult to cultivated taste, and yet of all the Impressionists Renoir was the most traditional. Even today we may misconstrue this canvas. Certainly it has now the look of an impression – a spontaneous reaction to a passing moment glimpsed on the spot in a theatre. It was in fact worked out in an entirely traditional studio manner, deliberately and calculatedly posed. The couple are Renoir's brother Edmond, and a Montmartre model called Nini. A sharp French eye would detect that the girl is palpably not of the high social class which her position in the box, her superb dress, her jewels, might lead one to expect, but a woman of the people, a girl such as Renoir indeed loved to paint all through his career.

THERE IS, THEN, MORE THAN MEETS THE EYE even in a picture apparently so direct and immediately seductive as *The theatre box*, and so it is with almost any painting or sculpture of high quality. It is the function – and privilege – of books such as this to bring out some of the resonances that might otherwise pass in works of art assembled from the four corners of the world, many of them less familiar and less accessible than Renoir's, but no less enjoyable. Very few, if any, will have the opportunity to devote in tranquillity to each of the originals reproduced in this volume the necessary minutes – or, more likely, hours – that it takes to enter and to explore, to commit to visual memory, a masterpiece. Indeed, the individual viewer at a major loan exhibition, or the diligent tourist in the holiday months, may find it difficullt, in a jammed picture gallery, to contemplate uninterrupted any one object for even a few seconds. The collection of reproductions that anyone can build up on private bookshelves – André Malraux's "Museum without walls" – can never displace the need to become familiar with the originals, the pleasure of confronting the works themselves. Yet books do act as reminders to fallible memory no less than as stimulants to the pursuit of the originals. They also set them in a context that can be profoundly enriching, offering comparison with other works of the same artist or the same period, and with works far distant in time or place.

Our ability to respond to a painting is often affected by its cultural context if only because, until the move away from figurative art in the twentieth century, many paintings had for subject matter some figure or event from myth, sacred writ, legend or idealized history. While a picture of a young man with a blue skin talking to a beautiful girl by a pool may seem bizarre to Westerners, a Hindu would have no difficulty recognizing the Lord Krishna conversing with a milkmaid. Even within a single historical tradition, common references may quickly become puzzling: a painter in seventeeth-century Rome, Madrid, Antwerp or London could expect his audience to know who Apollo was, what happened at Thermopylae, how Jacob treated Esau, what Zacchariah said to Mary or Christ to the Woman of Samaria – knowledge that cannot necessarily be assumed today. As well as such references, the political, social and economic forces that have in more or less degree conditioned works of art can be explained in a book; so too the technical constraints that have shaped them, and it seems axiomatic that the fuller the understanding of the original the richer and more satisfying the enjoyment of looking at it is likely to be.

It is, in fact, only by experience, by comparison, that an awareness of art can be tuned to its finest pitch of sensitivity. Certainly, just as there are those gifted with perfect pitch in music, some are born with an unerring eye for quality, but they are rare and for them, too, instinctive pleasure in quality is enlarged enormously by knowledge. One intention of this book is to make available a store of information and to present it in a way that can be understood by anyone interested in art. But the object always is to increase enjoyment, and discussion is based not upon theoretical aspects of art but upon individual works – the concrete objects themselves. The same principle is followed in sections of the book in which my colleagues discuss the materials and formal language of painting – the calculated or intuitive decisions artists make about tone or colour, viewpoint or proportion, as well as the physical means by which art achieves its effect, the media of tempera, oil paint, watercolour, ink or pencil, with their various creative limitations and possibilities. An artist's use of colour or light, perspective or pattern, works upon us in ways that are by no means obvious, and by understanding these underlying factors we are better able to appraise and enjoy paintings. In the final section of the book, the opportunity is taken to pause and contemplate nearly 50 single works of art. Whether a stupendous Michelangelo or a painting in quieter key such as Chardin's *House of Cards*, the aim is to convey the essential flavour of the work, sometimes to show why it was specially influential, sometimes to trace out the process of its creation, always to make readers look at it with deeper understanding. The works selected are not meant to represent the greatest paintings in the world. They do, however, mark significant stages in the long development of art. Where relevant to the theme, sculptures are also illustrated, but another book would be needed to do justice to three dimensional art, and here the focus is upon paintings, together with drawings and etchings.

THROUGHOUT, WE REFER BACK CONTINUALLY to specific works of art, for my part inevitably, as I am no aesthetician nor philosopher. Definitions of art have modulated through the centuries and across the world, according to the functions it has had to serve. By a modern European, paintings may be regarded as portable commodities bought for prestige or pleasure. In other times and places they have been magical signs, focuses of ritual, embodiments of myth or legend or aids to spiritual contemplation. They have also provided environments for escapist fantasy and instruments of education or propaganda to enhance the power and status of institutions, social classes or prominent and wealthy individuals. For St Bonaventura in the Middle Ages a picture was "that which instructs, arouses pious emotions and awakens memories", and we will look soon at a picture that is a call to prayer. For Zola, the nineteenth-century realist, a picture was "a bit of nature filtered through an individual temperament" ("un coin de la nature vu à travers un tempérament"). Only a few years after Zola, the twenty-year-old painter Maurice Denis, in 1890, formulated a tenet that was to be widely approved (though by no means universally) through the succeeding century: "A picture – before being a war-horse or a nude woman or some little genre scene – is essentially a flat surface covered with colours assembled in a certain order". Twenty years later, Kandinsky, followed rapidly by others, demonstrated that the war-horse, woman or genre scene could be dispensed with entirely, and in the West for a time it seemed that figurative or representational art, whether in painting or sculpture, was being obliterated in the flood of non-figurative or "abstract" art. It has now become clear that traditional forms are not so easily dispensed with, and they re-emerge, their horizons enlarged by the explorations of the abstractionists.

IF ONE IS TO SPEAK IN GENERAL TERMS OF ART, the analogy of music seems to become more and more relevant. Already Michelangelo claimed that "finally, good painting is a music and a melody which intellect only can appreciate". The suggestion implicit here recurred again and again, from Goethe's famous definition of architecture as "frozen music" to Walter Pater's scarcely less celebrated contention that "all art constantly aspires towards the condition of music". As the twentieth-century emphasis on the formal content of painting and sculpture increased, it began to seem that music was indeed the only viable analogy by which to describe or attempt to analyse the quality of much abstract painting. In the early years of abstract art there seemed (to the majority of the general public) no point of recognition from which to start an exploration. Time has brought its own solution to this, partly in a somewhat incestuous way, as the prolific expansion and diversification of abstract art has created its own internal body of reference and its own standards of quality, of good and bad, but also because it has gradually become clear that many of these standards relate very closely to those of traditional figurative art – to its basic ingredients of line and shape, rhythm and pattern, mass and space, light and shade, colour and texture. Even so, abstract art still evokes a less rich response from most viewers than does figurative art of comparable distinction, and it is indeed deprived of the immediate relationship to the life and flesh and blood that figurative art offers. Henry James, writing about Whistler's *Nocturnes* and *Arrangements* (to which he did not respond), asked that "a picture should have some relation to life as well as to painting". James had in fact earlier responded with delight to Whistler's portrait of his mother, but as "a masterpiece of tone, of feeling, of the power to render life", whereas Whistler, anticipating Maurice Denis, was to forbid assessment of the painting in terms of a portrait of a specific person and demand that it be known as *Arrangement in grey and black*.

The danger that threatens some non-figurative art is that it seems, and is often indeed asserted to be, art about art. To the public, even that part of it genuinely and sympathetically concerned with art, an obsessive concern among painters and sculptors with intellectual problems is frustrating, at least when that obsession leads to the sincerely held (but one hopes false) conclusion that figurative art is obsolete. When even the art object, the painting or sculpture itself, is jettisoned, artists' activities may come to seem to others mere narcissistic behaviour, posturing. The effective channels of communication available to the visual artist are sensual rather than conceptual, above all the sense of sight, but also, in sculpture, that of touch.

The ultimate feedback, however, from the exploratory investigations of the avantgarde to the mainstream of art is unpredictable; it has recently become increasingly evident that all kinds of art are pursued in all kinds of traditions, by dedicated men and women indifferent, sometimes heroically so, to the changing tides of fashion. The present uncertainty about the nature and function of art may derive from our inability, even after almost a century and a half, to come to terms with the consequences of one technical invention – photography. Its full effect on our attitude to man-made images is difficult to assess but has certainly been fundamental; for instead of being unique and finely-crafted objects, owned by few, or relatively costly engravings reproduced for wider dissemination, visual images now bombard us daily, reproduced by photographic techniques in colour and – in film and television – in motion as well. The devalued potency of the man-made image is felt at the most basic level: primitive amazement at the sight of reality's double has evaporated, and artistic illusion, which once could seem positively magical, supernatural, is commonplace and so ceases to be illusion.

PHOTOGRAPHY HAS INVADED THE TERRITORY of whole branches of art, of not only traditional, anecdotal, narrative painting but also, in films and television, the art of visual satire and social comment; few would now hang today's equivalent of Hogarth's savage "comic-history" engravings on their walls, and reproductions of Hogarth have been turned into picturesque decorations for pub interiors. The artist seems to have lost his most immediately obvious practical function as a unique recorder – whether of topography, human events or individual likenesses – a function now answered more quickly and cheaply by the camera. At the same time, many of the great traditional themes which have stirred artists to masterpieces are abandoned in a crisis of patronage: the Church is no longer a major patron, and the great works it commissioned in the past now turn many churches into museums. Visitors to the little chapel of Vence in the south of France come not to pray but to see Matisse's decorations, and so too, in the great old shrines of the West, it is to admire the architecture, or to pay homage to Giotto, to Michelangelo and Raphael, to Bernini, that the visitors come. In the museum and art gallery, twentieth-century art finds a purpose-built home but one that seems, to some artists, rather too final a shrine for their work, separated from life and no longer offering the satisfaction of creating a work for a particular person, or place, or purpose, as most artists have done throughout the history of painting and sculpture.

Photography, however, has not shrunk the possibilities of art; rather it has been the order of release from the slavery of imitation. Without it, the experiment of abolishing subject matter in abstract art might never have taken place. Photography has not only greatly extended our knowledge of the artistic traditions of the past, but also helped indirectly to change our approach to them – instead of dogma we look for humanity, instead of dwelling on subject matter we look for what makes it great art. The greatest artists have always been able to add something to life, a pattern or order, an emotion, a vision.

Major movements during the twentieth century have widened the freedom of artists to convey emotion through distortion, to re-create the landscapes and sensations of dreams, as well as to create abstract works that answer only to their own logic of shape, line, texture or colour. If it seems that artists today are still often caught off-balance by this revelation of imaginative freedom, and do not know what to do with it, it is also true that we, the observers, are still constrained by the expectations of lifelike imitation. In looking at traditional Renaissance art, we know the conventions and instant, if superficial, recognition allows us to respond and – if we have will enough and time – to become increasingly involved with its profounder depths. Each age selects from the past the art most relevant to its own needs, and it is only too true that we mostly like what we already know, simply because it is easier that way. Yet great art, even of the traditional kind, is not easy. To come to grips with it can mean the application of one's entire sensory, mental and imaginative faculties, and with a concentration suspiciously like that involved in hard work.

LIFELIKE IMITATION has never, in fact, been the only style of figurative art, and treatments by different artists of the same subjects vary enormously, even within a shared tradition. By way of illustrating this, and as visual introduction to the more technical and formal aspects of understanding art, we begin this book with a discussion of twelve great themes of painting and sculpture to which artists have consistently turned. Each discussion starts from contemplation of one single work, with a following commentary on just a few of the countless variations on the theme. As the commentary is necessarily brief, whereas the themes have produced not only a vast range of art but also a vast literature of criticism, the section is intended primarily as a picture gallery, an opportunity to compare and contrast paintings and sculptures of different eras in a manner impossible in a chronological history – though some will be discussed in more detail in their own historical context in the later sections.

We begin with the visible world – the individual, society, the material fabric of life – and end with the world of the spirit and the imagination. The thematic organization does not mean that the subject matter of pictures is the most important thing about them. Similarities between works on the same subject often reflect the fact that art is itself raw material for art – sometimes rather more so than the world of natural appearances. Yet it is the differences that are perhaps more striking, and these arise not only from variations of design, technique or medium but from fundamental differences of function. An art of emotion or persuasion is unlike that of sober, literal record, and each of these is different from the kind of art in which the wish to establish a formal order of shapes, colours, patterns for purely aesthetic ends overrides any attempt to imitate appearances. For the artist, a painting or sculpture usually has a personal function; it expresses a view of the world, an individual vision.

ARTISTS TURN TO PAINTING AND SCULPTURE because what they have to express is inexpressible in words; in spite of the superficial resemblances between photography and art it is equally inexpressible in photographs, which are products of a different creative process. What the camera records in the split second of the shutter opening is limited to the scene gathered in by the lens at that instant, and the range of choices the photographer can make about viewpoint, aperture and timing are necessarily limited; so too, in scale, colour and texture, the final positive image that can be produced is limited by the mechanical processes of printing. Artists stand between us and their subject matter in a different way, selecting at will the elements they feel are essential and transmuting them, often over weeks or months, into materials that record the mark of their hand and mind and which have a surface texture that can itself engage our feelings. The sterility of much academic art usually lies in the fact not that it is figurative but that it copies other art. What great paintings and sculptures have in common with great works of literature, with any form of great art, is their ability to create a fresh order from the flux of life. The pleasure we are given from looking at them is primarily that of having our view clarified, distilled, detached from the distractions that condition our everyday way of seeing. We are able to share a perception of the world different from our own, and more penetrating, to see a pattern that was not evident, or an attraction in things not ordinarily thought beautiful, or even a dimension in life that may be called spiritual.

Visual artists work with gross physical matter which, even when the medium is of stone or metal, is perishable, yet the greatest of them can transcend it, asserting the existence of a reality impervious to time and death. Years ago, a phrase from the conclusion of E.M. Forster's novel *A Room with a View* lodged in my mind. The heroine is expressing thanks to her mentor, an old man of experience and forthright wisdom: "It was as if he had made her see the whole of everything at once". Art, at that level of vision, can be a stimulus, a challenge, an inexhaustible enjoyment. The resonance of a dozen or so lines scratched by Rembrandt with pen and ink on a piece of paper may fill one with an astonishment different but no less intense than the wonder of his painting "*The Jewish Bride*", with all its elaboration of scale and colour.

Everything that follows is designed as aid to such enjoyment. I close this

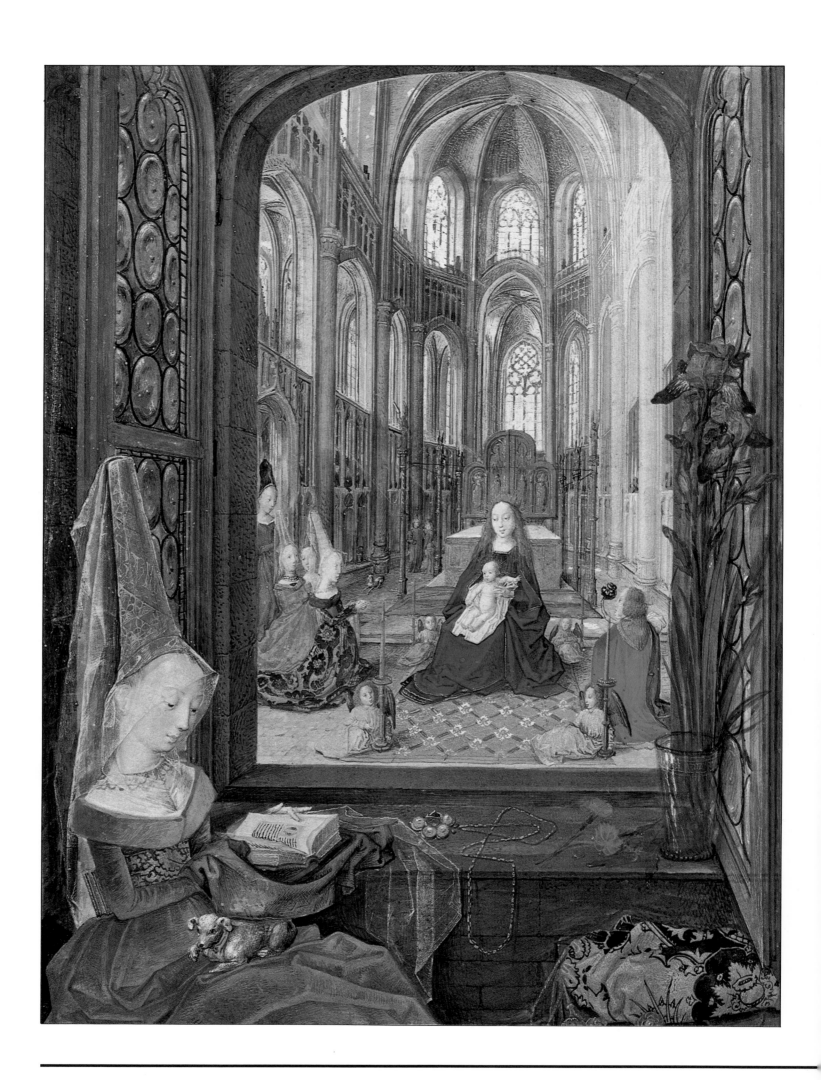

introduction with a little-known painting that has always delighted me. It may not be the greatest work of art among the hundreds we will show, but it contains within its small frame – only about the size of our reproduction – an unexpected richness. It demonstrates also the capacity of a book such as this to give access to branches of art that the ordinary gallery-goer can never be sure of being able to see – far less to handle, as this miniature was intended to be handled. It is one of the illuminations of a prayerbook, a so-called Book of Hours, painted for one of the great heiresses of Europe, Mary of Burgundy. The name of the artist is unknown, "the Master of Mary of Burgundy", but he is comparable in quality with any of the great followers of Jan van Eyck.

It is Mary herself who is shown here, gazing downwards on to a book in her lap – contemplative counterpart to her worldly sister in Renoir's *The theatre box* four hundred years later. The book she holds is perhaps the very same Book of Hours of which this is one page. To left and right, casement windows open – not on the outdoors but upon the interior of a great Gothic church in the centre of which Mary's namesake, the Virgin Mary, sits with the Child in her arms. Though the supernatural has entered into the scene in the choir it is painted with no less realism than the pensive lady whose vision it is. In a bewitching double-take she reappears, kneeling in front of the Madonna with her court ladies, and that red accent under her arm may be the same Book of Hours. The Mother of God is depicted as if she had just looked in on the church one silvery Flemish afternoon. There is a subtle play with illusion and reality in this image, and to scholars, a wealth of symbolic meanings in the objects and flowers displayed. The blue iris soaring from the vase is a flower sacred to the Madonna; it was also *gladiolus*, the sword-lily, and its prophetic presence alludes to a traditional representation of Mary after the Passion, her heart transfixed by a sword. It is the one dark note in the composition. The significance of the two carnations is less certain, but pinks or carnations were often allusions to betrothal – and if so the little painting should be of 1477, the year Mary married Maximilian of the great Hapsburg house of Austria. The illuminated initial at which the Book of Hours is opened is an "O", which has suggested to scholars that she is engaged with the popular prayer *Obscero te* ("I beseech thee"). If so, for Mary, invocation soon proved vain: she died in 1482, from a riding accident, only 25 years old. Yet the pervasive quality of the picture is serenity and peace, and to experience its mood we need no arcane knowledge, simply the time to look – to join Mary there in meditation on and within that beautiful synthesis of the natural and the supernatural, the human and the divine, the ephemeral and the eternal.

MASTER OF MARY OF BURGUNDY: *Maximilian and Mary of Burgundy before the Virgin, c. 1477*

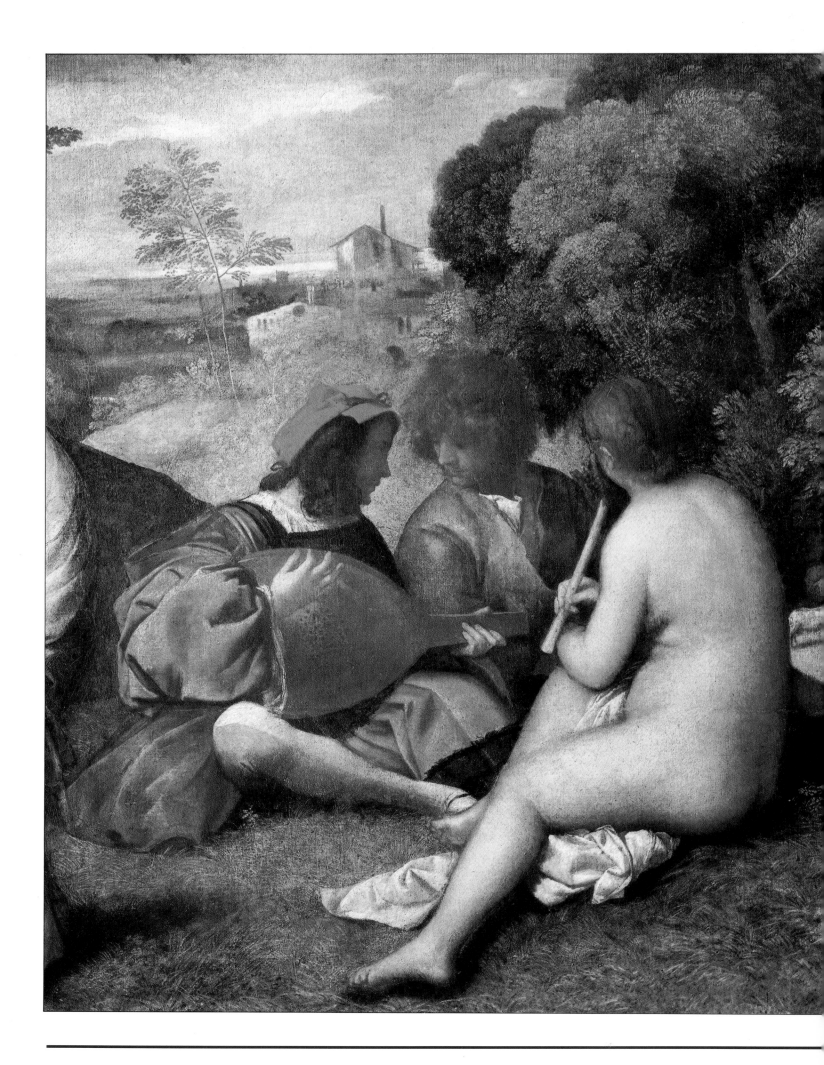

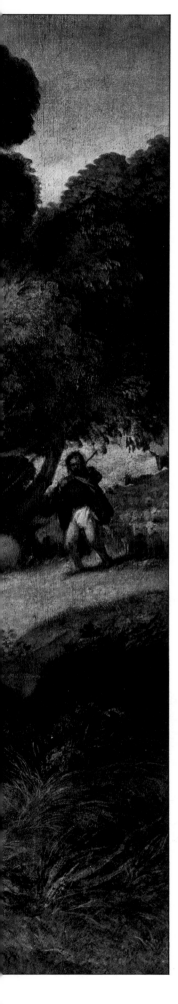

VARIATIONS
ON TWELVE THEMES

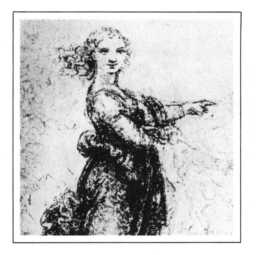

"The art of the Greeks, of the Egyptians, of
the great painters who lived in other
times, is not an art of the past; perhaps
it is more alive today than it ever
was. Art does not evolve by itself; the
ideas of people change and with them their
mode of expression." – PICASSO

(left) TITIAN: "*The Concert Champêtre*", detail, *c.* 1510; (above) LEONARDO: *A woman pointing*, after 1513

The Human Face

The human form provides the most enduring theme of art. And of all paintings, the most famous is Leonardo's *Mona Lisa* – so besieged by crowds in the Louvre as to be often almost invisible. It is further set apart by the armoured-glass-fronted shrine wherein it dwells in the dusk acceptable to scientists as a safe level of light – a submarine dimness in which, nevertheless, the eye observes that the painting is further obscured by old and discoloured varnish. On the other hand it is over-exposed in countless reproductions – postcards, posters, illustrations in books and periodicals all over the world. The spray of words that began to accumulate about it, from critics and writers through the centuries since Leonardo painted the lady while (they say) musicians sang to her, often mists rather than clears our view of the image.

Mona Lisa was the otherwise unremarked wife of Francesco del Giocondo, an influential merchant of Florence, yet not all agree that she was indeed the subject of this portrait. If, as seems probable, she sat for a portrait drawing Leonardo made in 1503 or 1504, the completeness and perfection of the final painting make it likely that he worked on it, as on all his important paintings, over a considerable period, and put into it more than could be discovered in the person of the Gioconda herself.

In revealing the formal potentialities of portraiture, the *Mona Lisa* is central to the whole development of that art. There are Flemish precedents for the beautiful, half-turned pose, but previous portraits had been in terms of a closed characterization – the sitter defined within a clear contouring line. By "melting" the contour so that the eye is led round it in imagination, Leonardo introduced new qualities – ambiguity of character and mood, the illusion of movement, and so of time passing – in short, the breath of life. The soft play of light and shade over the features, the hazy blending of the figure with an alpine landscape that suggests an organic unity of water, rocks and living things, the enigma of that famous, lop-sided smile, half lost in shadow, all create an elusiveness that is analysable to some degree in purely visual terms. At first it was the painting's technical mastery that awed observers – the delicacy of the chiaroscuro, the exquisite modelling of the lips, eyes, hands, the compositional harmony of it all.

The mysterious power of the portrait, its magical hold over the imagination of the viewer, is not finally explicable by formal means, however. Walter Pater's celebrated invocation: "She is older than the rocks among which she sits; like the vampyre she has been dead many times, and learned the secrets of the grave . . .", his equation of her with Leda, the mother of Helen of Troy, and with St Anne, the mother of Mary, may seem far from the reaction of Duchamp who, in our own century, drew a moustache on a postcard of her, subscribed by an obscene inscription. Yet both – Pater for a Romantic age, Duchamp for a sceptical one in which her defacement was the ultimate artistic sacrilege – acknowledged her as a lay icon, an image which remains, as it perhaps was for Leonardo himself, all things to all men.

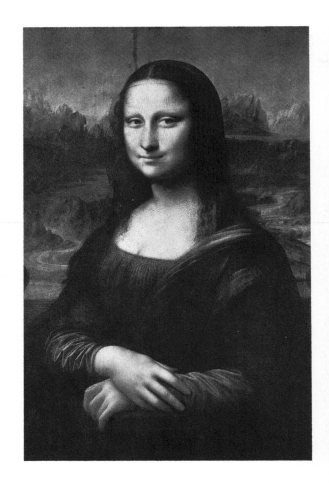

LEONARDO: *Mona Lisa*, c. 1503–06

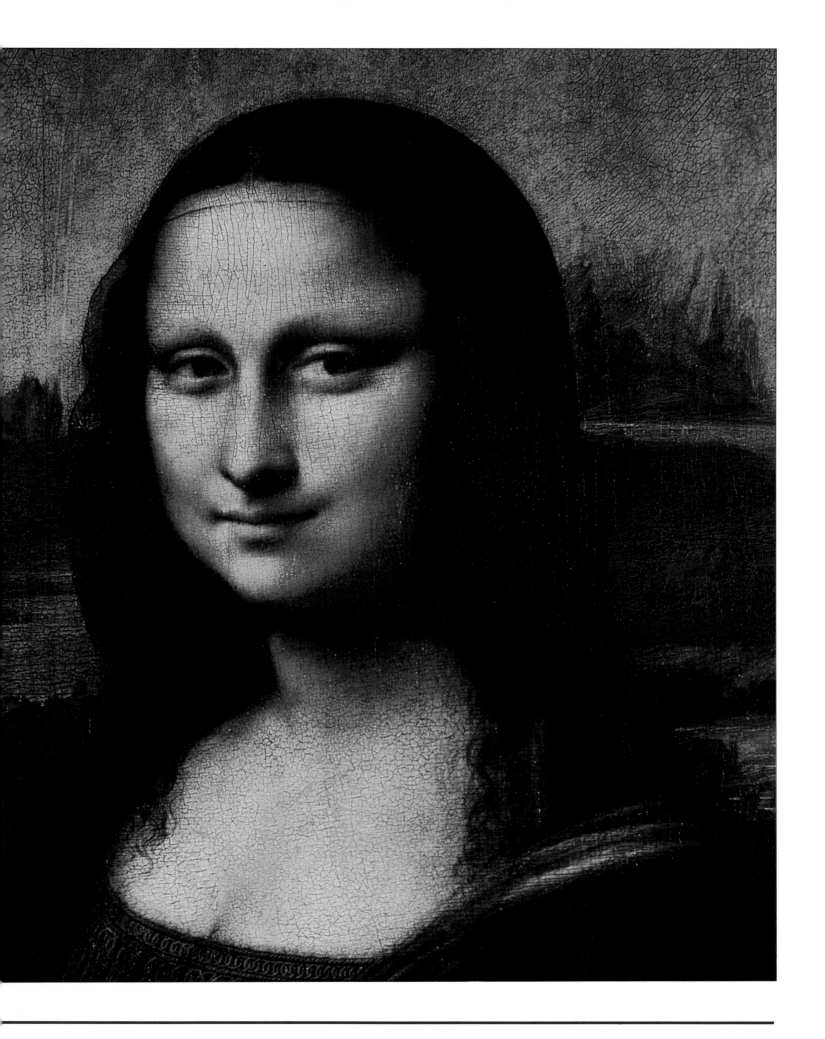

The Human Face

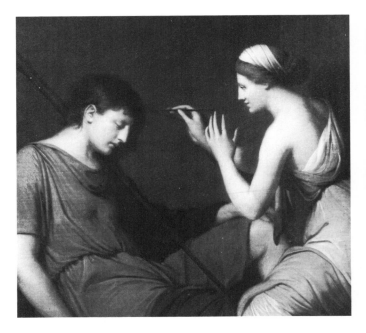

JOSEPH WRIGHT:
The Corinthian maid,
detail, 1784

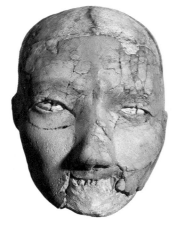

AMMAN: *Jericho skull*, c. 6000 BC

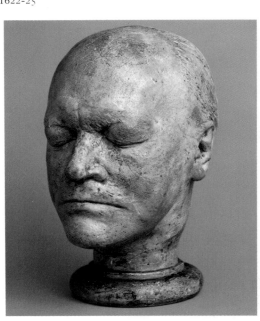

RUBENS: *Susanna Lunden*, c. 1622-25

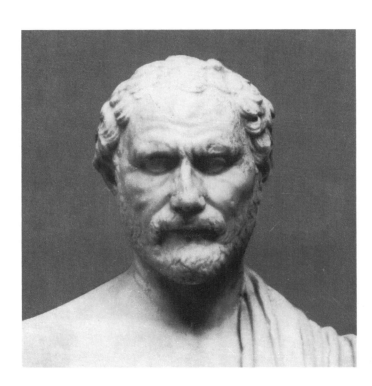

AFTER POLYEUKTOS:
Demosthenes,
original c. 280 BC

J.S. DEVILLE: Life-mask of William Blake, c. 1825

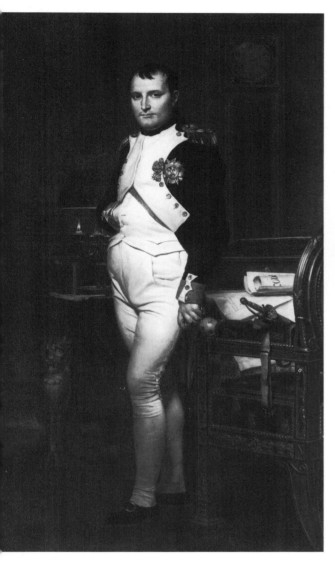

DAVID:
Napoleon in his study, 1812

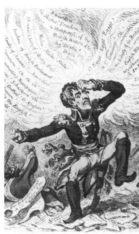

GILLRAY: *Maniac ravings*,
detail, 1805

DIX (below): *Sylvia von Harden*, 1926

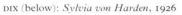

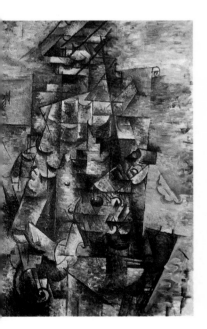

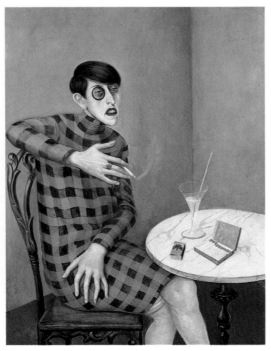

BRAQUE: *Man with a guitar*, 1911

Of all subjects of art, portraiture represents perhaps the most poignant attempt to retain something that cannot be retained, to deny the mortality of a unique human being. In a Greek myth (which later fascinated Joseph Wright), the Corinthian maid Dibutade, knowing her lover was about to leave her, traced his shadow on the wall. The same enduring concern reveals itself in primitive decoration of skulls, their skin rehabilitated with clay, their eyes with cowrie shells – from the Jericho skulls of 6000 BC to those of twentieth-century New Guinea. Such works seem intended to capture not only the likeness but also the spirit of the departed.

Aristotle distinguished between three kinds of portraiture – the idealized image of formal state portraits, the naturalistic mapping of the sitter's features and the satirical portrait. Yet Greek artists also attempted a psychological penetration that went beyond a mere likeness; the statue of the orator Demosthenes shows a remarkable introspective sensitivity. In its suggestion of a living presence this is not far from the force of personality inherent in the life-mask of the poet William Blake.

Christianity, with its emphasis on the spirit rather than on its mortal container, almost lost sight of portraiture for many centuries; only with the humanist and classical revival of the Renaissance did portrait painting revive and spread, growing in confidence and complexity. The range could extend from Netherlandish realism of an almost photographic fidelity to the ennobling idealism of Italian masters for whom dignity and decorum were tenets of artistic faith. In the wake of Leonardo's experiments with tonality and the capture of movement in human expression came seventeenth-century masters such as Rubens, who could make an informal record of a friend as affectionate, as perceptive, as glowing with life as his portrait of Susanna Lunden, whose sister he was later to marry.

At the other end of the scale from this freely-handled portrayal of a woman in the bloom of sensual youth is the official state portrait, didactic, clear-cut, with the sitter shown emblematically in the regalia of office, his bearing and surroundings projecting his authority. David's Neoclassical portrait of Napoleon splendidly answered his sitter's demand for portraits of great men in keeping with their greatness – an artistic licence that cartoonists carried to the opposite extreme.

The twentieth century has presented new variations, among them the use of portraiture as a foundation for formal experiment, hardly different in function from a still life. In the Cubism of Picasso or Braque the ever-present conflict between artist and sitter is won entirely by the artist, who, in disintegrating and reconstituting his subject, swallows his identity as ruthlessly as some spiders devour their mates. Expressionist portraiture offers another alternative to photography, using distortion to capture the human condition *in extremis*, as in Otto Dix's study of a German journalist, her features deformed by the violence, cynicism and isolation of our era.

The Human Face

Many artists have been praised for their ability to paint not only the face but the soul, though one of the finest of portrait painters, Reynolds, avowed that the artist could catch only so much of the inner character as was betrayed by the lineaments of the sitter. And as most people know to their cost, "face value" is not always reliable.

One form in which one might hope for a more than superficial assessment of character is the self-portrait, though most artists of the second rank in fact have tended to show themselves as vain as anyone else – if not more so – and as prone to paint their mirror-image in terms of the constraining fashions of their time. Self-portraiture can, however, provide artists with their most accessible and consistent source of personal and pictorial research. The narcissism essential to personal expression can here be focused most revealingly, whether to project an image of the artist in a certain guise for public view or to undertake an honest analysis for the artist's own satisfaction.

A startling example of honesty is the bleak, uncompromising account of his own person by Dürer, who seems to convey the sensation of the night of the soul in his own unidealized physique. Dürer was one of those few major artists who have left something approaching a pictorial autobiography (from which vanity was not always absent, as in one depiction of himself apparently as Christ). The broadest of all such autobiographies is that of Rembrandt – a life-long sequence of images of himself, sometimes role-playing but finally, in the last decade of his life, revealing through his own person the tragic destiny of all mankind, emerging from darkness into the light of life before receding into the final darkness. No one has rivalled Rembrandt in his ability to kindle the flame of the spirit on gross flesh.

Other formidable autobiographies include that of Courbet, boisterously extravagant compared with Rembrandt but aggressively asserting his artistic genius. Hokusai asserted himself unquenched at the age of 82: "At a hundred I shall have become truly marvellous". Van Gogh, in a whole series of concentrated head-and-shoulders studies, seems to attempt to establish his own identity, his precarious sanity; often they look like police photographs of suspects, if not of convicted criminals. Cézanne, too, scrutinized his features, not in search of spiritual essence but rather to crystallize a solid structure out of his own stubborn skull, foreshadowing the Cubists' concern with establishing a formal order. In contrast, the Expressionist Kokoschka's violent brushwork, proportional exaggerations and jarring colours display an almost accusing self-appraisal.

While photography has taken over much of the recording function of art, its own peculiarities have themselves become subjects for art. Chuck Close's gigantic self-portrait, nearly three metres (more than 9ft) high, embellishing in meticulously applied acrylics the camera's eye for detail, retains the impersonal neutrality of his source photograph and, in so doing, reveals its limitations – the extent to which it fails to represent form naturalistically and to capture the sitter's true character.

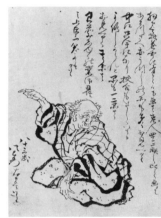

REMBRANDT: *Self-portrait*, 1669

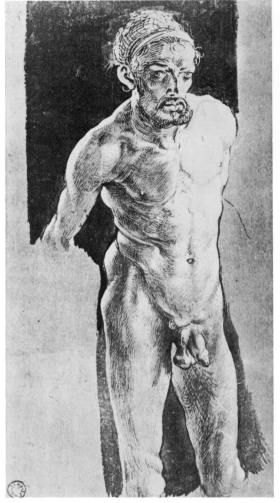

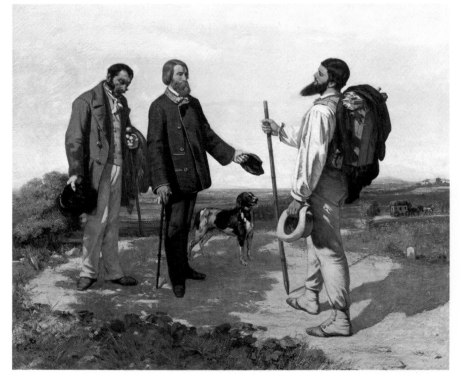

HOKUSAI: *Self-portrait, c.* 1843

DURER: *Self-portrait, naked, c.* 1510

COURBET (below): *The meeting,* 1854

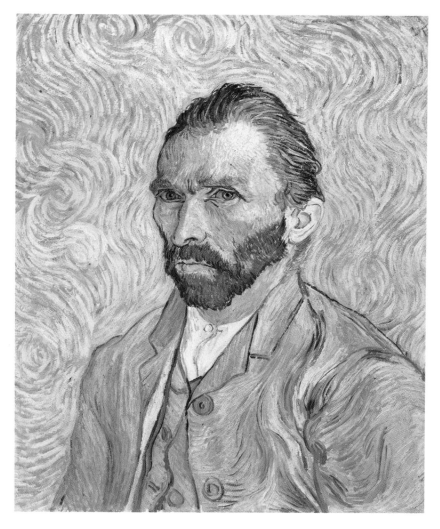

VAN GOGH: *Self-portrait*, 1890

CLOSE: *Self-portrait*, 1968

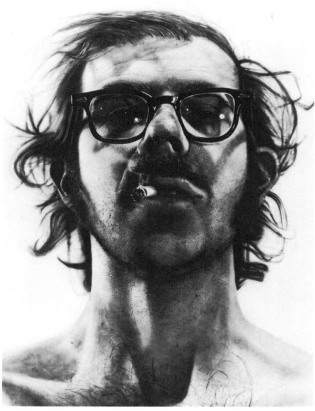

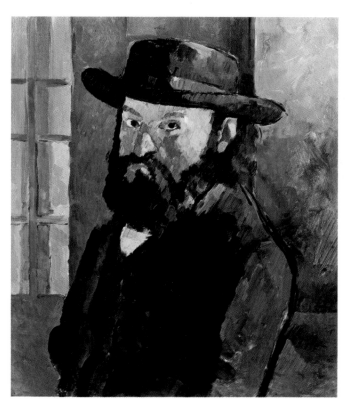

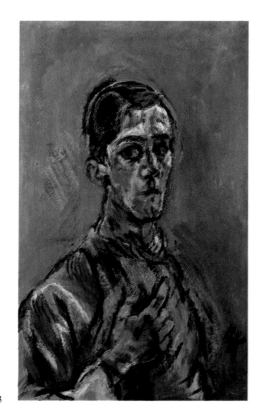

CEZANNE: *Self-portrait*, 1880

KOKOSCHKA: *Self-portrait*, 1913

The Human Figure

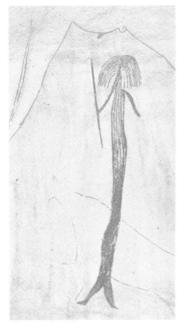

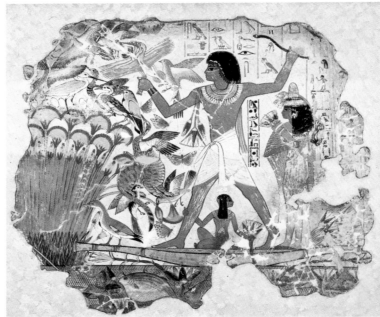

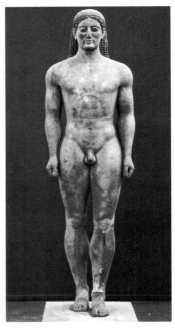

TANZANIA: *Rock-painting*

EGYPT: *Fowling in the marshes*, 1400 BC

GREECE: *Kouros, c.* 540-515 BC

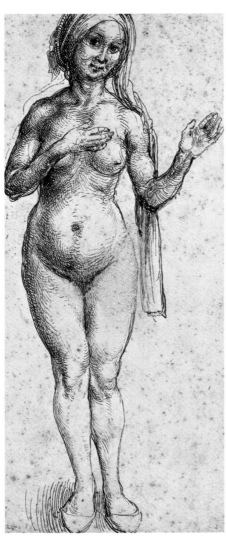

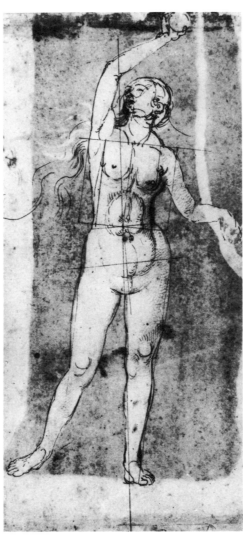

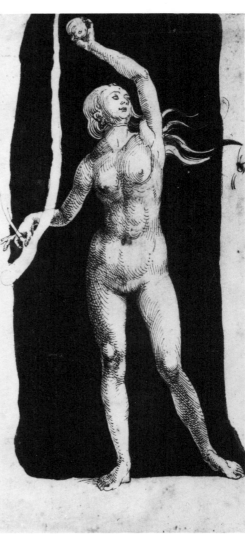

DURER: *Nude woman*, 1493

DURER: *Eve, c.* 1506

DURER: *Eve, c.* 1506

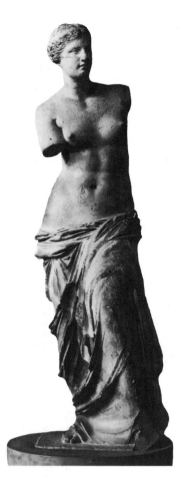

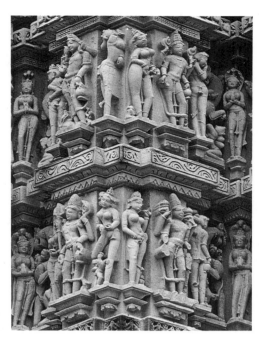

KHAJURAHO, INDIA:
The Kandarya Mahadeva temple, detail, *c*. 1000

GREECE (left): *"The Venus de Milo"*, *c*. 100 BC

Among the earliest representations of man are the matchstick figures of prehistoric cave-paintings, shorthand diagrams of the human physique, like those still to be found in the art of the South African Bushman and in the drawings of young children everywhere. Many cultures elaborated their own conception of the human figure from such elementary beginnings, the Egyptians introducing into their essentially linear portrayals a sense of movement by showing the body both frontally and in profile. Archaic Greek sculpture demonstrated a similar stiffness and stylization, but it is from the originally rigid and impersonal *Kouroi* that the classic Greek figure developed, based upon ideal proportions and quickening into life. For the Greeks discerned divinity in the harmony of the perfect naked body.

During the first millennium of Christianity reaction to the pagan celebration of physical form meant that the body again became a cypher, an expendable mortal shell whence the essential element, the soul, would soon escape to the true reality of life after death. When, after long estrangement and unease, European artists began to focus more closely on the body, it was at first not revivals of the Greek ideal they produced but much less flattering transcriptions from the actual configurations of normal – and fallible – human figures. The transition between medieval and Renaissance art is illustrated vividly in the development of Dürer, whose early drawing at Bayonne (1493) of a stocky peasant girl is entirely credible. Thirteen years later, in Italy, studies, one on each side of the paper, record a fundamentally different conception of woman. In one a geometric armature is traced within the figure. The second, more fully worked-out, image based on these calculated proportions becomes an enchanting compromise between real and ideal.

Dürer's slimly elegant figure refers back to classical interpretation of the human body as a module of proportion which could be related geometrically to the basic forms of square and circle – to the proposal of the Roman Vitruvius that architecture itself should be based upon the ratios of the human body. Greek sculptors of the Hellenistic period had already shown that such ideal proportions could be relaxed in more flexible and sensuous solutions, as in the famous *"Venus de Milo"* of about 100 BC. Almost comparably fluent expressions of the religious impulse in human form are found in Eastern art, never more enthusiastically celebrated than in the sculpture of India – the Hindu temple of Khajuraho teems with the voluptuous delights of Heaven. It was in the humanist culture of the West, however, that the nude would assume a central significance in art from the time of the Renaissance onwards. *The three Graces*, Raphael's study of the female body from three different angles, was painted at a time when it was still not permissible to draw naked women from the life. Yet it shows a confident assimilation of classical models in an idealized but sensuous image of physical perfection, a harmony that does not appear to proceed from calculation and which is both flawless and utterly convincing.

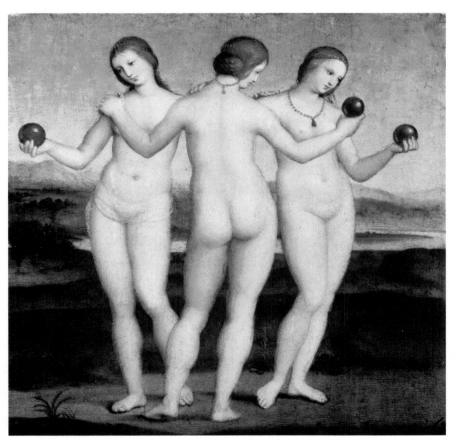

RAPHAEL: *The three Graces*, 1504-05

The Human Figure

Since the rediscovery of the human figure in the fifteenth century, Western artists have used the nude in enormously varied ways, as a theme on which to develop the original variations of their own time, their own interests, their individual styles. The range extends from the classical ideal to the literal recording of particular physical form, both traditions being aided by the developing science of anatomy and by the rapidly established academic tradition of drawing from life.

The delicacy of Raphael's *The three Graces* is far from the voluptuous, ripe radiance that Tintoretto was to infuse, later in the century, into *Susannah and the Elders*, an overtly erotic subject in which we, the spectators, are implicated as we spy with the old men upon Susannah's nakedness. In the large exuberance of her flesh, Tintoretto's nude is not classically proportioned but she is still idealized, a tendency which seems to diminish as one goes northwards: fascination with the reality of the flesh in all its imperfections increases from Umbria (Raphael) to Venice (Tintoretto) and then to Holland and the greatest master of the unideal, Rembrandt. His *Bathsheba* conveys, as perhaps no other nude in all art, the vulnerability of all mankind, not only woman, in the body. It is an image that is certainly erotic, but which rebukes the *voyeur*-spectator and demands love rather than lust; this nude is very far from being a sex object.

The great Baroque decorative painters of the seventeenth century, above all Rubens, must be open to the accusation of presenting women principally as objects for male desire, but the physical exuberance of Rubens' golden Amazons seems more accurately to be a natural outcome of the inexhaustible energy of his style. Eighteenth-century Rococo painters, such as Boucher and Fragonard, emphasized the erotic element above all else – Boucher's *Miss O'Murphy* seems overt invitation – and in much nineteenth-century academic art classical references became hardly more than a veneer of respectability over the eroticism of nymphs at play. Courbet, arch-enemy of academic classicism, used the nude more forthrightly as the focus of his allegory of modern life in *The artist's studio* – radiant at the centre of the canvas.

Only with the revolution against figurative art, signalled by Cubism in the first decade of the twentieth century, did the nude, and indeed the human figure, seem to lose its status as the centre of the world. First disintegrated by Picasso, it became in the hands of Boccioni a collection of planes moving through space, more a machine than an organism; it was abstracted to a study of pure cylinders by Brancusi. It vanishes entirely in the austere constructions of Mondrian – and yet it persists. From the formless welter of action painting in the 1950s there emerged, battling their way into ferocious presence, those elemental females, vital as Neolithic fertility figures, of De Kooning. The tradition of the human figure, of the nude in particular, has in fact never been lost; Picasso himself, in the midst of experimentation with light, form and line in *Nude in an armchair*, was able to reconcile non-literal representation with a voluptuous awareness of the body's opulence.

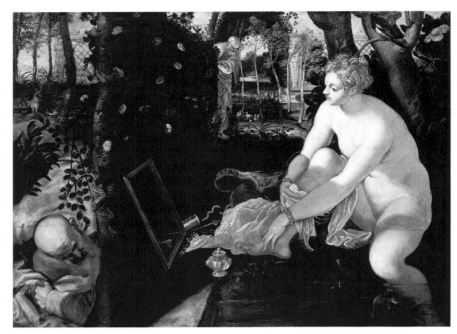

TINTORETTO: *Susannah and the Elders, c.* 1550

RUBENS: *Bathsheba reading David's letter, c.* 1636-38

REMBRANDT: *Bathsheba at her toilet,* 1654

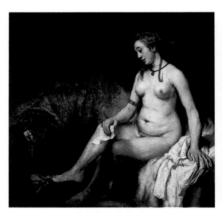
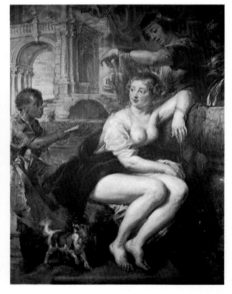

BOUCHER: *Miss O'Murphy,* 1732

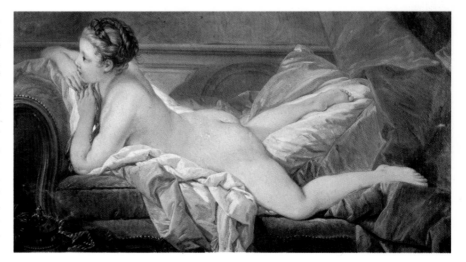

BOCCIONI: *Unique forms of continuity in space*, 1913

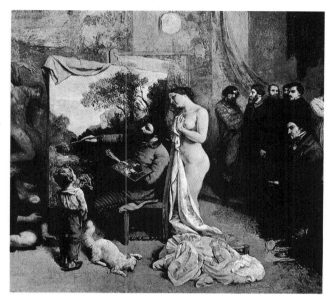

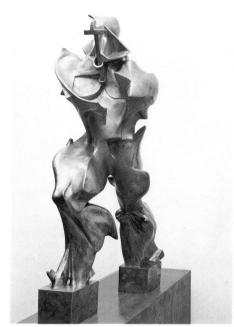

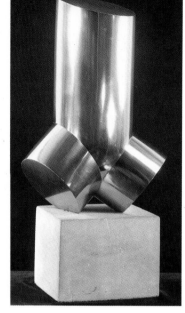

COURBET: *The artist's studio*, detail, 1854–55

BRANCUSI: *Male torso*, after 1924

PICASSO: *Nude in an armchair*, 1932

DE KOONING: *Woman IV*, 1952-53

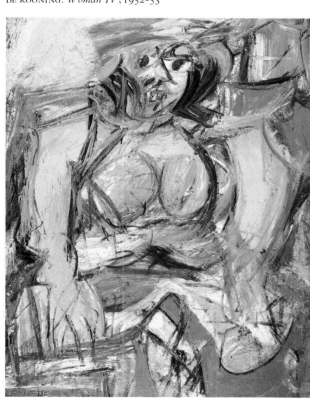

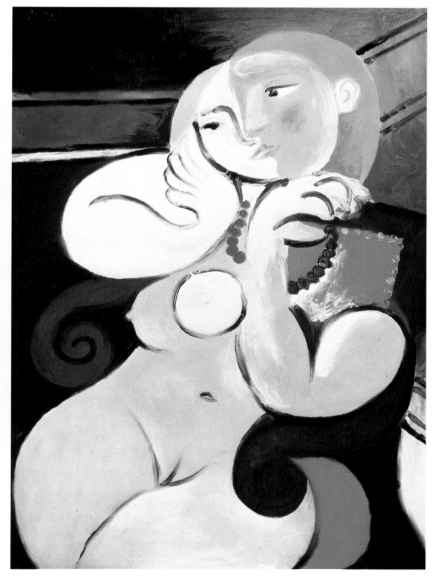

Couples

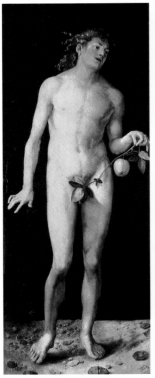
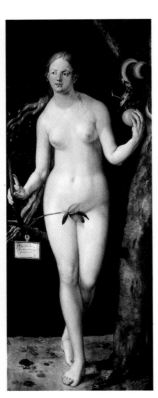

DURER: *Adam and Eve*, 1507

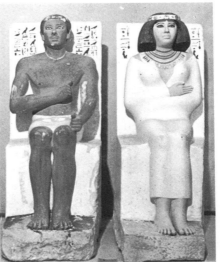
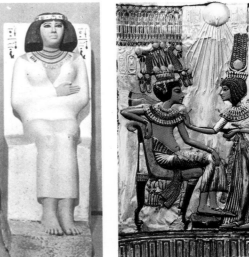

EGYPT: *Rahotep and Nofret*, *c*. 2550 BC; panel of Tutankhamun's throne, before 1361 BC

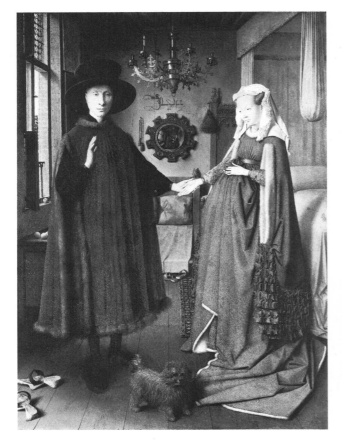

VAN EYCK: *"The Arnolfini Marriage"*, 1434

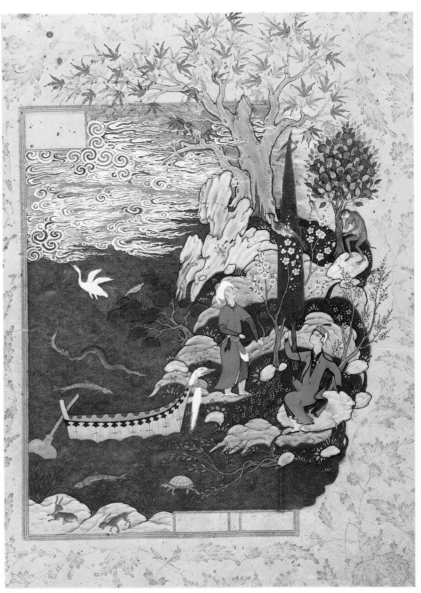

IRAN: *Salaman and Absal reach the shore of the sea*, 1556-65

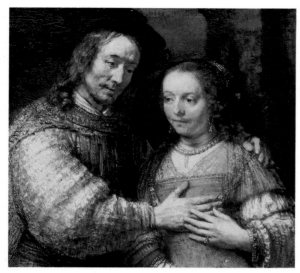

REMBRANDT: *"The Jewish Bride"*, detail, c. 1665

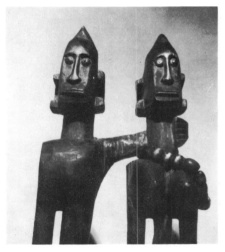

DOGON: *Male and female principles*, undated

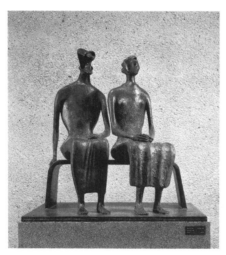

MOORE: *King and Queen*, 1952-53

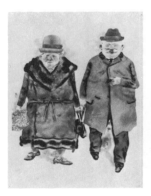

GROSZ: *A married couple*, 1930

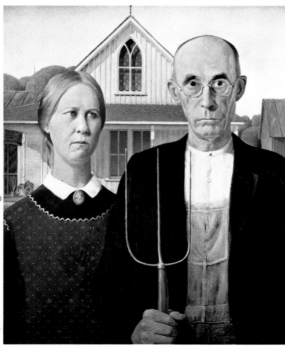

WOOD (right):
American Gothic, 1930

Doubtless from the very beginnings of human society, ritual and ceremony have attended the mystic union of male and female, whence all life continues, for even most animals and birds have established procedures at least in courting. So the story, in Christian art, of Adam and Eve tends towards the ceremonial; one of the most beautiful versions is Dürer's, classically perfect in body, serene in spite of the attending snake. Adam and Eve as a model of the union of any couple are translated into bourgeois terms in van Eyck's celebrated *"Arnolfini Marriage"*; though decorously clothed the couple are surrounded with the trappings of an earthly Paradise, inventoried in the lovingly detailed domestic setting, lucidly defined by the fall of light and by the exquisite symmetries of the picture's structure.

In a very different context, the twin Egyptian statues of Rahotep and Nofret confront eternity in their motionless four-square immobility, conveying to modern sensibilities perhaps a poignant impression of loneliness in togetherness. Yet Egyptian art could also capture tenderness, as witnessed in the delicate scene on the back of Tutankhamun's throne showing teenage royalty in playful intimacy. The dream of young love is apparently irrepressible, and not only in the culture of the West, influenced by the troubadour conventions of courtly love – the woman on a pedestal adored from afar. Persian and Mughal courtesies of wooing are amongst the most enchantingly poetic ever recorded, often enacted in gardens of exquisite artifice, where the lovers, dallying among flowers and shade coaxed from arid desert, seem woven into a decorative pattern of mystical beauty. The jewelled perfection of the example shown here reflects a cultivated society with sophisticated courtship rituals, but the innocent animation of the couple is entirely human.

Rembrandt's portrayal of love perhaps captures its sacramental essence more movingly than any other, in the tenderness of a simple yet profound gesture; the touch of hands and the downcast eyes of husband and wife in *"The Jewish Bride"* speak overwhelmingly yet with exquisite restraint. A similar universally understood gesture of affinity – a slight inward inclination of head or body – can be found in works of art utterly removed from European tradition, as in the culture of the Sudan, where male and female principles are figured with hieratic dignity, befitting a seminal mystery. The same movement may be discerned again in Moore's not so different *King and Queen*, whose regal status, conveyed in the upright, almost comic dignity of their figures, is underpinned by a private bond, hinted at in the closeness of arms, the merest tilt of heads.

Romantic or passionate love is not the only kind portrayed in art; Grosz views his squat, amiable couple with satirical good humour while not denying the strength of their relationship, and a subtle irony seems to pervade the title and whole composition of *American Gothic*, in which the prosaic pair yet emerge immortalized, as if hewn out of living timber, the very essence of frontier tenacity and rectitude.

Couples

If the ceremonies of love offer a subject on which art can most elegantly devise endless formal solutions, unbridled passion presents more thorny problems – at least, in the general tenor of Western conventions, even in the permissive society of the late twentieth century. The conventions of other cultures can be less inhibited, most remarkably in Hindu sculpture, in which the sexual appetite finds frank expression. In contrast, the sensuality of some of even the greatest Western artists may seem a little prurient – literally so for example in Titian's *Venus and the organ player*. Even though it is a superb celebration of the pleasure of the senses – rich in the sensation not only of colour and mass, but of almost audible music – the conventions of depicting love in terms of a ceremony are here gravely at risk; why is the decorously clothed gentleman playing thus to the naked lady? To render the actuality of physical love is even trickier for Western artists, tending to verge on the obscene or the merely ridiculous. The genius of Titian could, however, encompass passion itself in action, as in his formidably tumultuous drawing of Jupiter's assault on Io. Many other major artists have also executed erotic drawings but concealed them from public view. Few are so explicit as the art of the Japanese "pillow books", manuals of sexual instruction in which the act of love is depicted in graphic and elegant detail as a leisurely, sophisticated pleasure. Shame or melancholy as the consequences of the sexual act seem to be themes exclusive to Western art; the satirical eye of Hogarth caught the ludicrous and pathetic aspects of passion, the exhausting discrepancy between desire and satiation, in his *Before* and *After* – the seducer's eagerness turned to indifference, his coy victim now beseeching.

Courbet, however, with characteristic defiance, in *The sleepers* painted satisfaction without inhibition; his female lovers lie in a slumber as deep and abandoned as the passion (we can only assume) that went before. Taste has indeed changed since he painted this as a private commission – it has since become one of the most celebrated and exhibited of all his works. Less explicit and literal styles than Courbet's have been used by Romantic and Expressionist artists who wished to convey the turmoil of physical love. The erotic work of earlier artists may have been confined to sketches partly because oil-painting required a deliberation and finish inappropriate to the subject. The release of style from finish in the dynamic brushwork of Delacroix opened the way for the still more energetic methods of Munch and the Expressionists, who embodied in rich, jarring colours and savage brush-strokes desolate visions of the psychological relationship of man and woman. Munch's lover in *Vampire* appears the helpless victim of his mistress, merged with her predatory form as if the surrender of love meant the surrender of himself to an enemy. Indeed, remarkably few twentieth-century artists have portrayed the act of love without some undertone of violence or fear. In Schiele's painting, the naked couple huddling together in a storm of agitated lines seem, even in passion, desperately alone.

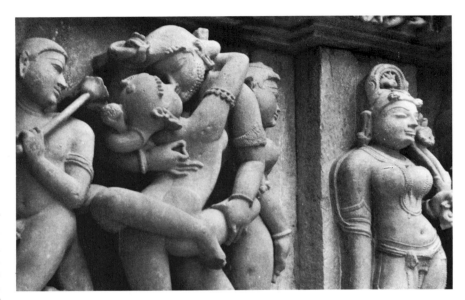

KHAJURAHO: *The Kandarya Mahadeva Temple*, detail, c. 1000

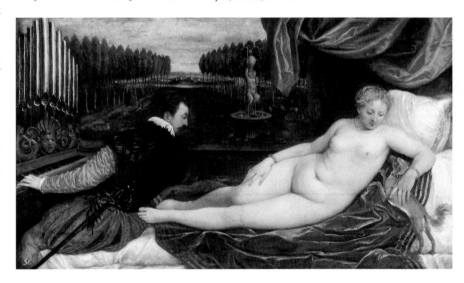

TITIAN: *Venus and the organ player*, c. 1550

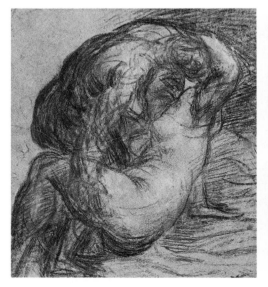

TITIAN: *Jupiter and Io*, c. 1560

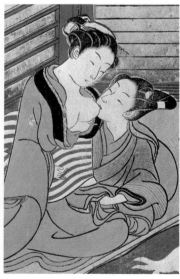

KORYUSAI: *Shunga*,
detail, second half of 18th century

COURBET: *The sleepers*, 1862

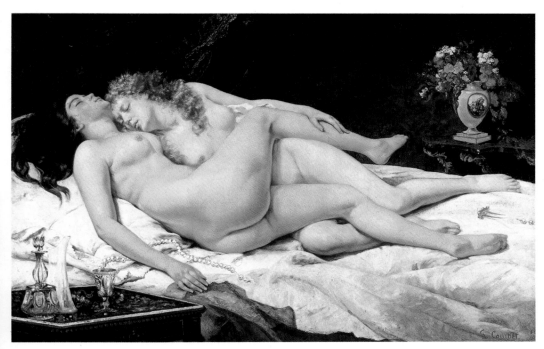

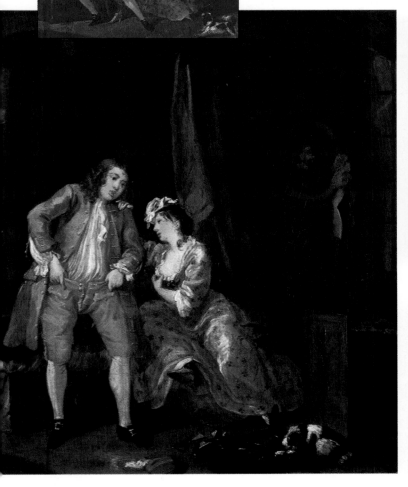

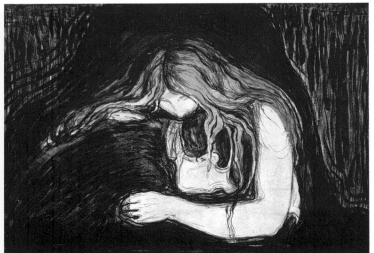

MUNCH: *Vampire*, 1895-1902

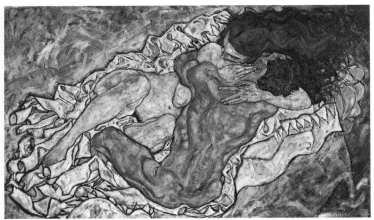

HOGARTH: *Before the seduction* and *After*, 1731

SCHIELE: *The embrace*, 1917

Life and Work

According to the legends that recur in many cultures there was a Golden Age, the lost Garden of Eden, in which the only work needed to produce a continual harvest of life-giving food (vegetarian) seems to have been a little genteel gardening. The reality of taming and working the soil – laborious, dirty, unglamorous – has, however, always been the privilege of the poor, of the peasantry. Scenes of such humdrum agriculture are found in ancient art, and the theme received increasing attention from the fourteenth century on, in the medieval Books of Hours. These prayerbooks, codifying a practice of devotion within a framework of ordered time, began with a Calendar tabulating saints' days and church festivals, and illustrating, month by month, the cycle of community life and work in a standard sequence of twelve themes.

In the great masterpiece of the genre, the *Très Riches Heures* of the Duc de Berri, begun by the Limbourg brothers in Burgundy in the early fifteenth century, a medieval innocence of conception, but also certain medieval formal conventions, fuse with that intense interest in the depiction of the natural world typical of Renaissance art to produce crystalline visions of a world strange as a dream yet sharply real as the waking from a dream. These twelve miniatures are, amongst other things, a major step in the evolution of landscape painting – they show an empirical understanding of perspective if not of the mathematical perspective of the Florentines, and, in some, sophistications adopted by later artists appear for the first time – the observation of the cast shadow, for instance. They illustrate two main facets of life, the courtly pleasures of the aristocracy, and then, as counter-theme, the peasants at their labours – both themes marking the changing rhythms of the seasons. In the semicircles above each one, the relevant phases of the Zodiac are calibrated and imaged.

In February – incidentally one of the first, if not the first, snow-clad landscapes in art – peasants sit about the fire, holding up their tunics to the grateful warmth (in a gesture that had sometimes to be modified for nicer tastes when reproduced later), while men are at work, cutting wood or slogging through the bitter cold outside. Some summer months show the elegant aristocracy at their pleasures, but March, June, October notably have accurately detailed accounts of labourers in the fields, ploughing and pruning the vines, then haymaking, then, in the autumn, harrowing and sowing as the cycle proceeds. These mundane activities are shown without overt comment, observed simply for what they are; yet the modern observer may diagnose an intrinsic irony. The foreground fields in which the peasants toil are set against a backcloth of turrets, pinnacles, castellations fretting the clear sky like story-book fairy castles. But they were real, the fantastic palace-castles of the fifteenth-century Burgundian aristocracy, and the foundations on which they rested were the labours of the peasants of the fields, here shown for the first time in such accuracy, establishing a theme of humble toil to be elaborated by many later artists.

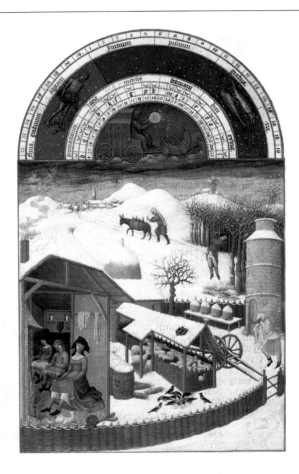

THE LIMBOURG BROTHERS: *February*

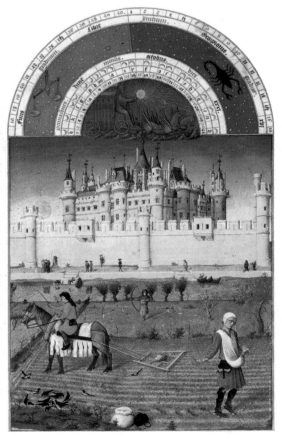

THE LIMBOURG BROTHERS: *October*

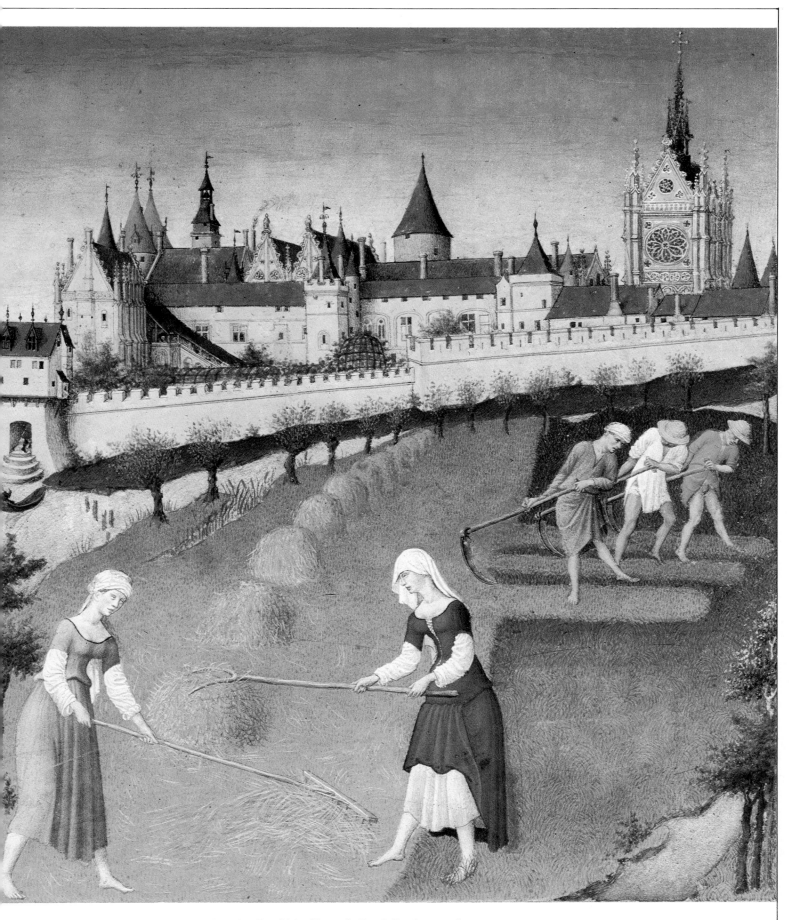

THE LIMBOURG BROTHERS: *June*, page from *Les Très Riches Heures du Duc de Berri*, 1413–16

Life and Work

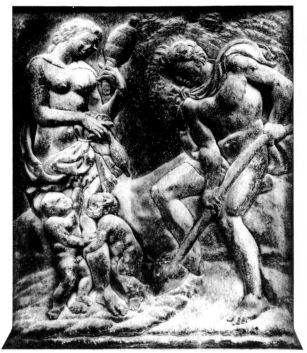

DELLA QUERCIA: *Labours of Adam and Eve*, c. 1428

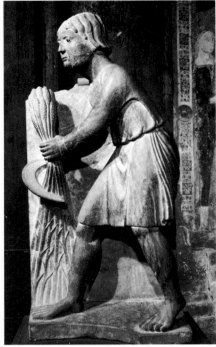

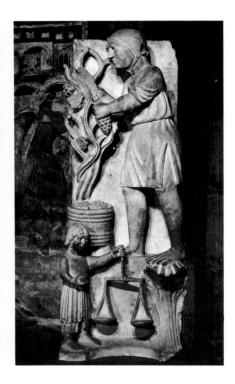

ANTELAMI: *June* and *September*, c. 1200

THEBES (left):
The tomb of Menna:
Harvesting, c. 1450 BC

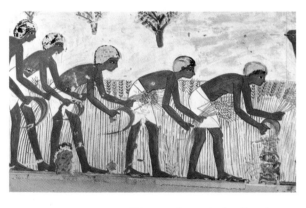

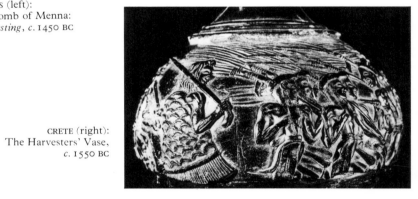

CRETE (right):
The Harvesters' Vase,
c. 1550 BC

BRUEGEL (below): *August* (The corn harvest), detail, 1565

STUBBS (below): *The reapers*, 1795

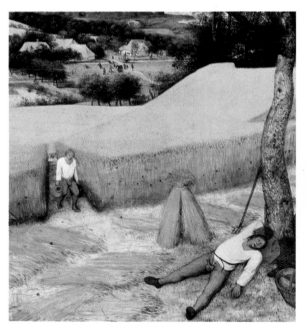

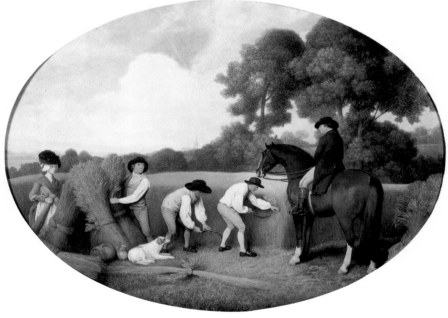

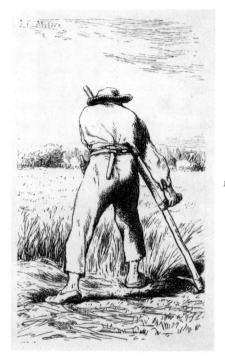

MILLET: *The reaper, c.* 1866-68

VAN GOGH (below): *The reaper*, 1889

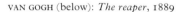

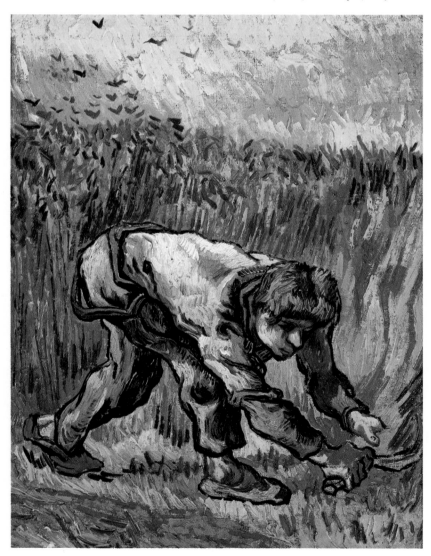

The biblical concept of labour as punishment for disobedience has profoundly affected its representation in Christian art, which frequently portrays it as painful thraldom. Jacopo della Quercia's powerful relief sculpture shows Adam and Eve reaping the fruits of their sin, Eve clutching her distaff and shackled by two squalling children – the infant Cain and Abel – while a grim-faced Adam, every muscle straining, tries to break the unyielding ground. A similar melancholy clouds the faces of labourers in the Baptistery in Parma; the garnering of bread and wine, staples of both physical and sacramental life, brings no flicker of joy to these earnest, stumpy figures, although their labour has a naive and touching dignity.

Other cultures were less inhibited and agricultural work is treated more lightly, even with humour, in Egyptian and Minoan art. A frieze from a tomb at Thebes depicts harvesting with vivacity and grace, while as early as around 1550 BC the famous late Minoan Harvesters' Vase from the Palace of Hagia Triada in Crete records an exultant harvest-home.

In Western art, agriculture was to remain a continuing theme especially, as we have seen on the previous page, in medieval Books of Hours. The calendar convention was to find its finest expression in Bruegel's series, *The Seasons of the Year* (see pp. 170–171). *August* is a wonderful evocation of sweltering summer heat, corn bleached by the sun, the spread-eagled figure of the worker expressing utter physical exhaustion. In marked contrast with this realistic portrayal of toiling peasantry is George Stubbs' view of eighteenth-century rural England, in which the workers are disposed across the foreground like figures in an antique frieze. Though the overseer on his horse reflects the notion of manual labour as being beneath a gentleman, his workers have a dignity of their own. Their clothes, seemingly quite unsuited to the dust and sweat of harvest, are hardly plainer than their master's and they stand or bend with a grace that derives partly, perhaps, from Neoclassical principles of composition – but only partly, for the landscape, though idyllic, is unmistakably English, and the unselfconscious harmony of the pictures seems rooted in acceptance of the natural and social order.

In the nineteenth century, with the awakening of a more sensitive social consciousness, labour began to be celebrated with a reverence once reserved for religious subjects. The noblest and most consistent painter of this theme was Millet, some of whose most famous images – *The Angelus* for example – reflect the romantic, pantheistic idea of a deep spiritual communion between man and nature. Others are of labour very much in action, like his *Sower* or *The reaper*; the latter captures back-breaking effort expressively but without comment. But the images of van Gogh, who copied several Millets and felt deeply for the sufferings of both industrial and peasant workers, are more overt in their fierce, heavy contours and distortions of feature into brutish near-deformity; his *Reaper* speaks without restraint of lives relentlessly exhausted in the battle for survival.

Life and Work

Memorable pictures of those kinds of work that do not involve muscular labour so much as skills of hand or mind are relatively rare. Apart from lacking the elemental drama of working the soil, such subjects present a difficult challenge simply because they often involve internal mental rather than external physical action.

In the materialist society of seventeenth-century Holland, business of all kinds provided subject matter for occasional anecdotal pictures, often of a fairly trivial kind. But there were also startling visions of intellectual discovery, among them *The anatomy lesson of Dr Tulp*, in which Rembrandt orchestrates the drama in strong contrasts of light and shade, the intent faces expressing the excitement of scientific investigation. The American Thomas Eakins later used chiaroscuro for similar ends in his *Gross Clinic*. The gruesome element was thought shocking at the time, yet it is the high tension of the operation that now compels our attention – the face of the surgeon rather than his bloodied hands.

In settled societies the traditionally feminine skills have been shown not as arduous labour (though arduous they often were) but as images of serene contentment. Vermeer, quietest of painters, was the master of such patient domesticities. In his hands a maid pouring milk becomes a profound, inexhaustible meditation on life itself, an everyday gesture taking on an almost sacramental quality, the mood evoked through a matchless handling of light, glowing like a pearl.

Except in the work of Chardin it was not until the nineteenth century that such subjects were again treated seriously, in Degas's scenes of women ironing. With an eye quick as a camera shutter in catching a momentary pattern in everyday life, Degas also succeeded in animating the traditional group portrait; his remarkable *Cotton Exchange at New Orleans* is the first to catch the flavour of a modern office at work. Its activity is suggested not by atmospheric lighting but by the seemingly random disposition of figures in a tightly organized design; within an asymmetrical perspective of steeply converging lines, workers are caught in mid-gesture, as in a photograph.

Reynolds, too, used an unconventional composition to revitalize the way in which intellectuals had traditionally been portrayed, eyes cast heavenwards, pen poised to write. He posed Dr Johnson with deliberate awkwardness, not simply for a true likeness of an ungainly man, but to convey the fact that great mental achievements come from human effort, not divine inspiration.

More recently, the idea of physical labour as heroic activity has been celebrated by Mexican painters such as Rivera and Orozco, and by the socialist-realist artists of the communist states. In the West, Expressionist artists have produced perhaps the most potent images of work, as in Ferdinand Hodler's stupendously emphatic *Woodcutter*. The artist, however, who has found the most satisfactory solution for a social and political philosophy is Léger – his workmen, integrated into a design of scaffolding and ladders, give a hieratic dignity to machine-age labour.

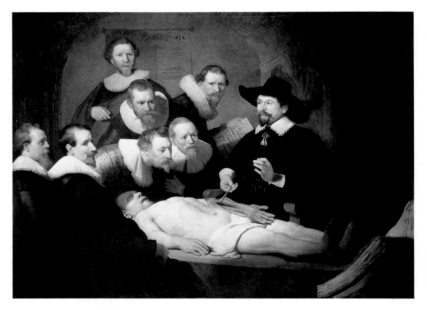

REMBRANDT: *The anatomy lesson of Dr Tulp*, detail, 1632

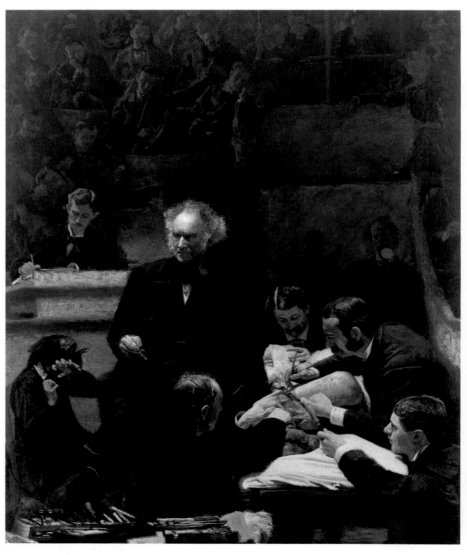

EAKINS: *The Gross Clinic*, 1875

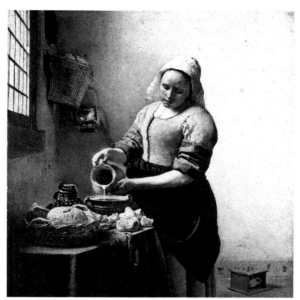

VERMEER: *Servant girl pouring milk*, detail, *c.* 1663

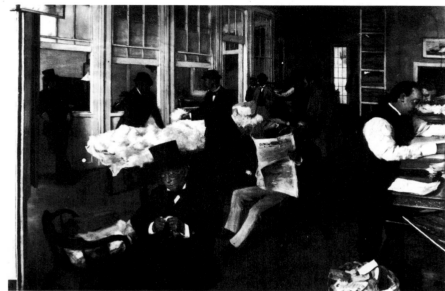

DEGAS: *The Cotton Exchange at New Orleans*, 1873

REYNOLDS (left):
Dr Johnson,
1756

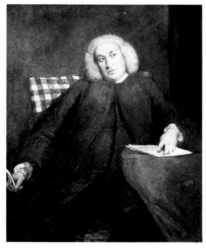

LEGER (right):
The builders,
1950

HODLER (below): *The woodcutter*, 1910

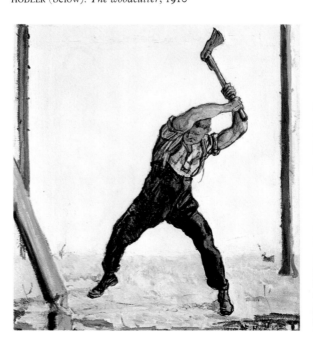

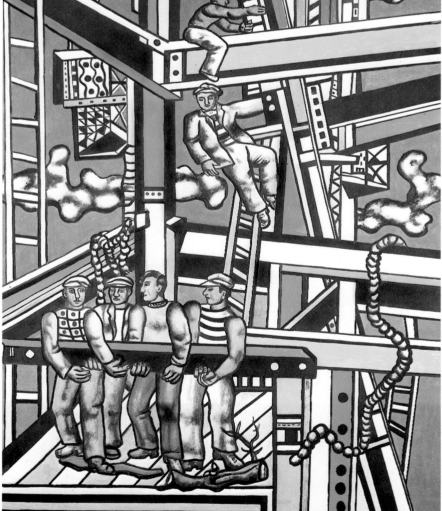

Life and Leisure

The summer afternoon is perfect. The Sunday lunch party is just beginning to break up; dessert and wine are still on the table. Utterly relaxed, well-dined, friends linger together; a desultory sparkle of gossip, of badinage, of flirtation, is almost audible. Soon, some decisions about what to do next through the long afternoon will have to be arrived at – but not just yet.

Renoir captured this moment, this eternity, of pure *joie-de-vivre* at the Restaurant Fournaise on the isle of Chatou on the Seine near Paris in 1881. This was one of the favourite weekend resorts for Parisians in the summer months – poets, artists, patrons; they came from the bourgeoisie and the fashionable world to enjoy themselves. Boating was in high fashion (hence the men in their singlets, though one landsman, Baron Barbier, retains the full formality of the top hat). Pretty women, as always, were also in fashion. That ripe pouting profile on the left under the hat is the first sight in Renoir's work of Aline Charigot; their love-affair was to consolidate into marriage. The girl raising a glass is "La belle Angèle", a witty and provocative professional model, and the enchanting figure leaning on the balcony rail Alphonsine Fournaise, daughter of the proprietor (Renoir painted her three times). The men, too, are mostly identifiable – Gustave Caillebotte, friend of Monet and Renoir, artist himself, and collector of their works, is the young man so casually, hat tip-tilted, astride his chair; seated next to him is an actress, Ellen Andrée, and the other young man, leaning over him but focused obviously on Ellen, is a journalist friend, M. Maggiolo.

The setting is a wooden dining-terrace built out from the restaurant, overlooking the river. It is high summer, not too hot, just right, the fringe of the terrace awning moving gently in the air. When he painted this idyll Renoir was 40, not in first youth but in the early maturity of his prime, beginning to enjoy the confidence of hard-won professional success. The picture is pervaded by his relaxed assurance; we sense that the artist is as much at ease as are his subjects.

Renoir had been foremost among Impressionists in experimentation with divisionist technique, juxtaposing strokes of pure, intense colour, eliminating black from his palette and contouring outline from his design. Yet he had already shown himself interested less in optical effects than in achieving the sensuous feeling of light and of fresh, moving air. In this painting, his later development is foreshadowed: theoretical considerations yield to his pleasure in his subject matter, in the pleasure of life itself. Foliage and background are handled in Impressionist technique but the foreground figures are fully solid in the flower of their flesh and the rich texture of his paint; his work would soon become ever more strongly a celebration of human happiness in the human form. As here, he could indeed paint idylls, but unlike the dreams of Watteau (whom he adored) it is the now – present laughter – that he recorded, not as a detached observer but as one sharing the tastes and sounds of that summer afternoon, its immediacy sharpened by the individual portraits of his friends.

Raoul Barbier

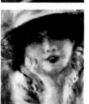

Alphonsine Fournaise

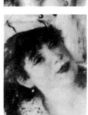

Ellen Andrée

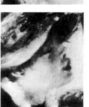

Aline Charigot

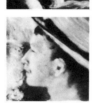

Gustave Caillebotte

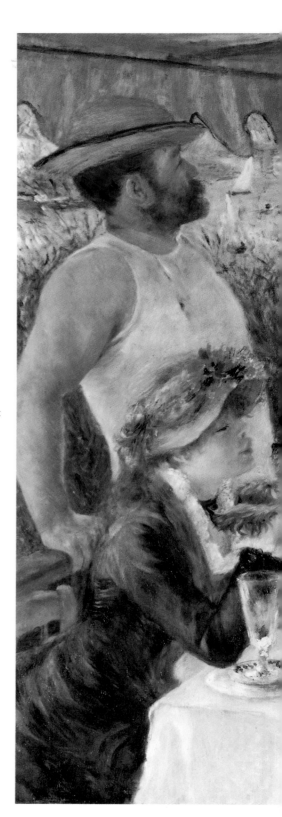

RENOIR: *The luncheon of the boating party*, 1881

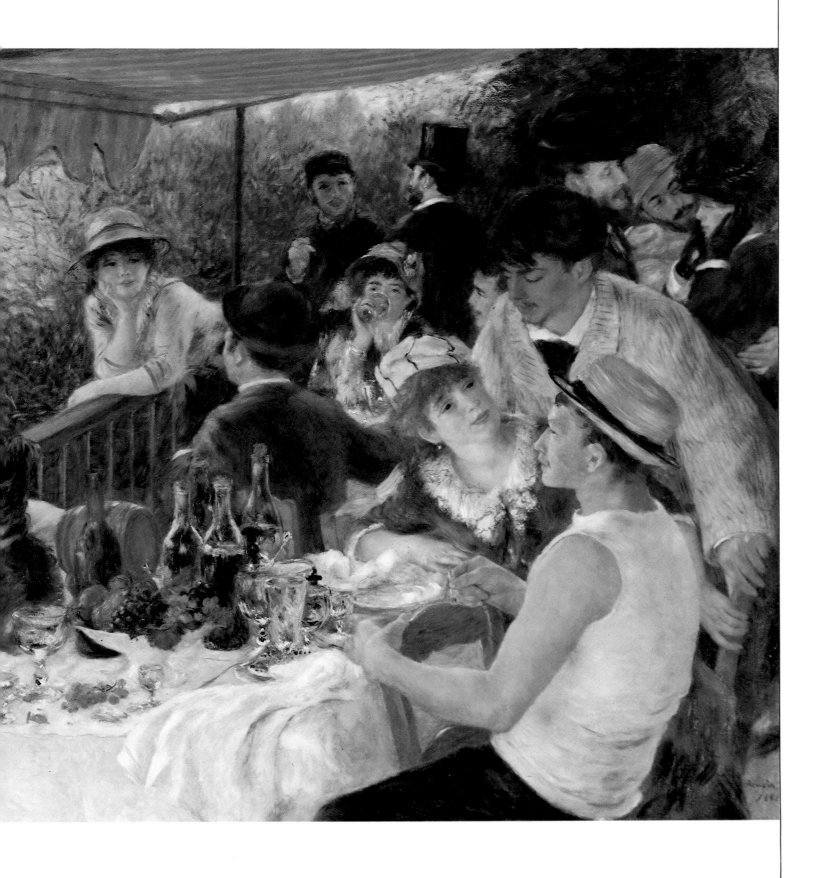

Life and Leisure

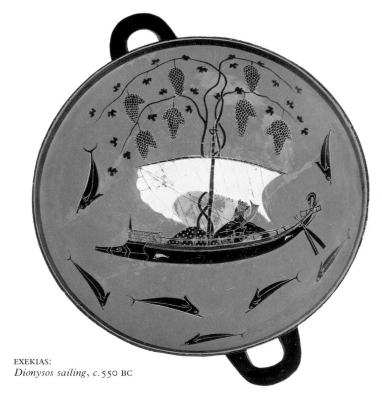

EXEKIAS:
Dionysos sailing, c. 550 BC

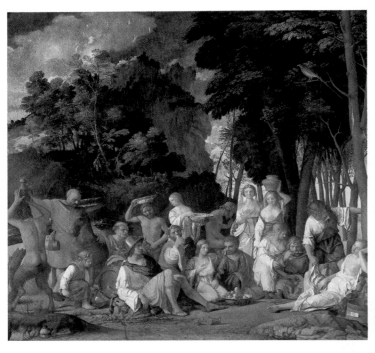

BELLINI: *The feast of the gods*, 1514

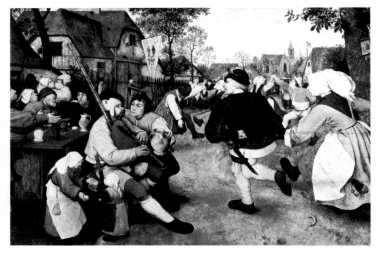

BRUEGEL: *The peasant wedding*, c. 1567

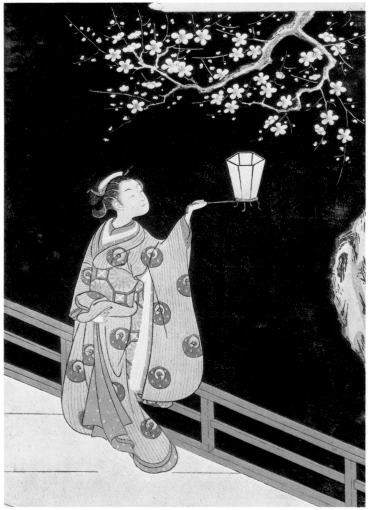

HARUNOBU: *Girl viewing plum-blossoms at night*, c. 1768

WATTEAU (right): *Les Champs-Elysées*, detail, 1717

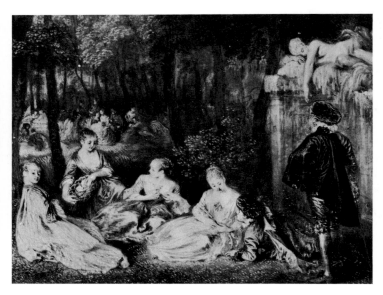

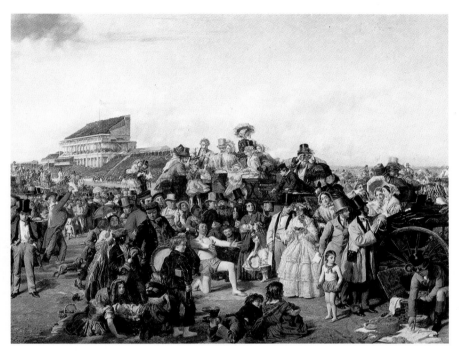

FRITH: *Derby day*, detail, 1856–58

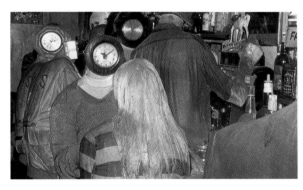

KIENHOLZ: *Barney's beanery*, detail, 1965

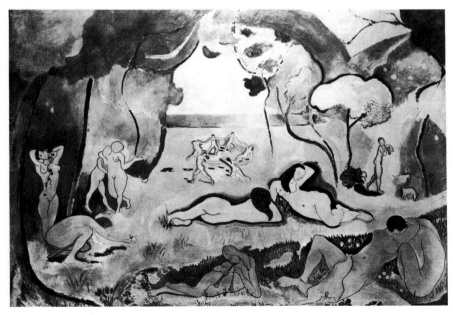

MATISSE: "*La Joie de Vivre*", 1905-06

One of the most complete, or replete, solo counterparts in all art to Renoir's orchestration of relaxed pleasure in *The luncheon of the boating party* is provided by the Greek potter Exekias in about the mid-sixth century BC. The wine-god, Dionysos, reclines on his barque; sea and sky have merged indissolubly into an infinite heaven in which dolphins sport. The ship's mast is also the support for a luxuriant grapevine. Form and decoration answer function perfectly (even the flaking of the white from the sail cannot spoil the harmony), for the composition is contained within the rim of a shallow drinking-bowl.

Pleasure is celebrated no less consummately, and with almost equal control of line and design, more than 2,000 years later and on the other side of the globe in Harunobu's exquisite print of a *Girl viewing plum-blossoms at night*. From classical Greece to eighteenth-century Japan – and since – the depiction of pleasure has been a constant theme, as if the ephemeral intoxication of the senses could be answered, renewed and even to some degree endowed with immortality by the rhythm of line and gloss of colour. Conviviality heightens pleasure, and feasts, parties, processions have all proved irresistible subjects for art. In one of the supreme masterpieces of the genre, *The feast of the gods*, painted by the aged Bellini and finished by the young Titian, gods and men, satyrs and beautiful girls consort in a picnic that seems both supernatural and real, set in one of the most idyllic landscapes ever painted. A little later, Bruegel recorded carousel of a more earthly kind; the stamp and huff of the dancers is all but audible, the movement of line and swirl of dress as vivid as if one were there. How different from the gusto of his cut-out shapes and emphatic colour contrasts is the approach and style of Watteau, who was painting with a different intention for a different social order. The airy, melting harmonies of his Rococo idyll capture the indolent sophistication of aristocratic eighteenth-century France – an eternal summer time of wine, lovely women and music in which leisure seems not something seized from life but its perpetual condition.

Beside the dreams of Watteau, Frith's view of a Victorian day out seems as matter-of-fact as a photograph, mere industrious craftsmanship. Yet documentary record has always been an important strand of art, and the pleasure Frith's panorama offers is close to that of sightseeing. We are sightseeing indeed in Edward Kienholz's surreal *Barney's Beanery*, a walk-in environment recreating, in a mixture of ghostly plaster casts and real, assembled trappings of bottles and glasses, the artist's own rueful nostalgia for a particular bar. The tyres and clocks and dingy clothes offer at the same time a commentary on the reality of plebeian urban leisure in the pressured twentieth century. It may be Matisse who, in an idiom of art far from this, abstracted not the reality but the spirit of leisure – Matisse who, after all, wished art to be, amongst other things, the mental equivalent of a comfortable armchair. In the suppleness of his linear rhythms he evokes an ideal leisure – one that is entirely relaxed and yet refreshingly vital.

Life and Leisure

Leisure, no less than work, becomes tedious if unorganized and without apparent aim. Sport is the work-out of leisure, first emerging clearly and becoming ritualized as one would expect in the context of the Greek culture of physical perfection and beauty. For sculptors, the body of the naked male athlete in action has been a supreme challenge – answered most famously by *The discus thrower*, modelled originally for bronze by Myron about 450 BC, though now known only in marble.

The controlling of the competitive aspects of sport, the imposition of order codified by often mysterious laws, proceeded in more settled and sophisticated cultures until, in Pieter de Hoogh's *Skittle-players in a garden* of the 1660s, it slows down into a social ritual as stately and ceremonious as a quadrille. The pattern of the play is answered by de Hoogh's assured grasp of the interrelationships of the standing figures (as if a free variation on the regimentation of the skittles) and of the tall verticals of house and trees.

It is more difficult for art to find a formal equivalent for the swifter, more violent outdoor sports: the attempts of the Italian Futurists, who made a fetish of movement, are not very convincing. Surely the most entrancingly absurd attempt at catching the spirit – or anyway, a spirit – of modern sport in motion is the Douanier Rousseau's vision, *The ball-players* of 1908, admirably self-satisfied, striped like technicolor, mustachioed tigers, gallivanting with a rather round rugby ball apparently in the depths of a thicket. One of the delightful attributes of so-called Naive art is its freedom from the constricting need to represent life with any kind of objective accuracy. The more successful literal attempts to show people at play tend to emphasize the ritual elements. A haunting example, *Memories* by the Belgian Symbolist Khnopff, 1889, is a very early salute to lawn-tennis, but the figures of these seven women, waiting perhaps for the nets to be raised before a game, evoke in their hieratic stillness something mysterious, as though each one, solitary, were in communion with some unseen elemental force. A more hostile presence seems to bear down on the awkward boys in Ben Shahn's *Handball*, accurately frozen by an artist whose eye is that of a social realist.

Indoor pastimes and games naturally captured the attention of many Dutch painters in the seventeenth century, and the best of them – Vermeer or Terborch, say – were able to catch in this stillness an echo of music: the music lesson, with its often slightly erotic overtones, was a favourite theme. Card-playing is another favourite, treated in almost as many ways as there are styles. In the anticipation of boys playing cards, a French follower of Caravaggio sensed explosive movement, and expressed it in the characteristic Baroque drama of contrasted light and shade. Cézanne, obsessed by the theme over some years, conversely painted two rather dour peasants into an elemental immobility; their individual feelings about the game are much less important than the part they play in building up a purely pictorial, almost monumental, structure.

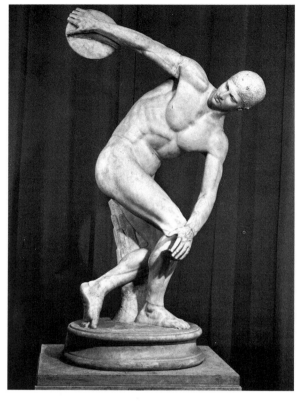

AFTER MYRON: *The discus thrower*, original *c.*450 BC

DE HOOGH (below): *Skittle-players*, *c.*1663-66

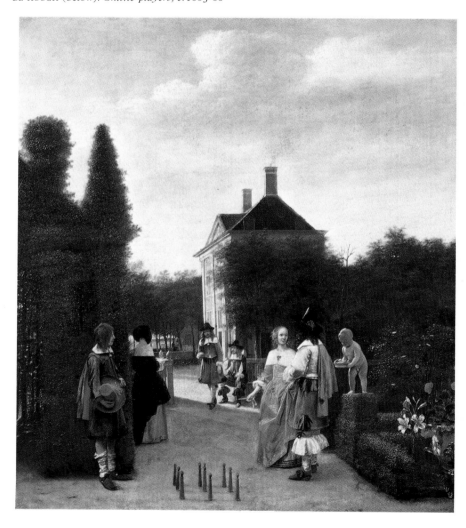

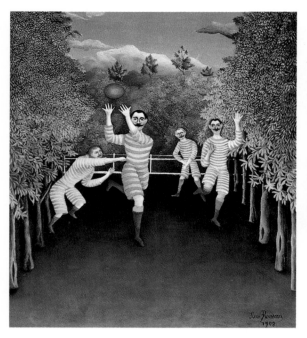

ROUSSEAU: *The ball-players*, 1908

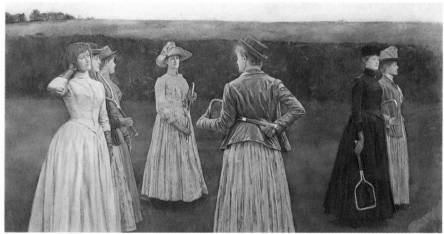

KHNOPFF: *Memories*, 1889

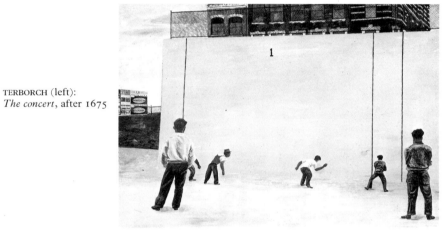

TERBORCH (left):
The concert, after 1675

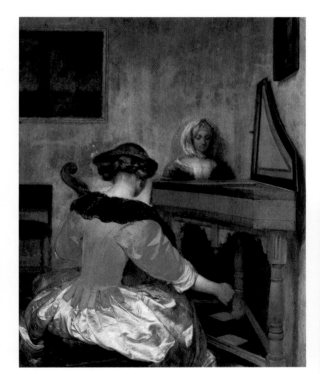

AFTER CARAVAGGIO: *The card-players*, detail, 17th century

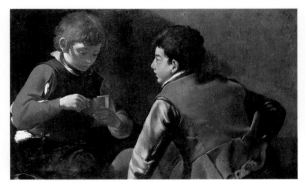

SHAHN: *Handball*, 1939

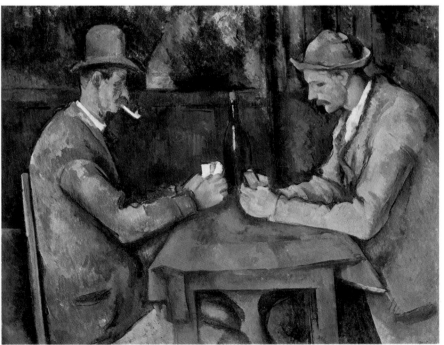

CEZANNE (above): *The card-players*, 1890–92

Narration

In 1528 Duke William IV of Bavaria commissioned eight large paintings of great battles of classical antiquity. The commission was entirely in key with the Renaissance discovery of antiquity; in Italy comparable projects were the series of *uomini famosi* (famous men) painted for state apartments. Just as these served as examples and inspiration to fame, so too legendary conflicts could serve as spurs to heroism and conquest. They had a narrative purpose, as much religious art had done, but the story was of human affairs and ambitions; the theme of each painting was probably laid down by the Duke's learned court historian, Aventinus. One of the painters employed was Albrecht Altdorfer, the most remarkable and genial of German painters after Dürer and Grünewald, and the most original landscape artist of his time.

Altdorfer's contribution was not just outstanding, it proved to be one of the most spectacular battle-pieces ever painted, with hundreds, or perhaps thousands, of warriors clashing in furious action within a frame only a little more than 1.5 metres (5ft) high. Its grandeur, however, does not rest on considerations of scale and detail but on an intensity of vision unique in his work. The battle portrayed is Alexander the Great's crucial defeat of the Persians under Darius III in 333 BC, but presented in terms of the massed clash of armies in Altdorfer's own time. Though Darius appears in an antique chariot, the armour and weapons, the splendid banners and pennanted lances, are those of sixteenth-century Europe, and there may be echoes here of the great battle of Pavia of 1525, only a few years before the artist was painting.

In the foreground the swaying tides of conflict are marshalled with extraordinary coherence, the lances like corn in the wind, the helmet plumes like foam on the sea. A surging rhythm pervades the entire composition, thrust and counter-thrust of armoured phalanxes subsiding in winding curves to the encamped tents, the turreted town at peace at the water's edge, only to pick up again, at first frozen in the alpine ranges and then galvanized into cosmic action in the vast turbulence of the heavens. Here, the symbolism becomes overt: the sun, signifying Alexander and Greece, rises through a vortex of cloud while the crescent moon, signifying Darius, Persia and perhaps, anachronistically, Islam fades. The lapidary inscription, miraculously but credibly afloat in the sky, suspends its tasselled cord over the press and shock of troops at the centre of action – Alexander on horseback, lance outthrust, tramples through a cleared ring of fallen bodies in hot pursuit of Darius, whose chariot is turned for flight. It is the turning point of the battle itself.

Human conflict here becomes as much a manifestation of the elemental force of Nature as the geological tumult that heaved up the mountains or the storm-tossed sky. As exultation of battle it has not been surpassed, and its quality was clearly grasped by Napoleon, who abducted it to hang in his bathroom at St Cloud, where he could contemplate over and over again its splendour, and no doubt identify satisfactorily with Alexander.

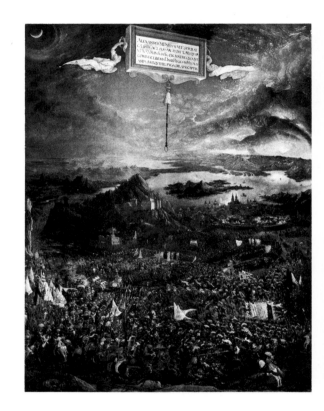

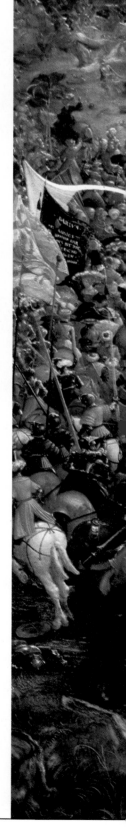

ALTDORFER: *The battle of Alexander and Darius on the Issus*, 1529

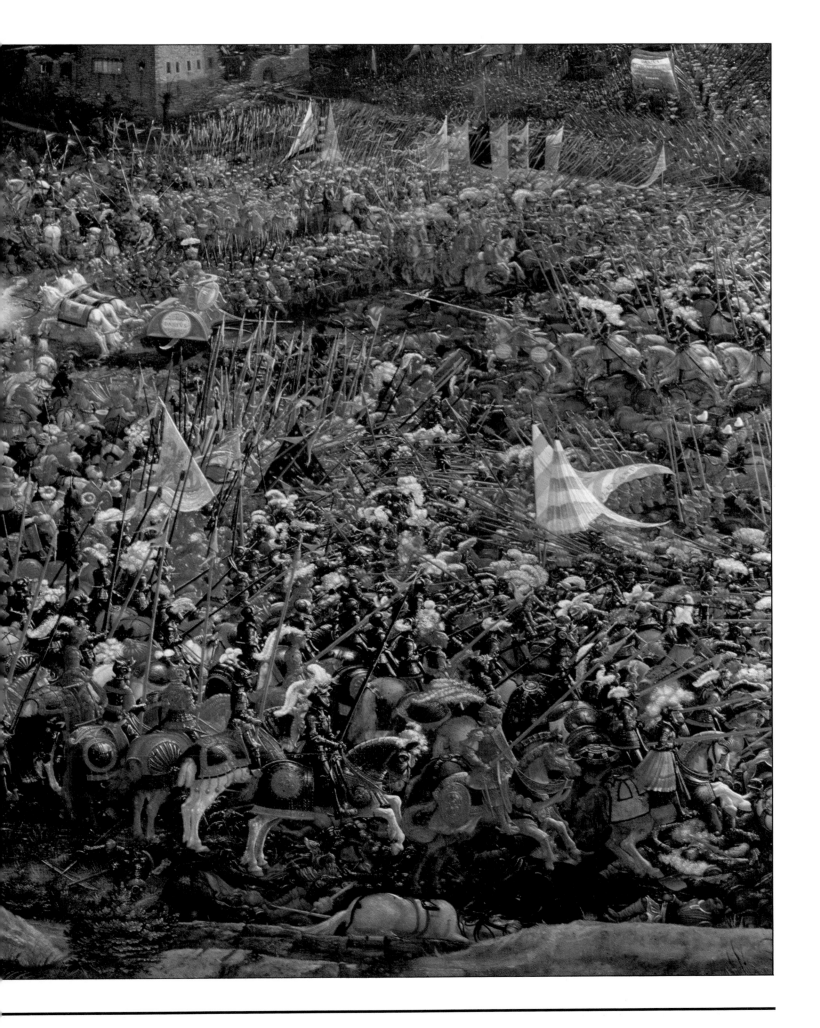

Narration

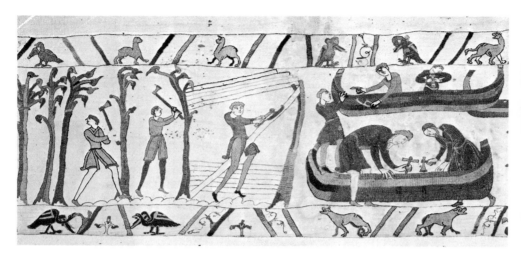

CANTERBURY: The Bayeux Tapestry, c. 1080

LICHTENSTEIN: *Whaam!*, 1963

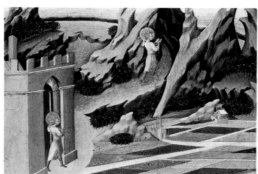

GIOVANNI DI PAOLO:
*St John entering the
wilderness*, c. 1450

HOGARTH: *The arrest* and *The prison*, from *The Rake's Progress*, c. 1733

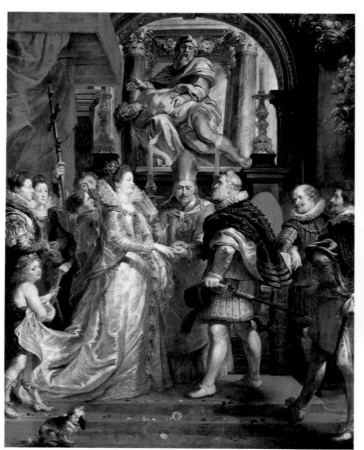

RUBENS: *The marriage*,
from the Médicis cycle, 1622-25

RIVERA (right): Detail from
a mural at the National School of
Agriculture, Chapingo, 1924-27

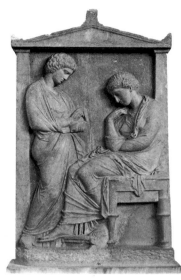

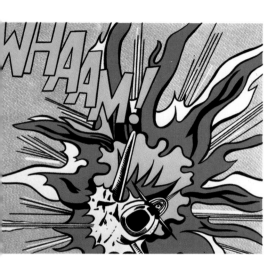

GREECE: Stela, 5th century BC

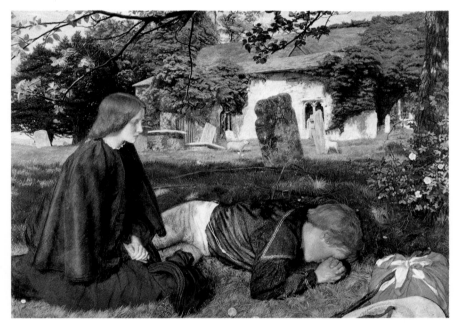

HUGHES: *Home from the sea*, 1862

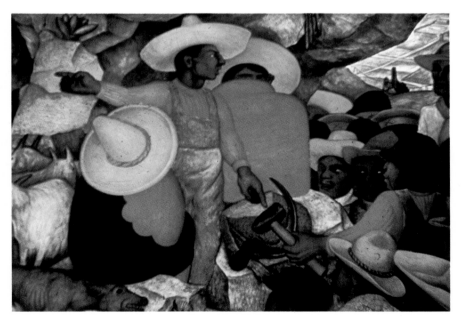

Narration, story-telling, implies a series of events and hence a dimension of real time with a beginning, middle and end, a dimension that paintings or sculptures may seem to lack by comparison with moving pictures. Yet artists who wish to tell a story may, as we have seen in Altdorfer's painting, choose an historical moment so crucial that its implications extend both before and after the event depicted, and concentrate the action so fiercely that the whole scene becomes impossible to take in at once, involving the viewer in minute exploration of the unfolding battle. Chinese scrolls provided a more ingenious method of presenting a pictorial sequence, so that even an unrolling landscape could become the story of a voyage down the length of a winding river to the sea. An early episodic example in Western art is the story of the Norman conquest of England told in the Bayeux Tapestry, ancestor of the comic strip and, in turn, of Roy Lichtenstein's *Whaam!* Here the brazen graphic energy of a mass medium is treated as art in two huge canvases placed side by side, so that we identify first with the pilot taking aim, then with his exultation.

Sequential narrative was common in medieval art – in manuscript illuminations, in the little predella panels showing the lives of saints at the bottom of altarpieces and, on a larger scale, in the fresco cycles and radiant stained glass of churches, the "Bibles of the poor", illustrating the Christian story in terms of a sequence of key events. Frequently, however, painters and stained glass illuminators felt under no constraint to observe the unities of time, place and action, and instead showed two or more stages of the narrative within a single frame. An enchanting example of such "continuous representation" is *St John entering the wilderness*, where the saint is seen emerging from the gate of a town and again halfway up the hill beyond it. By the sixteenth century this convention had given way to great, ambitious cycles of paintings by Baroque masters such as Rubens, whose allegorical evocation shown here of the marriage of Marie de Médicis is one of a sequence of 21 paintings depicting incidents from the life of the widow of Henry IV commissioned for her new Luxembourg Palace. Hogarth turned the method to satirical account in a number of narrative cycles including *The Rake's Progress*.

Equally with historical events, basic human emotions can have implications beyond the expression of a single moment; thus an austere relief of two figures in a Greek grave-marker can convey the echo of lost joys as well as a desolation shadowing the future. The popularity of Victorian narrative painting depended on a more explicit rendering of context and on titles which themselves told the story, as in Arthur Hughes' vision of a sailor boy prostrate on his mother's grave in a sunlit churchyard. In the twentieth century, narrative painting, where it survives at all, has been used mainly as an instrument of political persuasion or exhortation: Diego Rivera's vivid accounts of the history of the Mexican Revolution provide rare modern examples of the older tradition of fresco cycles.

Narration

Of all narrative topics, few have gripped the imagination of the artist so consistently and ubiquitously as battle, the struggle for survival. Men have always found in war a mixture of glory and horror, terror and exultant exhilaration. The visual dynamics of the subject – the hard, diagonal lines of flags, lances, brandished swords – can give even pictures of hand-to-hand combat a powerful urgency and realism, as in the detail from the Graeco-Roman mosaic of Alexander the Great; or again, the medieval manuscript illumination of the same hero, as if in ballet, unrelated to ground or sky but ferociously potent, painted with an astonishing energy and directness.

Some artists seem to have been born to paint the turbulence of full-scale battle; Rubens, for all his diplomatic efforts in the cause of peace, appears to have found in scenes of rape and pillage huge satisfaction for his copious vigour. Artists have been noble and persuasive propagandists, too, in the cause of freedom, of rebellion against tyranny – so the sculptor Rude, whose "*La Marseillaise*" is a call to arms as stirring as the anthem it interprets in stone on the Arc de Triomphe. The momentum of the winged figure is carried forward irresistibly by the wheel of figures turning below it.

From time to time, compassionate awareness of the pity and tragedy of war appears – in the etchings of Callot early in the seventeenth century, for instance – yet it is an awareness of a suffering implied to be inevitable. Stronger protest is first registered in great art in the paintings and etchings of Goya, whose horrific visions of the Napoleonic Wars are diametrically opposed to those of Rude or of Napoleon's own favourite painter, David. Goya spells out the full physical brutality of war, piling huddled figures together to suggest the helplessness of ordinary men, women and children against it. Nineteenth-century artists more often romanticized the subject, as in Leutze's vast canvas *Washington crossing the Delaware*, in which the privations of the American Army are subsumed in a dramatic image of Washington, posed in precarious, fully-accoutred glory on the gunwale of a pitching longboat.

It took the massacres of World War I for a more general admission of the unacceptable cruelty of war to materialize. Picasso's famous *Guernica*, painted in outrage at the bombing of a civilian town in the Spanish Civil War, shows the expressive power of his formal inventiveness, his capacity to take reality to pieces and construct an alternative reality from the splinters. In the great *Surrender of Breda* Velazquez had painted the magnanimity, the ceremonious stateliness of the humane victor, the battle over, all passion spent; the inclination of victor and vanquished towards each other is one of the most beautifully observed and rendered moments in art. In scathing contrast is the vision of Georg Grosz, satirizing the survival of militarist sentiment in the Germany of the 1920s. His mutilated manikins *Republican automatons*, faceless veterans in a sterile urban landscape but still wearing medals, waving the flag, offer eloquently dumb contradiction to Velazquez's view of the aftermath of battle.

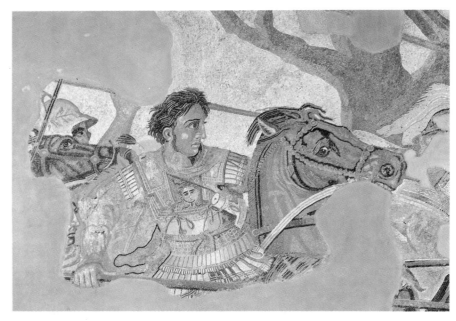

POMPEII: The Alexander mosaic, detail, original *c.* 300 BC

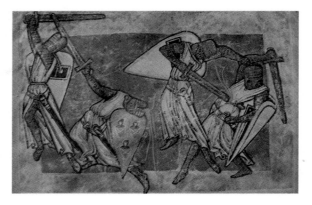

GERMAN MANUSCRIPT: *Alexander the Great in single combat*, 13th century

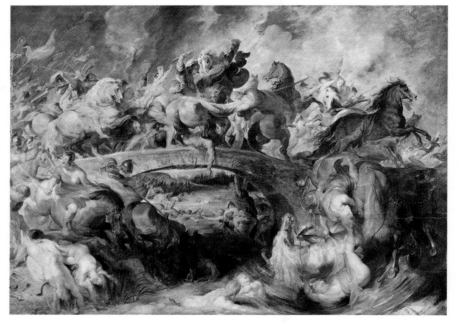

RUBENS: *The battle of the Amazons, c.* 1618

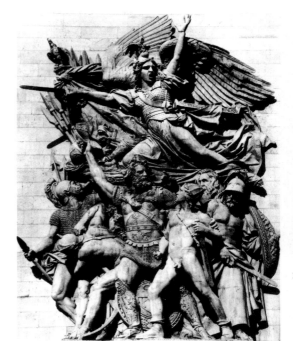

RUDE: *"La Marseillaise"*, 1833-36

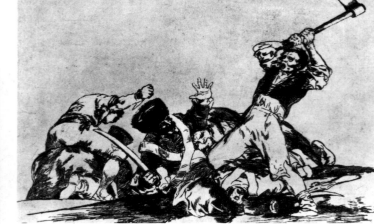

LEUTZE: *Washington crossing the Delaware*, 1850

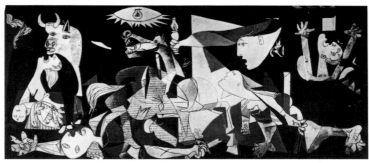

PICASSO: *Guernica*, detail, 1937

GOYA: *The same*, from *The Disasters of War*, 1810-15

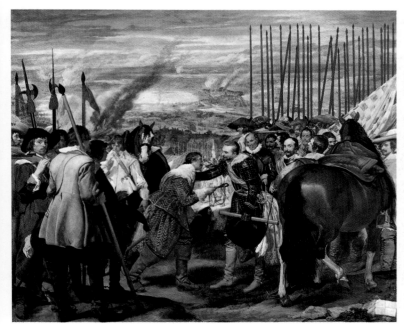

VELAZQUEZ: *The surrender of Breda*, detail, 1634-35

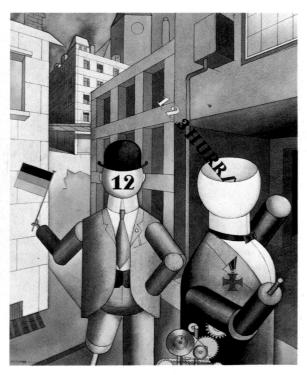

GROSZ: *Republican automatons*, 1920

Landscape

The curve of Mount Fujiyama starts long and slow from the left, almost accelerating to the climax of the peak on the right. The orangeish cone of the volcano, lifted clear of the stubble of the tree-line, is only just veined with snow at its peak. A flock, a shoal, of fleecy clouds moves horizontally from left to right across the deepening blue of the sky. Suspended in the sky on the left, the title – *Southerly wind and fine weather (Gaifū Kaisei)* – also suggests springtime or early summer, perhaps at dawn when the upper slopes, catching the rising sun, can glow red, suggesting the fierce inner life that once carried the volcano upwards in that matchless sweep.

No human being intrudes. The vision seems pure landscape, distilled to its essence. Yet it is preserved in one of the most fragile of mediums: coloured inks on a sheet, a mere 35 centimetres (14in) or so across, of that famous soft, almost transparent Japanese paper made from the fibre of mulberry tree bark – a woodblock print, in the "brocade" tradition, which reproduced, for the popular middle-class market of Edo (Tokyo) ephemeral images of *ukiyo*, the "floating world" of leisure. It dates from the late 1820s, and one of the inscriptions hung in the sky is its designer's signature: *Hokusai Aratame Iitsu Hitne.*

Hokusai (1760-1849) was then working at about the same time as his rather younger contemporaries, Constable and Turner, were revolutionizing the concept of landscape in the West. His own treatment was no less revolutionary, but very different, in terms of an abstraction from natural forms into a clarity that would have astonished and perhaps baffled them. It is only twentieth-century painting and printmaking that have accustomed Westerners to such grand simplicities of colour and design. This print is at one level a brilliant exercise in formal values. The symmetry of Fuji, set asymmetrically within the rectangle of the block, is balanced with the most delicate precision against the echoing shape, inverted, of the sky, and tuned to vibrant life by the subtlety of the contours, by the rhythmic shoaling of the cloud, and the modulation of the extraordinarily restrained range of colour. It is one of the most famous of Hokusai's most famous sequences, the *Thirty-six views of Mt Fuji*. They occur late in the development of a highly sophisticated tradition, though they are also a radical innovation.

Japan was at this time still a country forbidden to Europeans, but Hokusai was aware, through engravings, of Western traditions in art, and took something from them (shocking his compatriots) – thus the single, low viewpoint here is a departure from Japanese tradition, and Hokusai's devotion to landscape as such was also new. Yet the image – so superb in grandeur, so lyrical in its solitude – is wholly and quintessentially Japanese, and its intensity must owe much to the artist's obsession with Fuji as a sacred shrine, symbol almost of the Japanese national identity, even as Constable's intensity of vision of English landscape was fired by his Wordsworthian empathy with Nature, or as Cézanne's obsession with Mont Ste-Victoire answered some deep necessity of his imagination.

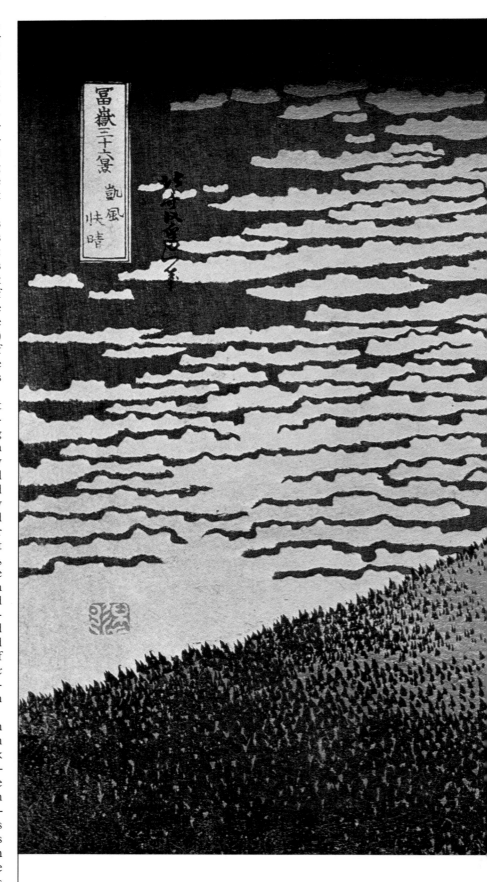

HOKUSAI: *Southerly wind and fine weather*, from *Thirty-six views of Mt Fuji, c. 1823-29*

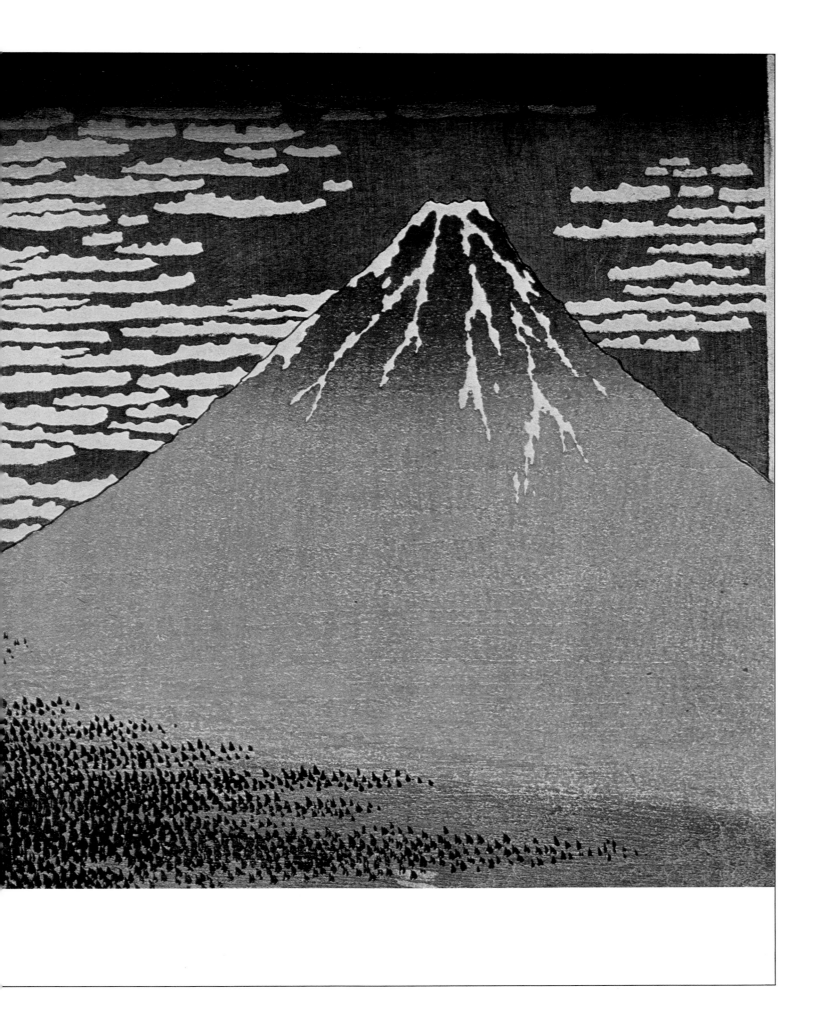

Landscape

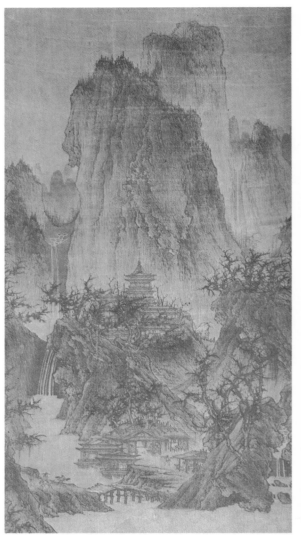

LI CHENG?: *Temple in the mountains after rain, c.* 1000?

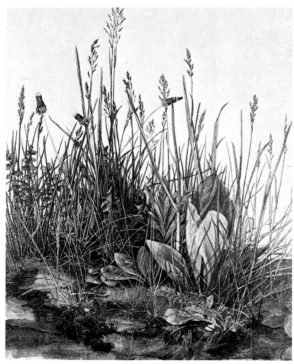

GIOVANNI DI PAOLO: *Madonna and Child in a landscape, c.* 1432

POMPEII (left):
Landscape with villa,
detail, *c.* 50 BC

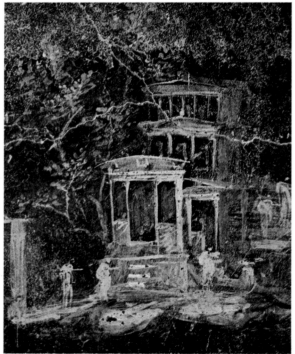

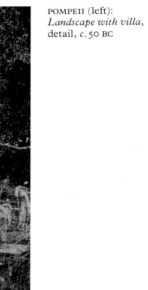

DURER (right):
The piece of turf, 1503

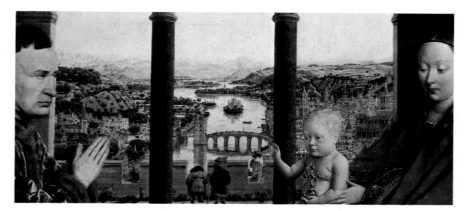

JAN VAN EYCK: *The Madonna with Chancellor Rolin*, detail, *c.* 1435

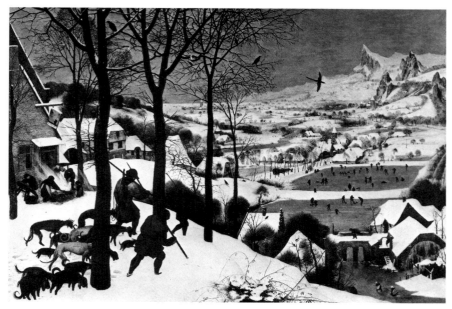

BRUEGEL: *The hunters in the snow*, 1565

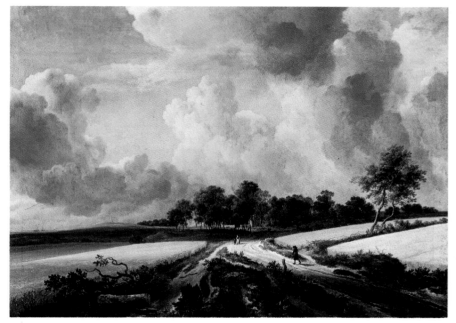

JACOB VAN RUISDAEL: *Wheatfields*, *c.* 1670

Landscape as the prime subject for a painting occurs perhaps earliest in China, during the Tang dynasty, and by Song times (tenth and eleventh centuries) the theme was being expressed in variations that would prove endless – dreamlike visions of the world emerging from mist, fantastic crags, rivers as long as time itself, and the dreamer man the poet, a minute figure almost invisible in the vastness of his imagination.

Such absorption in nature comes much later in the West; in the fourteenth century the poet Petrarch is recorded as the first European to climb a mountain for the sake of the view. Glimpses of landscape survive from the paintings of classical antiquity, treated relatively naturalistically, but strictly as background material. When landscape began to reappear in medieval art it was highly stylized and used for symbolic or decorative effect. The elements of landscape in Giovanni di Paolo's beautiful *Madonna and Child*, for instance, are clearly treated as decorative pattern, and are far removed from the remarkable study of botanical reality shown in Dürer's watercolour *The piece of turf*. Here, a single clump of grass is scrutinized with an intensity that seems to summarize a whole landscape. Dürer's studies were, however, closer to still life than to that interest in sheer space and the wonder of the natural world revealed in all its detail by light which was to characterize the great landscapes of the seventeenth to nineteenth centuries. The techniques – especially perspective – needed to realize such a perception in paint are in evidence by the time of the van Eycks. But their crystalline vistas, though integral contributions to the mood of the whole composition, are subsidiary to the human action. It is only in the sixteenth century, in that meeting-place of the north and south, Venice, and above all in the mysterious imagination of Bellini (see pp. 72–73) that man and Nature become equal partners.

With Bruegel, landscape has taken precedence over the people who humanize it, absorbing the tragic or comic concerns of life indifferently into its immensity. In his *The hunters in the snow*, the hunched figures trudging through snow or scattered upon the frozen river are turned into expressive cyphers of winter itself, the brittle stillness, the sharp clarity and stark contrasts of forms in raw air becoming the true subject of the painting. The exaltation of ordinary landscape as "hero" of the picture, and as a distinct and valid branch of art, was the achievement of the great Dutch masters of the seventeenth century who reflected, in their celebration of the material fabric of life, the independence, peace and prosperity of a new-born nation. A spirit of confidence invests their landscapes, ordered according to the demands of an agrarian economy, enclosed fields spreading under a vast summer sky or lying dormant in winter. Unlike Hokusai, Ruisdael, in a painting such as *Wheatfields*, dwells lovingly on detail. Yet for all its particularized appearance, the painting represents in fact a most skilful selection from the unconfined vistas of nature, orchestrated by the light into an overall harmony as grand and solemn as Hokusai's.

Landscape

The ability of an artist to grasp landscape, to order it into coherent and meaningful form, depends on man's ability to control his environment. The vision of Nature not raw and hostile but benign, tamed to serve human needs, is celebrated in many English conversation pieces of the eighteenth century – scenes of landed gentry who sit or stroll through countryside shaped by the hand of man, as ordered and harmonious as their own lives. Posed amid the evident prosperity of their own fields, Gainsborough's *Mr and Mrs Andrews* look out at us with unshakable confidence.

Gainsborough's picture derives from study of factual Dutch landscapes, but equally influential at the time were the Arcadian visions of the seventeenth-century French classicist Claude Lorraine who, with Poussin, gave landscape painting a dimension of poetry and a new artistic status. His mythical scenes, set in the idealized countryside around Rome, established a method of composing the elements of nature into a whole, suffused with a mellow, unifying light, which became a formula for many imitators who lacked his incomparable mastery of real effects in nature. Ideal landscape gave way to a greater realism with the rise of topographical or "view" painting – more or less comparable with a picture postcard – encouraged by travellers on the Grand Tour during the eighteenth century.

In the nineteenth century, it was the more awesome aspects of Nature, its power to transform landscape beyond the control of man, which seized the imagination of Romantic artists. Turner's extreme response was to lash himself to the mast of a ship in a gale, the better to observe its effects, and to spend hours at night recording the conflagration of the Houses of Parliament; here landscape virtually disappears into the volatile elements of fire, air and water. Yet Turner's visions were perhaps another aspect of the urge to control Nature – its fury tamed in a canvas.

Constable, with a fresh awareness of the way shifting light constantly fashions anew the physical world, developed a technique, anticipating the spontaneous directness of the Impressionists, which could capture in flecks of paint the very vibrancy of air and suggest the Wordsworthian vision of "the passions of man ... incorporated with the beautiful and permanent forms of Nature". The Realist Courbet was no less susceptible to such intimations of immortality, and his seascape is an eloquent salute to those timeless symbols of the infinite, the ocean and the horizon – symbols that still strike the onlooker with their profound simplicity.

Modern man's experience of the landscape is radically altered not only by flight but also by the spread of technology across the countryside, shrinking the world and creating new juxtapositions of form within it. Mondrian's distillation of a seascape to abstract, formal values acknowledges this as much as Hopper's inclusion of roads, railways and lighthouses in his matter-of-fact portraits of America's eastern seaboard – evidence of a continuing impulse to record the exact character of a specific place.

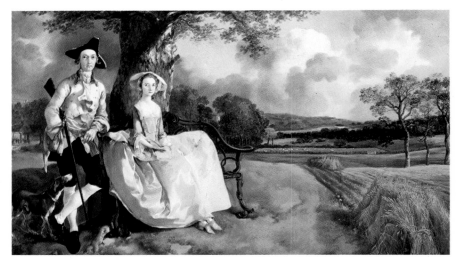

GAINSBOROUGH: *Mr and Mrs Andrews*, c. 1748

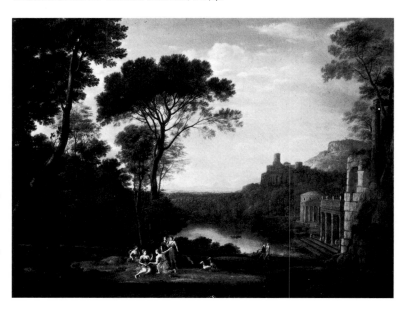

CLAUDE: *Egeria mourning over Numa*, 1669

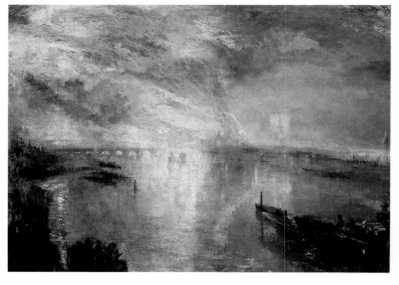

TURNER: *The burning of the Houses of Parliament*, 1834

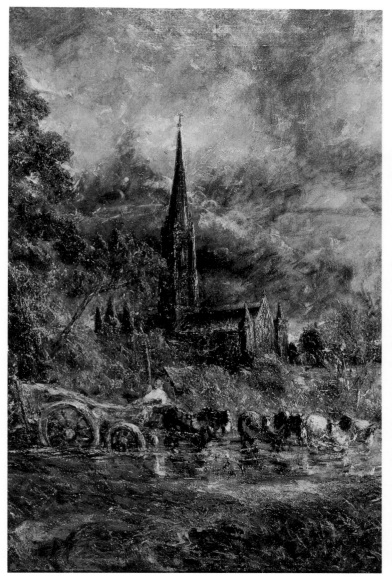

CONSTABLE (left): *Fording the river, showery weather*, detail, 1831

MONDRIAN (below): *The sea*, 1914

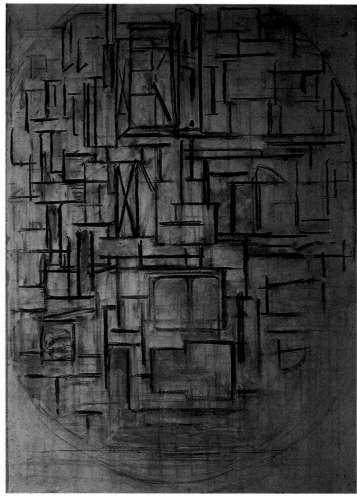

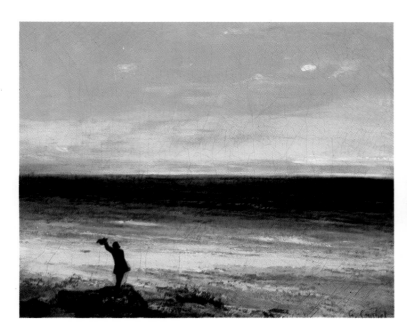

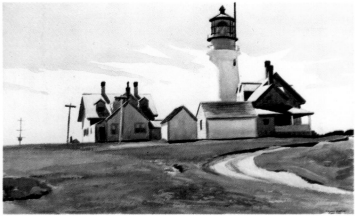

HOPPER (above): *Highland light*, 1930

COURBET (left): *Seaside at Palavas*, 1854

Animals

In 1940, boys in the French countryside of the Dordogne, at Lascaux, stumbled into a modest aperture in the earth that proved to open out into a series of caves. The limestone region of the Dordogne is very subject to internal erosion, and caves were no novelty, nor for that matter was evidence of prehistoric man – Les Eyzies, where years before Cro-Magnon man had been discovered, is near by. The calibre of the new find was, however, astounding, rivalled only by the famous Spanish cave of Altamira.

Across the rough, eroded walls and ceilings of the Lascaux caves rampage bulls, stags, bison, horses. They are drawn always in profile, painted direct on to the unprepared rock; sometimes, with a twist of body, an elementary effect of perspective is achieved. Moss or hair probably served as brush for the drawn outlines, but quite large areas are stained by a technique close to that of a modern spray-gun: colour blown on through a hollow bone. The pigments were mineral, the medium just water that soaked into the porous limestone. Anatomically, the delineation of the animals may not be literally precise, but in vitality and grandeur they have rarely been surpassed in the whole subsequent history of human art. Some are vast – more than four metres (13ft) long. What motives inspired their creation, what need they answered and what functions they performed, can only be a matter of speculation. Their intensity suggests a religious or magic relevance; sympathetic magic perhaps entered in – the notion that an image can provide power over the thing it represents; and these animals were mostly man's prey, his food and clothing. They express also, however, the irrepressible fascination of man – himself an animal – with the sheer vitality, the strength, speed and dangerous ferocity of animals, the exultation and at times the fear of their challenge to him – and also, surely, a profound sympathy in the blood with their beauty.

Man himself appears at Lascaux as a mere brittle symbol, vulnerable. The time range of the paintings is extraordinary: they are generally dated within some five thousand years round about 15000 BC, and all through that period men returned to add to them, sometimes superimposing but also sometimes respecting the existence of earlier images and not obliterating them.

The animals seem almost to float as in a dream across the depth of the rock and of time itself, unrelated to any landscape, silent yet suggesting the thunder of stampede. Or rather, they seemed. After 1945 Lascaux was opened up. Crowds thronged to see under modern lighting these marvels as the artists could never have seen them, working as they did in the faint flicker of oil-brand through the centuries, through the millennia, until for some reason the caves were abandoned and sealed in preserving darkness for 15,000 years or more. In a mere decade of exposure to light and the atmospheric pollution of mass curiosity the paintings deteriorated dangerously. Lascaux is now sealed off again, visited only by inspecting experts; its marvels seen by the ordinary viewer only second-hand, in film or, as here, in reproduction.

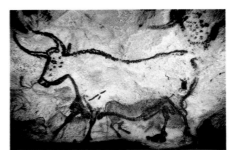

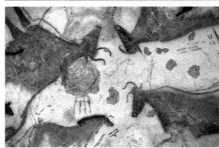

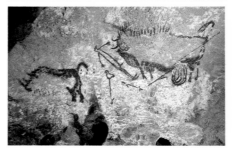

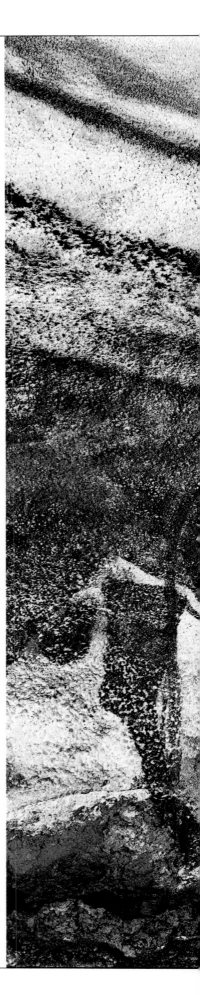

LASCAUX, FRANCE:
"The Hall of Bulls",
in use *c.* 15000 BC?

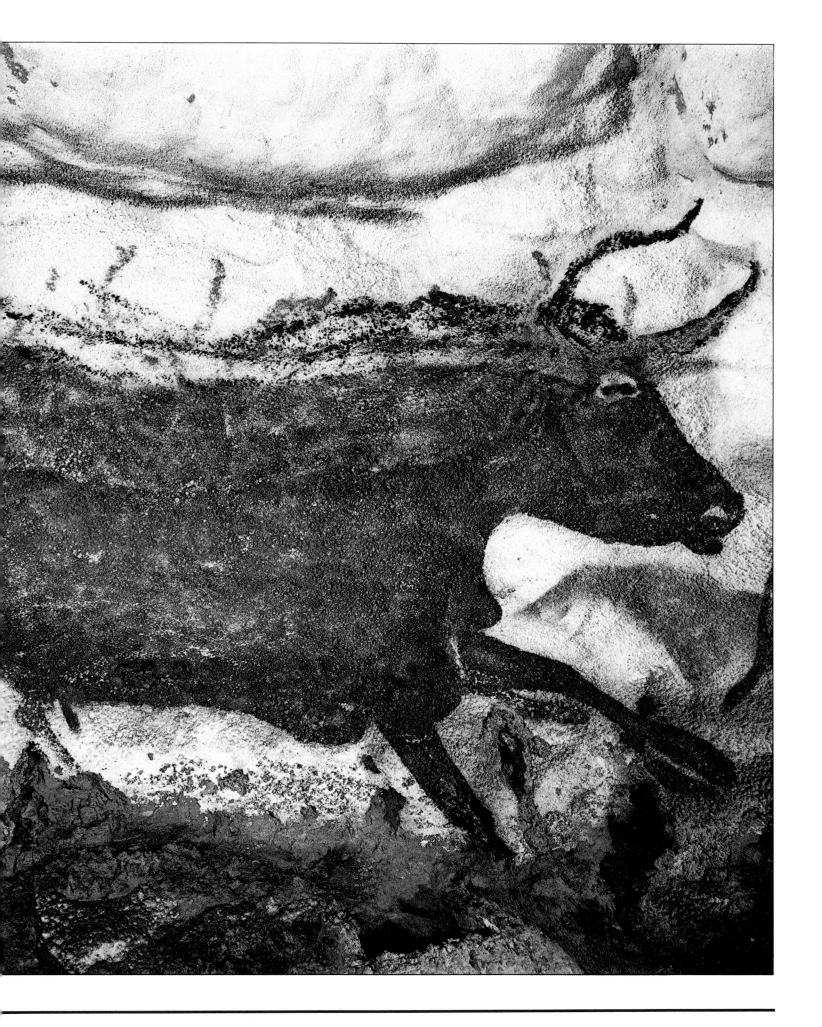

Animals

COURBET:
The death of the stag, 1867

CONSTANTINOPLE (below):
Adam naming the animals,
4th/5th century AD

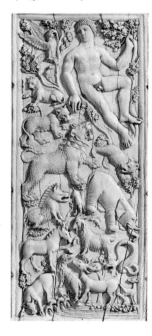

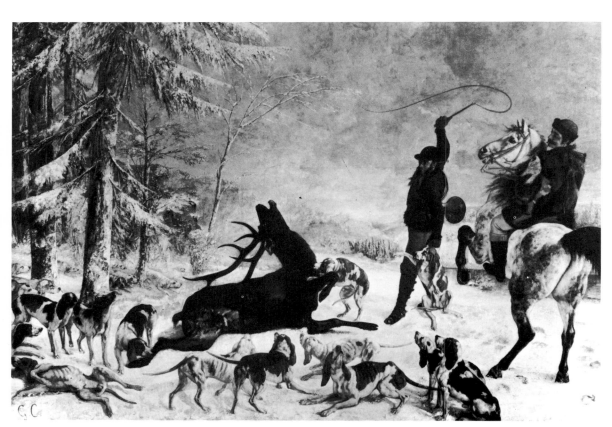

FRANCE (below): *To my sole desire*, detail from *The Lady of the Unicorn*, c. 1480–90

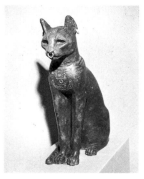

EGYPT: Bronze *Cat*, after 30 BC

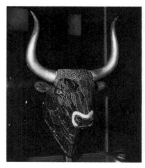

CRETE:
Bull's-head *rhyton*, c. 1500 BC

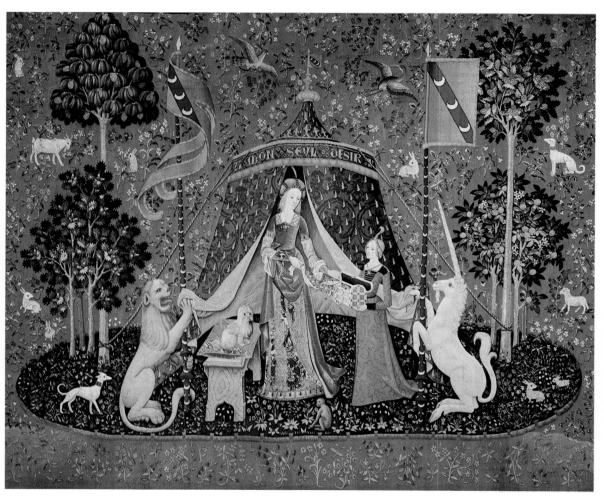

PICASSO:
Vollard Suite no. 85,
*Drinking Minotaur and
sculptor with two models*, 1933

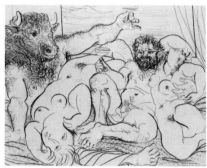

CANOVA (below):
Theseus and the Minotaur,
c. 1781–82

REMBRANDT (below): *Three elephants, c.* 1637

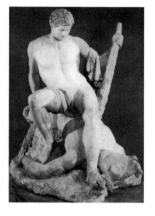

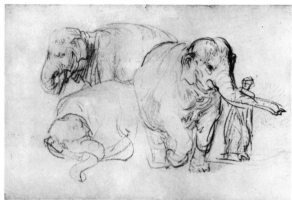

DÜRER (below): *The young hare*, 1502

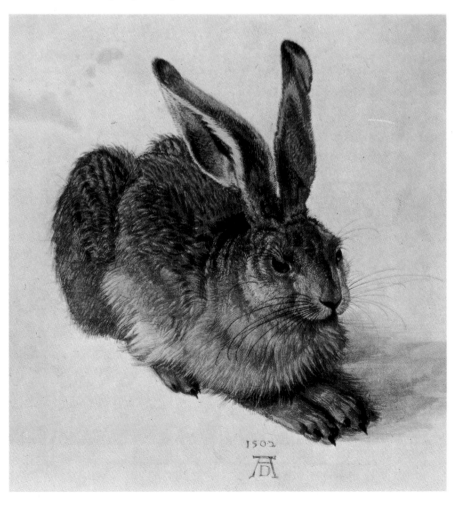

One of the most idyllic images of the relationship between man and animals is provided by a justly famous ivory panel of the fifth century: the subject is from Genesis, showing Adàm at ease in the fork of a tree naming the animals, from the eagle and lion down to the little sprawl of a lizard and even the dreaded serpent. Placid, highly formalized, it expresses a matter-of-fact vision of an amicable Paradise. More than 1,500 years later, Courbet's exultant painting celebrates the critical moment of a very different relationship, but one evidently unquenched since Lascaux: the electric vitality of its composition – the curve of the whiplash, the agonized straining of the stag's head – seems a visual equivalent of the triumphant paean of the huntsman's horn ringing in the cold air.

Man's ambivalent attitude towards animals, veering from pastoral care to the aggressiveness of the hunter, responds to the variety of roles animals play in human life. In art, however, it is their symbolic role that has most consistently provided painters and sculptors with rich subject matter. Akin to man, yet separated from him in the dumb, incommunicable mystery of their own lives, animals have always been endowed in art, literature and folklore with moral as well as physical attributes – admired, disliked or feared – and often, too, with god-like powers. Their identification with certain qualities, real or imagined, has profoundly influenced the way in which they are represented. In ancient Egypt, where the cat was sacred, images of this animal are remarkable not so much for their naturalism as for their aura of aloof power. Whilst cats are comparatively rare in art, the bull recurs again and again with divine or semi-divine attributes, its strength and potency identified with the life force itself, and frequently finding expression in sacrificial objects, as in the elaborate bull's-head vessel (*rhyton*) from Crete.

Artists have also given form and shape to many imaginary beasts – the dragons that romp and swirl through the art of China, for example, or, in the West, the enigmatic unicorn, originally perhaps derived from descriptions of the rhinoceros but taking on in medieval tapestries an elegant beauty as symbol of the courtly synthesis of spiritual and erotic love. Medieval art swarms with animals of all kinds – on the carved misericords under choir seats, in the lettering and margins of illuminated manuscripts and in the carving of architectural bosses and capitals – some representations semi-abstract, some fantastic, some naturalistic.

Animal mythology persists. The legendary Minotaur, a sculptural theme for Canova in the nineteenth century, reappears with characteristic gusto in the etchings of Picasso. Yet from early on, too, there is a strong tradition of objective observation, whether it be Rembrandt conveying with a few chalk-strokes the weight and presence of the exotic elephant, or Dürer tracing the quivering vitality of the hare in the minutest detail. Though Dürer's hare is probably the single best-seller of all animal portraits, the creature which has delighted artists more than any other, as we see on the next two pages, is the horse.

Animals

Artists have always found two contrary qualities in the horse – untamed elemental strength and speed, and the beauty of such power harnessed by man. Even when the horse as a working animal seems obsolete, the combination of horse and rider remains a formidable image of authority and power: thus the Romans portrayed the Emperor Marcus Aurelius, a precedent for Verrocchio to immortalize the military leader Colleoni in the emphatic arrogance of command. Baroque painters – notably Rubens – and Romantics such as Delacroix likewise fused both man and horse into a single compulsive rhythm of energy, as physically indissoluble as the centaurs of Greek myth.

Gods in horse shape may be rare (too useful, perhaps, as vehicles for other gods), but the mythical Greek winged horse, Pegasus, became the symbol of poetic genius. An intriguing parallel in China is the miraculous bronze of a horse rising from the wings of a flying swallow, modelled by an unknown sculptor in the early Han period, about AD 100. Leonardo, who improvised again and again on the theme of the horse alone, expresses in the dynamism of his line a similar sense of boundless energy, almost the force of the imagination itself. Humbler and quieter versions of the horse are among the many realistic pottery animals from the Tang tombs, and in the West, too, many artists have concentrated more upon the horse's solidity, stamina and strength; the patient endurance of the ordinary work-horse has never been portrayed more searchingly than in the studies of a saddle-horse – somewhat tired, nostrils slit, but ears and eyes showing willingness – drawn by Pisanello in the mid-fifteenth century.

The breeding of thoroughbred strains in eighteenth-century Britain inspired that painter of genius, Stubbs, who married the faithful likeness of such aristocratic beasts into a formal rhythm as satisfying as a Greek frieze. Géricault, who used form rather to express the impatient spirit, and whose empathy with animal vitality permeates his work, captured a horse galvanized by a thunderstorm as if the lightning had entered its very bloodstream. Later, Degas was fascinated by vitality of the racetrack, the shapes constantly created and recreated by nervous animal energy responding to the sensitive strength of a jockey's hands and feet. His intense observation and his awareness of the compressed forms of horses in motion paralleled (and perhaps responded to) the work of the photographer Eadweard Muybridge who demonstrated in 1878 that traditional depictions of the horse at full gallop with legs extended fore and aft were quite inaccurate.

Even through the increasingly formal preoccupations of the twentieth century the theme of rider and mount has sustained its fascination, reworked obsessively by the Italian sculptor Marini, whose most deceptively simple images contain harsh tensions, and translated by the Cubist Duchamp-Villon into a metaphor of brute mechanical power. We have yet to see those modern work-horses, the automobile and airplane, replace horse and rider as symbols of energy, grace and control in the imaginations of artists.

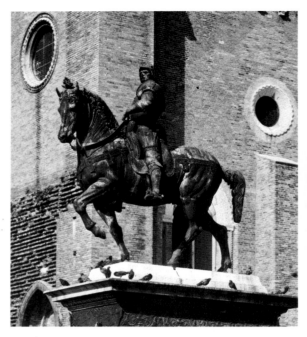

VERROCCHIO: *Bartolommeo Colleoni*, 1481-90

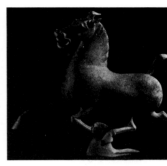

WUWEI, EASTERN CHINA: *"Flying Horse"*, 2nd century AD

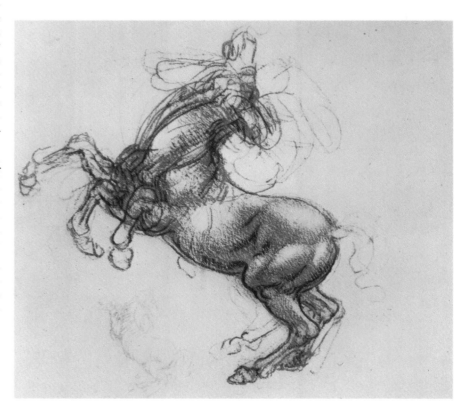

LEONARDO: *Study of a rearing horse*, c. 1498-90

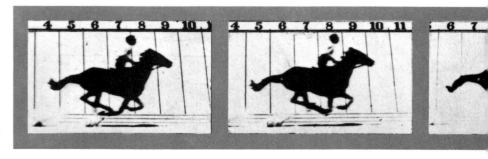

STUBBS (right): *Mares and foals*, 1762

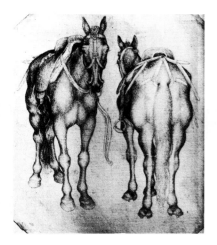

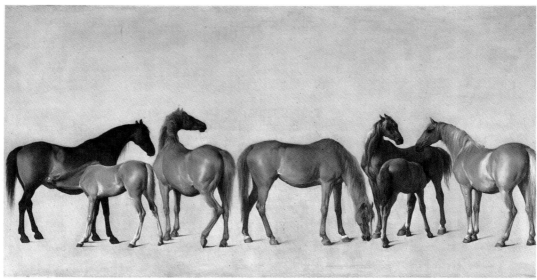

PISANELLO: *Horses, c.* 1433–38

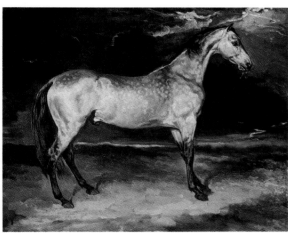

GERICAULT (left):
*A horse frightened by
lightning, c.* 1820

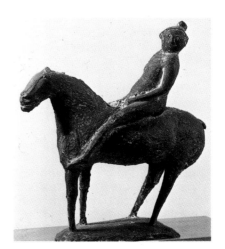

MARINI (right):
Little rider, 1946

DEGAS (below): *A carriage at the races*, 1877–80

DUCHAMP-VILLON (right):
The horse, 1914

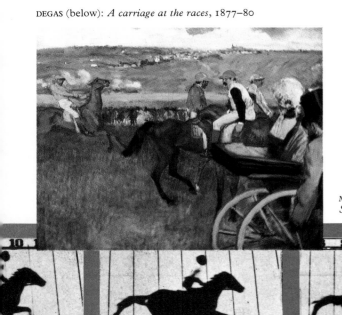

MUYBRIDGE (below):
Sally Gardner running, 1878

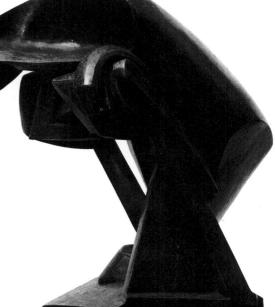

Still Life

Van Gogh's still life is not a large painting – only 63 centimetres (about 2ft) wide – but it is packed with meaning. The component items are arranged, not casually, but almost regimented, on the most important element of the painting: the drawing-board, its far edge precisely parallel with the top edge of the picture, the grain of the wood emphasized by the thrust of the brush on the thick paint. The subject matter is otherwise much as can be found at almost any time in the long history of still-life painting: pot, plate, bottle, candle, book, vegetables. This time, though, the items are positive characters, and the occasion of their being painted is crucial for the artist.

Van Gogh painted this in January 1889 – one of the first pictures he finished after his calamitous breakdown the month before, when he became finally alienated from his colleague Gauguin, who was staying with him in Arles, and ended up by depositing a severed piece of his own ear in a brothel. Dr Felix Rey, who treated van Gogh, encouraged him to paint as a therapeutic activity, and during the period between the first attack and his near-inevitable relapse in February, 1889, van Gogh appears to have been attempting to reaffirm both his style and his sanity. To his brother and his enduring pillar of strength, Theo, he wrote: "I'm so eager to work that it amazes me". He desperately reworked the famous painting of his chair, and painted a pair of portraits of Dr Rey and of Madame Roulin, together with two important self-portraits of his bandaged head which illustrated a direct confrontation with his sickness as well as his artistic aspirations. His inability to separate his art from his illness is evident in a letter to Theo: " . . . let me go on with my work; if it is that of a madman, well, so much the worse".

Still life with drawing-board becomes in this context an exercise in equilibrium. A virtual recipe or prescription for health, it details ingredients: food, drink, book and candle, and van Gogh's inseparable solace, pipe and tobacco. The letter asserts his identity from outside, the envelope legibly addressed to him and, no doubt, from Theo in Paris. The book is not any book, not even a novel by Zola, but titled as F.V. Raspail's *Manuel Annuaire de la Santé*, a treatise on health and hygiene. The vegetable heads shown may be garlic not onion; garlic is recommended by Raspail.

All these are set out on the drawing-board, the latter the arena on which, as on an easel, the painter has to resolve his disorientation. Formally, the picture's composition is strung taut on the thrust and counterpoise of almost exaggerated diagonals and plunging perspective; its tension is almost perilous, just held in check by the two strong assertive uprights of bottle and candle. The candle is lit, the flame alive. In van Gogh's hands the still life becomes a vibrant expression of his own personality, a testimony of faith and of hope. He may use traditional subject matter and devices (many earlier Dutch still lifes are signed thus on a *trompe-l'oeil* letter) but the total effect, and the whole significance of his picture, is entirely different. The still life becomes humanized, almost a psychological self-portrait.

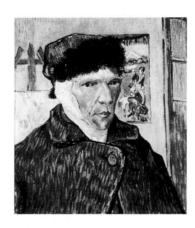

VAN GOGH: *Self-portrait*, 1889

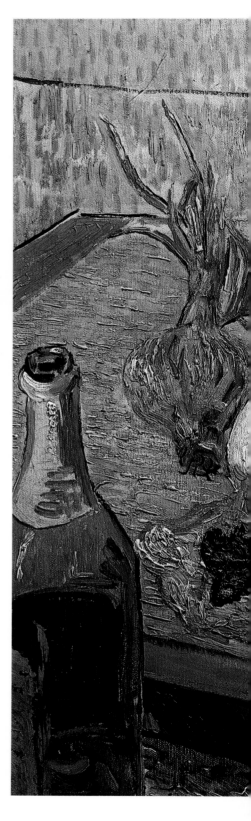

VAN GOGH: *Still life with drawing-board*, 1889

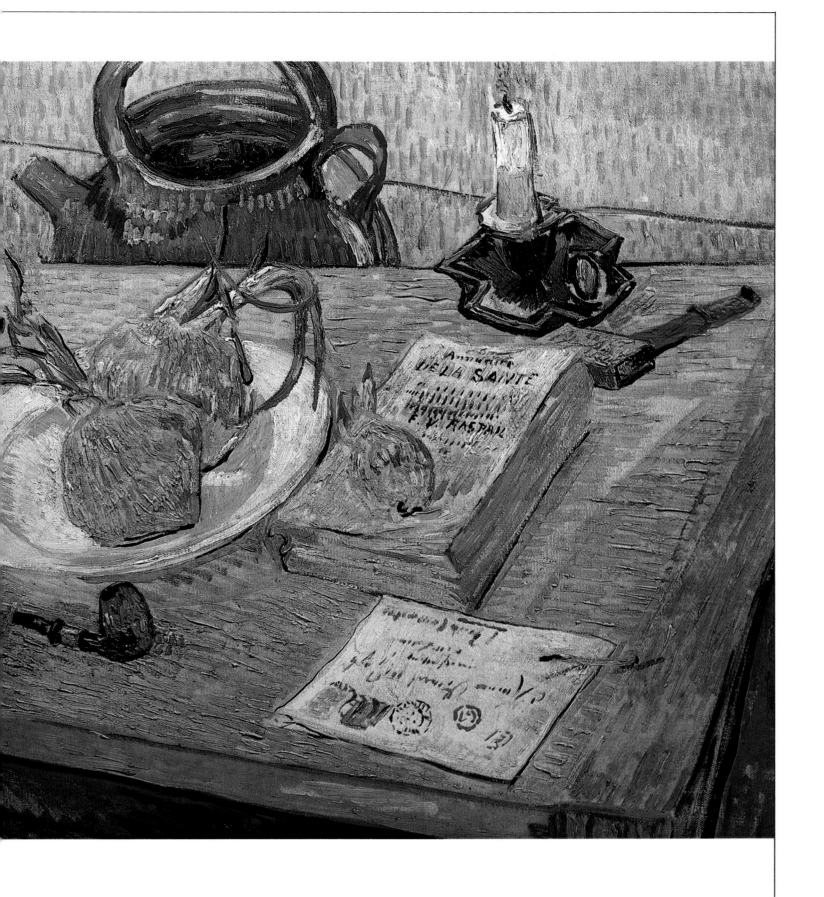

Still Life

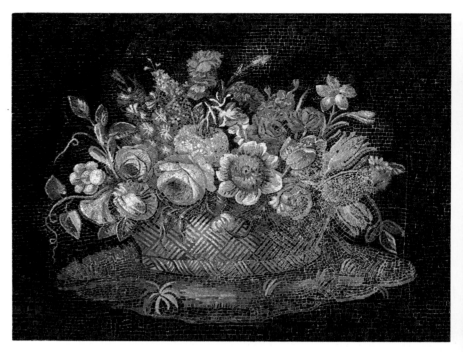

ROME: *Mosaic basket of flowers*, 2nd century AD

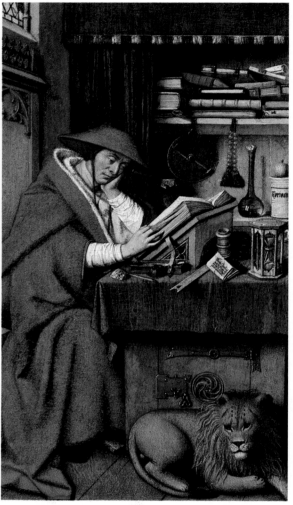

VAN EYCK: *St Jerome*, detail, 1442

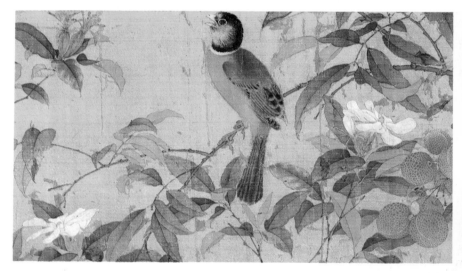

ZHAO JI: *Birds and flowers*, detail, 12th century

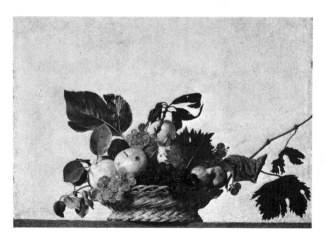

CARAVAGGIO: *A basket of fruit*, 1596

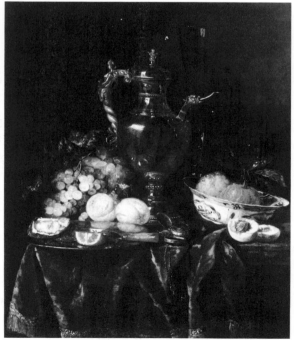

VAN BEYEREN: *Still life with a wine ewer*, after 1655

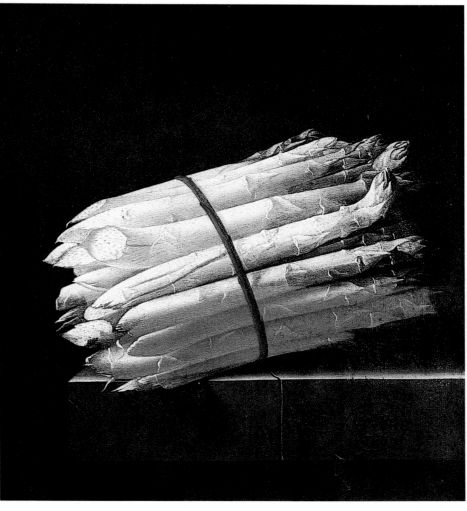

COORTE: *A bundle of asparagus*, 1703

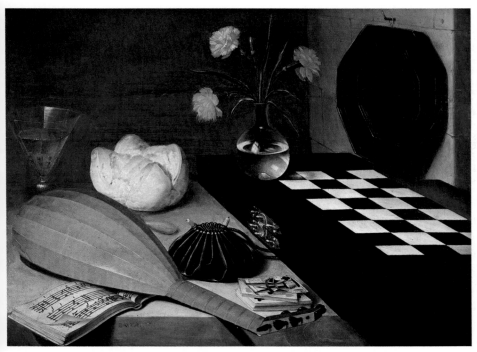

BAUGIN: *Still life with a chequer-board*, c. 1630

As we have just seen, a painting of still life may be more complex than it seems. The artist's state of mind is seldom as relevant to our understanding of a picture as it is in van Gogh's work, however; still lifes are more often painted – and intended to be enjoyed – purely as demonstration pieces which show off the artist's skill. Their history goes back to the legend of the Greek painter Zeuxis in the fifth century BC painting a bunch of grapes with such deceptive illusionism that birds tried to peck them. No early Greek still lifes survive, but examples recur in later antiquity, in wall-paintings, as at Pompeii, and in mosaics rendering fruit, vegetables and other staples of daily life in more or less naturalistic detail. In China, too, there is a long tradition of bird- and flower-paintings which capture with the greatest delicacy the subtle and evanescent beauty of fruit or petal.

The still life is, in large part, a salute to life, a celebration, and the persistence of the tradition may rely largely on the strength of man's reluctance to admit that, like life itself, the material pleasures of food and drink, the solid preciousness of silver and gold, of jewels and rich fabric are as transitory as flowers. Artists of the early Renaissance who, after the passage of centuries, began to take up again the theme of still life, were concerned to add a spiritual significance to their arrangements of objects. The items they chose often had some special, symbolic connotation (a lily for purity) and symbols of mortality, conventionally a skull, appeared among food or flowers as warnings of the passage of time, stern correctives to the vanity of life (*vanitas*). Yet we can see in the Eyckian depiction of St Jerome in his study that the books, hour-glass, writing instruments, glass vase, are described with the same loving scrutiny as the saint himself (and more convincingly than his lion).

It needed only for the artist to focus on the still-life elements alone, and indeed this began to happen during the fifteenth century. At the end of the following century the new naturalism of Caravaggio produced still lifes of startling virtuosity. A painting such as *A basket of fruit* does not depend on the narrative or symbolic significance of the objects displayed but bears out Caravaggio's own belief that the inanimate world was a worthy challenge to the artist and that it took as much skill to paint a good picture of fruit or flowers as of figures or faces.

The golden age of northern still life came famously in seventeenth-century Holland, whose citizens delighted in decorating their homes with technically flawless reflections of their own possessions. Artists such as van Beyeren, in his staggering accumulation of fruit, meat, fish, glass and silver on a banqueting table, or Coorte, who could deceive the eye with a simple bunch of asparagus, brought an astonishing illusionism to the genre. Yet profounder messages were often still concealed in even the most precise depictions of objects. The French painter Baugin's *Still life with chequer-board* is in fact an allegory of the five senses – sight, sound, taste, smell and touch – the transitory given a superb, formal permanence.

Still Life

From the seventeenth to the nineteenth century, Western critics and historians argued about the relative merits of the various branches of painting, from "history" painting at the top to, almost invariably, still life at the bottom. If history painting challenged the human imagination to its noblest achievements, still life was held to call on the imagination not at all, to be mere copying, servile imitation of superficial appearance – the basic prose of the inventory compared with the lofty poetry of the epic. Yet quite clearly many of the greatest artists have devoted exactly the same concentration of imaginative vision to still life as to any other subject. Rembrandt's still lifes are rare, but include masterpieces as extraordinary as his studies of the carcass of a *Flayed ox*, in which his characteristic drama of light and shade, of troubled and expressive movement of texture and colour, invests the butchered animal with an almost tragic quality.

Other painters of the period specialized entirely in still lifes, and included a few whose work has a contemplative poetry of form and colour that lifts it far above mere imitation. The eighteenth-century French artist Chardin showed what magical transformations could be effected in still lifes which are no longer cluttered inventories of luxuries but solemn, harmonious arrangements of everyday objects. Chardin's colour is rich yet muted, the texture of his paint revealing in the humblest ingredients nourishment for the spirit.

By the end of the nineteenth century, the Impressionists had shown that literally exact depiction of nature – live or still – was not necessarily the most effective way to capture a subject. Some of the most painstakingly exact still lifes of all were (and still are) of flowers – sometimes focused on an individual plant, essential illustrations to botanical and herbal studies. Yet it was Odilon Redon, Symbolist precursor of the Surrealists, whose flowers went beyond objective accuracy to penetrate the mystery of their ephemeral loveliness. His remarkable pastels can produce an electric, almost supernatural vibration.

Cézanne found in still life an ideal vehicle for pictorial research – for his patient reconciliation of the visible world with the flat surface of the canvas, revealing in his apples, his tilted table-top, a monumental solidity. The reality sought here does not seek to deny the reality of the paint and has nothing to do with sleight-of-hand illusionism; compare his table-cloth with the hanging sheet in Raphaelle Peale's *trompe-l'oeil*. The Cubists, following Cézanne, found in still life a captive for dissection and reconstruction, and then, beginning to turn full circle, used actual elements – packets, newspaper cuttings, as in Gris' *Breakfast* – as deliberate contrast between pictorial representation of reality and reality itself. This relationship has fascinated many twentieth-century artists, obsessed with the nature of perception and with the meaning (or validity) of art. Jasper Johns, transmuting the throwaway metal of beer-cans into the durable bronze of sculpture, seems concerned to make us think hard about the nature of the gap between the actual and the represented.

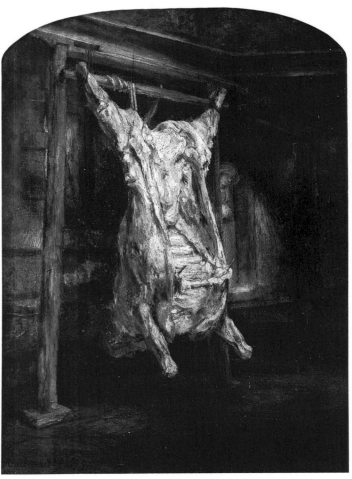

REMBRANDT: *The flayed ox*, 1655

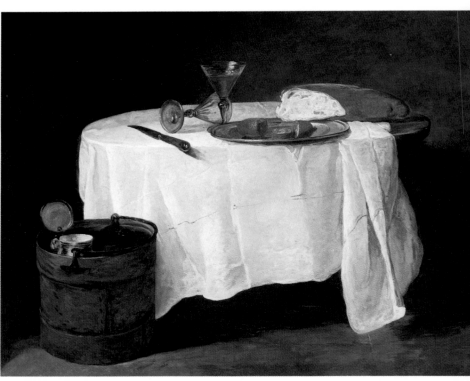

CHARDIN: *The white table-cloth, c.* 1737

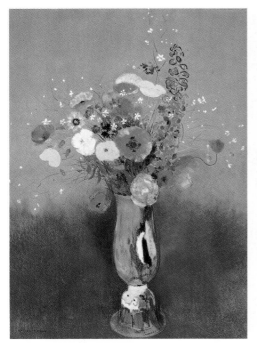

REDON: *Wild flowers*, after 1912

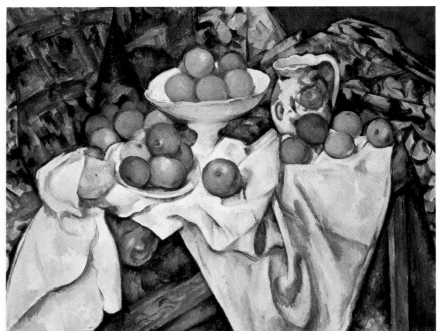

CEZANNE: *Still life with apples and oranges*, 1895-1900

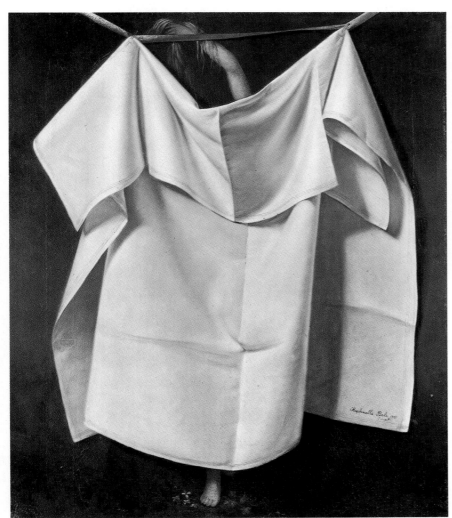

RAPHAELLE PEALE: *After the bath*, 1823

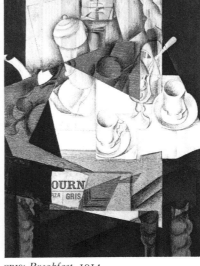

GRIS: *Breakfast*, 1914

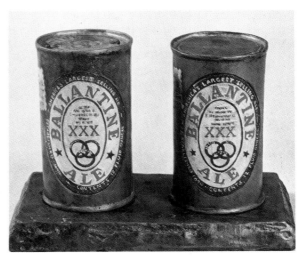

JOHNS: *Painted bronze II: ale-cans*, 1964

Images of Divinity

Rembrandt worked on this great etching in 1653, that is, when his genius was moving towards its last phase, as his vision became more sombre but also ever more profound. Then, later still, probably a few years·before his death in 1666, he worked the plate again, but he did not just "refresh" it where it was worn from heavy printing; he revised it so that its character in this state is quite different.

This etching is one of the grandest, most sublime of all his works, no less so than his greatest paintings. It is, to start with, one of the largest etchings – 38.7 × 45 centimetres ($15\frac{1}{4}$ × 18in). It responds to the account of the Crucifixion in the Gospel of St Luke: "And it was about the sixth hour, and there was a darkness over all the earth until the ninth hour. And the sun was darkened, and the veil of the temple was rent in the midst"; but it is as if, Christ having cried in a loud voice: "Father, into thy hands I commend my spirit", and died, the cloud has parted and light has cascaded from the heavens upon his body. About him, to left and right, the two crucified robbers are almost submerged in darkness, and at the foot of the Cross, from a disturbed medley of half-seen, half-felt figures, only the Roman centurion on his horse and a second mounted soldier with drawn sword emerge clearly defined. A commotion in the twilight on the left is a third horse, rearing in terror.

These last three elements, the horses and their riders, are entirely redrawn from their earlier state. The centurion must be he who, when he saw what was done, glorified God, saying: "Certainly, this was a righteous man". The figure is ambivalent, however, a profile antique yet familiar, and in fact borrowed from a medal by Pisanello of Gianfrancesco Gonzaga. This anachronistic, almost bizarre borrowing lends a further strangeness, a loneliness, a mystery to this already mysterious and emotionally supercharged setting.

Some prefer the clearer, more defined version, as in the second state of the etching, where the detail is controlled and gathered into the whole like the climax of a great Baroque organ fugue. This revised version, nevertheless, is a vision of tragedy in which the penetration of the natural order by the supernatural is rendered by the drama of light and shade with an intensity unparalleled in any other comparable work. In its inspiration, one may be reminded not of Bach's stately formal majesty but of the elemental pity and terror of Shakespeare's *King Lear*.

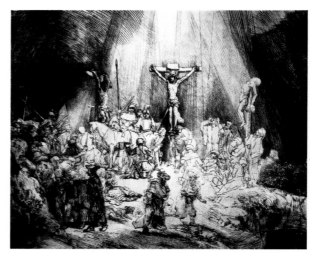

REMBRANDT: *The three crosses*, second state, 1653

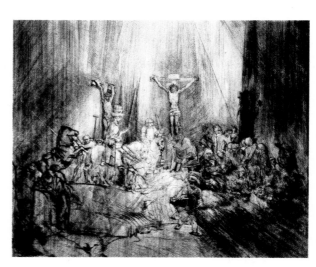

REMBRANDT: *The three crosses*, fourth state, *c.* 1662

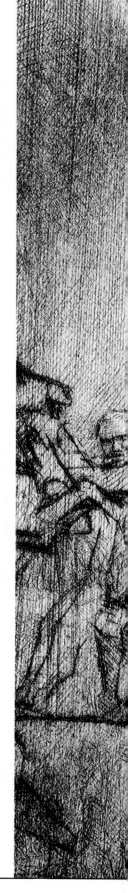

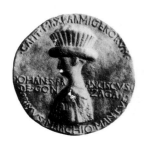 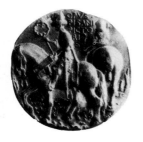

PISANELLO: *Gianfrancesco Gonzaga, c.* 1439

REMBRANDT: *The three crosses*, fourth state, detail

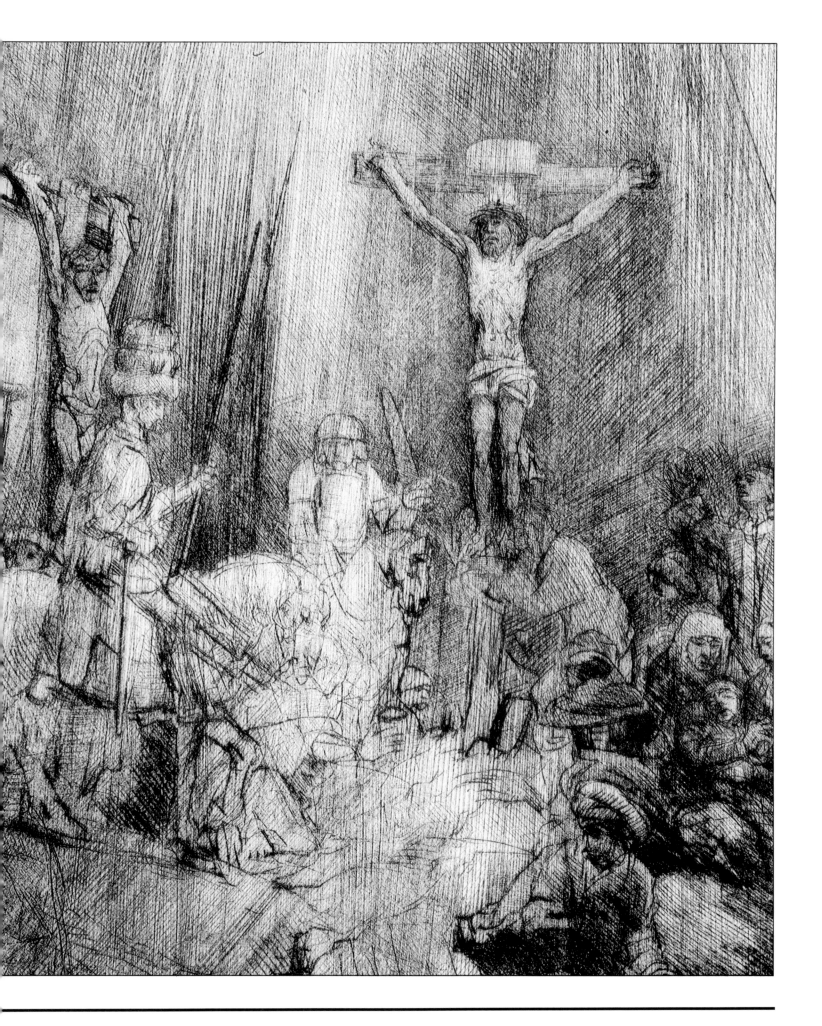

Images of Divinity

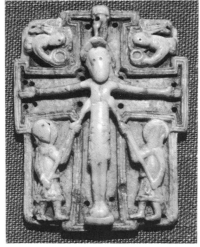 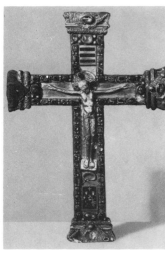 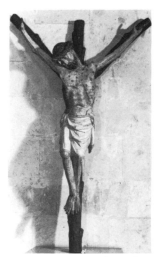

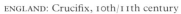 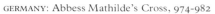 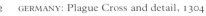

ENGLAND: Crucifix, 10th/11th century   GERMANY: Abbess Mathilde's Cross, 974-982   GERMANY: Plague Cross and detail, 1304

GRUNEWALD (below):
Isenheim altarpiece, 1515

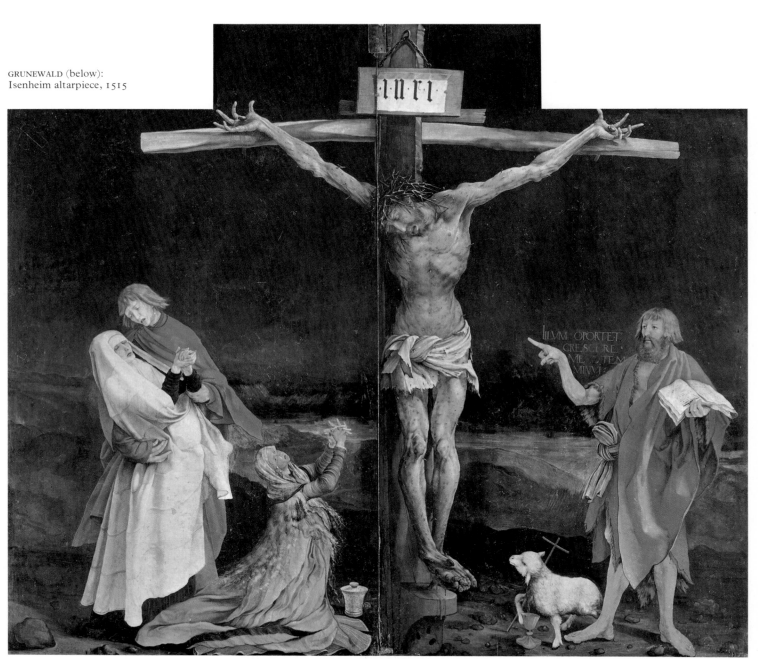

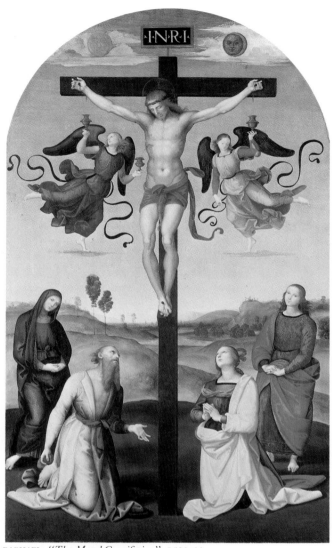

RAPHAEL: *"The Mond Crucifixion"*, 1502-03

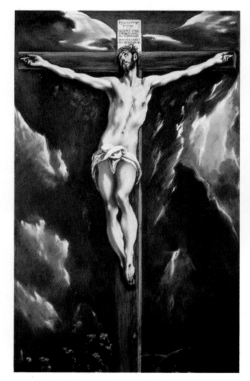

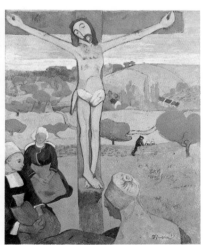

GAUGUIN: *"The Yellow Christ"*, 1889

EL GRECO (left): *Crucifixion with a landscape*, 1600-10

The image of Rembrandt's *Three crosses* is one of the most moving treatments of Christianity's central motif, the crucifixion of Christ and the Cross itself. As the focus of the Christian mystery and symbol of the faith, the subject has inspired recurrent interpretations, varying in style and approach according to the preoccupations of their artists' own times.

Early depictions of the Crucifixion tend to the schematic. Concentrated upon one of the most shameful forms of execution, reserved for slaves, criminals and agitators without civil rights, the theme must have been hard for many converts to accept when Christianity became the official religion of the Roman Empire, an Establishment creed. In early medieval art, the physical suffering of Christ tends not to be stressed. In some ivories, his body becomes essentially a second statement of the Cross itself, the horizontal of the arms crossing the vertical of the body, the face impassive, registering no pain or emotion. On processional Crosses such as Abbess Mathilde's at Essen, the body of Christ is a jewel, central but minute in the gold and enamel splendour of the crucifix; it disappears altogether on other Crosses which, whether unadorned and starkly geometric or richly elaborated, as in the great "carpet" pages of Celtic manuscripts, are used everywhere as the trademark of the faith.

In the Middle Ages, as interest in the physical world increased and Church doctrine emphasized the cult of Christ's body, the Passion came to be more realistically depicted, especially in the Gothic vision of northern Europe. The horrendous figure of the Plague Cross at Cologne, of 1304, responds to the anguish of the plagues already familiar in Europe and soon to devastate the continent. But the supreme example of the dolorous Crucifixion came later, in the famous Isenheim altarpiece by Grünewald of around 1515, where distortions of form and colour place almost intolerable stress upon Christ's agony. Although these methods were later to be revived by Expressionist artists, alternatives were at the same time being proposed in Renaissance Italy.

The composition of Raphael's early *Crucifixion* is classically serene, based on a scheme of intersecting circles, and radiating a serene, almost glad acceptance; salvation is assured. His solution, characteristic of the High Renaissance, states an ideal far removed from the reality of the Cross, emphasizing the spiritual in terms of physical perfection. A century later, in El Greco's version, Christ's bodily pain as he hangs upon the Cross seems almost transubstantiated into spiritual fire, a flame of ecstasy aspiring upwards, the reverse of the appalling collapse in Grünewald.

The theme endures. In Gauguin's *Yellow Christ* of 1889, the formal concerns of his revolutionary Symbolism are applied to the depiction of Breton peasants at their traditional devotions. A provincial Crucifixion of uncertain date from the little local chapel at Trémalo is here transposed through his highly personal style of flattened colour and decorative patterning into an image of a faith at once simple and profound.

Allegory, Myth and Fantasy

Allegory is the narrative description of a subject under the guise of another suggestively similar – a technique of ambiguity no less widespread in the visual arts than it is in literature. Artists in every culture have been able to convey layers of rich meaning by depicting figures of mythology or moral or religious allegory, often identified by conventional symbols (attributes). The themes acted out could be used for didactic purposes or simply as pegs on which to hang decorations – pliable raw material from which to shape satisfactory aesthetic forms. As the tradition behind such pictures decays, and as their decoding becomes subject for erudite debate, our enjoyment of them is likely to depend mainly on their visual qualities.

Giovanni Bellini's vision called *"The Sacred Allegory"* is one of the most fascinating and haunting of all, yet by no means untypical in that it is no longer capable of precise interpretation. Its attribution to Bellini, rather than to his brilliant pupil, Giorgione, is now generally accepted. Thereafter agreement ceases; it was long believed to have been conceived as an illustration to a fourteenth-century French poem on the pilgrimage of the soul. That may be part of it, but it is probably right to describe it specifically as a meditation on the Divine Incarnation.

The central figure, seated on a cushion, is certainly the Christ-child; he holds an apple, symbolic of the Original Sin from which he redeems mankind. The attendant little naked *putti* (one holding the Tree of Life) are doubtless angels, redeemed souls, but in form borrowed from pagan classical antiquity. There are further pagan echoes in the zone beyond the formal garden where beasts and even a centaur appear, and the waters, which in many mythologies represent immortality, also recall Lethe, the purging of earthly memories. The Virgin Mary, seated beneath a vine (symbolizing the blood of Christ) appears to judge between the crowned figure (Mercy/Peace?) and the woman on the left (Truth/Justice?). The sword is held by Simeon, who foretold the Passion. Next to him is Isaiah, who foretold the Virgin birth. The two figures on the right are Job and St Sebastian, here admitted to the world theologically conceived as in grace – the zone within the marble terrace.

The obscurity of the allegory to all but the most learned specialists (and even they disagree) is baffling, and yet the picture is spellbinding – inexplicable yet immediately acceptable as a reality in the setting of the north Italian landscape. It is the landscape, so tenderly and lyrically observed in the melting yet crystal-clear light, that was first established by the artist; the contemplative and now mysterious figures, each so solitary and yet linked by the web of some silent, blissful, communion, were then disposed on the marble terrace, the pattern of which is discernible through them in places. The whole has the irrational but compulsive logic of dream, structured on a beautiful counterplay of symmetry and asymmetry, and an underlying geometrically exact use of perspective. It has the intensity of a vision, of a divine order both informing and transcending nature.

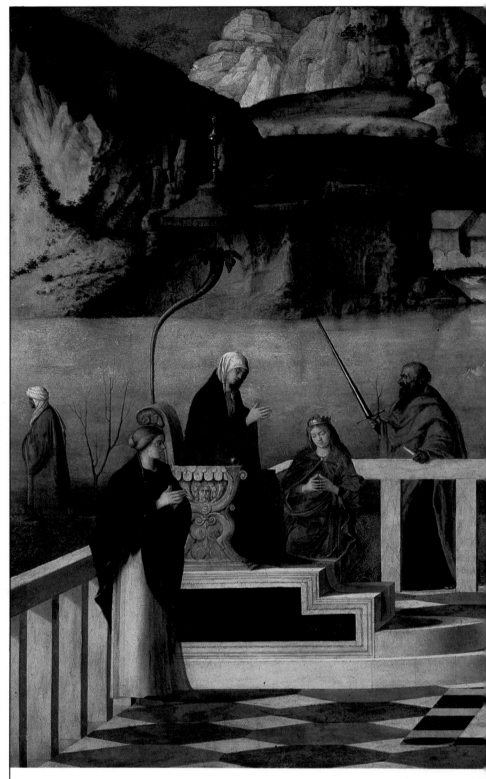

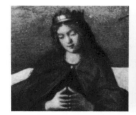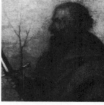

BELLINI: *"The Sacred Allegory"*, c. 1490   Mercy/Peace?   Simeon

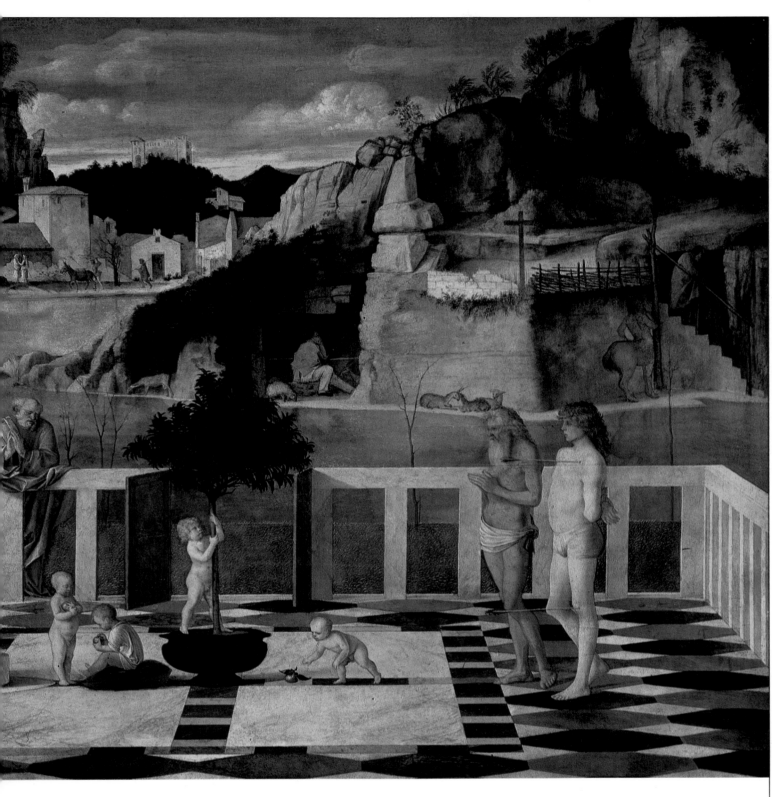

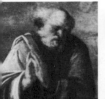
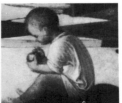

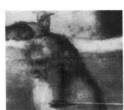
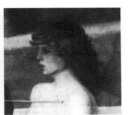

Isaiah   The Christ-child   Job   St Sebastian

Allegory, Myth and Fantasy

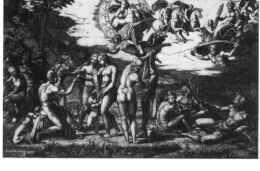

RAIMONDI: *The Judgment of Paris, c. 1516*

RUBENS (below): *The Judgment of Paris, c. 1632–35*

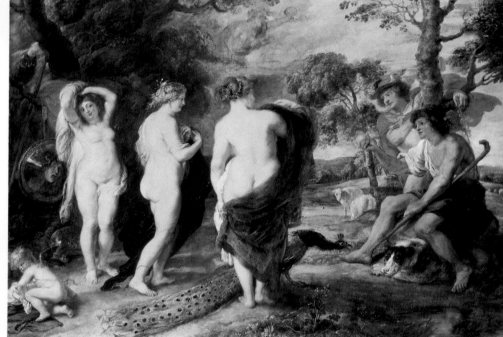

EWORTH (below):
Queen Elizabeth confounding the three goddesses, 1569

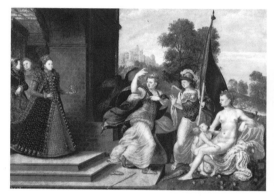

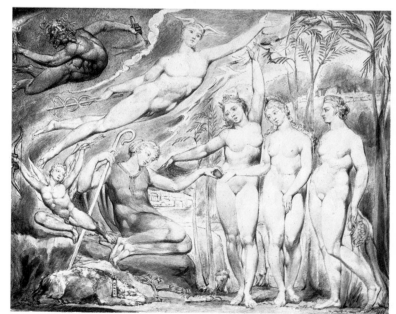

BLAKE: *The Judgment of Paris, 1817*

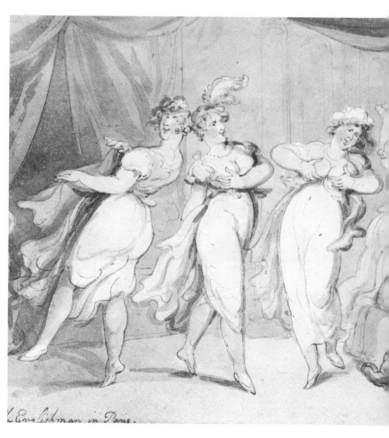

RAIMONDI: *The Judgment of Paris*, detail

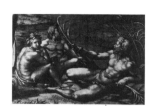

MANET (below):
"*Le Déjeuner sur l'Herbe*", 1863

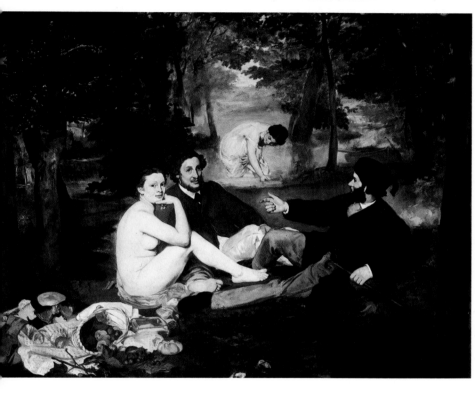

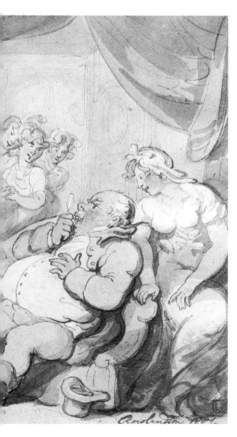

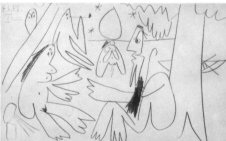

PICASSO: "*Le Déjeuner sur l'Herbe*", 1962

ROWLANDSON (left): *Englishman in Paris*, 1807

Many of the most persistent myths in Western culture evidently originated long before the first records of them in art and literature, surviving, no doubt, because they answered some profound need of the human imagination. Potent myths have endured even when the events they explained were forgotten, passing into the shared cultural heritage to be reinterpreted by subsequent ages.

One myth of perennial appeal is the story of the youth chosen by Jupiter to judge who was the fairest of three goddesses and to award her an apple. Paris' choice of Venus, which led to the seduction of Helen, the Trojan War and, indirectly, to the founding of Rome, was understandably popular in Greek and Roman art, but its continuing fascination surely depends on more than its symbolic or historical value.

Many versions exist in art, in part because of the opportunity afforded to paint nudes but also doubtless because the Judgment of Paris is about the irresistible appeal of beauty to the senses. Certainly, from the time of the Renaissance, artists have alluded to each other's versions of the myth, each rendering becoming richer by association with those that preceded it.

Marcantonio Raimondi's engraving is itself based on a lost design by Raphael, and includes divinities not directly concerned in the original story, perhaps water-nymphs and river-gods. In the sky ride Apollo in his chariot and Diana with the crescent moon in her hair, but the main centre of interest is the heroic treatment of the nude, the goddesses scarcely less muscular than the ideal male figure of Paris. Eroticism, entirely absent from this engraving, is the dominant strain in Rubens' version, which unashamedly invites male viewers to identify with Paris in contemplation of sensuously painted flesh.

In an ingenious adaptation of the story, a painter at the court of Elizabeth I allowed the Queen (decorously clad) to award herself the apple, suggesting that in Elizabeth Nature had surpassed the collective perfections of the routed goddesses. The Neoclassical revival of the eighteenth century brought renewed interest in the theme, though Blake's scorn for classical precedents is apparent in the leaping energy of his figures. His contemporary, Rowlandson, transformed the mood from an heroic to a ribald one: Paris becomes an old lecher, Hermes a procuress and the goddesses whores. Later, in one of the most controversial pictures of the nineteenth century, Manet omitted the central characters entirely and based his group on the reclining river-gods of Marcantonio's engraving. Whatever his private reasons for this quotation, the painting was a strong statement of artistic independence, setting free the academic studio nude in scandalous modern picnic with two clothed men. Picasso, in turn, exploited Manet's solution, claiming art equally with nature as raw material for the alchemy of his imagination. Here, with the accretions of the past almost evaporated, Picasso presents himself as a modern Paris, forced to choose the greatest beauty from the endless beauties of nature – an allegory of the creative process itself.

Allegory, Myth and Fantasy

Myths and folklore, whether Greek or biblical, the heroic doings of Persian kings in the *Shahnameh* or the vivid, semi-satirical versions of Samurai legend produced in nineteenth-century Japan by Kuniyoshi, have always provided artists with subjects recognizable and acceptable to their audiences, relevant to contemporary needs yet rich in tradition and echoes of the past. The creation of the work of art may even precede the decision to borrow the myth, as in one of the most famous masterpieces of Giambologna – conceived purely as a formal solution to three figures entwined in vigorous action. As he told his patron, "the subject was chosen to give scope to the knowledge and study of art"; only later was a suitable title added on the plinth: *The rape of the Sabine*.

Two centuries later Tiepolo was still drawing on classical myth for his *Apollo pursuing Daphne*, but, while the trappings of the story are faithfully recorded, with Daphne transformed into a tree before our eyes, the primary intention is erotic, a sunlit celebration of youth and the senses. To an educated audience the classical allusion added both respectability and an extra dimension. Knowledge of the story of Venus and Mars does not help us to interpret Botticelli's painting fully, however. There seems to be another meaning to this strange scene, other than the triumph of love over war.

The situation became more difficult still when the decline of classical education left audiences unmoved by even the clearest classical allusion. For the modern figurative artist who wants to convey more than surface appearances, the problem is to produce images in the absence of any spoken or written story to elucidate their meaning. Yet sometimes an invented mythology, however obscure, may impress us with its suggestive power while more explicable allegories fall flat. William Blake, at the end of the eighteenth century, drew not only upon traditional mythologies but also upon his own, and at his most intense succeeds in convincing us that the vision he records is of another reality. By comparison, the imagery of Ford Madox Brown, a nineteenth-century artist allied in earnestness of purpose with the Pre-Raphaelites, seems curious rather than convincing when he illustrates all kinds of labour in the setting of a suburban London street.

Modern revivals of classical myth have proved largely superficial. While Daumier in the nineteenth century could still parody a commonly accepted idiom for the purpose of social satire, more recent treatments of myth, by Picasso and Matisse, for example, have generally been decorative, if superbly so. It is the fantasies of the Surrealists, notably Magritte, that have most effectively challenged any easy assumption we may have that our feet are safely planted on solid ground; their images, often drawn from personal sources, record with painstaking precision events that we know to be utterly impossible. Less alarming, wholly captivating, are the poetic visions of Douanier Rousseau. Though his, too, were private fantasies rather than public myths, they convince us by their innocent beauty that the fairy story is alive and well.

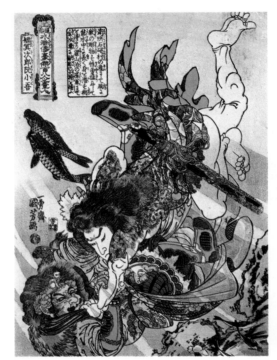

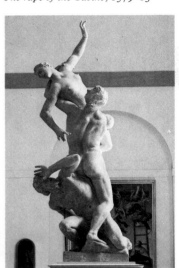

KUNIYOSHI (left): *Tameijiro dan Shogo grapples with his enemy under water*, 1828–29

GIAMBOLOGNA (below): *The rape of the Sabine*, 1579–83

TIEPOLO (below): *Apollo pursuing Daphne, c.*1755–60

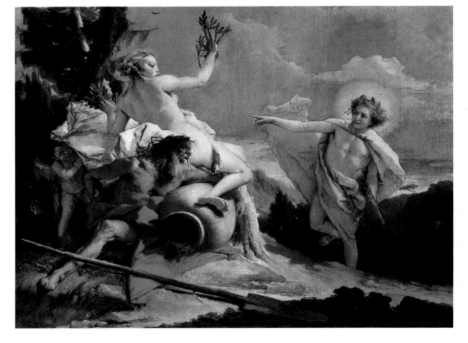

BOTTICELLI (below): *Venus and Mars, c.*1485

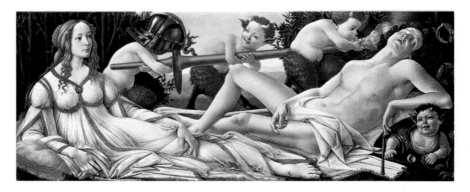

BROWN (right): *Work*, 1852–65

BLAKE (below): *The great red dragon
and the woman clothed with the sun, c.* 1800–10

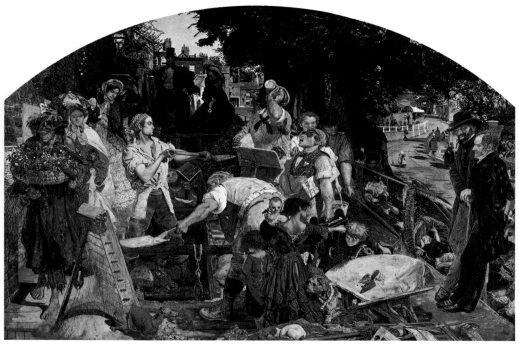

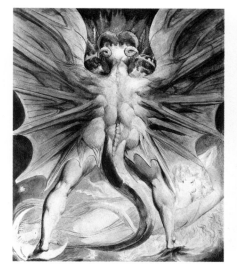

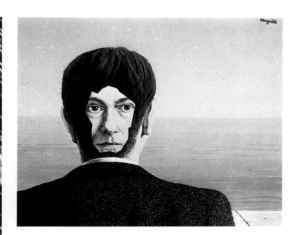

MAGRITTE (left):
The house of glass, 1939

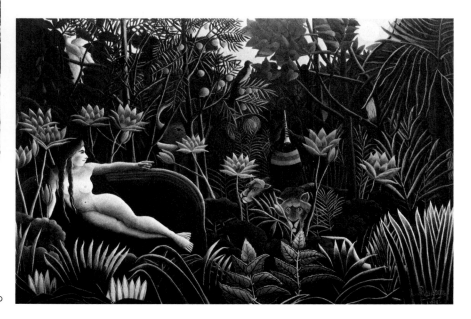

DAUMIER: *The triumph of Menelaus*, 1842

ROUSSEAU: *The dream*, 1910

The Inward Eye

At first sight, you might think perhaps, not much in it – a vast canvas, more than three-and-a-half metres (12ft) wide, covered with colour areas in maroon and dusty black. At the centre, two maroon rectangles of the same height but differing widths are set vertically, the edges soft, wavering, fuzzy. On closer inspection most of the canvas seems stained rather than painted, with only traces of the brush dragging black into the maroon. Everything is a bit hazy, the colour suffused, permeated with a gentle glowing. The precise colour of any one area is very difficult to define; there seem to be veils of colour behind colour, shifting like cloud in almost still air over the sun. The pale maroon darkens at the edges of the rectangles and again at the edges of the paintings. Nebulous, sombrely glowing, the colour gives the impression that the paint is generating its own light, as in the embers of a fire.

Rothko moved toward this, his late style, away from somewhat Surrealistic biomorphic imagery, through a long series of attempts to reduce his subject matter to the essential, in his own words: "toward clarity, toward the elimination of all obstacles between the painter and the idea, and between the idea and the observer. As examples of such obstacles I give (among others) memory, history or geometry, which are swamps of generalization ..." An American contemporary of Rothko's, and one who taught with him for a time, Robert Motherwell, observed that "the function of the artist is to make the spiritual so that it is there to be possessed".

Rothko came to work on a majestic scale – and the large scale is essential to his work. His huge paintings can create their most profound effect when a number hang together within an enclosed space, as in the Tate Gallery, London, or the chapel of St Thomas's Hospital in Houston, Texas. Then they produce a total environment in which the observer is enveloped, an impression different but comparable to that produced by the orchestration of space in great Baroque churches, or, in Gothic churches, by the magical suffusion of colour from sunlit, stained-glass windows. The chapel in Houston, with its great panels of glowing and shifting dusky red, invites the participant to silent and concentrated meditation. Some have even found, in contemplation of Rothko's work, the transcendental sensation of freedom from terrestial gravity which is the aim of many techniques of oriental mysticism.

This is remote from the traditional visions of Heaven recorded by most Western artists in figurative terms – or those of Hell either, for that matter. As some of the works on the following pages show, the artist's inward eye can define the most precise images as well as the most ineffable, giving them an hallucinatory clarity on the canvas. Rothko's own impulse was to reject definition, to strive for the universal rather than the particular, and there is an inevitable ambivalence in his paintings. The only valid subject matter, he wrote, was that "which is tragic and timeless. That is why we profess kinship with primitive and archaic art". Rothko in the end took his own life.

ROTHKO: *Black on maroon,* 1958

The Inward Eye

BOSCH (right):
The Garden of Earthly Delights,
detail, *c.* 1505-10

VAN DER WEYDEN (below):
The Last Judgment, detail, *c.* 1450?

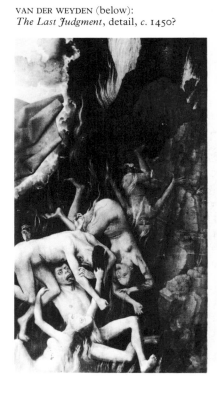

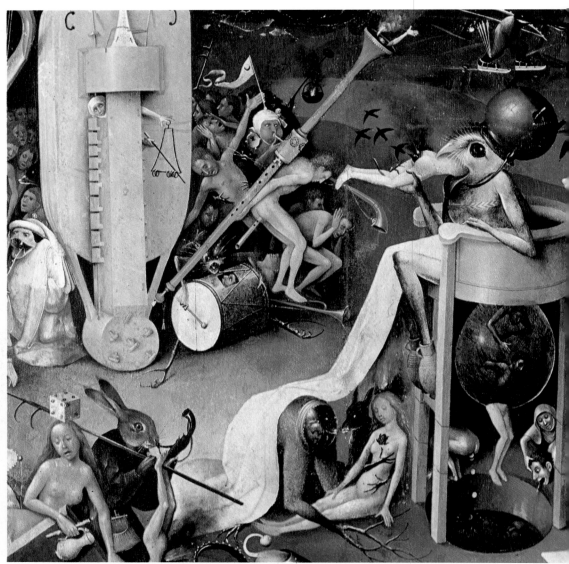

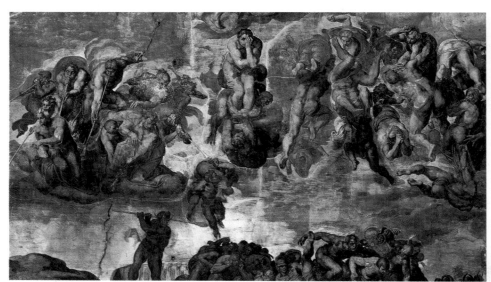

MICHELANGELO: *The Last Judgment*, detail, 1534-41

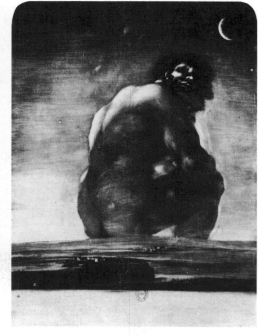

GOYA: *The Colossus*, 1808-12

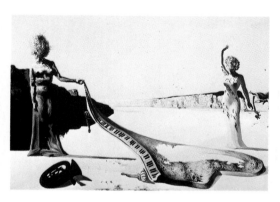

DALI: *3 young Surrealist women holding in their arms the skins of an orchestra*, detail, 1936

CHIRICO (below): *The enigma of the hour*, 1912

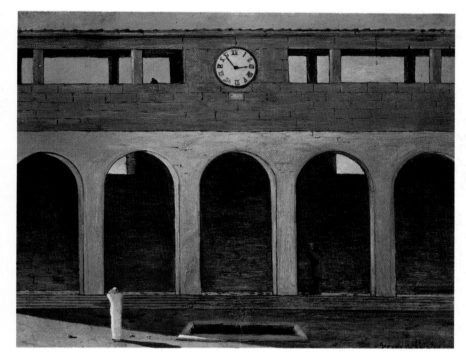

BACON (left): *Study after Velazquez*, 1953

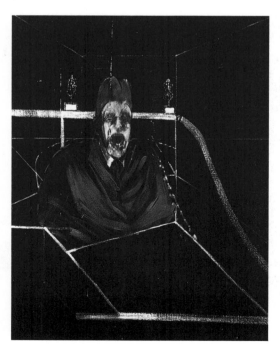

The feeling that the universe is divided into three zones persists, in spite of the explanations of modern astronomy and an almost universal scepticism of the biblical account of the Creation. Though we know the earth is not flat, nevertheless Heaven is still somewhere "up there" and Hell, though we may choose to ignore it, "down there".

Painters in a long tradition seem to have envisaged the torments of Hell with particular vividness. On the day of reckoning, a favourite subject for Christian artists, the lost souls are often shown spilling naked in a cascade down to their doom. The emphasis, though, differs remarkably; whereas despair is conveyed poignantly in the gaunt Gothic victims of a Netherlandish artist such as Rogier van der Weyden, Michelangelo's version calls attention, even at the Last Judgment, to the splendours of the human body rather than to spiritual damnation.

More effective in disrupting complacency are those visions of a Hell in which the artist's fantasy breeds distorted mutations of the natural world. To modern eyes, attuned to the irrational visions of the Surrealists, some of the paintings of Bruegel and Bosch strike home with a force in no way diminished by the obscurity of their imagery. The hybrid inhabitants of Bosch's Hell are horribly credible, detailing with ruthless clarity our profoundest apprehensions.

The twentieth-century concept of Hell as a state of mind rather than a zone of endless physical torment was prefigured during the Romantic age, above all in the nightmare visions of Goya. Images such as his *Colossus*, a vast figure silhouetted against a night sky as if brooding upon the destruction of all life, are characteristic of the mood of many etchings of his old age, and of the famous "Black Paintings" with which he decorated his house. The relevance of Goya's most extreme visions remained unrecognized until later in the nineteenth century, when some of the Symbolists explored the imagery of psychological states of mind and of the occult. The Surrealists were to exploit the Unconscious even more intensively and effectively; in Salvador Dali's imagination the world melts and sets in new, meaningless, yet sinister shape. Before him, Chirico in the baleful light of his deserted townscapes provided a modern urban nightmare of individual isolation and menace.

Less contrived than some of these images are Expressionist visions in which Hell resides within the human body, its contours distorted by the escaping screams of the damned. One of Munch's most famous prints is precisely that – a cry welling out, the solid world melting in its despair as if into lava. If some of the Expressionists seem to anticipate the holocausts of Nazi Germany, it is perhaps Francis Bacon who conveys most ferociously post-War man's realization of his potential for evil. Bacon's famous series of *Screaming Popes* takes a portrait by Velazquez of a man of great power in the splendour of life, of spiritual office – a picture notable for its humane understanding – and explodes it into the shuddering portrait of a soul in Hell on earth.

The Inward Eye

Heaven, no less than Hell, can be a state of mind, though in the nature of life perhaps less frequent. It is also less susceptible to visual expression: an eternity of rapture is difficult to imagine, much less to depict, and there is no heavenly counterpart so convincingly explicit as Goya's images of evil. Bernini's famous *St Theresa* captures the facial expression of ecstasy as almost no other image has succeeded in doing, but it is often claimed that the expression is one of physical rather than spiritual bliss. Likewise the marvellous vision of El Greco, *The Fifth Seal of the Apocalypse*, is ambivalent; its tremendous theme is the end of the world, but amidst the flaring colour and sinuous movement which, if any, are the damned, and which the saved, is arguable. Both the Bernini and the El Greco aspire upwards, and perhaps the most splendid Christian celebrations of Heaven do not attempt description of Paradise achieved, but of the ascent to it – the great Baroque vistas, in ceiling or dome, of Christ or the Madonna soaring into the empyrean from the attendant floating angels.

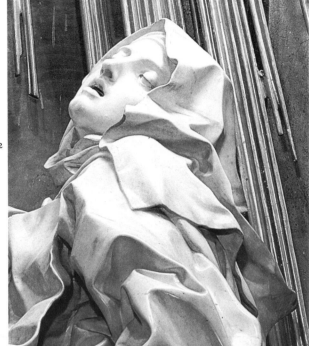

BERNINI: *St Theresa*, 1646-52

When literally envisioned Heaven often tends to be depicted in terms of the Garden of Eden, the Paradise (from the Persian "enclosed garden"), the Golden Age which must in the end return. In that first great monument of the northern Renaissance, the van Eycks' Ghent altarpiece, the Lamb of God is set on an altar before the source of the River of Life, the glory of God radiating over the landscape and the adoring crowds. Light is in most cultures associated with visions of beatitude, as is music also – the harmony of the spheres, the heavenly melodies of those elected to praise and serve God – a concept expressed most seductively by Fra Angelico's angels, whose lyrical, vernal colours seem felicity itself.

Later artists saw in idealized nature an allegory of eternal bliss, even without angelic hosts; such were Claude's idylls, bathed in serene golden light, and Constable's quick apprehensions of joy in the shifting weather (see p. 55). The most intense visions of the immanence of infinity in human life were provided by the German Romantic Friedrich, who combined sea, sky and isolated figures to produce a mood of contemplative awe.

Some artists have perceived the ethereal in the everyday, none more so than William Blake and, more recently, Stanley Spencer, who saw intrepidly literal visions of salvation even in the mass graves of a Flanders battlefield. The more general impulse of twentieth-century mystical art has been to abandon the human sphere in favour of a more abstract ideal – a balance of shapes, lines and colours visually analogous to musical harmony. The paintings of Mondrian were quite consciously spiritually motivated, providing in a sense a defined counterpart to Rothko's hazy, shifting shapes. Mondrian's clear, hard, geometric precision posits a clear order of things, immutable as the laws of the universe – the austere consolation of an order unaffected by mortal weaknesses and the miseries of the human condition. Though offering little hope to the individual, that is perhaps the only notion of Heaven available to the late twentieth century.

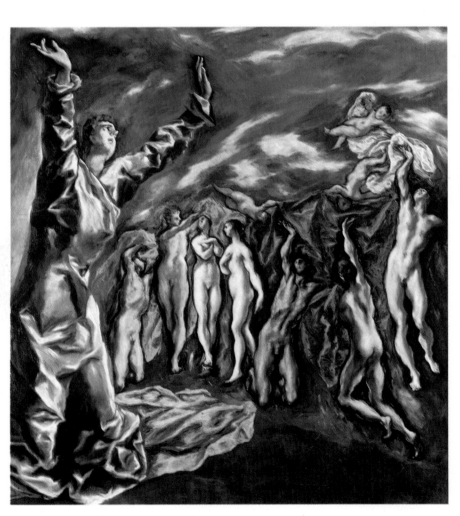

EL GRECO: *The Fifth Seal of the Apocalypse*, 1608-14

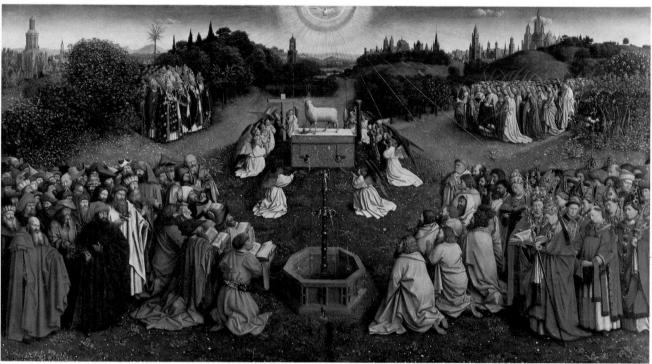

JAN AND HUBERT VAN EYCK: The Ghent altarpiece, finished 1432

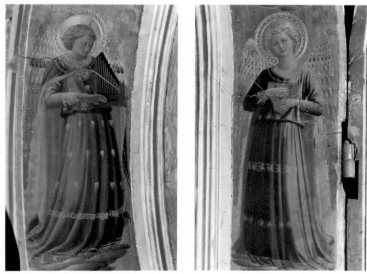

FRA ANGELICO: The Linaiuoli triptych, details, 1433

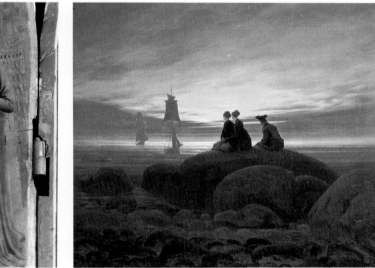

FRIEDRICH: *Moonrise over the sea*, 1822

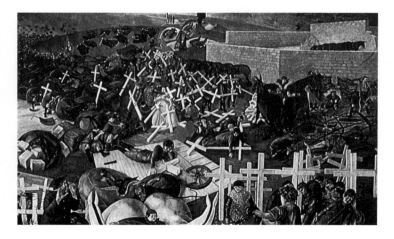

SPENCER (left):
*The resurrection
of the soldiers*,
detail, 1928-29

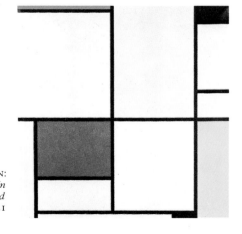

MONDRIAN:
*Composition in
red, yellow and
blue*, 1921

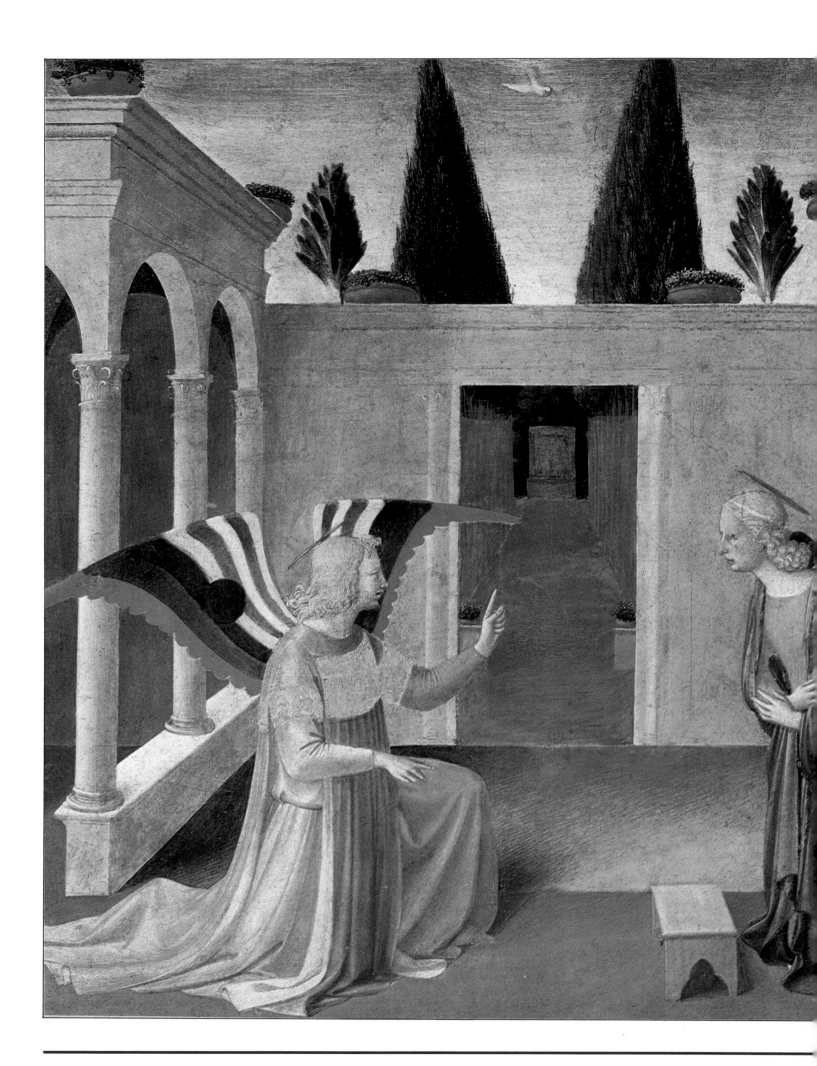

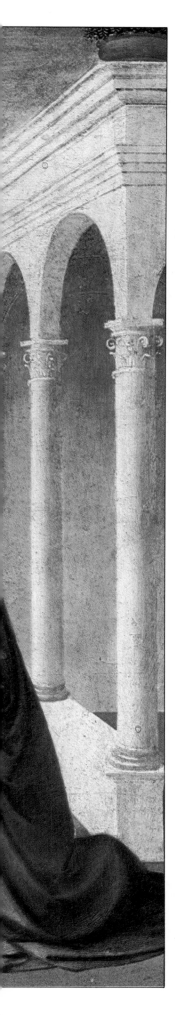

THE LANGUAGE OF PAINTING

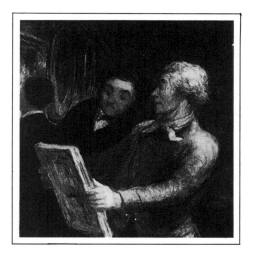

"Organized perception is what art is all about"
— LICHTENSTEIN

(left) FRA ANGELICO: *The Annunciation*, c. 1451-55; (above) DAUMIER: *The connoisseurs*, detail, c. 1860-63

Introduction

How much sense does it make to speak of painting as a language? At least this much: painting, like language itself, is a means by which feelings and thoughts can be transmitted, and there is a real sense in which we can speak of paintings being read by those who have the necessary familiarity with the tradition and conventions being used.

The preceding pages have dealt with the content of pictures, with the culturally determined meanings of the images they contain. Here our concern is with the factors in painting that are common to all pictures, whether figurative or abstract, whether Western or from any other part of the world; factors to which we would continue to respond even if we had no notion what the picture was supposed to represent.

Certain basic associations of colour, line or shape are not specific to time, place or subject matter and many qualities in a painting may remind us of things in the outside world. Smooth, undulant lines, for instance, tend to evoke water; jagged ones suggest crags or lightning. Again, all humans lie down to sleep and are awake when they stand up. Thus verticality and horizontality have opposite associations, and diagonal lines tend to suggest imbalance, movement or dynamism. Circles or ovals call up associations with eyes or breasts or, in other contexts, with the sun, the moon or the totality of the universe. A painting with bright, contrasted colours and angular shapes will set up a mood and suggest meanings vastly different from one having soft colours and gentle curves. The interaction of colours, shapes and lines also creates purely optical sensations, to which everyone can respond.

Paintings may also show distinctive or characteristic features which indicate that they are the product of a particular time or place, or mind or hand – qualities summed up by the word "style". Style (which will be considered in more detail later) is essentially choice of means, whether on the part of an individual or an epoch – conscious or subconscious choice of a particular way of using a number of elements, such as colour, texture, form or shape, each of which ranges between extremes.

Colour is often the most compelling of these elements, but in a definable sense may be secondary to form. The proof is that a black-and-white photograph of a painting that has sublime colour may still convey many excellences of the original, while a mere chart, no matter how accurate, of the colour used, would, when detached from the forms, be largely meaningless even if very agreeable. Therefore this section deals first with all those properties in painting to which a black-and-white photograph would do some justice – what might be called structural properties.

In representational painting the formal means can help to bring out the subject matter, but in abstract painting these means are themselves the subject matter. Just as a composer uses the raw materials of musical sound to generate meaning independent of representation (though association and evocation are often very much part of the listener's experience), so the abstract painter affects us by arrangements of "pure" form, colour,

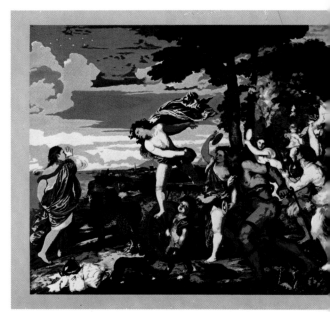

TONAL ANALYSIS
In all Old Master paintings from the High Renaissance until Neoclassicism, the distribution of light and shade is largely independent of, or contrapuntal to, the outlines of the solids, which therefore weave into and out of clear definition. In *Bacchus and Ariadne* light and shade imperceptibly merge, but in this simplified "map" only five degrees of tone are used, emphasizing the continual interplay of light and dark passages, which contributes so much to the painting's vitality, and simultaneously bringing out the subtle balance of its overall tonal structure – Titian's unity in variety.

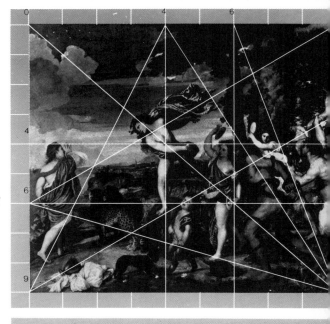

PROPORTIONAL ANALYSIS
There is documentary proof that Titian was interested in the use of geometry and numbers for the systematic division of pictorial space. In his time mathematics was part of the training of painters as well as of architects. Here Titian has divided width and height into nine units and placed the main divisions at 4:9 and 6:9 each way. This can be considered the spatial equivalent of the musical harmony of the double fifth. The bold geometric nature of the composition is further indicated by the diagonals which have been added to the basic grid pattern.

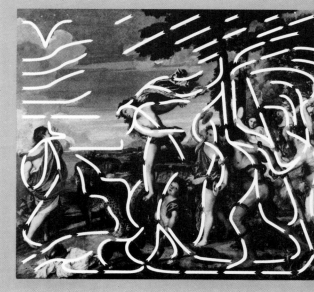

MOVEMENT ANALYSIS
Bacchus' desire for Ariadne and her startled reaction are expressed by Titian in vigorous, varied movement, the main axes of which are plotted here as white lines. The points indicate the direction in which we would normally follow them, though this is a variable since any axis, like any street, can be travelled two ways. But some of the readings are clear and unequivocal, for example that Bacchus' body moves towards Ariadne along the axis from his left foot to his head, whilst she twists spirally away from her right foot to right hand, checking and resolving the surging motion towards her.

shape or texture, which he might accordingly claim lie at the heart of the matter, since they are common to all painting, forming an underlying universal language.

The purpose of the following pages is to show how and to what extent it is possible to analyse this universal language by taking a painting to pieces and examining its distinguishing properties. In doing so, we should bear in mind that a thing dismantled is no longer itself. The parts of a motor-cycle laid out on the garage floor are not in a true sense a motor-cycle: they will not move us from place to place. A painting, when it moves us, does so not as a set of distinct elements but by virtue of the simultaneous interaction of a host of elements in a highly complex psychological event.

It may be argued that to analyse a work of art is to deprive it of a mystery that is its life. In opposition to this view the music critic Hans Keller asserts that "enjoyment is a function of understanding"; that the more we become aware of what are the affective elements in music the deeper and more total the communication and the more joyous in consequence. This section is written in conformity with Keller's view, and examines one by one the principal factors, elements or agencies that work on us in a painting. By way of sampling this approach, Titian's *Bacchus and Ariadne* is shown here along with three different analyses of it. It is a large and magnificent example of the work of one of Europe's greatest artists in his prime, and though Titian's mastery is so complete as to appear effortless the harmony it displays is the outcome of a very careful structural control which holds the dynamic movement in majestic balance. Knowledge of the formal language a painter has used can lead us to appreciate more clearly his intention as well as his achievement.

TITIAN
Bacchus and Ariadne,
1522–23

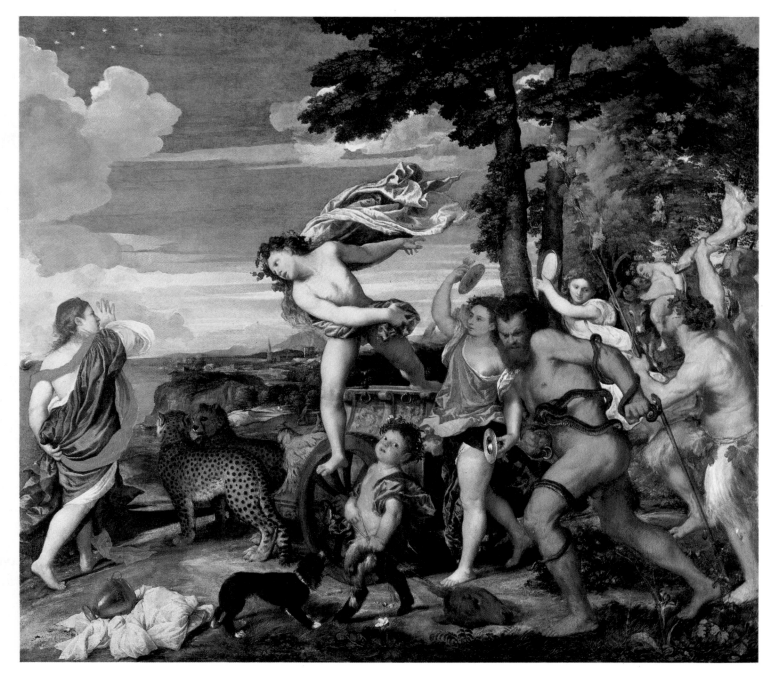

Scale and Space

Scale, which may be considered first in our list of pictorial values, is one of the most obvious qualities of a painting but by no means one of the most important. Sheer size can be impressive in itself, but no painting was ever good simply because it was large. Many very large paintings are pompous and empty; conversely, much can be conveyed in a very small area, as in a Vermeer or Hilliard.

The effects of scale on a viewer cannot be illustrated in a book and the main thing to be said about it is that it should suit the context, subject matter and purpose of the painting. The more public the destined role of the work the larger it normally needs to be. In domestic or non-public art a picture tends to seem big if it is two metres ($6\frac{1}{2}$ ft) or greater in its larger dimension and small if less than about 45 centimetres (18 in). At about 15 centimetres (6 in) it seems miniature. These, roughly, are the limits (judged very much in terms of human stature) within which a painter makes decisions about the size of a picture. Some mid-twentieth-century painters – Jackson Pollock was among the first – have used very big formats with the deliberate intention of preventing anyone at a normal viewing distance from taking the canvas all in one glance. The viewer is thus enveloped by the picture; being "in" almost more than looking at it – a drastically changed relationship.

With space we come to a category quite fundamental in the visual arts, whether two- or three-dimensional. The space of a painting is to begin with a blank, flat plane having two dimensions only. Normally, the plane is rectangular – a sheet of paper, a panel, a canvas. But if we make a mark of any kind on this plane – even a non-representational one such as a dash, a circle or a dab of colour – at once the surface is seen as having two generic elements. There is a "thing" and there is the space in which it seems to exist.

Perception psychologists use the word "figure" to denote what we perceive as thing and the word "ground" to denote the areas we read as surrounding air or void. They tell us that (largely for purposes of survival) we are programmed to perceive in figure-ground terms, and, as the diagrams here show, we instinctively read even the simplest visual images in this way. In situations where there are insufficient clues to indicate what is figure and what ground, our readings alternate, sometimes rapidly to give a sensation of flicker, as in Op Art.

The figure-ground interrelation is unambiguous and stable in nearly all figurative and much abstract painting. By symbolic extension, ground comes to stand for the entire set of circumstances in which a thing finds itself: and figure, therefore, tends to become the hero of the story, the creature in the predicament – indeed ourselves, to the extent that we identify with it. This is why the figure-ground, or spatial, relationship in a picture often betrays at deepest level the attitudes and outlook of the painter or the culture he represents. Lucid, orderly space, neither cluttered nor desolately blank, suggests a serene, balanced, optimistic personality or culture, whereas space that is confused, congested or

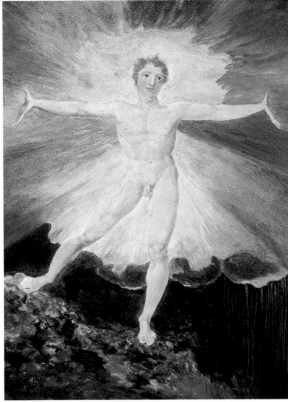

BLAKE (above)
Glad day, c. 1794
A mood of joy or optimism is irresistibly suggested in the relationship between the figure, dominating but not congesting the pictorial space, and the ground its energy seems to irradiate.

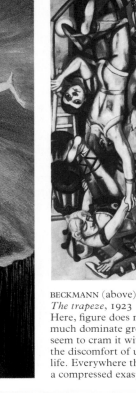

BECKMANN (above)
The trapeze, 1923
Here, figure does not so much dominate ground as seem to cram it with all the discomfort of urban life. Everywhere there is a compressed exasperation.

Our figure-ground readings often alternate: is (A) a black patch or square hole? (B) a white circle on black or square-plus-circle on white? (C) a white hook on black or black on white?

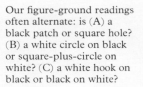

A   B

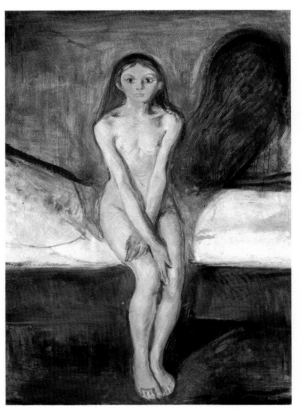

MUNCH (right)
Puberty, 1895
In opposition to Blake, Munch expresses a mood of anxiety and oppression by using ground (which stands for circumstance, life itself) to overbear and dominate figure. The girl intuitively foresees all the complexities and suffering ahead of her, and she cannot face them.

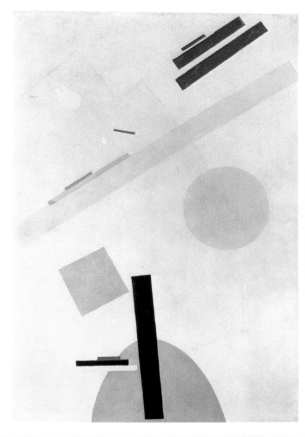

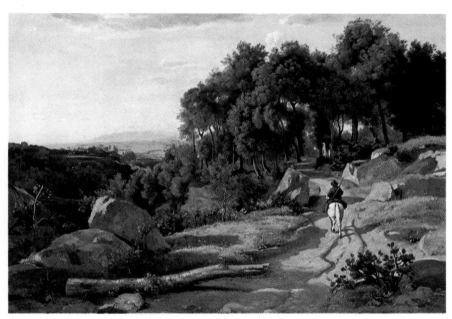

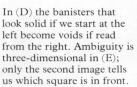

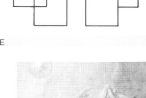

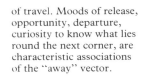

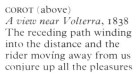

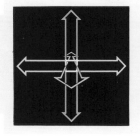

MALEVICH (left)
Composition, c. 1917
This is up-ness in abstract
form, offering release from
the implications of gravity.
A figurative example might
have been a soaring angel
or the resurrected Christ.

COROT (above)
A view near Volterra, 1838
The receding path winding
into the distance and the
rider moving away from us
conjure up all the pleasures

of travel. Moods of release,
opportunity, departure,
curiosity to know what lies
round the next corner, are
characteristic associations
of the "away" vector.

In (D) the banisters that
look solid if we start at the
left become voids if read
from the right. Ambiguity is
three-dimensional in (E);
only the second image tells
us which square is in front.

D   E

Height, width and depth
were the impersonal vectors
Descartes used to analyse
three-dimensional space,
but in pictorial space they
are charged with highly
differentiated meanings.

depopulated suggests anxiety, disturbance or neu-
rosis, whether individual or collective.

Mondrian observed, and we have all experienced, that vertical lines or shapes unrelieved by
horizontals, and vice versa, create a mood of
melancholy and oppression, while a balance between them is visually satisfying. The six major
directions in which figures can move or be aligned
in space – up, down, left, right, towards, away –
also have their own associations and moods. Up,
for instance, obviously evokes Heaven, exaltation,
aspiration, flight. Down, clearly, tends to the
opposite. Towards could be anything from a
threat to a welcome overture. In either case there is
a sense of intrusion or involvement, while away is
typically the direction of adventure and the unknown. Left and right are the comings and goings
we more or less detachedly observe around us:
though even these terms are not completely neutral or interchangeable: European paintings tend
to be read, like the written word, from left to right,
whereas in Chinese art the opposite holds true. In
paintings of the Annunciation, for example, the
angel almost always moved from the left towards
the Virgin on the right, although this can probably
be explained in terms of tradition and symbolism
as well as of fundamental pictorial psychology.

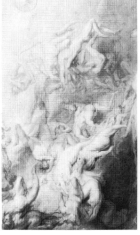

RUBENS (above)
The fall of the damned,
detail, *c.* 1614/18
Down, in the moral sense,
is the steep path to Hell
and damnation – a fall from
grace. But in principle
it could also symbolize
humility, earthliness or, in
other contexts, relaxation,
repose or weariness. It is,
at all events, a surrender
to gravitational force.

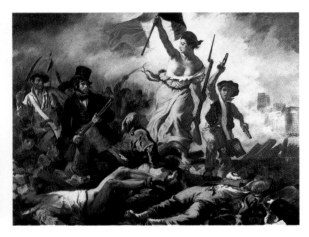

DELACROIX (above)
Liberty leading the people,
1830
The protagonists of this
superbly rhetorical picture
come unequivocally towards
us. With our personal space
thus invaded, we must
either turn and run (as
bourgeois reactionaries) or
join in (identifying with
the people's aspirations
for bread and freedom).

Types of Pictorial Space

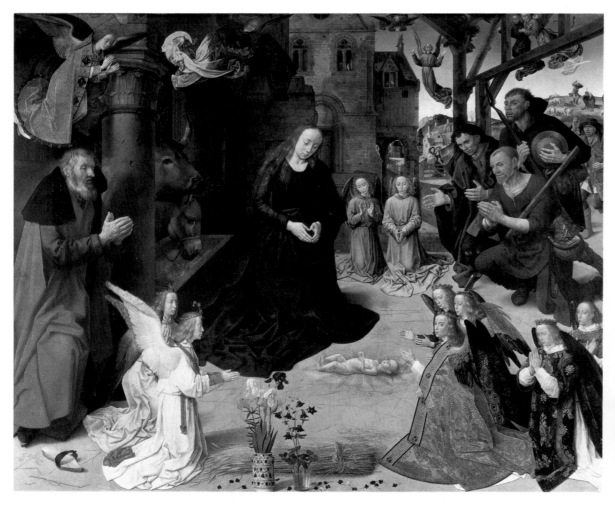

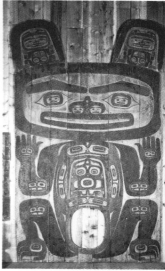

VAN DER GOES (left)
The Portinari altarpiece:
*The Adoration of the
shepherds, c.* 1474–76
This painting bridges the
Gothic and Renaissance
worlds. Its space is deep,
but the scale of the Virgin
relative to the angels is
medieval in conception.

NORTH AMERICA: TLINGIT
TRIBE
Bear screen, *c.* 1840
This is not so much a
mere picture of a bear as
a bear-like presence that
happens to be made of paint
and wood. Two dimensions
are all it needs to manifest
its totemic character.

There are many different ways in which space can be organized in paintings, but it may be helpful to classify them, however crudely, into three major modes. Not surprisingly, for reasons we have already discussed, methods of treating pictorial space tend to reflect the several ways in which reality is experienced by different artists.

The simplest kind of space is exemplified in the art of tribal cultures or in medieval heraldry, where the things represented are archetypal or conventional images rather than individualized representations of particular objects. The pictorial space in paintings of this kind – we might call it "totemic/magical/heraldic" space – is in essence two-dimensional. It cannot be quite strictly so, since "figure" (an heraldic lion for instance) must necessarily appear to be in front of "ground" (a field azure). But there is no illusory depth, much less perspective. There is little or no overlapping of shapes, and objects are presented in their most typical and informative aspect – frontal or side elevation or some combination of both. All shapes have definite boundaries completely filled with flat, clear, non-naturalistic colours: colours, that is, chosen for their symbolic significance and not transcribed from nature.

This kind of space shades off into a somewhat more complex kind that we might call "spiritual" space, for example that of Byzantine mosaics or icons. Here we find a greater degree of naturalism in the rendering of poses and drapery. Likewise there is more depth: objects overlap, and there is some modulation of colour from light to dark: they are no longer flat. The background, however, is unmodulated blazing gold, and does not represent any actual physical space; it is the space of hearing rather than sight – of attention to the word. In such paintings, the artist is concerned less with showing things as they might look in the everyday world than with making a visual list of things that belong together in the concept we are invited to meditate upon. To use Professor Ernst Gombrich's term, these are "what" paintings – mainly about what belongs with what in a certain hierarchy of ideas.

"Naturalistic or optical" space presents the "how" view: how things look or happen from a single point of view – more or less as we perceive them in everyday life. Apart from some fore-shadowings in Roman art, this kind of space does not occur in European painting until Gothic times. Giotto and Duccio grasped it, but did not as yet make it systematic. Early Renaissance painters perfected it as the science of perspective and it remained the norm until Cézanne modified it and the Cubists virtually attempted to abolish it. It is often, and for good reason, referred to as "Renaissance" space.

In the early Renaissance, space was organized

TINTORETTO (right)
Bacchus and Ariadne, 1578
Tintoretto's swooping and
spiralling figures, their
complex poses made to seem
effortlessly attained, are
typically Mannerist in the
way in which they move so
freely in depth as well as
across the picture surface.

AUSTRIAN SCHOOL (below)
*The Trinity with Christ
crucified*, 15th century
The space in this painting,
and in much other medieval
art, has a certain minimal
depth, but it is consecrated
space charged with spiritual
energies, with relationships
of scale quite different
from those of everyday life.

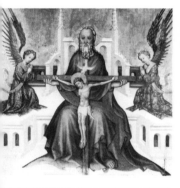

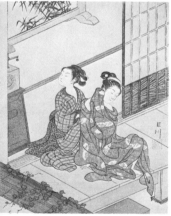

HARUNOBU (above)
*The evening bell of the
clock*, c. 1766
The space here owes its
character to diagonality. The
parallels do not converge
as in "correct" perspective,
and the two graceful ladies
seem almost to float, at one
with their surroundings.

TURNER (right)
Norham Castle: sunrise,
c. 1835–40
It is most unlikely that the
painter of the Tlingit bear
could have understood this
painting. With our cultural
background, however, we are
able to read these luminous
filmy washes and to feel the
depth they so subtly convey.

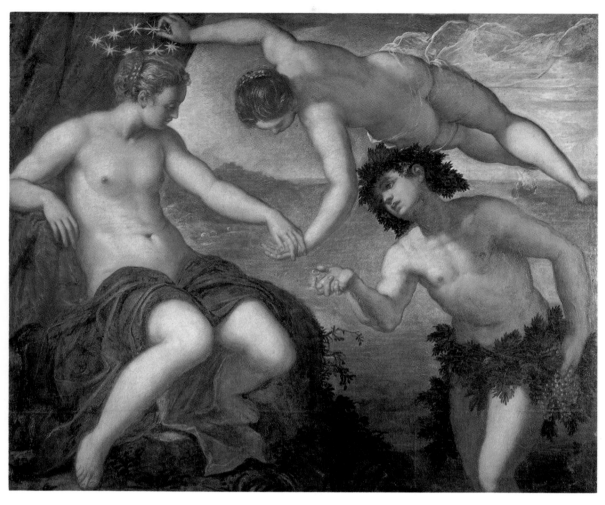

in layers parallel to the picture plane, normally in three distinct areas identifiable as foreground, middle distance and background, but during the sixteenth century this calm, lucidly articulated arrangement was increasingly abandoned in favour of slewed, oblique structurings in which the solids are dynamically diagonal to the picture plane and the viewer's line of vision. This is the space characteristic – though with different degrees of logicality – of the Mannerist and Baroque periods. It is highly illusionistic when compared with Byzantine space, and invites us to take off into heady, if always ultimately controlled, convo-

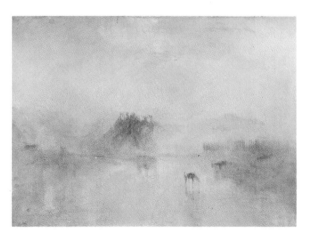

lutions in an apparently deep pictorial space.

A quieter kind of slewed or oblique space is frequently found in Japanese art, and often the effect is to make us feel that we have accidently happened upon an everyday domestic occurrence. It is the very opposite of the monumental, and sets up a mood of delicate casualness.

A painter has at his command, besides overlappings and diagonals, still further resources for the attainment of depth in pictorial space, another of which is called "atmospheric" or "aerial" perspective. This exploits the fact that, because of the density of the atmosphere, objects look paler and more bluish in colour the farther away they are from the spectator. Leonardo, who invented the term aerial perspective, was one of the first to explore its possibilities, although the phenomenon had been discussed by Ptolemy as early as the second century AD. The intensely blue distances found in the work of some of Leonardo's immediate followers often look artificial, but later painters, especially in northern Europe, where the atmosphere is generally hazier and the effects of light more varied, became much more subtle in their observation and depiction of the effects of aerial perspective. In some of Turner's most daring late works the atmosphere itself is almost the subject of the painting and the sole means of creating pictorial space.

Projection

All painters who seek to represent objects in three-dimensional space are confronted at the outset by a paradox. Unlike sculptors, they have at their disposal only a two-dimensional surface, so they must resort to one or another of a set of possible subterfuges that will describe three dimensions while using only two.

These subterfuges can collectively be called projections: "throwing forward", literally, of solids until they meet a plane surface and assume a flat shape. The mode of projection with which we are nowadays most familiar, optical perspective, is considered overleaf. It is a recent development in history, not having been systematically formulated until the early Renaissance in Italy, so we should, before coming to it, look at projection as it was practised before the Renaissance, and as it has once more been practised by modern painters who, impressed with the power and grandeur of primitive art, have abandoned Renaissance perspective in search of something more timeless, conceptual and archetypal.

To the right are set out, in diagrammatic form, the main *non-perspectival* types of projection. A simple chair-like object made of cubic blocks is taken as the test case, and placed upon its seat are a sphere and cylinder. It is drawn in seven logical and consistent projections and a final lawless and arbitrary one.

There are two criteria for assessing any of these methods. Firstly, one can consider its value as information: how much does it convey, and how clearly, about the object's shape; what items of information are concealed, distorted or ambiguous? Secondly, there can be an aesthetic appraisal: does a given method produce ugly shapes or awkwardness in "reading" it? This second kind of judgment, however, cannot be made in the artificial context of a diagram, but only in that of a work of art which uses the method in question. And in practice it is unusual to find a painting deploying a single method systematically. The Persian miniature reproduced here is parti-

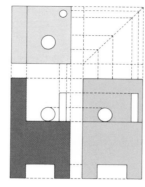
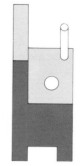
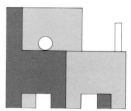

Strict plan, side elevation and front elevation give us accurate information about dimensions (hence their traditional use in architects' drawings) but here only side elevation conveys much about the *look* of the structure represented.

Here side elevation and plan are fitted together. The information has the same level of accuracy as before, but, because the side and top surfaces adjoin, the visual appearance of the structure is more effectively conveyed.

This is another combination of elements from the first group: side elevation combined with elevational views of frontal planes. This is more like the chair we might see, but strictly the sphere and the cylinder should each appear twice.

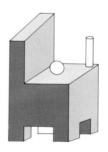
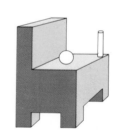
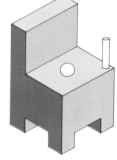

The side elevation is now combined with frontal planes which actively contradict a normal perspective view by diverging. The look is somewhat improbable, but this convention is often used in pre-Renaissance, modern and non-European art for the depiction of depth.

This is the reverse of the preceding system, with some convergence of the frontal planes as they recede. It is very close to orthodox perspective, except that the intervals between the horizontal planes are rather wider than they would be in a strict perspective drawing.

This is an isometric projection where both frontal planes and side elevation are shown at an oblique angle to the horizontal. It is frequently used by architects on account of its exceptionally high level of information and readability in three-dimensional terms.

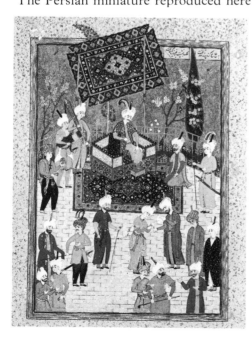

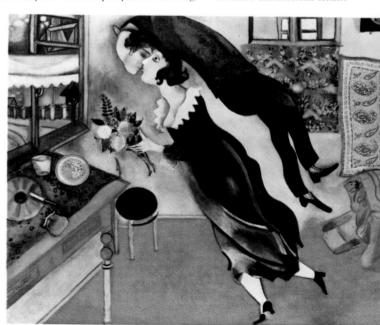

PERSIA (left)
Khosroe and his courtiers
1524/25
The painter of this miniature has suggested depth in a number of different ways. The varied methodologies are held together by a superb sense of texture, pattern and decorative placement to create pictorial unity.

CHAGALL (right)
The birthday, 1915
Chagall here uses, with wonderful freedom and confidence, as many kinds of projection as he chooses, creating a space which accords beautifully with the almost gravity-free choreography of the figures, in poetic disjunction.

culary rich in inconsistencies. The carpet on four posts which serves as a canopy is tilted obliquely to indicate that it projects over the throne, yet it is shown in full plan. The throne itself is partly in reversed perspective and partly in a convention resembling isometric. The floor tiles and the carpet on which the throne rests are in strict plan whilst the figures are shown in elevation. The Chagall painting also displays a wide variety of projection systems, and in Braque's painting we see several views of the violin from differing angles freely combined in one image. The Egyptian mural is comparatively restrained in that only two kinds of projection are used – strict elevation (trees, fish, people) and strict plan (the pond). In the Chinese example the idea of parallel lines being shown as parallels is applied throughout, but not with overall consistency, for there is no logical pattern in the differing angles of the lines of floor tiles and roofs.

What can be said in general about all the types of projections so far mentioned is that they give primacy not to what the artist optically perceives of the object represented but to what he may know of it – a knowledge gained not simply by standing in one place and looking at it, but by walking round it, touching it, measuring it, hearing it described, fully experiencing it.

The representation in art of this multi-sensory and multi-active kind of knowing tended to diminish after artists in Florence in the early fifteenth century began to observe and represent the world in a scientific way. Since the beginning of the twentieth century, however, artists have progressively resuscitated older modes, stimulated by revolutions in modern physics and cosmology, especially relativity and quantum theory, which have upset earlier certitudes about the nature of the universe. The first signs are observable in Post-Impressionism, especially in Cézanne. These insights were seized upon and developed by the Cubists, establishing new freedoms for themselves and for others such as Chagall.

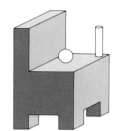

Here the side elevation is combined with an oblique presentation of the frontal planes. This recalls perspective, but the edges of these planes are parallel, not convergent, and thus in a sense give a truer image than linear perspective.

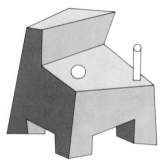

Whereas all the preceding projections adhered to a consistent policy, this one deliberately flouts all logic, but is still readable as a chair-like object. Distortions of this kind are common in the work of Picasso and other moderns as in the Braque opposite.

BRAQUE
Pitcher and violin, 1910
Braque's violin is a particularly clear example of the multiple viewpoints used by the Cubists to express the idea of an object rather than simulate its appearance. The scroll of the head is seen in side elevation, the far pegs in plan, the neck in three-quarter view, the near

shoulder or *bout* in frontal elevation – inconsistently with the amount of side planes visible – and so on. Thus might a fly see it if buzzing round it this way and that, up and down – a restless dynamic image, but rich in compositional value as well as in the amount of information it conveys about the third dimension without suggesting recession.

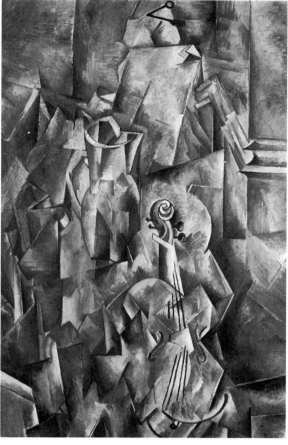

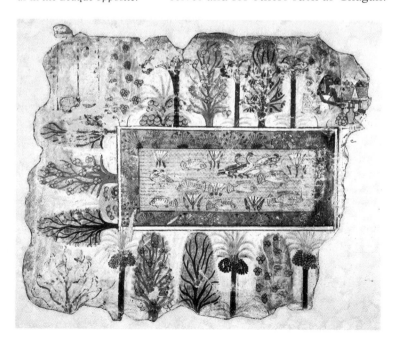

THEBES (left)
Garden with pond
XVIIIth dynasty, c. 1400 BC
Two kinds of projection, plan and elevation, are here used in what today might be considered mutual contradiction. Clearly it is a presentation not of how things look, but rather of what they essentially are.

CHINA (right)
From *The Mustard Seed Garden Manual of Painting; Winding veranda and porches of a palace*, c. 1679
A high viewpoint and what we might call "parallel perspective" were among the traditional conventions of Chinese painting in scenes involving buildings.

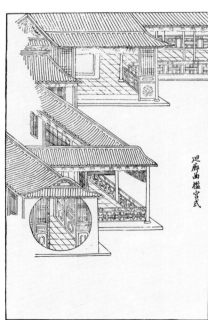

Perspective

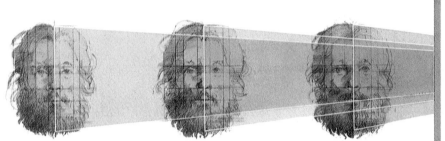

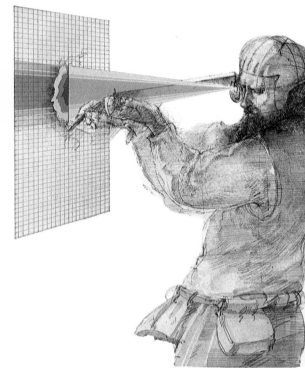

The term perspective is sometimes used in a broad sense to encompass projection systems in general, but here we are concerned with it in the narrow sense of what is sometimes called optical perspective. This quasi-mathematical system, invented in Florence in the early fifteenth century, uses as its basis the fact that parallel lines appear to converge and objects appear to become smaller the farther they are from the viewer. This "lie" does not trouble us in the least; we have been mentally adjusted to it all our lives, and it is impossible to imagine vision working at all if, for example, a horse three fields away appeared the same size as one we were standing next to. The perspective system of representing three-dimensional objects on a two-dimensional surface so as to give a naturalistic effect of spatial recession became one of the cornerstones of European painting for nearly five centuries.

Parallel lines that appear to converge, for example the margins of a straight highway when we look along its central axis, will eventually recede to meet at the level of our eyes. This is known as the horizon line, and the points at which any receding parallel lines appear to meet on it are called vanishing points. A form such as the block-chair we saw on the preceding page will, unless seen completely flat on, have one vanishing point to our left and a second to our right. Greek knowledge of vanishing-point perspective and foreshortening formed a basis for medieval artists who, during the fourteenth century, began trying to construct a realistic picture space with consistent recession from foreground to background. The placing and correct relative sizes of figures, especially in the middle distance, were a constant problem until Brunelleschi and Alberti formulated geometric rules for the convergence of parallels and the proportional reduction of objects.

Though "correct" perspective based on these strict rules can give a highly convincing illusion of three-dimensional space with the picture seeming like a window through which one looks, in certain

THE CONE OF VISION
Distant objects appear smaller than near ones, as light rays travel towards the eye in narrowing cones of vision – an effect shown by the image sizes on the glass screen upon which the artist is tracing. He is using a device described by Dürer to draw accurately by sighting a mark through a peep-hole attached to a line which ensures that his viewpoint remains consistent.

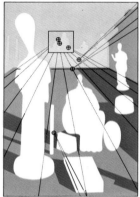

CHIRICO
Sinister Muses, 1917
This is the equivocal deep space of a dream, made disturbing not only by the imagery but by the lack of consistency in perspective convergence, despite the emphasis on it. As shown in the diagram, the vanishing points indicated by the box in the foreground, the shadowy *palazzo* on the right and the receding lines on the pavement are not mutually reconcilable.

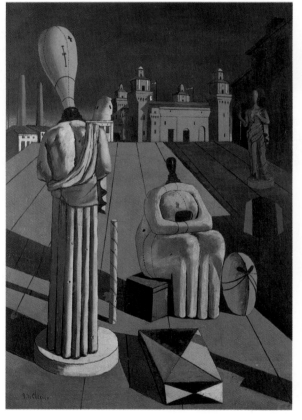

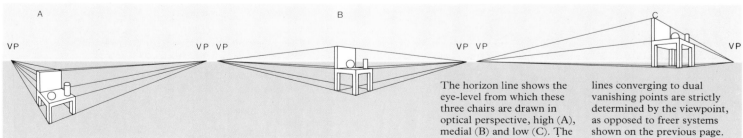

The horizon line shows the eye-level from which these three chairs are drawn in optical perspective, high (A), medial (B) and low (C). The lines converging to dual vanishing points are strictly determined by the viewpoint, as opposed to freer systems shown on the previous page.

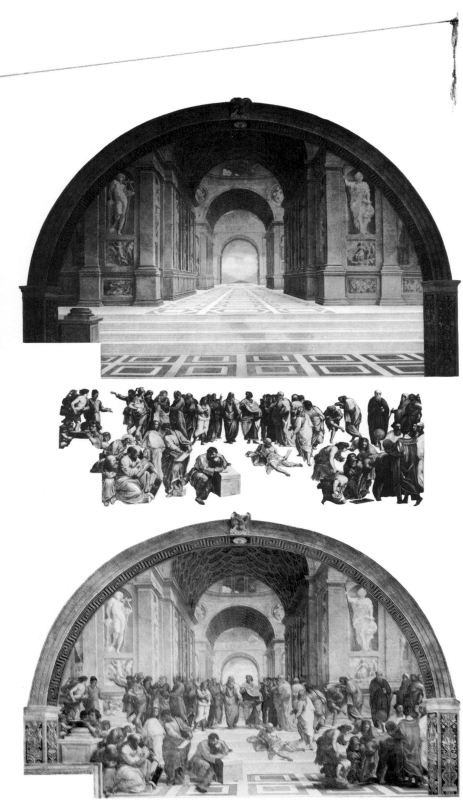

respects it is misleading, not least in that it is monocular. It assumes a viewer who has one eye only, held in a fixed stare straight ahead. This is what the artist in the illustration above is doing in order to plot his model accurately on the interposed transparent screen. He has rigged up a peep-hole almost like a gun-sight and has to shut one eye to look through it.

Anybody could similarly trace the view through a window by outlining it on the pane without changing position. But this, of course, is highly unnatural: we are endowed with binocular, hence stereoscopic vision; our eyes are continually and rapidly scanning our surroundings; and we move our heads frequently. Thus optical perspective from a fixed viewpoint can, unless carefully managed, seem quite out of accord with our experience. It is because the camera behaves like a single fixed human eye that amateurs are so often disappointed by prints of their earliest snapshot – an impressive building, perhaps, shrunk to the size of a pea in an acreage of boring foreground. Yet the camera has faithfully recorded what was in the viewfinder. The fault lay in the photographer's unawareness that seeing is at least as much a function of movement and selective attention as of optical laws or geometric plots.

In fact, few painters use perspective in a rigidly systematic way. In Raphael's "*The School of Athens*", for example, the architecture is seen from a central viewpoint and hence has a single central vanishing point, but each figure is painted as if seen from directly in front. The sphere which Ptolemy holds at the right of the painting would look like an ellipse if it were seen in the same perspective as the architecture, but such a distortion would look absurd in this context. Most artists work within a fairly narrow angle of vision, between about 30° and 60°, so the problems of marginal distortion are rarely acute.

Devices such as lessening convergence and spreading out vanishing points into vanishing areas can also help to soften the harsh effect of perspective – nowhere more so than in architectural scenes with large buildings close up on one or both flanks. Only too easily this produces sharp, stabbing diagonals and thin, mean shapes where there are doors and windows. At a philosophical level it could be argued that optical perspective implies a narrowing of outlook, an oversimplification of the complex and partly mysterious process by which we see the world, positing as it does optical experience as the sole source of visual art and implicitly downgrading other kinds of knowing, such as the evidence of other senses and knowledge built up over time.

These drawbacks notwithstanding, perspective has inspired and made possible – especially in the early Renaissance, when it was a new and exciting revelation – some majestic spatial compositions by painters such as Masaccio, Uccello and Piero della Francesca. Surrealists who have readopted it, even though often in breach of the rules, have been able to accomplish marvels in evoking the nostalgia or terror of the dream, the wistful strangeness of spatial recession.

RAPHAEL
"*The School of Athens*",
1509–11
Too obtrusive a perspective effect can punch such a hole in the surface of the picture that unless some counter-measures are taken to restore our sense of its real flatness we are left with a certain queasiness. When the group of figures is removed from Raphael's painting, the illusion of depth becomes disturbingly tunnel-like. Conversely, the removal of the architectural features deprives the figures of much of their solidity and depth. Raphael disposed them in a row parallel to the picture plane to maintain an appropriate balance with the architecture, and it is only when these two elements of the painting are combined that the composition comes together to create a sense of serene and monumental grandeur.

Line, Shape, Contour, Articulation

In the history of painting there is a significant dichotomy between artists who express themselves through line and those whose basic vision and pictorial construction is in terms of areas. The art historian and theorist Heinrich Wölfflin applied to these ways of seeing and creating the terms "linear" and "painterly": Botticelli well exemplifies the first type, Velazquez the second. Many other great European painters, most notably Rembrandt and Titian, also very clearly belong to the painterly category, especially in their mature work, but line undoubtedly has a kind of basic and primal quality, a descriptive power and magical intrigue which gives it unchallengeable importance in all visual art.

Line is intimately associated with motion, for in following lines with our eyes we tend to endow them with movement. We also judge lines in relation to the force of gravity, perceiving some to be in a state of equilibrium and others – diagonals for instance – to be dynamic. Even the simplest line or arrangement of lines, then, carries with it the suggestion of meaning and depending on the delicacy or force of the painter's brush may suggest anything from dawdling indolence to harsh, stabbing violence.

When a line turns and meets up with itself it generates shape, whether a frankly two-dimensional area like, say, the diamond on a playing-card, or the flat projection of a solid object, for example the man in the road sign warning us that works are in progress. "Contour" refers to the boundary of any such shape, or the outer limits of a three-dimensional shape as seen from any given angle. Broadly speaking we might say that all painting, however mass-based in conception, must arrive at a contour that satisfies our sense of shape. Mass, though often a powerful element in painting, is not a necessary one, being absent or understated in most pre-Renaissance, modern, and non-European art. The exquisite Roman fresco *Maiden gathering flowers* is a case in point. The girl has, it is true, a measure of weight and mass, but if she were reduced to contour alone, much of her enchantment would survive. Some forms of painting, for example certain types of Greek vases or Regency silhouettes, rely for their effect entirely on contour; its expressive power is superbly illustrated here by Modigliani's nude, whose swelling roundness is conveyed with a minimum of modelling.

By "articulation" we mean the manner in which contiguous shapes or forms join. This can vary a great deal from painter to painter. Buffet shows us a hard, brittle world where it seems some shock might cause everything to crack and fall, whilst Michelangelo joins form to form so toughly that nothing could shake them asunder. In a word, the dichotomy is between the inorganic on the one hand – or in our times the mechanical – and the organic and growing on the other. Hence the choice a painter makes in respect of these two extremes when he sets about joining forms is often, as with other kinds of option, ultimately philosophic, telling us something about his view of the world and relationship with it.

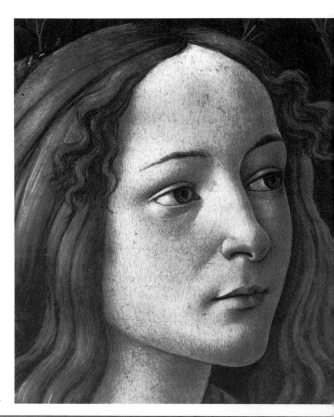

BOTTICELLI (near right)
Venus and Mars, detail,
c. 1485
VELAZQUEZ (far right)
Portrait of a man, detail,
c. 1640
Botticelli creates his forms with clear, precise lines, using only very slight shading to help indicate the roundness of the face. In the supremely painterly approach of Velazquez there are no outlines, and the forms merge imperceptibly with each other; the strong contour of the nose is suggested purely through the subtle modulations of tone Velazquez achieves with his unerring brushwork.

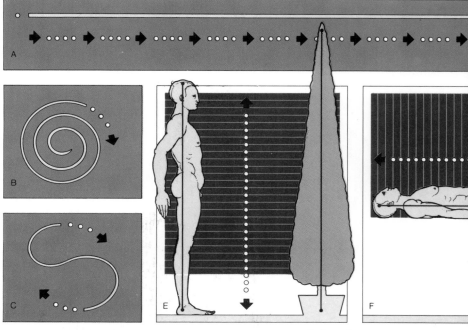

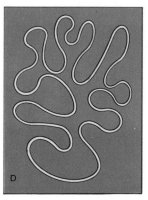

LINE AND MOTION
A line has traditionally been thought of as a trace left by a moving point (A) and we tend to follow lines with our eyes in one direction or another, and even mentally to continue them beyond the point at which they end (B, C); but if the movement of the line becomes too complex we tend to lose interest and cease to follow it (D). This sense of motion which is generated by line is intimately connected with the force of gravity, for there is a vast difference in association (and hence symbolic or expressive quality) between verticals, horizontals and diagonals. Verticality (E) is associated with alertness, daytime, potential activity, dominion; horizontality (F) with repose, night, sleep, submission. We associate diagonals (G) with imbalance, movement and energy, as in the dynamic art of the Baroque.

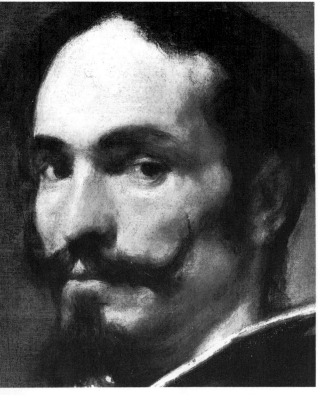

MICHELANGELO (below left)
The Sistine Chapel ceiling:
The creation of Adam, 1511
BUFFET (below right)
Artist and model, 1948
Michelangelo's tremendous
figure of Adam and Buffet's
stick-insect-like image of
himself represent opposite
extremes of articulation.
The fluent, cohesive rhythm
of Adam's body suggests his
wakening power, the resilient
knitting together of youthful
muscles, sinews and tendons.
Buffet presents himself
to us as a pathetic hinge-
jointed marionette, hardly
more substantial than the
easel at which he stands.
The confidence of the one
image, the anxiety of the
other, relate directly to
their differing articulation.

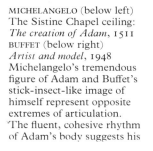

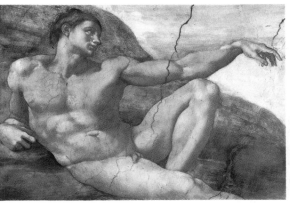

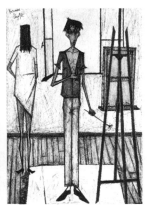

In nature forms rarely meet
at sharp angles: a gradual
merging of contours is
characteristic, as when a
tree spreads out into its
root formation. A roman
letter with its serifs, as
distinct from a modern block
letter, imitates this kind
of organic articulation.

MODIGLIANI (below)
Reclining nude, c. 1919
There is enough modelling
only to prevent the taut
outline from creating a
sense of flatness. Yet the
figure's flowing articulation
suggests the solidity and
suppleness of the forms.

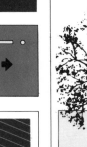

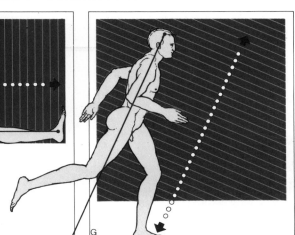

STABIAE, ITALY (left)
Maiden gathering flowers,
1st century AD
This mural, found near
Pompeii and one of the most
precious survivals of
ancient painting, is a
triumph of linear design.
The contour of the figure,
sometimes called *Flora* or
Spring, embodies graceful
contrasts between curves
of the arm and shoulder and
the rippling silhouette of
the drapery, creating a
mobile and expressive effect.

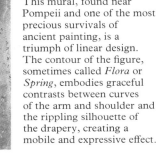

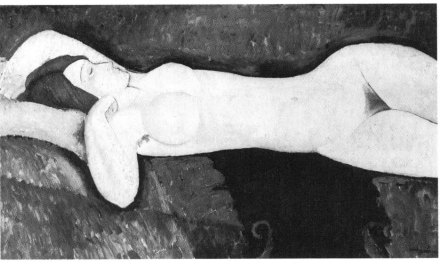

Movement

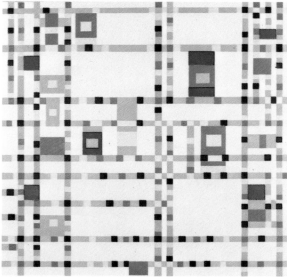

MONDRIAN
Broadway Boogie-Woogie,
1942–43
Mondrian was delighted by
the ordered animation of
New York. Here we might be
looking down on a grid of
streets, the small squares
representing the stop-go
of the traffic while the

larger rectangles are the
major buildings, monuments
or squares. Only verticals
or horizontals (the most
static of directions) are
used, but the restless
dance of our visual per-
ception from one coloured
patch to another gives a
sense of energy and motion.

The word movement, when used in the context of painting, can have a variety of meanings, few of them literal, because the contents of a painting do not move in reality; any appearance of movement must necessarily be illusory – a psychological or perceptual event rather than a physical one. On the other hand, looking at a painting can be – and is often designed to be – a highly active event as our attention is led from one area to another.

We have already looked at three kinds of perceptual events that imply some sort of movement: the tendency of our eyes to track along and even extend lines; the off-balance dynamism of diagonals; and the apparent spatial recession of objects drawn in diminishing scale. Many perceptual forces can be grouped together under the heading of visual dynamics, and dynamics of this kind are normally used by painters whenever they wish to convey impressions of motion and change. A glance at the pictures on this page will show a wealth of such activity.

Apart from the vitality generated by the thrusts and counter-thrusts of shapes or lines, the main kinds of pictorial treatment which in one way or another convey or evoke movement are five, beginning with the most obvious kind, depicted movement – the representation of things arrested in mid-action in such a way that we can tell they are in motion. Someone is shown leaping, running, dancing or making some momentary gesture; a cloud drifts by, a wave breaks, foliage is stirred up by the breeze. Such arrested movement may be represented two-dimensionally, and in pre-Renaissance painting, on Greek vases for instance, normally was. But by the time Tintoretto painted his *Bacchus and Ariadne*, depicted movement enjoyed the full freedom of deep space.

Implied or suggested movement of a slightly different kind occurs when a set of elements, in themselves abstract, is so arranged as to suggest

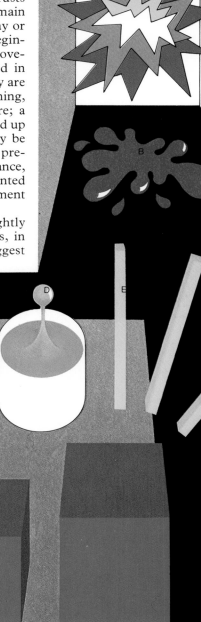

the vertical bar (and, by implication, also a stroboscopic illustration of something falling down). In (C) the radii of a set of concentric circles increase gradually, conveying slow movement outwards, as when ripples spread from a stone dropped in a pond. In (F) the size of the blocks and the intervals between them increase so that the eye is carried upwards and to the right. The visual gradient in (G) is from light to dark, or vice versa; in either case, the sequence impels us to move upwards or downwards progressively.

G

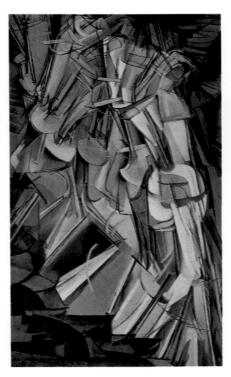

some kind of energized or kinetic event. For instance, the painting by Vasarély shown here is strictly speaking abstract, but can readily be interpreted as a hot-air balloon rising.

In stroboscopic movement the same action is shown at successive stages in a single image. There are hints of this in traditional painting – for instance in Goya's *Stilt-walkers*, where the leading walker is in a posture which the one following him will adopt a second or two later – but as a major resource it did not come into its own until it was vigorously exploited by the Futurists, influenced no doubt by the stop-frame photographs of walking figures by Eadweard Muybridge and by early cinematography. None of the Futurists, however, made more subtle and poetic use of it than did Duchamp in his *Nude descending a staircase*.

A fourth kind of movement is created by visual gradients – the increase or decrease of size, brightness, tilt, elongation, hue or any other measurable quality in regular sequence through pictorial space. We can scarcely avoid "reading" a sequence like those in the bottom diagram progressively, and feeling carried along as we do so.

A final category, induced eye-movement, depends on the fact that our eyes, as noted earlier, are intensely active and mobile organs, engaged in incessant scanning of our visual field. Moreover, there is a tendency on the part of the eye – or rather, of the perceptual system within which it works – to make myriad cross-comparisons hither and thither throughout the field between items which are in some way similar. Like is constantly associated with like, and the eye is forever jumping gaps in search of similitudes and analogies. The more it is persuaded to do so, the livelier the sense of movement we experience. It is this which animates Mondrian's *Broadway Boogie-Woogie*, for instance, in spite of its otherwise static configuration of lines and shapes.

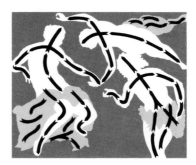

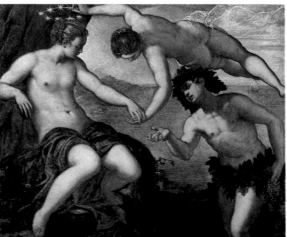

TINTORETTO (above)
Bacchus and Ariadne, 1578
The hurtling movement up from the right plotted in the diagram threatens to break out of the frame at top left, but Tintoretto, with the merest of swoops, brings the momentum back to the middle through the arms and shoulders of the flying figure. Energy thus controlled gives an enhanced sense of its potential.

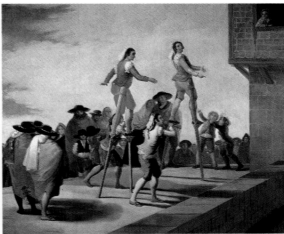

DUCHAMP (left)
Nude descending a staircase no. 2, 1912
This is stroboscopic movement, but not of a literal kind; it conveys the idea or feeling of descent. There are strong analogies with the machinery of the age – cylinders, pistons and connecting rods. That all is in motion is evident at a glance. Yet the diagonals lean together at the top in a manner that holds them within the picture space.

GOYA (above)
The stilt-walkers, c. 1788
Goya, himself an athletic man, had an unrivalled sense of the physical poise of dancers, bullfighters, acrobats and stuntmen such as these stilt-walkers. They are stylish and confident yet wary of their balance. The tilted axes move our eyes diagonally into the picture space but are then ingeniously held back on the far side by the angle of the building support.

Illumination and Tonality

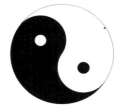

The dualism of light and darkness is summed up by the *Yin-Yang* symbol: each area contains the seed of its own opposite and each grows out of the other in unity and interdependence, as night succeeds day.

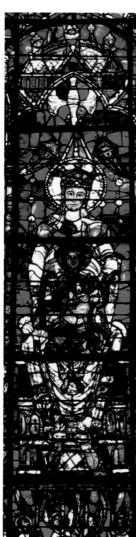

A picture's quality of light is amongst the most telling characteristics of a painter or a school of painting. For instance, the typical light of the Florentine early Renaissance is a cool, vernal, bright, all-revealing radiance; of Venetian painting a warm afterglow; of seventeenth-century Dutch landscape the clear but cloud-filtered midday light of the Lowlands.

At one level these characteristics reflect differences of climatic experience, but there are symbolic and indeed philosophical or religious issues at stake also. Obviously enough, light has in every age and place stood for that which is divine, holy, beneficent; and dark, for the unknown, for death, for evil, for spiritual anguish – "the dark night of the soul". Thus the dark-light dualism is as primeval and profound as any we could name, and the emphasis given to it by artists can tell us much about their individual temperaments.

At this point, with acknowledgments to Marshall McLuhan, the interesting distinction should be made between "light through" and "light on". Light through, in its more literal sense, is exemplified by a stained-glass window viewed from a church interior with the light coming from the sky outside. Nothing could better accord with the medieval Christian world-view, which held that the visible universe was a manifestation of the Divine will, hence man-made things both stood between us and celestial illumination (literally and

symbolically), and were also to varying degrees transparent (by the operation of Divine grace).

A similar but lesser quality of radiance is characteristic of most paintings until the Renaissance, when Leonardo and others introduced strong contrasts of light and shadow (chiaroscuro). Conceptually, it is true of nearly all painting before, and outside of, the High Renaissance and its aftermath, that the light comes towards us off the painting: we receive it rather than observing its effects within the painting. Conversely, "light on" implies luminosity coming from a specific source rather than an omnipresent metaphysical one. This in turn accords well with the new scientific world-view gaining ground throughout the Reformation and triumphant in the epoch of Descartes and Leeuwenhoek. By the seventeenth century, especially in the work of *tenebrist* painters, pictorial space is typically dark in tone, and objects are picked out by strong, often single-source light that strikes their top or side but leaves much of them unlit and causes them to cast deep shadows – the cast shadow, let us note, being virtually unknown outside the Western tradition.

The epoch of chiaroscuro gave birth to some of the greatest European painters – to Caravaggio, to Velazquez, Rembrandt and many others. A poetry of single-source illumination was brought into being, and with it a poetry of tonality exploiting the different expressive effects of slight or em-

VELAZQUEZ (below)
The water-carrier of Seville, c. 1619
It is a sense of the almost sacramental beauty of everyday, normally unregarded, experience that moves us. A shaft of strong daylight finds its way into a dark market-place, turning some facets of the solids into bright islands while almost losing the contours on the shadow side. The strength of the light and shadow structure is shown by the diagram, which simplifies the painting to only four tones without destroying it.

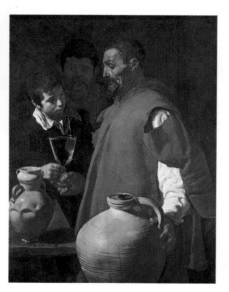

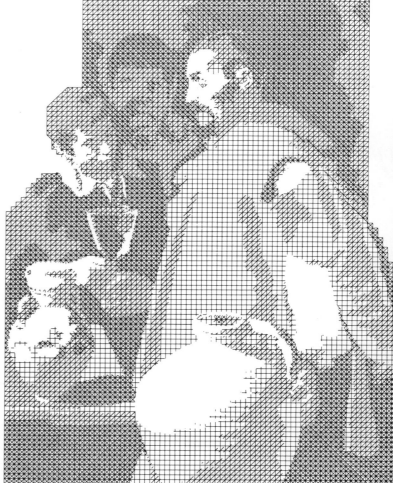

CHARTRES (above)
"*Our Lady of the Beautiful Glass*", mid-12th century. In the stained-glass image of Mary, "light through" has both metaphysical and literal meanings: as the vessel chosen to manifest the Divine on earth, she is someone through whom celestial light shines with especial brilliance.

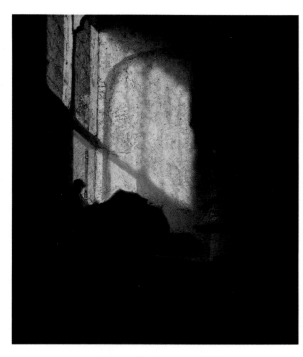

REMBRANDT (right)
A scholar, c. 1630
What streams through this
tall window is not so much
the Divine light that shines
through the Virgin Mary as
the fading (but returning)
light of day. The analogy
of the thinker wresting the
light of truth from a vast,
dark universe is tempting,
yet the artist may simply be
investigating the effects
of light through bottle glass.

CHARDIN (right)
Still life with a marmite,
c. 1762
In this beautiful instance
of "light on", the subtle
management of illumination
and design produces not a
photographically banal
account of light and shade,
cast shadows and highlights,
but a quiet, lyric poem in
praise of the daily miracle
of natural light falling on
a group of familiar objects.

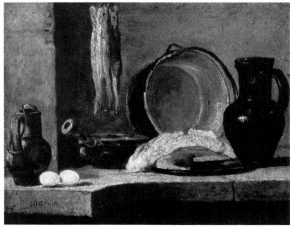

phatic tonal contrasts, of subjects hidden in shadow or theatrically spotlit. Gradations of tone as
surfaces turned away from the light became a
principal means of suggesting three-dimensional
form and volume. In addition to modelling forms
rather than simply delineating shapes, painters
used tone to indicate the spatial dimensions of
their pictures and to create rhythmic patterns of
light and dark, often running counter to the colour
pattern. In order to achieve the subtlest, most
poetic tonal rendering of the fall of light, intense
colour must be restricted or avoided: it competes
with and destroys the delicate play of tone. To a
great extent, therefore, a painter is obliged to make
the choice between full eloquence of tone, of "light
on", and the brilliance of colour so suggestive of
"light through". Only small areas, if any at all, of
strong colour are found in Velazquez, Vermeer,
Constable, Corot or Ingres.

At least in its silvery-grey seventeenth-century
sense, tonality began to evaporate with the onset of
Impressionism; and in Cézanne, Gauguin and van
Gogh, along with many of their contemporaries,
there seems to be a reversion in whole or part to
"light through"; a reversion which becomes still
more marked in the work of Klee and some other
abstract artists. With some exceptions – Super-
realism, for example, – it is in photography rather
than in painting that the nuances of "light on" are
now explored.

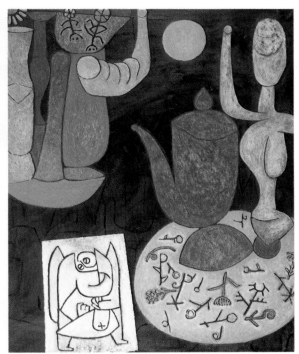

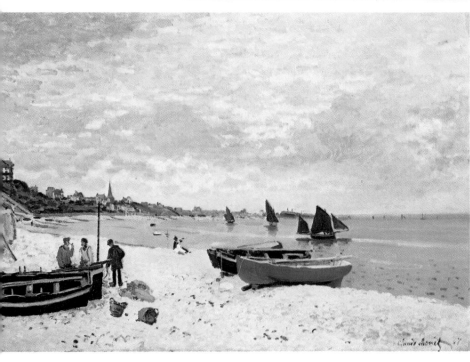

MONET (left)
Beach at Ste-Adresse, 1867
The luminosity that almost
warms our faces is arguably
a secular version of "light
through", since the sunlight
comes towards us directly,
filtered only by high cloud.
The few, fairly small solids
that obstruct the wash of
light suggest its strength
by their emphatic darkness.

KLEE (above)
Painting on black back-
ground, 1940
As with much of Klee's
work we have the impression
that light is coming through
the objects rather than
falling on them. There is
no lit or darkened side on
any shape and no cast
shadow. The black back-
ground enhances this effect.

Texture and Surface

Our response to texture in paintings depends in large part on the closeness of the link between our visual and tactile senses. The roughness of bark or the smoothness of glass are apprehended not only by looking but by many experiences of touching their surfaces, and it is the force of this tactile memory which, in painting, can make depicted textures seem almost as convincing as real ones. The distinction between the two needs to be understood. Even when the surface of the picture itself is almost smooth, a realistic and minute rendering of uneven surfaces may be achieved either by linear drawing – of wrinkles in a face or grain in wood, for instance – or, still more illusionistically, by using changes of tonality in a very meticulous way to indicate irregularities in a surface. This technique of depicting texture depends on the painting having a source of directional light which reveals more and more irregularities as surfaces turn away from it.

Jan van Eyck's "*The Arnolfini Marriage*" (see p. 152) is a supreme example of literal and exact textural representation: wood, metal, glass, cloth, fur, hair, lace are lovingly described in terms of their tactile and surface qualities as revealed by the light from a window. In the wake of this achievement came the great tribe of genre, still-life and flower-painters in the seventeenth-century Netherlands. *Trompe-l'oeil* painters of the eight-

CONSTABLE (below, with detail, below right)
The leaping horse, 1825
Constable expressed in a letter his involvement with natural textures and processes of time and wear: "Willows, old rotten banks, slimy post and brickwork, I love such things ... As long as I do paint I shall never cease to paint such places ... Painting is but another word for feeling. I associate my careless boyhood to all that lies on the banks of the Stour. They made me a painter."

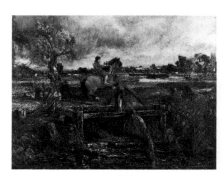

eenth century followed suit and so, in their own fashion, did the Pre-Raphaelites. The Superrealist school is the latest expression of a perennial human fascination both with mimetic skills and with the *frisson* of minute observation, exemplified here by Ralph Goings' trailer with its careful painting of reflections and of details as small as the rivet heads in the metal.

In this tradition, the quality of the paint surface itself tends to be smooth and anonymous, since fluid pigment and very fine brushes are the only means by which Eyckian or Pre-Raphaelite renderings are possible. Relatively smooth surfaces may also be found in some abstract paintings in which texture is predominant, as in much of Tobey's work, where the markings are too small and close to be read as distinct shapes yet not so

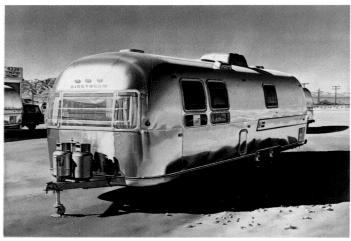

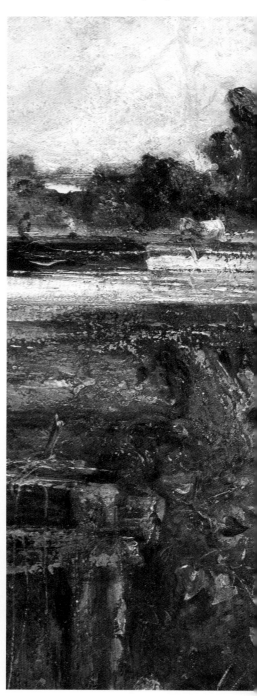

GOINGS (left)
Airstream trailer, 1970
The textural verisimilitude that may be achieved by a subtle and methodical handling of tone and cast shadow is seen in Goings' rendering of the polished aluminium sides of the trailer. Wavering shadow along the underside of the body explains every slight dent in the metal, and the hard shadow of the two canisters, the flare of light on the front, make the heat of the surface almost tangible. The painting retains the textual sharp-focus of the photograph on which it was based.

TOBEY (right)
Barth rhythmus, 1961
This is pure, abstract texture, the myriad hooks, squiggles and threaded trails of paint energizing a luminous surface which seems as impenetrable as quartz yet has depth upon depth of faceted colour.

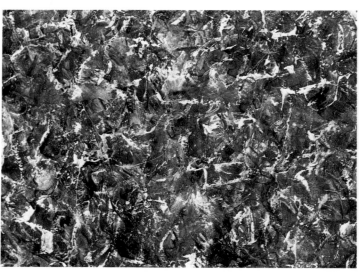

regularly spaced out that they form a pattern. It is quite otherwise with an Action Painter such as Jackson Pollock, whose pigment positively shouts out its own life-history – what kind of stuff it is and how it got there. Here we are confronted by the real texture of a worked substance – by the tangible qualities of impasto layers, glistening blobs or looping skeins, furrows, scorings or churnings of pigment. Pollock's intention is less to create textural interest for its own sake than to make explicit, by his handling of paint, the story of his own actions and state of mind.

Such evidence of the artist's hand is by no means the monopoly of Abstract Expressionism, however: it has been a powerful auxiliary in much figurative painting, as is clear from a study of the pictures here by Constable, van Gogh and Céz-

INGRES (below)
The spring, 1856
Clearly, the teased-up paint surface of Constable's landscape, perfectly suited to expressing the rough processes of nature in the Suffolk countryside, would be wholly inappropriate for the subject here. Discreet perfection of drawing, subtle tonality and creamy pigment all work together to convey a voluptuous and fluent serenity. Such contrasts of texture in painting are as delightful as textural variety in food.

anne. The quality of the paint surface – the real texture – in each case corroborates or may be even richer than the texture depicted. By his handling of paint each of these artists also makes eloquent the effect of time on the material world: wear and tear, erosion, crumbling, cracking, rotting away. For whereas smoothness speaks of newness, growth and resiliency, or of the durable hardness of machine-made products, uneven surfaces tend to be associated with wear, ageing, mortality – a tragic emotion but not wholly so, since decay implies regeneration. Most of us have felt some measure of agreeable nostalgia in contemplating the ravages of time: why else do we seek out weathered walls, sea-wrack, ruined temples and all those light-fracturing irregularities that the eighteenth century referred to as "picturesque"?

There is a second and more technical collusion between texture and time: quite simply, uneven textures of any kind – and patterns also – slow down our scrutiny of a picture. Their opposites, smooth surfaces and sinuous curves, those delectable attributes of youth which Ingres sets before us in *The spring*, allow our glance to slip readily from feature to feature. In contrast, Cézanne, by the manifold touches of his brush, obliges us to experience with him the heave and turn of the masses formed over slow geological time and analysed by him with such patience.

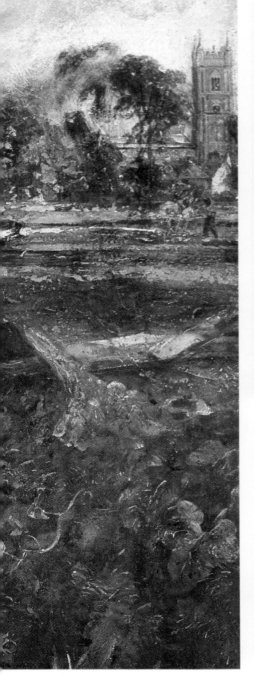

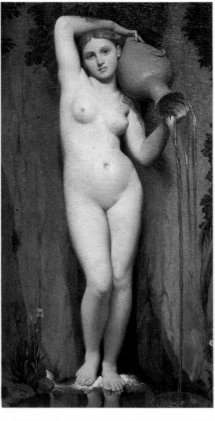

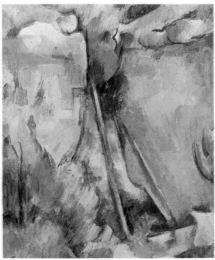

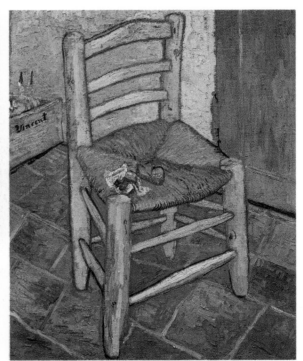

CEZANNE (left)
Mont Ste-Victoire from Bibémus Quarry, detail, 1898
Brush-strokes reminiscent of the marks left by a stonemason's claw chisel reveal the artist's slow assemblage of his pictorial architecture, his relish in the grand simplicities of mass – and something, too, of the quarryman's cleaving interventions in Nature.

VAN GOGH (above)
Chair and pipe, 1888-89
Thick, emphatic brush-marks tell of the rough workmanship of this chair and its long, sturdy service, the generations of scuffing and scrubbing undergone by the tiled floor, and the working man's consolation from the feel of his pipe. In both subject and handling, this is the poetry of use.

Edge Qualities

EDGE AND COLOUR
Quality of edge can have a
marked effect on tonality.
The two squares above are
objectively identical in
tint, but because the one

on the right-hand side has
a hard edge it makes a
sharper contrast with the
white background than its
neighbour, and consequently
we read it as being darker.

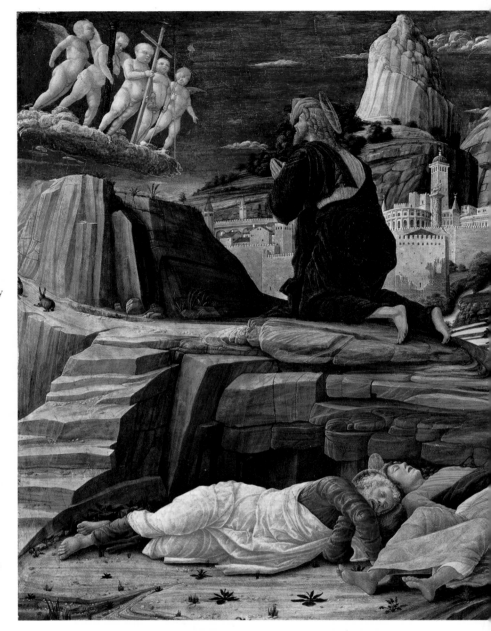

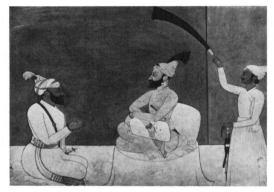

JAMMU, INDIA (above)
*Mian Brij Raj Dev with
attendants, c.*1765
Although this painting does
not wholly exclude volume
and depth, it relies for its
effects almost entirely on
the clarity and unwavering
grace of its contours.

MANTEGNA (right)
*The Agony in the Garden,
c.*1460
Mantegna's world is flintily
hard-edged, even the clouds
having explicitly defined
limits. But the number of
small clear steps around the
forms moderates the effect.

Painters today are often classified according to the
way they manage the contours or limits of their
colour areas: certain abstract artists, for example,
are said to belong to a "hard-edge school". It
would be entirely correct to infer from this that the
treatment of edge is very important aesthetically,
that is in terms of its effects, and also philosophi-
cally, in terms of the preferences and values one or
the other treatment reveals. In discussing line and
contour (see p. 96) we noted Wölfflin's distinction
between the linear and the painterly, and a
similar kind of polarity can be distinguished
between hard/continuous and soft/broken edge
quality. Hard-edge corresponds broadly with the
linear approach (a line, after all, implies continuity) and soft-edge with the painterly.

What is at issue here? Very largely it is a matter
of the painting's function. Totemic or heraldic
works, those that function almost as signs, will
invariably need hard edges for the sake of ready

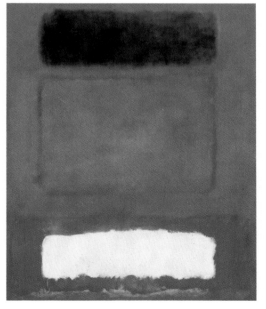

ROTHKO
Red, white and brown, 1957
If Rothko had given hard
edges to the shapes he uses
we might find this merely a
handsome abstract painting.
Its compelling quality comes
from subtle manipulations of
fading edges, and the glowing
vastness they make us feel.

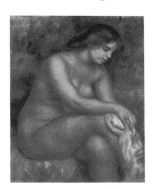

RENOIR (below)
Bather drying her leg, 1910
Renoir's edges, especially
when they enfold the
human figure, are the very
essence of softness. The
paint is fluidly touched
on to the canvas with a
soft brush, suggesting the
gentleness of a lover's
caresses – the poetry of
touch rather than sight.

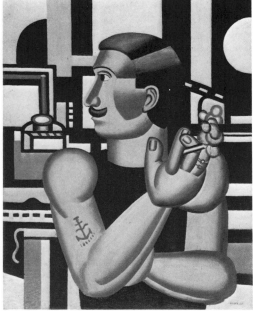

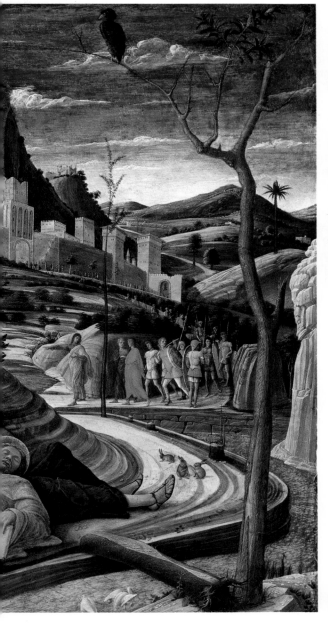

LEGER (above)
The mechanic, 1920
Léger gives us man re-created
in the image of a machine;
his limbs, like piston-rods,
shaped for work. This is
the hard-edge art born of
industrial civilization.

LEONARDO (right)
The Virgin of the rocks,
detail, *c.* 1505
Leonardo was a pioneer in
the modelling of forms in
light and shade. Here the
forms emerge from the deep
shadows of a rock grotto,
the contours dissolving in
a play of lost and found.

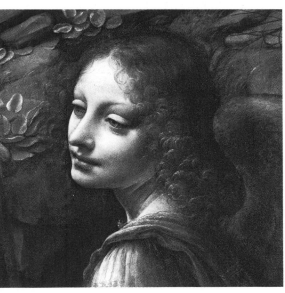

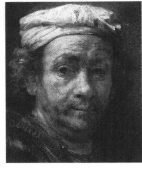

REMBRANDT
Self-portrait, detail, 1660
Rembrandt's edges vary here
from thin, sharp, clearly
formed accents, where light
strikes his cap, eyelid and
collar, to contours so deeply
sunk in shadow that they
are almost blended with
their neighbouring areas.

decipherability. In more recent history hard edges have corresponded with an intellectual, structural, architectonic approach, as against a sensory or intuitive one. Hard-edge art is strongly visual: it is the outcome of clear illumination and accurate focus. Soft-edge, by contrast, is tactile and caressing, conveying the roundedness of things and the way curved surfaces fade gently off at their contours. It marks, too, a response to the effulgence, the glow of objects in light, and how the impact of light seems to fracture and modify the sharpness of their silhouettes; or how, as can be seen here in the heads by Leonardo and Rembrandt, envelopment in deep shadows causes a local "lostness" of contour and elision of shapes.

Generalizing still further, we could say that hard edges are usually chosen whenever separation of parts, categorization and intellectual analysis are the aim; whereas if an artist is concerned primarily with unity, integration and

fluency, then softness or brokenness will typically be preferred. As intellectual clarity is at the heart of classicism, classic art inclines strongly to the hard side. The pursuit by Romantic artists of unity and totality has often – though by no means always – propelled them towards a soft-edge treatment.

To some extent, indeed, we have here an antithesis between the rational or commonsensical and the imaginative or visionary. While it is probably true that supreme mystical experience is accompanied by great clarity and that linearity is characteristic of many visionary painters, notably Blake, nevertheless imagination is often freed by images which are suggestive rather than specific. Hence, perhaps, the soft edges of the rectangular forms in Mark Rothko's paintings, typical as they are of what the critic Robert Melville has called "the abstract sublime", in radical contrast to the literal quality of many American hard-edge paintings of the 1960s, with their clean severity.

Pattern

As soon as leisure and skills have been available, people everywhere have wanted to decorate surfaces – those of their bodies, clothes, utensils, carpets, walls, weapons – with ornamental patterns of frequently breathtaking beauty and ingenuity. Elaboration and artistry by no means always correlate; there are many instances of patterns becoming too intricate and garrulous for an educated taste, and conversely, of simple but subtle ones (on much Song dynasty pottery) which are of the highest quality.

In painting, patterns can be formed by any repetitive sequence of lines, shapes, tonal accents, colours or even brush-marks. Figure/ground ambiguity can occur in abstract patterns, a chessboard being a simple example; are the white squares on a black ground, or vice versa? Most patterns in figurative art are unambiguous, however, and painters have traditionally delighted in them: one thinks, for example, of the costumes in Japanese prints; the textile and architectural decoration in Persian and Indian miniatures; the damask hangings of Crivelli or Veronese; the spots on Titian's leopards; the wall-papers and cretonnes of Vuillard and Matisse; the bold decorative passages in Picasso and Braque from Synthetic Cubism onwards.

What lies at the root of this seemingly unconquerable urge, and what does pattern do in painting? It has already been suggested that pattern, like texture, serves to slow down our eye as it traverses the picture surface, much as repeated ridges on a road would slow down a car. But whereas natural texture is often an index of wear and tear through time, a patterned surface, by contrast, whether it is the work of nature or of human hands, speaks of a sense of constructive purpose or design and often, too, of exuberance, vitality, relish, the determination to enjoy and to enrich life.

In the early twentieth century, pattern in the sense of surface ornamentation for its own sake fell into disrepute among some critics of art, architecture and design – largely in reaction against the indiscriminate application of decorative motifs, plundered from every culture, to every available surface in the homes of the newly affluent classes in the late nineteenth century. Following the precepts of Adolf Loos in architecture and the Bauhaus in industrial design, there emerged a positively puritanical disdain for any surface treatment that had no "functional" purpose. But the

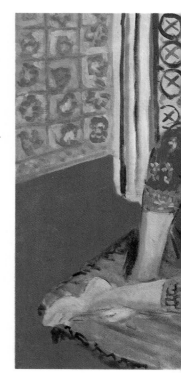

BRAQUE (left)
Still life on a red table-cloth, 1936
Addicted both to texture and to pattern, Braque has woven at least six motifs, in repetitions sufficiently regular to qualify as pattern, into one of the handsomest of all Synthetic Cubist still lifes. He can create a monumental grandeur from elements as banal as the Christmas tree motif on a piece of oil-cloth, which can be discerned when the picture is held upside down.

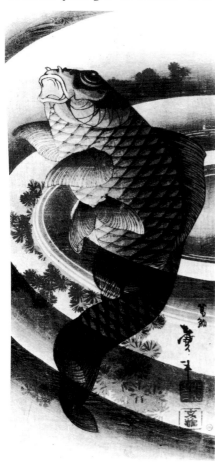

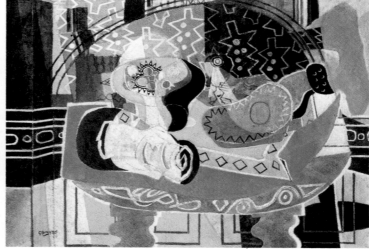

HOKUSAI (left)
Carp leaping in a pool,
late 18th century
Without any loss of truthfulness to nature, the maker of this woodcut manages to confer upon his representations of the ripples, the water-weed, the fins and the scales value also as pattern. Nature and stylization (the concentric rings depicting water), the momentary and the deliberately organized, are miraculously at one.

HILLIARD (right)
Young man in a garden,
c. 1588
The bold pattern on the doublet of the dreaming youth lends piquancy to the smoothness of his white hose, and the entwining leaves and flowers among which he is posed are so delicately formalized that they, too, fall within the definition of pattern, even though their repetitions are not strictly regular. As with Hokusai's stylized carp, natural appearances have been vividly rendered and at the same time fully exploited for their pattern potential – their value as sensuous ornamentation.

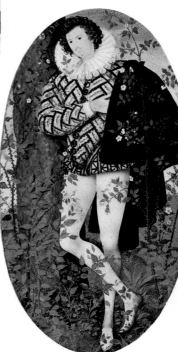

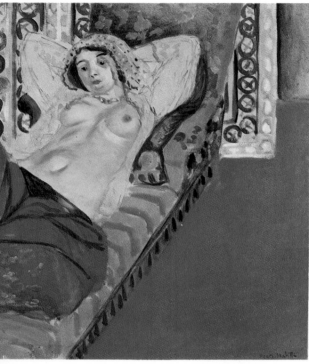

SPENCER (right)
Swan-upping, 1914–15,
finished 1919
Spencer celebrates a unity
between the natural patterns
of the cedar, the vine and
the wavelets, and man-made
patterns in the roof tiles,
the bridge parapet, the
cushions, the timbers of
punts and landing stage.
These are played off against
each other but together
enhance the plain areas
of the foreground and the
metal plates on the bridge.

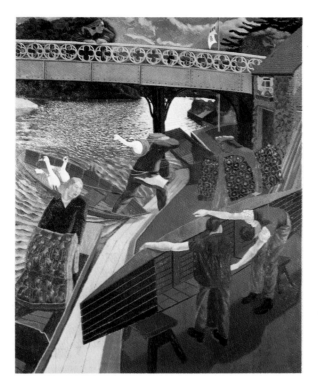

MATISSE (top left)
Odalisque, 1922
The Middle Eastern theme
reflects Matisse's lasting
fascination with Islamic
traditions of rich and
variegated pattern. Apart
from its decorative value,
pattern often enabled him
to suggest form by linear
changes of direction rather
than by modelling in tone
and losing the purity and
brilliance of his colour.
In the small copy shown
below Matisse's picture, the
patterning has been replaced
by colours that approximate
the effect of the combined
hues; the bed which seemed
to rise so solidly becomes
flat and formless. At the
same time the liveliness
of the picture is depleted.

demand for austerity and economy of means did
not reduce the allurement of symmetrical pattern,
as Mondrian's abstract work shows. To this day
we have Minimal painters such as Frank Stella,
who is decorative before he is anything else, and
modular or "serial" art in which painters and
sculptors are concerned above all with regularity
and repetition, and on achieving an almost mathematical objectivity within a closed system.

Pattern is not "merely" decorative; as well as
being a primeval human pleasure, not lacking in
deeper implications, it can be used to convey
symbolic meaning, as in the stylized patterns of
much Islamic and Eastern art, and can also serve a
range of formal uses. It may provide a sense of
continuous visual harmony and order or, when
combined with·unpatterned areas, satisfy our wish
for visual variety. How delectable it is to savour, in
simultaneous contrast, the slipperiness of butter
with the crunchiness of toast. The pleasure derived from looking, for instance, at the contrast
between the plain and patterned areas in the
pictures by Matisse, Hilliard and Braque shown
here is not dissimilar; an effect of mutual enhance-
ment is taking place, and we can see, in the altered
version of the Matisse, what a loss is suffered when
pattern is eliminated.

If we concentrate on a patterned area in a
painting – say the striped counterpane on which
Matisse's odalisque reclines, or the deep buttoning
of the cushions in Stanley Spencer's riverside
scene – we may become aware also that we are
being offered an enriching double experience – a
sensation of surface regularity together with a
realization that its departures from regularity (the
curvature of the stripes in the Matisse) signify
changed orientation in space; we have two readings for the price of one.

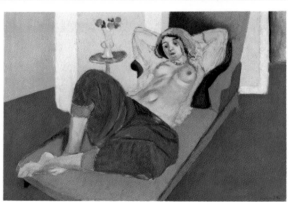

WARHOL (right)
Marilyn Monroe, 1962
Here is repetition far more
blatant than can be found
in Braque or Spencer, its
few variations suggesting
rather the accidents of
screen-printing than any
deliberate intent. It is
precisely the monotony of
mass-produced glamour that
is being – not celebrated,
for that would imply some
delight – but methodically
rehearsed in the paradoxical
context of highbrow art.
Obviously enough, pattern
is one inescapable result,
but it is questionable
whether Warhol seeks to
please us by it, as do the
other artists represented.

The Dimensions of Colour

Colour has become, for many twentieth-century abstract artists, the most essential attribute of painting, a means not simply of enriching a design but of creating space, volume and movement and of expressing and even inducing emotional states. The main dimensions of colour are hue (the spectrum name), intensity or saturation (degree of purity), tone (degree of lightness or darkness) and temperature (relative warmth or coolness). A vast number of variables comes into play when colours are used together in the restricted space of a picture, however. As everyone knows who has tried to paint, each addition or extension of colour alters the total equation in ways very hard to predict, so that any good painting is a prodigy of only partly conscious calculation.

Three colours – red, yellow and blue – are primary in the painter's spectrum. These form the basis of all others, countless pure chromatic hues being made by mixing any two primaries in varying proportions. When these hues in turn are shaded by the addition of black or grey, tinted by the addition of white, or overlaid by other colours in semi-transparent glazes, the permutations of hue become infinite. Their mutual behaviour – how they consort together – may depend on another variable, the relative sizes of colour areas. "A metre of green is more green than a centimetre of it", said Gauguin; conversely, a small accent of red in a field of green can have an impact out of all proportion to its size. By conjuring with the relationships between adjacent hues, artists can make colours that objectively are muted appear

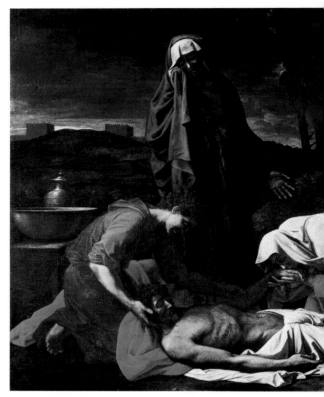

THE COLOUR WHEEL

Colours differ from each other not only in hue (red from orange) but also in tonal value, their lightness or darkness. The tonal range charted by the grey segments on the wheel shows that yellow is inherently much brighter than violet and that bluish hues are darker in general. Each hue could be made tonally lighter or darker by tinting or shading to produce, say, a dark yellow and a light violet. But the chromatic purity or intensity would then diminish. Between each of the three primary hues (yellow, red and blue) are shown three intermediate colours. Complementaries lie opposite each other on the wheel and form strong contrasts of hue – red with green or blue with orange – while those that are close to each other harmonize. Hues also have a perceived "temperature"; we feel that reddish-yellow colours are warm, the blue-greens cool.

MATISSE (below)
The red studio, 1911
Matisse's commitment to strong, pure colour without light and shade is daringly expressed in a picture which seems deliberately to challenge the convention that colour used as a background must necessarily be neutral in tone and hue. The huge field of warm, rusty red dominates all,

advancing to flatten a space which is nevertheless indicated unmistakably by the delicate linear sketching and the angles at which frames lean against the walls. The painting is also an inventory of his own work disposed about the studio, the picture on the right showing the direct, flat, contrasting colours of his early Fauve period.

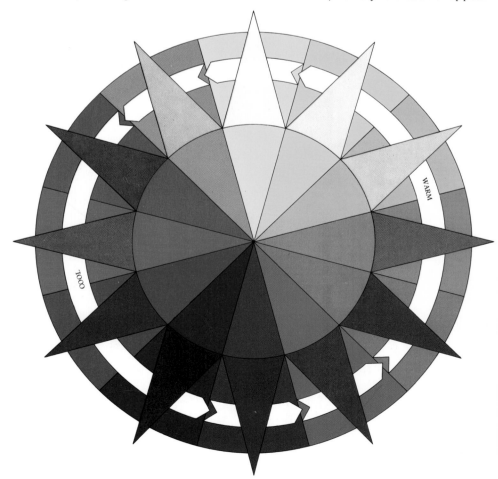

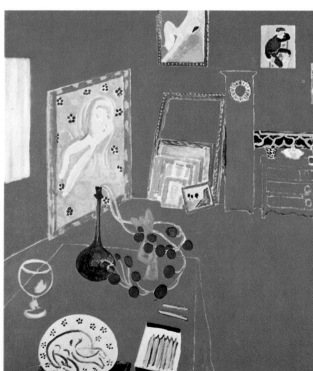

pure and glowing. "Give me mud", wrote Delacroix, "and I will make the skin of Venus out of it if you will allow me to surround it as I please."

Because of the elusiveness, subtlety and complexity of colour, systems of mapping or calibrating it, as on the colour wheel shown here, can do no more than establish basic terms and indicate some of the main options open to painters. A picture with colours from opposite sides of the wheel (complementaries) juxtaposed at full chromatic strength will tend towards powerful, perhaps disturbing effects as each colour competes for attention. Optical vibrancy is reduced when colour contrasts are slight, inducing, perhaps, a more contemplative mood. Subtly differentiated chords can be struck within these extremes, however, and the strongest contrasts can be controlled by the mediating effect of neutral areas.

Similarly, while the red-yellow side of the wheel suggests the warmth of fire, and the blue-greens the coolness of ice, such psychological perceptions of "temperature" are highly relative. Just as hues degraded towards grey can be made to seem pure, so cool colours may sometimes look warm against others. The spatial aspects of colour are no less subtle. Fields of pure, unvarying hues jostling each other tend to flatten a painting and have been exploited most vigorously by modern colourists who have discarded illusionistic depth. Yet even without modelling in light and shade, the differing tonal values and relative temperatures of colours can be used to give convincing effects of depth and volume, the light, warm colours tending to advance, the dark, cool ones to recede, an effect used by Cézanne to create an extraordinary three-dimensional solidity. Matisse and the Fauves went even further in discarding conventional tonality and expressing form simply by combining line with rich, forceful colours.

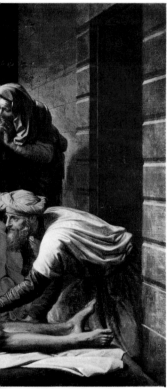

POUSSIN (above)
Lamentation over the dead Christ, c. 1655
The wide range of colours strikes a plangent chord which is nevertheless made harmonious by greys, near-whites and other mediating neutral areas. An emphatic light-and-shade structure crossing the colour areas also helps to offset the intensity of colour contrast.

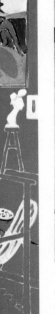
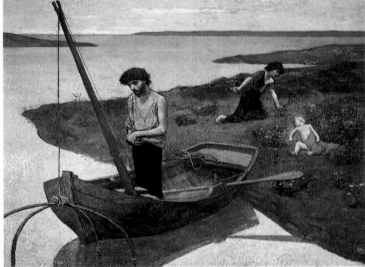

PUVIS DE CHAVANNES
The poor fisherman, 1881
The melancholy power of this picture depends not on strong contrasts, as in the Poussin, but on muted, near-monochrome tints, subtly

modulated and in balance with the linear design. When colour is used in this restrained manner, even a small increase in intensity – the purple of the distant headland – registers in full.

BONNARD
Self-portrait, 1940
Unlike Poussin, Bonnard reduces light and shade to a minimum and chooses a fairly narrow range of hues

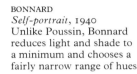
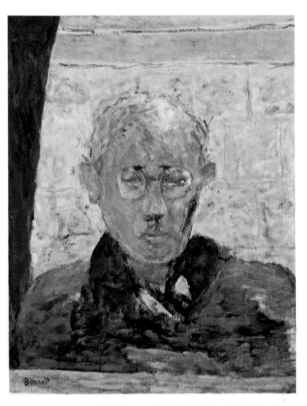

to suggest the pervasive yellow of reflected sunlight. The head is less three-dimensional than Cézanne's but the picture is suffused with warmth.

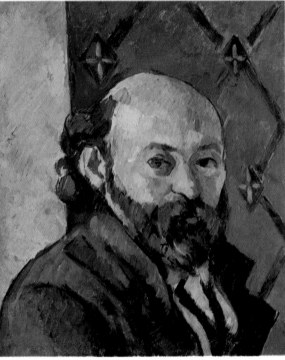

CEZANNE
Self-portrait, c. 1880
Brush-strokes of mutating colour make both a web of harmonic changes across the surface and an analysis of volume and space. Light

hues used for the advancing planes are further projected by the complementary action of the darker, cool colours – and opposites in the spectrum wheel – chosen for the receding surfaces.

Ways of Using Colour

In a simple way we have already charted the basic colour and tone keys that are at the painter's disposal. The question remains why a painter or school of painting may habitually prefer one rather than another and what social, personal or aesthetic intentions are revealed by these choices. The main typical ways of using colour are discussed below. But first another distinction must be made, this time between local and atmospheric colour.

In a local-coloured picture a red garment is more or less fully red from edge to edge: and the same would apply to a green tree or a gold throne. Atmospheric colouring, on the other hand, acknowledges that although a red garment is predominantly red it may have, broken into its red hue, tints and reflections of other colours from the environment, modulating it here and there towards purple, say, or brown or grey. Obviously enough, local colouring generally corresponds with concept (what a thing is thought of as being) and atmospheric colouring with observation (how it may really look at a given moment). To appreciate the difference, we have only to glance from the Archangel Michael on this page to Seurat's seascape and back.

Local colour in a painting tends to be flat, of one hue and tonality throughout. St Michael's wings and the gold background are quite flat, for instance, though his green tunic has slight modulations and highlights. Atmospheric colour is by definition modulated: it must necessarily change from one tint to another across small distances (the shadow side of Seurat's jetty) and may have declensions of tone as well.

With these antitheses in mind we may now distinguish several significantly different ways of using colour, beginning with its heraldic or symbolic use in paintings produced within well-established stylistic conventions. Such paintings

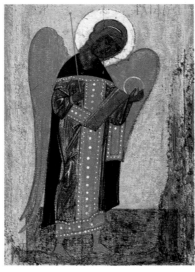

NOVGOROD SCHOOL
The Archangel Michael,
early 14th century
In the tradition of icon painting stemming from Byzantium, verisimilitude must be kept at bay, since the object is to present sacred figures as living in a transcendent world rather than the everyday one. The icon painter intended to hold the eye of the faithful by strong and simple beauties of shape and colour, not to render symbolic red wings, for instance, as they might look in a given light. This is different from atmospheric colour, shown in the lower part of the diagram, where red and green are modified by both light and proximity.

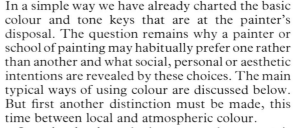

TIEPOLO
The marriage of Frederick and Beatrice, 1753
A great master of swagger, Tiepolo courts verisimilitude – the blue of Beatrice's train is modulated to render its surface quality – but his clear, local colours are deployed with decorative intent, to create a lively, stylish, worldly atmosphere.

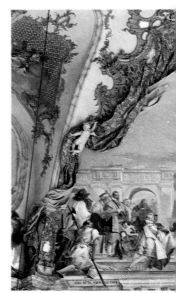

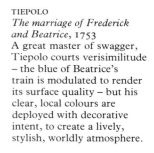

TISSOT (below)
The ball on shipboard, 1874
Balanced to a nicety, with asymmetrical neutral areas played against clear, local colours (little modified by the light), the composition conveys the passing moment with snapshot-like realism.

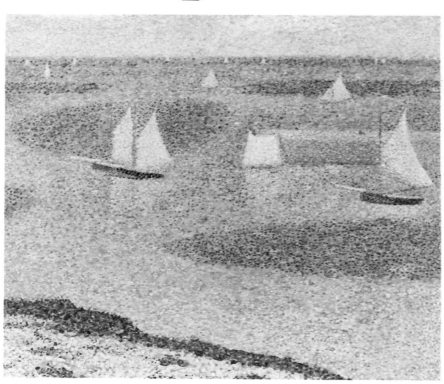

SEURAT (left)
Fishing fleet at Port-en-Bessin, detail, 1888
Seurat uses the vibrancy of pointillism, dots of separate colour interacting in juxtaposition, to define and celebrate everything that, in Auden's words, "the leaping light for your delight discovers". He is acutely aware of a need to render the essential and typical in terms of the optical and the transient. At the same time his use of atmospheric colour has a structural intention; he locates carefully selected and simplified solids with extreme precision to realize a volume of deep space.

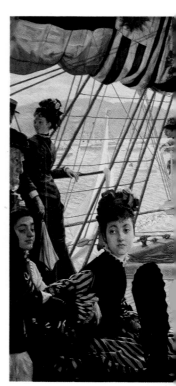

PIERO DELLA FRANCESCA
(right) *The baptism of
Christ, c.* 1440–50
The calm equilibrium, the
grave, exalted atmosphere,
are achieved with a limpid
chord of colours, a hybrid
between Byzantine formality
and subtle naturalism. The
colours are treated as local
but modulated by a clear,
vernal light from the right.

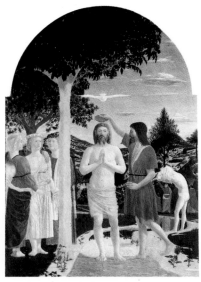

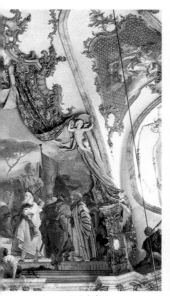

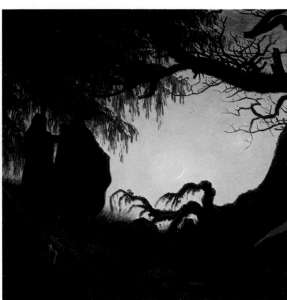

FRIEDRICH (right)
*Man and woman gazing at
the moon,* detail, *c.* 1830–35
Friedrich's choice of a
sombre, near monochrome
scheme of greenish browns
and salmon pinks enfolds us
irresistibly in an elegiac
mood of dusk and moonrise.

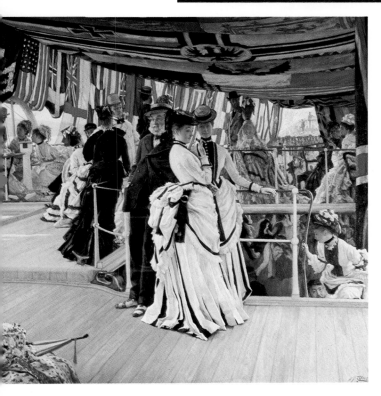

have an assigned function, often a ritual one, involving colours with known symbolic connotations (the Madonna's blue robe in Western painting or Krishna's blue skin in Indian art). Colour tends to be local, edges hard.

Decorative colour, on the other hand, is intended to provide an agreeable background to daily living or to draw attention to the person who has commissioned the work. It could be himself, in the case of an African tribesman painting his hut, or a prince, as in the Tiepolo shown here. Colours tend to be chosen for their restful, pleasing or stylish properties, and to be local rather than atmospheric, very often painted rather flatly.

Realistic colour is chosen when the painter is making a documentary record of contemporary life, normally in an easel picture, as in the genre paintings of nineteenth-century salons and academies. Colours tend to be literal and descriptive: often local rather than atmospheric (see the Tissot on this page).

In Impressionism and Divisionism, "realistic" colour is reinterpreted; the painter's preoccupation is with the visible world as manifested by light in atmosphere. Small touches of relatively pure and often complementary colours are juxtaposed, almost mixing in the viewer's eye, thus creating vibrancy: yellow and blue touches combine as optical green, for instance, as in Seurat's seascape. Colours are based on the pure hues of the spectrum: black and greys are eliminated, except greys made by juxtaposed hues cancelling each other out. A significant extension of this principle is the use of colour for analytical-structural purposes: the painter selects and modulates colours to help create pictorial space and light in the manner of Seurat or to bring out aspects of volume and mass as Cézanne did by using light, warm colours on advancing planes, cool dark ones to suggest recession (see preceding page).

Symbolist colour moves sharply away from realism; the painter's overriding aim is to express his feelings about the theme of the painting, and colour thus becomes a powerful symbol of emotions, thoughts, aspirations, recollections, moods. Whistler's *Nocturnes* and Picasso's "Blue" period paintings are typical. A single mood-colour often dominates, as in the Friedrich shown here. Expressionism, a more extreme manifestation of Symbolism, has very much the same intentions but shows still more marked departures from realism and often much more saturated colour (see, for instance, the Chagall on p. 92).

Finally, the abstract painter, being under no constraint to render appearances, concentrates on choosing colours that will create movement, space or structural form, or "sing together" the pictorial tune he has in mind, as in the Mondrian on p. 98. It is important to emphasize that these usages are not always mutually exclusive: Tissot, for instance, is firmly realistic but also very decorative; Piero's *Baptism* embodies aspects of heraldic, decorative and symbolist colour and perhaps a foretaste of Impressionism. Yet the recognition of a dominant colour mode can tell us much about an artist and the meaning of his work.

Abstraction

Nobody expects music to be "of" something, said the founders of abstract art; why then should any such demand be made on paintings? In a sense, this whole section of the book has shown that, as the pioneer abstractionists contended, spaces, shapes, lines, tones, patterns or colours can indeed work on us emotionally and, in a sense, intellectually as well, even when we encounter them unattached to any recognizable image – just as do melody, harmony or rhythm in music.

Without the yardstick of truthful representation that marks out a skilful figurative work from a clumsily executed one, we may find it hard to explain why one abstract painting is completely satisfying while another is unconvincing or simply messy. On the other hand it can be claimed that the depiction of objects according to strict rules of perspective was a false and restrictive yardstick in the first place.

This argument, though valid in its own terms, does not close the controversy, since there is obviously loss as well as gain involved in the abandonment of representation. Nor does the infinite freedom of abstraction mean that certain major trends or traditions cannot be distinguished in abstract painting. A bipolarity suggests itself at once between the impulsive and the calculated, the rough and the tidy. While some abstract paintings succeed by intuition, risk, gesture, free handling and the rich, unforeseeable textures and edges that result, others are measured, deliberate, neatly finished and usually hard-edged.

A broad analysis of these two trends must begin with Kandinsky's painterly "writing down" of

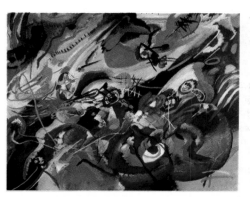

KANDINSKY (left)
Study for *Composition no. 7*, 1913
This might be called the landscape of Kandinsky's (evidently turbulent) psyche at the time he painted it, and is typical of his early expressionist style. The strong drive travelling from lower left to upper right leaves whirlpools in its wake. Colours are intense, edges often broken and blurred, yet there is much forethought.

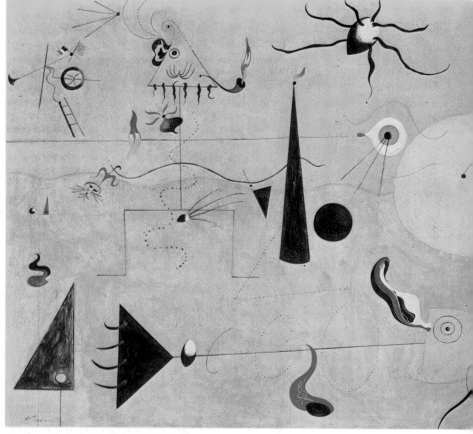

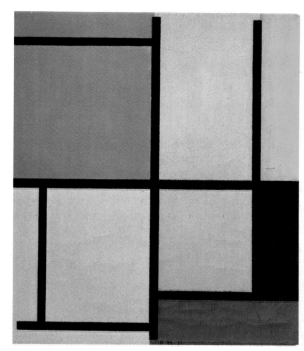

MONDRIAN (above)
Composition, 1921
Subjectivity, caprice and accident are banished from Mondrian's mature art; the whole of reality as he experiences it is reduced and compressed within an austere structure of black bars with infillings of white, grey and the three primary colours of yellow, red and blue. These were the elemental constants.

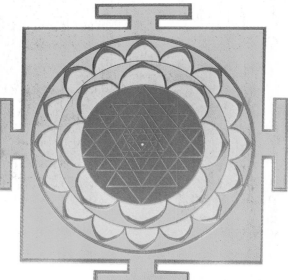

RAJASTHAN, India (left)
Sri yantra, 18th century
The *yantra's* formal pattern of outer gates and petals, overlapping triangles and central point provides a visual focus for meditative concentration. In both its abstract simplicity and its optical effects there are analogies with American hard-edge abstractionists such as Noland who have sought to conjure away therapeutically the fuss and complication of modern life.

MIRO (below)
Catalonian landscape (The hunter), 1923–24
Though more playful than Kandinsky, Miró was no less interested in what he called "the golden flashes of the mind". Nature is the point of reference for an impulsive abstraction in which appear "Monstrous animals and angelic animals, trees with ears and eyes, a peasant in his Catalan beret holding a shotgun and smoking his pipe".

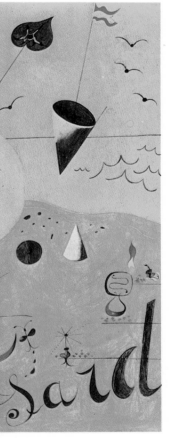

form and colour equivalents for his feelings, since this was historically the first kind of abstraction and, by virtue of its individualistic gestural character, points straight towards all subsequent kinds of painterly and expressionist activity, most notably that of the New York School in the 1940s. Kandinsky also pioneered a more controlled idiom whereby small, clearly defined but non-specific shapes float in abstract space, an idiom adopted by several painters on the abstract wing of Surrealism, in particular, Miró, though much of his imagery has associations with the natural world.

The more premeditated kind of abstraction may be subdivided into two categories. Suprematism, as developed principally by Malevich (see his *Composition* on p. 89), reveals a search for pictorial equivalents of psychological states akin to Kandinsky's, but the forms used are more sparing, more geometric and measured, and further from any suggestion of the real world. Malevich aimed, he said, at the "feeling of true being", and his art influenced Kandinsky himself to move towards more geometric forms. Almost simultaneously, Mondrian was developing a geometric abstraction arrived at by analytical reduction of natural forms, as in his celebrated apple-tree sequence (see p. 231). While the eventual "pure plastic art" of Mondrian and his De Stijl colleagues has a meta-

LOHSE (below)
30 vertical systematic shades with red diagonals, 1943–70
Richard Lohse's picture calls to mind the analogy between structured abstract painting and music with its permutations and combinations occurring across a regular matrix or "beat". It can be read in many different ways, some melodic, some chord-like, some syncopated, some on the beat. The use of similarity factors and cross-groupings is complex and fugue-like; the total effect both intellectually satisfying and formally grand.

physical significance, the move away from expressionist tendencies has become clear: the search is for fundamental principles of order, expressing not individual feelings but a universal coherence. This category of abstraction points towards the wholly impersonal art of the recent Minimalists. Like the more spatial and three-dimensional approach of Constructivism, its concern with formal structure makes it a natural ally of architecture.

The second major category of abstraction proceeding from premeditation rather than impulse is more diverse; it is based on experiments in geometry, mathematics, optics and theories of colour, proportion and perception (exemplified here by Lohse). The categories are not mutually exclusive; some optical paintings, for instance, are not simply concerned with visual phenomena in an objective, unemotional way but are intended to induce states of mind, almost in the manner of *yantras*, which, in Tantric art, seek to concentrate cosmic energies. Yet the dichotomy between the impulsive and the tidy is clear enough, and corresponds loosely with that noted earlier between the painterly and the linear, the romantic and the classical. It is possible, therefore, with some exceptions and hybrid forms, to boldly divide twentieth-century abstraction into the two camps of romantic/painterly/expressionist as opposed to classical/linear/hard-edged. Each has its own potentialities, and the recognition in each of a continuing artistic tradition provides some means of guidance through the frequently confusing crosscurrents of modern art.

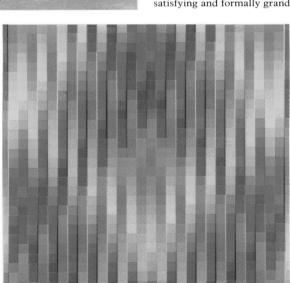

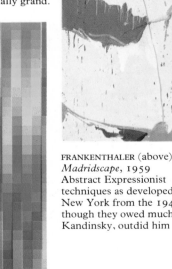

FRANKENTHALER (above)
Madridscape, 1959
Abstract Expressionist techniques as developed in New York from the 1940s, though they owed much to Kandinsky, outdid him in audacity and in unquestioning obedience to impulse. An initial gesture started off a dynamic dialogue between artist and canvas which had to be discontinued before it went dead, and in which drips, slashes, splatters, wipings, were as far as possible dictated by the painter's Unconscious. Here a kind of order emerges: repeated sickle shapes, "eyes", bunched verticals.

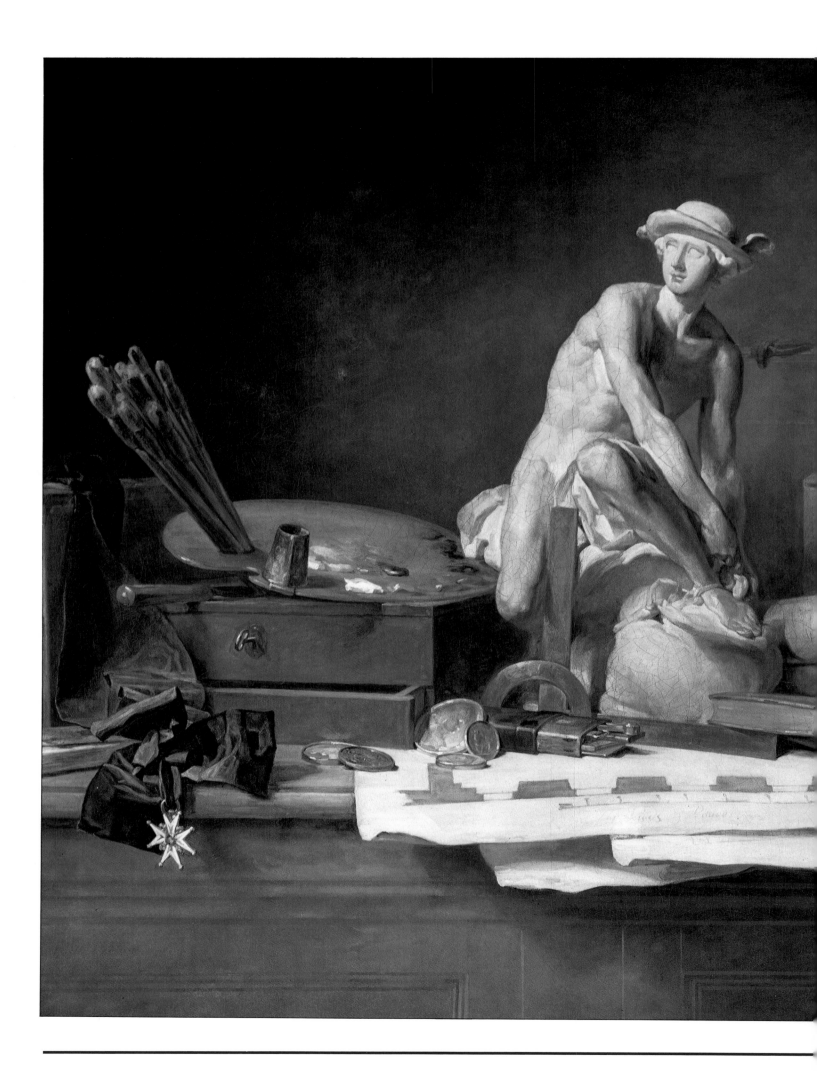

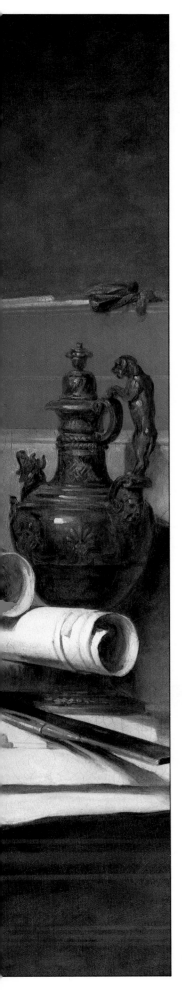

MATERIALS AND METHODS OF PAINTING

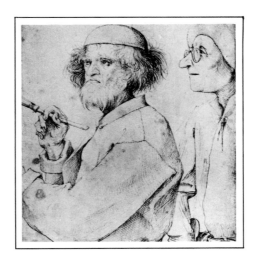

"The supreme misfortune is when theory outstrips performance" – LEONARDO

(left) CHARDIN: *The attributes of the arts*, 1766; (above) BRUEGEL: *The painter and the connoisseur*, c.1566-68

Introduction

We have already seen how widely paintings can differ according to the context in which they were created and the artist's individual approach to composition. But their appearance may be influenced equally by the techniques used to make them. Each medium of painting, drawing or printmaking has its own possibilities and limitations, and the purpose of this chapter is to bring out the expressive characteristics of each.

For anyone who has tried to draw or paint, and knows something of the difficulties, it is impossible to watch an image take shape beneath the hand of an adroit artist without a sense of wonder at what seems a kind of alchemy. The analogy is particularly apt for European painting, which for centuries was linked to chemistry and to the craftsmen's guilds of metalworking and dyeing. It was a skill laboriously learned, using materials that were often expensive or difficult to obtain and techniques (sometimes jealously guarded) which determined the character of the painting within fairly strict limits. The development of a wide range of vivid colours in tubes and of other equipment that makes possible rapid, direct painting is comparatively recent in the West, and has influenced the kind of painting produced.

As art terminology is often ambiguous, a few basic definitions will be helpful. The word "medium", for instance, is used sometimes to mean the water, oil, turpentine or synthetic resin added to bring paint to the consistency the artist wants. But in its wider sense it means the different painting methods in general – tempera, encaustic, fresco, oil, acrylic, ink, watercolour, gouache, pastel and also the various drawing and printing methods. The basis of all painting media is powdered pigment – colouring matter, which may be produced chemically or derived from coloured earths and crushed minerals or plants. It is bound together and made adhesive by a "vehicle" – glue, casein, egg, oil, wax or resin – except in fresco, where the pigment, dispersed in water, is bound simply by chemical action with the damp lime-plaster wall on which it is laid. By adding water, oil, turpentine or synthetic resin, artists can further extend the paint, thin it and influence its speed of drying and matt or glossy appearance. The dry media used in drawing may also be coloured, but of these only pastel is considered a painting medium because it can be spread: the others are basically linear methods. Finally, the term "support" refers to the surface on which the image is made – usually wood panel, canvas, paper or wall plaster.

The tools, technique or support employed by an artist can extend the inherent expressive and textural range of a medium, but the characteristic qualities of one medium cannot always be achieved with another. Of the quick-drying water-diluted paints, tempera and gouache favour linear designs with sharply defined images, relatively flat colours and decorative textures; the special fluidity and transparency of watercolour and ink demand swift execution and facilitate imperceptible tone and colour gradation and soft, atmospheric effects; oil-paint allows illusions of volume and

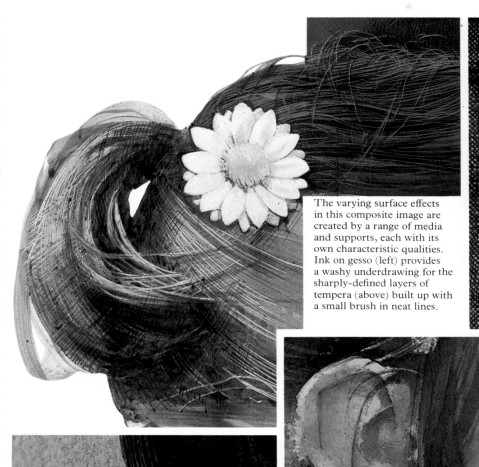

The varying surface effects in this composite image are created by a range of media and supports, each with its own characteristic qualities. Ink on gesso (left) provides a washy underdrawing for the sharply-defined layers of tempera (above) built up with a small brush in neat lines.

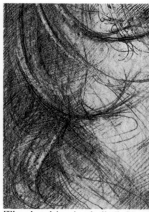

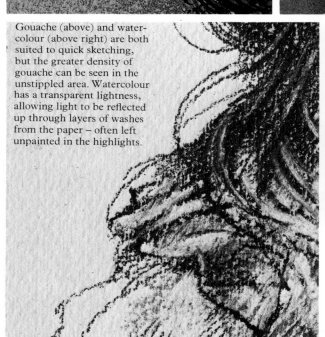

Gouache (above) and water-colour (above right) are both suited to quick sketching, but the greater density of gouache can be seen in the unstippled area. Watercolour has a transparent lightness, allowing light to be reflected up through layers of washes from the paper – often left unpainted in the highlights.

The sketching in chalk (left) and pencil (above) is done on the same coarse paper but the more friable chalk gives a denser, grainy line and can more easily be used to create tonal depths by smudging or drawing with a broad surface – so also can charcoal and pastel.

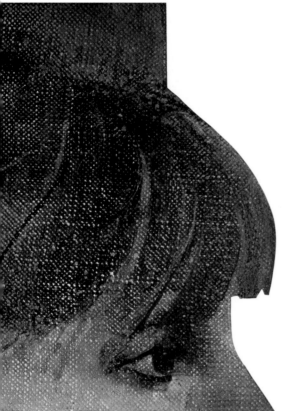

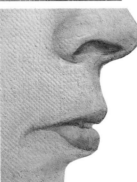

The more tractable medium of oil, which dries slowly, can be used to blend tones and colours in successive layers, beginning with thin underpainting blocking in the hair and establishing the design (above), then with glazes and touches of local colour translating the canvas weave to softer skin, and finally with thicker paint laid on with a palette knife or loaded brush (below).

space to be created by subtle fusion of tones; acrylic paint is still more versatile, combining the plasticity of oils with the precision and quick-drying capabilities of tempera and gouache. Texturally, the tiny cross-hatched brush-strokes of tempera or the broad washes of fresco or water-colour create effects quite different from oils, where brush-lines may range from blade-sharp contours made with pointed sable hair to the rougher, whiskery marks of a hog-bristle brush or the heavy slabs created with a painting-knife.

Similarly, a painter's use of tone and colour depends largely on the materials at his disposal. Tempera and fresco colours dry to relatively light tones; only with the development of an oil medium was it possible to achieve the darker and richer shadow depths of a Caravaggio or a Velazquez. Movements such as Impressionism and Fauvism which astounded contemporaries by the way they exploited colour as a means of expression were not technically possible until the researches of nineteenth-century chemists and dyers made available permanent pigments along the full spectrum. Before this, the range of colours expanded only gradually. The brilliancy of some pure colours available now could not be obtained from natural substances; other vivid mineral colours were expensive and sometimes unobtainable, and large canvases of the sixteenth century onwards were painted primarily in cheaper and readily available earth colours, artists relying on the optical effects of overlays or colour contrasts for subtlety or illusionistic intensity of hues.

The nature of some techniques can be only surmised and rash restoration or alteration have meant that many great works cannot be appreciated in the original form. Recent advances in historical research, however, allow a deeper appreciation of the skill of those who painted them and a better understanding of the complex interaction between medium and meaning, technique and expression.

BOTTICELLI (below):
Venus and the Graces bringing presents to a bride, detail, c. 1486
The grandeur and simplicity of Renaissance frescos came from quite a limited range of colours mixed in water and flooded with large brushes on to damp plaster which bound the colour as it dried. Less arduous ways of creating large-scale works superseded this technique.

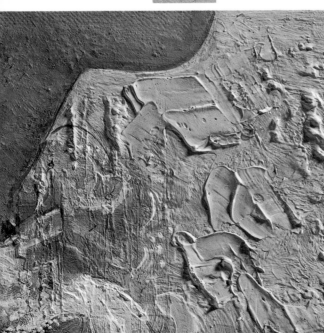

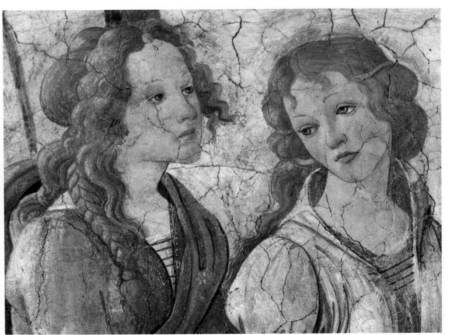

Tempera and Encaustic

Tempera was known to the Egyptians, Greeks and Romans but was fully developed during the Byzantine period to become the main process used for small-scale painting until the development of oil-paint in the fifteenth century.

Originally, tempera was a term given to all colours "tempered" with a vehicle to make them workable; the early encaustic medium, for example, was pigment tempered with hot, liquid wax. Encaustic colours and brush-marks were fused, and the pigment driven into the wood panel surface, when a heated spatula or a metal plate was passed across the completed painting. The ancient Greeks probably invented encaustic, and it was used most skilfully by Egyptians in mummy portraits of the second century AD. Their smooth finish contrasts with the rough surface of modern wax-emulsion paintings, in which a wax vehicle is used intentionally to retain a texture of brush and spatula marks, as in the *Flag* and *Target* Pop Art works by Jasper Johns.

In traditional casein, or "cheese-painting", techniques, pigments were tempered with liquid milk-precipitate. Casein paints dry quickly to a matt finish, and it is not easy to blend tones and colours, but impasto textures can be made with a spatula or a stiff brush. Modern artists such as Matisse and Motherwell have used these paints, which are now manufactured ready-mixed in tubes. Modern gouache paints (see p. 138) are also often wrongly described as "tempera colours".

The true tempera medium is pigment mixed with the yolk or the white of egg, and thinned in use with water. It is so fast-drying that the technique of painting with it is not unlike drawing. The linear nature of the medium is reflected in the neat, delicate, stylized and unambiguous work

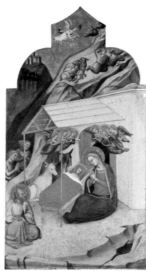

STYLE OF ORCAGNA (above)
The Adoration of the shepherds, c. 1370–71
The angels shown in the retouched detail (right) are taken from this gabled tempera panel, part of a large altarpiece with an elaborate frame, probably fitted before painting began.

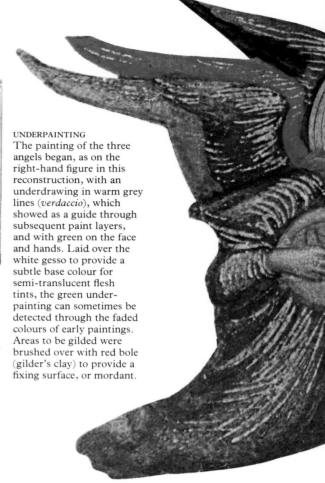

UNDERPAINTING
The painting of the three angels began, as on the right-hand figure in this reconstruction, with an underdrawing in warm grey lines (*verdaccio*), which showed as a guide through subsequent paint layers, and with green on the face and hands. Laid over the white gesso to provide a subtle base colour for semi-translucent flesh tints, the green under-painting can sometimes be detected through the faded colours of early paintings. Areas to be gilded were brushed over with red bole (gilder's clay) to provide a fixing surface, or mordant.

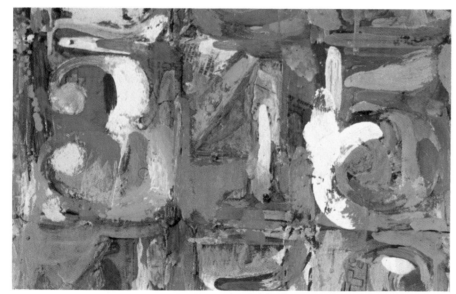

JOHNS
Numbers in colour, detail, 1958–59
The ancient wax medium, encaustic, has been used here in a modern form, on crinkled newspaper stuck to canvas (the print is visible in places). The uneven ground, combined with swashy brush-strokes of quick-setting encaustic colour, demonstrates that familiar images – letters, numbers, flags or maps – may acquire the status of fine art when rendered in such a painterly manner.

ANDREA PISANO (below)
Painting, c. 1431
The intent attitude of the panel painter depicted here suggests the painstaking nature of tempera. He may be using a stylus to incise the outlines of a halo against the gold-leaf background. On the work-stool beside him stand jars of pigment ready for use. Colours were mixed with egg and a little water and lightened by the addition of white, producing smoother paint with more covering power. Small brushes were hand-made by inserting sable hairs tied with waxed string into a quill, which was then mounted in a cane or wooden handle. Since the shape and thickness of the tip helped to determine the character of the brush-stroke, the brushes were individually trimmed to suit the needs of the painter. Preparatory work, including gilding, was often done by work-shop apprentices.

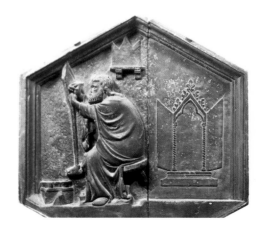

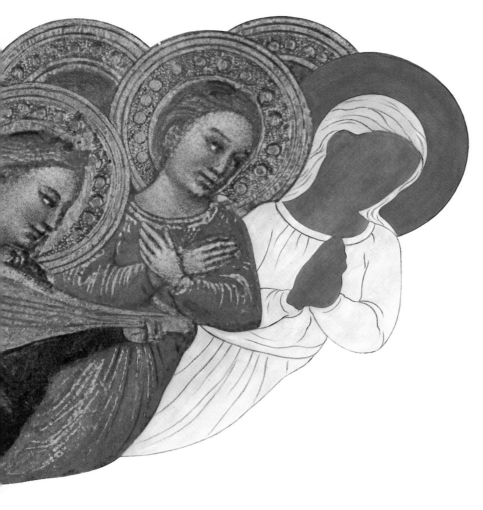

GILDING
The gold-leaf of the haloes
was fixed to the red bole
in small squares of paper-
thin beaten gold which was
then burnished with bone,
ivory, agate or even the
back of a spoon. Smoothed
down into a hard lustrous
coat by the burnisher, the
gold could be incised with
a stylus (A) or compass
(C), or impressed with a
punch (B) or die stamp
engraved to the artist's
design. Drapery could be
embellished with highlights
and tiny stencilled patterns
by using gold powder in a
thin solution of egg, which
stuck only where glue was
applied to form a mordant
and brushed off elsewhere.

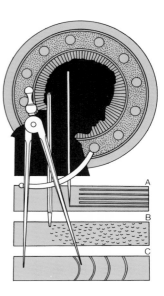

typical of medieval and early Renaissance artists.

The luminous quality of many tempera paintings depends on a ground of brilliantly white gesso
(gypsum mixed with glue) which carries the paint.
Successive layers of gesso were applied to the
support – traditionally a well-seasoned wood panel
– and the final layer was burnished for an enamel-
smooth surface. The design could be drawn free-
hand with charcoal directly on to the gesso, but for
larger works might be traced on to greased paper
and transferred by incising the gesso with a metal
stylus or by dabbing carbon through the perforated design. There was relatively little scope for
corrections in the course of the work.

Gold-leaf decoration was an important element
of panel painting until the middle of the fifteenth
century, used for backgrounds as well as haloes
and drapery details. Icons and altarpieces were
gilded not only to enhance their value but to
symbolize divine radiance and to catch the light in
churches. Medieval manuscripts on vellum (animal skin) were also enriched with gold-leaf; the
tempera was usually bound with white of egg.

Tempera painting involves adding colours over
a light ground; after the initial monochrome
drawing describing the forms a green (terre-verte)
underpainting was laid on in some areas to provide
a neutral base for flesh tints. Much of the painting
was done in earth colours, which could be successfully applied in one coat. But for the more precious
pigments – such as vermilion, ultramarine and
malachite – a glowing intensity and characteristic
sheen might be achieved by building up as many as
ten layers of thin colour. The paint was laid on in
swift, successive strokes of the brush. Tempera
dries too quickly for brush-strokes to be blended
but details such as drapery could be further
modelled by a series of fine brush-strokes hatched
and interwoven on the surface.

During the Renaissance, tempera was gradually
replaced by the more flexible medium of oil. But
the traditional tempera technique has been revived
by such modern artists as Ben Shahn, Edward
Wadsworth and Andrew Wyeth, who have exploited its linear precision and clarity.

SHAHN (right)
Handball, detail, 1939
Many of Shahn's tempera
paintings are political or
social commentaries. The
medium's precision suits
his interpretation of bleak
city settings, texturally
enlivened only by stark
patterns of wire netting,
brick or crude graffiti.
His flat, shadowless forms
and reliance on contour have
affinities with the work
of early tempera painters.

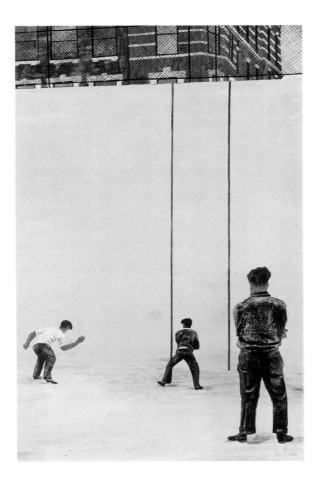

Wall-painting

Wall-painting is one of the oldest and noblest traditions in the history of art. Where tempera demands precise craftsmanship, the sheer scale of most murals, and their public rather than private nature, challenge the artist to create correspondingly powerful works in which the overall breadth of the conception is usually more important than meticulous detail.

The earliest of all paintings were drawn in charcoal on cave walls and coloured with raw earth pigments, taking on the contours of the rock itself. In the ancient civilizations of Egypt, Greece, India and Asia, enormous murals covering the temples, tombs and palaces were conceived as an integral part of the architectural decoration. Some Roman murals in private houses featured *trompe-l'oeil* effects. The Byzantines preferred to enliven the interiors of their churches and monasteries with glittering mosaics, but the older tradition of mural painting was continued, particularly in Italy, leading to great picture cycles in churches of the Gothic period.

Fresco, meaning fresh, was the major Renaissance method of wall-painting. It developed gradually from the technique, chiefly used until the thirteenth century, of painting on walls *a secco* (on dry plaster) in egg or glue tempera. This was a straightforward and reasonably durable process in which the colours were applied to a slightly dampened wall and adhesion was provided by a binder of egg or glue. Wax was sometimes laid over the paint to preserve it from humidity, which might cause flaking, and to give lustre to the characteristically matt colours.

The true fresco method (*buon fresco*) is difficult but rewarding. Pure pigments, mixed only with water, were applied directly to fresh, damp plaster which absorbed and bound them as it dried. The range of colours was limited to those that were lime-resistant, such as the ochres and umbers, chalk and charcoal, and the pinks and greens that occur naturally in clay. These earth colours tend to be subdued, producing the airy and muted harmonies characteristic of most frescos. Vivid mineral colours, particularly the blues, could only be added in tempera over areas painted in earths that were already dry.

The whole work had to be conceived clearly in advance. From preliminary sketches, the main axes of the composition were marked out and the design sketched on a coarse plaster layer (the *arriccio*). This was the first opportunity for both painter and patron to see the work in context and assess the relationship of the design to its architectural setting, often a fundamental compositional aspect of wall-painting.

The thin top coat of plaster on which the painting was done (the *intonaco*) was laid an area at a time according to the artist's estimate of how much he could paint in a day. The day-piece (*giornata*) therefore varied in size according to the amount of detail it covered. The artist might have had to do the final plastering himself to achieve the surface he wanted. When he came to paint, the drawing showing at the boundary of the new day-piece served as a guide in relating the different

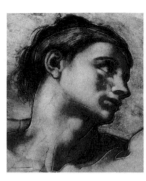

MICHELANGELO (above)
Head of Adam, detail from the Sistine ceiling, 1510-12. Michelangelo used a full-size plan, called a *cartoon*, to trace his design on to the plaster with a stylus. The resulting score lines are still visible in the head of Adam. He worked unaided, on high scaffolding with his head thrown back and his brush held up at arm's length. The discomfort and eye strain he suffered were bitterly described in a poem and a caricature of himself as a hunchback.

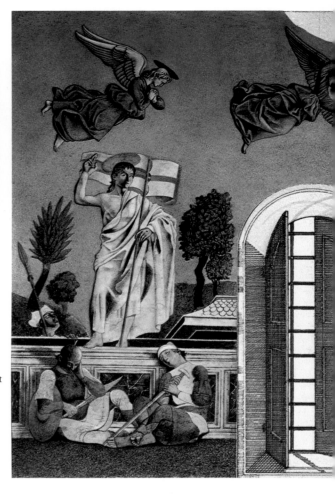

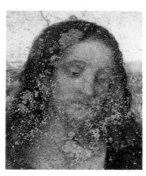

LEONARDO (above)
The Last Supper, detail, c. 1495-98
Damp can ruin murals, particularly if the artist's technique is faulty. Seeking a less piecemeal method than fresco, Leonardo invented a process that was perhaps designed to allow him to work over *The Last Supper* at leisure and as a whole, uniting the tones of the composition. He tried oil on a resin undercoat which failed to dry out. The surface of the painting quickly began to deteriorate.

elements in the composition. Colours were not easily matched with those of an adjacent day-piece, however, which would have dried matt and lighter in tone than newly-applied paint. For their work to stand out in the dim natural light or candlelight of interiors, artists often used a range of pale shades, mixed with white, giving cool, rather high-key colour schemes.

Fresco painters laboured for long hours in tiring, often badly-lit conditions and needed physical stamina as well as skill and decisiveness. Mistakes were not easy to rectify as the brush-strokes were absorbed rapidly into the plaster surface. Retouching could be done *a secco* but major corrections were possible only by hacking off dried plaster and starting again.

The beauty of the method lay in its freedom and scale. The little sable brushes commonly used in tempera were employed only for finishing *a secco*. As fresco paint was made up in quantity and spread like watercolour it was easy to cover large areas quickly, using big brushes in sweeping strokes. This encouraged monumental settings and figure groups, and impressionistic rather than detailed handling of distant scenes. The use of fresco declined after the sixteenth century, partly because of a growing demand for intimacy and naturalism but mainly because oil and canvas provided a more versatile and convenient method of painting, even for large-scale works.

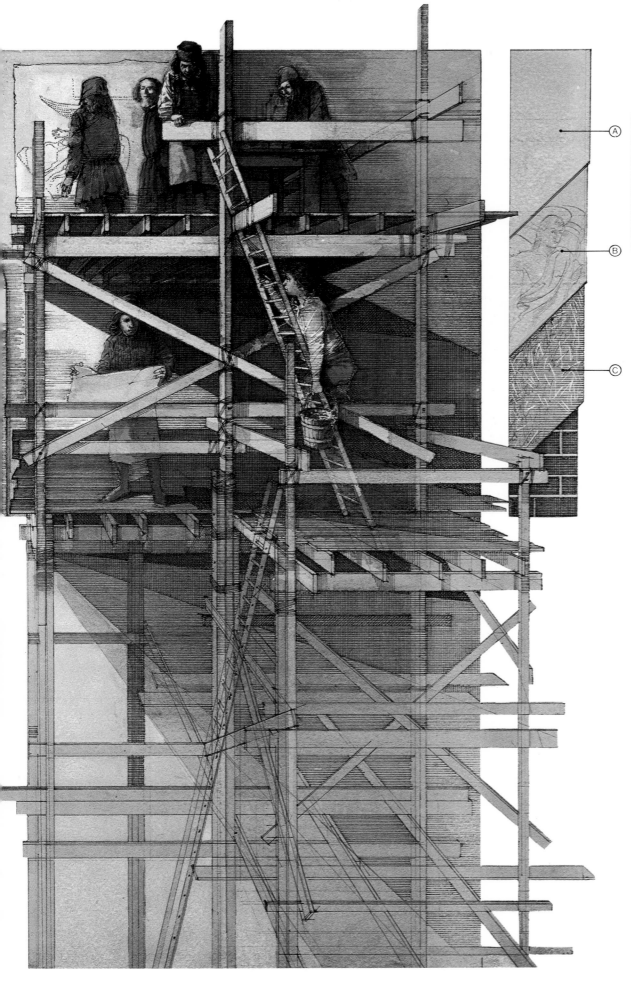

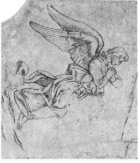

STAGES OF A FRESCO
The reconstruction (left)
shows how Andrea del
Castagno and assistants
may have worked on the
*Crucifixion, Deposition and
Resurrection of Christ*,
c. 1445-50, in the Convent
of St Apollonia, Florence.
He worked up from an underdrawing in red paint, the
sinopia (detail above) to
finished sections such as
the left-hand *Resurrection*,
shown here as it may have
looked when first completed.
The entire *sinopia* was
sketched out on coarse
plaster, the *arriccio* (B),
covering the wall plaster
(C). The original design
was transferred to the
arriccio by using a full-
size paper pattern fastened
to the wall over a blank
sheet, the outlines being
perforated with a tailor's
tracing wheel. With the
pattern removed, charcoal
dust was dabbed (pounced)
through the holes in the
blank sheet to provide the
basis for the underdrawing
in red earth pigment. This
sinopia was covered by
the *intonaco* (A), the thin
section of fresh plaster on
which the artist painted
his day-piece, but Castagno
reused the pattern to map
out the design in charcoal
again (as illustrated here)
before he began to paint.
His method of drawing up
his design on the wall was
exceptionally thorough;
most artists began painting
directly on the *intonaco*.
Assistants had to haul up
large tubs of water to
thin the ready-mixed paint,
keep brushes clean of lime
and wet out the *intonaco* as
the day-piece proceeded.
The scaffold was secured to
the wall by crossbeams.
Castagno's fresco, in the
refectory of the convent,
was discovered in 1890
under a layer of whitewash.

Early Oil Techniques

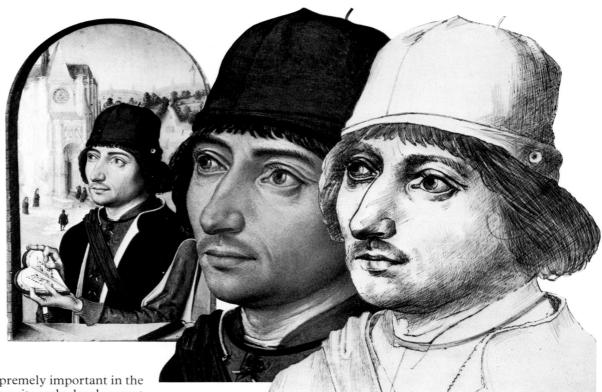

MASTER OF THE VIEW OF SAINT
GUDULE (immediate right)
A young man, c.1480

Although oil has been supremely important in the history of Western painting, its early development as a vehicle for colour was slow, difficult and tentative. Oil was used from ancient times for tinting and varnishing, and as a medium for colouring Egyptian mummy cloths, Roman shields and medieval processional banners. Among medieval panel painters who employed oil varnishes to preserve their work or give it a surface sheen, there were those who perceived the potential usefulness of a vehicle which would allow colours to be blended and tones to be deepened without recourse to the minute hatched brush-strokes of tempera. Ways of mixing pigment into oil were discussed in treatises on painting from the late thirteenth century, but it was found difficult to control the drying process or to develop an oil vehicle suitable for delicate work. Much experimental work has deteriorated or been lost. Florentine painters of the fourteenth and early fifteenth centuries restricted the use of oil-paint to less detailed parts of the composition where fine work was less crucial.

It was left to northern European artists, notably Hubert and Jan van Eyck, to turn to account the gradual refinement of the oil medium. In their painting technique during the early fifteenth century, they and other early oil practitioners followed closely the careful, considered approach of the tempera masters, laying colour in a thin, transparent glaze of oil and resin over a detailed underdrawing in a water-based paint – a method not unlike the tinting of a black and white photograph. Gesso grounded panels were still used as supports and the smooth white surface of the ground helped to give clarity and brilliance to the subsequent colour layers, which could be further lightened by applying a thin layer of white tempera over the oil glazes.

Early oil-glazed temperas are characterized by glowing colour and incisive draughtsmanship;

The reconstruction (above) of the underdrawing, beside the finished head, is based on the method of Jan van Eyck, whose realistic draughtsmanship set a precedent. The drawing medium was a glue tempera, applied with the tip of the brush. This could be employed directly by following a preliminary design, or used to reinforce a preliminary sketching out in charcoal. Individual styles varied between highly detailed and summary work. Pencil-thin strokes served to outline forms and define shadows. When the drawing was dry, areas of colour could be blocked in, the brush-strokes blending easily, owing to the spreading power of the oleo-resin medium. The final stage, once the colours were established, was to work up highlights and details with dabs of varnish, to make them glow with colour or reflect light.

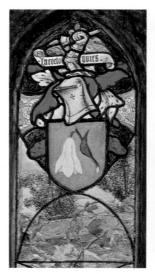

MILLAIS
Mariana, detail, 1851
In true Pre-Raphaelite tradition, Millais painted with close attention to naturalistic detail. Work such as this fastidious copying of the stained glass at Merton College, Oxford prompted a critic to compare Millais with van Eyck.

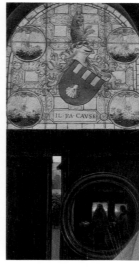

MEMLINC
The Nieuwenhove diptych, detail, 1487
The fish-eye mirror, the crest in the window and the slit opening on to a glimpse of the garden indicate the delight with which this Netherlandish artist, an early master of oil-painting, observed and recorded detail.

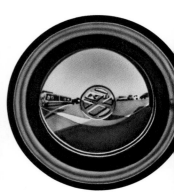

EDDY
Untitled, detail, 1971
Don Eddy's interest in the literal, impartial quality of found images leads him to copy from his own black and white photographs, which provide an even tighter basis for the picture than could be achieved by a meticulous underdrawing. Here, he uses oil to create a flatly-painted, illusionistic surface, adding colour which is realistic but not necessarily true to the original source.

lines were drawn with the precision and control of a master heraldic sign-writer. Successive colour overlays fused the cross-hatched tempera shading into imperceptible tonal gradations, extending the scope for varying effects of lighting, so that the picture space might seem to be illuminated by diffused light – a flickering candle or supernatural glow – or by harsh, direct light. Subtle modulations of light and shade combined with skilfully simulated cast shadows brought a magical solidity to the volume and weight of things. But since the whole design had been determined by the underdrawing, the completed picture retained much of the compositional character of medieval panels. Figures and background features were usually drawn in meticulous detail and, whatever their spatial position in the picture, defined in sharp focus – then separately identified by colour, with map-like clarity. The systematic technique brought a still grandeur to the formal portraits and to the frozen tableaux of statuesque figures. The sense of emotional restraint was reinforced by the faultless finish of the paint surface, which dried without any evidence of the artist's brush-marks.

Subsequent developments in oil-painting technique established a variety of painting methods and a greater spontaneity of brushwork. Yet many later painters have followed self-imposed technical limitations. Using close-weave canvas and fine brushes, Neoclassicists such as David and Ingres returned to a systematic painting procedure controlled by precise underdrawing. The nineteenth-century Pre-Raphaelite school found inspiration in temperas executed "before the time of Raphael", and employed painstaking oil techniques to seek "truth to nature". More recently, Surrealist painters such as Dali and Magritte, concerned with expressing the persuasive clarity of irrational dream images, have suppressed the expressive brushwork and texture available to the modern artist, using an even application of paint which gives their surfaces an anonymous, illustrative quality. Photo-Realist painters, while pursuing very different aims, have used oil-paint to achieve an intensely objective detail derived directly from photographic sources.

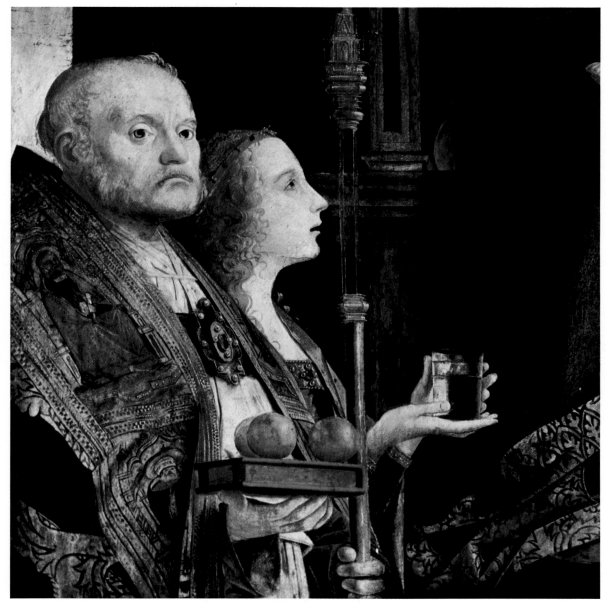

ANTONELLO DA MESSINA
S. Cassiano altarpiece,
detail, 1476
Antonello's deft handling of light and colour opened the eyes of other Italian Renaissance painters to the new possibilities of oil-paint. The solidity of the book, the volume of the spheres, the contrasts of textures and the luminosity trapped within the glass are simulated with a skill that owes much to Netherlandish techniques. If Antonello did not himself visit the north, he could certainly have seen Netherlandish work in Naples, where he studied under Colantonio, who worked in the style of van Eyck. This altarpiece, painted in Venice and now surviving only in fragments, may have been executed in an egg/oil emulsion or in oil glazes over tempera. Its subtle modelling and glowing colour decisively influenced Giovanni Bellini and the whole future course of Venetian painting.

Oils on Coloured Grounds

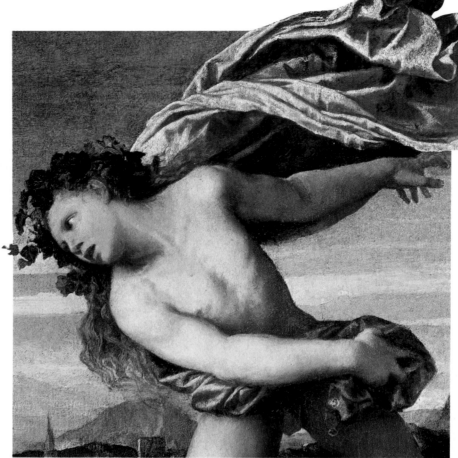

From the early fifteenth century painters were using canvas as a support for paintings and this gradually became standard, as international patronage brought demands for large pictures and transport abroad. Whereas even strongly braced panels might warp or split with a change of climate, canvas could be rolled for shipment, and its lightness made it convenient for large-scale works. The suppleness of canvas and its woven surface facilitated a wider range of textures than the smooth, inflexible panels; sharp contours of rocky or metallic forms, for example, could be contrasted with blurred edges of fleecy clouds and soft velvets.

With the development of oil-painting, gesso was found to be unsuitable as priming on canvas, and in Italy the practice evolved of priming the canvas with an oily paste. From the beginning of experiments with oil-painting, some painters had spread a thin layer of colour (*imprimatura*) over the white ground to establish an overall tone for the composition, either before or after the underdrawing was complete. In the late sixteenth century the Venetians developed the use of coloured oil priming for canvas, actually mixing the pigment into the priming layer. Working on a coloured ground prepared by one or other of these techniques was the standard method of oil-painting for more than three hundred years.

With the development of the paper industry from the fifteenth century onwards, paper became cheaper and more freely available, enabling artists to build up a body of reference drawings and to try

ZURBARAN (below)
A painter at the foot of the Cross, detail, *c.* 1635-40? The immediacy of oil-paint is well suggested by the loaded brushes held by the artist (possibly Zurbaran himself) and by his palette with its colours arranged neatly to hand in two tiers and in order of decreasing tonality. The brushes seem to carry colours from the lower tier, probably used for glazing and for the final highlights and dark accents that intensified his dramatic chiaroscuro.

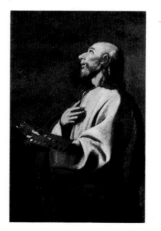

out ideas before starting the actual painting. The oil on tempera technique of carefully colouring in a linear underdrawing gave way to less formal preparatory work; richer, more painterly methods of underdrawing in oil-paint were used on the coloured grounds, including a liberal use of white to give body to the form and establish areas of light and shade. This was similar in principle to *grisaille* (literally a painting in tones of grey), where the composition was laid out in wash rather than line and highlights applied with opaque white paint.

The colours chosen for the *imprimatura* or for the priming layer were various and had a significant effect on the final painting. Artists of the Italian school, notably Caravaggio, who wished to establish a rich depth of tones, often worked from a dark red or brown priming. Dutch landscape painters of the seventeenth century continued to use white grounds, laying over them a variety of cool greys and ochres, according to the depth of tone they hoped to achieve in the most luminous details of sky or water. The English school of the eighteenth century favoured warm grounds which had a reddening effect on subsequent colour layers, while the French, admiring the airy qualities of pastel drawing, preferred light tints tending towards bluish tones.

With the tonal basis established by the coloured ground and the underpainting, subtle modulations could be achieved through careful handling of the brush when colour was applied. By lifting or depressing the brush it was possible to achieve a wide range of tonal variation and degrees of colour

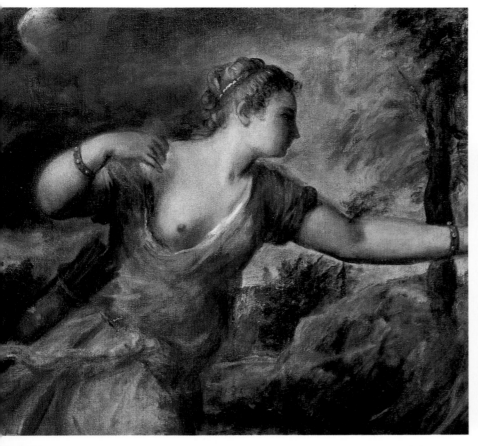

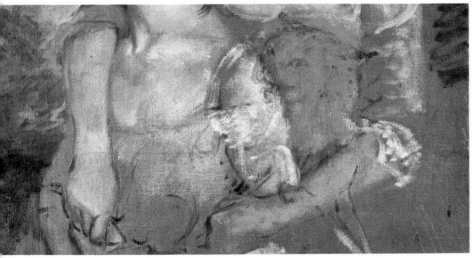

The technique of *grisaille*,
here used by Rubens in a
preparatory sketch for a
ceiling painting, became
for some northern painters
a convenient means of
underpainting the full work,
allowing the composition
to be worked out swiftly in
monochrome oil. Rubens laid
a streaky brown *imprimatura*
over a white, gessoed panel
to provide the general tone
and indicated volume rapidly
with strokes of loaded white
and thinned grey umber.
Grisaille was often used to
indicate relief before the
advent of chiaroscuro.

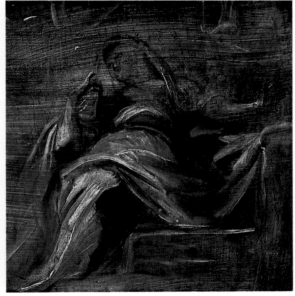

intensity in one application. Pressing the loaded
brush firmly on the canvas left colour at full
opaque strength, while if it was skimmed lightly
across the tinted canvas weave it would produce
scumbles – broken passages of less intense, semi-
transparent colour, optically influenced by the
ground tint beneath. The colour range could be
increased further by the free application of alternate glazes of warm and cool colour, overlapped to
produce harmonious transitional mixtures or juxtaposed to create optical contrasts. Strong colour
accents and definition of detail could be clarified in
the final stages of painting.

These procedures helped to overcome the limitations of the relatively small range of colours
available to painters until the nineteenth century.
Initially paintings were executed primarily in
earth colours and it was necessary to exploit
properties of complementary contrast to achieve a
real intensity of hue. Earth red could take on an
intensity similar to vermilion when juxtaposed
with *terre verte*, and yellow ochre gained a golden
brilliance against a field of blue.

Even though the development of a full range of
painters' colours was very gradual, the free techniques of oil-painting and scope for improvisation
demanded that the painter had all his available
colours to hand, and a palette became essential
equipment. Powdered pigment was mixed with oil
on the palette with a spatula and, until satisfactory
methods of storing mixed paint were invented,
pigments were ground fresh each day and colours
mixed as required.

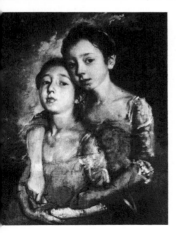

GAINSBOROUGH
*The painter's daughters with
a cat*, unfinished, *c.* 1759
The use of a coloured
ground to provide a middle
tone can be clearly seen in
unfinished 18th-century
portraits where the standard
procedure was to complete
the sitter's head, leaving
the ground empty or perhaps
with shapes indicated only
sketchily. Gainsborough has
used a red-brown priming,
and sketched in the figures
in iron oxide red, blocked
in with an admixture of
white. His characteristic
rapid, grainy stroke is
shown in the detail, with
some scribbling at the right
in what looks like pastel.
The cat has been partly
obliterated by a patch of
yellow ochre. Gainsborough
might have excluded the cat
in the finished picture and
he would probably have
cooled and greyed the
background to add, by
contrast, translucency and
warmth to the flesh tones.

Oils: Surface Effects

As oil-painting techniques developed, artists began to exploit the plasticity of the paint itself and to achieve a wide range of surface effects by varying its opacity and thickness. Although oil-paint eventually oxidizes to form a tough skin, its fluidity and slow-drying properties allow changes to be made by scraping, wiping or reworking while the picture is being built up, making possible an improvising spontaneity of style and composition. For some styles of painting it is necessary to let each layer of paint dry before applying subsequent colours, but there are early instances of artists painting swiftly into wet layers (*alla prima*) to achieve the final effect in one operation. Freedom and speed of attack were further encouraged by the development during the late seventeenth century of ready-mixed paints stored in bladders.

The surfaces of paintings worked over in successive layers had a richness and luminosity unknown in earlier mediums. Glazes allowing light to be reflected back from lower layers were played against soft, textural scumbles and impasto areas in which paint was laid on with a thickly loaded brush or with the spatula. Forms could be shown submerged in shadow or suffused with light, compositions made in dramatic tonal patterns of woven light and dark masses.

Painters established individual styles according to their intentions; it was possible for the Dutch still-life painters, for example, to build up carefully detailed, illusionistic works in which a range of textures and surfaces were simulated, while artists such as Velazquez and Hals, both of whom sometimes worked wet-on-wet, developed a characteristically personal use of the brush, where a dextrous shorthand of dots, loops and dashes sufficed to suggest the glitter of metal or the sheen of satin, the droop of a mouth or eyelid and the weight of tumbling hair. Rembrandt's mature works demonstrate most clearly the expressive textural range of oil-paint; pigment is spread with rag and spatula, smeared with thumb and palm or scraped with brush handle, with crusty, pitted mounds of paint forming a sculptured infrastructure for final colour glazes. His method of working is so complex – and varied – as to defy precise analysis, but the effect is one of unparalleled subtlety, depth and richness.

HALS
A member of the Coymans family; and detail, 1645
Hals' assurance enabled him to dispense with laborious underpainting or multiple glazes and to achieve his effects at the surface. Most of this portrait is painted wet-on-wet over a very thin brownish ground. The detail shows the confidence with which shadows and lights are brushed into the grey of the sleeve. Final accents of black and yellow were then dashed on to define the folds and to suggest the texture of the brocade.

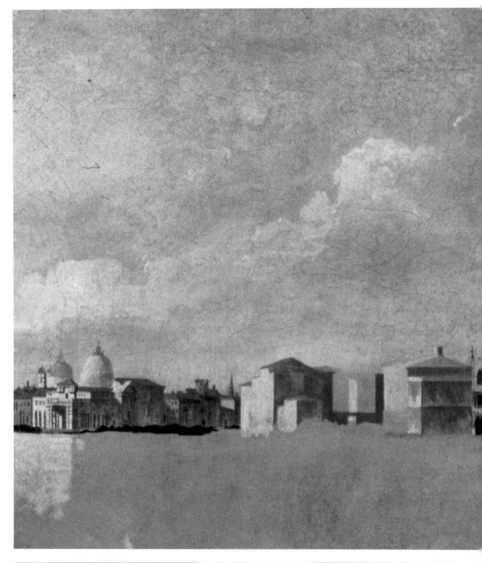

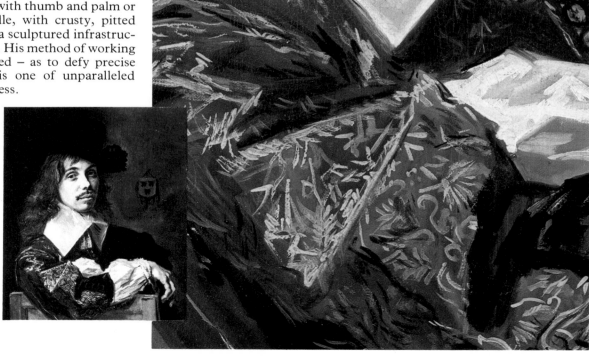

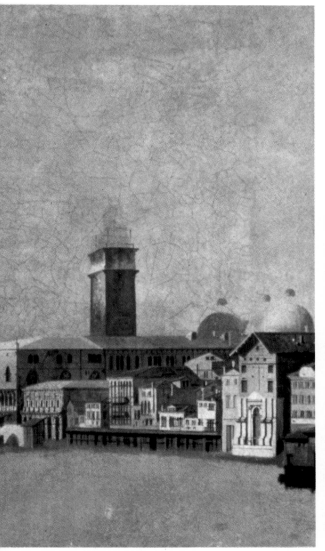

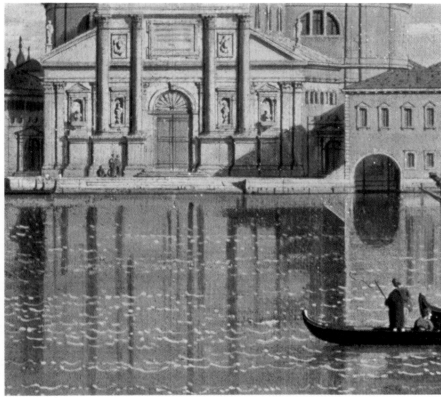

CANALETTO
(left) *The harbour of St Mark's towards the west,* unfinished, *c.* 1760-66?
(below) *The harbour of St Mark's from the east*; detail of S. Giorgio Maggiore, 1740
Working from a ruled-up ink-and-wash drawing mapping the view, Canaletto proceeded towards a free handling on the surface of the picture. The unfinished oil shows that a fluid sky colour has been washed over a warm brown *imprimatura*, with hazy clouds and tonal gradations added while the pigment was wet. The lit sides of the buildings have been blocked in with opaque tints, the ground colour retained as shadow. Patches of the ground also appear through the greyer blue of the water. The reflection of a building is dragged vertically in a semi-opaque scumble. The detail of a finished view shows the use of a fine brush to sharpen features, and white highlights flicked in with tiny strokes on the water to give a scalloped pattern suggesting lapping waves.

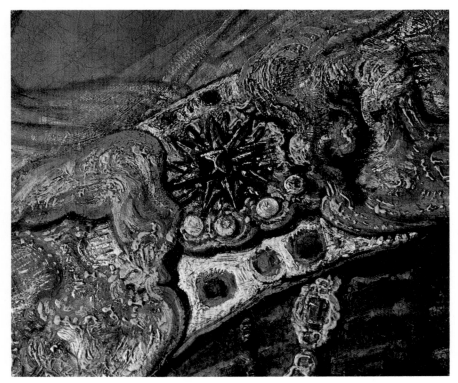

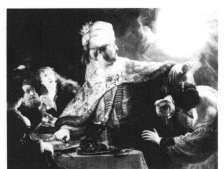

REMBRANDT
Belshazzar's feast; and detail, 1635
Reproached for building up his pictures so heavily, Rembrandt said he was no dyer but a painter. Unlike Hals, he developed his rich effects through a heavy structure of underpainting and glazes, using unusually thick oil, which dried quite quickly, and resin varnishes which preserved the body and texture of the paint. Except in final glazes, he rarely blended different applications of paint. The jewel-encrusted brocade of Belshazzar's cloak is built up over a layer of umber which is allowed to show through in some areas, and at the cloak edge seems to have been scratched with the brush handle or a finger-tip. The surface is covered with thick blobs of yellow paint like golden snail trails. In parts, the paint is visibly raised, giving the surface a real, not illusionary texture and, by catching the light, adding to the overall sparkle.

Oils: Direct Methods

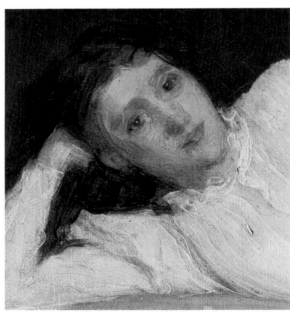

During the nineteenth century events conspired to encourage direct methods of painting in which the use of coloured grounds was abandoned and the hand of the artist became more visible and assertive. Scientific research introduced intense, permanent pigments that made it possible for painters to achieve, in an initial application of paint, hues earlier approximated only by the optical effects of overlays and complementary colour contrasts. Portable equipment and the development about 1840 of commercial paints in soft metal tubes increased the mobility of artists and freed them from the strict traditions of studio practice. At the same time, the invention of photography, which threatened to usurp the painter's function as a literal recorder of people, places or events, provided a spur to experimentation and to a redefinition of the artist's role as expressive creator rather than as dutiful illustrator.

Constable and Delacroix, in the energy and spontaneity of their brushwork were among the forerunners of a growing interest in the textural

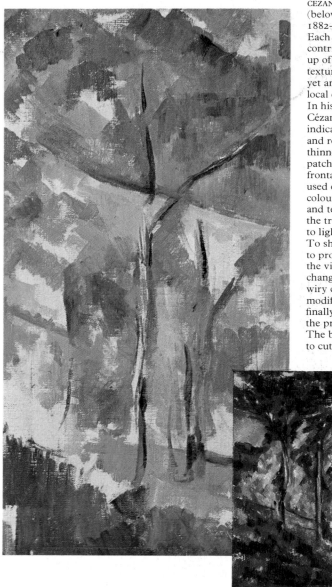

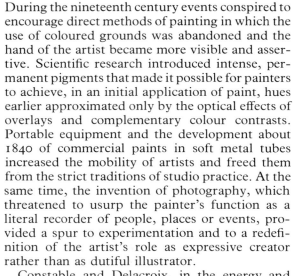

CEZANNE
(below) *Woodland scene*,
1882–85; (left) detail
Each deliberated brush-mark
contributes to the building
up of volume, structure,
texture, space and light,
yet an overall pattern of
local colour is maintained.
In his mature technique,
Cézanne began by loosely
indicating main contours
and receding planes in
thinned blue. Retaining
patches of white priming as
frontal planes, he then
used overlapping strokes of
colour, modulated in tone
and temperature, to establish
the transitions from shadow
to light in faceted planes.
To sharpen these transitions,
to project forms towards
the viewer and to imply a
changing viewpoint, nervous
wiry contours were drawn,
modified, obliterated and
finally determined throughout
the progress of the picture.
The brush-marks seem almost
to cut into the canvas.

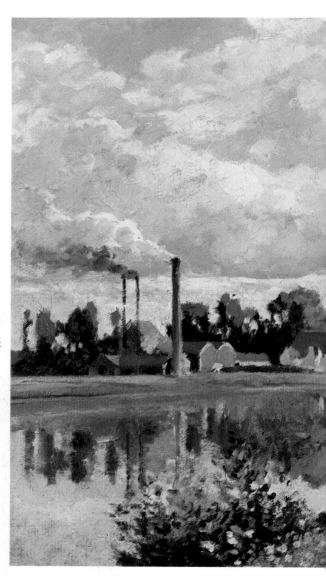

qualities of oil-paint itself, an interest also championed by Whistler, whose paintings emphasized formal, decorative values, his composition and technique reflecting the influence of Japanese prints and brush drawings. Trends towards spontaneity and away from the smooth finish of salon art culminated in the work of the Impressionists, many of whom regarded photography more as a stimulus than a rival. They were excited by the unconventional viewpoints of arbitrary snapshots and by the camera's ability to capture transitory effects of light and weather, which they set out to render with vibrant brushwork.

Plein-air Impressionists such as Pissarro exploited the colour strength of the new pigments by painting in direct, unmodulated strokes on white-primed canvas. Illusions of volume and the simulation of tactile surfaces gave way to sensations of shimmering light suggested by a vivacious handling of juxtaposed colours. Impressionist techniques demanded a rapid, skilled judgment of a landscape's shifting tones and colours as they appeared under momentary lighting conditions. Monet advised: ". . . you must try to forget what objects you have before you – a tree, a house, a field – merely think, here is a little square of blue, here an oblong of pink, here is a streak of yellow, and paint it just as it looks to you".

Cézanne and Seurat attempted to bring a classical order to Impressionist discoveries – Seurat by a scientific analysis of colour, Cézanne by more intuitive methods which evolved slowly and with great effort into a technique of rendering form by using his brush almost as if it were a chisel. The plasticity of oil-paint was employed more passionately by van Gogh, who vividly represented space, volume, texture and light with writhing streaks of unmerged pigment, and by the Expressionists who followed Munch. In the twentieth century this interest in the gestural, emotive and textural possibilities of oil-paint has been carried further, most vehemently in Abstract Expressionism which often became an explosive celebration of the act of applying paint.

PISSARRO
The Oise near Pontoise, 1873
Solid forms are summarily treated and detail kept to a minimum in short, broad strokes of thick paint on the boat and buildings. Glints of light are suggested with dabs, flecks and dots. To retain full intensity of colour and a sense of the immediacy of application, Impressionist paintings were usually left unvarnished.

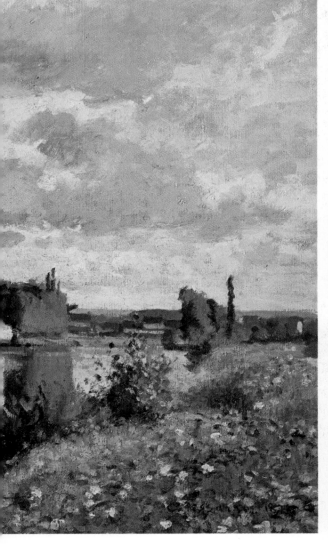

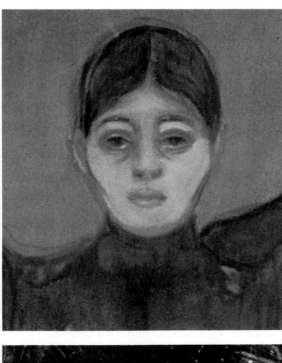

MUNCH (left)
Death in the room, detail, 1892
Technical refinement is subordinated to an anxious mood helped by map-like patterns in which traces of preliminary drawing are incorporated. Lapped by swirling tides of greenish colour, the woman's face is insubstantial, haunted.

JORN (below)
Green ballet, detail, 1960
In the apotheosis of direct painting methods – Abstract Expressionism – colour may be squeezed straight from the tube, splattered or dripped from a can on to raw canvas and spread with knives, trowels or hands. The Danish painter Jorn manipulates oils savagely to create a maelstrom of brilliant colour, looping contours and impasto skids.

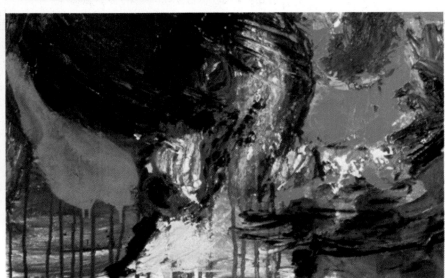

Twentieth-Century Developments

The physical nature of paint, and its collaboration with other materials, together with the texture and shape of the painting's support, have become formal elements in the design of many modern pictures; in some they constitute the very theme of the work. The rejection of the long Western tradition of spatial illusionism in painting – accelerated by the prankish works of Duchamp and other Dadaists early in the twentieth century – went hand in hand with a willingness to experiment with new techniques of handling and combining different media. Braque and Klee both delighted in original picture-making recipes. More recently, Dubuffet, Tàpies and others have expressively mixed pigment with materials ranging from tar and gravel to sand and mud.

The central place of brushwork has itself been questioned by artists such as Ernst, who created forms and textures by scraping a wet painted canvas (*grattage*), by rubbing impressions from textured relief surfaces (*frottage*) or by decalcomania techniques – pressing tacky painted shapes against dry canvas or alternatively pressing materials against wet canvas and then lifting them to produce partly accidental patterns and images. Others have gouged or slit the canvas, or built up projections to introduce an element of real space and cast shadows into an art once considered essentially two-dimensional. Painters have also countered the "window" effect of the framed rectangular canvas by the use of shaped canvases or boards, often unframed, which austerely emphasize their own flatness or suggest spatial extensions beyond the edge of the picture.

The freedom of modern artists to work rapidly and experimentally, often on a large scale, has been increased by technological advances, including the development of acrylic and vinyl paints, the first new painting medium for some 500 years. These are refined forms of industrial paints – pigments bound with synthetic resin, most of which can be thinned with water or given greater plasticity by the addition of various media. They dry quickly to form a waterproof and tough yet flexible skin. The hues are characteristically clear and intense, including a range of fluorescent and metallic colours, and it is claimed that they will not yellow with age as oil-paints tend to do. Acrylic paintings are also easily cleaned and less susceptible than oils or tempera to heat and damp.

Acrylics can be applied to almost any surface in a variety of ways – with a brush, sponge, rag, air-brush or spray-gun (normally used with masking tape or some form of stencil), or flooded directly on to the canvas – and can be used in any form varying from liquid to a thick paste. Their drying speed allows successive coats of paint to be applied almost immediately without smudging or colour change. For colour blending, drying can be retarded with additional resin medium. Surface textures range from thin, vibrant stains of colour to smooth hard-edged areas of opaque paint or heavily brushed impasto. The effect is sometimes indistinguishable from that of oil-paint and the choice of medium in recent styles of painting has been largely a matter of personal preference.

DUCHAMP (right)
Tu m', 1918
The emergence of the canvas as an art object in its own right was heralded by the works of the Dadaists. This mocking summary of traditional illusionistic devices includes deft examples of linear and atmospheric perspective, systems of portraying form and volume in terms of tonal modelling, cast shadows and colour contrast, and a *trompe l'oeil* tear "mended" with a real pin. The pin, together with the pointing hand (added by a professional sign-writer Duchamp hired), seems to challenge the artistic value of technical virtuosity.

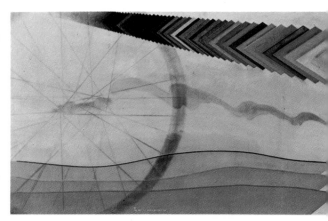

TAPIES (right)
Ochre gris, 1958
Primeval earth textures are implied by the parched, pitted ground where a putty of oil-paint, mixed with shredded sponge and marble dust, is spread across the canvas, impressed with pieces of rope and card and gouged in scored tracks.

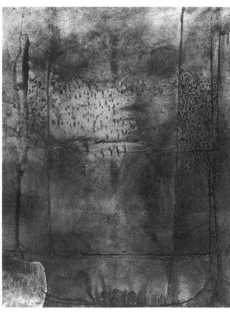

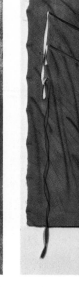

ERNST (below)
Forest, 1929
Natural shapes and textures (including wood and leaves) are imprinted in black. Over these, Ernst stained counterpoint areas of transparent colour, then used opaque paint to suggest figures and foliage texture.

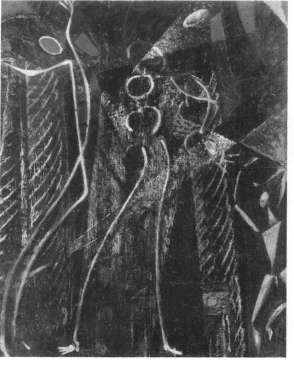

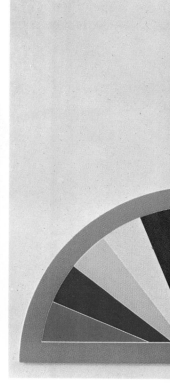

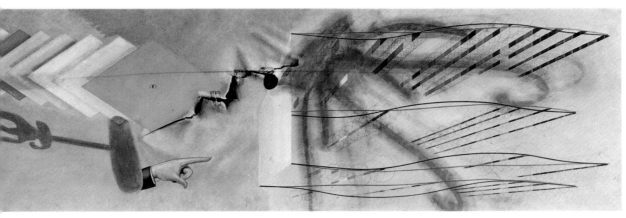

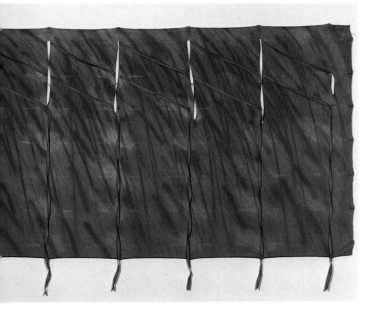

RICHARD SMITH (left)
Sudden country, 1972
Smith's canvas, delicately
streaked in fluid acrylic,
is loosely tacked and laced
with limp fabric ribbons.
The soft, threaded colours
suggest grass, trees, drifting
rain, but illusionism is
countered by the slackness of
the canvas, hinting at
practical uses – kites, sails?

HOYLAND (right)
Drape, 1978
Acrylic is the natural
medium of an artist who has
said that paint should be
put on "the way water
flows, and if there is an
accident it must be con-
trolled". Over initial
colour stains Hoyland uses
rollers, spatulas and broad
brushes to build contrasting
layers of heavy impasto.

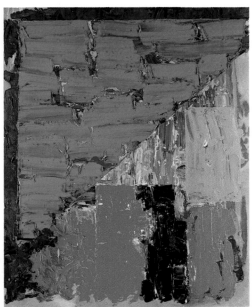

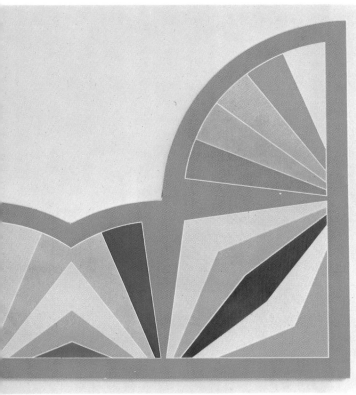

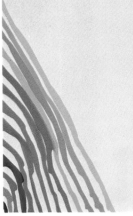

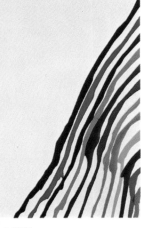

FRANK STELLA (left)
Agbatana 3, 1968
Stella wants his canvases
to be regarded primarily as
coloured objects. His
respect for pure shape, his
antagonism to illusionism
and nuance are emphasized
by the severity of the
geometric design and by the
clear, luminous acrylic and
fluorescent polymer colours,
mixed by the artist himself.

LOUIS
Theta, 1960
The manual dexterity of the
traditional artist is here
replaced by the flow of
thinned paint down a tilted
surface of raw canvas.
Louis retains an interest
in pictorial depth; his
painting engulfs the viewer,
its size making it difficult
to focus on both banks of
acrylic colour at once.

Mixed Media

St Peter, detail of the
Demidoff altarpiece, 1476
Continuing a medieval
tradition of decorative
embellishment, Crivelli's
"assemblage" includes
raised ornament in gesso
(on the cloak border and
bands of the crown), wood
(the keys) and pieces of
red, green and clear glass.

SCHWITTERS (below)
Opened by Customs, c. 1937
"What nectar and ambrosia
were to the Greek gods",
said Arp, "glue was to Kurt
Schwitters". His subtly
beautiful *merz* (rubbish)
collages were composed of
debris from the street – here
overlapping, pasted fragments
of cut and torn stamps,
envelopes, adhesive tape,
newsprint, newsphotos and
paint-scribbled paper.

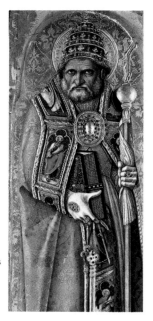

Collage and assemblage – techniques of building
up a picture wholly or partially from found or
manufactured pieces of material – have enabled
modern painters to cross the boundaries between
one art form and another, and also between reality
and representation. Early mixed-media works
were often made as precious devotional objects,
embellished with gold-leaf, beaten metal or gems.
Sources for the imagery and materials of
twentieth-century assemblages have been more
often the junk-yard, sidewalk and supermarket.
Responding to a flood of new visual stimulation,
artists have shown that an almost limitless range of
ingredients can provide the formal elements of line
or shape, colour or texture. The creative ability to
organize these ingredients into effective images
does not depend on the laboriously acquired
technical skills needed for representational painting, and the ease with which pieces can be tried,
moved, discarded or reassembled makes the contrast with any earlier artistic discipline all the
sharper. Matisse, himself a superb draughtsman,

WESSELMANN (below)
Bathtub collage no. 3, 1963
Posed amid the sanitary
trappings of a partly
real bathroom, the figure,
depersonalized and flatly
painted, seems to throw
doubt on the actuality of
assembled real materials –
the curtain, wall-tiles, mat,
radiator and door with
hanging towel. Though it is
life-size, the assemblage
is only 45 cm (18 in) deep.

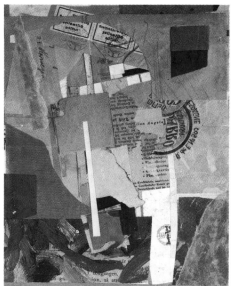

HAMILTON (below)
My Marilyn, 1965
In a montage based on
contact prints of Monroe
(some crossed out by her)
Richard Hamilton comments
on the repetitiveness of
mechanically-produced
images by overprinting
hand-drawn marks and
stencilled shapes to show
"art obliterating reality".

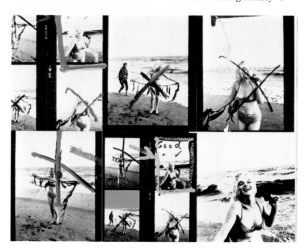

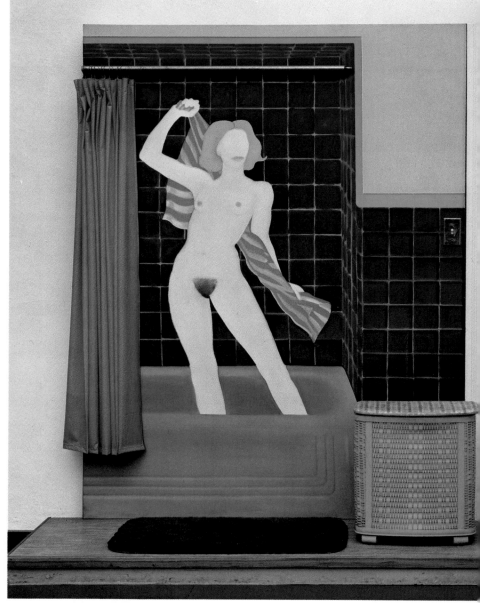

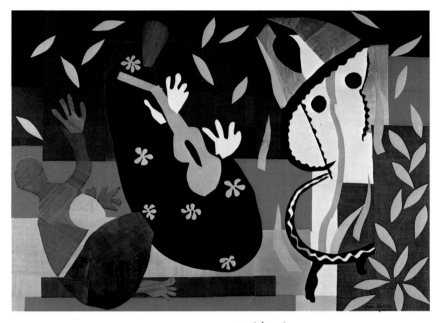

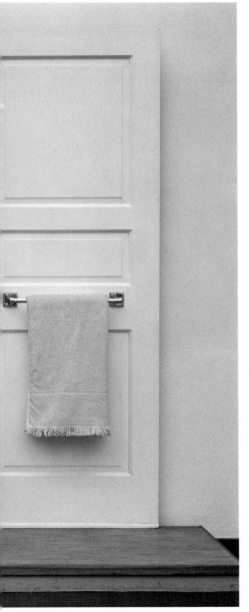

MATISSE (above)
Sorrows of the king, 1952
After 1950, confined by
arthritis to a wheelchair,
Matisse created joyous
gouaches découpées – works
composed entirely of shapes
cut from gouache-coloured
paper and pasted on a paper
ground. He called this
"cutting the colour out
alive". These flat collages,
often of mural size, became
progressively more abstract.

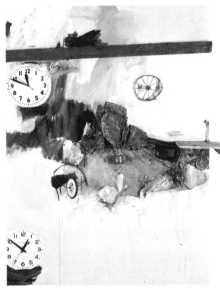

RAUSCHENBERG (above)
Reservoir, 1961
A provocative and poetic
scavenger whose works are
almost inventories of city
life, Rauschenberg seems
fascinated by the way in
which the ephemeral may be
transfixed by glue, nails
or paint into art. He set
the upper clock going when
he began this painting, the
lower one when he finished.

put the case for a free choice of means with
characteristic directness when he said: "Composition is the art of arranging in a decorative
manner the various elements at the painter's
disposal for the expression of his feelings".

The materials of a collage are glued in place,
usually remaining virtually flat. An early example
is the traditional Chinese craft of pasting together
intricately cut shapes of transparent coloured
paper. Collage became a major art form in Europe
when Picasso and Braque began to introduce a
greater variety of colour, texture and references to
real objects in their Cubist works by combining
found materials with painted and drawn areas.
Newspaper, muslin, textured card and patterned
papers, cloth and cane gave way to more three-
dimensional objects in the work of the Dadaists.
The materials in some of Kurt Schwitters' magpie
nests included wire, string, nails, cork, rusted
metal, splintered wood and worn rag.

While collage materials are often combined for
their emotive, political or comical connotations
they may also be arranged for purely formal, non-
literary reasons. Sonia Delaunay composed her
Orphist abstracts in geometrical shapes cut from
flatly coloured paper and worked over in chalk and
watercolour. Arp's Dada collages were created
"according to the laws of chance" in arabesque
patterns dropped at random on colour-stained
paper and pasted where they fell. At the end of
their lives Mondrian and Matisse made major
abstract compositions from coloured paper alone.

Montage, a collage technique incorporating
prints or photographs, was exploited by the Surrealists to produce absurd, amusing, disturbing or
lyrical fantasies, and photographs became a major
element in the work of some Pop artists. The
introduction of mirror glass or other reflective
materials into collages is another Surrealist device
taken up by more recent artists, some of whom
have used areas of polished steel or aluminium in
combination with painted or collaged figures. The
visual texture of paintings has been further enlivened by the revival of word imagery in Synthetic Cubist collages, and in the stencilled sign-
writing of Pop artists such as Indiana.

Combine paintings, or assemblages, are an
extended form of collage where a part or all of the
finished object is essentially three-dimensional,
fastened in place. "I am a painter and I nail my
pictures together", said Schwitters. In the combine
paintings of Rauschenberg painting "becomes
an adventure, like walking down the street".
Shattered road signs, buckled metal plates,
burning electric lights, stuffed birds, radios or
ticking clocks may be combined with screen-
printed images of ball games and moon landings,
advertising   symbols   and   famous   faces.
Rauschenberg's use of gestural brush-marks to
subdue, isolate or integrate such disparate com-
ponents preserves a link with the traditional
concept of painting, but the tendency has been for
modern artists to reject limitations of space and
time and progressively to dismantle the barriers
between painting, sculpture, architecture, theatre
and life itself.

Watercolour

Watercolour has a fluency and adaptability which most other art media cannot match, and its exacting simplicity has challenged many artists who have painted chiefly in oils. The basis of the medium is powdered pigment bound with a solution of gum arabic which is thinned with water and laid on paper or card with pointed and square-ended brushes of soft squirrel or sable hair. Its special quality of luminous delicacy arises because light reflects back from the paper through the colour, making the whole vivid and translucent.

Dürer was probably the first to exploit the fluid immediacy of the medium in the atmospheric studies of lakes and mountains he made on his travels through Europe to Italy. But for the next three hundred years it was to be employed mainly for colouring prints and tinting botanical and architectural line-drawings. During the eighteenth century it came to be favoured by travelling topographical artists for its quick-drying properties and light, compact equipment. Paper quality was an important element in the development of the technique by English masters at the end of the eighteenth century, when a range of tough, absorbent paper, hand-made from linen rags, which could stand repeated flooding with water, was available. To prevent its cockling during painting, the paper was pasted to card, or dampened and stretched over a board, or frame.

In order to express the evanescent qualities of colour and light in a landscape and to retain the freshness of the completed watercolour, certainty and swiftness of execution were essential; all stages of the painting were carefully planned and corrections and second thoughts avoided. The picture progressed from light to dark: the taut sheet was sponged with water and the pale sky tints washed over the entire picture surface; next the colour silhouettes of the main landscape features were superimposed. Tints were obtained by diluting the pigment with water, highlights and white forms made by leaving patches of the paper untouched, giving watercolour's characteristic sparkle. Hues could be intensified or deepened in tone by applying successive transparent stains and

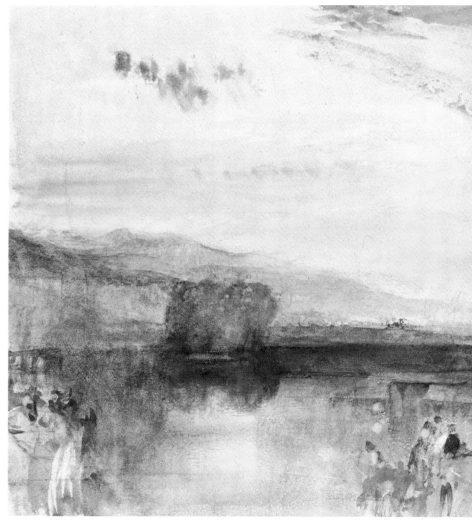

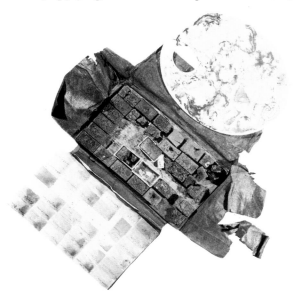

TURNER
(above) *Sunset on the Jura*, 1841; (right) *Tintern Abbey*, 1794
Turner's early watercolour is really a tinted drawing, the colour washes clarifying landscape features already outlined in pencil, in the manner of topographical artists of previous eras.
In his later, almost abstract work, he moves beyond even the direct techniques of his contemporaries, resorting to thumbnail and knife-scratches or flecks of opaque white to create effects of suffused atmosphere and dancing highlights. Turner's 36 cakes of watercolour (left) were carefully preserved and recorded, after the artist's death, by his influential champion, the critic Ruskin.

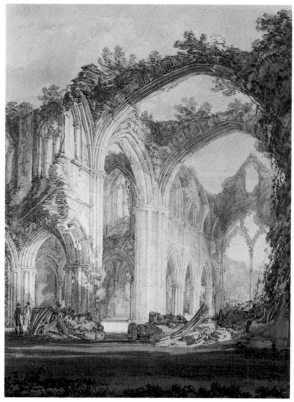

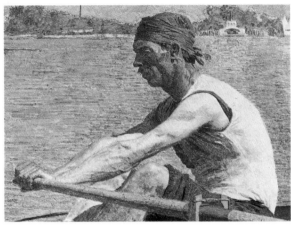

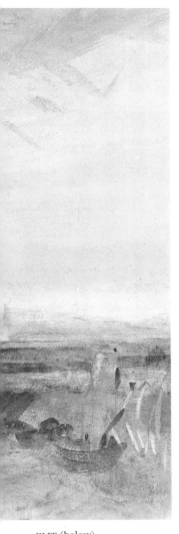

colours were often blended in the same way rather than by mixing them first on a palette. Progressive thinning with water made tonal gradations almost imperceptible, though to blend these wet bands of colour required considerable judgment and skill. Undispersed particles of pigment in the crevices of the rough surfaces of the heavier hand-made papers produced effects of broken colour, and coarse textures, such as bark, brushwood and tufted rock, were suggested by dragging a wide-ended brush of drier pigment across the irregular surface of the paper. Details could be added and focal points in the design sharpened when the paper dried. Leading exponents of this near-Impressionist, "direct" manner were John Robert Cozens, Thomas Girtin, and Richard Parkes Bonington. Though less purist in technique, Turner exploited the full range of the medium in watercolours ranging from studies centimetres across to paintings the size of large oils and meant to hold their own beside them in a gallery.

English watercolours of the nineteenth century often became little more than showy displays of bravura handling, but in America a vigorous tradition of fluidly expressive marine painting developed with the watercolours of Thomas Eakins and Winslow Homer and later of the expatriates James Whistler and John Singer Sargent. More recently, the emotive character of buildings and interiors has been a particular theme in American watercolours – Charles Burchfield's eerie windswept streets painted in sinister drips and spooky squiggles, or Edward Hopper's shadowed rooms and shuttered shopfronts, expressed in neat clear washes. Although gouache has been the preferred medium of most European artists, watercolour has also been brilliantly employed in the twentieth century by Kandinsky, Klee, Dufy, Picasso and Nolde.

The medium is often expressively combined with others – ink, crayon, body-colour and pencil. Cézanne, for instance, used pencil concurrently with wash in the manner of his line and colour-plane oil method, combining an exploration of structure with a sense of transitory effects of light.

EAKINS (above)
John Biglen in a single scull, detail, 1876
A systematic technique of tiny overlaid brush-strokes and streaks of bare paper gives sharp-focus realism, yet the direct handling and accurate tonality sustain the medium's freshness.

NOLDE (below)
Summer flowers, detail, c. 1930
Nolde's approach is spontaneous rather than calculated: across dampened paper, he laid flat glowing patterns of colour, gradated and intensified with deeper hues dropped from a full brush.

KLEE (below)
Hamammet motif, detail, 1914
Klee exploits the fissured quality of the paper itself, creating rich contrasts in texture between lightly painted squares and those with more depth of paint.

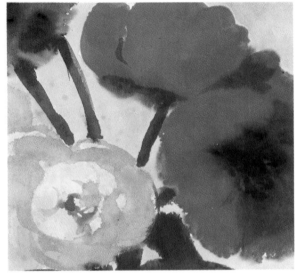

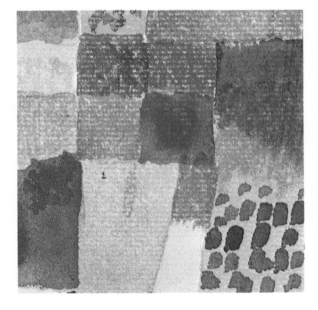

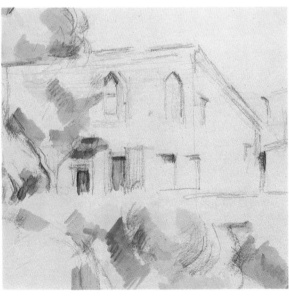

CEZANNE (left)
The black château, detail, c. 1895
Much of the paper is left untouched and pencil used to demarcate the main forms in terms of frontal planes and projecting and interlocking surfaces; this outline is then enlivened by deft, transparent strokes of watercolour, which give the building, despite the light handling, a feeling of depth and carved solidity.

Ink

Ink is a principal medium in Far Eastern painting, which relies on line and tone as the main expressive elements. Oriental artists attempt to capture a sense of cosmic unity through harmonious communion with the spirit of Nature – the Tao; the very act of painting becomes a spiritual exercise in which the controlled handling of the brush demands an apprenticeship as exacting as that required from a ballet-dancer or a pianist. A traditional choreography of brush-movements (learned from standard works of instruction) is practised with extreme dedication, giving basic formulae of prescribed brush-sequences.

Chinese and Japanese painting cover a wide range of subjects: nature and the changing seasons are central to both traditions, though history, genre and portraiture were very popular. There are important differences in design and interpretation: the Chinese style of composition is generally linear, the mood classically disciplined and austere; Japanese artists emphasize silhouette-pattern, the approach is more emotional and subject matter is often dramatic and, at times, humorous. The technique used is basically the same, however. The ink, known as "India" or "Chinese" ink, is made from wood or vegetable soot, mixed with animal glue into a paste which is formed into sticks and tablets and dried. In preparation for use, the hardened ink is rubbed on a rough stone as drops of water are added. By diluting this dense black ink with varying amounts of water, a range of grey tones is prepared. Paintings are executed on absorbent paper made from pulped bamboo, hemp, reed, cotton or mulberry bark, and on silk, sized with a solution of

HAN GAN (right)
Night shining white,
8th century
Brushes of wolf, goat or deer hair, tied in a conical shape and set in a bamboo tube, were the only tool of Chinese painters. Effects range from the needle-point brush-strokes conveying the tension of the horse's harness to the soft shading which defines the muscular forms and accentuates the nervous head and dancing hoofs.

XIA GUI (below)
Landscape, c. 1200-25
An exponent of the "boneless" technique (painting without contours), Xia Gui creates a landscape from flecked, hooked and writhing strokes which seem blown across the surface of the picture.

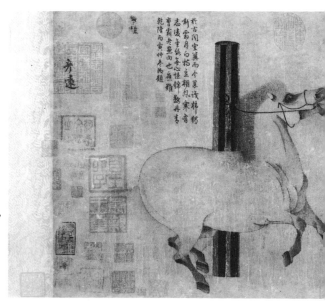

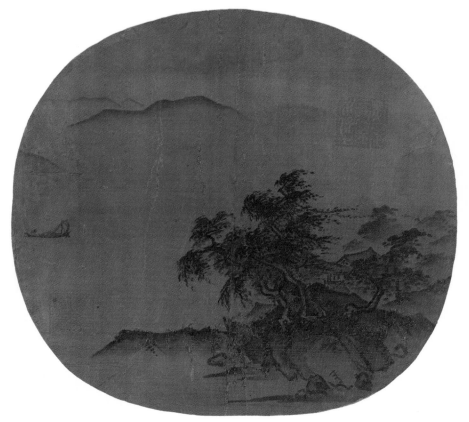

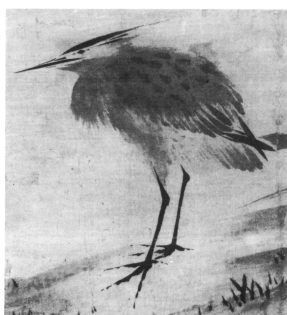

TAN-AN (above)
Heron, detail, *c.* 1570
Eastern brushes respond to the slightest pressure; a lifted brush produced the fine or "bone" line of the heron's bill, a depressed brush the fat, or "flesh" strokes of the feathers.

TOSA MITSUYOSHI (right)
The battle of Uji river,
detail, 16–17th century
Clan struggles are a popular theme of Japanese handscrolls; the narrative essentials were outlined in ink and the scene enriched with gold, silver and colour.

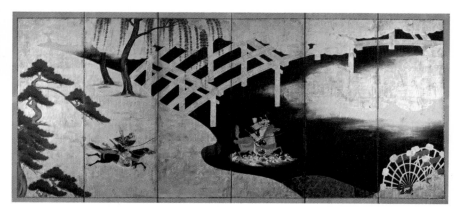

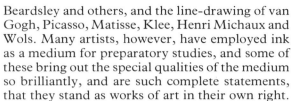

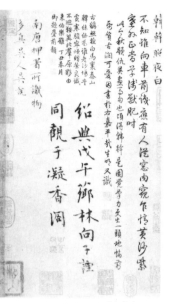

alum and glue. In traditional procedure, the paper or silk is spread across the floor or table, and the brush poised vertically above. The artist never paints confronted with his subject. Instead, after a period of inward contemplation, he sees clearly in his mind what he wants to paint; he is "moved by the spirit" of the subject, and begins to "write" its image with swift, rhythmic movements of the flexible arm and hand. His control is such that his palm never rests on the paper; this would "earth" the spirit of his theme, which is felt to be passing through the brush. A calligraphic panel with a poem or a piece of narrative often accompanies the painting, carefully placed to provide a textural and harmonious element in the design.

In Western art, watercolours or gouaches are often outlined first in ink or completed by pen, but ink has seldom been used as an independent medium. Among the few examples of autonomous works in ink are some of Rembrandt's drawings, the black and white book-illustrations by Aubrey

Beardsley and others, and the line-drawing of van Gogh, Picasso, Matisse, Klee, Henri Michaux and Wols. Many artists, however, have employed ink as a medium for preparatory studies, and some of these bring out the special qualities of the medium so brilliantly, and are such complete statements, that they stand as works of art in their own right.

A range of inks has been used in the West. Medieval manuscript illuminators used a dense black ink extracted from the gallnut which, in time, turned brown. India ink, formerly imported from the East in sticks and bars, began to be made in liquid form in Europe from the fifteenth century. Although India black has been the most popular, brown inks have also been used, alone or in combination with black. Rembrandt, for example, drew in bistre, a yellowish-brown ink made from the soot of burnt wood, in the nineteenth century, Goya, Constable and others made brush-drawings in sepia, a cooler brown extracted from cuttlefish. Chinese white, applied with a fine-pointed brush, has also been used, generally on tinted paper and in conjunction with black and brown ink, to produce illusionistic effects of space and sculptural volume.

Pens, the conventional Western tools for ink, have an ancient ancestry. The reed is the oldest form, and artists such as Rembrandt and van Gogh superbly exploited its characteristic angular and staccato strokes. The quill pen used in manuscript illumination, cut from the wing-feathers of swans, geese and other birds, is more responsive and springy, moving easily across the paper; it has lately been superseded by the cheaper steel nib, in different widths and strengths.

CLAUDE LORRAINE (right)
Port scene, 1649–50
Claude has ruled up this small working drawing for transferring to canvas. Pen and wash are complementary: pen is used to establish spatial perspective, planar relationships and the main divisions of the composition; loosely applied washes indicate the final picture's dramatic tonal contrasts and magical watery light.

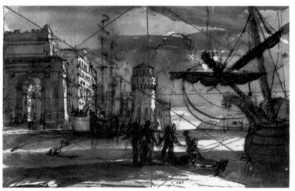

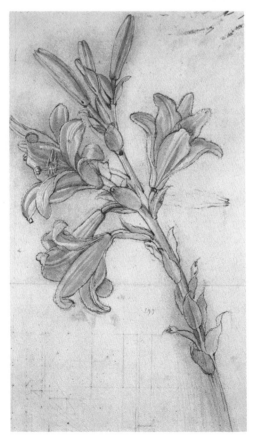

LEONARDO (left)
Lily, c. 1475
The pen is used like a scalpel to expose the plant's organic structure: fine brush-strokes define the lithe stem and blooms; white accents sharpen the petals' curling edges and project the floating pistils. The whole is washed over with a delicate sepia.

VAN-GOGH (right)
Washerwomen on the canal, 1888
Van Gogh invented a supple calligraphy of dots, dashes, streaks, stabs and cross-hatchings in preparatory studies for oils. His reed-strokes expressing texture, tonal relationships and structural forms are also used to indicate reflections and radiating light in the manner of his impasto oils.

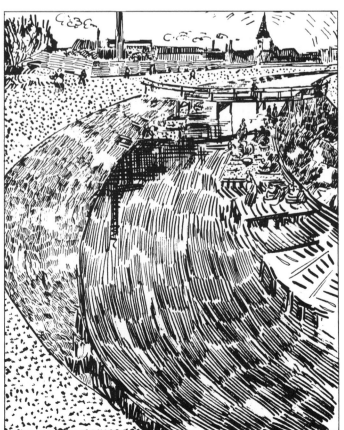

Pastel and Gouache

LIOTARD
Self-portrait with beard, 1749
The blunt pastel he holds is
for colour masses, but for
his prodigiously wiry beard
Liotard has used a pencil-
sharp edge. The alertness
of the pose reflects the
immediacy of the medium:
textural contrasts help to
offset the limited depth of
tone and the flat colours.

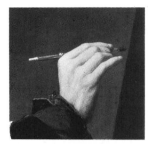

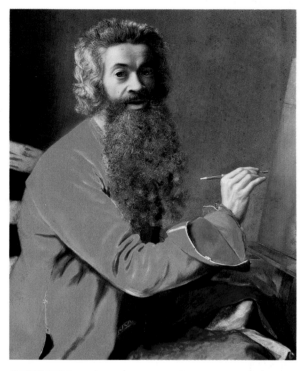

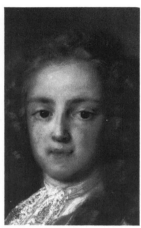

CARRIERA (above)
Louis XV, detail, 1720
Blending subtly to eliminate
individual chalk-strokes,
Carriera portrays the ten-
year-old king with exquisite
simplicity, the granular
nature of the pastel giving
his face a powdery softness.

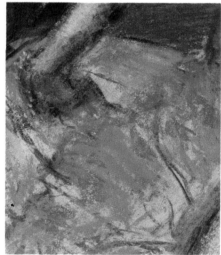

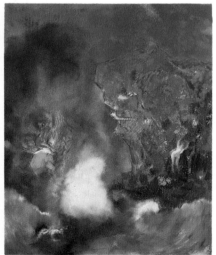

DEGAS
(right) *Dancers in the wings*,
c. 1900; (above) detail
Abandoning the orthodoxy
of soft, waxy gradations,
Degas used a rough, tense,
linear handling to suggest
effects of movement and
light. The surface becomes
a vibrating patchwork of
dashes and scribbles, of
tracks crossing in slanting
diagonals and clashing hues.

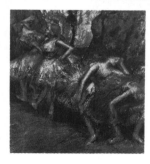

REDON (above)
Roger and Angelica, c. 1910
Like Degas, Redon extended
pastel techniques by varying
his handling of the medium,
though to softer effect. He
gives shape to his ambiguous
visions by counterpointing
blocky contours and dense,
rich, chalky colours with
downy, smudged areas where
the side of the pastel is
rubbed deep into the paper.

Pastel chalks are the most easily applied and responsive of all painting materials, putting pure colour literally at the artist's fingertips. The chalks are made by mixing ground pigment with water and a binding agent to produce a stiff paste which is then pressed into tubular moulds and dried; white or black is added for tints or shades. The medium is particularly associated with France and the chalks are often called French pastels. They can be used on any surface with sufficient tooth to hold the pigment particles, but the medium is fragile since the colour adheres only as a dry dust. Varnish fixative diminishes the characteristic granular freshness and pastels are therefore best displayed within a deep mount and behind glass.

Although the opaque nature of the medium restricts the range of tone and colour that can be achieved, the ease and speed of execution and the simplicity of its equipment made pastel a popular portrait medium in eighteenth-century France and Italy, especially with travelling professionals. Pastel portraitists such as Nattier and Quentin de La Tour achieved the fused, waxy softness of highly-finished oil-paintings, blending the colours by gentle rubbing with soft suede, a stump of coiled paper, or with the thumb and fingers. The spontaneity of the medium was exploited more expressively by Chardin, Liotard and Rosalba Carriera. But it was during the late nineteenth century, in the individual experiments of Degas, Toulouse-Lautrec and Redon, that the medium was most brilliantly employed. Working on raw strawboard or tinted, abrasive paper, they extracted a full range of tints, shades and hues with the use of a few chalks. The influence of the tinted ground was controlled by varying pressure on the pastel; heavy strokes obliterated the ground colour, lighter touches allowed it to show through in degrees and affect the colour of the chalks. Degas's most vivid pastel works are perhaps those in which his handling is most direct.

Degas and others also used pastels in combination with other media, and sometimes fixed the chalk by working on turpentine-soaked paper or over a pastel layer fixed with varnish. The more recent development of oil pastels has enabled artists to achieve the colour depth and adhesion of wax crayons without losing the subtlety of pastels; they can even be spread by washing over the chalk-marks with brush and turpentine.

Gouache is a water-diluted medium which is made, like watercolour, from powdered pigment bound with gum arabic but is an opaque, denser paint; the colours dry slightly lighter in key. As with pastel, it is both a traditional material for making life studies for paintings and a picture medium in its own right. It, too, is a swift and convenient method. Sometimes loosely termed tempera, it is also marketed as "poster" and "designer's" colour. Drying speed can be retarded with the addition of honey or an acrylic medium but, like tempera, gouache dries too quickly for reliable tone and colour fusion. Instead, optical blending is obtained with a pastel technique of cross-hatched and overlapping brush-strokes of different hues, often over a tinted ground. Impasto

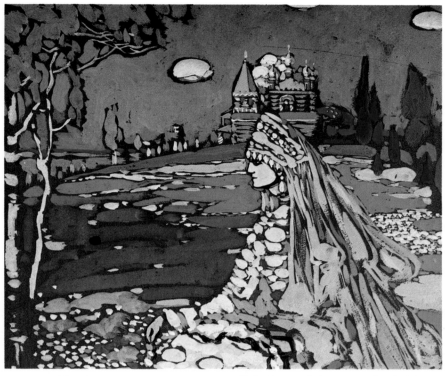

ridges and whiskered colour boundaries are characteristics of gouaches painted with brushes of stiff hog bristle on canvas or rough paper. When the paint is prepared to the consistency of thin paste and applied directly with a broad, soft sable brush, flawless fields of unvarying colour can be achieved.

Until recently in Western art gouache has been generally used for preparatory sketches for oils. Among notable examples are the cartoons and colour sketches for tapestries and paintings by Raphael and Rubens. Since gouache is capable of delicate detail when applied with a fine pointed sable, it was the medium of the sixteenth-century miniaturists and was also used in France and Italy during the eighteenth century for fan decorations – Rococo pastoral scenes painted on paper, card and silk and mounted on exquisitely fretted sticks of ivory or wood. Modern artists who have used gouache as a picture medium for its qualities of rapid drying and application include Kandinsky, Picasso, Klee, Rouault and Sonia Delaunay. In his "Rose" period, Picasso often relied on gouache because it was cheap, but he continued to use it throughout his life and executed many of the sketches for his famous mural-size oil *Guernica*, in a monochrome gouache medium.

Gouache was the medium of Indian, Persian and Turkish "miniatures" – the court portraits and decorative illustrations to religious, historical and romantic narratives. Early album pictures were painted on palm leaves bound between wooden covers. The technique and approach of Hindu Indian painters, though influenced by the formal, ornate styles of Islamic manuscripts, were less inhibited, as demonstrated in the exuberant calligraphy of the Rajasthan schools.

KANDINSKY (above)
Russian beauty in a landscape, detail, 1905
Kandinsky has allowed the black paper ground to show through in places to provide contours and enhance the delicate harmonies of dry gouache colour. The blobs of quick-drying, flat paint create a shimmering mosaic.

RAJASTHAN, INDIA *(below)*
Raja Umed Singh of Kotah shooting tigers, c. 1790
Although gouache lacks the translucent softness of watercolour, its opacity and drying speed are advantages in elaborate decorative work such as this, where flat colour enhances a lively linear pattern. After the design was outlined with a fine-pointed brush, a semi-transparent coat of white was laid over the whole and colouring and details were added, sometimes by a team of specialist artists. Apart from some softer areas where a swift wet-into-wet technique was used, brush-strokes are laid side by side, unblended.

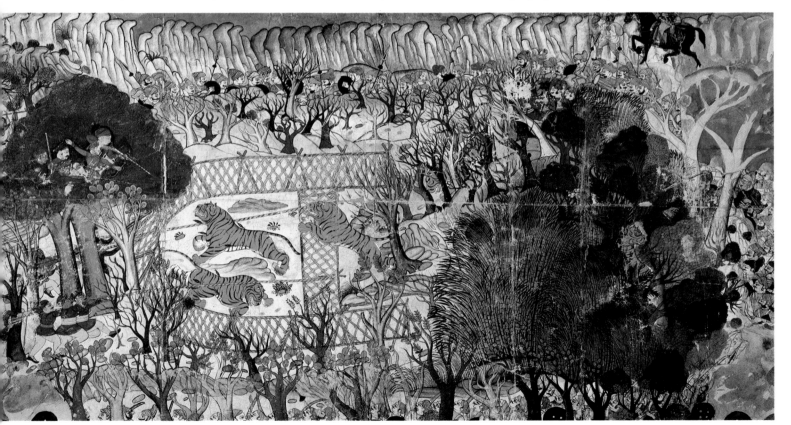

Drawing

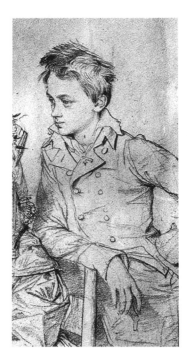

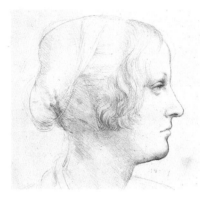

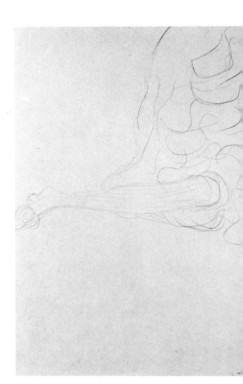

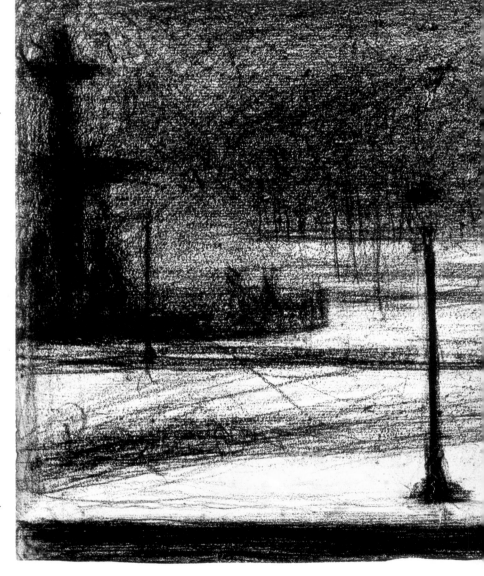

Drawing is associated intimately with painting, both as a means of sketching or establishing the design of a painting and as an independent medium which can clearly reveal the creative process and the artist's temperament or sureness of hand. Principal drawing media (apart from ink and pastel) are charcoal, metal point, graphite pencil, Conté crayon and chalk. The very limitations of the materials used – their lack of fluidity and restricted colour range – mean that drawing is perhaps the most abstract medium of art, the least illusionistic. Yet it is also the quickest and most economical method of giving visual information, developing concepts and expressing emotions.

A special aesthetic quality in a drawing may be the conscious or intuitive placing of an isolated image in relation to the frame or edge of its ground. The empty spaces surrounding the image contribute to the overall pattern on the support (usually paper) as "negative" shapes, and can also suggest spatial recession. These spatial effects are not only implied in representational drawings but seem to occur, by optical effect, in non-figurative works also, since all marks made on a bare surface appear to advance from it. However, a drawing is not always linear; when a massing of dark shapes leaves isolated white patches of paper, these become the advancing planes.

Broad tonal masses are not easily achieved with some drawing media, but linear hatching techniques can be used to create tonal patterns and provide precise and subtle means of indicating planar relationships and surface textures. Continuous, unvarying contours are used when an accurate representation is required of sharp-edged forms and interlocking flat planes. Illusions of light, shade and substantial volume can be achieved with chalk or charcoal by using the side of the stick or smudging with the fingers.

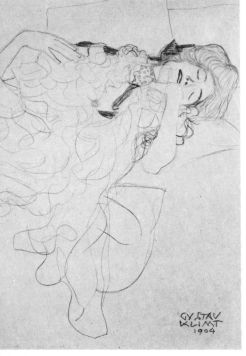

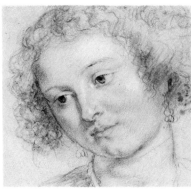

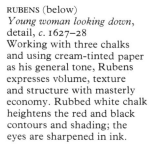

RUBENS (below)
Young woman looking down,
detail, *c.* 1627–28
Working with three chalks
and using cream-tinted paper
as his general tone, Rubens
expresses volume, texture
and structure with masterly
economy. Rubbed white chalk
heightens the red and black
contours and shading; the
eyes are sharpened in ink.

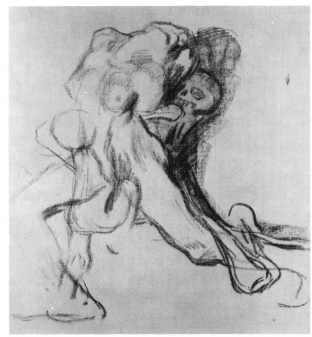

KOLLWITZ (above)
Woman and Death, 1910
Emphatic contours, breadth
of modelling, and contrasted
grainy and smudged textures
are characteristic qualities
of charcoal drawings. The
medium is impermanent and
fragile, but its range of
effects – from thin, sharp
lines to broad, smoky
masses – and its erasability
enable it to be used with
unique expressive freedom.

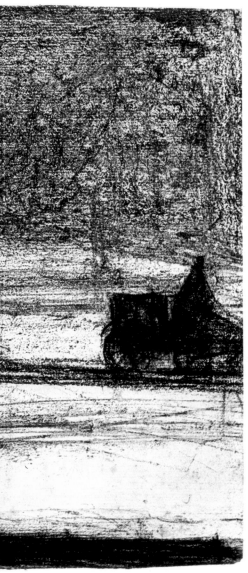

Whether the primary expressive element is line
or mass, the physical presence of the drawing
surface is always apparent. Tinted paper and a
combination of coloured chalks facilitate a convincing rendering of space and solid form, the
paper tint being retained as an intermediate tone
between white highlights and darker chalk shading. The best papers are hand-made from hemp
and linen rag, as woodpulp paper soon yellows.
For smooth surfaces, suitable for the harder
grades of graphite pencil, the paper is dipped in a
glue solution.

Contributing to the comprehensive language of
drawing are the first, sketchy jottings of an idea,
experimental variations on a design, creative doo-
dles, calligraphic records of momentary movements, and incisive, investigative studies of form,
space and structure. Many drawings are made
solely for the artist's practice or pleasure; others
are executed as autonomous works of art or as
"presentation drawings" for a friend or patron.
The purpose of the drawing may determine the
artist's choice between various drawing materials,
some being suited to swift technique or broad
statements, others to fine detail and considered,
incisive execution.

Charcoal (charred willow twig is preferred) was
the earliest known drawing material. Metal point
(lead or silver) derived from the ancient stylus
technique and was primarily a linear Renaissance
medium; it has largely been supplanted by graphite pencil, in varying degrees of hardness and tonal
range. Conté (named after its eighteenth-century
inventor) is a grease-free, hard crayon, useful for
studies of tone and texture, and made by mixing
powdered graphite with a clay coloured with red
ochre, soot, or powdered blackstone. Chalks were
popular with Baroque and Rococo artists, who
achieved striking volumetric effects with red, black
and white chalks on a background of tinted paper.

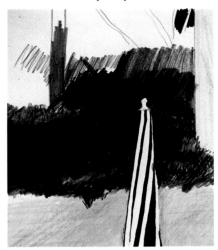

HOCKNEY
Beach umbrella, Calvi,
detail, 1972
Directly and forcefully
used here for a finished
work, coloured pencil-
crayons are, like the felt-tip
pens and oil pastels, a rapid
means of colouring sketches
and preparatory designs.
They are made up from a
mixture of wax and powdered
pigment or dyestuff, with a
binder of gum or cellulose.

Painters and Printmaking

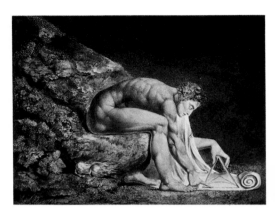

Until fairly recently, printmaking was usually regarded more as a means of reproducing paintings and drawings or illustrating books than as a unique fine art form in its own right. Until the end of the nineteenth century, the artist, or his printer, pulled as many prints as could be sold. Prints are now considered "original multiples" and are collected as works of art for the very qualities which distinguish them from other forms of expression. Limited editions are individually signed and numbered by the artist and when the print or "run" is completed, the printing surface is spoiled, to ensure the commercial value of the edition.

There are three main groups of printmaking process: relief, intaglio and surface, described in greater detail overleaf. Relief methods (most commonly wood and linoleum-cutting, or wood-engraving) involve the removal of some surface areas, leaving raised areas to be inked with a roller. Conversely, in intaglio techniques (metal-engraving, etching, mezzotint and aquatint) the ink is worked into lines and pits incised, or etched with acid, into a metal plate. Surface (or plano-graphic) methods include lithography, screen-printing and monoprints, where the image is drawn on to a flat plate or stencilled on a fabric screen. Each print process has different characteristic linear and textural qualities, with distinctive expressive possibilities. As in the history of painting, printing techniques have, from time to time, been revitalized and given new directions by individual artists.

In early European printmaking practice, the plate or block was generally made, to the artist's design, by craftsmen. Many of the Old Masters, however, were themselves virtuoso craftsmen who prepared their own printing surface, choosing the medium and process which best enabled them to extend particular expressive characteristics of their painting. So, qualities of linear precision and full tonal modelling in the paintings of Dürer, Mantegna and Pollaiuolo are emphasized in the hard, incisive line and elaborate cross-hatching of their metal engravings; Rembrandt and Goya used the very limitations of monochrome etching in order to develop the dramatic chiaroscuro design of their oils; The German Expressionists exploited the raised long grain of wood to gouge splintery cuts in character with the aggressive brush-strokes of their oil-paintings.

BLAKE
Newton, 1795
Blake developed his painting from a monotype, beginning with a design, in reverse, painted on board in tacky glue-tempera. From this he took a print impression, enriching it further while it was still wet. Finally he worked over the dry monotype in pen and water-colour, wholly overpainting some areas but retaining the mottled and pitted print impression where this could suitably represent natural surfaces. As the detail shows, he used pen, brush and ink to discover and emphasize marine imagery – sea-urchins, anemones and seaweed trailing across the rock.

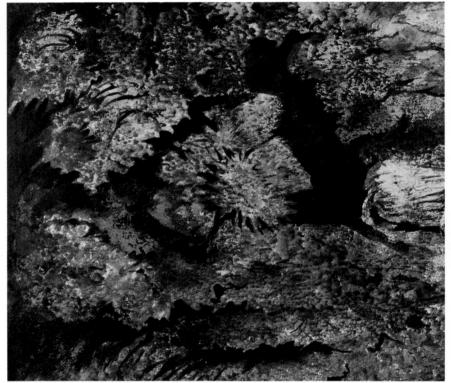

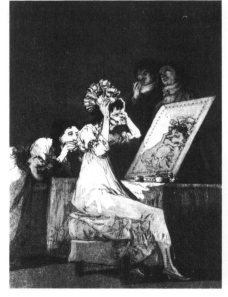

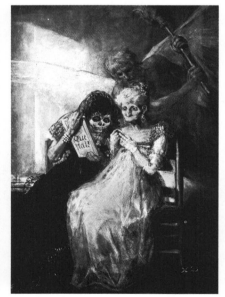

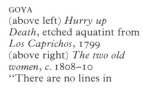

GOYA
(above left) *Hurry up Death*, etched aquatint from *Los Caprichos*, 1799
(above right) *The two old women*, c. 1808–10
"There are no lines in nature", Goya said. His prints and paintings were both designed in broad shapes of light and shadow. While details were brought into sharp focus by etching, the first print impression was made in aquatint (see over) to produce a pattern of harsh white and smoky black masses. In a similar way the painting began as a stark design of scumbled lights and glazed shadows.

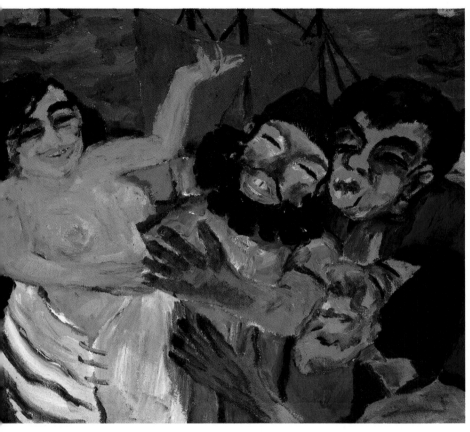

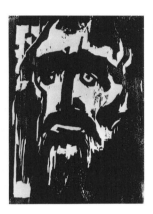

NOLDE
(left) *The life of St Mary Aegyptiaca*, detail, 1912
(right) *The prophet*, 1912
The fierce colour conflicts of Nolde's oils parallel the harsh black white contrasts of his woodcuts. His direct and deliberately crude handling of tools denotes a frank acceptance of the physical nature of the two media: both the canvas weave and the wood grain are visible; the brush attacks with the savagery of the wood gouge.

Lithography can reproduce almost any kind of drawn mark and provides the widest range of gestural textures. Daumier (see over) pioneered the medium. His near-monochromatic oils and watercolours, essentially graphic in character, share with his prints qualities of calligraphic line drawn in counterpoint with powerful patterns of light and shade. The recent Abstract Expressionist lithographs of de Kooning and Motherwell extend their impetuous handling of oils and casein into skidding sweeps and explosive blots and splatters of fluid ink. In contrast, screenprints by Vasarély or Bridget Riley, with their precise knife-cut stencils, parallel some of their smaller Op Art paintings.

Painters have often used printmaking to work out problems met in their painting – either through the discipline imposed by a particular process or through the opportunities it offers for experimentation and unpredictable effects. A monotype, or decalcomania print, the single impression taken from a design painted on a flat surface, has provided the starting point for some paintings. William Blake's tempera monotypes created mottled textures he preserved in paintings completed with ink and watercolour. Other artists have employed monotype methods to experiment with various tone and colour schemes by painting over a preparatory sketch placed beneath a sheet of clear glass and then taking impressions to be worked over in their pictures. Degas kept some of his "one-off" prints in their original state; others he developed, with oil and gouache, working them up as finished paintings.

Just as the character of early European prints was governed largely by current styles of painting, prints and their characteristic effects in turn have affected the composition and textural range of many paintings and design forms. Japanese woodblock prints, for example, strongly influenced Impressionist painters such as Degas, Whistler and Monet, the book illustrations of Beardsley and Greenaway, and the poster designs of Toulouse-Lautrec, Bonnard, Vuillard, Steinlen and the Beggarstaff Brothers. Modern mixed-media painters have also combined different processes in mixed-media prints, juxtaposing shapes and textures created by relief, intaglio and stencil methods with images printed by commercial photographic processes.

HIROSHIGE (below)
The plum-tree garden, 1857
Many of the qualities that made the Japanese woodcut so influential in late 19th-century painting are seen here: flattened forms, broad colour areas, unorthodox use of empty space.

VAN GOGH
Oil based on Hiroshige's *The plum-tree garden*, 1886
Van Gogh has made an interpretative version of the print rather than a true copy. The tender optimism of the print, with its pale sky and soft explosion of

buds, is replaced by a more uneasy mood, a sense of forced and painful growth. The dominant silhouette of the foreground tree has been further thickened, and the abrupt tonal contrasts introduced in the sky hint at an approaching storm.

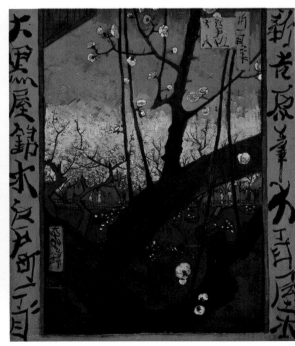

Printmaking Techniques

RELIEF PRINTING

Blocks for relief prints are cut away in the blank, or "negative", areas of the design, leaving "positive" lines and shapes standing proud for inking. The woodcut, made from a block sawn plank-wise, along the grain, was the earliest form of relief print, first developed in China, and fully established in Europe by the fifteenth century with the manufacture of paper and the introduction of typographical printing. Once the design is cut, the surface is rolled or dabbed with sticky ink and the paper print is pulled under a press or burnished by hand. Linocut prints have a softer appearance. The third major relief technique, wood engraving, which uses a small block of hardwood sawn across the grain rather than along it, can give finer detail and was widely used for book and magazine illustration before the introduction of photo-mechanical printing processes.

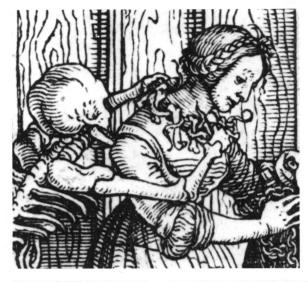

WOODCUTS, distinguished usually by a bold, forceful line, as in Holbein's *The Countess* (detail, left) from *The Dance of Death*, 1538, are gouged with "v" and "u" sectioned blades set in wooden handles. Wide-ended chisels remove the larger negative areas. Fine details, lines, and the contours of images are first incised with a knife to avoid whiskered or splintered edges where they cross the direction of the long grain. Progress impressions can be taken with wax rubbings on paper. Hardwood is preferred for fine details, though modern woodcutters have exploited raised grains of softwood.

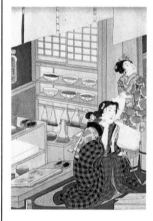
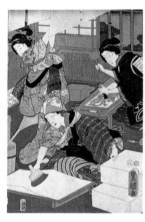
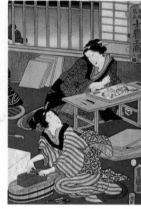
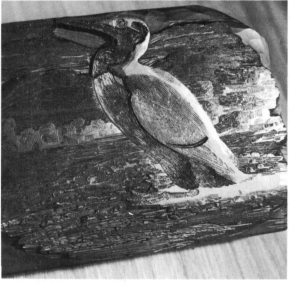

JAPANESE COLOUR PRINTS were taken from a number of woodcut blocks (one for each colour) cut through a key-block proof on which the artist indicated colour positions. Mulberry paper was then laid over each inked block in turn and rubbed with a twist of hemp, colours being modulated by varying pigment strength and pressure. Kunisada's triptych (1857) shows, from right to left, the key-block being cut, paper being soaked and hung to dry, and printing-off about to start.

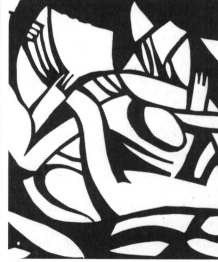
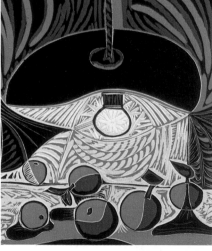
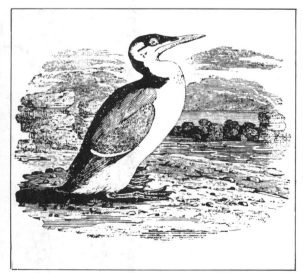

LINOLEUM allows the artist to cut a freer, more spontaneous line than wood and to work unhampered by grain. In Gaudier-Brzeska's *Wrestlers*, 1914 (detail, above left), the cut-out areas print white. Picasso's exuberant lino-cuts, such as *Still life under the lamp*, 1962 (detail, above right) have helped to raise the status of the medium. By progressively removing areas of the design after completing each colour run, he was able to produce a number of polychrome prints from a single block.

WOOD ENGRAVINGS, on smooth, uniform end-grain, allow delicate detail and tonal cross-hatching. The block and print (above) by Thomas Bewick in his *History of British Birds* (1797) shows atmospheric effects created by chiselling down the block in background areas so that details cut on it took less ink and printed more lightly.

INTAGLIO PRINTING

An intaglio press forces dampened paper into ink-filled channels or pits in a metal plate that has been either directly scored with a tool or else etched with acid. Direct methods include engraving (the deeper the cut the wider and darker the printed line), drypoint, where the needle used leaves a fine, burred line, and mezzotint, where the effect is tonal rather than linear: the whole plate is burred and selected areas are smoothed down to print lighter. Etching, the other major intaglio technique, is often combined with the toning method known as aquatint. An acid bath is used to bite out the design drawn on an acid-resistant wax ground, the acid biting only where the metal plate has been exposed. The depth of line varies with the time and solution strength of the acid bath; the deeper the line the darker it will print. Etching allows more spontaneous handling than engraving.

METAL ENGRAVINGS are usually cut in copper, as in the detail of a lion by Dürer which shows the hard linear clarity of this slow and demanding technique.

MEZZOTINT plates are first uniformly roughened with a serrated "rocker". This ground prints as the overall soft, dense black seen behind the tiger by

Stubbs. Tones ranging from grey to white are managed by varying the degree to which the burred surface is then smoothed down with a burnisher or scraper.

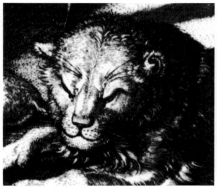

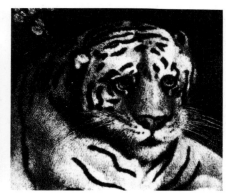

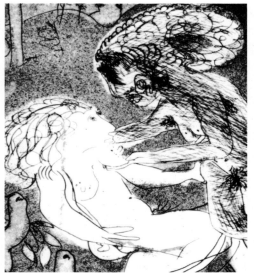

ETCHING requires a metal plate (copper, zinc or aluminium) coated with two hard, acid-resistant grounds: wax on the working surface, varnish on the back. Designs are drawn by scratching the wax ground with a blunt steel needle set in a wooden holder. The plate is then immersed in a bath of acid solution, where the exposed lines are etched. The ground is removed with a solvent, but repeated "bites" can be taken by laying a new ground. The final print may be the last of many trial proofs. For printing, the inked plate is placed on the bed of a heavy intaglio press and covered with a sheet of damp paper, followed by felt blankets. Pressure

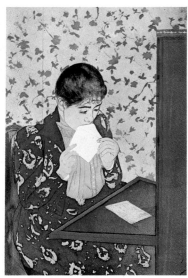

forcing the paper into the inked lines produces a slightly embossed surface. Etched line is combined with aquatint in both Arthur Boyd's *Lysistrata*, 1970 (detail, far left) and Mary Cassatt's *The letter*, 1891 (detail, left); a separate plate was used for each colour and another for the etched lines. Aquatint is a quick way of creating broad dark-toned areas. Powdered rosin is dusted over the plate and fused by heating; the acid bites only between the dust particles, giving a pitted surface and a soft, granular tone when the plate is printed. In pure aquatint, without etched lines, the design is brushed over with stop-out varnish.

SURFACE PRINTING

The most direct surface prints are monotypes (see previous page), unique originals taken from a design painted on a non-absorbent plate. A more versatile planographic technique is lithography, which can give a number of prints. An alternative surface method is stencilling, the direct printing on to paper of an image formed by pushing ink through the open areas of a cut or painted mask, giving emphatic, hard-edged images.

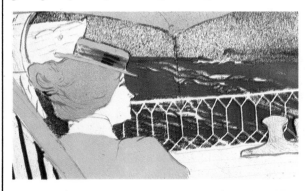

LITHOGRAPHY can produce effects ranging from the soft granularity of the detail (top right) from Daumier's *The legislative paunch*, 1833-34, to the contrasted clear and stippled colour areas in Toulouse-Lautrec's *The passenger in cabin 54*, 1896 (detail, left). The process works by the natural antipathy of oil and water. The design is drawn with a greasy crayon or paint directly on a lime-stone block, a zinc or aluminium plate, or a sheet of coated paper. This greasy image is fixed with gum so that when water is sponged on the surface the unworked areas are dampened but the image remains dry. An oil-based ink is then rolled on and adheres only to the image. For colour lithography, separate stones are made for each colour run.

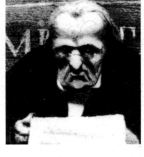

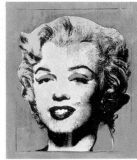

SILK-SCREEN PRINTING, or serigraphy in its fine-art form, uses a stencil made of paper or lacquered film stuck to a fine-mesh fabric stretched over a wooden frame. The printing ink is forced through the screen with a rubber squeegee. Cut stencils produce sharply defined images, but chalky lines and granular textures can be created by drawing on the screen with a waxy or waterproof medium. The mesh is then coated with gum and the medium in the image area is dissolved to allow the ink through. A design can also be painted directly on the screen with gum, varnish or plastic emulsion paint which masks negative areas. Warhol's *Marilyn*, 1962 (detail, left) is printed in acrylic ink using a stencil made from a half-tone film positive.

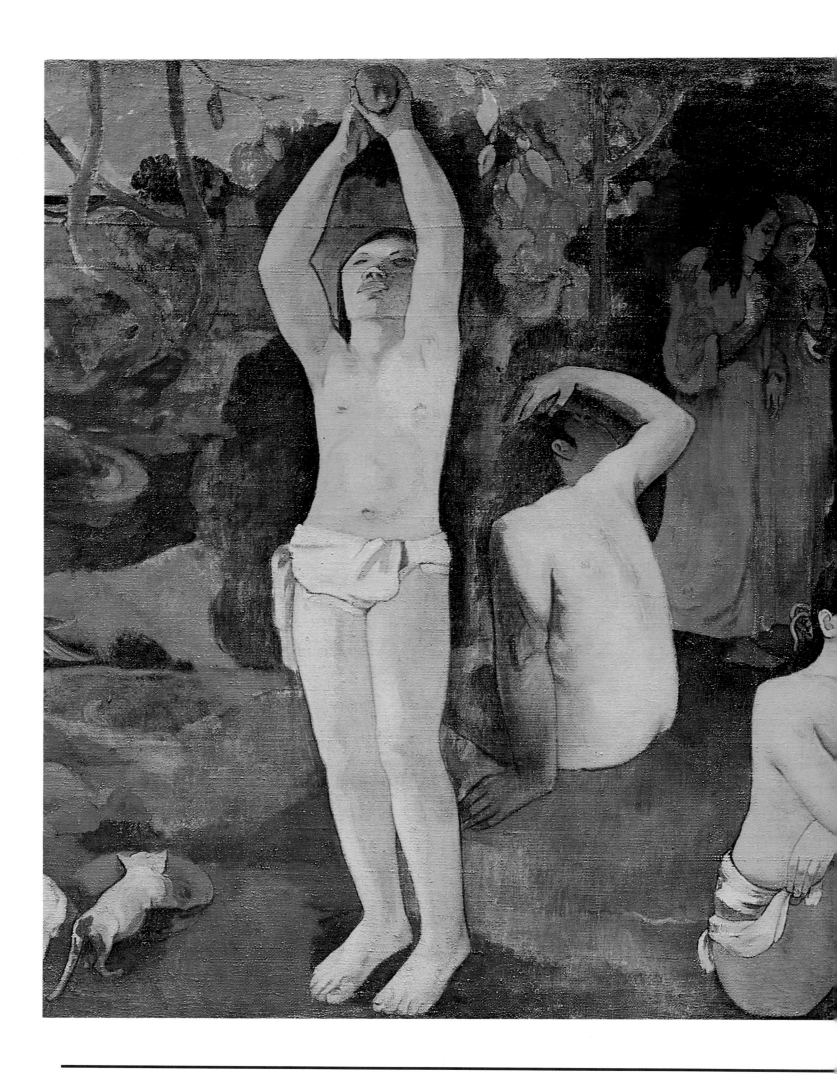

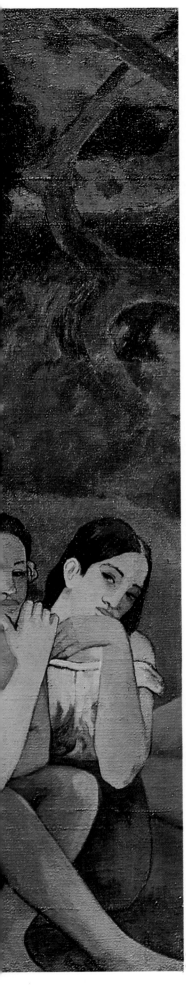

LOOKING AT PAINTINGS

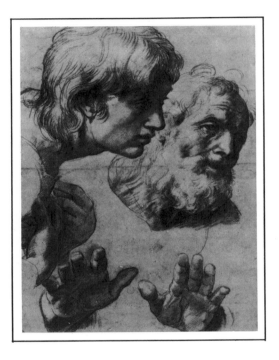

"I have tried to vindicate the right
to dare anything" – GAUGUIN

(left) GAUGUIN: *Where do we come from? What are we? Where are we going?*, detail, 1897
(above) RAPHAEL: study for *The Transfiguration*, 1520

The Virgin of Vladimir

Icons, generally small and so easily transportable, are the best-known form of Byzantine art. A tradition persists that the first icon was painted by St Luke the Evangelist, showing the Virgin pointing to the Child on her left arm. However, no examples that date from before the sixth century are known. Icons became increasingly popular in Byzantium in the sixth and seventh centuries, to some degree precipitating the reaction of iconoclasm. Although the iconoclasts asserted that icons were being worshipped, their proper function was as an aid to meditation; through the visible image the believer could apprehend the invisible spirituality. Condensed into a small compass, they fulfilled and fulfil the same function in the home as the mosaic decorations of the churches – signalling the presence of divinity. The production of icons for the Orthodox Churches has never ceased.

Dating of icons is thus fairly speculative. The discovery at St Catherine's monastery on Mt Sinai of a number of icons that could be ordered chronologically with some certainty is recent. Many different styles are represented. An early *St Peter* has the frontal simplicity, the direct gaze from large wide-open eyes, that is found again and again in single-figure icons. It also has an almost suave elegance and dignity, allied with a painterly vigour that imparts a distinct tension to the figure. There is a similar emotional quality in a well-preserved *Madonna and saints*, despite its unblinking symmetry and rather coarser modelling. Both surely came from Constantinople.

Immediately after the iconoclastic period, devotional images in richer materials, in ivory, mosaic or even precious metals, may have been more popular than painted ones. From the twelfth century painted icons became more frequent, and one great masterpiece can be dated to 1131 or shortly before. Known as "*The Virgin of Vladimir*", it was sent to Russia soon after it had been painted in Constantinople. The Virgin still indicates the Child, as the embodiment of the divine in human form, but the tenderness of the pose, cheek against cheek, is eloquent of the new humanism.

From the twelfth century the subject matter of icons expanded considerably, though the long-established themes and formulae, important for the comfort of the faithful, were maintained. Heads of Christ, Virgins and patron saints continued, but scenes of action appeared – notably Annunciations and Crucifixions; later, for iconostases, or choir-screens, composite panels containing many narrative scenes were painted. Long after it had ceased in Constantinople with the Turkish conquest, production continued and developed in Greece and (with clearly discernible regional styles) in Russia, and in modern Yugoslavia, Romania and Bulgaria. In Russia individual masters emerged even before the fall of Constantinople. The most famous of them was the monk Andrei Rublev (*c.* 1370-1430), whose masterpiece, *The Holy Trinity*, is the finest of all Russian icons. He transcended the Byzantine formulae, and the mannerisms of the Novgorod school founded by the Byzantine refugee Theophanes the Greek; Rublev's icons are unique for their cool colours, soft shapes and quiet radiance.

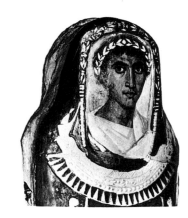

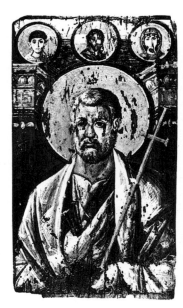

FAYOUM, EGYPT (left)
Artemidorus, portrait on a mummy-case, 2nd century AD
Fayoum has yielded some of the best-preserved painted portraits from classical times. Early icon painters were recognizably schooled in the same tradition: the hypnotic eyes of the icons are already found here, and the *St Peter* (right) was painted in the same technique, using encaustic paint – coloured wax applied while hot.

CONSTANTINOPLE (below)
The Madonna among saints, 6th century
SS. Theodore and George flank the Virgin, who seems withdrawn and preoccupied, and the archangels behind look fearfully up to God.

CONSTANTINOPLE (right)
St Peter, early 7th century
St Peter's pose and format, and the roundels up above, recall consular diptychs, perhaps deliberately. Note how freely the drapery is painted, with bold strokes.

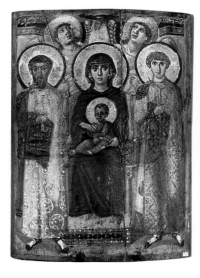

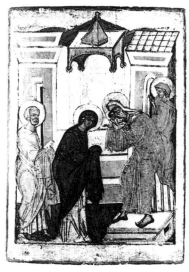

NOVGOROD SCHOOL (below)
The Presentation in the Temple, 16th century?
Typical of the Novgorod school are such tall, rather wooden figures, in cramped poses. The drawing is jerky and the drapery geometric.

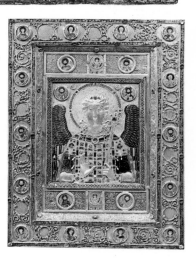

ANDREI RUBLEV (above)
The Holy Trinity, *c.* 1411
The three angels who were entertained by Abraham, as Genesis relates, became symbols of the Trinity in art. The firm and unifying symmetry of the meek but aristocratic figures is softened by the subtle play of shape and colour.

CONSTANTINOPLE (right)
St Michael, *c.* 950-1000
The Frankish Crusaders who sacked Constantinople in 1204 destroyed the city's treasures barbarously; the Venetians, equally piratical but more discriminating, preferred to loot. This icon in gold and silver, inset with jewels and enamels, was part of their booty.

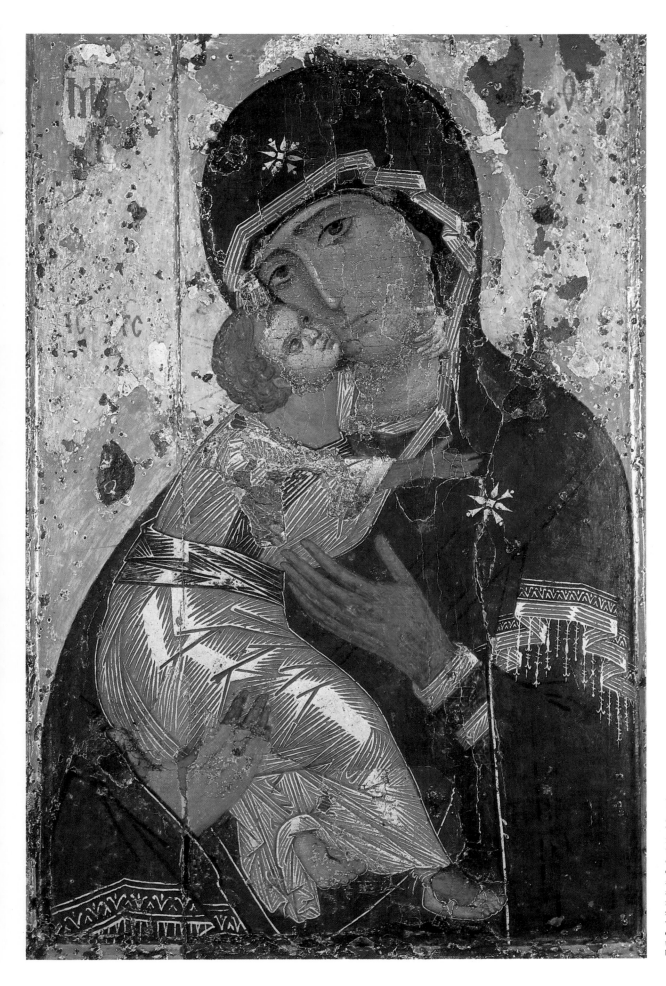

CONSTANTINOPLE
"The Virgin of Vladimir",
c. 1131
The icon has been care-
fully cleaned, but little of
the paint now left is
original – with the great
exception of the Virgin's
and Child's faces. Almost
all early icons have been
repainted not once but
several times. Because it
was abraded by a silver
cover, or *oklad*, the rest of
the icon was damaged too
badly to be restored.

AMBROGIO LORENZETTI:
The Good Commune

The lively, independent mercantile republics of central Italy were growing both in size and prosperity during the thirteenth century. Among them, Siena is the most brilliant example of a community rebuilding and adorning its communal heart, the city. In Pisa, Florence, Siena and elsewhere the cathedrals were already well advanced; now the streets and squares were levelled and paved, and meeting places, halls and government buildings erected. Siena's new fabric was planned as the visible expression of the city's order and harmony – even as a mirror of the City of God described by the theologians. Its most significant enterprise was the Palazzo Pubblico, or Town Hall, begun in 1284 and largely completed by 1310; from 1315 the nine elected city consuls undertook to fill the huge bare walls of its interior with a remarkable series of frescos, expressing communal aspirations.

In 1315 Simone Martini was commissioned to paint a *Maestà* (Madonna in majesty) in the room where the general council met: there the Madonna presided as patroness and divine ruler of the city, her message spelled out in an inscription. In the adjoining room where the Nine met, Ambrogio Lorenzetti was commissioned in 1338 to paint a series of frescos: on one wall, an allegory of Good Government, of Justice and the Common Good; on the second, an allegory of Tyranny; on the third wall, 12 metres (40ft) long, a vision of the city of Siena and its countryside enjoying the benefits of Good Government. The inclusion of Siena Cathedral, its campanile and the streets and houses around it, brought home the meaning of the allegory to the spectator personally.

The main allegory of Good Government on the north wall is expressed in solemn seated figures representing various virtues, moral, political and administrative. Each figure is named, and its significance spelled out in rhymed inscriptions. The enthroned figure on the left is Justice, linked by a cord to the largest figure on the right, Common Good, or Good Commune. The group of citizens below all face their elected choice, the Common Good; on the right, soldiers securely guard wrong-doers. On the opposite wall is the alternative, a group of vices about the throne of Tyranny – Cruelty, War, Treason and Division. The overall message is clear, an exhortation to the citizens and a call to unity; and it was urgent: the government of the Nine, though unusually durable, was constantly threatened by tension and violence between rival factions.

On the east wall the hieratic range of Virtues adjoins an astonishing city and landscape, unrolling beneath the hovering figure of Security. City and countryside are recorded with an attention to their physical reality in a way never attempted before, although two little panels ascribed to Ambrogio (the first pure landscapes in Western art?) foreshadow his achievement in the frescos. The peasants had carried out their same Monthly Labours on Cathedral portals; but they work now in a real landscape, indicated not by a token rock or tree but by an undulation of hills, winding roads, water and cultivation shaping the earth as it is still shaped about Siena today. The sky, however, is a grey-black blank.

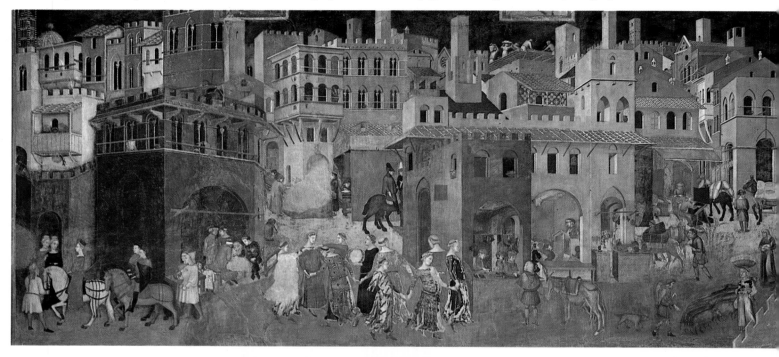

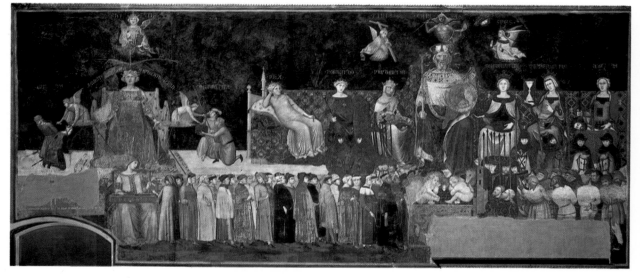

AMBROGIO LORENZETTI (above) *The effects of Good Government on town and countryside*, 1338
Siena Cathedral is on the far left; other buildings, not identified, suggest real structures, with known Sienese features. Ordinary activities such as building a house and washing at a communal fountain are truthfully observed. This realism, so different from the conventions of previous painters, is apparent also in the landscape beside.

(right) *Allegory of Good Government*
The row of citizens pass a symbolic cord running from Justice on the left, with Concord beneath her, to Common Good, throned with sceptre on the right.

SIENA (below)
Winged Victory, 2nd century?
Known to have been in Siena in Ambrogio's day, the Roman arch relief may have inspired his figure of Security, guarding the landscape in *The effects of Good Government*. The original has a suppleness Ambrogio does not match.

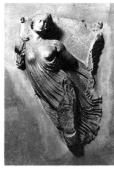

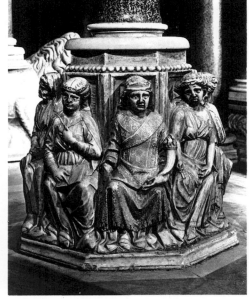

NICOLA PISANO (left)
The Liberal Arts, detail of the Siena Cathedral pulpit, 1265-68
Nicola's matrons were prominent monuments in the heart of the city.

AMBROGIO LORENZETTI (below) *Grammar*
The influence of Pisani sculpture on Ambrogio is apparent in the drapery and mass of *Grammar*, shown teaching a child, but is less so in figures that are not allegorical.

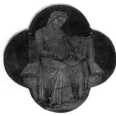

The reality rendered has been carefully interpreted. Central in the city dance maidens, the focus and symbol of the harmony of the whole: the light radiates from them to left and right, the buildings recede obliquely from them, and the scale of the figures behind them diminishes. This compositional unity had its counterpart in the deliberate disorganization of *The effects of Bad Government* (much damaged; not shown) where there was no clear focus of attention, and no coherent light.

A whole summary of medieval thought is completed in the medallions that border the frescos; these include symbols of the Liberal Arts and Sciences, the seasons and the planets. In representing these allegorical figures, Ambrogio was clearly stimulated both by contemporary sculpture and by antiquity.

A decade later Siena was to be overwhelmed by a disaster of which the Palazzo Pubblico programme had taken no account – the Black Death, which perhaps killed both Ambrogio and his brother Pietro about 1348, and, in a sense, served to delay the Renaissance.

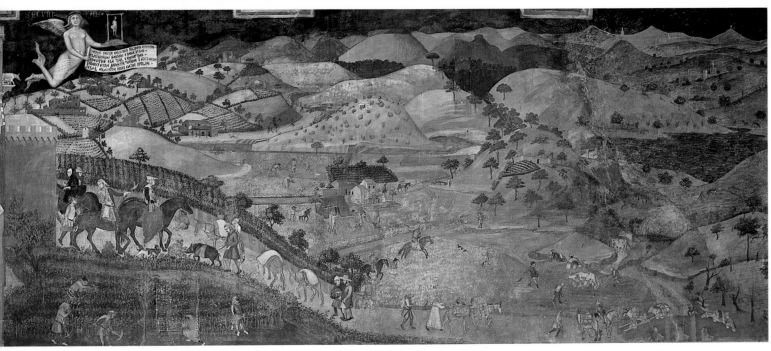

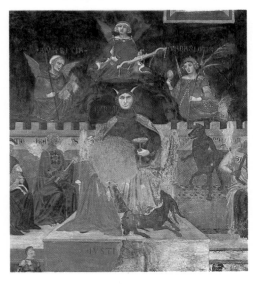

AMBROGIO LORENZETTI (left) *Allegory of Bad Government*, detail
This fragment from the now badly damaged fresco shows horned Tyranny, negative counterpart to the Common Good, with some of her cohorts.

AMBROGIO LORENZETTI? (right) *Landscape*, c.1335?
This, and another similar panel, are probably the two earliest pure landscapes in Italian art. In its uniform bird's-eye view this differs from the very much larger Palazzo Pubblico landscape, which is seen from a view much closer to eye-level. Had Ambrogio seen a Roman landscape fresco that no longer survives?

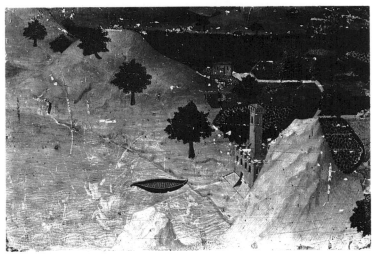

JAN VAN EYCK:
The Arnolfini Marriage

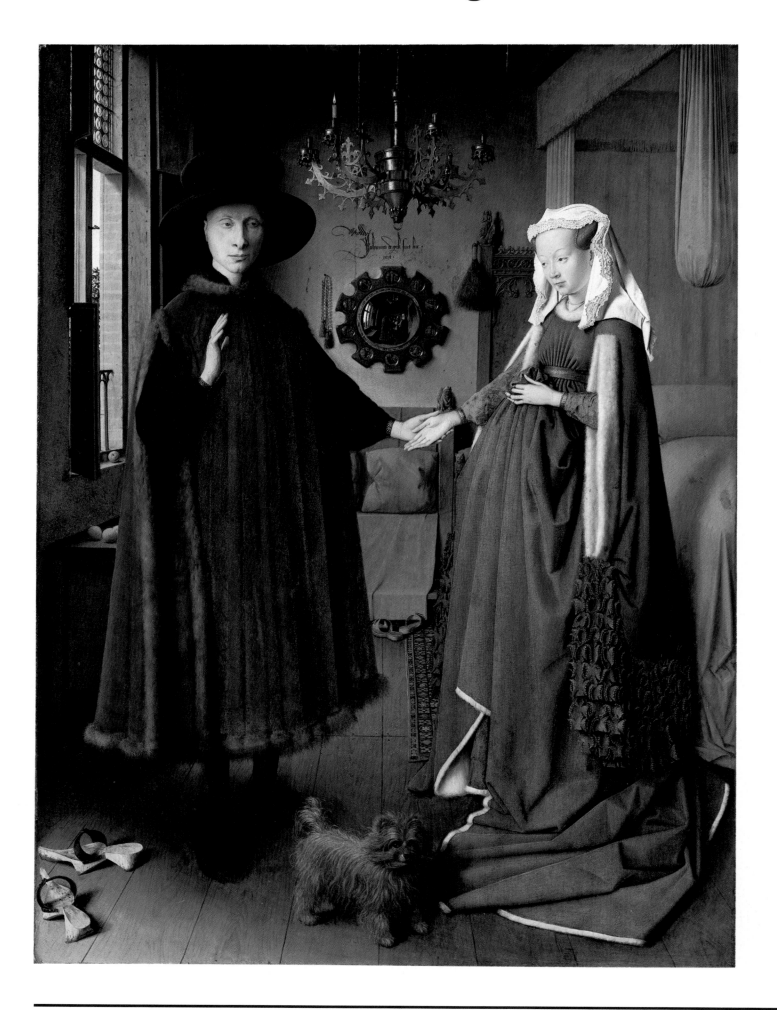

JAN VAN EYCK (right)
Giovanni Arnolfini,
c. 1437
Arnolfini's modest but
warm attire (van Eyck
superbly conveys the
texture of heavy wool)
marks him as a prosperous
bourgeois merchant. He
had court connections,
through which he must
have met and become
friendly with van Eyck.
He became a counsellor
to the Duke of Burgundy,
and advanced him money.
(It is generally accepted
that the sitter here and in
the *Marriage* is Giovanni
Arnolfini, but this is not
absolutely certain.)

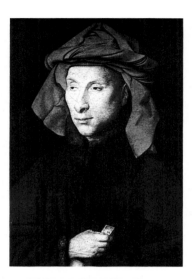

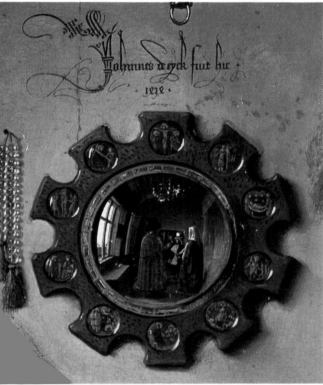

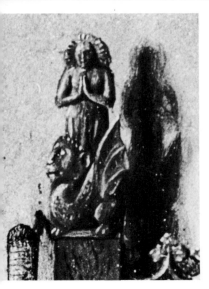

JAN VAN EYCK
(opposite page) "*The
Arnolfini Marriage*", and
details: (above) the mirror;
(left) *St Margaret*, 1434
St Margaret was said
to have escaped from the
belly of a dragon: hence
her role as patron saint
of childbirth. (Giovanna
is quite possibly pregnant.)
The ten roundels of the
mirror show scenes from
Christ's Passion, solem-
nizing the oath-taking.
The mirror indicates
things existing outside
the picture's limits, and
in the 17th century, when
van Eyck's picture was in
Madrid, Velazquez saw
and used the device in his
"*Las Meninas*" (see p.182)
– complicating further
van Eyck's metaphysics
of illusion and reality.

Within a room of some luxury, Giovanni di
Arrigo Arnolfini and Giovanna Cenami stand
side by side. Her right hand rests on his left,
and his right hand is raised as if to confirm a
vow. They are being betrothed, or perhaps
married. The year is 1434.

It seems that the painter Jan van Eyck, a
friend of Giovanni Arnolfini, a silk merchant
from Lucca in Tuscany who had settled in
Bruges, attended, and recorded the event with
documentary, even legal precision. The signature, *Johannes de Eyck fuit hic 1434* (Jan van
Eyck was here 1434) is written in a careful
Gothic script, as though he were inscribing his
name as an official witness to the ceremony,
and it is placed above a mirror in which two
figures are reflected, one presumably the painter, the other a second witness. It is as if the
picture were painted for posterity, as if the
artist knew full well that in 1534 or 1634 he
would not be there, but others would be.

The painting is not, however, a literal record
of a real event, for it is rich in symbolism,
unobtrusive but explicit, though more readily
understood by his contemporaries than by us.
Many details illuminate the significance of the
event, the married state as a continuing human
sacrament. The candle, lit in full daylight, was
not only a necessary prop in the ceremony of
oath-taking, but was a "marriage-candle", a
flame emblematic of the ardour of newly-weds.
The dog was a symbol of marital faith. The
fruit on the window-sill and the crystal beads
beside the mirror are taken over from the
symbolism surrounding the Virgin Mary. The
little figure carved above the back of the chair
is St Margaret, patron saint of childbirth.

This little painting, about 80 × 60 centimetres (32 × 23½in), has become one of the
most famous masterpieces of Western art, a
celebration of a human relationship as vital
today as it was five and a half centuries ago. It
was then astonishingly original – in presenting
full-length portraits confronting the onlooker;
in siting them in a domestic interior without a
religious context; in introducing narrative, and
even genre, elements into a double portrait.
For the picture is also an inventory of objects
lovingly described – the discarded shoes, the
little dog, the fruit; the planked floor, the
grandly intricate brass candelabra; the rich
texture and glowing colours of materials. All
these, ranged in immutable order, comple-
menting the calmly tender central figures and
extending their symmetry, are fused into the
serene composition of the whole by that pervasive light, welling from the window.

The picture is the summit, but not the
whole, of van Eyck's revolutionary achievement in portraiture. His single portraits reveal
a human approach that is quite new; with
modestly posed head and shoulders, the sitters
are seen for themselves and themselves alone.
Their faces (that of the *Man in a turban* may be
van Eyck's own) are intensely scrutinized –
one, at least, preceded by a silverpoint drawing
of vivid delicacy, certainly from the life – but
again the inventory of detail is modelled into
harmony, each item precisely related to the
others. The secret is the accuracy with which
the light is realized, with a subtlety and
flexibility which the refinement of the oil
medium allowed for the first time.

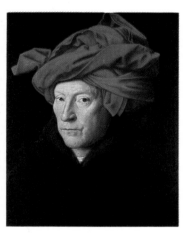

JAN VAN EYCK
A man in a turban
(Self-portrait?), 1433
The day, month and year
are written on the frame,
with van Eyck's motto
"Als Ich Kan" – as I
can (but not as I would).
He seems conscious
that his art will outlive
him – reviving a theme
of classical poets.

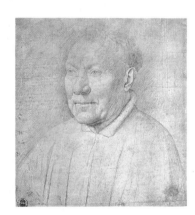

JAN VAN EYCK
(above and below)
Cardinal Albergati,
*c.*1432
The study for the oil
portrait is a drawing
in silverpoint, that is,
using silver wire on
paper specially prepared
to take its impression.
Notes for the colours are
on the drawing; has the
oil been slightly idealized?

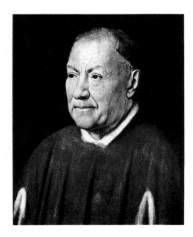

MASACCIO:
The Holy Trinity

Masaccio (1401-28?) probably completed his fresco *The Holy Trinity* in the north aisle of the church of S. Maria Novella in Florence at the age of 27, in the year when (so far as we know) he died. Who ordered this fresco and why is unclear, though the Lenzi family, corn chandlers, are believed to have been the donors. The fresco has been bruised by time, but five and a half centuries have not blurred its unmatched and magisterial statement of the fundamental principles of the early Renaissance.

The picture has a carefully organized perspective system on the lines first set out by Brunelleschi. The modelling and characterization of the figures have parallels in the sculpture of Donatello. But specifically Masaccio's is the exact control of directed light that unifies the whole, and the indivisible majesty of the conception. The composition is designed to be seen from eye-level as we stand in front of it. Nearest is the skeleton, stripped and stretched in its niche, with an inscription in Italian reading *I was once that which you are; and that which I am you will become.* Slightly above, and set back, kneeling outside the architectural frame, are the two donors in prayer. Above them again, and set back this time within the vault, the Virgin and St John attend the Cross planted on its outcrop of rock. The crucified Christ is supported by the outstretched hands of God the Father, looming majestic behind, who is the only figure seen foursquare in frontal view. Between the heads of Father and Son, in the image of a dove, hovers the Holy Spirit.

The perspective plotting is geometrically exact, the lines converge on a single vanishing point still visible to the searching eye, scored into the plaster beneath the paint. The architecture seems as real as the church in which it is painted – or, as Vasari put it, the painted chapel looks as if it opens through the wall. The classical detail – Corinthian pilasters that frame Ionic columns supporting a coffered vault – is worthy of Donatello or Brunelleschi, and the chamber so well planned in three dimensions that it could be built in stone.

In siting the Christian Passion within classical architecture, not against a Gothic gold background or in an insubstantial landscape, Masaccio suggests that its mystery is not only a matter of faith but is also penetrable by human reason. By his use of perspective, Masaccio anticipates the argument of Nicholas of Cusa, cleric, mystic, geometer and astronomer, that mathematics is the most certain of the sciences, a reflection on earth of heavenly light. The truths of mathematics are not subject to change; neither individual death nor the fall of empires can affect them; natural laws are the reflection or symbols of eternal laws, and it is within their logic that Masaccio's masterpiece is constructed.

Specifically invited into the picture by the Virgin's direct gaze and beckoning hand, the beholder becomes involved in the illusion, calculated to his own human measure, and appearing to his eyes exactly as does any earthly phenomenon. All, divine and human alike, living and dead, share here and now in an immutable eternity, through the mediation of Christ central on the Cross.

MASACCIO: *The Holy Trinity*, 1428

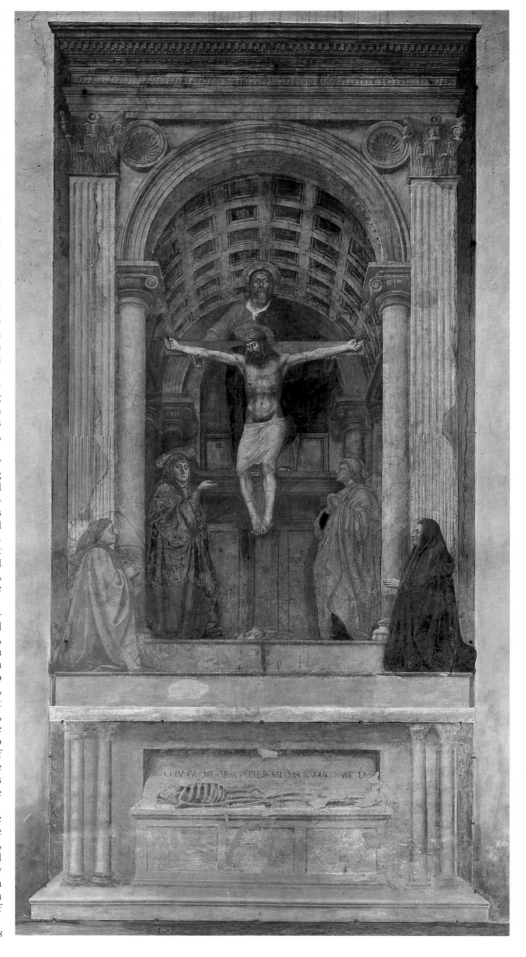

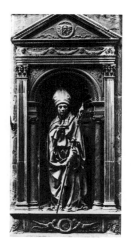

DONATELLO (left)
St Louis, c. 1422-25
These classical columns
between pilasters were a
rare precedent for the
Trinity architecture. It
is known that Donatello
and Masaccio were friends,
since Donatello received
on Masaccio's behalf in
1426 money due to him
for his Pisa altarpiece.

BRUNELLESCHI? (below)
Crucifix, *c.* 1412
It is rather appropriate
that the *Trinity* Christ
should have been based
on a work in the same
church by that pioneer
of Renaissance art in
Florence, Brunelleschi.

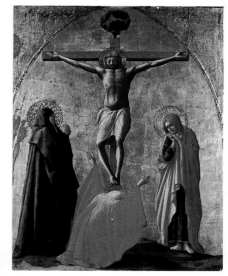

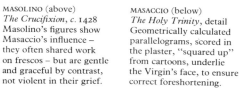

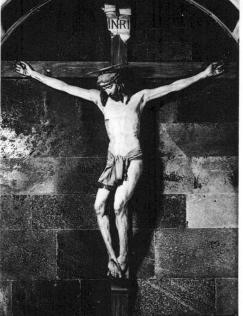

MASACCIO (above)
The Crucifixion, fragment
of the Pisa altarpiece, 1426
Christ's raised chest is
very forcefully modelled,
perhaps so as to stress his
asphyxiating agony. The
figures are strong, simple
shapes, highly expressive;
but note how solidly St
John's feet are planted.

LORENZO DI NICCOLO
GERINI (right)
The Holy Trinity, late
14th century
In other pictures of the
Trinity, God the Father is
shown enthroned; save for
Masaccio's this is the only
known example in which
He stands. Christ's Cross
rests on a rock with a skull,
Adam's skull; his blood
falling on it redeems the
human race. In Masaccio's
fresco the skull has been
replaced by a skeleton.

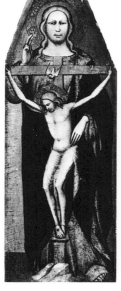

MASOLINO (above)
The Crucifixion, c. 1428
Masolino's figures show
Masaccio's influence –
they often shared work
on frescos – but are gentle
and graceful by contrast,
not violent in their grief.

MASACCIO (below)
The Holy Trinity, detail
Geometrically calculated
parallelograms, scored in
the plaster, "squared up"
from cartoons, underlie
the Virgin's face, to ensure
correct foreshortening.

MASACCIO'S PERSPECTIVE
The left-hand diagram
reveals the logic of the
perspective Masaccio used:
seen here as it were side-
on, the figures are placed
back in explicitly defined
layers of depth. The line
(AA) marks the picture
plane, the window through
which the viewer sees the
illusion, standing a few
paces back. The floor of
the chapel is tilted down
out of sight, since it is
above the observer's viewpoint; the viewpoint is in
fact precisely level with
the top of the altar: the
skeleton under it is seen
from above. None of this,
however, is permitted to
interfere with the impact
of the figures, who are all
of the same size and who
all seem to press against
the picture plane. This
play of flat surface and
illusory space is typical
of early Renaissance art.

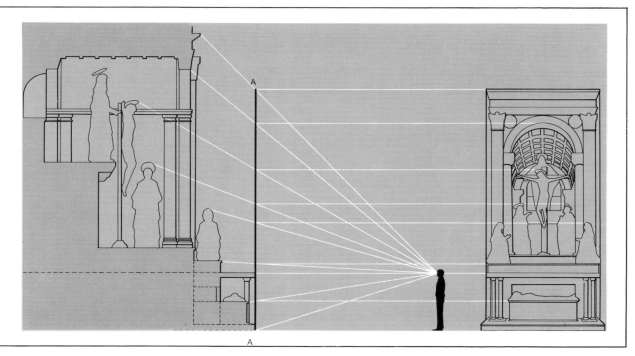

FRA ANGELICO:
The San Marco Annunciation

Fra Angelico (born *c.* 1395 or 1400; died 1455) is quintessentially part of early Florentine Renaissance painting, and yet an individual and untypical personality. The critic Ruskin termed him "not an artist properly so-called but an inspired saint", but he was very much a professional, running a workshop, aware not only of his predecessors but of contemporary trends in art, and taking up commissions in Florence, Cortona, Orvieto and Rome (where he died). In early youth, however, he entered the Dominican monastery at Fiesole, just above Florence, and thereafter led the pious life of a friar.

The Observant Dominicans whom Fra Angelico joined were a reforming movement within the order, emphasizing the need for direct and simple preaching, and rejecting mystic emotionalism. Giovanni Dominici, former Prior of Angelico's convent, had stressed that, steeped in the study of the natural world and inspired by love, the mind of man could grasp the nature of the heavenly world. Fra Angelico's painting is correspondingly clear, direct and optimistic; the certainty of his line-drawing, the radiant light of his pictures and their lucid, shining colours all express this, and also convey irresistibly the painter's own sweetness of nature.

Even when Angelico's subject is high tragedy, the message is not of horror or grief – or even sadness. His *Deposition*, the dead body of Christ being taken down from the Cross, is a *magnificat*, a serene hymn of praise and thanksgiving. The format was not determined by Fra Angelico, but he was able to dispose his imagery very happily within its three divisions: in the centre the body of Christ is displayed with ceremonial gravity; on the left the holy women, with the shroud, are gathered about the kneeling Mary; on the right Florentine worthies in contemporary dress stand in contemplation. On the left, it has been said, the religion of the heart; on the right, that of the mind. To left and right recede landscapes of magical beauty, which have elements still of International Gothic – the flights of angels, the Jerusalem built rather fantastically in Florentine architecture – but they are handled with a sophistication hitherto unseen in Florentine painting. The broad treatment of the draperies, and the figures modelled by light, recall Masaccio (and also Giotto); the tender delicacy of Christ's nude body indicates awareness of Ghiberti's sculpture. The sense of ritual, the singing colours, the flood of heavenly light – these, however, are unmistakably Fra Angelico.

Masaccio had painted chiefly for the Carmelites, who even earlier than the Dominicans had realized the use of naturalism in stating their message with force and immediacy. It is not surprising to see Masaccio's influence already in Fra Angelico's early *Annunciation* for Cortona, although it is tempered by the gentler vision of Masolino. Here also is Brunelleschi's classicizing architecture and his perspective system, characteristically applied towards doctrinal ends: the recession leads from the Virgin, the new Eve, back to the little figures of Adam and the old Eve: Paradise lost is linked to hope of redemption. Fra Angelico's style is always governed by the doctrinal

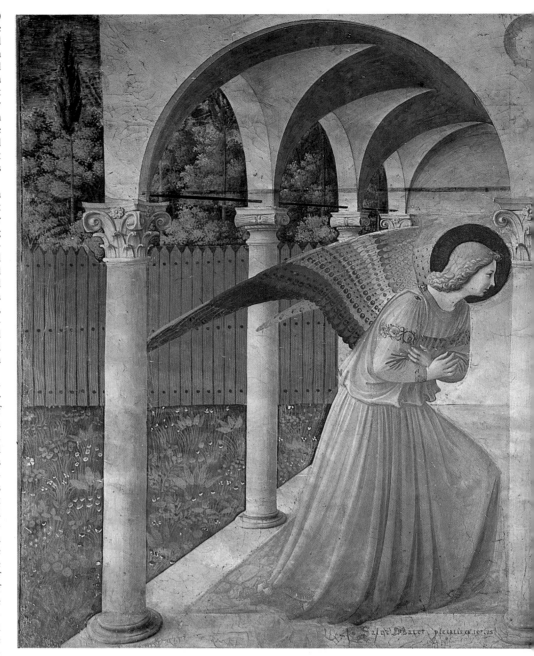

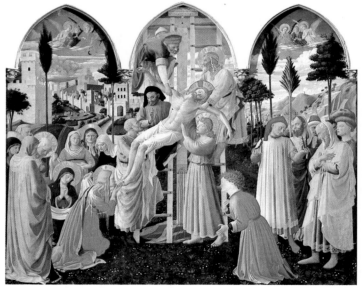

FRA ANGELICO
The Deposition, *c.* 1440?
Fra Angelico took over the commission from the Gothic master Lorenzo Monaco, who died in 1425, having already prepared the panels in their present shape, and partially painted the frame. Fra Angelico divided his composition according to the format, but joined the three panels in a single coherent space. St John, in blue beneath the Cross, closely resembles the St John painted by Masaccio in the *Tribute money*. Nicodemus, in the red cap on the right showing the crown of thorns and the nails, is said to be a portrait of Michelozzo, the architect who designed the new buildings at S. Marco.

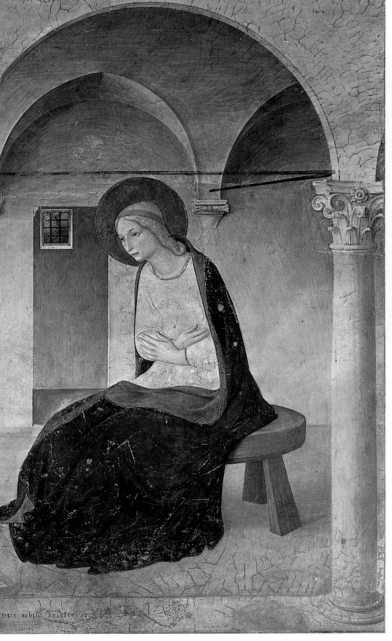

FRA ANGELICO (left)
The Annunciation, at the
top of the dormitory stairs
in S. Marco, *c.* 1450?

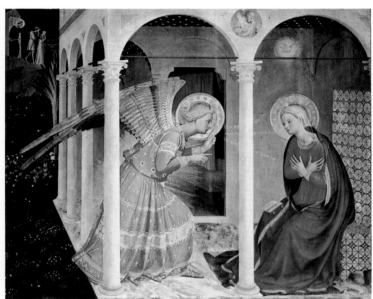

FRA ANGELICO
(above) *The Annunciation*,
for S. Domenico, Cortona,
c. 1428-32
The silhouettes of the
figures and the spatial
structure are subtly co-
ordinated, so that the tip
of the angel's wing is on
the picture's centre line.
In the left half, doom; in
the right half, hope of
redemption. This work
formed the basis for many
later *Annunciations*.

(right) *The Annunciation*,
in Cell 3 of the dormitory
of S. Marco, *c.* 1441
St Peter Martyr looks
on, motionless in prayer.
The corridor in which the
figures stand is closed; the
import is concentrated in
the pose and placing of the
Virgin and the angel.

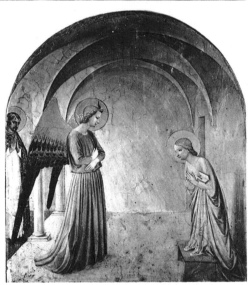

function of his art. Its development can be traced in two other *Annunciations*, both frescos painted in the dormitory of the monastery at S. Marco in Florence where the Fiesole Dominicans moved in about 1437.

Fra Angelico and his assistants painted the chapels, refectory, cloisters and the cells of the dormitory of the new premises. Each cell had one window, and one fresco as a window on the divine world. In these little chambers of utter simplicity the paintings are entirely austere: the *Annunciation* in cell 3 presents the scene in its most essential terms, pared down from the Cortona version. Fra Angelico's masterpiece, the *Annunciation* at the head of the dormitory stairs, was painted probably after he had been in Rome, at the cultured court of Pope Nicholas V. The Virgin's humility is both plainer and more haunting than before; the articulation of space is exquisite and yet grand. The balance of shapes and structure in the picture is delightful in purely abstract terms.

FRA ANGELICO (right)
*St Stephen preaching and
addressing the Jewish
council, c.* 1447-49
St Stephen's preaching
caused him to be
summoned before the
council, and his profession
of faith there caused him
to be stoned. The two
episodes form part of a
cycle of scenes from the
lives of SS. Stephen and
Lawrence, painted in
fresco in the private chapel
of Pope Nicholas V in the
Vatican. Their wealth of
detail and rich colouring
set them apart from Fra
Angelico's S. Marco
frescos – reflecting the
difference between the life
of humble monks and the
procedural pomp of the
papacy. The spatial clarity
and solid figures directly
recall the work of Masaccio.

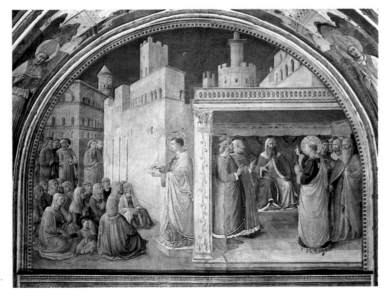

PIERO DELLA FRANCESCA:
The Flagellation

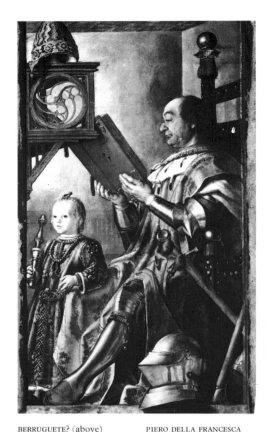

The dukes or despots ruling the local centres of power in northern and central Italy were always on the lookout for artists to adorn their courts and enhance their prestige. In the mid-fifteenth century they turned most commonly, as one might expect, to the Netherlands or to Florence. The Este in Ferrara briefly obtained Rogier van der Weyden about 1450; Sigismondo Malatesta, tyrant of Rimini, had a classical, humanist monument to himself, the Tempio Malatestiano, designed by Alberti, and his portrait painted by Piero della Francesca in 1451. Alberti moved on to build for the Gonzagas in Mantua; Piero went to Urbino, to the court of Federigo da Montefeltro. In Federigo's magnificent palace, denuded of most of its treasures in the sixteenth century, now resides one of Piero's finest paintings, the small panel of *The flagellation of Christ*.

Piero's picture is not a straightforward representation of an episode in Christ's Passion, since the Flagellation is relegated to a secondary position in the middle ground. Dominant are the three figures in the foreground, on whom the further meaning of the picture must depend, but their identification still poses puzzling questions. Though it no longer exists, in the nineteenth century a phrase from Psalm 2 was written beneath the picture – *Convenerunt in unum* (They met together). Those who met together were princes and kings of the earth, with the purpose of stirring up war against the Lord and his Christ. The Psalm is quoted in the Acts of the Apostles, where the princes are identified with Pontius Pilate, seated here in judgment, and Herod, perhaps the man in luminous grey who directs the flagellators. Grouped together by some com-

BERRUGUETE? (above) *Federigo da Montefeltro*, 1477
Soldier, diplomat, scholar and informed patron of the arts, Federigo, Duke of Urbino, was a Renaissance "complete man". He wears the Garter awarded by the King of England and the Ermine bestowed by the King of Naples; the mitre is from the Pope. His son Guidobaldo is beside him.

PIERO DELLA FRANCESCA (below) *Federigo da Montefeltro, c.1472-73*
On one panel of a diptych Federigo looks towards his wife, profiled on the other. Behind them atmospheric, panoramic views suggest that Piero learned from Netherlandish painters. On the back of the two panels Federigo and his wife are shown seated in allegorical triumphal cars.

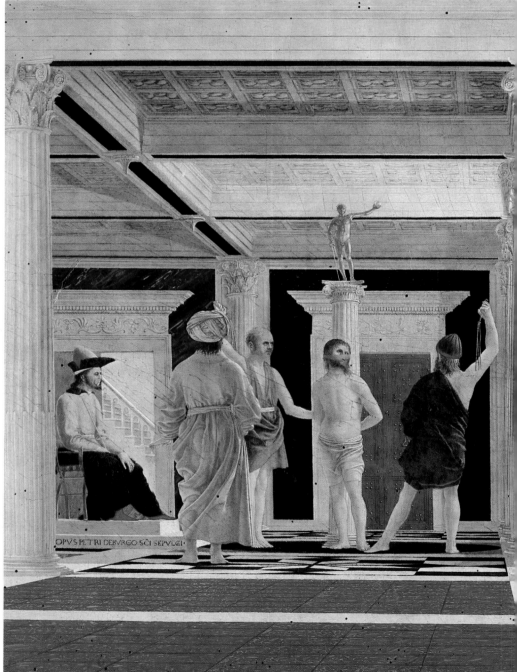

PIERO DELLA FRANCESCA (right) *The flagellation of Christ*, undated

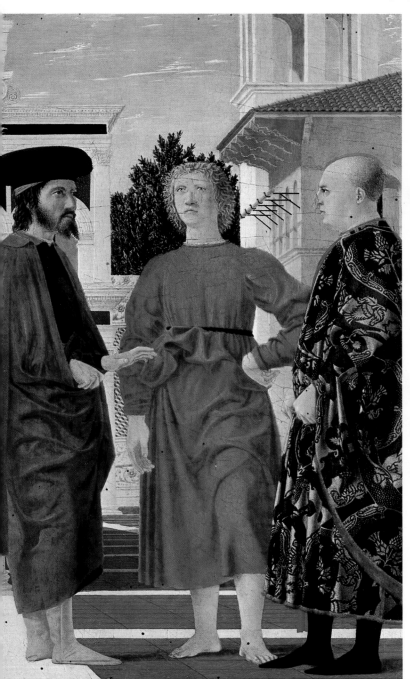

pulsive force stronger than ordinary conversation, the three foreground figures may on one level represent the Old Testament, prefiguring the torment of Christ in the New.

The emphatic placement of the three figures, however, suggests also a topical reference, and the strong individuality of the two flanking figures makes it likely that they are also portraits – the man in profile on the right bears some resemblance to Ludovico Gonzaga of Mantua, who had close connections with the court of Urbino. The austerely beautiful youth, however, whose hair is as blond as a halo, framed by the laurel-tree behind, who stands in a pose so close to that of Christ, left foot forward, his hand at his waist, must be allegorical: it would be bold to represent even the most blameless youth as a larger reflection of Christ.

The picture is divided into two halves, into two theatres of being, by an elaborate perspectival system, mathematically so precise that the plan and elevation of the Hall on the left can be deduced exactly. The loggia, constructed with a perfect command of its classical elements, strongly recalls Alberti's architecture; the design is not perhaps arbitrary, but based on reports brought back from Jerusalem of the surviving buildings there, including Pilate's Judgment Hall. Alberti's Holy Sepulchre in the Rucellai Chapel in Florence, with which Piero's Hall has some details in common, was probably based on the Holy Sepulchre in Jerusalem. The area on the right, however, the real world contrasted to the divine one, is fragmentary in plan. The two areas are lit by different sources of light, but are linked indissolubly by the reiterated elements of the composition, by the harmony of colour, and by Piero della Francesca's extraordinary still and solemn mood. The timeless Christian Passion is reconciled with the topical likenesses of Piero's contemporaries in an immutable formal framework.

The *Flagellation* was painted for the appreciation of learned humanists – not least among them Federigo (who wrote superb Latin). Besides painters – not only Piero but the Netherlandish Justus of Ghent and the Spaniard Pedro Berruguete – visitors to Urbino included the leading intellectuals of the day, among them Alberti. It was in Urbino that Castiglione was to set his famous account of cultured courtly life, *The Book of the Courtier*, and in Urbino that Bramante, the High Renaissance architect of St Peter's, was trained, and the great Raphael born.

UNKNOWN ARTIST (below) *Ludovico Gonzaga, c.* 1450 The man in profile on the right in the *Flagellation* closely resembles Ludovico, Marquis of Mantua, as he appears in this bust by a court sculptor.

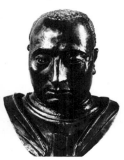

URBINO, DUCAL PALACE (right) The *Cappella del Perdono*, 1468-72 The tiny remembrance chapel is comparable to Alberti's structure (below right). Perhaps like Piero's picture it served some private, learned piety with personal references.

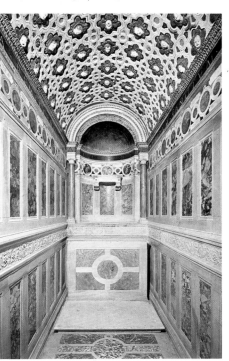

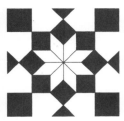

PIERO'S FLOOR PLAN (above) This is a flagstone of the loggia of *The Flagellation*. The paving, and the whole ground plan of Piero's picture, can be precisely reconstructed – such is the complexity and accuracy of his perspective geometry.

ALBERTI (right) The Holy Sepulchre in the Rucellai Chapel, Florence, 1467 Alberti's building and Piero's painting share the idiom of their classical ornament and the motif, perhaps symbolic, of a star.

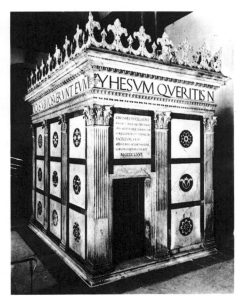

MICHELANGELO:
The Sistine Chapel Ceiling

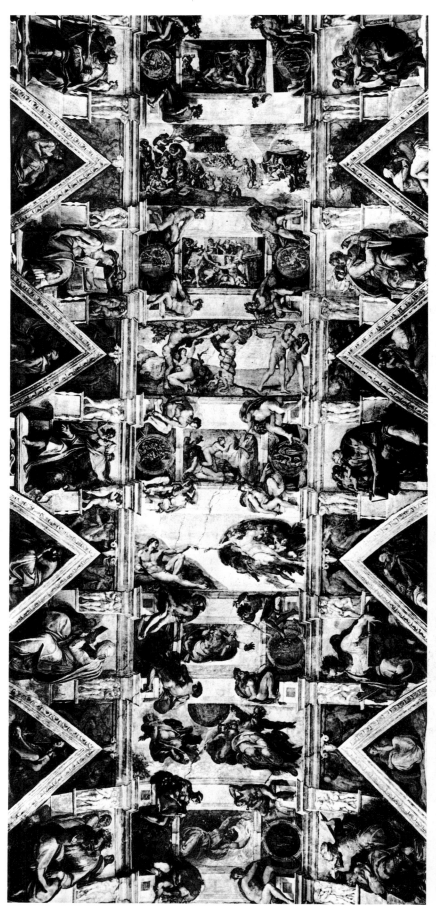

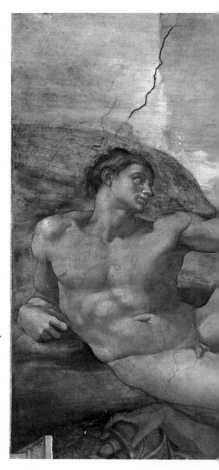

MICHELANGELO
(left) The Sistine Chapel
ceiling, 1508-12
The narrative is contained
within the long central
strip of the barrel vault.
It consists of nine scenes
from Genesis, three for
The creation of the world,
three for *The creation
of Adam* (detail, right),
The creation of Eve and
The Fall, and three for
The story of Noah. The last
scene, *The drunkenness of
Noah*, above the entrance,
shows man in weakness
but implies his redemption.
Along the sides are figures
illustrating the indissoluble
concordance of Old and
New Testaments, the Old
foreshadowing the New:
The ancestors of Christ
listed in St Matthew's
Gospel, and pagan *Sybils*
and Hebrew *Prophets*, who
foretold Christ's coming, in
the triangular spandrels of
the vault. Separating the
nine central scenes are the
famous *Ignudi* (male nudes),
whose meaning is unclear.
Perhaps, though wingless,
they are angels, but their
vivid force far exceeds the
needs of their function, to
support fictive medallions
and sprays of oak (emblem
of Julius II's family); they
culminate the Renaissance
adaptation of classical
modes to Christian use.

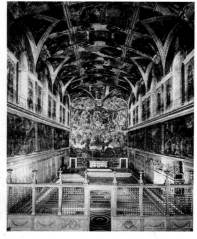

(left) The interior of the
Sistine Chapel
When Michelangelo painted
the ceiling there were two
frescos and an altarpiece
by Perugino at the end, and
windows like those down
the sides. These, and two
lunettes of Michelangelo's
own ceiling, were removed
when he came to paint *The
Last Judgment*. In 1519
tapestries by Raphael were
hung round the lower walls.

(below) *The Libyan Sibyl*
The huge Sibyl, painted
after the break of 1510, is
in the more monumental,
later style. Her figure is an
idealization synthesizing
the beauty of both sexes.

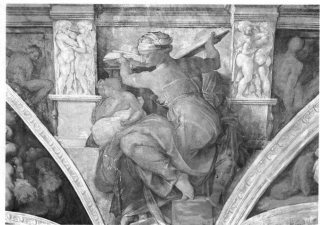

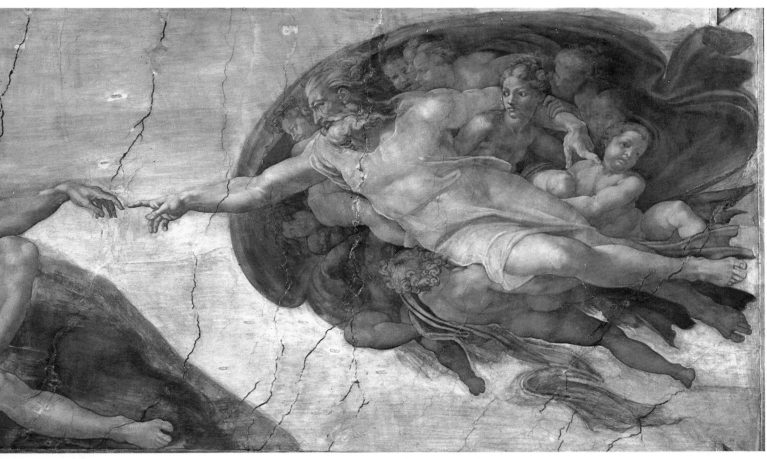

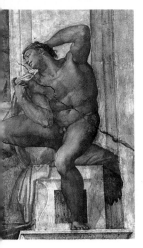

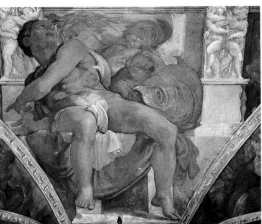

(left) *Ignudo*
The *Ignudi* can be interpreted as a series of formal variations on the classical Hellenistic "*Belvedere Torso*". They also strongly express Michelangelo's individual genius – almost art for art's sake; in this and in their strain, thrust and counter-thrust of pose, they were an inspiration for succeeding generations of Mannerist artists.

(below) *The prophet Jonah*
Vasari called it the peak of genius in this supreme work that Michelangelo could paint on a forward-sloping surface a figure that apparently falls backwards.

The Sistine Chapel in the Vatican, begun by Pope Sixtus IV in 1473, was and is a place of worship, but it is also the setting for certain extraordinary functions – notably the conclave of cardinals for the election of a new pope. The decorations of the 1480s – frescos by Perugino, Signorelli, Botticelli and others girdling the walls – had illustrated the basis of papal authority in the Old and New Testaments. When he commissioned Michelangelo to paint the ceiling in 1508 Pope Julius II probably wished to assert not only the Christian faith and his role as its leader, but also papal independence from such temporal powers as Louis XII of France, with whom he was embattled. Once entrusted to Michelangelo, however, the scheme became one primarily of Michelangelo's devising.

The commission to paint the ceiling came to Michelangelo at a point when he was obsessed with the design for Julius II's tomb, that is, with sculptural problems, and at first he seems to have fiercely resented the imposition. Julius II was an impatient and demanding patron, while Michelangelo's temperament was often neurotic or moody. In a poem written in 1510 Michelangelo bemoaned his lot – "I am not in a good place, and I'm no painter". But in the event the ceiling was to prove a more satisfactory project than the tomb.

The vast area of the Chapel ceiling, 38.5 × 14 metres (118 × 46 ft), took four years to paint, and was unveiled in part in August 1511 and completely on October 31 1512. It was Michelangelo's first major exercise in fresco, for the *Battle of Cascina* project had never passed the cartoon stage. After un-satisfactory trials with assistants he locked himself away in the Chapel, and virtually single-handed, on dizzy scaffolding of his own design, worked slowly across the expanse of the ceiling, through the days and months, often in acute discomfort. It was an heroic feat never to be surpassed by himself or another.

The extraordinary programme of the ceiling evolved from very simple first ideas – figures of the twelve apostles in an ornamental setting. But once the project had seized hold of his imagination, Michelangelo emended and aggrandized the first conception beyond recognition, though he must have discussed his ideas with learned churchmen – the Vatican was certainly not lacking in theological expertise. Formally, the imagery used clearly reflects the sculptor's frustration: the figures of the *Sibyls* and *Prophets* are variations on the theme of the great statue *Moses* for the tomb of Julius II; the famous *Ignudi* (nudes) likewise take up the mood of the so-called "*Slaves*" intended for the tomb. Michelangelo's style evolved as he progressed from the entrance to the Chapel, with its complex *Story of Noah*, towards the altar wall, and, especially after the break of 1510 when the scaffolding was removed, he simplified the compositions and form, reduced the details, and made the images ever bolder and more dynamic. One of the first images Michelangelo painted when he resumed work in early 1511 was the most famous scene in the Chapel, its climax, *The creation of Adam*, with its electric charge passing from the outstretched hand of God to the hand of the awakening Adam – an unsurpassed image of the most profound human mystery.

GIOVANNI BELLINI:
The S. Zaccaria Altarpiece

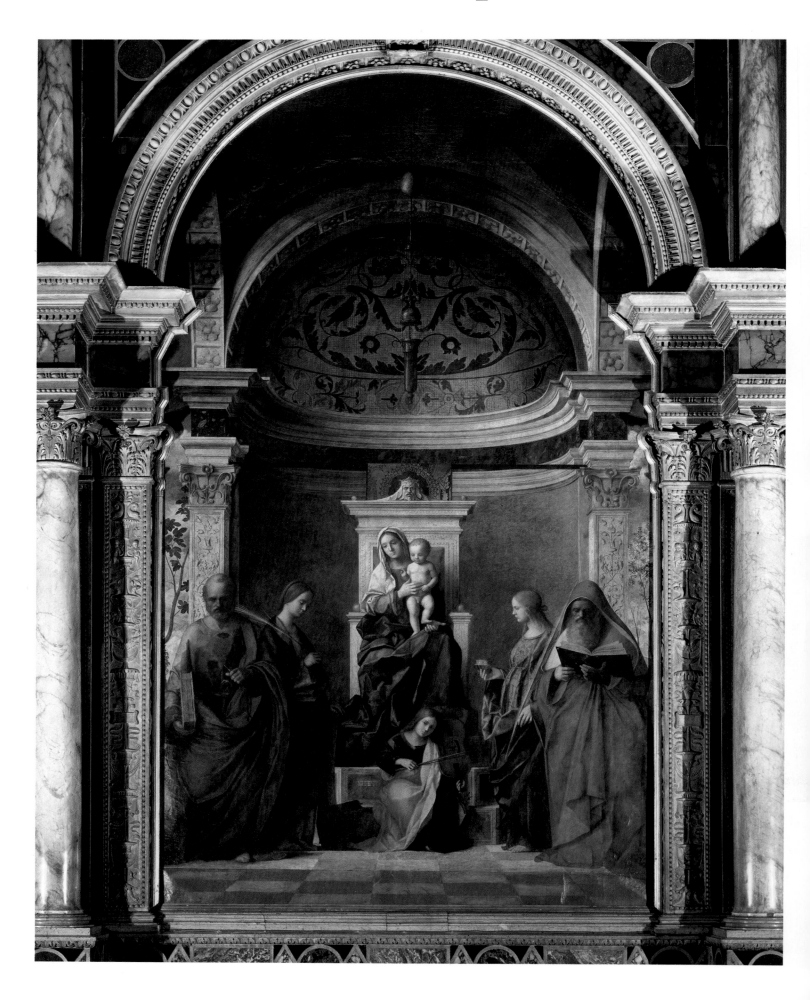

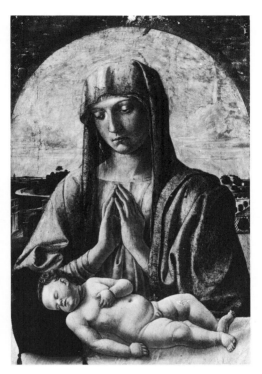

GIOVANNI BELLINI (above)
The Madonna and Child,
c. 1465-70
Giovanni's early *Virgins*
often have a distinctly waxy
texture; ideal images, they
have a precisely sculptured
form, an almost geometric
neatness. The light is still
hard and dry; the breath of
air which relaxes his later
work has not yet arrived.

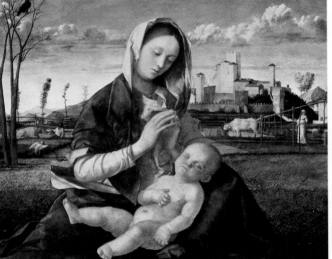

GIOVANNI BELLINI (above)
"The Madonna of the
Meadow", c. 1501
The supernatural is hinted
at both in symbolic details –
the stork battling with the
serpent, beneath the eagle
in the dry tree; the monk in
his white robe – and, above
all, in the serene calm.

GIOVANNI BELLINI (left)
The S. Zaccaria altarpiece:
The Virgin and Child with
saints, 1505

GIOVANNI BELLINI (right)
The S. Giobbe altarpiece,
c. 1490
The painted architecture
correlated with the real
altar, probably designed by
the architect of S. Giobbe,
one of the first Venetian
Renaissance churches.
The space is an extension
of the spectator's world –
and to be seen from below.

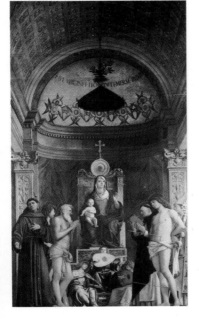

GIORGIONE (right)
"The Castelfranco
Madonna", c. 1504
Giorgione's only altarpiece,
painted for his native town
of Castelfranco, is so dated
because it seems similar to
the S. Zaccaria altarpiece,
and it seems to confirm that
Giorgione at first worked
in Bellini's studio. The
strange proportions, how-
ever, with the Madonna so
high, and the moodiness, are
Giorgione's own (see over).

Giovanni Bellini's great altarpiece in S. Zaccaria in Venice was painted for that church
in 1505; it is signed and dated IOANNES
BELLINUS MCCCCCV, and has been there ever
since. It represents *The Virgin and Child with*
saints, and it is perhaps the most perfect
realization of the *sacra conversazione* theme in
all Western painting. In 1506, the year after it
had been finished, the greatest artist of the
Renaissance in northern Europe, Dürer,
visited Bellini in Venice and noted: "He is very
old, and is still the best in painting". Possibly
Dürer was thinking of this painting when he
wrote that; and this work of a man in his
seventies was judged by the critic Ruskin to be
one of the two best paintings in the world (the
other was also by Bellini).

The S. Zaccaria altarpiece is the climax of a
long series of meditations by Bellini on the
theme of *The Virgin and Child.* Especially
early on in Bellini's career his *Madonnas* were
generally smallish panels intended for domestic devotion, continuing the tradition of Gen-
tile da Fabriano and of Giovanni's father
Jacopo. The earliest are still very much in the
early fifteenth-century tradition, hieratic and
quite austere, but very soon human tenderness
between a flesh-and-blood mother and her

child becomes apparent. The slightly melan-
cholic mood could be that of a woman consumed with wonder at the miracle of birth, but
also apprehensive, since the infant in her lap is
a hostage to fortune; yet simultaneously the
image is divine. Divinity is indicated not so
much by the halo (not always present) or by the
hands joined together in prayer, as by that
heavenly radiance and solemnity with which
Bellini imbued his women. Often, when the
Child is recumbent, there is a haunting foreshadowing of the *Pietà,* of the dead Christ
supported by his mother. Bellini developed
and enriched the still charm of his *Madonnas*
throughout his career, and in the very late
ones, such as *"The Madonna of the Meadow",*
the image of the Madonna is merged convincingly into one of the most beautiful of
Giovanni's landscapes, serene in the cool light
of spring, with the little village clear-cut on the
rise beyond. The Mother of God is brought
into direct relationship with day-to-day life.

Bellini's sequence of more monumentally
scaled *sacre conversazioni* began with one, now
lost, painted about 1475, related to a famous
one by Antonello da Messina painted in Venice
about the same time. From the fragments of
this work, and from Bellini's surviving S.
Giobbe altarpiece of about 1490, it can be
deduced that the architectural frame was conceived as integral with the painting, thus tying
the image bodily into the structure and presence of the church as a whole. In the S.
Giobbe altarpiece, the sense of space, the
relative relaxation of the figures, the glowing,
translucent colour all speak of Antonello's
Netherlandish-oriented vision, and probably
of his technique. The composition, however, is
a little busy, even claustrophobic (it is the only
one of Bellini's compositions entirely enclosed
in an interior). The gain achieved through
simplification in the S. Zaccaria altarpiece is
subtle but substantial.

Here the five figures are almost life-size and
the viewpoint is higher, the spectator closer,
while there is a hint of landscape and open air
at each side. The Virgin is seated, with the
Child blessing, amongst attendant saints – St
Peter with his key, St Catherine with her
martyr's palm, St Lucy, and St Jerome with
his open book. The draperies and the heads are
softly modelled in the fall of a unifying light
(the head of St Jerome, in its pensive meditation, seems already tinged with the mood of the
young Giorgione, whose *"Castelfranco Mad-*
onna" is thought to have been finished in the
previous year). The colours glow in a rich
harmony, and the serene symmetry and balance of proportions exist in a silence that
somehow is full of music – the music indicated
by the angel with the viol on the step of the
Madonna's throne. The figures, as in most of
Bellini's mature work, have an ample ease
both monumental and peaceful.

Bellini's painting is already of the High
Renaissance. The composition unites in harmony the primarily Florentine concern for the
logical, even mathematical, control of space
and proportion with the typically Netherlandish interest in the rendering of light, while
there is more than a promise of the revolutionary colourism with which Bellini's pupils
and followers were to startle the world.

GIORGIONE:
The Tempest

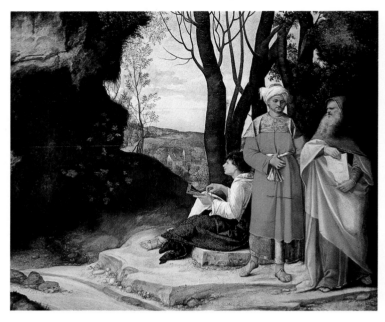

GIORGIONE (above)
"The Three Philosophers",
after 1505?
The enigmatic figures are
set before a mountain cave,
a dark chasm symbolizing
birth? Or the unknown? If
they were Magi, Christ's
birth could be meant. The
figures and landscape are
still reminiscent of Bellini,
but Bellini is always clear:
Giorgione escapes analysis.

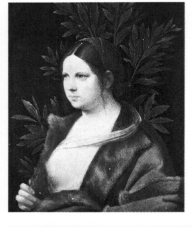

GIORGIONE (left)
"Laura", 1506
What exactly the laurels
signify is unknown. The
sitter's gaze is veiled and
introspective; the *sfumato*
also recalls Leonardo's
Mona Lisa. Is this woman
the one in the *Tempestà*?

GIORGIONE (below)
Venus, c. 1509-10?
A tiny cupid, later painted
out, played at Venus' feet.
She lies improbably but
convincingly in a superb
landscape (the picture is
perhaps in need of cleaning,
however). Titian reworked
the theme in his *"Venus of
Urbino"* (see p. 167).

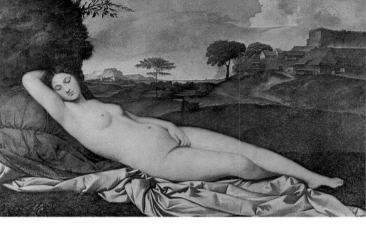

The brevity and obscurity of the career of
Giorgione (died 1510) are no index to his importance in the history of art. Although only
some 20 paintings are generally associated with
him, of which only about six are attributed
without dispute, his originality was so potent
that these few works have come to stand for an
enduring quality of the Western imagination.

Surviving documentation on his life and
work is sparse: the main reflection of his
personality is that recorded in a brief *Life* by
Vasari, who visited Venice about half a century
after his death and talked with Giorgione's
early collaborator, Titian, and others who may
have known the young painter years before.
Giorgione was clearly a phenomenon, of a kind
new to Venice if not to humanist circles in
Florence – a creature endowed with unusual
physical beauty as well as grace and wit; gentle
and courteous, "always a very amorous man";
a brilliant singer and lute-player. Not least, he
had an instinctive gift for the visual arts. He
was associated with the humanist circle of the
poet Bembo, and with a sophisticated group of
private patrons, for whom he painted generally
small-scale pictures. Giorgione's only public
commissions in Venice were paintings, now
lost, in the Doge's Palace, and frescos, now
something less than ghostly fragments, on the
exterior of the Fondaco dei Tedeschi, the
important trading centre (just by the Rialto
Bridge) of the German community.

Significantly, Vasari, himself a master of
esoteric allegory, was unable to understand the
meaning of the figures on the Fondaco dei
Tedeschi ("nor, for all my asking, have I found
anyone who does"). A certain hermetic mystery is a characteristic of virtually all the
paintings ascribed to Giorgione: his characters
are engaged in some concern of unworldly
significance, in a mood so intense that it verges
on the mystical, which no prosaic explanation
can ultimately elucidate. Beneath what Vasari
called "a harmonized manner, and a certain
brilliance of colour" there is an underlying
tension, and in this, and in the softness and
subtlety of his modelling, Vasari recognized
the influence of Leonardo. The emotional

vibrancy of his colour, however, is Giorgione's
own, although he could never have achieved it
without earlier developments in the flexibility
of the oil medium. Vasari observed that he
worked directly from nature – and surely
swiftly, directly on to the canvas, without the
elaborate structural preliminaries that were a
necessary part of Florentine *disegno*.

The famous *Tempest* is a key work among
Giorgione's few paintings, and a turning-point
in the history of art. It is confidently identified
with a painting inventoried in 1530 as a "small
landscape ... with the storm, and the gipsy and
the soldier". Significantly, hardly 25 years
later the compiler of the list did not know what
the subject of the painting was, and, significantly also, it is described as a "landscape".
For the modern observer the picture must be
primarily a meditation, a "mood painting"
needing no explanation, exciting chiefly an
emotional response. That the story, if any, was
never specific seems indicated by the changes
Giorgione made as he went along: X-rays have
revealed that before the "soldier" existed there
was another figure, a naked woman, seated by
the river. The mood, however, reflects the
recent humanist discovery of a lyrical pastoral
world in the Latin and Greek poets. The
Renaissance mind also delighted in symbolism
and allegory: broken columns may stand for
Fortitude, while the naked mother with the
child at her breast is an image of Charity, a
secularized echo of the Madonna. The male
figure may be a soldier, and so personify
Fortitude again: his breeches are like those of a
German mercenary, but he appears to hold a
staff rather than a lance. Pervading all is the

atmosphere created by the impending storm.
It is extraordinarily real – the lightning is
indicated not as a notional zigzag but as the
retina flinches at it; the buildings of the town
loom in the weird stillness of the thunder-light;
the storm has not yet broken in on the en-
chanted, mute dialogue of the two figures.

Hints of Giorgione's achievements are to be
found in Giovanni Bellini's work – the stillness
and, more pertinently, the feeling for landscape (it is probable that Giorgione worked in
Bellini's studio). But Giorgione united landscape and figures in one mysterious whole as
Bellini never quite did, and he achieved a new
harmony between man and Nature, in which
one appears to reflect the mood of the other. A
similar mystery and harmony of figures with
landscape is achieved in the so-called *"Three
philosophers"*. There is enigma even in
Giorgione's portraiture, in the so-called
"Laura" of 1506, his single firmly dated work,
and in the strangely chaste sensuality of
Giorgione's *Venus*, the "founding mother" of
generations of recumbent nudes.

Giorgione was snatched to his death by
plague in his early 30s, and the *Venus* is one of
several paintings of his that are known to have
been finished by other hands – the *Venus* by
Titian. Giorgione's hold over Titian's imagination seems for a period to have been complete, and the famous *"Concert Champêtre"* in
the Louvre (see p. 16) is now more generally
ascribed to Titian than to Giorgione. In this
and in other works Titian realized again
Giorgione's magical coherence of figures with
landscape, that mysterious sense of music
unheard – the essence of his enchanting vision.

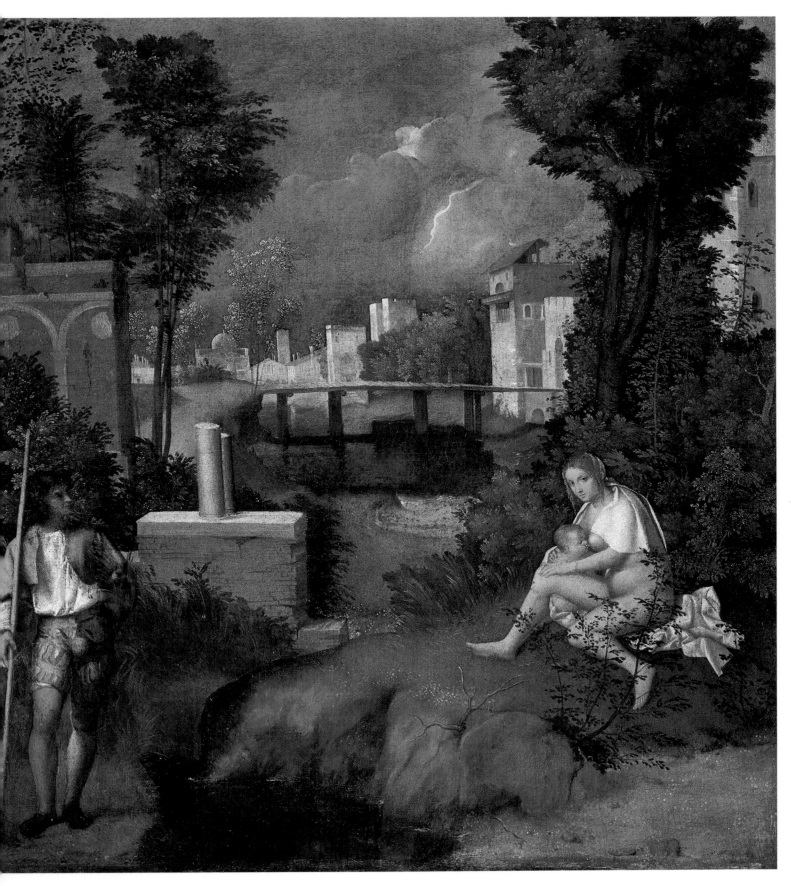

GIORGIONE
The tempest, 1st decade
of the 16th century

TITIAN:
The Rape of Europa

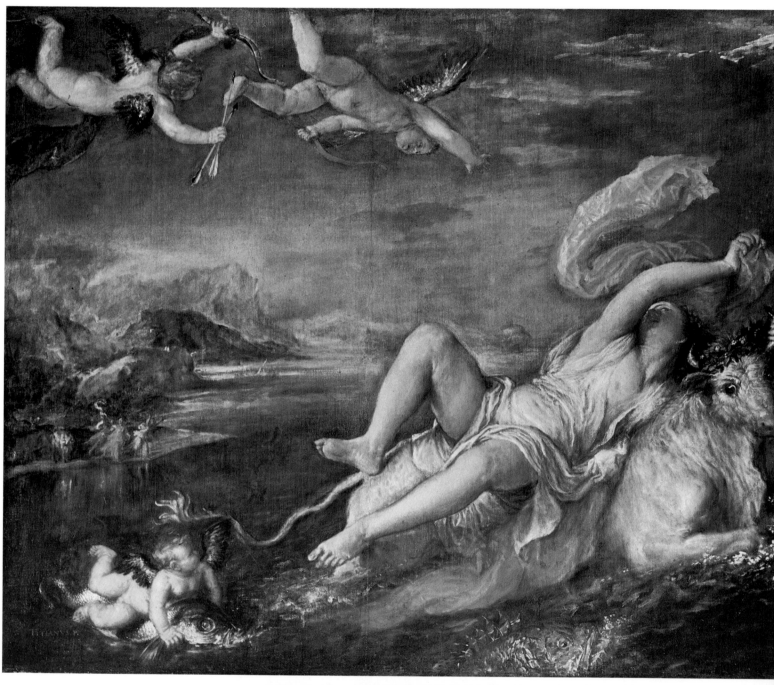

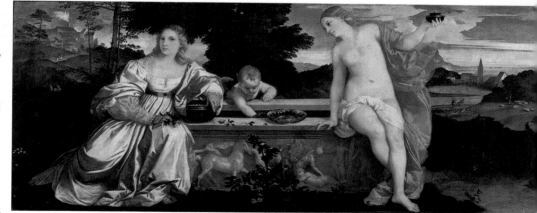

TITIAN (above)
The rape of Europa, 1562
The pagan sensuality of the *poesie* Titian painted for Philip II was surprisingly contrary to the spirit of the Counter-Reformation. It was equally at odds with the religious austerity and melancholia that overtook Philip II at the end of his life. It is clear that Titian's mythologies, especially the *poesie*, in all their inventive vigour and uninhibited but controlled splendour, were fired by personal passion – as other works were not; in contrast his religious works can often seem superb ceremonial formalities.

TITIAN (right)
Sacred and Profane Love,
c. 1514
The "meaning" of the two Venuses has aroused much learned argument. It is now generally accepted that the naked figure is celestial Love, the divine Venus, while the clothed woman is earthly Venus, representing the generative forces of Nature. The sculpture on the sarcophagus, the distinct landscapes and many other quiet details, seem to indicate an elaborate humanist allegory. What no one questions or denies is the supreme beauty, the elegiac mystery of the work.

In his great series of mythological paintings, continuing throughout his career, Titian's dominant and ever-recurrent theme is the female nude. Although they often illustrate subjects from classical literature, especially Ovid, and adapt poses and motifs from classical sculpture, these paintings are sometimes so overtly erotic – though rendered with the greatest subtlety and skill – that they disturbed nineteenth-century critics, and their greatness has been fully acknowledged only recently.

One of Titian's most celebrated early essays in the theme is the *Sacred and Profane Love* of about 1514. Its dreaming landscape still echoes Giorgione's, but its celebration of the female figure is much more overtly sensual. Titian's famous *"Venus of Urbino"* of about 1538 has none of the delicate, vernal chastity of Giorgione's sleeping *Venus* (see p. 164) and in later variations he even introduces a male figure contemplating the naked Venus, in some of them a lute player – creating an additional dimension, joining the idea of music to the voluptuous visual harmony. The direct appeal to the senses, as distinct from the more intellectual approach of the Florentines, seems essential not only to Titian but to Venice.

Early in his career, between 1516 and 1523, Titian had painted a magnificent suite of three mythological subjects for Alfonso d'Este of Ferrara. But his greatest mythologies are the seven paintings painted in his old age for Philip II of Spain, called by Titian *poesie* (poetries). The commission probably came when artist met patron at the court of Philip's father, the Emperor Charles V, at Augsburg in 1550-51. Except for the unfinished *Death of Actaeon*, they had all been shipped to Spain by 1562.

The last to be shipped, *The rape of Europa*, is the most joyously sensual of them all. Jupiter, disguised as a white bull, has enticed the unsuspecting maiden Europa to climb on his back; Titian depicts the moment when Europa realizes that the bull has ceased its playful meander in the shallows of the tide, and is taking off for deep waters where she cannot escape. Her perilous, open-bodied pose, with one hand's grasp on a horn so inadequately securing her to her steed, is one of the most breathtaking in all Renaissance art; its inspiration goes back no doubt to the maenads' abandoned Dionysiac dance in reliefs of classical sarcophagi, but it conveys with remarkable naturalism both the ripeness and the frailty of human flesh. Even this picture has been read as tragic, but it is surely not: the lady is no doubt alarmed, reasonably enough, and her companions, gesturing far behind on the shore, are astonished, but ecstasy is promised by the volley of cupids above and the marine cupid riding the great gold fish. The picture has also been called "hilarious", but it is one of the greatest masterpieces of European painting, the dazzling climax of the optimistic side of Titian's late style. The splendour of its colour is matched by the subtlety of its handling – for example, in the play of tones of white in the woman, her draperies and the bull. The iridescence of sea, distant mountains and sky suggests not solid form, but its dissolution in veils of colour: such an illusion of space and atmosphere remained unparalleled until Watteau. Its virtuosity has never been surpassed.

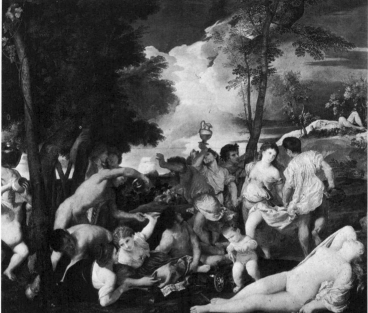

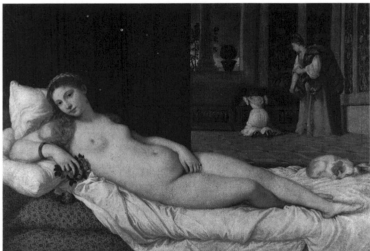

TITIAN (left)
The Andrian Bacchanal, 1518-23
The Andrians, The worship of Venus (both in Madrid) and *Bacchus and Ariadne* (now in London) constitute the three large and complex mythologies Titian painted to hang in Alfonso d'Este's *studiolo* (study). Alfonso chose the subjects from the descriptions of imaginary paintings in the 3rd-century classical writer Philostratus: *The Andrians* has Bacchus and his followers drinking from a stream of wine on the island of Andros. The naked Ariadne on the right comes from a figure closing the angle in just the same way on a classical sarcophagus. The *Andrians* is a splendid rhythmic evocation of a Bacchanalian romp: all its dancing, carousing and swaying and falling revelry are caught in a suspended motion, epitomized in the half-empty jug held tipsily askew against the clouds.

TITIAN (right)
"The Venus of Urbino", c. 1538
Unlike Giorgione's *Venus*, Titian's nude is aware of her own beauty and invites appraisal from admiring eyes. She is, of course, far more than a "pin-up", not only in the harmony and brilliance of the colours but also because there are allusions to marital love and fidelity. The little dog symbolizes faithfulness, and the chest being opened in the background perhaps contains a trousseau. The painting may specifically refer to the marriage of the Duke of Urbino, who bought the painting, and has lent it his name. But its eroticism is unexcused by a mythological setting.

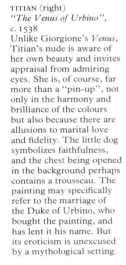

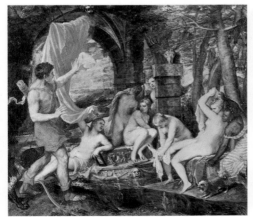

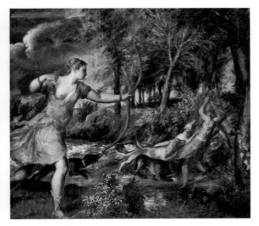

TITIAN
Diana and Actaeon, 1558
The *poesia* is based upon Ovid, who describes the hunter Actaeon surprising Diana and her nymphs bathing: he was punished by being transformed into a stag and killed by his own hounds. Titian's painting is an unabashedly erotic celebration of the female body, though hints of Actaeon's fate are clear – for example the little symbol of fidelity that yaps at his intrusion. Titian's play of white on black flesh, in Diana and her maid, has since held the Western imagination.

TITIAN
The death of Actaeon, after 1562
In most of the *poesie* for Philip II there are tragic overtones, though no other is so sombre as this, the last in the series, which Titian never dispatched. Its vibrant, brusque contours, the almost palpitating forms, offer a striking parallel to the contemporary late work of Michelangelo. The striding Diana avenges her discovery by Actaeon, who, transformed into an animal, in Titian's interpretation sinks into the landscape, and becomes one with it.

HOLBEIN:
The Ambassadors

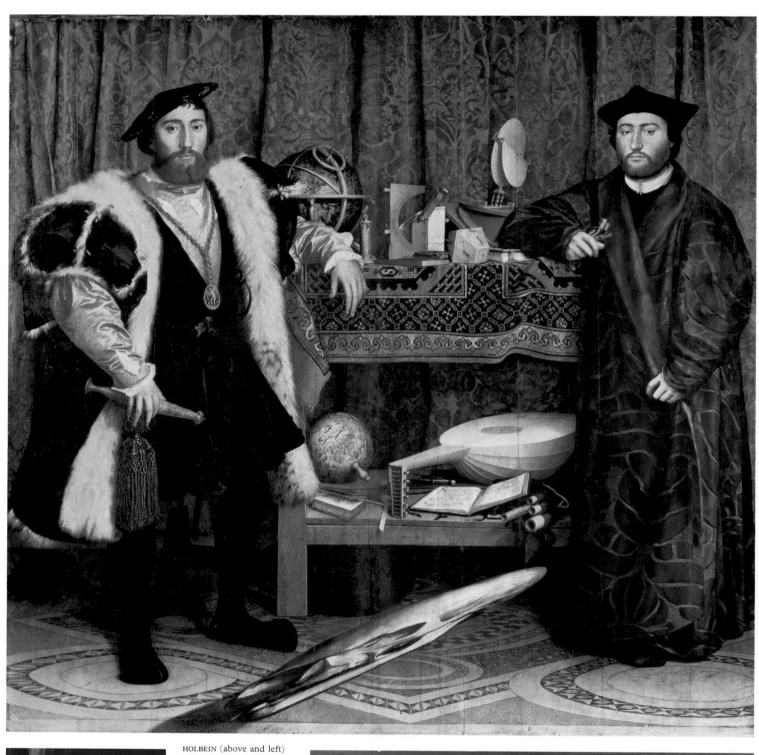

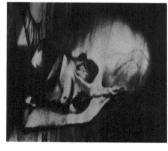

HOLBEIN (above and left)
"The Ambassadors", 1533
This is one of the earliest
portraits to show two men
full-length, life-size. They
are as close to real life
as the artist could make
them – illusionistic in every
particular, the picture is a
replica of an instant. It
was perhaps placed (at the
top of a great stair?) where
it could be seen either from
straight on or obliquely –
the angle at which the skull
takes on its true shape
(detail, left). When it is so
seen, the two men blur, and
eternal death overtakes all.

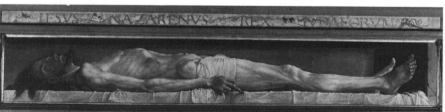

HOLBEIN (above)
The dead Christ, 1521
Though clearly influenced
by Grünewald's *Christ*
in the predella panel of the
great Isenheim altarpiece,

Holbein here depicts the
body of Christ rigid in
death with an exactitude
that deprives the image of
all spiritual comfort: the
tomb imprisons the body

in its *rigor mortis*. Before
this painting, Dostoevsky
cried: "This picture could
rob a man of his faith". It
perhaps belonged to a lost
altar with *The Deposition*.

The men represented are French, Jean de Dinteville and Georges de Selve, Bishop of Lavaur, but Hans Holbein the Younger (1497/8-1543) painted their portrait in 1533 in London, where Dinteville was on a diplomatic mission to Henry VIII of England. Shown life-size, full-length, the two are depicted with exact realism down to the details of their very opulent costumes. The green damask curtain behind and the inlaid marble floor (based on one in Westminster Abbey) are equally scrupulously portrayed, while in the centre, on a two-tiered table, is displayed an elaborate still life – on top, instruments of science and astronomy; below, more earthly interests – a terrestrial globe, an arithmetical textbook, a lute, but also an open hymnal (the text is Luther's revised version). The composition seems to be a Reformed version of the traditional *sacra conversazione*, in which the still life, rather than the Madonna, is the focus of the two figures' intellectual and spiritual commitment. At the same time, in their paired placement, and impassive stillness, the figures are like "supporters" in a massive coat of arms.

Closer inspection, however, reveals an underlying disquiet: the minute badge in Dinteville's cap is a skull; a small crucifix is almost hidden away at the top left; a string of the lute is broken. Most strikingly, but also most enigmatically, the yellowish smear tilted across the foreground reveals itself when seen at an acute angle from the left below (or from the right above) as a skull, distorted by a mathematically exact trick of perspective. And the central still life is also a vanity, a *memento mori*. Dinteville's age is given, on his dagger, as 29; Selve's, on his book, as 25; dials indicate the time to be 10.30 am, the date April 11th; the two men are in the prime of life and health, of material and intellectual accomplishment. But the reality of the stated moment, the instantaneity, is undermined by the omens of mortality, above all by the added dimension of the distorted skull, which the sitters cannot see, and all their science cannot understand. This ambiguous picture, realized with scientific precision and consummate art, combining monumental realism with complex symbolism, is one of the most ambitious and successful achievements of Renaissance art.

Holbein's own name is, literally, a synonym for a skull, and his obsession with human mortality lasted throughout his career, from even earlier than his woodcut designs for a *Dance of Death* (not shown) about 1525. He was born in Augsburg and trained by his father Hans the Elder; he was fully established in Basel by 1520, and there came to know, through the printer Frobenius, a remarkable humanist circle including Erasmus. His early work reflects many influences and was in many media – portraits, designs for engravings, altarpieces, large-scale mural decorations – but common to all was his astonishing technical virtuosity. His *Dead Christ*, in its starkness, may be influenced by Grünewald's expressionism, but its detached, exact observation has a very different effect. A probable visit (or visits) to northern Italy was more fundamental; some paintings seem to acknowledge Leonardo's example very closely, but in his *Madonna and Child with the Meyer family* he

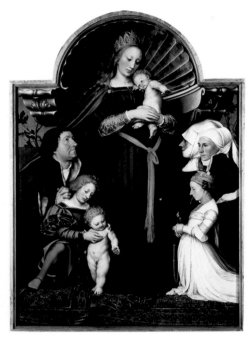

HOLBEIN (above)
The Virgin and Child with the Meyer family, c. 1528
Between 1528 and the death of Meyer in 1531, a portrait of the patron's second wife was added. The Virgin with her lively Child perhaps reflects local sculpture.

HOLBEIN (below)
Sir Thomas More, 1527
Holbein developed to a perfect realism the type of humanist portrait Massys had pioneered in Antwerp. The expressive, sensitively modelled hands are typical of Holbein's minute skill.

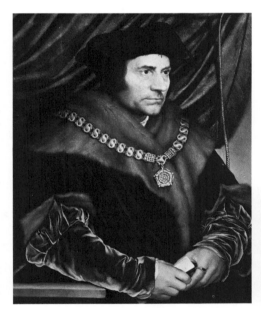

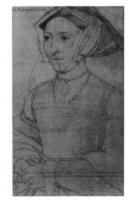

HOLBEIN (left)
Jane Seymour, preliminary drawing, *c. 1535*
Apart from a few details of dress, the finished portrait closely copies the drawing, indicating that, for Holbein, the basis of art lay above all in precision of outline.

HOLBEIN (right)
Henry VIII, 1542
In an image originated by Holbein, and repeated endlessly by copyists, the figure of the King already shows signs of an advanced obesity, skilfully hidden under a bell-shaped surcoat.

fused the principles of both Leonardo and Raphael with northern literalness into a magisterially monumental image. No one, not even Dürer, had achieved such a synthesis.

After an initial visit to London (1526-28) he finally settled there in 1532, and from about 1536 until his premature death from the plague in 1543 he was court painter to Henry VIII. His personality and his personal convictions remain elusive, but he was clearly sympathetic to the Reformation, even though the shrinking of religious patronage in the Reformed climate of Basel was certainly a strong reason for his move to England. On his first visit, he became attached to the circle of Sir Thomas More, Erasmus' humanist friend: his portrait of More is one of the most gravely humane portraits of the whole Renaissance, and his group of More's family – now lost, but known from a preliminary drawing (not shown) sent to Erasmus – was one of the first "conversation pieces". Like "*The Ambassadors*", it turns a traditional religious format to secular ends.

Soon after his arrival in London for the second time, Holbein painted some superb portraits of members of the German Steelyard, a merchant community. His painted portraits depended on studies from the life made with the aid of some form of perspective aid, such as a *camera obscura*, but the resultant drawings, of which a series has miraculously survived, show no trace of mechanical dependence; they include some of the most delicate but sure reflections of the human face ever made, captured within a contour line quick with life. Holbein established a tradition and standard of quality in miniature to which English practitioners constantly referred, especially the greatest Elizabethan miniaturist, Nicholas Hilliard. From his meticulous drawings Holbein could project the images without any loss of quality to any scale – he is most famous for his awesome straddling life-size image of the King. In his state portraiture the static, linear quality became more marked, and he achieved images of cool, aloof splendour that were perhaps matched but not surpassed by Bronzino.

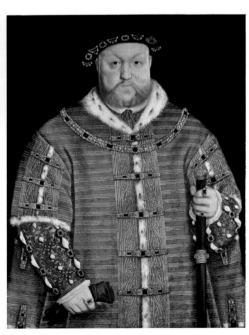

BRUEGEL:
August, or the Corn Harvest

Pieter Bruegel (*c.* 1525-69) worked in Antwerp and then in Brussels, but early in his career travelled extensively in France and Italy, between about 1551 and 1553. Unlike almost all his northern contemporaries, he took from Italian art virtually none of the surface trimmings, though he surely developed in Italy his sense of space, his organization of majestic compositions in depth and the density of his human figures – though very different in effect, his broadly conceived peasant figures have a physical gravity like those of Giotto. From his journey through the Alps, however, he drew one enduring inspiration – mountains: views from the heights are recurrent in his work.

The most important early influence on Bruegel in Flanders was clearly the work of Bosch. This is apparent not only in the many designs that he made for engravings, but also even in quite late paintings. Many of his pictures illustrate proverbs and parables, most of them depicting humans as creatures of appetite subservient to the whims of nature or to their own folly. Bruegel's religious subjects are usually set in a contemporary context, almost submerged in the ebb· and flow of everyday life about them; so in *The procession to Calvary* the spectator has to search amongst the teeming throng across the panoramic landscape, to discern Christ. Nor are his religious characters idealized: indeed, in the London *Adoration of the Magi*, not only Joseph but the three kings are portrayed much like the shepherds and attendant soldiers – in fairly brutish terms. Bruegel's grimmest works, such as *The triumph of Death* (not shown) with its serried legions of skeletons, date from around 1562, during the Spanish persecution of a large Protestant minority in Antwerp. Bruegel removed that same year to Brussels, but his own

BRUEGEL (right)
August (*The corn harvest*), 1565
This is probably the first picture in the history of art to transcribe the heat of high summer into paint. A group of peasants take a midday break in the shade of a tree, eating, drinking – one is sprawled in sleep. Others are still at work, scything, stacking the corn, carrying sheaves. Through trees on the brow of the slope is glimpsed the village church; in the valley below, close to a farm, other small figures are at work in the fields. Beyond, the landscape melts shimmering away for miles; land and the watery expanse of the estuary merge in haze into the opaque sky. The working figures move with a torpid sluggishness. A man arriving from a path through the dense, shoulder-high corn, bearing liquid refreshment – the sweat that trickles down his chest is not visible but it seems to be there. The extraordinary colours, the dominating hot yellow and green, reverberate through the picture.

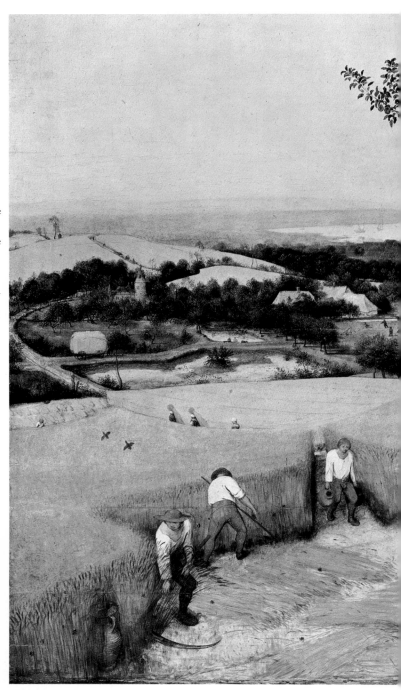

BRUEGEL (below)
January (*The hunters in the snow*), 1565
If *August* is heat itself, then *January*, in its whites, greys and blacks, is the very rigour of iron winter.

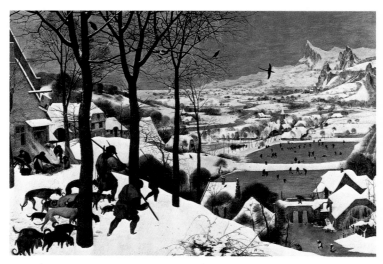

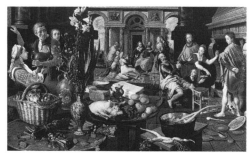

AERTSEN (left)
Christ in the house of Martha and Mary, 1559
Interposing huge piles of food and flowers between the observer and the central scene, Aertsen anticipated pure still life, seen for itself.

BRUEGEL (right)
The peasant wedding, *c.* 1567
Drawings of peasants from the life underlie the incisive characterization and detail.

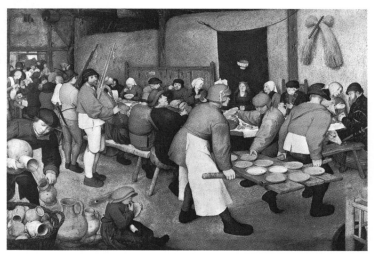

political or religious convictions are not clear; in Brussels the Spanish President of the Council of State, Cardinal Granvella, was an important patron. Despite his nickname, "Peasant Bruegel", Bruegel was a man of culture and discrimination, and a close friend of the great geographer Ortelius.

Quintessential in Bruegel's work is his "close-up" masterpiece of peasant life, *The peasant wedding*. Here composition, wit, and acute observation are superbly fused. Echoes of religious themes may linger – the Feast at Cana, even the Last Supper – but Bruegel's work is entirely of this world. His supreme achievement is *The Months of the Year*, a series painted in 1565 for the villa in Brussels of his patron Niclaes Jonghelinck; there are five survivors, astonishing in their range of mood, of which the most famous are *August* (*The corn harvest*) and *January* (*The hunters in the snow*). Their predecessors are the brilliant miniatures of the changing months by the Limbourgs, in which any religious significance was already peripheral, though the theme of annual rebirth and change always had astrological relevance and allegorical undertones of good and evil, light and dark, life and death. Bruegel's peasants, however, squat, tenacious and unlovely, work the world for survival. Food, its getting and its consuming, is one of Bruegel's preoccupations; no one has surpassed the sensitivity and skill with which he evokes the beauty of the earth that provides. His true subject is Nature herself, with man an integral part of her growth, decay and rebirth.

Bruegel's compositions were repeated by his son Pieter II, but the only painter to deal with similar subjects with originality and more than average competence was Pieter Aertsen (1508-75), working in Antwerp and Amsterdam.

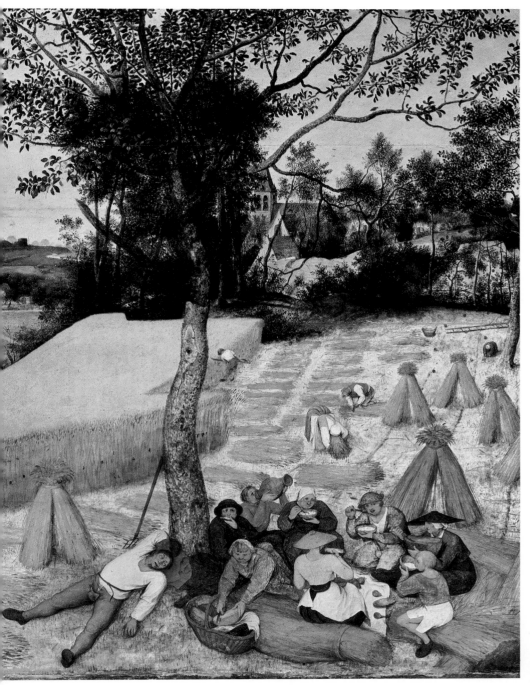

BRUEGEL (right)
The procession to Calvary, 1564
The crowded panorama is full of telling episodes condemning human folly – the moralism of Bruegel's engravings transferred to a religious setting. As an example of hypocrisy, his wife attempts to detain Simon of Cyrene, called to assist the fallen Christ, although a crucifix hangs at her belt. There are also topical references, and the Roman soldiers wear the uniform of the "Habits Rouges" who kept order in Flanders for the Spanish. *The triumph of Death* is in composition quite similar, teeming with corpses hung in attitudes of agony.

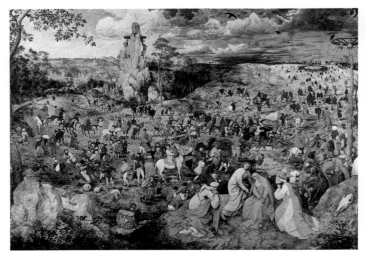

BRUEGEL (below)
The Adoration of the Magi, 1564
There are perhaps traces of Schongauer and of Italian influence in the grouping of figures, but the grimacing onlookers themselves are a clear reference back to those of Hieronymus Bosch. The view of humanity is not kind; nor is it didactically moralistic; Bruegel's realism can be monumental, serene.

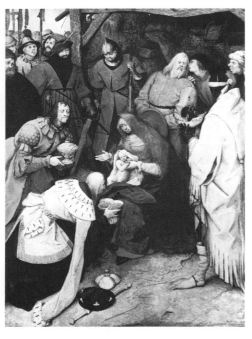

TINTORETTO:
The Scuola di San Rocco Crucifixion

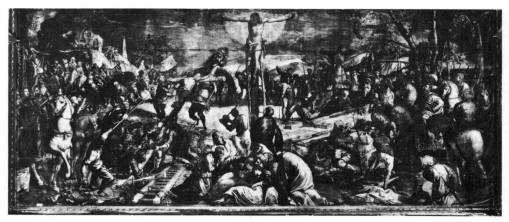

Between 1564 and 1587 Tintoretto virtually took over the building in which the Scuola, or Confraternity, of San Rocco was housed, and decorated its two storeys, both the walls and the ceilings, not with frescos but with canvases, many of them large, some huge – *The Crucifixion*, the largest of them all, is some 12.25 metres (40ft) across.

The Venetian Scuole were charitable organizations, rather like clubs or unions, each linked with a particular saint, and each with a strong *esprit de corps* motivating artistic patronage, often on a large scale. The Scuola di San Rocco, of comparatively recent foundation, in 1564 invited a number of painters, including Veronese and Tintoretto, to submit sketches in competition for the decoration of the smaller hall in its upper storey, the Council Chamber. Tintoretto assured himself of the commission by a trick: instead of a small sketch, he installed a full-scale painting surreptitiously *in situ*, which he then revealed to the astonished committee. He clinched the commission by suggesting that he present the painting to the Confraternity free – an offer which could not be refused, apparently, according to the Scuola's constitution.

The first phase involved the decoration of the Council Chamber only, but included *The Crucifixion*, 1565, and *The road to Calvary*, 1566. The second phase (1575-81) decorated the larger, main hall on the same floor – 13 Old Testament scenes on the ceiling in concordance with New Testament ones on the walls. The final phase, 1583-87, in the Lower Hall, was devoted to scenes from the life of the Virgin. The canvases, virtually encrusting the walls and the heavily coffered ceilings, do not make up a formally coherent whole, though they are disposed symmetrically, but through them all pulses the uniting rhythm of Tintoretto's formidable, rushing style.

The huge panorama of the *Crucifixion* occupies the whole wall facing the door of the Council Chamber. The impact is overwhelming, as it is impossible to get back far enough to take in the whole composition at once. The stark austerity of its central focus – Christ suspended over the huddle of his shattered followers beneath him – contrasts with the radiance ebbing from the Cross itself out to the edges of the composition. There ordinary folk, some interested, some not, set a context of both immediacy and enduring relevance, an effect that the wide screen of the cinema has yet to surpass. In the larger halls, Tintoretto created a wholly new range of imagery to rekindle the traditional stories, but his strange lighting – or lightning – is the essential agent that lifts them into the highest realism of visionary art. It is sometimes complemented by an unreal, hallucinating space and a disdain of mere physical possibility, so far from Renaissance principles as to seem almost medieval in some elements. Yet Tintoretto's vision is not necessarily so stupendous: *The Flight into Egypt*, ghostly in the weird moonlight, is set in a lyrical, rural landscape, and the handling of the Holy Family shows a tenderness quite rare in Tintoretto. In *The temptation of Christ*, in contrast, the luscious image of seduction embodied in Satan has been compared in its imaginative power with Milton's Satan in *Paradise Lost*.

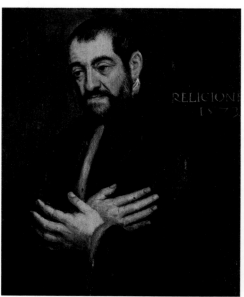

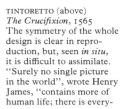

TINTORETTO (above)
Self-portrait, 1573
The humility of this *ex voto*, which hung to the right of the entrance to the Council Chamber in which *The Crucifixion* hangs, does not seem quite to dispel Tintoretto's reputation with his fellow-artists as a ruthless undercutter.

TINTORETTO (above)
The Crucifixion, 1565
The symmetry of the whole design is clear in reproduction, but, seen *in situ*, it is difficult to assimilate. "Surely no single picture in the world", wrote Henry James, "contains more of human life; there is every-

thing in it, including the most exquisite beauty." Perhaps only Rembrandt equalled the cosmic power of this Christ (detail right), swaying forwards towards the onlooker vertiginously, both victim and redeemer: "And I, if I be lifted up, will draw all men unto me."

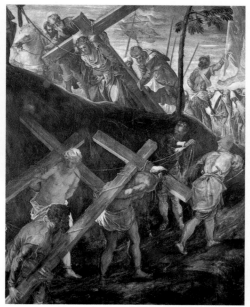

TINTORETTO (right)
The road to Calvary, 1566
The terrible lurching of the crosses and arduous ascent of the figures has the effect of forcing the spectator into the picture space, a characteristic of all Tintoretto's work. The *Calvary* is placed directly opposite *The Crucifixion*.

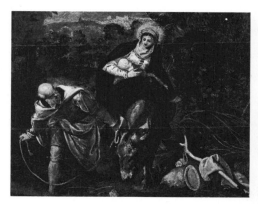

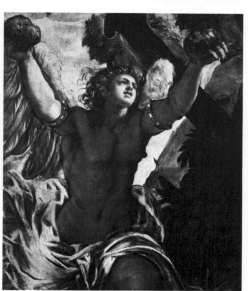

TINTORETTO (above)
The Flight into Egypt, detail, 1583-87
The Holy Family is placed before a wide landscape, sombre, but romantically echoing the tenderness of Mother and Child.

TINTORETTO (right)
The temptation of Christ, detail, 1579-81
Satan, whose demonic nature is hinted at only by the fire's reflection which reddens his cheeks, extends himself alluringly.

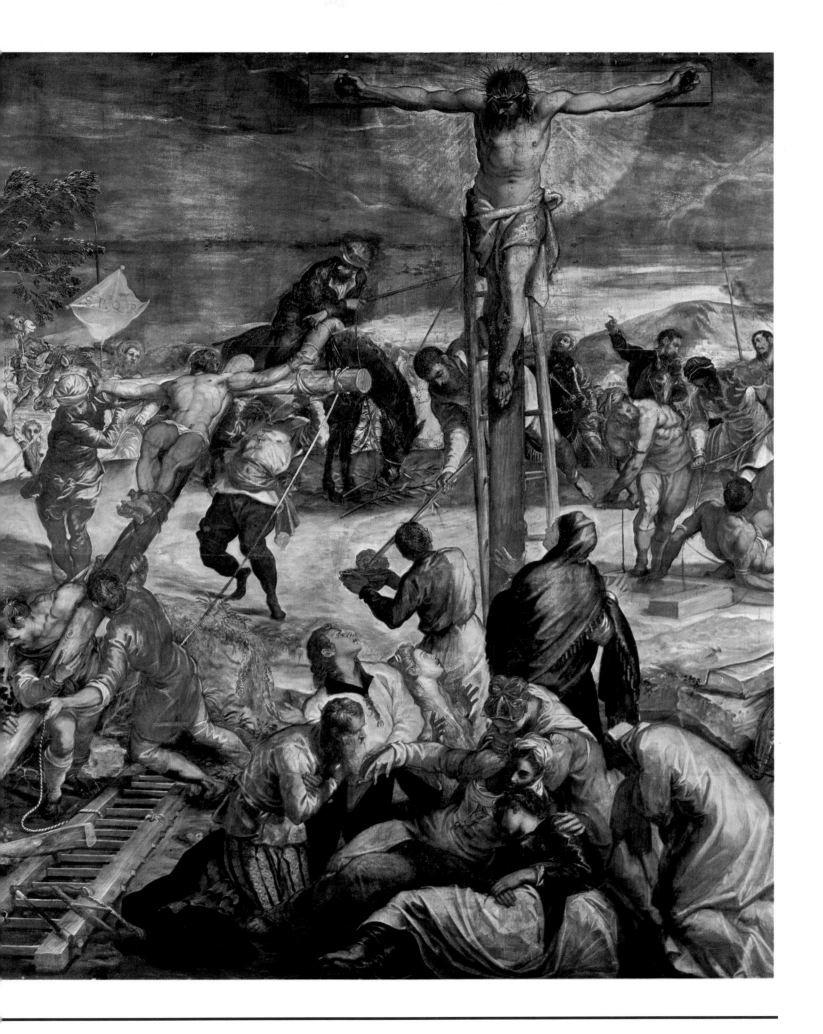

CARAVAGGIO:
The Conversion of St Paul

In July 1600 the papal treasurer Tiberio Cerasi acquired, for his resting place, a chapel in S. Maria del Popolo, Rome, and shortly afterwards commissioned the two outstanding (but very different) painters in Rome to decorate it: Annibale Carracci to paint the altarpiece and Michelangelo da Caravaggio to provide two paintings for the side-walls.

Caravaggio's subjects were the conversion of St Paul and the crucifixion of St Peter. His first versions were not satisfactory – whether to the client or to himself is not known; the second versions were paid for in November 1601. The Carracci altarpiece, *The Assumption of the Virgin*, had probably been finished before then, likewise the ceiling decoration, painted to Annibale's design by an assistant. The St Paul subject was already fairly popular, the St Peter one less so, but they are the two subjects of Michelangelo's last paintings, in the Cappella Paolina in the Vatican, which must have been in Caravaggio's mind, though his solutions are very different.

The large difference reflects not only Caravaggio's profoundly personal view of the world but also the shifting attitude, within the Catholic Church, to the function of religious painting and consequently its style. Faced with the division of Europe between primarily Protestant north and primarily Catholic south, the Catholic Church had reasserted its doctrines and against the Reformation proclaimed the Counter-Reformation: the rigour of the Inquisition was only one aspect of a movement of self-examination, of confirmation of faith and of positive propaganda. This new and active fervour was fuelled by direct and personal appeal to the faithful through the arts; Caravaggio strengthened the meaning of St Peter's martyrdom and St Paul's conversion by telling their stories in contemporary idiom and down-to-earth detail – even if the staider clergy felt he pushed realism too far.

The conversion of St Paul could represent a man tripped over backwards in a stable, but even before the viewer recognizes the subject he is aware of the electric potency of a supernatural event in this mundane image. Like Michelangelo, Caravaggio has chosen the moment when Saul was flung to the ground blinded, as if by lightning, and accused by God: "Saul, Saul, why persecutest thou me?" But there is in the Caravaggio none of the supporting cast of airborne Christ and angels present in the Michelangelo. The bucketing steed has become a rather heavy hack, and the agitated crowd is replaced by one solitary baffled groom, an old peasant with a varicose vein; these two have heard nothing. The source of light is not shown; but the violent, even awkward foreshortening of the figure hurled down expresses an impact of huge energy, and the outflung arms embroil the whole in the vortex of a blinding miracle.

For contemporaries, this must have been a stunning vision. Formally, Caravaggio has exploited already known methods – even more dramatic foreshortening occurs for example in Mantegna and Tintoretto. But the overall assault on the beholder's emotions in such concentration was unparalleled. The courtly elegance of the still prevailing Mannerist style seems both esoteric and effete in contrast.

CARAVAGGIO (below)
The crucifixion of St Peter, 1600-01
No earlier painter had made the focus of this subject so emphatically the action and effort of raising the cross. St Peter appears the more helpless – an ordinary, perplexed, suffering old man, though still robust and dignified. The composition seems more effective from an oblique viewpoint, from outside the chapel.

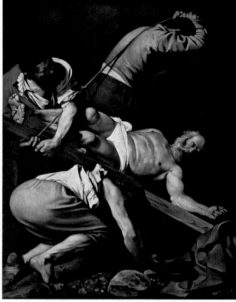

ANNIBALE CARRACCI (above) *The Assumption of the Virgin*, 1600-01
The Carracci altarpiece is flanked by the two Caravaggios; the artists worked in their studios probably without close knowledge of each other's designs. Neither was likely to compromise for the sake of the other, anyway, even though in many respects *in situ* their pictures clash. Annibale's forms are pale-coloured in a serene, diffuse light, against Caravaggio's luminous browns and blacks. Yet in both the figures are life-size, solidly modelled, and crowded against the frame.

MICHELANGELO (right)
The conversion of St Paul, detail, 1546-50
Here drama is conveyed by the seething energy of crowds in movement and a rearing horse, whereas Caravaggio concentrated on Saul's own sensation.

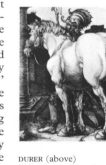

DURER (above)
"*The Large Horse*", 1505
Engravings by northern artists were an inspiration for Caravaggio's own vision of common-life realism. Dürer's stolid animal was perhaps the prototype of the nag in the *Conversion*.

MANTEGNA (right)
The dead Christ, c. 1490
Mantegna's picture is an early precedent for the use in the *Conversion* of extreme foreshortening for emotional effect.

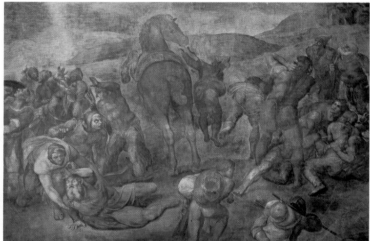

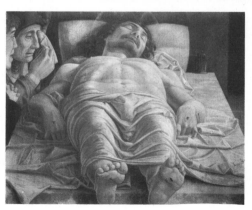

CARAVAGGIO (right)
The conversion of St Paul, 1600-01
The picture is a masterpiece of simple, forcefully stark, concentrated drama. The unbalanced composition, in which the massive, unmoved figure of the horse fills almost the entire canvas, makes all the more emphatic the prostrate Saul's shock. He falls back thunderstruck almost out of the picture frame, involving the viewer as a witness.

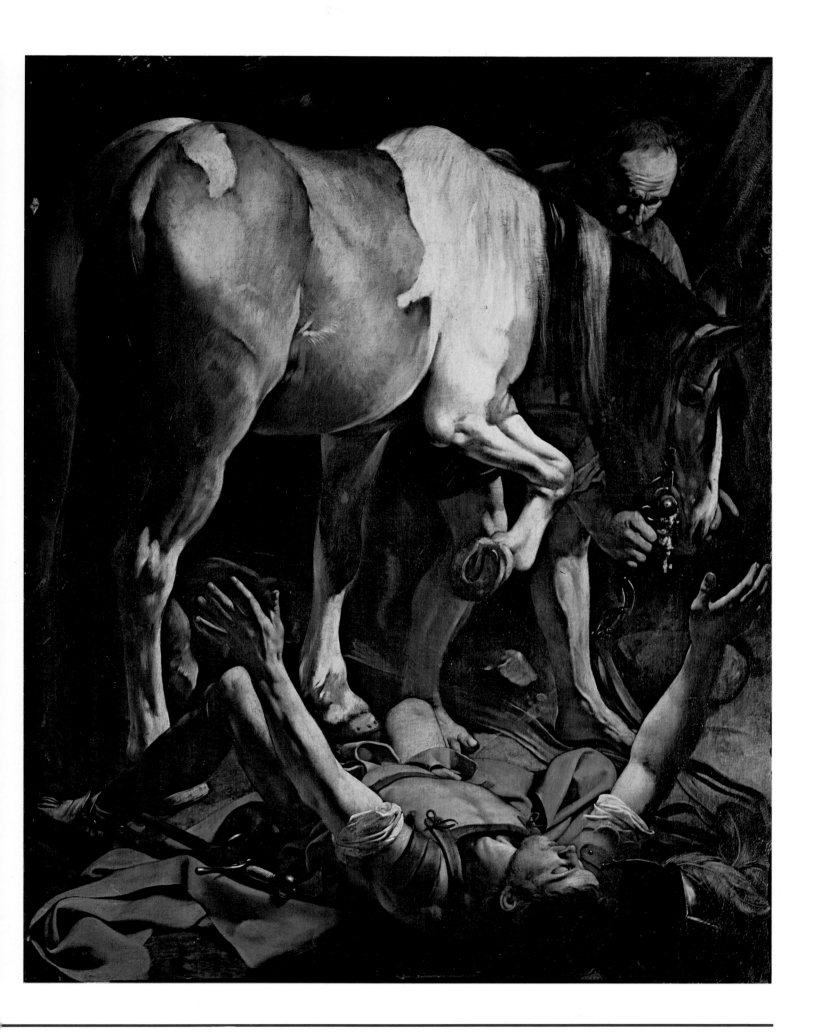

ANNIBALE CARRACCI:
The Farnese Gallery

The Gallery of the Palazzo Farnese is the last of the three great classic decorations in Rome, following Raphael's Stanze in the Vatican and Michelangelo's ceiling in the Sistine Chapel. The Palazzo is a building of much grandeur, the creation of a succession of famous architects, including Michelangelo and Giacomo della Porta, who built the Gallery, with its three tall windows overlooking the garden to the Tiber beyond, in 1573. The palace was the Rome headquarters of the great patrician dynasty of the Farnese, used by various members of the family, including the very young Cardinal Odoardo Farnese, who summoned Annibale Carracci from Bologna in 1595.

Annibale's first decorations were in Odoardo's study, the Camerino (1595-96, not shown). Painting began in the Gallery about 1597, and the frescos of the vault were finished in 1600. Annibale's brother Agostino played some part in these, but the overall design and the bulk of the work were Annibale's. The Gallery has noble dimensions – 20 metres (66 ft) long by 6.5 metres (21 ft) wide, its coved and vaulted ceiling ten metres (32 ft) high. Its function, which conditioned Annibale's design, was both for receptions and for the display of classical statuary in the Farnese collection (now in Naples).

The programme – subject matter and storyline – of the decoration was probably provided by Odoardo's learned librarian, Fulvio Orsini, in consultation with the painter. The preliminary workings were exhaustive, involving more than one thousand drawings. The theme – odd for a cardinal, however youthful, but natural enough for lay members of the family – is pagan, profane and erotic: scenes taken from classical mythology to illustrate the power of love, the exalted but very physical love of the gods – even if some discern a deeper Christian message of Divine Love pervading the whole. The scenes are not linked in any continuous narrative progression, but echo and respond to one another in form and composition.

The idea of opening up an enclosed space by means of illusionist painting was already well developed, and Annibale had several examples before him in Bologna. But he chose the system

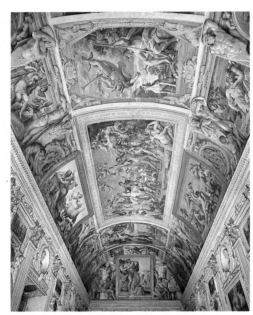

ANNIBALE CARRACCI (above) The Farnese Gallery: *The loves of the gods*, 1597-1600 Everything above the cornice is painted, even the frames of the pictures. At the end *Polyphemus* hurls a rock at Acis, whom he had caught in the arms of his love Galatea. Other panels illustrate similar stories, culled from Ovid.

(below) *View of the inner wall of the Farnese Gallery* The figures of the ceiling were a foil to the classical sculpture originally set in niches below, as Giovanni Volpato's engraving shows. Over the central door is Domenichino's *Virgin and unicorn*, painted, like the other wall panels, a little after the vault (*c.* 1604-08).

used by Raphael and Michelangelo, which was to build (or rather paint) a framework containing either paintings or illusory visions of the open sky above. However, the way in which illusionistic features are conjoined with real ones in the Gallery is much more complex than in earlier examples, and seen from a point central in the room, with one's back to the windows, the illusion of a picture gallery continuing above the cornice and carrying right across the vault is vivid – though the effect cannot be captured in photographs.

The colour is strong and lucent; the bodies of the participants are modelled densely, with a sculptural clarity, to answer the real antique marbles that once stood below. Their forms echo and restate precedents from the great masters of the Renaissance – the theme of the naked youths is obviously inspired by Michelangelo's Sistine *Ignudi* – and from classical antiquity. But their vitality springs from the fact that each is also studied from the life, and the central "framed painting", *The triumph of Bacchus and Ariadne*, which owes much to the study of reliefs on Roman sarcophagi, has a richness and fluency not to be found either in antiquity or in the High Renaissance. In the rhythm of this procession, at once measured and exuberant, both the classicism of Poussin and the surge of Rubens are heralded, and, although Annibale's compartmental solution for ceiling painting was not often followed, his mastery and delight in illusionism speak already of the High Baroque.

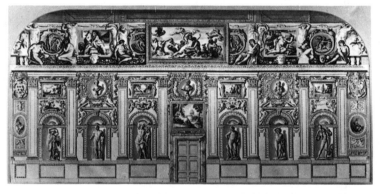

RAPHAEL (below) The ceiling of the Villa Farnesina *loggia*, detail: *The marriage of Cupid and Psyche*, 1518 Raphael's *loggie* in the Vatican and his ceiling in the Farnesina (across the Tiber from the Farnese Palace, and visible from its windows) were important precedents for Annibale, in both their style and their compartmental scheme. Raphael's vision of pagan deity, executed perhaps wholly by his assistants, clearly inspired Annibale.

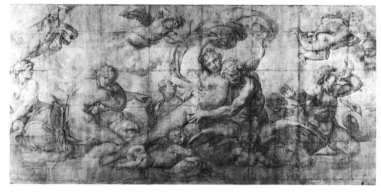

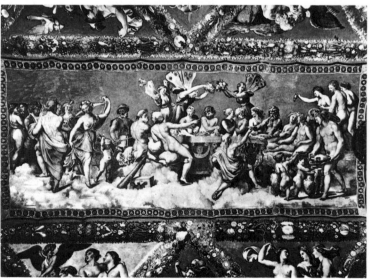

AGOSTINO CARRACCI Cartoon for *Glaucus and Scylla* on the inner wall of the Farnese Gallery, *c.* 1597-99 Though Annibale no doubt sketched the preliminary design, the scale cartoon is the work of his brother and assistant Agostino. Conception and pose are magnificently robust, and the triton blowing a conch in the (modified) painting probably inspired Bernini, who must have visited the Gallery; he used the motif in his *Neptune*.

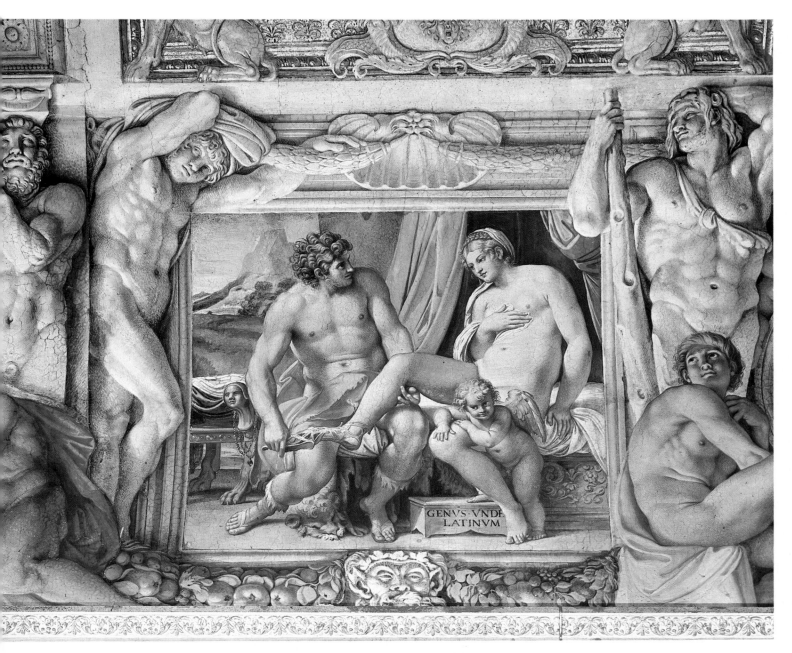

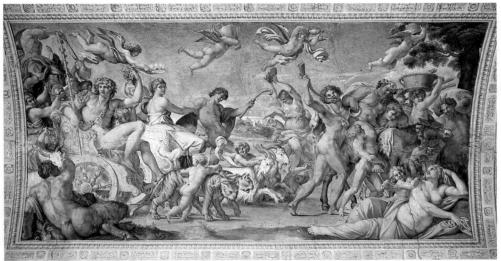

ANNIBALE CARRACCI (above)
The Farnese Gallery,
detail: *Venus and Anchises*,
1597-1600
From the union of Venus
and Anchises was born the
founder of Rome, Aeneas,
as the inscription on the
footstool, a quotation from
Virgil's *Aeneid*, indicates.
Surrounding the pair are
illusionistic stone "Atlas

figures" and busts called
"terms" – both classical
architectural ornaments.
In front of them, in vivid
contrast, are illusionistic
fleshy figures, based on the
Ignudi of Michelangelo's
Sistine ceiling. Further
details reproduce yet other
textures, and the illusion
of planes lapping and overlapping is very successful.

ANNIBALE CARRACCI (left)
*The triumph of Bacchus
and Ariadne*, 1597-1600
The *Triumph* is the centrepiece of the ceiling and
of the whole Gallery. The
idealized forms are derived
from Raphael, though their
heaviness and musculature

echo Michelangelo; the
reclining goddess filling
out the right-hand bottom
corner comes from Titian's
Andrians (see p. 167). This
classicist formula still has
energy, a disciplined richness and – despite lengthy
preparation – real warmth.

POUSSIN:
The Holy Family on the Steps

The classical strain in French art found its greatest exponent in Nicolas Poussin (1593/4-1665) – though Poussin's working life was spent almost entirely in Italy. For subsequent generations, not only in France, he gave classicism a definitive form – one that was at the same time so vital and rich in possibilities that Cézanne, prophet of the revolution in painting more than two hundred years later, sought "to do Poussin again, from nature", envying his perfect clarity of form and structure. Poussin sought the ideal synthesis of form and subject matter, of landscape with figures, of light with colour and mood, and in the noblest works of his maturity, between 1630 and 1660, achieved

it. In them he refined his early sensuousness, freely inspired by Giovanni Bellini, Giorgione and Titian, with a high seriousness, sobriety and linear perfection in the tradition especially of Raphael, from whom Poussin inherited the formal preoccupations of *The Holy Family on the steps* (1648) in particular.

Poussin's *Self-portrait* is sumptuous but severe, set against an almost abstract composition of rectangular picture frames. It is the portrait of a man who expressed visually a Stoic philosophy of self-control and self-sufficiency, perhaps more deeply than he transmitted the Christian faith or ethic. In seventeenth-century Rome, where he lived

from 1624, he found a learned and sensitive society that nourished the artistic expression of this temperament. A brief spell (1640-42) in Paris was unhappy; he worked habitually alone, painting what he wanted to paint, and he was ill at ease with the large-scale mural decoration and workshop management required of him at the French court.

Even in Rome, Poussin's cool severity, achieved by the rigorous elimination of all inessential detail, was in striking contrast to the emphatic art of his great Baroque contemporary, Bernini. The difference between Poussin and the swirling rhythms of the art being produced all around him seems extra-

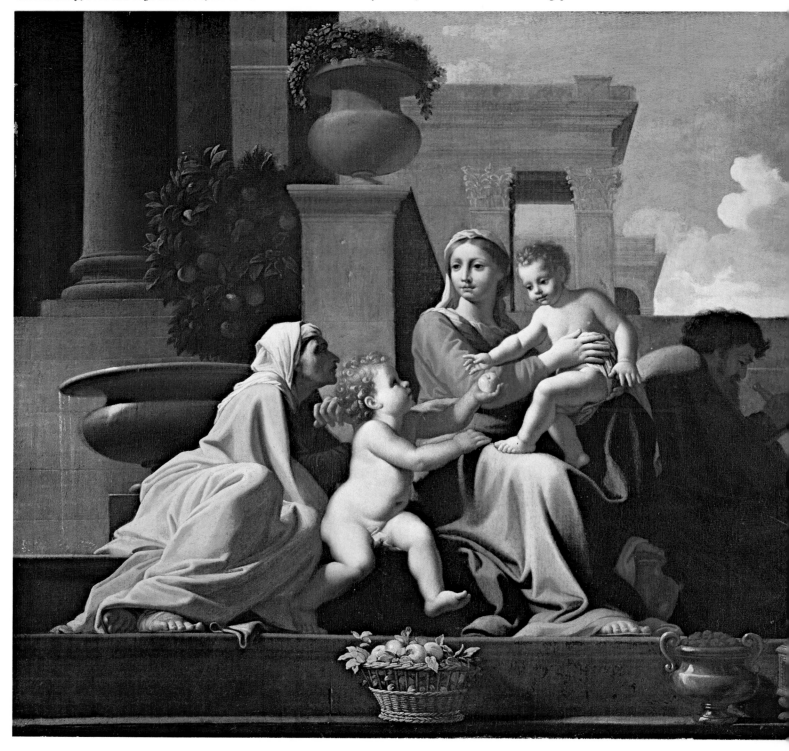

ordinary. Yet it was a logical enough development of that ordering of the picture space already achieved in the work of the Carracci and Domenichino. Although the theme of the *Holy Family* is entirely Christian, it has little in common with the propagandist emotionalism of the Counter-Reformation Baroque. Like Poussin's idealised landscapes the *Holy Family* reads not as a mystical vision but as a superb effort of will, eye and intellect to extract an enduring order from the transitory world of life. Bernini realized Poussin's achievement when he tapped his forehead when looking at one of his paintings and said: "Signor Poussin is a painter who works up here."

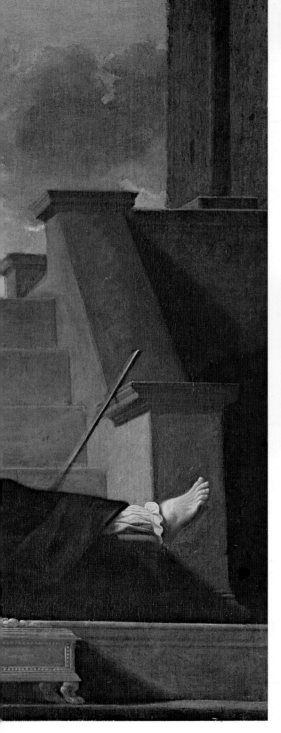

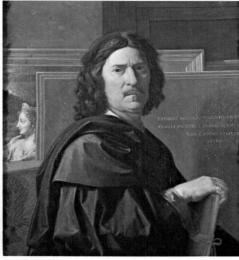

POUSSIN (above)
Self-portrait, 1649-50
Poussin painted only two, very similar, portraits, both of himself, as favours to friends. In recording his likeness he stated his principles, those of an austere and profoundly cultivated man, versed in the classics and in the Stoicism of Horace and Cicero. The female bust signifies Painting, her diadem Perspective.

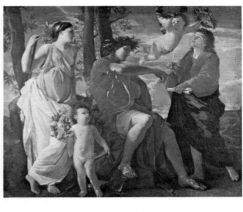

POUSSIN (above)
The poet's inspiration,
c. 1628-29
This early work shows the young Poussin's sensuous
delight in Venetian colour and atmosphere. The poet, watched by the Muse of Epic, presents his work to the seated Apollo.

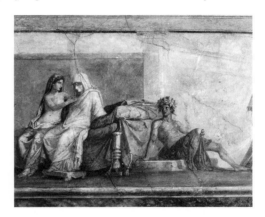

ROME, ESQUILINE (right)
"*The Aldobrandini Marriage*", detail,
1st century BC
Found in a house on the Esquiline Hill, this is one of the few Roman frescos of the highest quality that survive. It inspired Poussin's general composition, and St Joseph's pose with outstretched foot seems a conscious reference to the reclining youth here. In Rome Poussin drew and studied classical remains avidly, so as to found his art on antique principles.

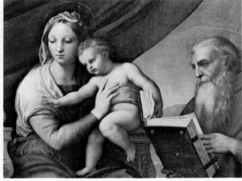

RAPHAEL (left)
"*The Madonna of the Fish*", detail, *c.*1513
Raphael's altarpiece was almost a proto-Baroque composition, not least in the use of a sweeping diagonal backdrop. It comes late in a series of Madonna compositions by Raphael, Leonardo and Michelangelo, to which Poussin's *Holy Family* is a deliberate coda. The pose of his Mother and Child is based on Raphael's; his Madonna's face has the same abstract purity.

POUSSIN (below)
Preparatory drawing for *The Holy Family*, 1648
The figure group has been resolved almost in its final form, but the two middle background buildings that help to centralize the composition round the Virgin, and to suggest great depth, have not been determined. The way in which Poussin blocks out the figures in light and shade shows him thinking in sculptural terms, of solid forms displayed in an almost abstract harmony.

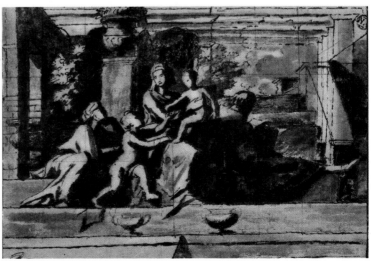

POUSSIN (left)
The Holy Family on the steps, 1648
Though Poussin avoids Venetian colourism, the mask-like solidity of the Virgin's face recalls the *Madonnas* of Giovanni Bellini. Raphael, the Antique and Michelangelo all contibute to a work full of symbolic allusions to the Old and the New dispensations. There are few better examples, even in Poussin's varied range, of Baroque synthesis or of 17th-century classicism.

RUBENS:
The Descent from the Cross

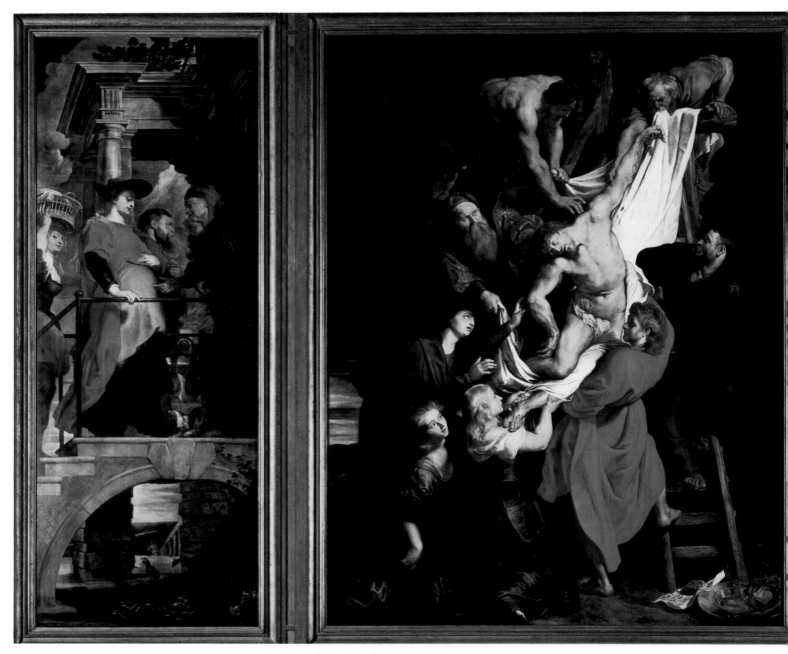

In the early phases of Rubens' career, after his return from Italy in 1608, two masterpieces are supreme. Both are large altarpieces, both now hanging in Antwerp Cathedral, but they were not painted as a pair. The first, *The raising of the Cross*, painted in 1610-11, was commissioned for the church of St Walburga in Antwerp, now demolished; the second, *The Descent from the Cross*, completed in 1614, was always intended for Antwerp Cathedral. Although Rubens had been appointed (in 1609) court painter to the Viceroys of the Netherlands, these commissions came not from that quarter, but from the merchant classes.

The Descent established Rubens then and there as the greatest painter in northern Europe but, though it was less well received, the muscular and emotional turmoil of *The raising* is closer to the subsequent trend of Rubens' work. In its original form, *The raising* had an old-fashioned, complex framework involving not only closing wings but predella

panels below, and God the Father with angels above. The central triptych, to which it was reduced in the eighteenth century, was far from old-fashioned. It was emphatically Baroque, and violent in action, treatment and expression – in the straining muscles of the men heaving up the Cross, in the deep, thrusting diagonals of the composition, in the anguish of the crucified figure. The two wings extend the action and the emotion: on the left, the Virgin and St John look on in a group of horrified women and children; on the right, a mounted Roman officer controls the preparations for the two thieves' execution. On the outer panels were four saints connected with the original church.

In contrast, *The Descent* appears calm and classical. Now the agony is past; the mood is of the most profound sorrow, almost elegiac in the superbly controlled decline of the dead Christ's body down the diagonal white fall of the winding-sheet, caressed by the eloquent

hands that guide it. The design is unforgettable, reused by Rembrandt and many others.

The subjects of the two wings are complementary in theme to the central panel, but do not extend the action as do those of *The raising*. *The Visitation* and *The Presentation in the Temple* on the inner surface of the wings, and a colossal *St Christopher* and a *Hermit* carrying a lantern, the light of the world, on the outer panels, are all linked by the Greek meaning of Christopher, "Christ-bearing", the patron saint of the commissioning guild.

The Descent from the Cross was a not uncommon subject both in northern and Italian painting, though Rubens' interpretation is influenced most clearly by the Italians – works by Caravaggio and the sixteenth-century painters Daniele da Volterra and Il Cigoli all provided ideas for Rubens' composition. Many of the working stages towards *The Descent from the Cross* survive, and illustrate Rubens' methods clearly – first drawings di-

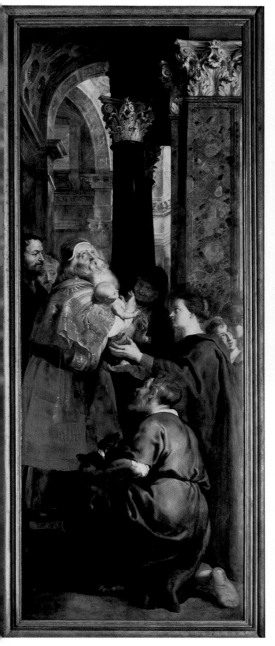

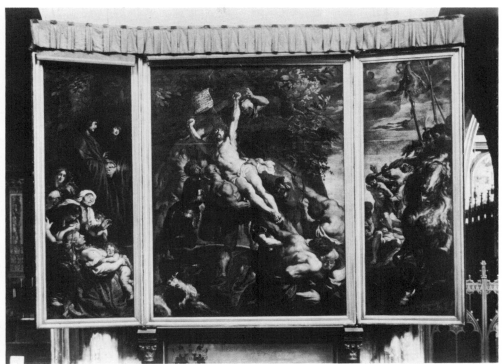

RUBENS (above)
The raising of the Cross,
1610-11
The realism of the action,
the lighting and the solidity
of the bodies show the
influence of Caravaggio,
but Rubens has introduced
passion and bravura, and
exaggerated everything –
the paint itself seems now
to shimmer and vibrate.

DANIELE DA VOLTERRA
(right) *The Descent from
the Cross*, begun 1541
The scale and spectacle
of Daniele's painting had
early showed the trend of
Counter-Reformation
taste. Rubens preserved
the strong diagonals, but
reworked the composition
to achieve greater unity
and dramatic coherence.

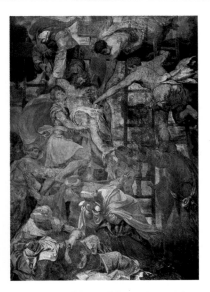

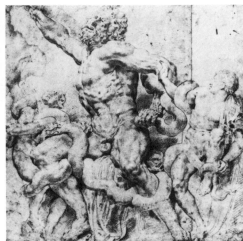

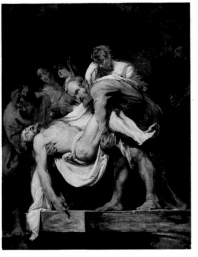

rected towards a resolution of the composition;
then an oil-study, sometimes very fully worked
out, as is that for *The Descent* (this was probably submitted to the client for preliminary ap-
proval); then a reference back to detailed chalk
studies from the life; and finally the execution
of the full-scale painting itself. The imagery is
rich in references not only to Italian masters
but also to classical motifs – St Christopher
clearly echoes "*The Farnese Hercules*" with his
club, while the pose of the dead Christ reflects
closely (in reverse) that of the late Hellenistic
statue of *Laocoön*.

When Rubens' pictures were finished, the
studio often produced replicas, and through
engravings the design was broadcast to a far
wider audience. From an engraving of *The
Descent*, Gainsborough – to take an example –
made a free copy in oils, and then, fascinated
by its formal rhythms, transposed it into the
merry bucolic group on the cart in *The harvest
wagon* (not shown), one of his best landscapes.

RUBENS (above)
Drawing of the *Laocoön*,
c. 1606
Rubens' sketches of the
works of art he had seen
in Italy were an abiding
inspiration – he used them
rather as Rembrandt used
his hundreds of drawings
from the life. Rubens was
a superb draughtsman, and
often infused his drawings
with greater vividness than
the original had.

RUBENS (right)
Copy after Caravaggio's
The Entombment, c. 1605,
reworked c. 1613
When he reworked the copy
of Caravaggio he had made
in Italy, Rubens probably
had in mind the design of
his own *Descent*. He has
heightened the luminosity
of Christ's white body, and
introduced more sorrowful
feeling into Caravaggio's
rather aggressive realism.

VELAZQUEZ:
Las Meninas

Diego Rodríguez de Silva y Velásquez (1599-1660) was trained and began his independent career in Seville, painting mainly still lifes and scenes of peasants, who sometimes play a part in a religious story. His early works exhibit the Caravaggesque influence dominant in Spain, without the emphatic tonal contrasts of such *tenebrismo* painters as Zurbarán.

Almost abruptly, in 1623, he became court painter in Madrid, and thereafter until his death his prime concern was portraiture. He admired Rubens (who with characteristic generosity seems to have persuaded him to go to Italy in 1629-31), and was the exact contemporary of van Dyck and of Bernini, yet his portraiture in its sobriety is the antithesis of their Baroque rhetoric and elaboration. Velazquez extracted the essence of aristocracy – or, for that matter, of childhood or dwarfdom – in simplicity and dignity. He worked directly on to the canvas, usually, it seems, without preliminary drawings, realizing the physical form of his subject not so much in rhythmic line (as Rubens did) as by an immensely subtle tonal analysis in little touches – observe the smallness of the brushes on his palette in *"Las Meninas"*. His art is one of meditative observation rather than of overt expression or energetic composition – he admired Titian, but apparently actively disliked Raphael.

He himself summarized the complexity of his art in his famous *"Las Meninas"* (The maids of honour, finished in 1656). Here, seemingly, we have the painter at work in his studio, which has been invaded by the little Infanta (momentarily poised for admiration) with her suite – her attendant maids and her dwarf, who echoes the royal child so grotesquely, and a great dog. At the far end of the room, an enigmatic figure turned against a flare of light looks back as he mounts the stairs beyond an open door. Beside this figure are the framed images, shadowy and silvery, of the King and Queen, with two large paintings hung above. Each and every one is solidly there, established unerringly back from the foreground light into the shadowed depths of the great room, set in pyramid groupings interlocking across the surface. *"Las Meninas"* was once known as *The family*, and seems to be an assertion of the artist's pride and right of place in the royal hierarchy. But if you ask what is on the front of the huge canvas he is painting, or where the King and Queen in the mirror are standing, then the picture reveals ever richer ambiguities, in subject matter as in formal construction.

"Las Meninas" owes much to Velazquez's second stay in Italy, 1649-51, which forged his mature style. Freshly inspired by Venetian painting, he reached a new command of singing colour and a brilliant, liquid handling revealed in the portrait he made in Rome of Pope Innocent X (reproduced on p. 240) or in another set piece, probably painted before *"Las Meninas"*, *The tapestry weavers*, which again has layers of meaning.

Manet and the Impressionists would be fascinated by the way in which Velazquez could catch with unerring accuracy not the mere physical substance, say the hairs of a dog, literally recounted, but the essence of its appearance in light, its gleam in the eye.

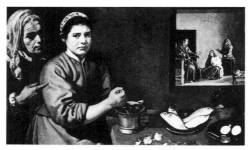

VELAZQUEZ (left)
Christ in the house of Martha and Mary, 1618
The figures and objects are observed with close intensity in strong light, but even in this early genre scene Velazquez was already conjuring with his subject matter, with small but vital ambiguities: is the background scene a picture on the wall or a glimpse through to a second room? The serious and enigmatic expression of the younger woman and the clear gesture of the older – echoing that of Martha in the scene behind – suggest that this is a meditation by two servants on a Gospel story intimately related to their calling. The objects may then take on symbolic meaning, and the work is deepened, enriched.

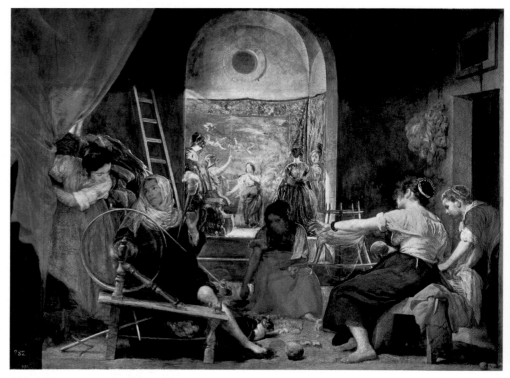

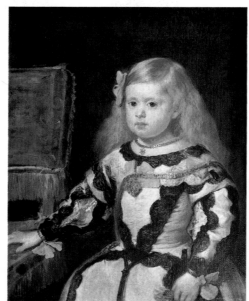

VELAZQUEZ (above)
The Infanta Margarita, c. 1656
The portrait of the little royal princess who is seen again in *"Las Meninas"*, painted at about the same time, shows a similar pose without repetition: the fall of light and the textures are observed entirely afresh. It is easy to see how much Velazquez could offer the Impressionists – the bold pattern, the liquid purity and truthfulness of colour.

VELAZQUEZ (above)
The tapestry weavers, c. 1654
Beneath the realism of the picture (in his rendering of the spinning-wheel's blurred spokes Velazquez anticipates photography) there is a tacit reference to the myth of Arachne, who boasted her spinning was the equal even of the goddess Athena's. Note the interplay of separately lit spaces, and the movement.

VELAZQUEZ (below)
Philip IV, 1634-35
Like Rubens, like van Dyck, Velazquez based his royal portraits on Titian's prototypes – there were many Titians in the Spanish royal collection. Velazquez's less flamboyant portraiture expresses much the same ideal of a Baroque monarch as do his great contemporaries – splendour and decorum achieved with perfectly relaxed ease.

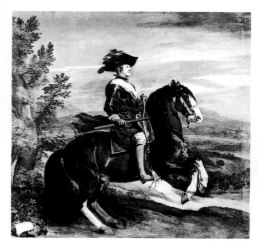

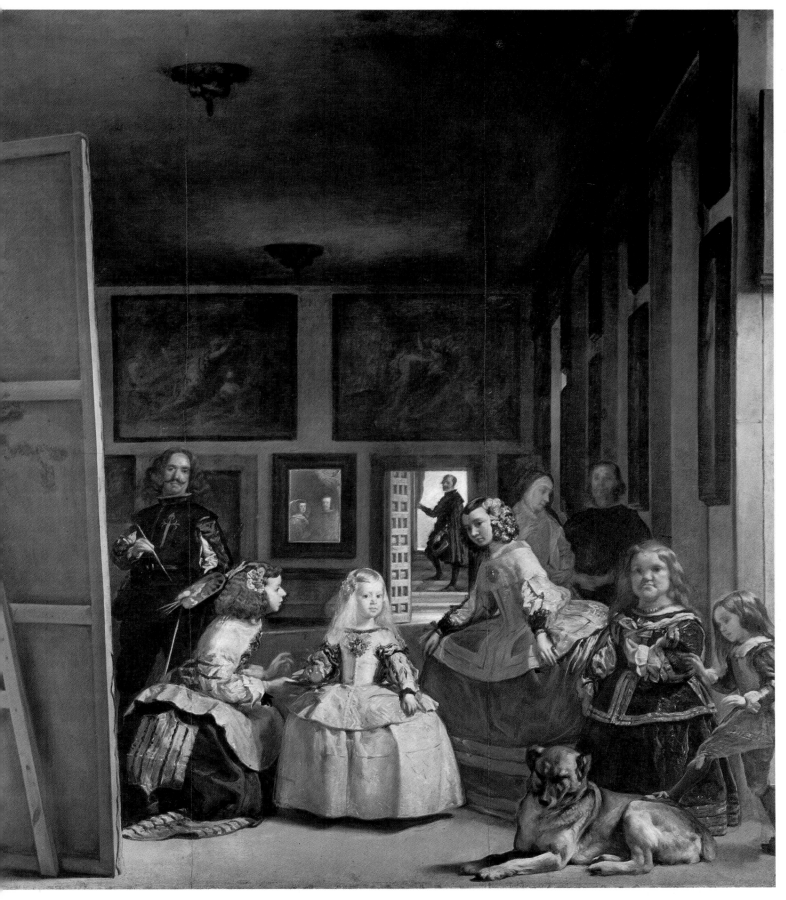

VELAZQUEZ: "*Las Meninas*" (The maids of honour), 1656

HALS:
A Banquet of the St George Civic Guard

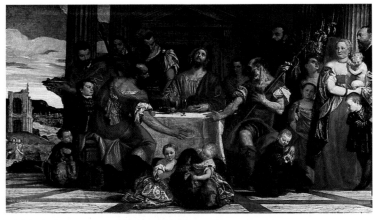

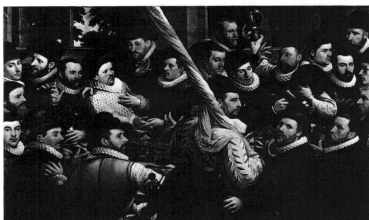

CORNELIS VAN HAARLEM
(left) *The banquet of
Haarlem guardsmen*, 1583
Cornelis has introduced
variety, but the twists
and turns of the figures
add up to no concerted
unity. The traditional
elements which Hals was
to transform are clear.

FRANS HALS (below)
*The banquet of the St
George Civic Guard*, 1616
There are clear lines of
direction articulating the
whole, and the officers are
convincingly grouped in
starts of movement or in
natural conversation.

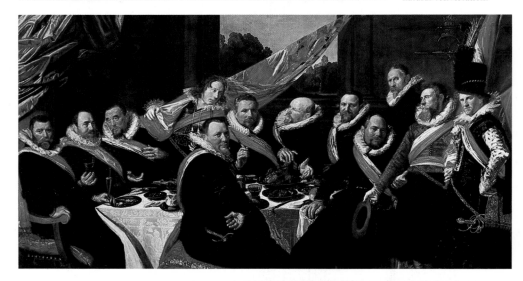

FRANS HALS (right)
*The regents of the St
Elizabeth Hospital*, c. 1641
The restricted colours,
the subdued mood and the
isolation of the figures
are characteristic of the
painter's late style. It
was to culminate, in the
portraits Hals painted
in his 80s, in canvases
constructed virtually
in monochrome, except
for a few colour accents.
Though his exuberance
vanished, Hals never lost
his touch, and he painted
freely and boldly, with
ever increasing directness,
until his penniless death.

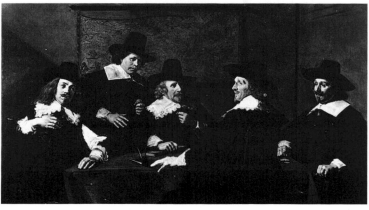

The work of Frans Hals (*c.* 1581/85-1666) is
one of the inexplicable miracles of the great
surge of Dutch painting in the seventeenth
century. Hals was Flemish-born (which perhaps explains something of his bravura) but
spent virtually his whole life in the small town
of Haarlem, painting the locals. The sparse
records of his career – a series of financial,
domestic and legal disasters – indicate a
failure to cope with life entirely at odds with
the exultant vigour and spontaneity of his art.

Hals worked almost entirely in portraiture;
even his genre subjects read as portraits. Hals –
though it took centuries for this to be fully
realized – turned mere likenesses into great
pictures. His particular genius was not for
"psychological insight" but the ability to capture the individual presence of his sitters and
almost fling them alive on to the canvas. This
he achieved by a swift, very free technique:
working often with a restricted palette, he
modelled, not by rounding off and smoothing
out, but by a sequence of dabs, dashes and
slashes that close-to can look haphazard, but
then at a distance cohere into images vibrant
with life. No drawings can be firmly attributed
to him – he worked directly on to the canvas.

Hals' instantaneous technique and immediacy of effect make the unerring control
and organization of his compositions all the
more incredible. Everything is subordinate to
the impact of the whole image. Consider the
famous "*Laughing Cavalier*". What lingers in
the memory is that not altogether explicit
smile, yet the costume and all its detail is a
marvel of laundering. Nowhere is Hals' spontaneous orchestration of detail better shown
than in the great group portraits – Hals, as
Vincent van Gogh remarked, "painted a
whole glorious republic".

The group portrait of civic bodies was a
Dutch speciality, beginning well back in the
sixteenth century with stiff rows of individual
heads. Cornelis van Haarlem (1562-1638) had
succeeded in enlivening their composition,
but it was Hals alone who could catch alive
the brash, brilliant, vulgar ostentation of the
Civic Guards at their junketing. The Civic
Guards clung dearly to their memories of
heroic resistance against the Spanish, but by
1616, when Hals painted his first group, their
gatherings were more like the outings of a
social club than military parades; although
martial dress, banners and equipment were
splendidly displayed, the main focus of their
meetings was food and drink – consumed in
indefinite banquets (the authorities tried to
reduce them from a week to three days).

Hals painted the Company of St George at
Haarlem three times, in 1616, in about 1627
and finally (not shown) in 1639. The 1627
composition is the most splendid: it is resolved
into two groups, linked by the flash of the
furled flag and by the marvellous invention of
the genial and tipsy captain turning his glass
upside down in the right centre. There is an
explosion of colour against the purplish curtain in the background – a surf of blues, whites,
reds, yellows and greens. Amidst it all each
participant is sharply individual. It is a truly
Baroque composition – the swirl, the emphatic
diagonals; the direct technique, the colour and
excitement; the naturalism and illusionism.

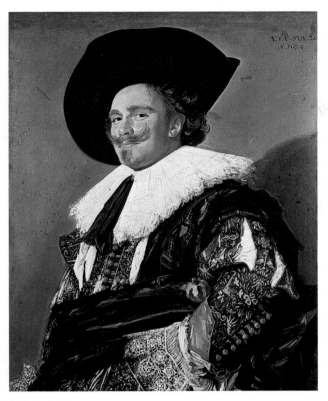

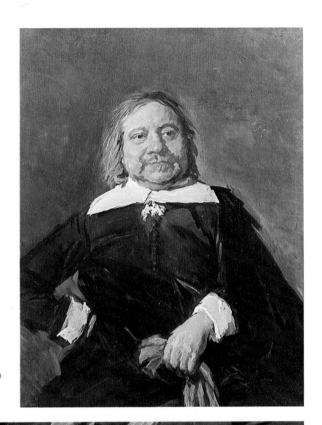

FRANS HALS (left)
"*The Laughing Cavalier*",
1624
Only Velazquez can rival
Hals for brushwork that
seems to live a life of its
own on the canvas. Yet
the figure is solid: the
elbow seems to jut out,
and the torso to pivot
against the background.

FRANS HALS (right)
Willem Croes, c. 1660
In his later paintings
Hals avoided complexity
of pose or brilliance of
colour, and the presence of
the sitter emerges the more
forcefully and frankly.

FRANS HALS (below)
*The banquet of the St
George Civic Guard,
c.* 1627
Each officer has more
character, and the whole
has a greater ease and
more natural variety than
had the earlier *St George*
group portrait. There the
interruption of the spec-
tator is clearly felt; here
there seems to be too much
din, the officers seem too
involved in their feasting
to pay much attention.

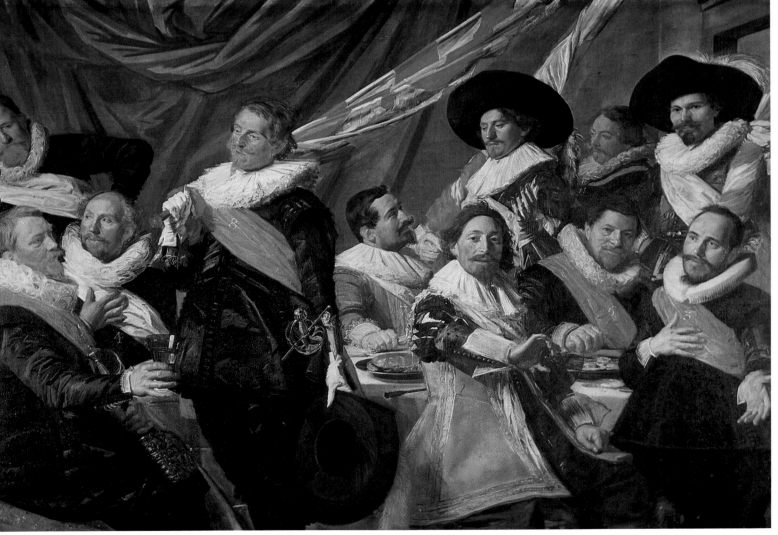

REMBRANDT:
The Self-Portrait at Kenwood

The main course of Rembrandt's life is fairly clear – his birth in Leyden in 1606; his early success (with pupils even in his twenty-first year) in his home town; in the 1630s, fashionable prosperity in Amsterdam; then the decline in popularity, the death of his wife Saskia in 1642; financial mismanagement, culminating in bankruptcy and the enforced sale of his superb art collection in 1656/57; the deaths of his common-law wife Hendrickje Stoffels in 1663 and of his only son Titus in 1668; his own death in 1669.

The recorded facts reveal little about one of the greatest artists in history, rivalled in scope of imagination and universal appeal perhaps only by Shakespeare. But the skeleton provided by the documents is endowed with both flesh and spirit by the sequence of *Self-portraits* – more than 100 drawings, etchings or paintings, ranging from his beginnings as an artist to the last year of his life. They constitute the most remarkable autobiography ever painted, and culminate in the searching self-interrogations of Rembrandt's last decade: amongst these the three-quarter-length portrait at Kenwood, London, is one of the most impressive and haunting.

In almost all the late *Self-portraits*, the demand that the spectator identify with the artist is irresistible: he looks at himself, searching; you look at him; he looks at you. In some of these portraits, Rembrandt is very much the Protestant, holding his human identity clear of the dark as if by sheer will-power – alone with himself, uncertain perhaps if man is made in the image of God but determined to find out. The search for identity is there even in the earliest portraits, though these are often clearly studies, exercises in capturing momentary expression. The Dresden double portrait with Saskia, of his brash middle years in Amsterdam, is also a brash image, Rembrandt exultant at his fortune and rather vulgarly unconcerned with the dignity of his station as the leading Dutch artist of his day. The element of role-playing, as in the London National Gallery portrait, where he is posed and clad like a Titian portrait then believed to represent the prince of poets, Ariosto, persists almost to the end. But in one of the last of all (also in the London National Gallery) Rembrandt, hands folded, quietly resigned on the threshold of death – but in his paint still vital with life – records simply himself.

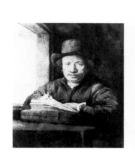

REMBRANDT (above)
Self-portrait drawing by a window, 1648
The pose and setting recall the many paintings and etchings Rembrandt made of scholars or of saints seated in a room by a window: in comparison and contrast the artist appears as an earnest, prosaic burgher – his hat completes the image.

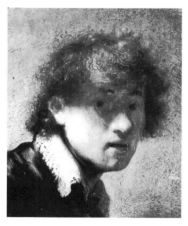

REMBRANDT (left)
Self-portrait in Munich, detail, *c*. 1629
Like Caravaggio before him, Rembrandt wants to catch a momentary start in paint, and exploits sharp contrasts of light and shade to do so – but also introduces mystery.

REMBRANDT (right)
Self-portrait in Berlin, detail, 1634
The somewhat mysterious drama of the portrait (left) is retained; there is now more of a swagger: the boisterous youth yields to a romantic, but hardly less truculent, young man.

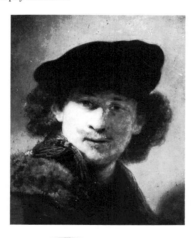

REMBRANDT (right)
Self-portrait at Kenwood, London, *c*. 1665
Against the predominant dark brown to red of the whole, the focus is on the lighter key of the face, the grey hair, the cap almost slashed on to the canvas. The face is old, seen without vanity or flattery. No one knows the meaning of the semicircles incised on the background: if they hint at a possible ideal order, the ruggedness of the face contradicts them sharply. There is paradox again in the rich fur of the robe and the workaday context. Tools of the trade are perfectly legible from a distance, but closely inspected become ambiguous. Seen closer still, they are like pure paint energized, and the hand holding them is just a brusque zigzag of paint dragged down, diminishing as the brush unloads. Rembrandt had no truck with the kind of art that conceals the art: he left his workings bare and one of his few remarks on record is a warning to connoisseurs not to expect high finish: "Don't poke your nose into the painting or the smell will kill you."

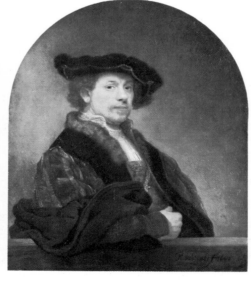

REMBRANDT
Self-portrait with Saskia, c. 1635
Of the bold self-conscious bravura there is no doubt; but beyond that the interpretations vary: is there some unease? What does Saskia think of it all? The still life and raised glass recall genre tavern scenes, with a moral undertone.

REMBRANDT
Self-portrait after Titian's "*Ariosto*", 1640
Both Titian's "*Ariosto*" and Raphael's similar *Castiglione* had passed through the Amsterdam sale-rooms in 1639. The more mature Rembrandt's interest in Renaissance art was increasing, and was to be reflected in his painting.

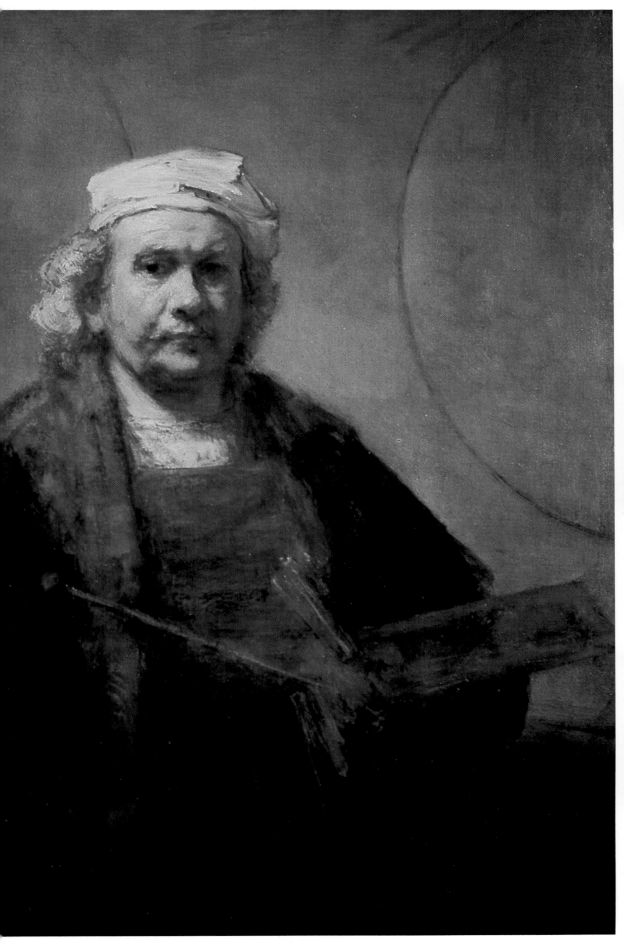

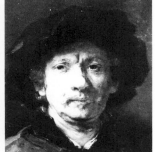

REMBRANDT
Self-portrait in Vienna,
detail, 1652
The later self-portraits
are mostly frontal – the
painter face to face with
himself. Rembrandt by this
time was painting probably
more for himself than for
clients or on commission.

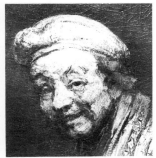

REMBRANDT
Self-portrait in Cologne,
detail, *c.* 1669
The image is undeniably
grotesque – Rembrandt as
a genre old man. However,
he peers from the shadows
with a bruised grin: the
vigour and freedom of
the impasto asserts life.

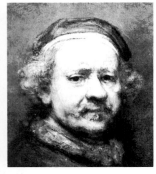

REMBRANDT
Self-portrait in London,
detail, 1669
The lonely suffering of
Rembrandt's last years
(with Hendrickje dead, his
son Titus dead, aged 27)
is never more than hinted
at even in his latest *Self-
portraits*. Their dignity is
powerful, utterly honest.

RUISDAEL:
The Jewish Cemetery

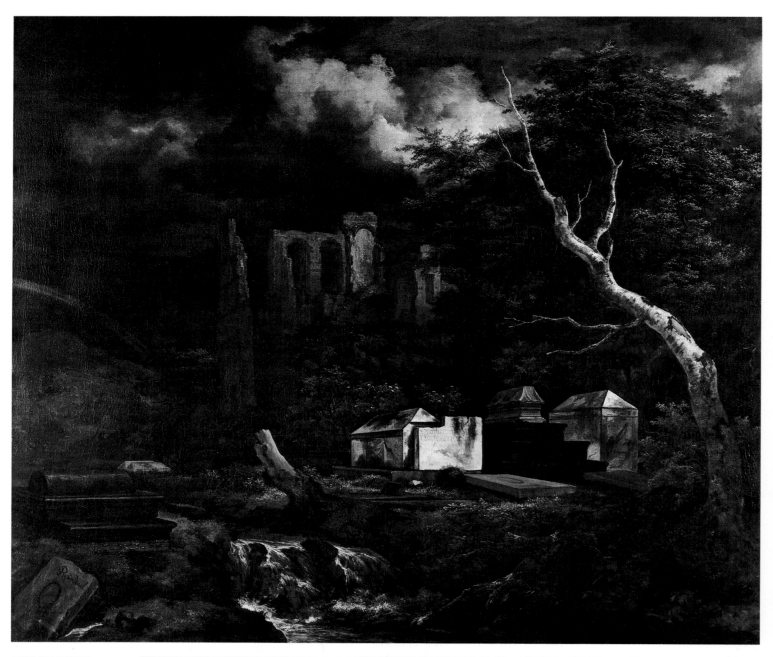

JACOB VAN RUISDAEL
(above) The Dresden
Jewish cemetery, 1660s
There are no figures, no
animals: the tombs are the
central characters; trees,
buildings, sky, a stream
and the changing light are
the supporting cast. Each is
charged with an animating,
transfiguring atmosphere.

JACOB VAN RUISDAEL
(right) The Detroit
Jewish cemetery, 1660s
In this version the mood
seems warmer: the trees,
for instance, are less stark;
the desertion is not quite so
absolute: there is a cottage
amid the ruins, and two
small, black-robed figures.

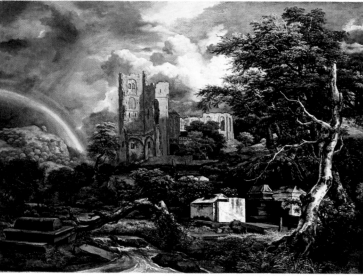

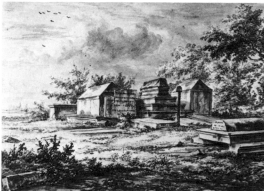

JACOB VAN RUISDAEL
*Tombs in the Jewish ceme-
tery at Ouderkerk, c.* 1660
The positions of the tombs
have been slightly altered
in the paintings, but they
retain their striking shapes.

So, too, the other elements
were no doubt closely based
on observation from life,
though even the drawing
has been organized into a
composition – the birds in
the sky, the placed trees.

The tragic drama of nature is felt in most of the paintings of Jacob van Ruisdael (1628/9-82), but only in the two versions of *The Jewish cemetery* is it so explicit, and the symbolism so overt. The strongest accents in the composition, in each case, are the tombs, painted "from the life", as is proved by two drawings and by the tombs themselves, still to be seen in the Jewish cemetery at Ouderkerk near Amsterdam. They catch the eye not only because of their near-central position, but because the light of the lowering sun picks them out and a tree almost points to them. Simultaneously amid the dark rain clouds kindles a rainbow – the age-old symbol of hope and Resurrection.

In both versions, the cluster of the tombs is identical, but otherwise the paintings vary considerably, in the whole and in the rest of the details. The surrounding landscapes, for all their vivid presence, are fantasies. Both versions are presumably of the 1660s, though which is the earlier is uncertain. The Dresden version is the more sombre, the rainbow more tentative, the ruined church a different building much further gone in decay, sunk deeper in oncoming night. (Note, however, how important in each version is the vertical accent of the ruined flank of the building, holding the light and stabilizing the whole composition.) As Constable was to observe, Ruisdael enveloped the most ordinary scenes with grandeur, and in his work as a whole – with its evocation of melancholy and its drama of light and shade – the Romantic movement would find a prophet of its own feelings towards Nature; Goethe, however, analysed a profounder poetry in this composition: "Even the tombs themselves, in their state of ruin, signify something more than the past: they are tombs of themselves".

Ruisdael developed that combination of realism and romanticism found in a greater or lesser work in all his mature work from the example of his predecessors and contemporaries. His fascination with trees is reminiscent of the late Mannerist follower of Coninxloo, Savery; his ability to consolidate the facts of earth, foliage, water into classical compositions surely owed something to the Italian example filtered back to Holland chiefly by painters from Utrecht. His delight in mountainous spectacle, in crags and waterfalls alien to his native Dutch landscape, was formed perhaps by the Scandinavian visions of Allart van Everdingen (1621-75); in contrast, his panoramic sweeps of the true ·Dutch plains doubtless owed something to the great horizontal sweeps of Philips de Koninck (1619-88). Finally, his compulsive effect on the spectator's imagination demands comparison with Rembrandt. But, though in a few instances Ruisdael produced visions very close to some of Rembrandt's rare painted landscapes, no specific influence from Rembrandt can be seen. Ruisdael's technique, which derives much of its impact by marrying a broad, majestic massing of forms with a very detailed characterization of individual elements, could certainly be called Baroque; however, in realizing landscape as an equivalent of the tragic human condition, Ruisdael was profoundly original, and his empathy with the rhythm of transient and inexorable Nature is akin to that of Romantic poets such as Wordsworth.

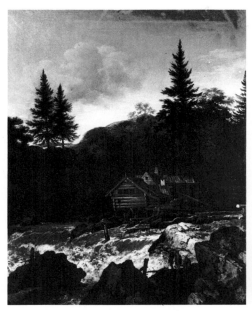

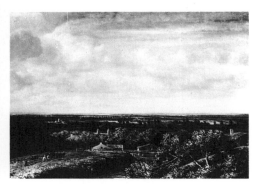

EVERDINGEN (left)
A waterfall, 1650
Everdingen was probably taught by Savery, who had travelled in the Tyrol. He himself travelled to Scandinavia with a patron in 1640, and in the 1650s he introduced into his pictures the waterfalls and log huts he had sketched there.

KONINCK (below)
View over flat country, 1650s or 1660s
Typical of Koninck is the bisecting horizon: no house or church joins land and sky. The slightly raised viewpoint stresses the endlessness of the plain: and Ruisdael, too, was to exploit such an effect of panorama.

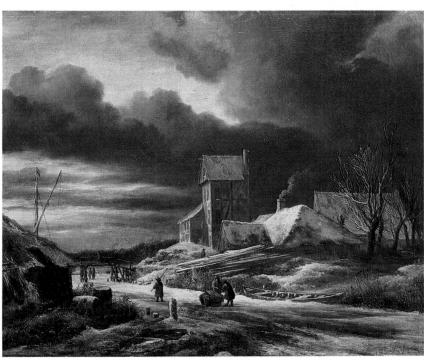

JACOB VAN RUISDAEL (above) *Winter landscape*, c. 1670
Desolate figures tramp the frozen river in the freezing dusk. The river slants against an ominous counter-diagonal into a void: even in this homely scene there is a sense of the insignificance of man.

REMBRANDT (right)
The stone bridge, c.1637
The lighting is not naturalistic: it erupts into the dark of the painting, and blanches the tree it strikes. It is a theoretical landscape, like those of Seghers, not a sublimation of natural landscape like, for instance, Ruisdael's picture (above).

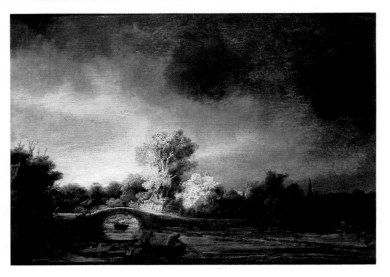

VERMEER:
The Artist's Studio

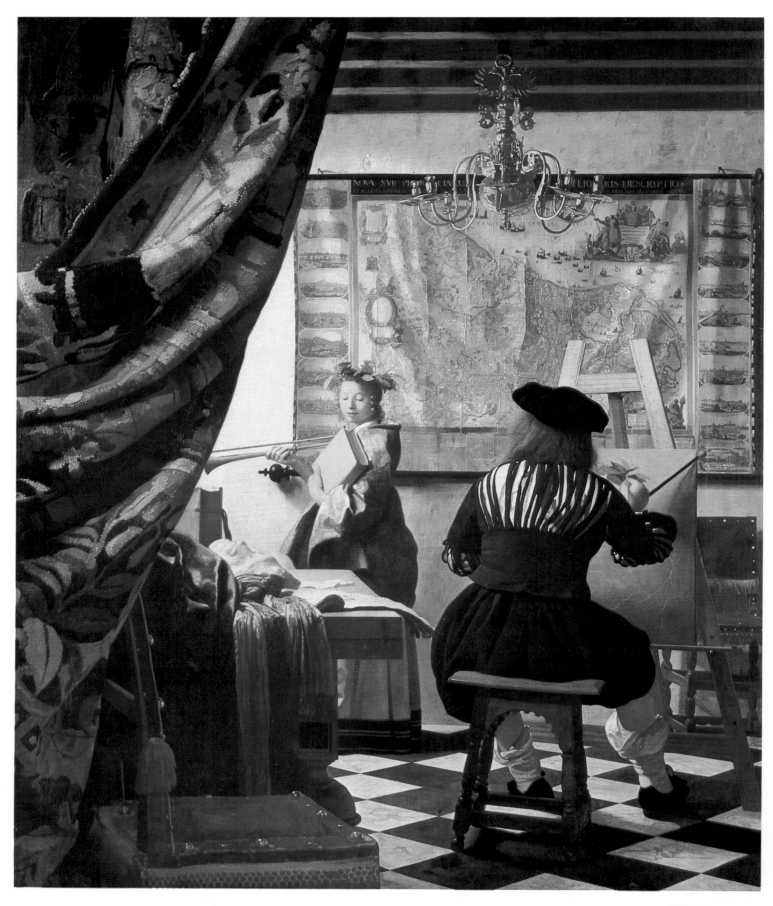

VERMEER
"The Artist's Studio"
(The art of painting),
c. 1665-70

The subject matter is detailed with all Vermeer's firm modelling and luminous, cool serenity: a painter, seen from behind, is in the act of painting on the easel before him the figure of a young girl who stands in the gentle light of a window in the corner of the room. It is a rich and typically Dutch interior – the black and white marble pattern of the floor; the sumptuously textured curtains; the fine brass chandelier; a map of Holland on the wall – inhabited by an inimitable element, Vermeer's pervasive and all-creating light.

On inspection, however, several questions about the picture begin to arise. This is no ordinary working painter's studio, cluttered and untidy; the painter is dressed in a costume that is certainly not studio garb. His model's shoulders are clad in a rather indeterminate drapery; her head is wreathed with what seem to be laurels, and though she has the features of a typical Vermeer girl (a daughter perhaps) she is accoutred with a fine trumpet and a large tome (that will soon surely be uncomfortably heavy). She must represent either a Muse – the Muse of History, Clio – or Fame, both of

whom earlier artists had shown with these accessories. Vermeer painted other allegories, and his widow is known to have referred to this painting under the title *The art of painting*. But this work celebrates the triumph of the painter's art far more movingly and convincingly than any Baroque contrivance of allegorical females could ever do, partly just because Clio, or Fame, is also a simple Dutch girl, dressed up rather touchingly and awkwardly; the artist in the picture, however, has not yet started with her person, he is beginning on his canvas with the laurels of fame.

But then, how did Vermeer himself set about the painting we see? There is no evidence in this or in any other painting that he worked otherwise than *alla prima*, directly on to the canvas, without preliminary studies or drawings – and this in spite of the absolute certainty with which the very elaborate structure and detail of the picture is established. He could, however, have framed his composition on a two-dimensional surface – ready to trace as it were – by the ingenious disposition of two mirrors, one behind the artist, the other in

front, so placed as to include the image of his own back as he painted. If so, this is a self-portrait, characteristically rejecting any self-revelation. There is still some ambiguity about the exact scope of the painting, a query, for example, as to whether the foreground curtain and chair are inside or outside the main subject of the picture. There are also ambiguities in the significance of the subject matter – the map of Holland, for instance, so ostentatious on the wall, looks like an assertion of Dutch national pride, but is beyond doubt of the Dutch provinces under the old Spanish rule.

The painting is signed (though for long it was attributed to de Hoogh), and is thought to be late within Vermeer's mature period, somewhere between 1665 and 1670. Some elements restate established motifs: painters at work (and seen from behind), the transitional device of the foreground curtain drawn back between the picture and the spectator – these occur in Rembrandt or in masters such as Dou or Mieris. What is unique to Vermeer is the monumental whole into which they are bound – entirely credible and yet unfathomable.

VERMEER (below)
*The head of a girl, c.*1666
Though the girl may well be Vermeer's daughter, it is an impersonal portrait.

It seems to have been made chiefly to experiment with a favourite colour contrast, or to explore a fascination with the behaviour of light.

VERMEER (left)
An allegory of Faith,
*c.*1669
This seems stilted. "*The Artist's Studio*" is instead really a genre picture of an artist painting an allegory: hence its greater success.

VERMEER (below)
Diana and her nymphs,
*c.*1654
The subject, like that of the *Allegory* (left), is essentially Italian; classical myths and theatrical allegories were not main Protestant themes.

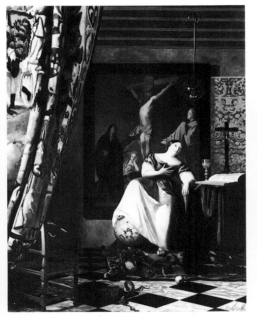

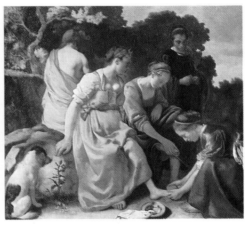

REMBRANDT (right)
The artist in his studio,
*c.*1628-29
There is no high-flown allegory about this little genre work – it is hardly even a self-portrait. In Rembrandt's picture there is both a comic element and a debunking realism – the opposite of Vermeer's quiet, high seriousness.

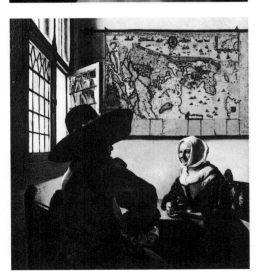

VERMEER (left)
A soldier and a laughing girl, c. 1657
Both the Italianate subject and the composition of "*The Artist's Studio*" owe much to the Utrecht school – even if the Utrechtian device of silhouetting a foreground figure against the light in the picture is more bluntly used in this early work.

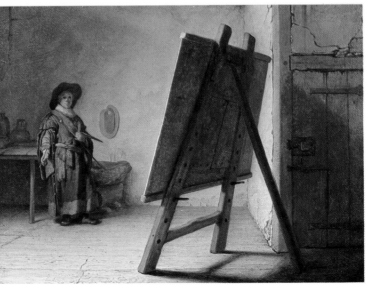

WATTEAU:
The Embarkation for Cythera

Men and women in pairs, almost afloat in their silks against the haze of the sunset sky and the distant misty peaks, ebb down from the right of the painting, where stands a sculptured bust of the goddess Venus wreathed with roses and convolvulus, towards a boat awaiting them at the shore of an inlet of the sea. The picture is all autumnal gold, with a certain lilt of melancholy, a dying fall of farewells, and echoes of unheard music.

Of the two slightly different versions of "*The Embarkation for Cythera*", one in Berlin and one in the Louvre, the earlier one in the Louvre was the enrolment picture which Jean-Antoine Watteau (1684-1721) deposited with the Académie in 1717 – a little belatedly, as he had become an Academician in 1712. He called it originally *Le pèlerinage à l'Ile de Cythère*, translatable as "the pilgrimage to, or on, or towards the island of Cythera". The title by which it has long been known, "*The Embarkation for Cythera*", came later, and, though it was universally adopted, it is surely wrong, as has recently been shown. In legend, Cythera is the island where Venus rose from the sea, and here indeed she is, in statue form. But clearly the pilgrims are not setting off for the island but about to leave after a day's enchanting dalliance on it.

Fêtes galantes, showing lovers in a pastoral setting, sometimes banqueting, often with music, had attracted painters since the sixteenth century at least: an obvious prototype for Watteau's version is Rubens' *Garden of Love*,

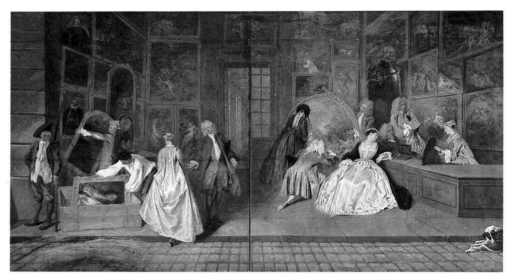

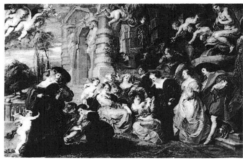

RUBENS (left)
The Garden of Love, c. 1632
Rubens' *fêtes galantes* (but not yet called that) were an inspiration to Watteau and other 18th-century painters – although they transposed his extrovert sensuality into an intimate, more graceful, Rococo key.

WATTEAU (above)
"*L'Enseigne de Gersaint*" (Gersaint's signboard), 1721
Watteau's "shop sign" has a greater realism, a more specific setting than his earlier pictures. Flemish artists hang recognizably on the walls; the man in the middle may be Watteau.

WATTEAU (below)
The Louvre "*Embarkation*

for Cythera", properly *The pilgrimage to Cythera*, 1717

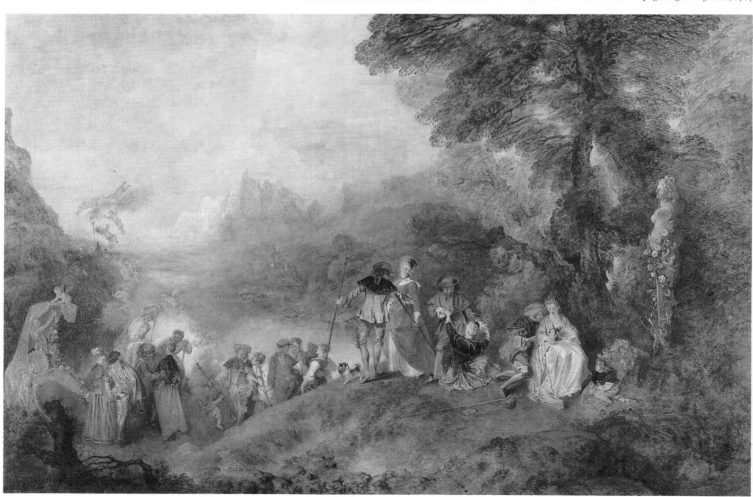

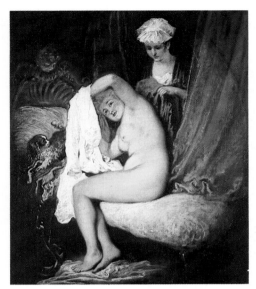

WATTEAU (below)
The Berlin *"Embarkation
for Cythera"*, 1718
Here the moral lurking in
the first version is made
explicit: lovers turn to leave
with a more obvious regret.
The lyric haze of the first
version has turned to a
brighter clarity. The lady
with the fan beneath the
statue of Venus (now *"The
Medici Venus"*) has a face
of clearly Rubensian type.

WATTEAU (above)
"La Toilette", *c.* 1720
The picture is superbly
ambiguous: the lady seems
to have been surprised in
the privacy of her chamber,
but is she undressing or
dressing? Her pose reveals
as much as it conceals.
Why the onlooking maid, if
not to reinforce the erotic
atmosphere? The moral
laxity, the shell couch-head,
her body's oval, are Rococo.

which Watteau certainly knew. His literary
source was probably a musical entertainment,
The Three Cousins, by Florent Dancourt,
which appeared in 1700. It had pilgrims jour-
neying to a temple of Love in Cythera, whence,
a couplet pointed out, no girl returned without
a lover or a husband. In Watteau's picture –
which is very like a stage presentation, almost
an opera – this consummation has clearly been
brought about, as the couples turn lingering to
the boat; yet pleasure is shadowed by the
approach of evening. Time is not to be denied,
and the transience of youth, the bittersweet of
love itself, is only just below the surface.

The inspiration of the stage is obvious in
most of Watteau's work, and in particular that
of the Italian *Commedia dell'Arte*, with its
costumed stock characters, of whom the best-
known is Pierrot – he typifies its element of
pathos and its occasional edge of satire. These
qualities are indeed almost always present in
Watteau's painting. But the enduring fascination of his artificial never-never world must
be due in great part to the brilliance of his
technique. From his very early days, he kept
sketchbooks with swift notations of figures
from the life, and these he used again and again
in his paintings. He is one of the world's most
bewitching draughtsmen, marrying strength
and fragility, power and delicacy into his
swallow's-wing line; this quality he transposed
into his painting with no loss of grace. Over an
underpaint of pearly white, sometimes hazing
to blue or palest pink, he drifted on trees in

washes of green and golden brown; then the
figures, in a thick impasto modelled with
incisive gesture; over this, transparent glazes,
in a technique based on that of the sixteenth-
century Venetians, so that the overall impression is of shimmering depths. His Flemish
origins, however (he was born in Valenciennes,
which until a few years before his birth was
part of Flanders), are apparent in the rhythm
and colour of his compositions, and his debt to
Rubens was never forgotten. When Watteau
arrived in Paris in 1702 the argument among
French painters between "Rubenisme" and
"Poussinisme" (see p. 178) was already swaying back towards Rubens.

The tinge of melancholy in Watteau's work
is matched by his life. His health was undermined by early hardships, and he had less than
ten years left when he became an Academician.
In 1719-20 he was in London, partly in hopes
that the famous Dr Mead might cure his
consumption, partly perhaps from a desire to
extend his sphere of action. He was already,
however, fatally ill. On his return to France, as
his death approached, he destroyed a large
number of his more erotic paintings. One of his
last paintings, however, *"L'Enseigne de Gersaint"* (Gersaint's signboard), for a picture
dealer called Gersaint, who looked after him,
was a new departure.

After his death, Watteau's style in *fêtes
galantes* was carried on by Jean-Baptiste Pater
and Nicolas Lancret, both of whom had competence but not Watteau's unique magic.

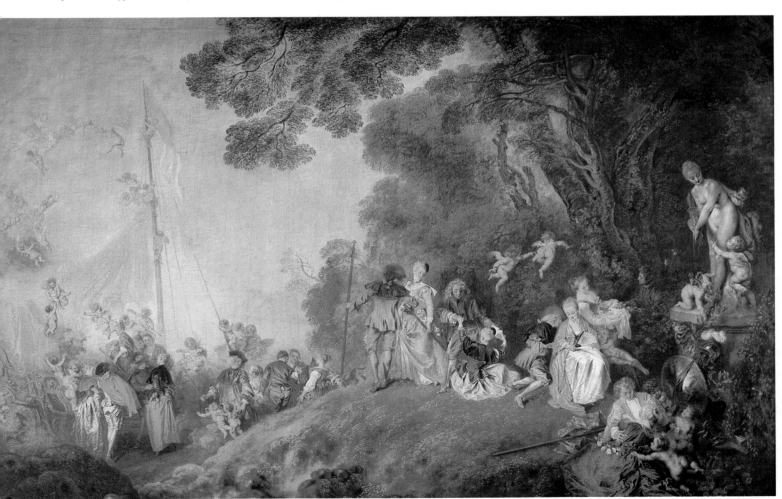

CHARDIN:
The House of Cards

Jean-Baptiste-Siméon Chardin (1699-1779) developed only two main themes throughout his long career – still life, and domestic genre subjects. The still life is usually observed in the kitchen, rather than in the opulent dining-room implied by so many Dutch and Flemish still lifes; the genre scenes, too, are often sited "below stairs" – servants about their chores or – a favourite focus – children at play.

The boy building a house of cards is a subject to which Chardin returned several times. The concentration of the child, the delicacy of the operation on which he is engaged, are matched by the painter's concentration and subtlety. The image is essentially of transience, expressing the brevity and innocence of childhood: the cards will collapse and be put away in the half-open drawer; the child will grow up. This is observed with the utmost objectivity, though bourgeois values are implicit – a leisured society in which a house of cards is practicable, a secure family context. But there is no moralizing intent, as in Greuze; no sly overtones, as in Fragonard; and no trace of Boucher's Rococo fantasy.

Chardin's approach to his subjects was direct, relying not on preparatory drawings but on painting from nature straight on to the canvas: the density and richness of his paintings comes from an elaborate building up of the paint itself. For this there were precedents (there was the example, for instance, of Rembrandt's impasto), but it was noted by contemporaries as entirely new. The arbiter of contemporary taste, Diderot, commented: "There is a magic in this art that passes our understanding. Sometimes thick coats of colour are applied one above the other so that their effects seep upward from below. At other times one gets the impression that a vapour has been floated across the canvas, or a light sprayed over it. Draw near, everything becomes confused, flattens out, disappears, but step back and everything takes shape again, comes back to life" – effects achieved by a combination of broad and very fine brushwork, sensitive both to the textural qualities of the objects and to the pictorial qualities of the canvas. But the handling is supported by an ability to select a composition in which modern eyes can diagnose an abstract structure underlying the vivid reality of the images.

Chardin's beginnings were unorthodox: he did not pass through the Academy, and he had difficulty in establishing his artistic status. He was constantly being compared with Dutch and Flemish predecessors. The move from still life to scenes of domestic genre was prompted in part by this need to "elevate his art" and his prestige. For a time he further expanded his range to paintings that have elements of portraiture, but characteristically his subjects perform some undramatic, domestic action. Although these seem not to have met with such general favour, all aspects of his work were very successful, not so much among the middle classes as among his fellow-artists and with aristocratic connoisseurs. He repeated many subjects in replicas, and there was a widespread demand for engravings of his work, surpassing, it was noted at the time, the demand for the hitherto more fashionable allegorical and historical pieces.

CHARDIN (below)
Skate, cat and kitchen utensils, 1728
Exhibition of this early still life led to Chardin's election in 1728 to the Académie Royale. It shows, consummated for the first time, a sensuous pleasure in the substance and texture of paint which soon became characteristic of the French school. Chardin lies behind the still lifes of Courbet, Manet, Monet and Cézanne.

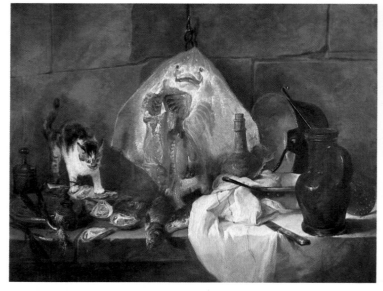

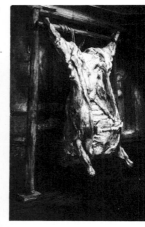

REMBRANDT (above)
The flayed ox, 1655
Rembrandt's picture was surely known to Chardin, and probably a precedent for the aggressive realism of Chardin's lurid *Skate*, disembowelled and bloody on its hook. Rembrandt's glow of light against dark was a more lasting lesson.

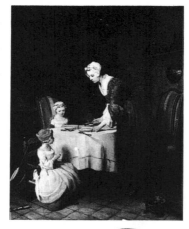

CHARDIN (left)
Saying grace, c. 1740
Chardin's modesty seems stark beside Boucher's sparkling gaiety (right). Perhaps he needed such unassuming, uninteresting domestic settings (so they perhaps appeared to those who preferred Boucher) to set off the voluptuousness of his paint. He depended, as Boucher did not, on the perspicacity of connoisseurs.

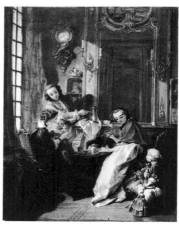

BOUCHER (right)
Breakfast, 1739
The very close similarity in composition between the two pictures emphasizes the difference in approach.

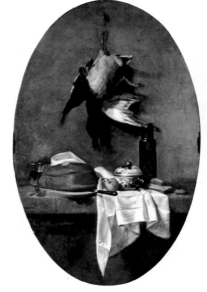

CHARDIN (above)
Still life with a wild duck, 1764
Chardin's reversion to still lifes in his latter years was due perhaps partly to his second marriage, to a rich wife, who brought him a new financial independence and thus artistic freedom.

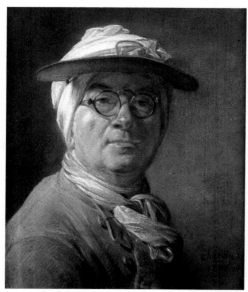

CHARDIN (above)
Self-portrait with an eyeshade, 1775
Neither illness nor failing eyesight stopped the aged Chardin painting, though he was forced to work in pastel. His very late *Self-portraits* are outstanding in their naked directness.

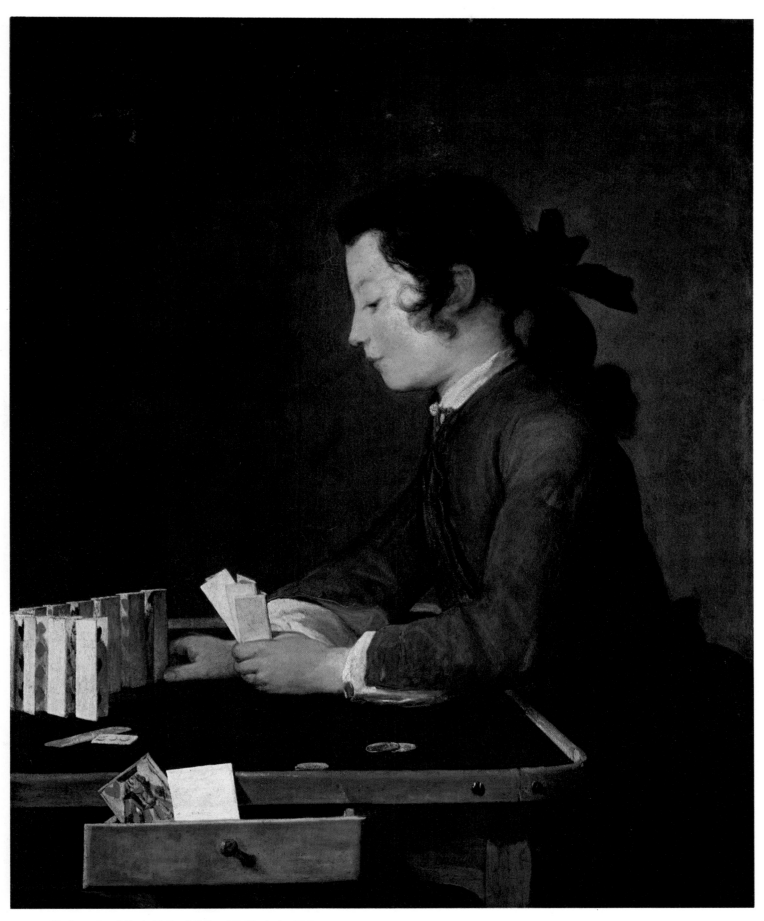

CHARDIN: *The house of cards* (in the National Gallery, Washington), *c*. 1741

TIEPOLO:
The Residenz at Würzburg

One of the most spectacular achievements of eighteenth-century art is the decorative ensemble of about 1750 in the Prince-Bishop's Palace, or Residenz, at Würzburg. It is the work of the great German architect Balthasar Neumann and the last of the great Venetian painters, Giambattista Tiepolo (1696-1770), and its two main elements are the staircase, or *Treppenhaus*, and the salon, or *Kaisersaal*.

In the *Kaisersaal* marble, gold, stucco and glass come together with the colour, light and fluency of Tiepolo's paint to achieve a masterpiece of *Gesamtkunstwerk*, that union of the arts that lacks only music to become opera. On the ceiling are painted incidents from the life of Emperor Frederick Barbarossa, who had invested the Bishop of Würzburg in 1168 – almost in the Dark Ages. In Tiepolo's interpretation the action is transported into the sixteenth century, into the Venetian costume of Veronese, and has been rendered incandescent with light. The ceiling shows an exultant Apollo conducting across the heavens a triumphal chariot bearing Beatrice of Burgundy towards Frederick, her husband-to-be, who is enthroned on a steeply towering edifice on the other side, while Glory with a flaming torch hovers above. The *Treppenhaus*, with its complex iconography, *Olympus with the four quarters of the Earth*, is hardly less luminous.

Tiepolo's art in his maturity was the consummation of Baroque fresco, as complex and inventive as that of any of his predecessors, yet controlled and disposed with crystal clarity. The illusion in the *Kaisersaal* is complete – from the real, solid floor the eye travels up into the intricacies of art and so to the apparent dissolution both of the real and of art: the gilt stucco, now real, now a painted imitation indistinguishable from the real, melts into a heaven flooded with light and with an air that is almost breathable. Tiepolo's magic is most telling in the foreshortened horses that surge across the sky; their ancestors are to be found in the work of Reni, Guercino or Giordano, but only Tiepolo could inspire the spectator with a sense of almost interplanetary "lift-off". The glorious white creatures retain all their physical and massive presence, yet are superbly and triumphantly indifferent to gravity. In the frescos on the walls Tiepolo had less scope for such aerial heights of fantasy, and presented the scenes on stages revealed behind heavy curtains raised by angels; yet the quality of painting is equally high, and illusion interpenetrates reality equally deftly.

Tiepolo's earlier work had been influenced by the sculptural modelling and heavy chiaroscuro of his older contemporary Piazzetta, and was mostly in oil. Fresco, with the opportunity

for working over vast areas at great speed, released his genius, and for it he developed his characteristic high tonal key, within which he could make even his shadows glow with light. His frescos, whether religious or secular, are so joyfully radiant that to some nineteenth-century critics they seemed intolerably frivolous. There is no doubt, however, of Tiepolo's religious sincerity. Later in his life a strain of melancholy became stronger and his altarpieces could strike a grave and elegiac mood, for instance in the ashen blues of the *modello* for an altarpiece of *St Thecla* for the Cathedral at Este. Yet the overwhelming impact of his art is its heart-lifting colour and light.

At the end of his career, in the service of Charles III in Madrid, his aerial perspectives became even more free, his figures sporting in their heavens became as light as bubbles in champagne, but this climax was attended by indications that new fashions were on the way. His almost equally brilliant son and collaborator, Domenico, painting in fresco what was in fact genre at the Villa Valmarana in Vicenza was by 1757 "burying the Grand Manner right under his father's vigilant eye", as the historian Wittkower has put it, and the end of Tiepolo's life in Madrid was clouded by lapse from favour, when the King came to prefer the Neoclassical manner of Mengs.

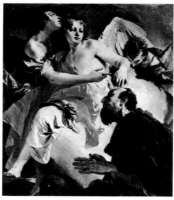

TIEPOLO (below)
Abraham visited by the angels, c. 1732
Even after Tiepolo had developed his light-filled fresco style, he retained a more sombre and emphatic approach (conditioned in part by the medium) in his large-scale canvases in oils.

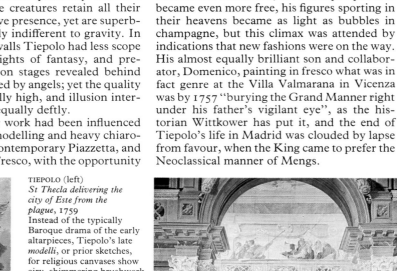

TIEPOLO (left)
St Thecla delivering the city of Este from the plague, 1759
Instead of the typically Baroque drama of the early altarpieces, Tiepolo's late *modelli*, or prior sketches, for religious canvases show airy, shimmering brushwork. (He left the full-scale work to be done by assistants.) They are, however, more solemn than his frescos – in approach recognizably Counter-Reformation art.

TIEPOLO (right)
The banquet of Cleopatra and Anthony, detail of the Palazzo Labia ballroom, 1745-50
The greatest influence on Tiepolo was Veronese: his complex illusionism at the Villa Maser, Venice, and the animated spectacle of his famous vast *Banquet* pictures lie behind the Palazzo Labia frescos.

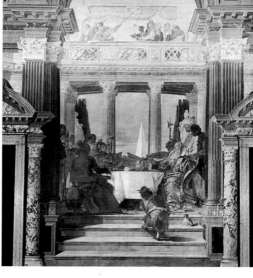

TIEPOLO (right)
Olympus with the four quarters of the Earth, detail of the ceiling of the *Treppenhaus*, Würzburg, 1752-53
Tiepolo exalts the four continents then known – Africa, Europe, America, Asia – in a cosmorama of races, costumes, flora and fauna, in which mythical and allegorical figures commingle with living persons. Apollo, in the middle, pays homage before the portrait of the Prince-Bishop. The group below, symbolizing Europe, includes the artist and his son Domenico.

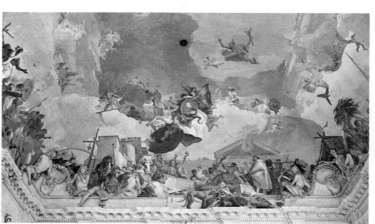

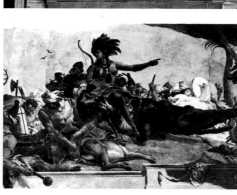

TIEPOLO
America, in the *Treppenhaus*, Würzburg
On each of the four walls is represented a continent: this splendid woman in a feathered head-dress is the personification of America.

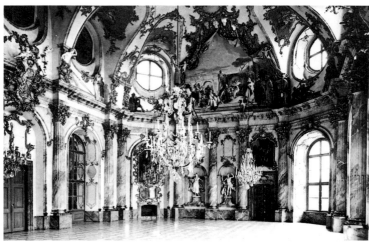

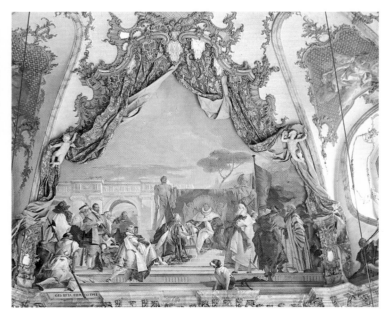

NEUMANN AND TIEPOLO
(above) The *Kaisersaal* in
the Residenz, Würzburg,
1751-52

TIEPOLO (below)
*Apollo leads Beatrice
to Barbarossa*, in the
Kaisersaal, Würzburg

TIEPOLO (right)
*The marriage of Beatrice
and Barbarossa*, in the
Kaisersaal, Würzburg

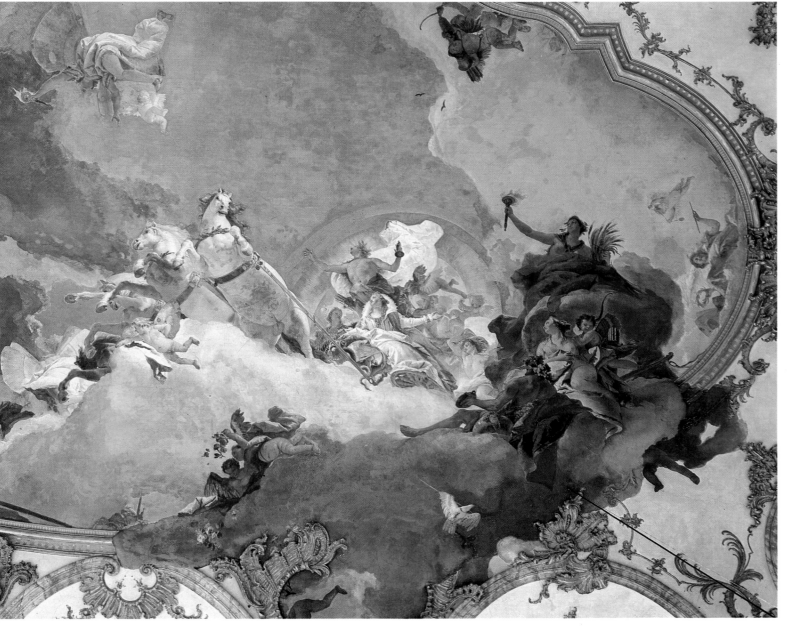

GAINSBOROUGH:
Mary, Countess Howe

Thomas Gainsborough (1727-88) painted Lady Howe's portrait about 1763-64. The sitter, the wife of a naval officer later to become one of Britain's heroes, was in her early thirties, the painter a little older, just settling into his assured maturity. The portrait was painted in the fashionable spa of Bath, where Gainsborough had moved from his native Suffolk in 1759. His early portraits in Suffolk had been of the provinces, a little naive and tending to the awkward, but both direct and delicately sensitive. He had already produced masterpieces with these qualities, such as the small-scale *Mr and Mrs Andrews* of about 1748, doubtless a marriage portrait, which unites the vivid young couple with an equally vivid portrait of the fertile sunlit Suffolk corn country. For the fashionable clientèle of Bath a more fully resolved sophisticated elegance was necessary, and for it Gainsborough deliberately evolved an appropriate style, inspired above all by the example of van Dyck.

In a very early portrait of his Bath period, the *Mrs Philip Thicknesse* of 1760, the pose is developed from a precedent by van Dyck into spiralling Rococo movement. Original and essentially informal compared with most society portraiture, it was disconcerting as such to some contemporaries. "A most extraordinary figure, handsome and bold", commented one, "but I should be very sorry to have anyone I loved set forth in such a manner." Four or five years later the image of Lady Howe, no less original and equally paying homage to van Dyck, is stabilized in a more orthodox decorum, but with that bewitching ease of informality within formality, in which none have surpassed Gainsborough. The difficult marriage of a literal likeness ("the principal beauty of a portrait", said Gainsborough once, perhaps in peevish response to his rival Reynolds' insistence on generalizing) with the urgency of his almost fluid handling of colour in paint is here magisterially consummated. Lady Howe is at once of flesh and blood, and a shimmering cascade of pinks and greys. The hat, so lovingly dwelt upon, adds a touch of chinoiserie. The landscape has dissolved away from the factual account of the Andrews painting, and is perhaps the least satisfactory part of the composition: the silver birch, a complementary vertical to the sitter's figure, is an afterthought.

A little later, in his most famous portrait, "*The Blue Boy*", Gainsborough made his most explicit homage to van Dyck. It was painted not as a commission but for the artist's own pleasure, though he showed it at the Academy in 1770. The subject was a friend, Jonathan Buttall, the dress a van Dyckian studio prop –

the fancy dress fashionable with sitters at the time and used by many painters other than Gainsborough, including Reynolds. The result, a sophisticated romantic vision, shows all the fluency with which Gainsborough's style was opening out. Here landscape and figure are fully integrated, echoing each other in their rhythm. Gainsborough had a passion for music, and in contrast to Reynolds' more theoretical and literary bent, his genius demands a musical analogy. "One part of a picture ought to be like the first part of a tune ... you can guess what follows, and that makes the second part of the tune." Reynolds, in his tribute to Gainsborough after his death, indicated much the same, praising "his manner of forming all the parts of his picture together; the whole thing going on at the same time, in the same manner as Nature creates her works".

In the final phase of Gainsborough's career, in London, where he moved in 1774, his style became ever more fluent, free and open. His loyalty to the likeness remained – as in *Mrs Siddons*, seen as an imperious lady of fashion in remarkable contrast to Reynolds' apotheosis of the same sitter as a tragic heroine. Gainsborough at his most inspired, his most original, as in the flickering, shimmering vision of "*The Morning Walk*", seems to merge his sitters into the landscape as in a happy dream.

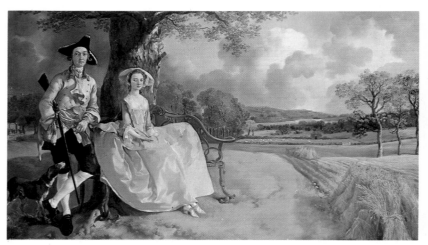

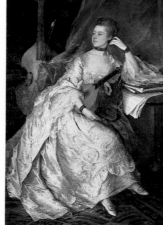

GAINSBOROUGH (left)
Mrs Philip Thicknesse, 1760
Gainsborough's style was nourished by van Dyck and some French Rococo. This portrait could be set beside Boucher's images of *Mme de Pompadour*, but its nervous intensity differentiates it.

GAINSBOROUGH (below)
"*The Morning Walk*" (Mr and Mrs Hallett), 1785
Gainsborough's animated brushwork drew comment from Reynolds – "those odd scratches and marks ...this chaos which by a kind of magic at a certain distance assumes form".

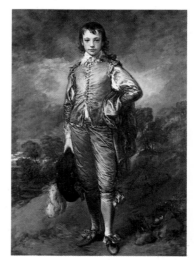

GAINSBOROUGH (above)
Mr and Mrs Andrews, c.1748
At heart a landscapist who earned his living "in the Face way", Gainsborough started his career painting precise conversation pieces closely comparable with the work of Devis.

GAINSBOROUGH (left)
"*The Blue Boy*", c.1770
Gainsborough worked with very long brushes, in oils thinned to the consistency of watercolour, to achieve his shimmering effects.

GAINSBOROUGH (right)
Mrs Sarah Siddons, 1785
"Damn the nose, there's no end of it", Gainsborough is reported to have remarked. He uses it to enhance the presence of the sitter, shapes it into the nature of her imposing beauty.

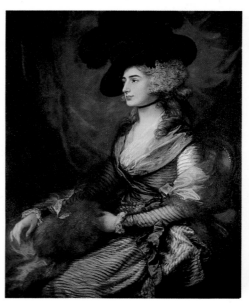

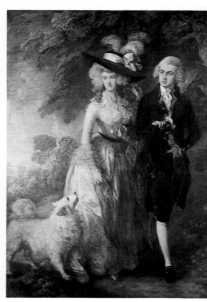

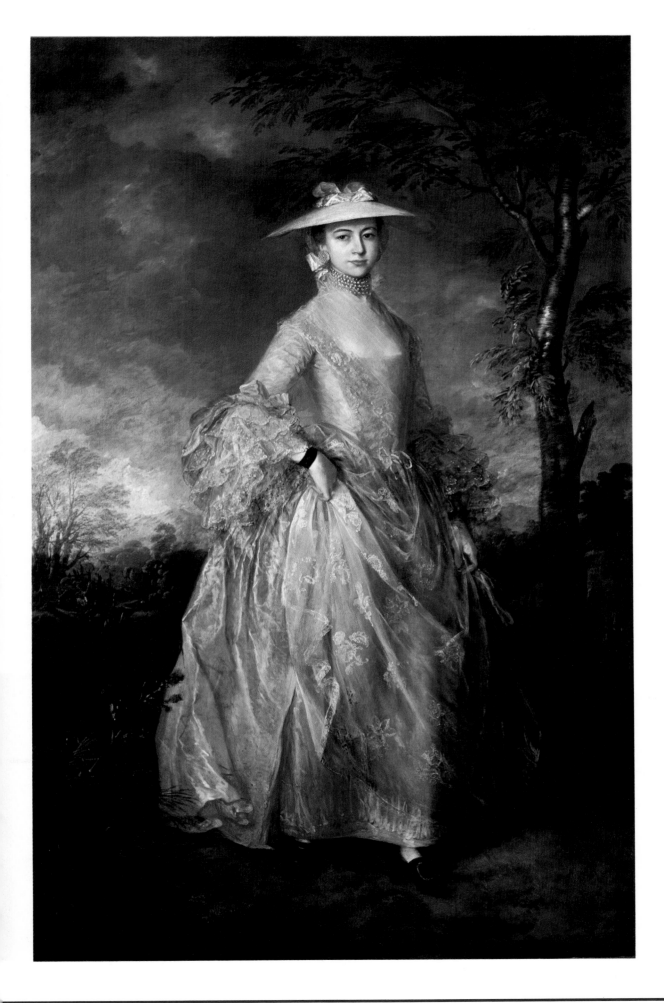

GAINSBOROUGH
Mary, Countess Howe,
c. 1763-64

GOYA:
The Colossus

GOYA

The Disasters of War:
(right) *This is how it is;*
(below) *This is worse,*
*c.*1810-15
Goya's mixed technique
of etching and aquatint
produced the equivalent of
a pen-and-wash drawing;
by drawing the human body,
dead or mutilated, in the
unimpassioned idiom of
Flaxman's illustrations to
the classics, he intensified
the horror. Certainly the
war brought atrocities, but
these etchings (first published after Goya's death)
seem as much a reflection
of a personal sensibility as
anti-war propaganda.

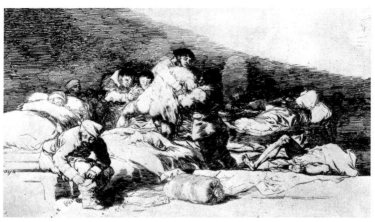

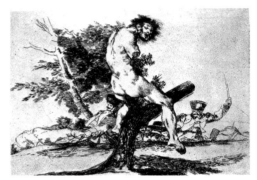

GOYA (below right)
Los Caprichos, plate 43:
The sleep of Reason, 1799
A preliminary drawing has
apparently direct echoes
of Fuseli's *Nightmare* of
1781, but these do not
persist in the etching. The
table on which the figure
rests is inscribed: *The
sleep of Reason produces
monsters*; and the message
is defined in the subtitle:
*Imagination abandoned by
Reason produces impossible
monsters; united with her,
she is the mother of the arts.*

It is a visionary image;
its subject is creativity,
and in theme and import
the image is quintessentially
Romantic: reason is a vital
control but the life-giving
impulse is imagination, here
breeding unchecked, with
no hint that the sleeper will
awake, and the monsters be
dispelled. The sole fact
alleviating the pessimism is
that the artist, Goya, could
realize and control this
vision in such memorable
form within the symmetry
of a rectangle of paper.

GOYA (right)
The straw manikin, 1791-92
Even before his illness, and
in public commissions, hints
of his "black" imagination
appear in Goya's art. *The
straw manikin* was one of
a series of cartoons for
tapestries to be woven in
the royal factory. Scenes
of pastoral country life
were required, and Goya
shows women performing a
ritual in a peasant festival.
Yet the manikin looks like
a human victim, and in the
faces of the women there is
something quirkily inhuman.

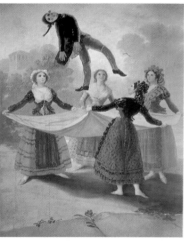

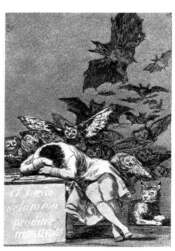

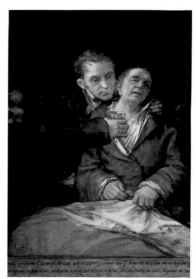

GOYA (right)
Saturn, 1820
In the "Black Paintings"
Goya realized in paint the
unelucidated visions of his
private infernal mythology
on the walls of his living-
rooms. He chose to paint
in his dining-room Saturn
devouring his offspring
(a rare classical subject
amid what baffled visitors
described as *caprichos*).

GOYA (left)
*Self-portrait with Dr
Arrieta*, 1820
Compassionate, but blind to
Goya's demons, the doctor
holds up the glass with a
firm, supporting right arm
(emphatically horizontal).
Goya inscribed his gratitude
on the painting and gave it
to his doctor, but also made
copies of it for himself.

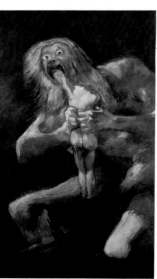

Goya painted *The colossus* (originally called
The giant) in the years 1808-12, that is in the
period when Spain took the full brunt of the
Napoleonic Wars for the first time. Characteristically enigmatic and mysterious as the image
is, there are grounds for thinking it as much a
reflection on war as his famous etchings, *The
Disasters of War*, the first of which date from
about 1810. Lines from a poem by Juan
Arriaza about the wars have been identified as
a possible stimulus for Goya's image: "On a
height above yonder cavernous amphitheatre a
pale colossus rises, caught by the fiery light of
the setting sun; the Pyrenees are a humble
plinth for his gigantic limbs." *The colossus*
may represent the emergent spirit of a defiant
Spain against French invasion, but, if so, the
people in the picture do not seem confident of
success. A related mezzotint (not shown) of a
giant seated solitary on a low horizon, brooding, dates from about the same period or rather
later. Otherwise *The colossus* must speak for
itself. The painting is not physically colossal
(some 1.5 metres (5ft) high), but its impact
certainly is, achieved by the dramatic clash of
opposing scales and values. Probably, as in so
much of Goya's work, it is more a general, non-
partisan statement on the human condition, an
allegory of human impotence.

In a famous plate in the series of etchings *Los
Caprichos* (or Phantasmagoria, 1796-98), there
is a similar clash of reality and surreality. The
artist is seen slumped in sleep, and surely
nightmare, with a host of bat-winged monsters
battering at him. A grave illness in 1793 had
left Goya virtually stone deaf; turned inwards
by the consequent isolation upon the tumult of
his own mind, he became increasingly obsessed with the spectres that thronged his
imagination. *The Disasters of War*, in which
the most appalling miseries and tortures that
man can inflict on man are vividly and ruthlessly rendered, conveys not so much com-
passion or anger or patriotic fervour as an
appalled fascination and a resigned horror:
This is how it is, read several captions. But then
the plate showing a man impaled on a splintered tree-trunk, his arms severed, has the
laconic subscription: *This is worse*.

Goya's addiction to the abnormal and violent expressed itself elsewhere, in his scenes of
asylums, of religious flagellants, of witchcraft.
The accumulating agony and exhaustion of
Goya's inner world are mirrored vividly in a
late *Self-portrait* showing the artist in the arms
of the doctor who nursed him during a second
crucial illness in 1819, with omnipresent demonic figures hovering in the murk of the
background. The last manifestation of his
morbid obsessions was the famous "Black
Paintings" Goya concocted to adorn the interiors of his own house on his retirement. To
be condemned to live surrounded by these
paintings would be a fearsome sentence, but
Goya chose as it were to paper his house with
them. Painted very broadly, often with the
palette knife rather than the brush, in dark and
sombre tones, they closely anticipate in their
mood and hideous violence the savage pessimism of twentieth-century Expressionism.
Goya's genius was recognized again in the age
of Manet and Baudelaire, but his "Black
Paintings" appeal specifically to our own.

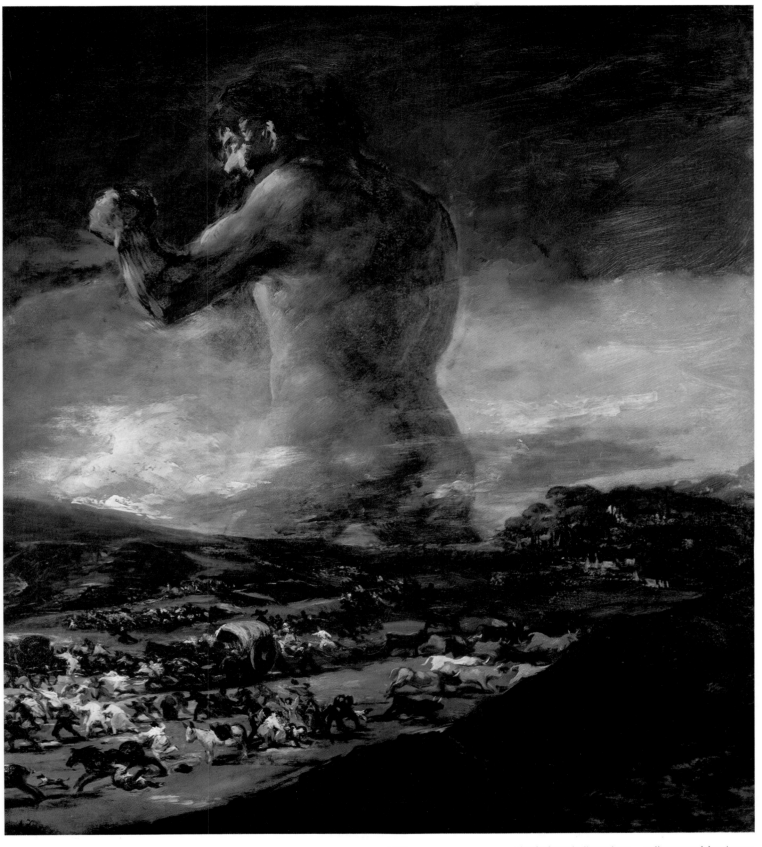

GOYA
The colossus, 1808-12
The naked colossus is from
one world, the scattering,
running figures in the foreground belong to our puny
planet (only a donkey is unmoved by the panic). Yet the

giant's threat is directed not
overtly against the men and
women below, but against
a force, presumably on his
own scale, out of view on
the left. Superhuman forces
engaged in their own titanic
conflict disrupt and destroy

ordinary people's existence
almost haphazardly. Painted
in a very free technique,
the giant looms upward
phantom-like through cloud,
while the fleeing men and
animals are shaped more
solidly in a swift impasto.

CONSTABLE:
The White Horse

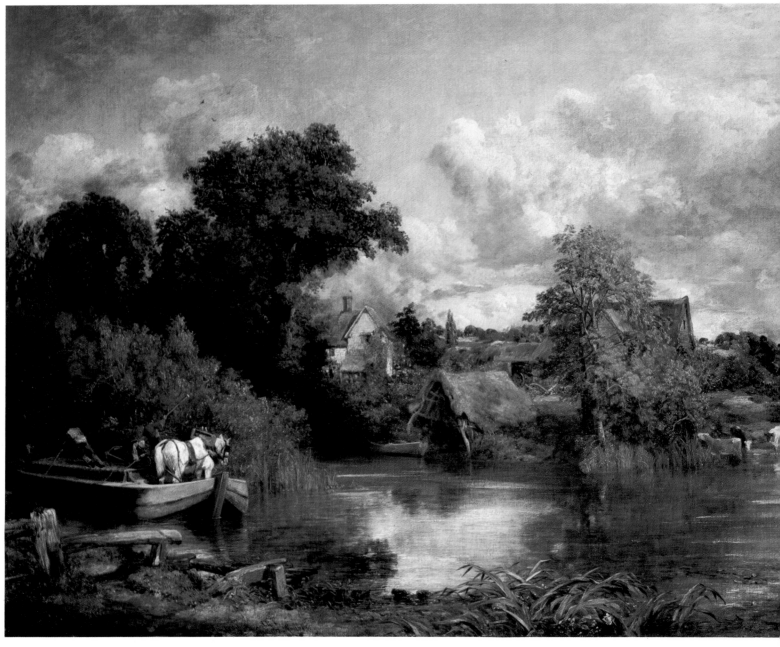

In late 1819 John Constable (1776-1837) was at last elected an Associate of the Royal Academy and was able to sign his latest work, now known as *"The White Horse"*, as A.R.A. The painting remained one of the artist's favourites throughout his life, and in 1829 he bought it back from its first buyer. When exhibited in 1819, it had been greeted with enthusiasm by the critics – "what a grasp of everything beautiful in rural scenery", wrote one, predicting that "this young artist" would soon be at the top of his profession. The "young artist", however, was already 42, and success was coming late. Full membership of the Academy came only in 1829, after the most fruitful decade of his life had come to a close with the death of his wife in 1828, and he himself died nine years later.

Constable had been a slow starter. Son of a Suffolk mill-owner of some substance, he began full training at the Royal Academy schools in London when already 23. Although he always deplored the imitation by artists of earlier painters, he loved and often copied them, Claude as well as Gainsborough, though his affinity to the Dutch masters, to Ruisdael and Hobbema, is perhaps greater.

Constable insisted that the essential source for any original painter must be Nature itself, and that there was no alternative to drawing directly from Nature. His conviction was the foundation of his art, and of his own highly personal style, which became mature only by about 1810, when he was in his 30s. It did not mean that all his work was done in the open air, but he made endless studies, in pencil, in watercolour or in brilliantly free impressions in oil on paper or small wood panels, directly from his subject. Afterwards he used their material in building up his large compositions (what he called his "six-footers"), and for the famous *Haywain*, begun in 1821, he worked through a whole series of compositional variations, from a miniature scale to sketches equal in size to the finished painting. It was an experimental, pragmatic process, and the interrelationship of all these variations is often unclear, but Constable was adamant (though posterity does not always agree) that the finished painting was the climax of the process.

His longing was always to distil the eternal from the ephemeral, and to reveal what he loved to call the chiaroscuro in Nature, the interlocking harmony of the elements. Constable knew Wordsworth, whose poetry answered his painting, and quoted a phrase of his when describing his wish to make monumental "one brief moment caught from fleeting time". Empathy with Nature in all its moods informed them both, though Constable found his inspiration in the domestic, man-made landscapes of his native Suffolk, of Hampstead Heath or in the beaches of Brighton, rather than in the mountains and lakes Wordsworth loved. If there is ever an awesome quality in Constable's work it is in the skies, and in the

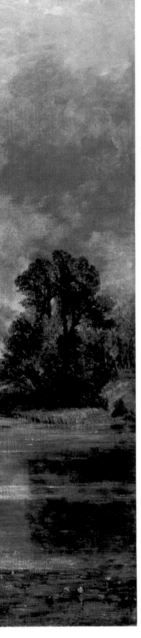

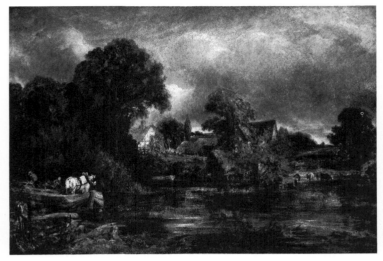

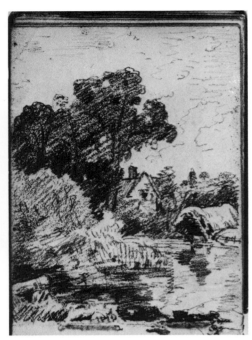

CONSTABLE (above)
Oil-sketch for *"The
White Horse"*, c. 1819
Constable made a full-
scale study in oil before
painting his Academy
entry – a procedure he
later elaborated. This
sketch corresponds less
closely to the finished work
than the several oil-studies
for the later *Haywain*, and
less closely also to prior
studies made from Nature.

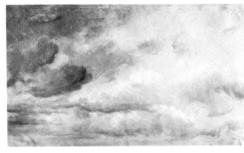

CONSTABLE (left)
"The White Horse", 1819
The first of Constable's
"six-footers" – huge works
devoted to mundane rustic
scenes – the picture com-
pelled immediate attention,
if only for its size: such a
humble subject had never
before been presented on
such an heroic scale. It was
shown under the title *A
scene on the river Stour*,
"a placid representation
of a serene, grey morning,
summer". The barge-horse
is being ferried across the
river between Flatford
and Dedham in Suffolk at
a point where a tributary
interrupted the towpath.

CONSTABLE (left)
Clouds, Sept. 5th, 1822
Constable's series of
cloud studies typifies his
almost scientific attempt
to capture permanently
the momentary in Nature.

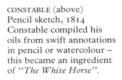

CONSTABLE (above)
Pencil sketch, 1814
Constable compiled his
oils from swift annotations
in pencil or watercolour –
this became an ingredient
of *"The White Horse"*.

CONSTABLE (left)
The haywain, 1821
Constable's view of the
house of a close friend, on
the Stour near Flatford
Mill, was distilled from
long acquaintance, from
studies made over many
years, proving his heartfelt
attachment to the scene.
His emotional involvement
with landscape was intense:
he wrote: "The sound of
water escaping from
milldams, etc., willows, old
rotten planks, slimy posts,
and brickwork – I love
such things. . . . Painting
with me is but another word
for feeling." The lavish
scattering of highlights,
"Constable's snow", which
give vibrancy to the work,
puzzled contemporaries.

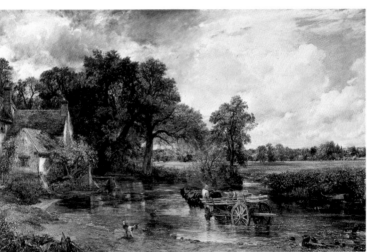

mood created by qualities of light – as in the
small watercolour of *Stonehenge* with its
double rainbow. Constable's love of Nature
was both intense and true and faithful: he
wrote: "Painting is a science and should be
pursued as an enquiry into the laws of
Nature". His "experiments" included studies
of types of cloud formations, and his results
were attempts to establish, in free, swift, open
brushwork, the equivalent on canvas of English sunlight running through moist air, the
wind rustling foliage and wimpling the water.

Constable's deepest impact, and his warm-
est reception, was in fact in France. *The
haywain* was singled out by Géricault at the
Academy in 1821 and in 1824 French critics
acclaimed his work at the Paris Salon. Delacroix, entranced by Constable's light aerial
key, reworked the background of his *Massacre
at Chios* (see p. 209), and Constable's poetry of
the ordinary later had effect on the rural
meditations of the Barbizon school.

CONSTABLE (right)
Stonehenge, 1836
Ever more vigorous and
masterly effects are evident
in Constable's later works,
especially in this water-
colour view of the inher-
ently dramatic "Druidic"
megaliths of Stonehenge.
A gleaming sky highlights
the grey stones, revealing
the artist's aim "to give
'to one brief moment caught
from fleeting time' a lasting and sober existence, and
to render permanent many
of these splendid but evanescent exhibitions, which
are ever occurring in the
changes of external Nature".

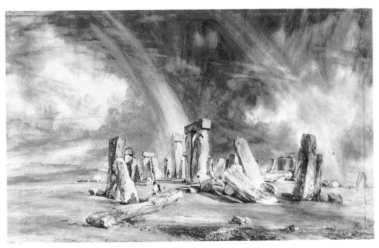

TURNER:
Dawn after the Wreck

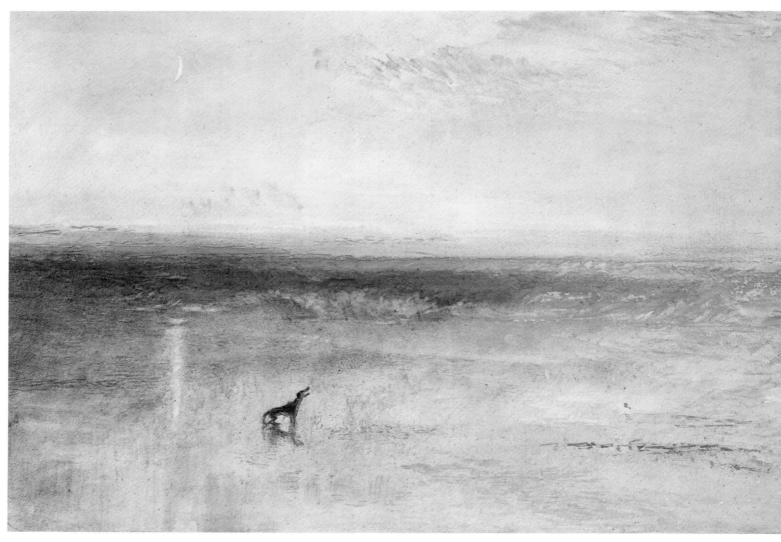

The sea, stretching to the horizon and beyond, illimitable as the skies above, is one of the elemental images of Romanticism. It compelled many artists to paint it, yet remained essentially indefinable – seeming, in an evening calm, to suggest a peace beyond understanding, but in storm one of the most formidable agents of inhuman, destructive power in Nature. The career of Joseph Mallord William Turner (1775-1851) was a long one, but through almost all of it he was obsessed by the sea in all its moods, though most of all by its more violent aspects.

Dawn after the wreck is a watercolour painted with the full freedom of Turner's later years, probably about 1840. It belonged originally to a friend, the Rev. Kingsley, but it may well have started as one of what he called his "beginnings", and not necessarily with the idea of being worked up into a "finished" picture for framing and hanging on a wall. Turner kept sketchbooks all his life (all left to the nation, amongst 19,000 or so watercolours, and now in the British Museum). In the later books, hundreds of colour sketches record atmospheric effects, many of which may read to the modern eye as pure abstracts; already in 1799 he told a colleague he had "no settled process", but "drove the colours about till he had expressed the idea in his mind". *Dawn after the wreck* may well have started with

Turner snatching at an effect of turbulence of light and colour and painting very fast, perhaps with the aid of the sharp end of the brush, even fingers. The stability of the composition hangs on the strong yet disturbed horizontal of the horizon, transfixed by the tremulous reflection suspended from the frail sickle of the new moon, which together with the flecks of cloud defines the sky as sky. Then the addition of the title spelled out the Romantic desolation; the sea, the victorious destroyer, subsides, passion all but spent. And possibly after that came the shivering dog with its almost audible howl of mourning.

Turner was very precocious. He started traditionally, as a travelling topographical draughtsman and watercolourist. He exhibited *Tintern Abbey*, a drawing of literal linear accuracy and great accomplishment, in the Royal Academy in 1795, when he was only 20. Unlike Constable, he was able to make himself acceptable to the art establishment and public very early: he was a full Academician by 1802 – a recognition denied Constable, born one year later, until 1829. Gradually, however, as he developed towards an ever greater freedom, his work began to mystify most people. His later pictures were called "fantastic puzzles", but were nonetheless based on the faithful observation of Nature. The first of his famous vortex compositions, *Snowstorm: Hannibal*

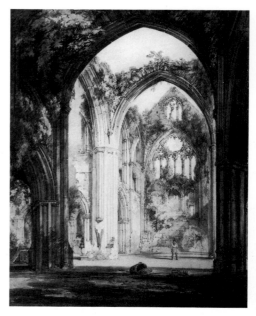

TURNER (above)
Tintern Abbey, c. 1795
Together with Girtin, Turner had copied watercolours by John Robert Cozens – *Tintern Abbey*

reflects the influence of Cozens' wistful tonalities. Such Picturesque views contributed significantly to Turner's income, and first made him known abroad.

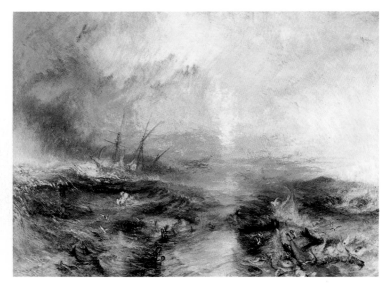

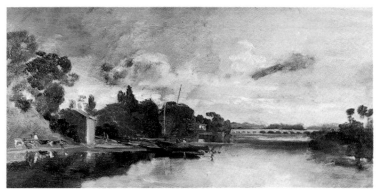

TURNER (left)
The slave-ship, 1840
Turner reacted emotionally
to a recent scandal in which
a slave-ship's captain had
thrown overboard those of
his "cargo" dying of fever.

TURNER (below)
*Snowstorm: Hannibal
crossing the Alps*, 1812
Turner attempted to show
the truth of natural fury,
rather than exaggerating
its scale, like John Martin.

TURNER (above)
*The Thames near Walton
Bridge*, c. 1807
Turner seldom sketched
in oil in the open air. This
exception may pre-empt
innovations by Constable.

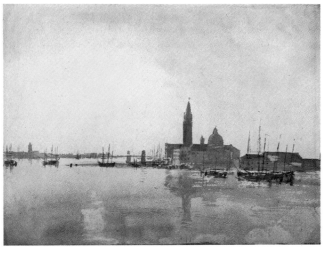

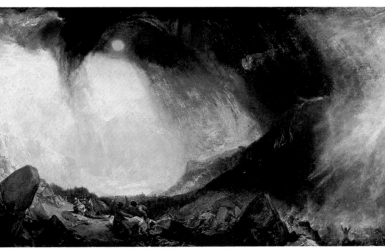

TURNER (below)
*Sun rising through vapour:
fishermen cleaning and
selling fish*, 1807
The seascapes and harbour
scenes of Cuyp and van de
Velde challenged Turner at
the beginning of his career.
Determined not just to rival
but to excel these masters,
he adopted similar subject
matter, but introduced his
own concern with elusive
effects of natural light.

TURNER (above)
*Venice: S. Giorgio
Maggiore*, 1819
Turner's first visit to Italy
in 1819 was a revelation of
light and colour, a decisive
event in his career. The
freedom of these water-
colours indicates a direct
and revolutionary response
to the haunting, luminous
atmospherics of Venice,
held in pure transparent
tints on a white ground.

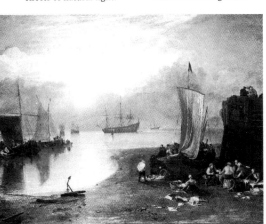

crossing the Alps, 1812, was based on a violent
storm he had witnessed two years before in
Yorkshire. In an overarching, overwhelming
paroxysm, Nature rears in all its blind force, in
the biting fury and flurry of snow, cloud and
ice. At the other extreme, his *Burning of the
Houses of Parliament* (1835; not shown) shows
light and fire threatening to consume not only
the centre of Government but the earth and
water as well. Gradually his basic theme
became light itself, in an almost Shiva-like
capacity as creator and destroyer – creator, by
revealing the physical world, destroyer, by
dissolving solid form in luminous veils of
colour. Already in 1816 the writer Hazlitt
complained that Turner's paintings were "representations not properly of the objects of
Nature as of the medium through which they
were seen". It was part of Turner's achievement successfully to transpose into oils the
technique of watercolour, with all its lightness
and fluency, and ability to capture the most
fleeting, evanescent atmospheric effects.

Though the public found such works eccentric ("pictures of nothing, and very like it"),
Turner painted a whole series of pictures,
spread over many years, in which he self-
consciously and provocatively allied himself to
the European tradition, challenging Claude
and Poussin, Cuyp and van de Velde, Wilson,
even Titian, Veronese and Rembrandt. In

paintings such as *The slave-ship*, 1840, he
evoked marine catastrophe in terms surpassing
Géricault's celebrated *Raft of the Medusa* –
here the tormented seas are laced with human
blood. In contrast, his paintings (not shown) of
Norham Castle, made in the early 1840s, are
rich with a radiant serenity, and make a
fascinating comparison with the very similar
viewpoints he had selected at the same site in
the late 1790s: these early watercolours had
been romantic enough, but in the late full-scale
oils the subject is dissolved into insubstantial
mists of glowing, shimmering colour, in which
castle or cattle are mere accents subsumed into
emanations of light.

In his lifetime Turner was recognized as a
genius who might be criticized but not denied,
and in John Ruskin (1819-1900) he found a
sympathetic critic and panegyrist of genius. In
Modern Painters, 1843, Ruskin placed Turner,
as the artist who could most stirringly and
truthfully measure the moods of Nature, at the
culmination of a tradition stemming from
Dürer and the Venetian colourists. Turner and
Constable dominated the subsequent course of
landscape in England, and both were acclaimed in France, though Turner rather later.
The Impressionists took respectful note, if
with reservations; and his work has continued
to have reverberations, not least in the abstract
painting of the later twentieth century.

FRIEDRICH:
Man and Woman Gazing at the Moon

Caspar David Friedrich (1774-1840) has shown the man and woman from behind, beheld by us as they themselves behold the moon. Our own position is uncertain, since we see them from above; no stabilizing foreground links us. They are alone together, as almost all Friedrich's figures are alone, as if alienated, silent, their faces unseen. Beyond them, the moon rides remote in infinity.

The picture is replete with Friedrich's personal symbolic imagery. Thus, for him, the moon represents Christ. The pine trees (Christian faith on earth) are traversed by a stony path (the path of life) winding uphill (towards Christian redemption). The shattered and dying oak tree and the dolmen represent transience and paganism, while the dark abyss falling away to the right shows the way down to temptation and unbelief. However, the impact of the picture is far from being entirely dependent on the spelling out of its symbolism. The success of Friedrich's finest paintings rests on their vivid visual coherence, their credibility as real topographical sites.

The painting is a variation on a design which obsessed Friedrich throughout his career, and which had been established in the haunting solitudes of *Moonrise over the sea* of 1822, in which Friedrich repeats with only slight variations a version of 1819, *Two men contemplating the moon*; here the two men of the *Moonrise* are replaced by the artist himself and his wife. The theme reached its most complex elaboration in *The stages of life* of 1835.

All Friedrich's work is religious, the most astonishing example coming early in his career, *The Cross in the mountains* of 1808, known as the Tetschen altar. It was in fact used as an altarpiece, though it is a landscape, which caused controversy. The sun sets, the old order passes, its last gleams transmuted in the golden figure of Christ on the crucifix, while the rock symbolizes steadfast faith in Christ. The mood has a serene, even optimistic quality unusual in Friedrich's work. The famous *Abbey graveyard under snow*, with the gaunt Gothic choir rising in a snowy graveyard amongst shattered trees, is more typical. Terrifying in its bleak mystery, it is one of the most haunting images of European Romanticism.

Friedrich's predilection for Gothic forms has no doubt some nationalistic significance, and his work included positive references to the German struggle for freedom against Napoleon. But Friedrich's art was essentially nontopical, visionary. "The artist should not only paint what he sees before him, but also what he sees within him. If, however, he sees nothing within him, then he should also omit to paint what he sees before him".

In the 1812 painting of Friedrich by Georg Friedrich Kersting (1785-1847), the artist is seen in an austerely empty studio, summoning up his picture from within himself rather than from outside. Friedrich was nevertheless a close and precise observer of Nature, as a great many drawings make clear. The detailed precision of his drawing reinforces his startling contrast of the mundane with the unearthly. His people may appear in frock-coat or dress and bonnet – dressed, as it were, for office or shopping – but poised on the brink confronting eternity. Usually his figures are unemphatic, often seen from behind. They are simply and exactly described, yet such is their still intensity that the effect is transcendental.

Friedrich's technique could seem somewhat dry; painterly virtuosity, the sensuous delight in the painter's materials, was always strictly subordinated to the image to be produced, in a style descriptive rather than expressive, so that he was for long condemned as a literary painter. Many of his paintings are of twilight or dusk or moonlight, but in fact he was a most subtle colourist. He lived out his life quietly in Dresden, and the considerable attention that his work had at first attracted dwindled, until at his death he was almost neglected – and so he remained until the 1890s, when the Symbolists rediscovered the formidable potency of his imagery. Indeed, echoes of Friedrich are to be found in the greatest of the northern Expressionists, Edvard Munch. Friedrich's art, in fact, was no less revolutionary than the very differently generated landscapes of Constable and Turner. The analogy of his art with Chinese landscape painting, though it cannot be pressed too far, is striking – the vision of man alone in the immensity of a natural world that is the symbol of an infinity beyond.

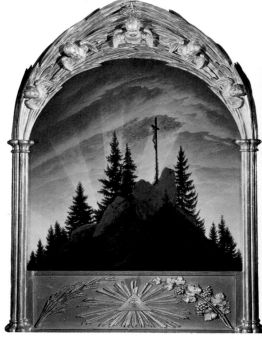

FRIEDRICH (above)
The Tetschen altar: *The Cross on the mountains*, 1808
Friedrich himself designed the gold frame. On the base, shafts of light around the eye of God echo the rays of the setting sun, while the wheat-ear and grapes refer to the Last Supper. The star above symbolizes both death and resurrection.

FRIEDRICH (below)
A dolmen near Gützkow, c. 1837
These prehistoric burial stones, stranded like wrecks in the sea of time, fascinated Friedrich: they suggested at once human transience and eternity. A dolmen occurs in the left foreground of *Man and woman gazing at the moon*.

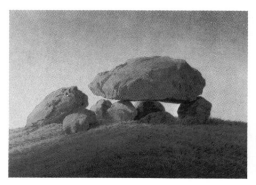

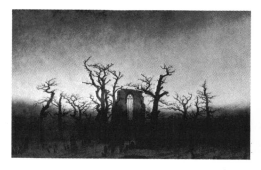

FRIEDRICH (above)
Abbey graveyard under snow, 1810
The way in which the once Picturesque attractions of the Gothic past are raised into mystical symbolism is typically Romantic. The skeletal trees and the Gothic ruin endure against time in transcendental melancholy.

A German Romantic poet, Körner, had described a similar, earlier picture as a *Totenlandschaft* (a landscape of the dead). Indeed the monks appear to be carrying a bier into the "bare ruin'd choir" of the church. A mist completes the sense of sepulchral mystery and lost faith.

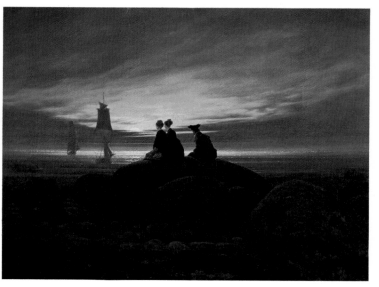

FRIEDRICH (left)
Moonrise over the sea, 1822
Though ostensibly closely observed and naturalistic, the canvas takes on a near-abstract appearance, with its vertical and horizontal axes and colour contrasts – the reddish browns of the land and the suffused bluish-purple sky. The sea without any horizon, a recurrent motif, suggests infinity and the unknown, against the familiar, homely silhouettes of the gazing townspeople.

FRIEDRICH (below): *Man and woman gazing at the moon, c.1830-35*

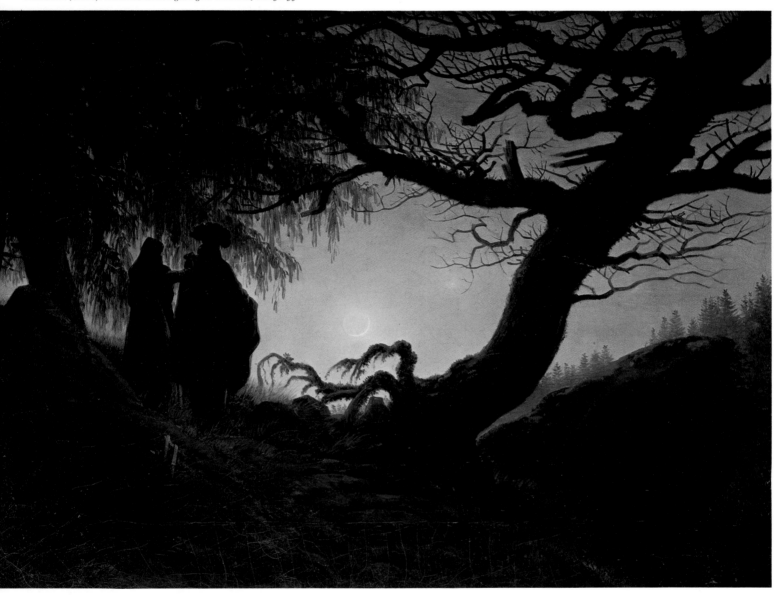

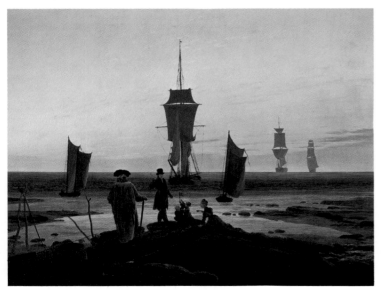

FRIEDRICH (left)
The stages of life, c.1835
This is perhaps the most
personal of all Friedrich's
images of transience. Sea
and sky shine luminously,
but soon after he painted
them Friedrich had a stroke
from which he never fully
recovered. The painter is
the old man confronting
infinite spaces, while his
children and grandchildren
stand, sit or play close by.

KERSTING (right)
*Caspar David Friedrich
in his studio*, 1812
The painter has shuttered
the lower part of his studio
window, blocking out the
world, the better to visu-
alize his inner world as he
broods over his canvas.
The bars of the window
form a Cross in the sky,
like a delicate blessing.

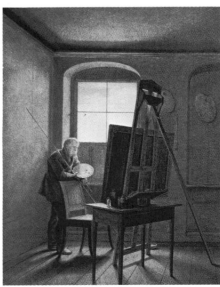

DELACROIX:
The Death of Sardanapalus

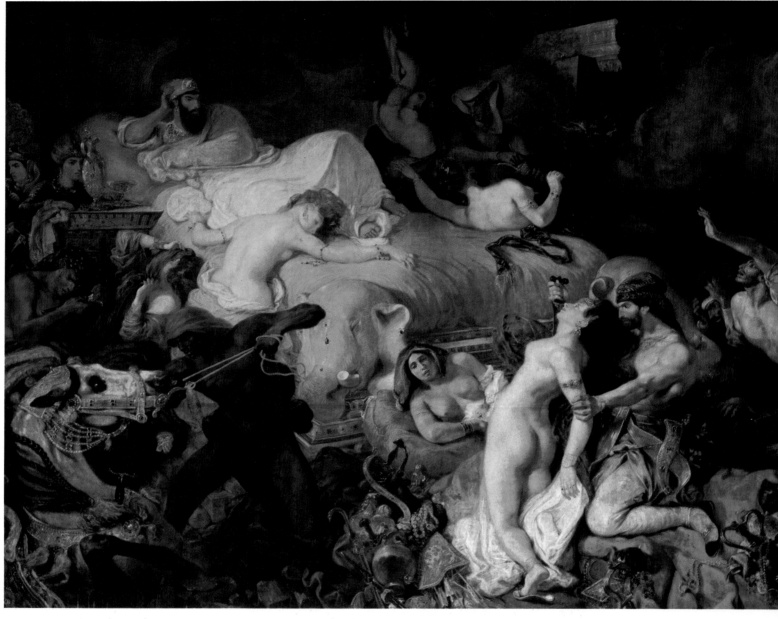

The first painting Eugène Delacroix (1798-1863) exhibited at the Salon in Paris was his almost Michelangelesque *Barque of Dante*, clearly influenced by Géricault and equally clearly in the Grand Tradition. Though it provoked some criticism it was bought for the royal collection. In 1824 he showed *The massacre at Chios*, which owed something to Gros's *Plague at Jaffa* in its heroic glamour; but while Gros had celebrated Napoleon serene in the midst of pestilence, Delacroix's *Chios* was a lament, or perhaps a celebration, of defeat. Although it was criticized for its "unfinished" quality, and its bold juxtaposition of colours seemed crude to contemporary taste, it was nevertheless bought by the state.

The death of Sardanapalus was a very different matter. It coincided in the Salon of 1827-28 with Ingres's *Apotheosis of Homer* (see p. 211) – confronting the Neoclassical principles of clarity and nobility with dynamic bravura, colour, violence, exotic subject matter, sensual passion and morbid despair – a manifesto of extreme Romanticism. Delacroix

himself called it "an Asiatic feat of arms against David's Spartiate pastiche".

Sardanapalus is from Byron's drama of the same name. Byron's hero, though certainly of a voluptuous temperament, had in fact committed a heroic, self-sacrificial suicide, but Delacroix described him thus: "Besieged in his palace by insurgents . . . Reclining on a superb bed on top of a huge pyre Sardanapalus orders the eunuchs and palace officers to cut the throats of his women and his pages, and even of his favourite horses and dogs; none of the objects that have contributed to his pleasure must survive him." Hence, a self-indulgent, almost bored figure presiding impassively over a sensual abandon of destruction, in a clash of resonant colour and collapsing shapes.

Sardanapalus represents the climax of Delacroix's developing obsession with death and pessimism, and of his pictures of doomed heroic figures in despair and defeat; and his style was now fully evolved to deal with them – the movement of the paint itself, the chords of colour, being integral to the expression of the

artist's emotion. Delacroix clearly identified himself very closely with Sardanapalus; unlike Géricault's *Raft of the Medusa* (based on a real event) this is a work of personal fantasy, and ultimately remote from reality – no drop of blood obtrudes, for all its violence. Yet it is typical of Delacroix that the artist's involvement is balanced by a disciplined detachment, and the whirl of flesh and pleasure and colour spinning out from Sardanapalus is held within a controlled composition. But public reaction was violently hostile, and Delacroix himself had doubts, referring to the painting as his "retreat from Moscow" and keeping it thereafter unseen in his studio until his death.

In 1830 Revolution displaced the last of the Bourbon monarchs and installed the so-called "citizen-king" Louis-Philippe. Delacroix was a conservative in politics, a cool, impeccable dandy in society, and not one to participate on the barricades, but he painted the spirit of revolution, *Liberty leading the people*. The picture found favour: henceforward he was relatively secure in official patronage.

DELACROIX (left)
The death of Sardanapalus,
1827

DELACROIX (below)
The massacre at Chios, 1824
Byron, whom Delacroix
admired, had passionately
identified with the cause
of enslaved Greece; and yet
Delacroix shows an episode
from the War of Liberation
with a curious ambiguity:
the Turks' indifference is
as striking as the inertia of
their victims. Fatalistic
figures mostly recline in
a fresh, brilliant landscape.

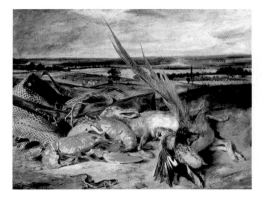

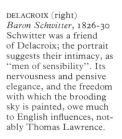

DELACROIX (left)
Still life with a lobster,
1827
The conjunction of still
life and landscape is somewhat bizarre: exhibited in
the Salon in the same year
as *Sardanapalus,* it seems
to intend another kind of
antithesis to Neoclassical
theory and practice. The
tartan plaid among the
disparate objects reflects
Delacroix's current anglo-
philia: he had spent some
months in England in 1825.

DELACROIX (right)
Baron Schwitter, 1826-30
Schwitter was a friend
of Delacroix; the portrait
suggests their intimacy, as
"men of sensibility". Its
nervousness and pensive
elegance, and the freedom
with which the brooding
sky is painted, owe much
to English influences, notably Thomas Lawrence.

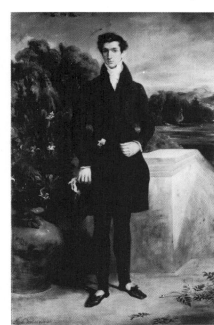

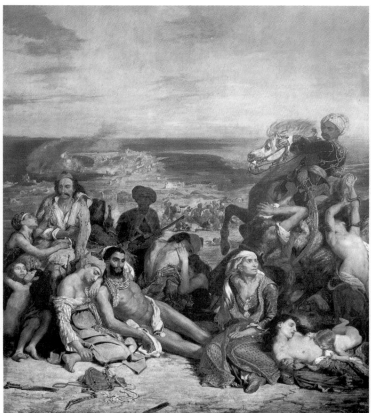

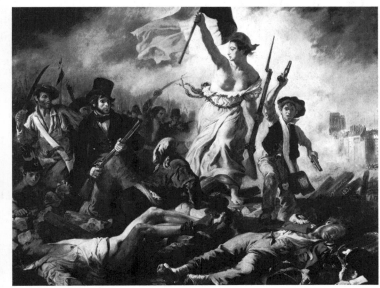

His voyage to North Africa in 1832 has been
likened to other artists' voyages to Italy. It
provided him with a source, recorded in many
sketchbooks, of exotic sensuous imagery and of
glowing colour. Its impact is summarized
in his small, famous and influential painting,
Women of Algiers, a memory of a harem
interior into which he had managed to gain
entry, a vision of languor half-asleep in voluptuous, floating colour. Violence however, was
still the theme of much of his later work, and in
an impressive series of small-scale paintings he
depicted horses, lions and tigers, symbols of
power and passion, with a vigour and intensity
rivalling Rubens. However, in his large official
commissions, he moved away from his more
Romantic obsessions. His aloof temperament
had always made him suspicious of the
publicity-conscious postures of militant Romanticism, and it may be that he is equally
significant as the writer of the most elegantly
styled and perspicacious journal in the history
of art, and as the subject of an apologia by
Baudelaire, as for the bulk of his paintings.

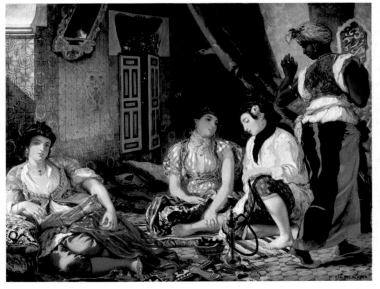

DELACROIX (above)
Liberty leading the people,
1830
Although Liberty is more
than a frigid abstraction,
and the People are workers,
not the bourgeoisie who
were in fact triumphant,
this is more a patriotic
than a specifically socialist
work. If it is restrained in
key and composition beside
Sardanapalus, it epitomizes
Romantic rebellion: per-
sonal protest has replaced
David's corporate idealism.

DELACROIX
Women of Algiers, 1834
The surface is patterned in
a close and intricate harmony
of colour, suggesting a new
attention to current theories
on colour complementaries.
The intensity of the almost
abstract design enhances
rather than dominates the
mood of subdued eroticism.
The Impressionists took
note, and so did Matisse.

INGRES:
La Grande Odalisque

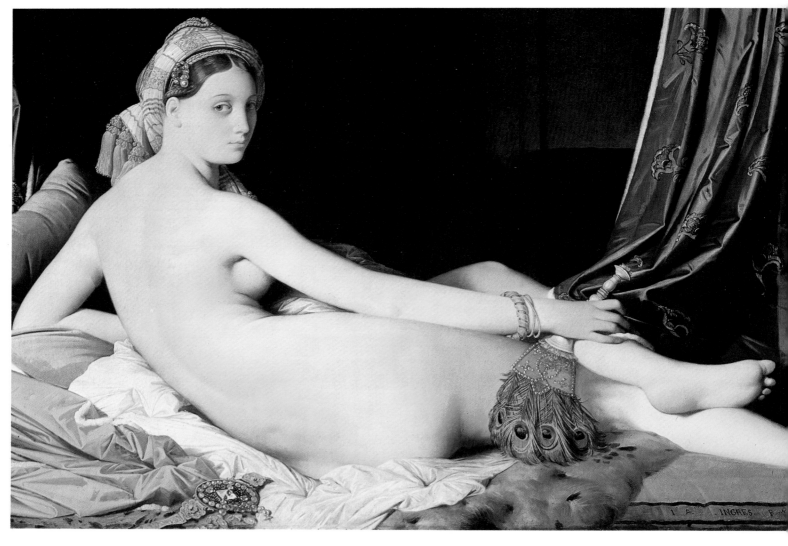

Jean Auguste Dominique Ingres (1780-1867), a pupil of David's, is said to have assisted in the painting of the famous reclining *Madame Récamier*, for which David himself seems to have made a nude study, and the pose is echoed in Ingres's own *"La Grande Odalisque"* (The concubine), painted in Rome in 1813-14. It is an essay in the long tradition of recumbent female nudes that stems from Titian's *"Venus of Urbino"* (see p. 167), and is one of many variations on Ingres's personal and so successfully realized vision of the nude. Of these the most natural and, in the objective precision of its drawing, the most classical, is the earlier *"Valpinçon Bather"* of 1808, a superbly cool study in pale flesh colours and tones of white, yet also in its secretive way intensely erotic. Ingres's famous command of line is already completely assured.

The domination of contour is in accordance with the Neoclassical principles of David, but the total impression of the *Odalisque* is of a nude seen for its own sake rather than as an illustration of any ideal or heroic theme. It departs from strict Neoclassic canons, both in subject matter and in the way it is handled. Though preceded by many assiduous studies from the life, the anatomy is unnaturalistically modified for the sake of the composition – contemporary critics observed disapprovingly

INGRES (below)
"The Valpinçon Bather",
1808
The effect of suspension of time and gravity is achieved by the diffusion of light, the insistent verticals and the refined contour of the sitter's untroubled repose.

INGRES (above)
"La Grande Odalisque"
(The concubine), 1814
The *Odalisque* was commissioned by the Queen of Naples, Napoleon's sister, but never delivered, since the Emperor's fall intervened. Ingres remained in

Rome but sent the picture to the Paris Salon of 1819, where one critic wrote: "Sworn enemy of modern schools, and infatuated with Cimabue, he has taken the dryness, crudity, simplicity and all the Gothic traits with a rare talent."

INGRES (below)
The Turkish bath, 1859-62
A description of a women's bath in Istanbul, and illustrated accounts of oriental travels, inspired Ingres's complex composition, which includes several portraits, though not of Easterners.

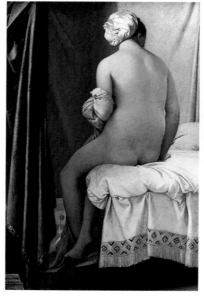

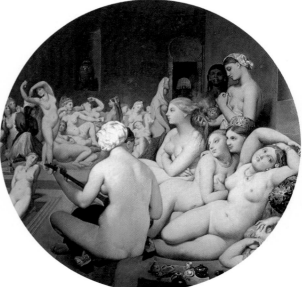

INGRES (below)
Oedipus and the Sphinx,
1808, reworked 1825
Ingres enlarged the picture
in the 1820s, filling in the
figure of the Sphinx and
adding the fugitive man,
thereby investing it with
immediacy, and stressing

the element of terror –
the horrible fate of those
who failed to solve the
riddle. Oedipus is posed
apparently in imitation of
the Antique, but Ingres
was not just a stylist: he
wrote: "I copy only from
Nature and never idealize."

INGRES (below)
*Joseph Woodhead, his wife
Harriet and her brother
Henry Comber*, 1816
Each figure is drawn with
admirable precision, each
face carefully portrayed,
traced without shading in
Ingres's unfaltering line.

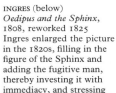

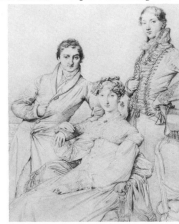

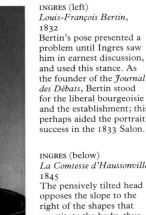

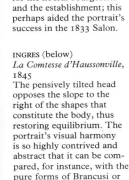

INGRES (left)
Louis-François Bertin,
1832
Bertin's pose presented a
problem until Ingres saw
him in earnest discussion,
and used this stance. As
the founder of the *Journal
des Débats*, Bertin stood
for the liberal bourgeoisie
and the establishment; this
perhaps aided the portrait's
success in the 1833 Salon.

INGRES (below)
La Comtesse d'Haussonville,
1845
The pensively tilted head
opposes the slope to the
right of the shapes that
constitute the body, thus
restoring equilibrium. The
portrait's visual harmony
is so highly contrived and
abstract that it can be compared, for instance, with the
pure forms of Brancusi or
Hepworth without ridicule.

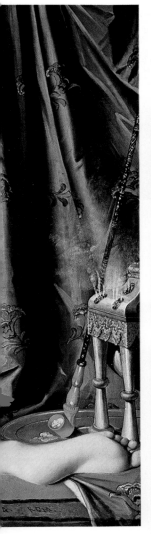

INGRES (below)
The apotheosis of Homer,
1827
Ingres attached considerable
importance to this work
(for a ceiling in the Louvre
but conceding nothing to its
position), and was hurt by
the lack of due appreciation.

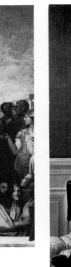

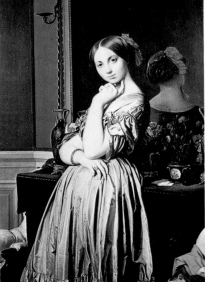

that the back had been elongated by the
equivalent of at least two vertebrae. The effect
is more closely related to the cool, smooth
eroticism of much sixteenth-century Mannerist painting than to Ingres's beloved Raphael.
When finally exhibited in Paris, the *Odalisque*
was found eccentric and bizarre. Only with
"La Source" of 1856 did Ingres produce an
image of the nude that responded entirely to
popular taste.

Ingres's obsession came to a remarkable
climax in the famous *Turkish bath*, completed
when he was 83 (as he noted beside his
signature with a natural pride). This extraordinary welter of nudes, the highly refined
result of a series of searching studies, appears
in the abstract view as a remarkable resolution
of swarming curving forms within a tondo
form. Admired by Prince Napoleon, it was
painted only a year before Manet's notorious
Olympia. Ingres's vision was apparently acceptable partly because it was clearly placed in
an exotic fantasy world.

Ingres's early career was far from an un-
mitigated popular success. Even in lucidly
drawn classical subjects, such as the *Oedipus
and the Sphinx* of 1808, there is something
strange, and the painting was criticized for
being flat and shadowless; he was accused of
being Gothic, of being *un Chinois égaré*, a
Chinaman who had lost his way. Alienated by
French censure, he spent many years in Italy
(1806-24), but in mid-career he became established and returned to Italy (1835-41) as
Director of the French Academy in Rome.
Although artists of opposing views never quite
reached the point of pitched battle, as factions
of writers did at the famous opening of Victor
Hugo's Romantic drama *Hernani*, their anta-
gonisms were ferocious, and Ingres was a man
of high and stubborn temper. At a Salon show,
after Delacroix had left, it is reported that
Ingres demanded that the windows be opened:
"I smell sulphur."

Ingres's influence was extensive and enduring over successive academic generations (but
also on Degas and even on Matisse). The vast
Apotheosis of Homer, 1827, was to remain the
model for many frigid murals. It is a response
to Raphael's *School of Athens*, laboriously and
efficiently executed as if expressly to illustrate
Winckelmann's description of "noble simplicity and calm grandeur"; but its artificiality
discourages the modern spectator.

Arguably, Ingres's most purely successful
work is that in which he was most closely
committed to his own contemporary reality.
The exquisite delicacy of his early pencil
portraits, mostly done in Italy, has rarely been
surpassed, while in minutely detailed and
highly finished parade portraits he was to
mirror the sumptuous material prosperity of
the Parisian bourgeoisie of the mid-century,
and create images of formidable monumentality. Few portrait painters illustrate better
Dostoevsky's note that the portraitist's job was
to catch his sitter at the moment when he
looked most like himself – most individual, yet
representing a whole human social type.
Baudelaire praised the *Monsieur Bertin* of 1832
and the later *Comtesse d'Haussonville* as "ideal
reconstructions of individuals".

COURBET:
The Artist's Studio

Gustave Courbet (1817-77) painted his huge *Artist's studio* (it is nearly six metres (20ft) wide) in 1854-55. He subtitled it *A real allegory, determining a phase of seven years in my artistic life* when it was first exhibited in his independent "Pavilion of Realism" at the Universal Exhibition in Paris in 1855. The critical reception was very mixed, but the 40 or so works displayed established Realism, or Courbet's personal vision of it, as a powerful movement that could not be ignored.

Courbet himself gave a long, detailed account of this painting, starting: "It is the moral and physical history of my studio." On the right are "all the shareholders, that is my friends the workers, the art collectors. On the left, the other world of trivialities – the common people, misery, poverty, wealth, the exploited, the exploiter; those who thrive on death". It is not clear either from the individual characterizations, or from Courbet's own description (intellectual rigour was never his *forte*), which represent good and which bad

in the left-hand group, but an acquaintance of Courbet's said that the seated huntsman with his dog and the farm labourers behind him stood for healthy country life. Others in the group included workers representing poverty and unemployment in the urban working classes; a destitute old republican of 1793 – all that was left of the heroic legend of Revolution and the Napoleonic Empire – a curé, an undertaker, and a pedlar hawking rubbish. The group on the right includes Courbet's loyal patron, Bruyas, the philosopher Proudhon, the writer Champfleury, and the poet and critic Baudelaire with open book. But the focus of the picture is the artist himself at work, attended by a superbly painted nude (Naked Truth), and a child (Innocence), though it is a landscape of his native Ornans region that is depicted on the easel.

The composition can be construed as a secularized *sacra conversazione* in triptych form; the plaster figure with adjacent skull, behind the canvas, appears to be a crucified

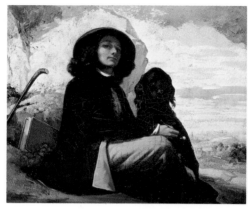

COURBET (above)
Self-portrait with a black dog, 1844
In this, Courbet's first accepted Salon picture, the subject – an informal figure in a rural setting – is in the tradition of van

Dyck and Gainsborough, but the self-assurance of the face, compounded by the low viewpoint, establishes the young man's individuality. This initiates a series of robust, extrovert *Self-Portraits* of some power.

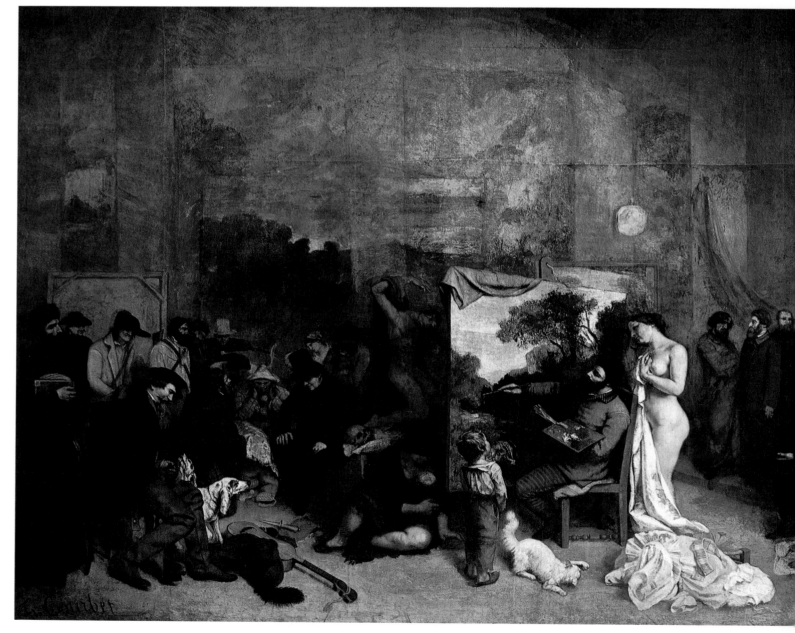

Christ. It also invites comparison with that Neoclassical manifesto, Ingres's *Apotheosis of Homer* (see p. 211), but Courbet's central figure of artistic genius (himself) is set in the context of real people from contemporary life ("society at its best, its worst and its average . . . my way of seeing society in its interests and its passions"). The theme has been interpreted in terms of Fourierist socialism – a personal, concrete expression of an association of Capital, Labour and Talent, an ideal harmony of society. Yet the picture also expresses alienation in a way that Baudelaire himself might have approved: there is scarcely any communication between the three groups, or even between some figures in the groups. The artist in the centre is the hope of communication.

As "real allegory" the picture's internal contradictions baffled contemporaries. The people are all real, faithfully and vividly portrayed, but as an event the gathering is impossible, and even its setting, the walls of the studio, is vague and unidentified. The choice of characters is also far from an adequate representation of contemporary society. However, it made an impression (Delacroix considered it "one of the most outstanding paintings of the times") and it has since continued to fascinate. Not least, it opens a doorway to modern art: here the artist is shown dominant at the centre of the world. In *The studio* not just the artist, but for the first time the "activity of creating art" becomes the subject. In Courbet's self-portraits and in his portraits of his friends, too, the artist as maker assumes heroic stature, even when surrounded by children, as is *Proudhon*.

Courbet had come to Paris from his native Ornans, in the mountainous Jura of France, in 1840. His early *Self-portrait with black dog* suggests his flamboyant and truculent character, though not his lifelong social and political commitment. Even though *The studio* was the last major work in which he tried to programme his political, social and moral ideals, he continued to participate in politics, taking a prominent part in the Commune of 1871, until, following a brief imprisonment, he was forced into exile in Switzerland, where he died. His artistic and social sympathies are strikingly expressed in the unemotional but monumental *Stone-breakers* (1849; destroyed) – two men shown simply at their dehumanizing task. In the same year he also depicted a small-town funeral, *A burial at Ornans*, on an heroic scale. He always drew on the real, but with great variety and with a brilliantly broad and free style, often laying on with a palette-knife. Courbet's still lifes have a density, a weight of presence comparable with those of Chardin or, for that matter, of Cézanne. His nudes were of a veracity, sometimes unflattering but often also startlingly erotic, that many found offensive. *The bathers*, again a life-size genre subject, allegedly provoked Napoleon III to assault it with his riding whip at the Salon of 1853. Perhaps, however, his landscapes of the Jura are the best examples of the beauty, the rich, sombre colour, of his paint.

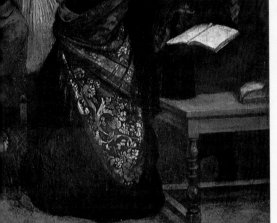

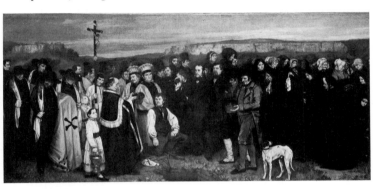

COURBET (left)
The artist's studio,
1854-55
Courbet's great manifesto rejects both academicism, represented by the dusty plaster figure, and Romanticism, symbolized by the plumed hat and the guitar. Champfleury, Baudelaire and Proudhon, however, who are shown in it, expressed dislike of the work, finding Courbet's vanity and the autobiographical tone of the painting distracting. It is in fact the true subject.

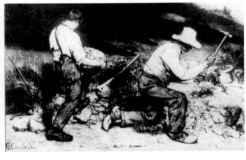

COURBET (left)
The stone-breakers, 1849
Courbet wrote to a friend: "I stopped to look at two men breaking stones on the road. It is rare to find an expression of such utter and complete misery; and at once I had an idea for a picture." It was neither expressionist nor sentimental, however.

COURBET
A burial at Ornans,
1849-50
All sorts of people from Courbet's native town posed for this vast canvas, a mirror of provincial life and death. The onlookers' grief, fear and indifference are dispassionately noted; the faces struck Parisian critics as shockingly ugly.

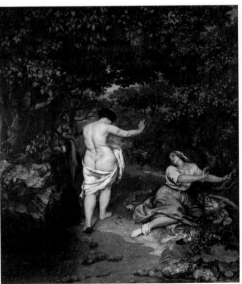

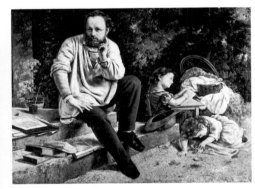

COURBET (left)
The bathers, 1853
The scandal of the 1853 Salon, *The bathers* attracted universal odium. It is an incongruous picture: even if the women are earthily mundane, their extravagant gestures are reminiscent of the nymphs and goddesses of 17th- and 18th-century art, but almost violent.

COURBET (above)
Pierre-Joseph Proudhon and his family, 1865
Proudhon's "thinker" pose and books indicate a larger reality than the man amidst his family (the portrait is set in 1853). Details such as his worn shoes and his daughters' toys enable the viewer to reconstruct the sitter's situation, though.

WHISTLER:
Falling Rocket

James Abbot McNeill Whistler (1834-1903) was a true international – born in Massachusetts, brought up early on in Russia, then at West Point (failed in Chemistry); as a Navy cartographer he learnt the techniques of etching, before his definitive expatriation in 1855, first to Paris, and, in 1859, to London. Wit, dandy and aesthete, he provoked outrage and astonishment in the sedate worlds of High Victorian art and society.

On his arrival in Paris in 1855, as a student, he was struck by Courbet's forceful denunciations of the official art of the Paris Salon after visiting his one-man show, the celebrated "Pavilion of Realism". In 1859, rejected by the Salon, Whistler, with Manet, showed in a later, comparable "counter-exhibition" where Whistler's *At the piano*, modelled by mass and colour rather than line, was approved by Courbet; subsequently, Whistler was profoundly influenced by Courbet, and at times worked alongside him, although his admiration for the tonal subtleties of Velazquez's paintings in the Louvre and for the flattened, schematic patterning of Japanese prints was to prove more enduring inspiration. (Japanese prints began to arrive in numbers in Paris in the 1850s, and in the 1860s Whistler built up a considerable collection of Japanese art.)

From 1859, with his move to London, Whistler fought off the influence of Courbet. His famous *White girl* of 1862, a *succès de scandale* (alongside such landmarks as Manet's "*Déjeuner sur l'Herbe*") at the Salon des Refusés in 1863, reflects something of the wistful characterizations of young women painted by the Pre-Raphaelite Rossetti. It is an exquisite modulation of tones of white, and Whistler later added the definition *Symphony in white no. 1* to the title. This is symptomatic both of his increasing dedication to the subtle gradations of tonal painting and of his belief in the importance of purely formal pictorial values – overriding that of literal representation. His musical titles – *Symphony, Arrangement* and later the famous *Nocturnes* – stress his notion of the harmonics of tone, colour and line – the equivalent of a kind of mood music. Even in portraiture he claimed the supremacy of abstract form over naturalistic representation. His preferred title for *The artist's mother* (1872), one of the most famous of nineteenth-century portraits (and paradoxically, it seems, a most faithful one), was *Arrangement in grey and black no. 1*. In its subdued delicate tonalities it echoes Velazquez, but its flattened space, its exquisitely calculated disposition ("arrangement") across the picture plane – these qualities anticipate the abstract preoccupations of much twentieth-century painting; they also affected younger Impressionists, and indeed Seurat, when the painting was shown in Paris in 1882, and later they were adapted by Intimistes such as Bonnard and Vuillard. As to the subject of the portrait, Whistler provocatively denied the right of the public to be concerned with it; an arrangement in black and white was what it was – "To me", he said, "it is interesting as a picture of my mother, but what can or ought the public to care about the identity of the portrait?" However, in spite of the emphasis here on purely formal values, and elsewhere in his work on instantaneity, Whist-

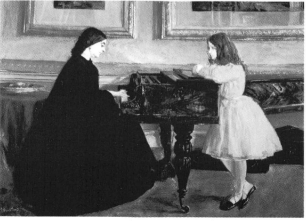

WHISTLER (above)
Falling rocket: Nocturne in black and gold, c. 1874
In Whistler's words, "The masterpiece should appear as the flower to the painter ... with no reason to explain its presence – a joy to the artist – a delusion to the philanthropist – a puzzle to the botanist." Aestheticism had no room for art expressing the goodness of Nature, as Ruskin saw it.

WHISTLER (left)
At the piano, 1858-59
The counterpoint of black and white already suggests an association of tonality with musical harmonics.

ler was never really at one with Impressionist theory or practice: he was essentially subjective rather than objectively descriptive. His work, however, was equally incomprehensible to his contemporaries.

His confrontation with established British art and the public came to a climax in 1876 with the exhibition in London of *Nocturne in black and gold: Falling rocket*. Painted about 1874, it is a lyrical exclamation of delight at the effect of fireworks, raining coloured fire through the night at a display in a London pleasure garden. The English critic John Ruskin was revolted by it, for reasons that are not entirely clear (for Ruskin had been the champion of the late work of Turner). Then at the height of his prestige as national moral, no less than artistic, prophet, Ruskin in a famous article denounced Whistler for flinging "a pot of paint . . . in the public's face". Whistler sued for libel. The resulting trial was (in retrospect) one of the most entertaining in legal history. Whistler's wit coruscated, even more brilliantly than his painted fireworks. Some of the phrases used have passed into the language. Asked how long he had taken to "knock off" the painting", he answered, "About two days"; asked then if it was for two days' work that he asked 200 guineas, he replied: "No. I ask it for the knowledge of a lifetime". It is a response, provoking applause in the courtroom, that still echoes today. Whistler won, but he was awarded only a token farthing damages, and the costs led to his bankruptcy.

Whistler's harmonics were usually more subdued than those of the *Rocket*, above all perhaps in his twilight meditations on the Thames, transmuting its industrial daytime prose into mysterious dreamy poems – drifts of shadow glinting here and there with reflected lights. Such works as his *Cremorne lights: Nocturne in blue and silver*, 1872, pre-date Monet's mist-hazed accounts of Rouen Cathedral by nearly 20 years.

Delighting in controversy, deliberately provoking antagonism, Whistler was not the ideal propagandist to reconcile British taste with the new values of French art, although towards the end of his life his influence, especially on Sickert, was decisive. His prolific and delightfully sensitive etchings found an appreciative public, however, and his influence on interior decoration was also important; he was a pioneer in simplification, sweeping out Victorian clutter, using clear and plain colours.

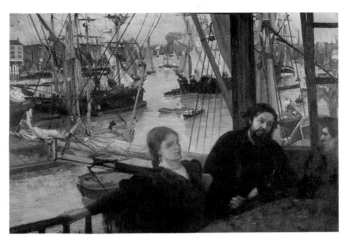

WHISTLER (left)
Wapping-on-Thames,
1861-64
The limited colour range may owe a debt to Manet, but the silvery tones and the almost abstract design of masts and rigging behind the obliquely-angled foreground figures are wholly original.

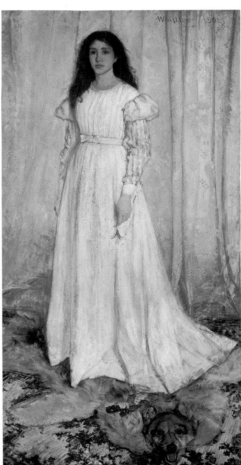

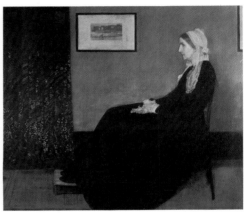

WHISTLER (left)
The white girl: Symphony in white no. 1, 1862
The critic Castagnary thought she was a girl on the morning after her wedding night. Her soulful look, the drooping lily and contrast of pale and vivid colours perhaps suggested his interpretation: the picture seems an elegy for lost innocence.

WHISTLER (above)
The artist's mother: Arrangement in grey and black no. 1, 1862
Whistler's affection for his mother, a devout woman, was deep. Working rapidly, he refined each application of paint to reach a delicate, almost transparent harmony of tones, evoking the gentle resolve of his subject.

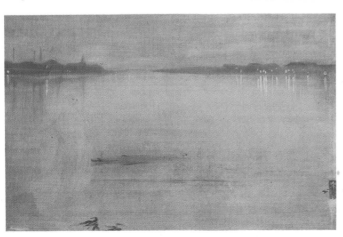

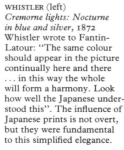

WHISTLER (left)
Cremorne lights: Nocturne in blue and silver, 1872
Whistler wrote to Fantin-Latour: "The same colour should appear in the picture continually here and there . . . in this way the whole will form a harmony. Look how well the Japanese understood this". The influence of Japanese prints is not overt, but they were fundamental to this simplified elegance.

WHISTLER (right)
Venetian palaces: Nocturne, 1879-80
The shimmering etched lines make mystery out of nuances of reflected light.

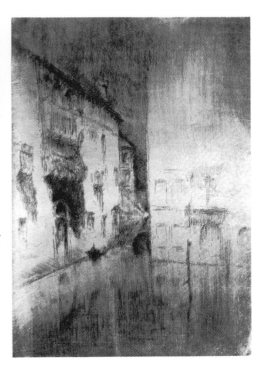

MONET:
Rouen Cathedral

In 1892 and 1893, the French painter, Claude Monet (1840-1926), settled into Rouen from February till April, and there day after day painted the formidable series of more than thirty studies of the vast front of the Cathedral. Though the view remains much the same in each, he worked from three slightly different positions; in one, a boutique for "lingerie and fashion", a screen had to be erected to preserve the modesty of the clientèle.

Monet was then in his early fifties, at the height of his powers, and enjoying a public acceptance and fame, and some financial secur-

ity that had long been denied him. Brought up in Le Havre, his remarkable sensitivity to light may well have been fostered by the open marine skies of Normandy, and later by Algerian sunlight during his military service. The artists who primarily influenced him as a young man were Eugène Boudin (1824–98) and J.B. Jongkind (1819-91), both first-rate practitioners based in the tradition of landscape painting of the Barbizon School, but with an increased vivacity and sparkle of colour, and accustomed to working directly from nature in the open air.

As a student in Paris, Monet, though attached to the studio of the academician Gleyre, associated with young contemporaries who were later to become famous with him as the masters of Impressionism – Renoir, Sisley, Pissarro. His own work, which had reflected Courbet's style, began to answer to the example of Edouard Manet, in increasingly bold and free interpretations of the transient effect of light on form and colour. After the mass rejection of work by himself and his friends from the Paris Salon of 1867, he drove these investigations still further, using pure colours in sometimes almost staccato brushwork. Atmospheric conditions fascinated him to a point at which physical objects became essentially a medium in which light could discover its own shape.

In 1870-71 Monet, like his friend Pissarro, took refuge from the Franco-Russian war in London, where he saw work by both Constable and Turner that interested him. Back in Paris, he was, with Pissarro, a prime mover in an independent exhibition in 1874; from a canvas entitled *Impression: Sunrise*, he and his colleagues were dubbed "Impressionists". By 1877 Monet had begun to develop his obsession with recording serial studies of a single motif. He continued, however, a predilection for themes from contemporary life – railway stations, for example - and also for the humblest, apparently least spectacular objects, as the "heroes" of his work – such as the famous series of haystacks. During the

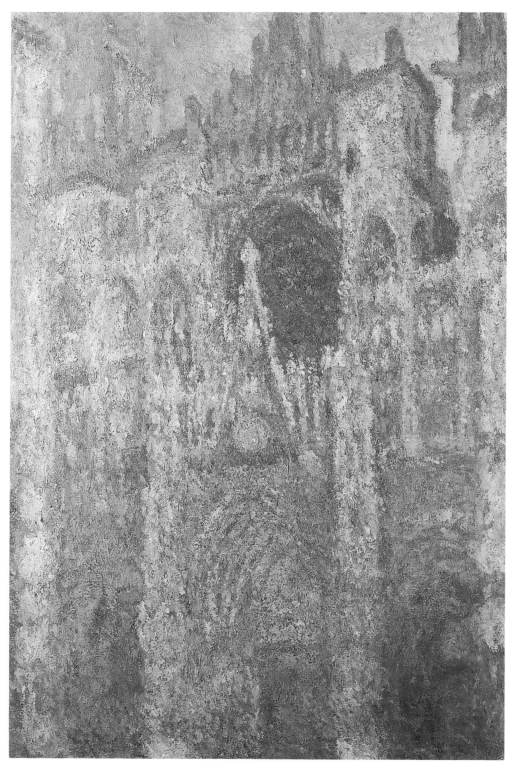

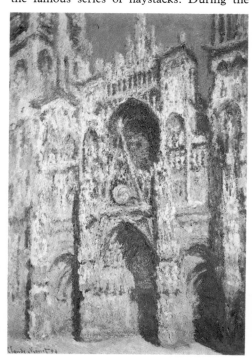

MONET (left)
Rouen Cathedral: morning sunlight, 1894
After his series of *Haystacks* and *Poplars*, Monet embarked on more than 30 canvases studying the west front of Rouen Cathedral. In this series, he took a technique of building up colour in rich, dense paint further than ever before.

MONET (above)
Rouen Cathedral: full sunlight, 1894
The intricate forms of the decorative Gothic stonework dissolve in the play of light, and the Cathedral seems to lurk only nebulously behind the clotted brushwork. In this reduction to the purely optical, Realism is fulfilled – and undermined.

1880s Monet travelled extensively, sometimes using a portable "canvas box"; in this he would slot a number of canvases so that he could shift from one to another as the day wore on and the light changed. But sometimes, lapsing from absolute naturalism, he began to modify the image in front of him in the interests of realizing a more satisfactory colour structure.

These serial exercises found their ultimate subject matter in the legendary water-garden which he created at his house at Giverny, with its "Japanese" bridge and its constellations of waterlilies in the pond. Although at one time threatened by blindness from cataract, after a successful operation he continued his painting of the lilies almost until his death in 1926. In these, some of them on huge scale, the subject becomes increasingly primarily the harmonious modulation of colour.

Twenty of the Cathedral series were shown in Paris in 1895. (They are almost all dated 1894, when Monet, ever reluctant to consider his paintings as "finished", put the final touches on them, in his studio.) It is in this series that the tension between the physical reality of the subject – in this case a major monument in enduring stone of Gothic architecture – and light that transposes that solidity into something quite other but no less real, is most sensible.

It was probably the great canvases of waterlilies, *Les Nymphéas*, that were to have the greatest effect on the painting of the second half of the next century – notably in the large-scale abstractions of the New York school of "action painters", like Sam Francis. Yet Monet himself would never have agreed that his painting was abstract; it is precisely in the alchemy by which his brush both preserved and transfigured the natural world that his enduring power to delight succeeding generations resides.

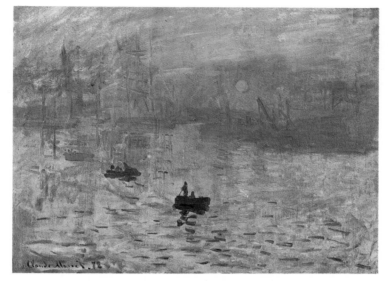

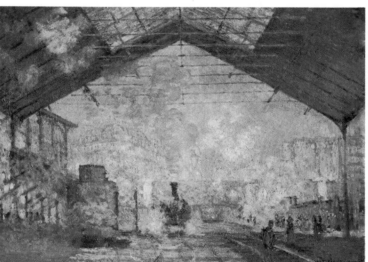

MONET (left)
Impression: Sunrise, 1872
This was the painting that earned the Impressionists their name. "What freedom, what ease of workmanship", wrote one sarcastic critic. The title acknowledges that the work is a sketch; Monet exhibited it since it caught as well as any reworking the effect he sought. The lack of "finish" or labour, to which the critics objected, made possible its instantaneity. Between 1874 and 1886 there were seven further exhibitions by the group, though the only important member to exhibit at all of them was Pissarro. By 1880, Monet's personal relationships with the other Impressionists were beginning to fade.

MONET (left)
Gare St Lazare, 1877
Monet here explores the vaporous effects of steam and smoke within a light-filled but confined space. This was the first of a long series of studies of a single motif shown at different times of the day and under different conditions. The choice of subject continued the emphasis on themes from contemporary life that characterized Realism. In another sense, however, it was a new departure in naturalism, an attempt at absolute loyalty to the ephemeral effect at a given moment. Monet was to develop these series into the equivalent of musical variations on a theme.

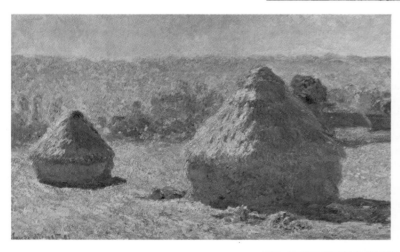

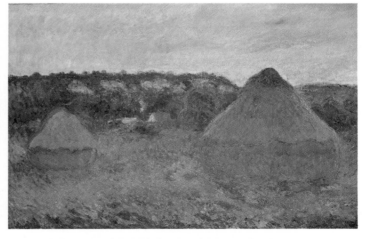

MONET (above)
Two haystacks, 1891
The *Haystacks,* with their glowing changes of colour (here from broad daylight to sunset) were hailed by Kandinsky as the inspiration of modern abstract painting. "Unconsciously, the object was discredited as an indispensable element of the picture" he wrote.

MONET (right)
Waterlilies, after 1900
Though the growing formlessness of Monet's late works is partly explained by his failing vision, more significantly they represent the ultimate development of Impressionism into subjectivity. They invite the viewer to contemplate pure colour harmonies.

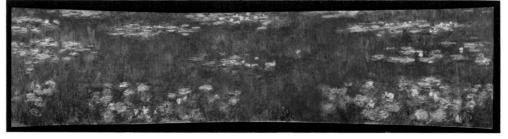

SEURAT:
La Grande Jatte

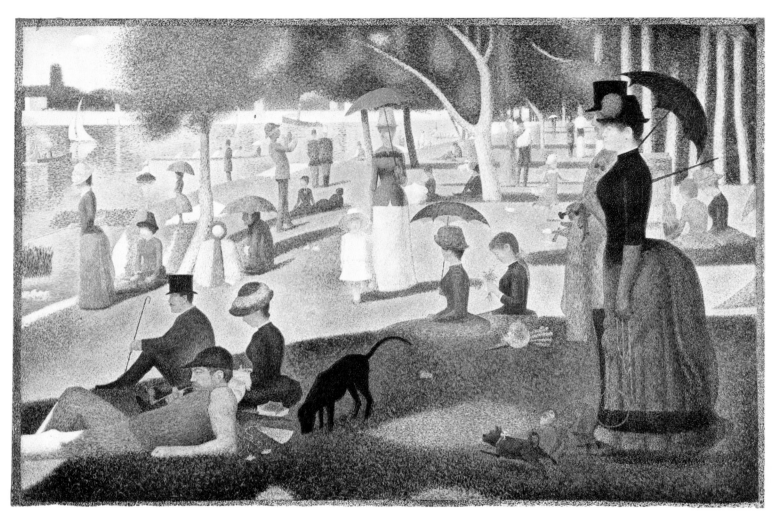

La Grande Jatte, named after a weekend resort on the banks of the Seine popular among Parisians, was begun in 1884 and finished in 1886, and exhibited in that year in the last Impressionist exhibition. Seurat's admission to the show, due largely, it seems, to Pissarro's championship, caused dissension among the original Impressionists. Indeed this picture is obviously at variance in very important points from the practice of Impressionism – so much so that subsequent historians distinguish the style evolved by Seurat with the label "Neo-Impressionism". The interest in light, in colour created by light, and in a very high key of colour, is still dominant, but the technique is both more fragmented and more precisely (even at times mechanically) worked out. In its contemporary subject matter *La Grande Jatte* is still Realist, but the effect in sum and detail is as if the Impressionist vision had frozen: the sense of implicit movement, the feeling for ephemeral effects, are rejected in favour of a timeless, highly formalized, monumental quality. Realist in some aspects the image may be; it is in no sense naturalistic.

Georges Seurat (1859-1891) was a seemingly orthodox, docile student at the Ecole des Beaux-Arts in Paris, 1877-78, working a great deal in the Louvre, studying there intensely the masterpieces of traditional art from Greek classical sculpture to the Italian and northern Renaissance. However, he extracted his own conclusions from them, and was probably already interested in theoretical writings on colour, such as those published by Michel-Eugène Chevreul and others, leading to the demonstration that juxtaposed colours mix in the human eye, and that the colour so mixed is purer than any pigments mixed on the palette. By 1881 Seurat had developed a highly original drawing technique in black crayon, extracting simplified and very solid figures by the subtle and exact control of tone. His early painting in colour always tended towards a similar simplification: even his small oil-studies, painted in the open, direct from the subject, moving gradually towards the lighter palette of the Impressionists, demonstrated his primary interest in an exactly articulated composition, plotted with equal emphasis across the picture plane, using simplified silhouetted shapes, and increasingly shallow space.

By 1883, he was developing the technique known as pointillism, a system of applying paint in isolated dots of pure colour. His first major work in this technique, on the grand scale of ambitious Salon pictures, "*Une Baignade, Asnières*" (A bathing scene at Asnières), was finished in 1884. The subject, urban recreation at the riverside, was an Impressionist one, and the innumerable preliminary studies likewise reflect Impressionist practice; but their integration into the whole was a studio process, and an austere call to order of the chaotic, multitudinous impressions with which nature assails the eye.

The exhibition of *Asnières* in 1884 and of *La Grande Jatte* in 1886 established Seurat as the spearhead of the new avantgarde. The exponents of Neo-Impressionism, Pointillism or Colour Divisionism were supported by critics such as Fénéon and the Belgian poet Verhaeren, but older Impressionists (with the exception of Pissarro) read *La Grande Jatte* as a counter-Impressionist manifesto.

For Seurat, "the purity of the element of the spectrum is the keystone of technique", and he continued to work with tireless industry towards the perfection and simplification of his system until his premature death from an unidentified illness in 1891. He had continued to produce *grandes machines*, major exhibition pictures, extending his subject matter to further aspects of modern urban life, even adapting motifs from the abstracted imagery of posters and fashion plates, but always resolving his pictures into immobile patterns, even when his subject was the sea or his theme motion, as in his last big canvas, *The circus*. "I want", he said, "to make modern people move about as if they were on the Parthenon frieze, in their most essential characteristics."

Apart from his impact on Pissarro's style in the 1880s, Seurat's work inspired only one disciple of significance, the prolific Paul Signac (1863-1935), who remained to the end faithful to the divisionist principle and technique, although his vision was less subtle and more coarsely handled.

SEURAT (left)
La Grande Jatte, 1884–86
Seurat's biographer, the
critic Fénéon, described the
picture: "It is four o'clock
on Sunday afternoon in the
dog-days. On the river the
swift barks dart to and fro
... A Sunday population has
come together at random,
and from a delight in the
fresh air ... Seurat has
treated his figures in a
summary or hieratic style,
like a Puvis de Chavannes
gone modern."

SEURAT (right)
The yoked cart, 1883
The rich colour and the
seemingly casual design –
cutting off the cart at the
edge of the canvas – re-
call "pure" Impressionism.
Seurat, however, achieves
a still image purged of all
superfluous detail, evoking
a mood of calm expectancy.

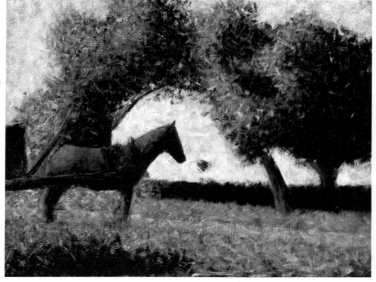

SEURAT (below)
*Seated boy with a straw
hat*, 1883-84
Seurat liked to sketch in
black crayon on thick white
paper; its textured surface
enabled him to achieve the
fine tonal gradations which
characterize his atmospheric
drawings. Sometimes, like
this one, they were studies
for larger pictures (this is
the youth on the left in the
Asnières canvas); yet they
possess all the qualities
of finished works of art.

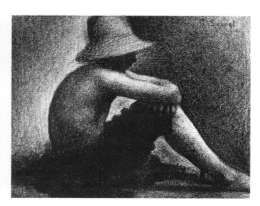

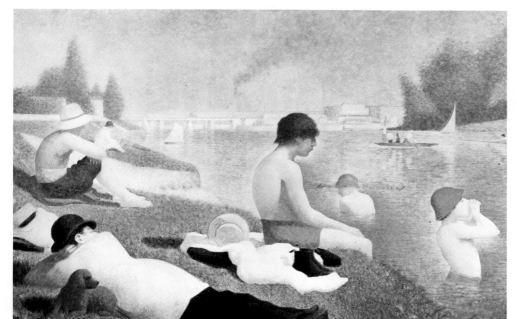

SEURAT (above)
"*Une Baignade, Asnières*"
(A bathing scene at
Asnières), 1883-84
Seurat's method was based
on contemporary scientific
theory, even if the separate
dots of colour are not small
enough to blend in the eye,
as presumably he intended.
(This was pointed out only
some 40 years later.) But
Seurat's "scientific" basis
helped to justify his artistic
aim, to capture on canvas
the essence of appearances.

SEURAT (right)
*The "Bec du Hoc" at
Grandchamp*, 1885
The dynamic mass of cliff
against calm sea and sky
rears imposingly; Seurat's
dots and strokes vibrate
before the eye, enlivening
the surface – much as the
less regimented brushes of
Monet or Renoir also did.

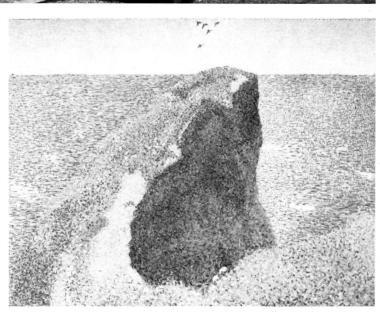

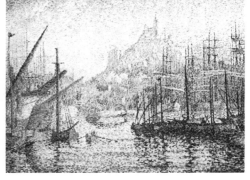

SIGNAC (above)
*View of the marina at
Marseilles*, 1905
Seurat's divisionism and
deliberated arrangement
of forms is here enlivened
by vibrant "Fauve" colour
(Matisse was a friend).
Signac had earlier painted
working-class or industrial
scenes, perhaps with implicit
social comment; he was a
professed anarchist. Seurat's
politics were less definite.

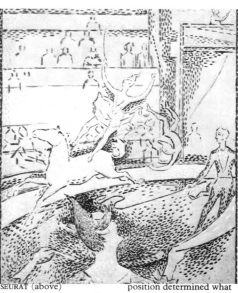

SEURAT (above)
Study for *The circus*, 1890
Seurat was later influenced
by the philosopher Henry,
who proposed that certain
analysable factors in a composition determined what
emotional message it had:
upward curves and leaping
forms here signal gaiety.
He sought "to do Poussin
again", but from science.

CÉZANNE:
Mont Ste-Victoire

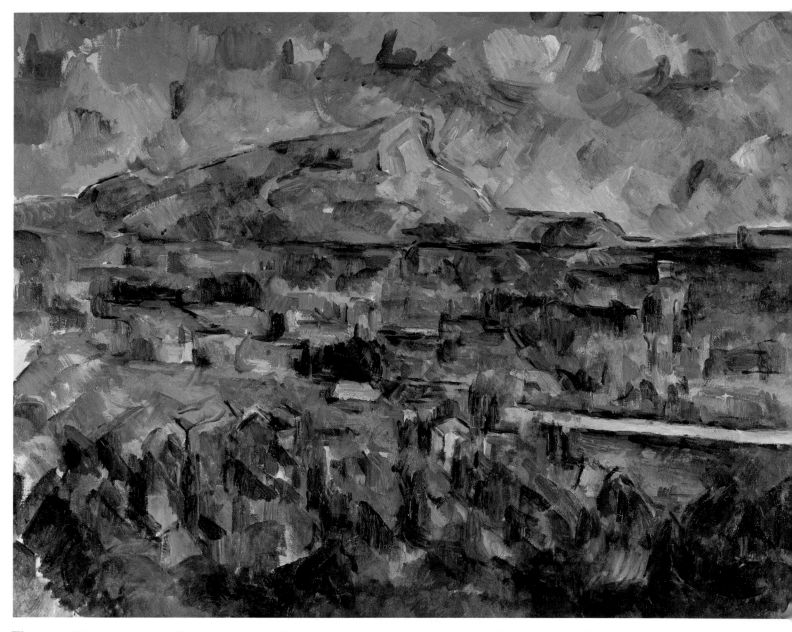

The year 1886 was crucial for Cézanne, then aged 47. His father died, leaving him a comfortable fortune, and he was at last able to seal with marriage his 17-year-old liaison with Hortense Fiquet. In the same year his friendship with Zola, dating from their school-days, came to an abrupt end, and in the 20 years remaining to him he left home in Provence increasingly rarely. He became more and more touchy and suspicious, almost a recluse, even after long-delayed recognition came rapidly, indeed spectacularly, after the dealer Vollard's exhibition of about 150 of his paintings in Paris in 1895. His life was concentrated on the stubborn battle with his art – the battle to achieve a reconciliation of the three-dimensional world confronting him with the two-dimensional limitations of his canvas. In 1903 he wrote: "I am beginning to see the Promised Land"; in 1906 he wrote: "I am old and ill and have sworn to myself to die painting". In October 1906 he collapsed after being caught in a storm while painting outdoors, and died a few days later.

These later years were occupied with still lifes, figure painting – ranging from portraits to more general, monumental themes – and landscapes. Still lifes enabled him to structure his compositions before painting; even so in the finished work traditional perspective and true shapes were distorted in answer to the needs of harmony and the stability of the whole. The portraits were painted, like the still lifes, in a long process of profound analysis: giving up his portrait of the dealer Vollard after 115 sittings Cézanne was "not altogether displeased with the shirt". Yet in some portraits, built up laboriously touch upon touch like all the late work, the response to individual character can still be almost lyrical.

Cézanne was also preoccupied especially with the theme of nude, female figures in a landscape, or *Bathers*. The subject is still surely Impressionist, stemming from Manet's "*Déjeuner sur l'Herbe*" (see p. 75), but the picture goes much further, not just in its distortions, but in Cézanne's attempt to create something durable, "like the art of museums".

Most of all in his last years Cézanne painted landscapes, which allowed him the greatest breadth for the development of his style and necessitated working from and with nature. He had several chosen local views to which he returned, but the favourite – and one that has become almost as much a cult image as Mount Fuji in Japanese art – was Mont Ste-Victoire. His technique, building up a pictorial structure by the schematic overlay of colours applied mostly very thinly in short, square strokes of the brush, had been developing during the 1870s, at its peak in watercolours. In the London *Mont Ste-Victoire with a great pine*, 1885-87, the composition, though framed by the arabesque of a foreground tree, is determined by the logical recession of the planes or blocks of colour. Even the outline contours usually reveal themselves on close inspection to be built up of crisply defined patches of colour, of astonishingly subtle and varied shades. In the silence, the frontal monumentality of the scene, Cézanne surely achieves his avowed wish, to do Poussin again

CEZANNE (below)
*Mont Ste-Victoire with a
great pine,* 1885-87
In the early days of the
long struggle with Mont

Ste-Victoire, details of
the landscape survive the
artist's attempt to translate
his sensations into paint
and so achieve a "harmony

parallel to nature". In a
related watercolour, these
details are clearer still,
and the diagonals sharper,
the frontality less firm.

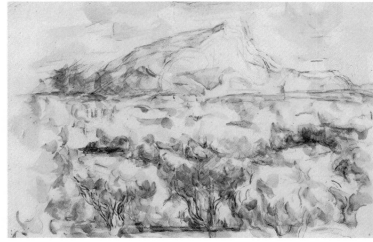

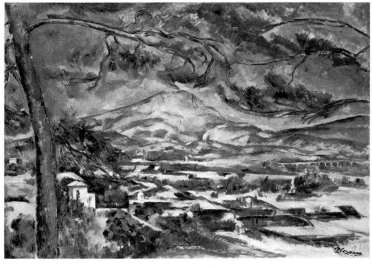

CEZANNE (above)
Mont Ste-Victoire,
watercolour, 1906
In the late paintings, oil
or watercolour, detail is
unimportant; it is unclear
precisely what – a house or

a tree – is represented by
any given patch of colour.
The patches, overlapping
and interlocking, build up
their own coherent form.
It was Cézanne's belief
that "in the contrast and

connection of colours –
there you have the secret
of drawing and modelling"
There is a great variety
in the brushwork and the
tones of colour, sometimes
gentle, sometimes savage.

CEZANNE (left)
The Philadelphia *Mont
Ste-Victoire,* 1904-06
Rich colour applied in a
mosaic-like pattern builds
up and integrates the land
and sky, held on the canvas
with hallucinatory power.
Cézanne's conversation in
these years revealed that he
felt that in his later views
of Mont Ste-Victoire he was
coming close to his goal.

CEZANNE (right)
Still life with onions,
c. 1895-1900
Form and colour echo each
other across the canvas;
greens complement pink
onions, the rim of a glass
is tilted up, a plate bent,
in the interests of overall
harmony. Cézanne took so
long painting that fruit
and vegetables shrivelled;
he used wax substitutes.

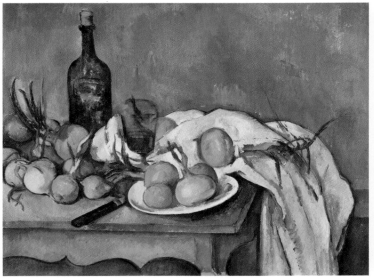

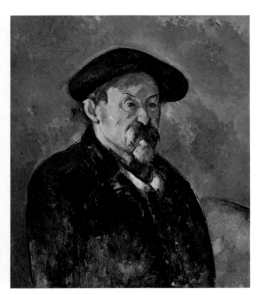

from nature: this is classical form. In his final
contemplations of Mont Ste-Victoire, he used
the same method still more austerely to extract
– or abstract – his picture from the mass and
profile of the landscape. The version in Philadelphia of 1904 may or may not be unfinished –
Cézanne tended to advance work over the
whole canvas simultaneously, so that, whenever he stopped, that stage cohered as a whole;
this is faceted by those square brush-strokes,
those sharp, even harsh, edges or planes of
colour, into unconsoling yet majestic solidity –
even in the sky. Yet there is, too, a sense of
urgency: the silhouette of the mountain has
become a beak or prow – aggressive or defiant.
Cézanne's analytic-synthetic method was also
a transposition of his own temperamental
reaction to the sensation ("*ma petite sensation*") the landscape aroused in him.

Indefatigable as he was in his search for
objectivity, Cézanne's example in paint nevertheless went far to establish the supremacy of
the modern artist's subjectivity: the world is
his, to translate into his own terms as he will.

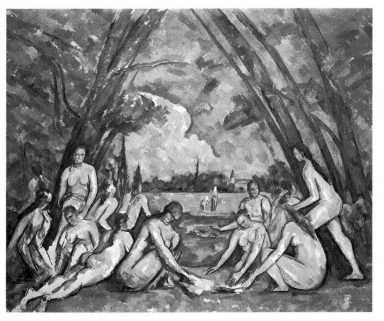

CEZANNE (above)
*Self-portrait with a
goatee, c.* 1906
In his last *Self-portrait*
Cézanne treats himself as
dispassionately as a still
life – in contrast to van
Gogh's or Gauguin's self-
expressive images. In the
reduction of his head to a
compendium of hollows and
planes of colour, the basic
grammar both of Cubism
and of Fauvism is implicit.

CEZANNE (left)
"The Great Bathers",
1898-1905
Whereas the early *Bathers*
are often relatively static,
rhythmic forces permeate
the huge canvases of later
years. These nudes seem to
be primeval, fashioned of
stone or wood, part of the
cathedral-like structure
of the forest. The picture
is constructed with colour
– pale shades of blue, ochre
and green dappled by light.

NOLDE:
The Last Supper

"With light strokes I traced 13 figures on to the canvas, the Redeemer and the 12 Apostles seated at a table in the warm spring night, the night before the Passion. This was the occasion when Christ revealed His great idea of redemption to His beloved disciples. I obeyed an irresistible impulse to express deep spirituality and ardent religious feeling, but I did so without much deliberation, knowledge or reflection ... While working on *The Last Supper* and *Pentecost* I had to be artistically free ... These paintings marked the transition in my development from reliance on external optical stimulus to that of experienced inner value."

When Emil Nolde (1867-1956) painted his *Last Supper*, the genesis of which he was later to describe, as above, in his memoirs, he was already 43. He had been a slow developer. Brought up on a farm in Schleswig-Holstein, in the remoteness of north-east Germany, he always remained a somewhat solitary figure in the German Expressionist movement, with an almost hermetic, mystical dedication to his artistic vocation. He became a full-time painter only in 1894, but he had nevertheless by 1900 acquired considerable experience, in Munich, in Italy and in Paris, and had worked at Dachau in the school of Adolf Hölzel (1853-1934; not shown), whose use of symbolism and of expressive colour was probably very important for Nolde. Nolde's style evolved through Impressionism, but his real mentors were to be Munch and Ensor.

Nolde discovered or consolidated the themes that would preoccupy him for the rest of his life between 1900 and 1910 – religion, Nature (especially the wilderness of northern plains or the elemental forces of the sea), figure painting and, not least, flowers. These, however, he painted according to his inner vision: "All the free fantastic paintings of this period came into being without any prototype or model, without any well-defined idea ... a vague shape of glow and colour was enough. The paintings took shape as I worked." From such conceptions there evolved his idea of "passive artistic creation", defined in 1942 as "the moment when a spark glows in the

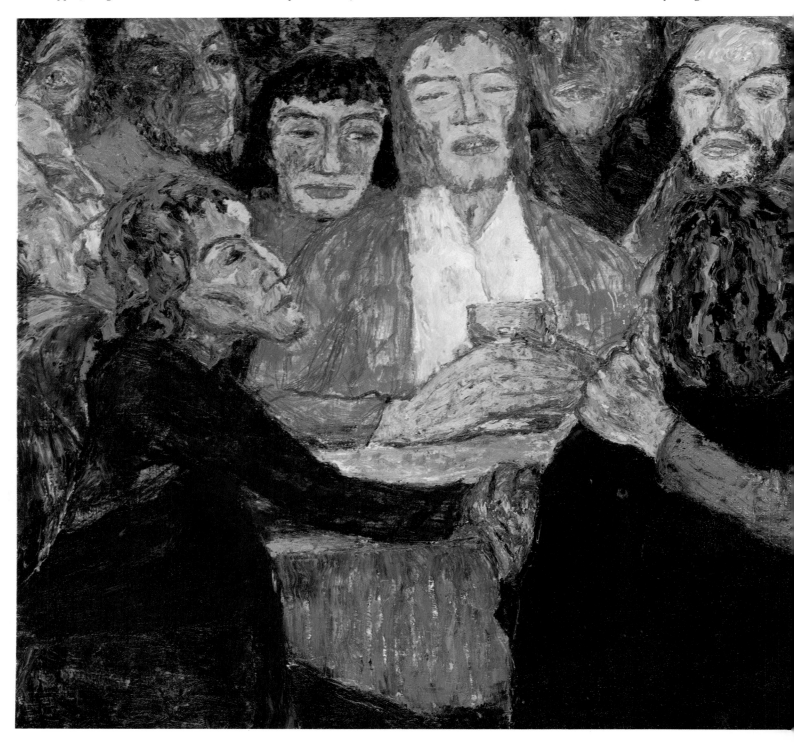

darkness and grows, if the circumstances are right, into a leaping flame."

The handling of Nolde's *Last Supper* is indeed a far cry from the traditional formulae evolving from the famous prototype by Leonardo da Vinci of this subject, though the force behind it owes something surely to the tortured anguish of Grünewald's religious painting. In its harsh, summary drawing, in its echoes of tribal African or Oceanic sculpture, in the strident reds and yellow greens and the compression of figures within the picture space, the painting is unequivocally in the mainstream of German Expressionism. But the religious impact is Nolde's own, and his only peer as a religious artist in the twentieth

century is Georges Rouault, also a great master of glowing colour. Nolde, however, lacked Rouault's sexual disgust, and also his formal restraint, for Nolde could unleash his brush in a wild gaiety of swirling paint in which the figures dissolve.

As a prolific printmaker, exploiting the technical potential of both woodcut and lithograph, Nolde had an importance in the development of Expressionist graphics. Yet perhaps his most remarkable achievements were in watercolour: in this medium, in the incandescent intensity with which he could kindle colour into blaze on paper, he has no peer in the twentieth century.

After he had briefly, in 1906-07, been a

member of Die Brücke, Nolde withdrew to a farm in the northern German fastnesses at Seebüll (where a foundation now houses much of his work); and became more and more a recluse. The Nazis (of whom Nolde at first approved) declared him a "degenerate" artist, but, though he was officially forbidden to paint, he produced innumerable compositions in miniature (his secret "unpainted pictures") during World War II, and subsequently, in an astonishing burst of energy before his death, painted full-scale versions of a great many of them. Well aware of the example of van Gogh, Gauguin and Munch, he rivalled them in the intensity of his vision, in which he formulated an original, elemental imagery of great power.

NOLDE (left)
The Last Supper, 1909
Early in 1909 Nolde had been dangerously ill; on his recovery he began painting a series of religious works – *The Last Supper*, *Pentecost*, *The mocking of Christ* and *The Crucifixion*. He said: "I stood almost terrified before my drawing, without any model in nature – I was about to paint the most profoundly significant episode in the Christian religion! ... Had I felt bound to keep to the letter of the Bible or dogma, I do not think I could have painted these deeply experienced pictures so powerfully."

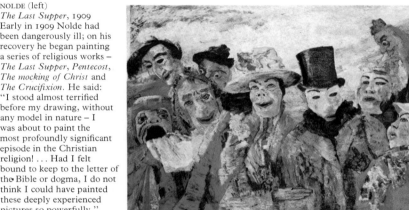

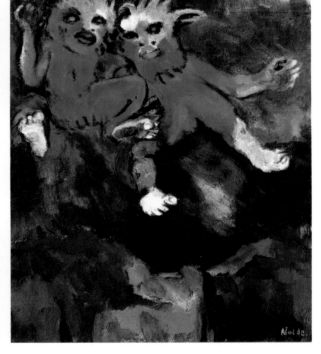

ENSOR (left)
Intrigue, 1890
Ensor was one of the first European artists to break traditional constraints on expression – turning to use the ugly and disturbing. In what seems to be a carnival there is here no festivity; the masks reveal an inner evil; the smiles are leers. Nolde, trying to give form to a personal vision, took up Ensor's example, conveying his emotion through garish colour and coarse features.

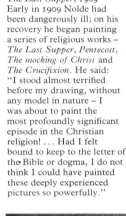

NOLDE (above)
A Friesland farm under red clouds, c. 1930
The wild and desolate landscape of Seebüll with its vast expanses of sky suited Nolde's fervent, solitary nature. A visit to China in 1913 perhaps stimulated the vivid hues and liking for pattern typical of his later watercolour style.

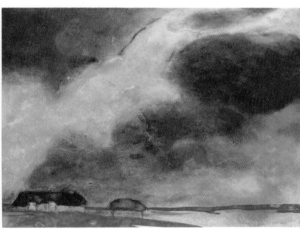

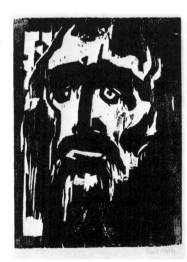

NOLDE (right)
The prophet, 1912
This is one of a series of woodcuts that Nolde made in 1912. He had earlier been associated with Die Brücke and he, too, was attracted by the German origin of the technique, and the powerful crudity of the kind of image it produces.

NOLDE (above)
Early morning flight, 1950
Nolde's late oil-paintings are all enlarged versions of watercolour improvisations, with glowing colours, free brushwork and a dreamy or mystical quality. Perhaps these are spirits heralding the coming of morning; the subject matter is usually fanciful or fey, expressing a joyous vivacity that had seldom appeared earlier.

KANDINSKY:
Study for Composition no. 7

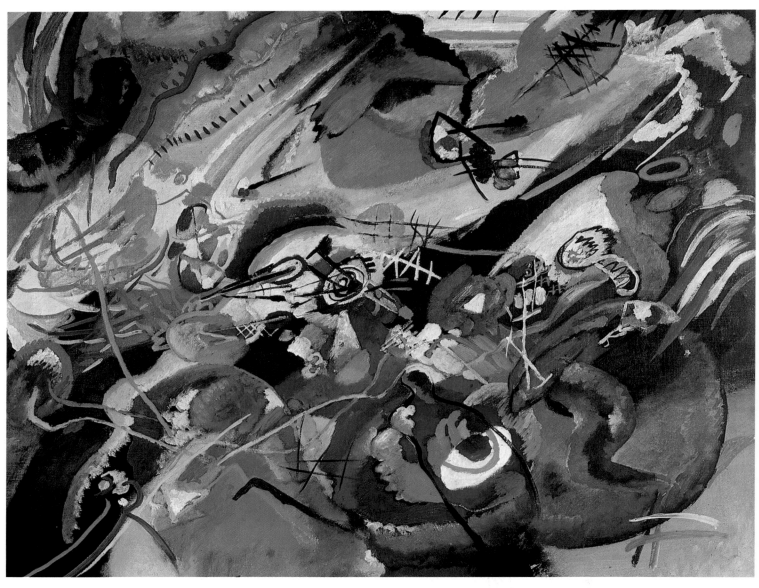

Composition no. 7 is one of the largest and most elaborate of the series of *Improvisations* and *Compositions* in which Kandinsky moved gradually, between 1910 and 1914, towards the elimination of all figurative or representational elements in his work. This study, of 1913, at first sight seethes, a hurly-burly of colour in conflict – colour that in places melts tenderly, even amorphously, and in others is hot, sharp and strident; here and there are sharp scratchy scorings or criss-crosses of lines. On longer inspection, the implications of the title, a *Composition*, may seem more valid. There is a main focus of attention in an emphatic clench of forms, of thunderous blue and of heavy black left of centre, while the rectangle of the painting is divided by a diagonal from lower left to upper right. Below this is relative calm, above it all is turbulence. The onlooker's first impression may be of uncontrolled explosion; longer acquaintance reveals that the explosion is profoundly excogitated.

Wassily Kandinsky had already completed his fundamental treatise *Uber das Geistige in der Kunst* (Concerning the Spiritual in Art) in 1910, though it was not published until 1912. In this, and his other theoretical writing, the argument is often obscure, but he was grappling with the huge difficulty of explaining the inexplicable, the unanalysable – the abstract values of colour and form completely detached from all representation of nature or objects. Very conscious of the danger of non-figurative art becoming mere vapid decoration, Kandinsky nevertheless believed that in pure colour and pure form the artist could find direct and valid expression of his mind or spirit. "The harmony of colour and form must be based solely upon the principle of proper contact with the human soul." Towards this end he worked out definitions of the qualities of colours and forms, but these, when not patently obvious, are generally highly subjective. One ready parallel with the art to which he aspired was, however, music: his own comments, and titles – *Improvisation, Composition* – indicate this clearly. For all his legal background, Kandinsky was always attracted by mysticism (particularly the theosophy of Madame Blavatsky), while his faith in materialism, in the value of the object, had been undermined by scientific revolution – the splitting of the atom.

Kandinsky's distrust of subject matter goes back to his student days in Moscow, when he saw one of Monet's *Haystacks* (see p. 217), in which the subject was dissolved into shimmering light and colour. Then in Munich, probably in 1910, he saw in one of his own paintings lying the wrong way up, in a subdued evening light, an apparition, a harmony of colour, line and form "of extraordinary beauty, glowing with an inner radiance"; and this precipitated the final conversion to non-figurative art: "Now I know for certain that subject matter was detrimental to my paintings." Kandinsky claimed to have been the first to paint purely abstract pictures – or rather non-figurative ones. The Cubists and others likewise "abstracted" their compositions from their subject matter, but never became completely detached from the object. Kandinsky's claim can be and has been contested, but it is clear that he was indeed the first to establish abstract art as a consolidated and valid mode of expression.

Following the revelation of his upside-down painting, Kandinsky did not proceed immediately to absolute non-figuration, nor did he altogether abandon landscape or other subjects even when he had. Figurative motifs, while becoming increasingly schematic or ves-

KANDINSKY (left)
*Study for Composition
no. 7*, 1913
Kandinsky found "vistas
of purely pictorial possibility" in the "shock of
contrasting colours, the
checking of fluid spots
by contours of design, by
the mingling and the sharp
separation of surfaces".

KANDINSKY (right)
*Composition no. 7,
fragment no. 1*, 1913
Apocalyptic struggles have
been seen in these studies;
but also the first visual
equivalent of "conscious-
ness on a psychic level".

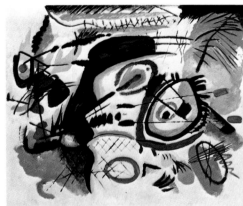

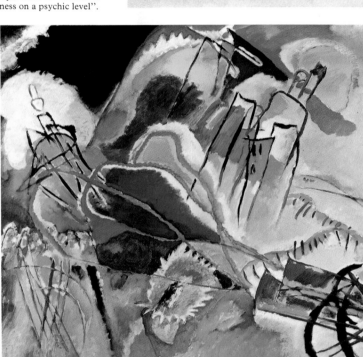

KANDINSKY (below)
*The first abstract
watercolour*, 1912
Is Kandinsky's title true?

There are rival claimants.
The difficulty is that all
the short-listed works were
long in the artists' hands

and might well have been
repainted later. This is the
favourite, as it seems fully
balanced, not an experiment.

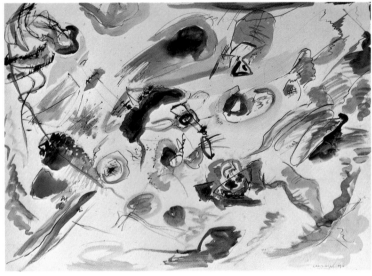

KANDINSKY
(left) *Improvisation
no. 30 – Cannons*, 1913;
(right) *Black lines*, 1913
Both works are abstract,
though Kandinsky agreed
that his own title *Cannons*
and their clear intrusion
might reflect the constant
war-talk of the time; and
Black lines seems eerily
prophetic of aircraft being
strafed in bursts of fire.

KANDINSKY (below)
Two poplars, 1913
Kandinsky did not become
an abstract painter over-
night; the landscapes he
continued to produce until
1914 reveal no impassable
gulf between painting the
soul and painting trees.

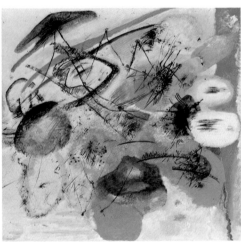

tigial, persist in some of his paintings as late as
1920. Before 1914, however, he had already
singled out the Unconscious as the mainspring
of his work. Thus of *Improvisation no. 30 –
Cannons* he wrote that it was "painted rather
subconsciously in a state of strong inner tension. So intensively did I feel the necessity of
some of the forms that I remember having
given loud directions to myself, for instance,
'But the corners must be heavy'." This may
suggest a closer parallel with the Abstract
Expressionism of American artists in the 1950s
than is really justifiable. Kandinsky's workings, his intuition, were always controlled by
an inner discipline, and there are more than 12
preliminary studies for *Composition no. 7*; the
final painting took three days.

World War I disrupted Kandinsky's career.
Returning to Russia, he painted relatively
little, and after the Revolution was busily
employed as an artistic administrator, although his work found no favour with the
young Constructivists. During this time, however, he was refining his practice towards the
geometric, "hard-edge" style that he was to
develop fully on his establishment, in 1921, in
the Bauhaus.

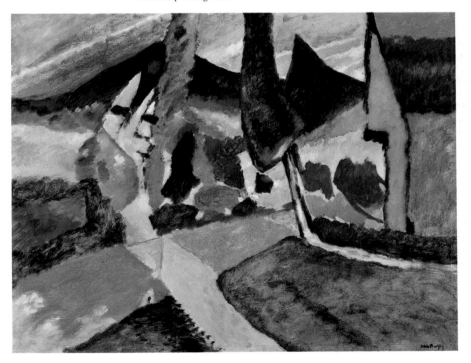

MATISSE:
Le Luxe II

"With '*Le Luxe II*'", George Heard Hamilton has observed, "Matisse completed and closed the Fauve revolution." By the time the painting was finished, in 1908, Henri Matisse (1869-1954) was no longer young, but in the previous years he had refined, consolidated and then unleashed his feeling for the expressive possibilities of luminous colour, first fostered in Moreau's studio ten years earlier.

Unlike his fellow-Fauve Vlaminck, Matisse was a conscientious student of the art both of the past and of his contemporaries: "I have never shunned outside influences. I should consider that an act of cowardice, and bad faith towards myself. I believe that the struggles that an artist undergoes help him assert his personality." In the late 1890s he was painting landscapes very much in Impressionist terms, with, however, at one stage (sometimes called "proto-Fauve") greater audacity of colour contrast than the Impressionists had ever shown; in 1900, though he was then quite the reverse of rich, he bought Cézanne's *Three bathers* (not shown), and certain compositions on the same lines show Matisse thereafter grappling with problems of form as well as colour. A crucial lightening and kindling of colour seems then to have been sparked by a summer spent at St-Tropez with Signac.

Matisse painted "*Luxe, Calme et Volupté*" in 1904-05, applying the divisionist technique in almost doctrinaire fashion, producing a mosaic of short stabs of colour. The result is somewhat stilted and inert, but it is nevertheless the point of departure for "*Le Luxe II*" (a shortened version of the first title, which was a phrase from Baudelaire) and for much of Matisse's future career. It states above all the theme of the female nude, but also the artist's mature quest for "an art of balance, of purity and of serenity devoid of troubling or disturbing subject matter ... like a comforting influence, a mental balm – something like a good armchair in which one rests from physical fatigue". Nothing, perhaps, could seem further from that ideal than the Fauve explosion of colour that came in 1905 (see preceding page), but in the great canvas "*La Joie de Vivre*", nearly two and a half metres (8ft) wide, which he finished in the following year, that aim is almost completely achieved. The divisionist technique has yielded to clear contour, curvaceous line – though there is little depth; the scenery seems composed of stage flats. Perspective is abandoned, and the figures and their scale are arbitrary, attenuated or distorted as the rhythms of the design may require. Technically, the picture owes much to Gauguin, and much also surely to the sinuous linearism of Art Nouveau. Its theme is Arcadian – such a vision as has haunted European fantasy since Titian's *Bacchanals* (see vol. 2 p. 145), a terrestrial paradise that not only Signac and Derain but also Renoir, Gauguin and Cézanne had glimpsed.

Then "*Le Luxe*" *I* and *II* come as the climax of this development – the process of reduction and elimination of inessentials in the design, the distillation of Matisse's art to its characteristic flat colour and line. The theme is still *Bathers*: indeed the two major figures are adapted from two on the left edge of "*La Joie de Vivre*". In the study, "*Le Luxe I*", the brushwork is relatively loose, the colours broken, the contours tentative, and auras, or penumbras, around the figures, though diminished, are present here and there. In the final version, "*Le Luxe II*", the clarity of contour is final, the penumbras eliminated; the ragged edge of the cloud is now smooth. The line is comprehensive, incisive, incomparably economic. The colour is lucent.

Matisse did not share Vlaminck's urge to translate impression into instant expression. "I want to achieve that state of condensation of sensations which makes a picture ... a representation of my mind." The sentiment may suggest a close relationship between Matisse and the early Cubists, but the *Luxe* series and *The dance* of 1910 could be read almost as anti-Cubist manifestos. Although Matisse's painting subsequently went through a phase sometimes described as "constructivist" – a sharp disciplining of the lyrical curve of his line – his pure singing colour and his characteristic fluent arabesque line were to be reasserted in his work during the 1920s and 1930s and not least in the remarkable colour cut-papers he made in his 70s and 80s.

MATISSE (below)
"*Luxe, Calme et Volupté*", 1904-05
The title is a phrase from Baudelaire's *Invitation to the Voyage*: "There, all is order, beauty, luxuriance, calm and voluptuousness." Cézanne's *Bathers* theme is treated in Signac's style.

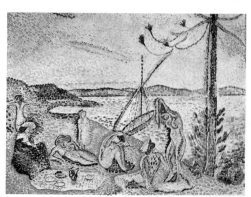

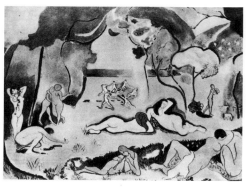

MATISSE (above)
"*La Joie de Vivre*", 1905-06
Here Matisse reached an expression unmistakably his own (greatly disappointing his mentor Signac). His soft, flat tints and strong curves exhale a serene bliss; some of the nudes retain from "*Luxe, Calme et Volupté*" their penumbras, on which they recline pneumatically.

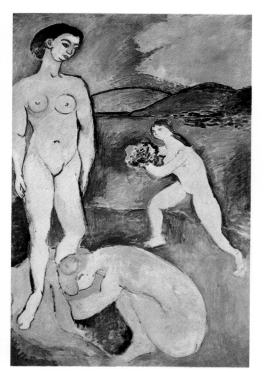

MATISSE (right)
The dance, 1910
Matisse detached the group of dancers from "*La Joie de Vivre*", transforming the distant, relatively loose-knit circle into a tighter design, a fully independent picture. The fast tempo of a *farandole* performed at the famous Moulin de la Galette inspired him. The rhythmic lines of the figures are even bolder than those of "*Le Luxe II*", a lithe pattern in themselves – the rapid development of Matisse's flat colour and flowing line reaches culmination.

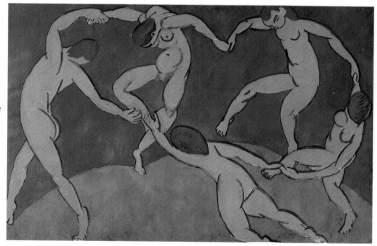

MATISSE (above)
"*Le Luxe I*", 1907
Viewing the full-scale oil-sketch for "*Luxe II*" the critic Barr felt that, after study, "the earlier picture ("*Luxe I*") grows on one despite its faults or perhaps because of them. The sense of experiment and struggle sets up a tension that holds the interest by comparison with the decorative grace of the second version." The light is unnatural, but the colour more realistic than in Fauve paintings, the forms more modelled.

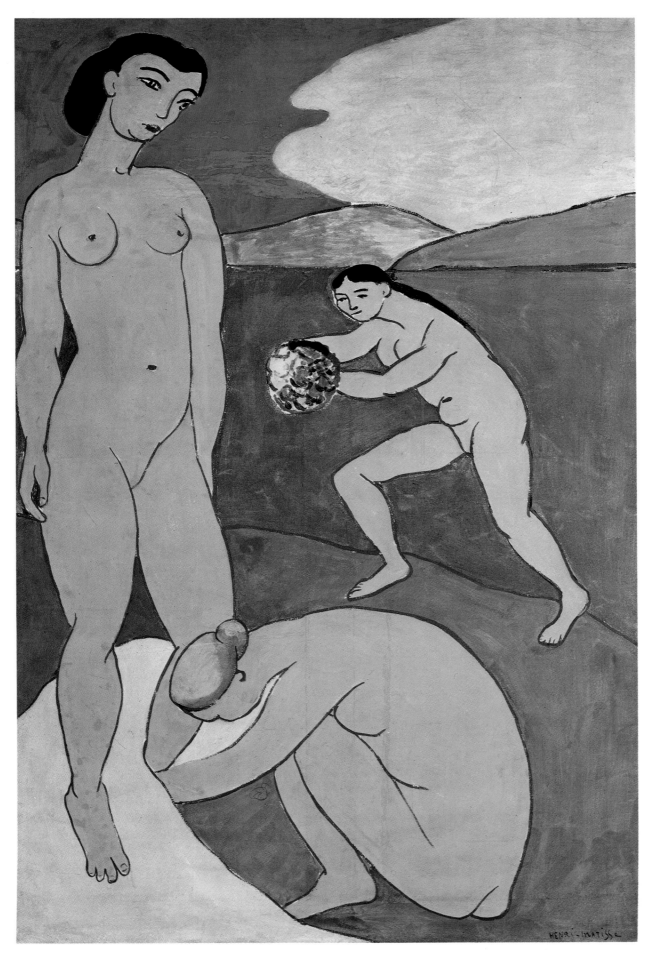

MATISSE (left)
"*Le Luxe II*", 1907-08
Matisse's teacher Moreau
is said to have remarked:
"Henri, you were born
to simplify painting."

MODIGLIANI:
Chaim Soutine

In 1917 in Paris Amedeo Modigliani (1884-1920) painted Chaim Soutine. Modigliani and Soutine were colleagues and drinking companions. Modigliani set his friend within the rather narrow compass of a tall canvas, which he had by then established as his chosen format for single portraits. Cézanne had used a similar scheme, and Modigliani had been impressed no doubt by Cézanne's example, his unflinching confrontation with his sitters; but the format also accentuates Modigliani's characteristically elongated, attenuated vision. His subject is reduced to an almost schematic formula of a long oval (the body, with the hands looped to clasp somewhat primly) linked to a second, smaller oval (the head) by an elongated neck (when his sitter was female, it grew sometimes swan-like). In Soutine's portrait there is a minor elaboration in the formula, provided by the compartmentation of the picture space by the corner of the room and by the rudimentary table with the glass, perhaps witness to their shared interest. However, the variations that Modigliani achieved within this simple, almost monotonous scheme were remarkable: Chaim Soutine is subtly but strongly characterized, an individual human being. Details are subordinate to the painter's need for a certain balance and rhythm in the composition, but the likeness is there, even though the neck is long and the eyes somewhat eccentrically aligned. There is surely a reflection of Soutine's character in the handling, and especially in the choice of colour. In his early paintings, Modigliani relied on a very limited, rather sombre palette of ochres, greys, browns and beautiful muted reds (with a pale fluid blue glint for the eyes); the strong colours used here may acknowledge the violence of colour of Soutine's own painting.

Modigliani's colours may well have been influenced by the similar palette of Cubist painting, or even by that of Cézanne, but otherwise, apart from occasional angular distortions (which as much reflected the idioms of African art), Modigliani's style was not fundamentally affected by the Cubist revolution. His work vividly illustrates just how cogent traditional figurative painting can be in the hands of a great talent, taking what seemed profitable from avantgarde explorations and proceeding along its own course. Modigliani, from an Italian Jewish family, academically trained in Italy, came to Paris in 1905 or 1906. He rapidly established the Douanier Rousseau and Picasso as his idols, but his dependence on Italian tradition was ineradicable, and his linear fluency, his elegance, seem to echo Florentine Mannerist art, or Botticelli.

One might not perhaps guess from this portrait that both Modigliani and Soutine belonged to that group of artists sometimes known as *les peintres maudits* – doomed or accursed painters, the archetypal Bohemian artists of popular legend. Modigliani, however, was fatally infected by tuberculosis even before he came to Paris, and there his excesses of drink and drugs, combined with extreme poverty, hastened his death at the age of 36; the macabre coda to which was the suicidal fall of his mistress Jeanne Hébuterne with their baby daughter from a fifth-floor window the following day.

His legend, and the strict, even mannered limitations within which he worked, have in part obscured the remarkable strength and subtlety of Modigliani's work. Besides portraits, he also painted nudes, again in the same sinuous elongations, but with a freshness both pristine and evocatively sensuous. His modelling is achieved by the subtlest gradation of tone and hue; the dominant quality is always linear, and some of his prolific drawings are masterpieces of comprehensive economy. His ambitions as sculptor were furthered by Brancusi's example; he created in a series of tall enigmatic stone heads, in which an African mystery is combined with that of Archaic Greece or Egypt, some of the most haunting "archetypal" images of modern art.

MODIGLIANI (below)
Reclining nude, c. 1919
So harmonious and graceful is the line that one does not at first notice a dislocation of hip and torso as radical as any to be found in Matisse. Though the older man exercised a profound influence over Modigliani, studies such as this seem also to refer back to the great European tradition of reclining nudes, to Giorgione and Ingres – more sensuous than Manet.

MODIGLIANI (below)
Head of a young woman, 1907
The cool, subdued tones are typical of what the artist later liked to dismiss as his "Whistler period". His work became brighter and more sculptural after the major Cézanne exhibition of 1907.

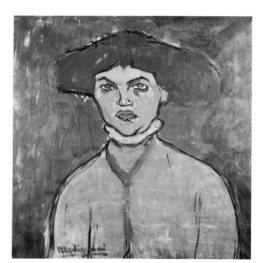

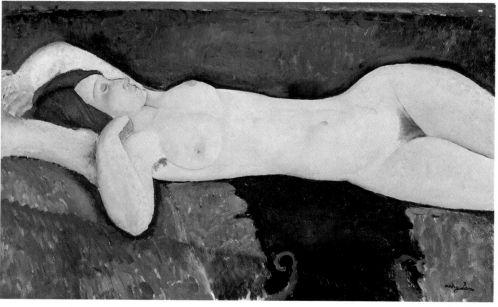

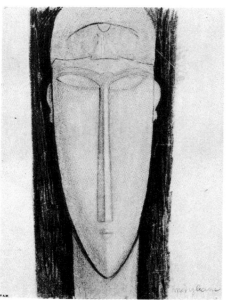

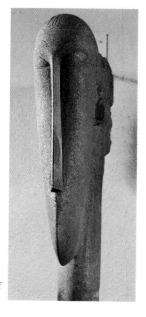

MODIGLIANI (left)
Study for a stone *Head,* 1909-15
The severely simplified shapes give the impression of being exercises in pure geometric drawing which, almost fortuitously, come together to suggest a human face. Within this reduction of form to essentials there is also a cool spirituality that is even more apparent in the carved stone *Heads.*

MODIGLIANI (right)
Head, 1911-12
Tuberculosis forced the artist to abandon sculpture in 1915; however, in a few years he had created from a knowledge of West African figures and Greek *Kouroi* some immensely powerful images. These heads have a refined monumental grandeur, confuting any notion of Modigliani's art as slight.

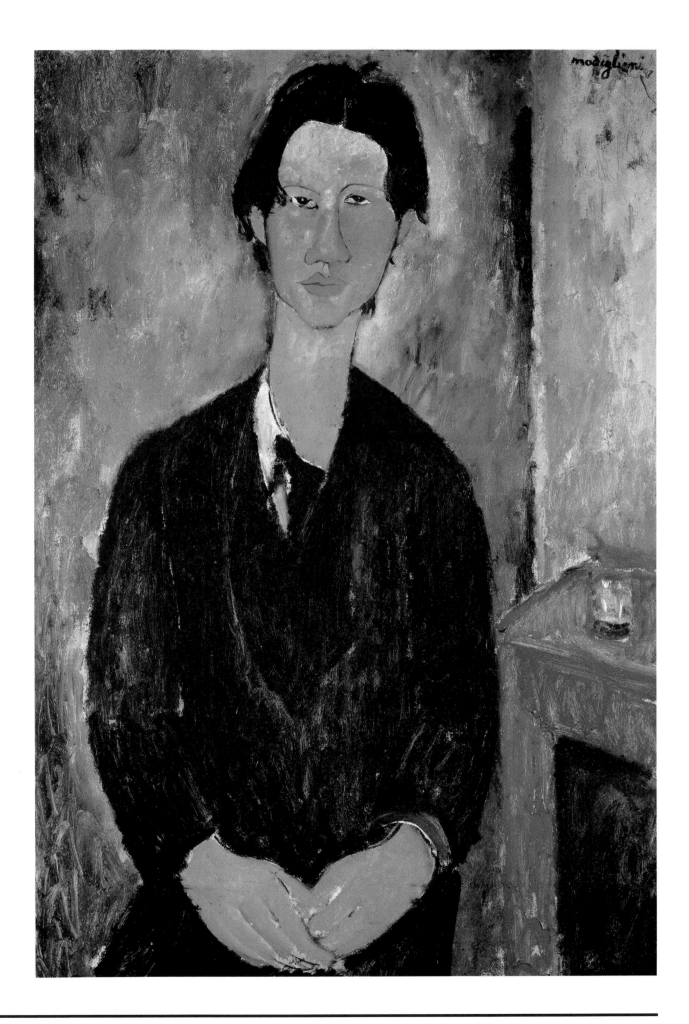

MODIGLIANI
Chaim Soutine, 1917

MONDRIAN:
Composition in Yellow and Blue

Towards the end of his life Piet Mondrian wrote: "It is important to discern two sorts of equilibrium in art – (1) Static balance (2) Dynamic equilibrium ... The great struggle for artists is the annihilation of static equilibrium in their paintings through continuous oppositions (contrasts) ... Many appreciate in my former work just the quality which I did not want to express, but which was produced by an incapacity to express what I intended to express – dynamic movement in equilibrium." At first glance *Composition in yellow and blue*, a classic specimen of Mondrian's most successful period, the 1920s and 1930s, may indeed impress the spectator as a precisely static balance; only on longer contemplation does the

tension between the component forms become more positive and vital. The forms – seven rectangles, one yellow, one blue, the rest pure white, compartmented by black lines of varying thickness – are a consequence of Mondrian's early discovery "that the right angle is the only constant relationship, and, through the proportions of dimension, its constant expression can be given movement, that is, made living". Mondrian's ability to avoid inertness in the most austere designs becomes clear when successive variations on a compositional theme are considered together: though the basic formula in each case is the same, the number of satisfactory resolutions appears infinite.

Piet Mondrian, born in Amersfoort, near Utrecht, was trained in Amsterdam in the prevalent Dutch naturalist tradition, but was soon affected by modern trends – Symbolism, Neo-Impressionism. Almost from the start a pronounced feeling for linear structure and a strong contrast between horizontal and vertical shaped his compositions; constant throughout his career was the ascetic austerity of his spiritual quest for essential truth. (It owed much no doubt to his strict Calvinist background; he was a committed theosophist, and deeply influenced by the philosophical writings of Schoemaekers.)

In 1911-14 Mondrian was in Paris, and was attracted by Cubist theory and practice, but

"gradually I became aware that Cubism did not accept the logical consequences of its own discoveries, it was not developing abstraction towards its ultimate goal, the expression of pure reality". Mondrian's urge to extract the essence is illustrated in variations on several themes early in his career, of which those on the tree are the most famous – moving from relatively naturalistic drawing, through vividly unnaturalistic and expressive colour, to linear and faceted simplification, resolved in nearly complete abstraction.

In Amsterdam, during World War I, Mondrian found sympathetic support for his views especially from Theo van Doesburg; De Stijl was established under their leadership. In 1919

Mondrian moved back to Paris, where he remained until another war drove him first to London, then to New York. His living quarters in Paris were eloquent of his commitment to De Stijl theories – floor, walls and furniture were all integrated into a unity of design, a total environment. It was in Paris that Mondrian pared away his compositions to their utmost simplicity, reducing the number of elements, using a square rather than a rectangular canvas, banishing grey from his palette as too indecisive. He made diamond-shaped canvases from 1919 onwards, their diagonals acting as taut stays against the vertical and horizontal thrusts of the black lines: many paintings are in black and white

alone. *Fox-trot A*, 1930, is one of the most austere but also vital examples of his "dynamic movement in equilibrium". The title reflects another aspect of Mondrian's character; he was addicted to dancing and to jazz, and the theme recurs in the latest development of his style, in the four years in New York (which he loved) before his death in 1944.

Mondrian sought a completely objective quintessence in his art, and yet his paintings are not analysable or translatable in terms of scientific or mathematical formulae. They remain in the end a subjective statement, their success dependent on the exquisite sensibility with which the dynamic equilibrium is poised – his "equivalence of opposites".

MONDRIAN (left)
The red tree, 1908
The desire for order is implicit (as in Cézanne, as in Seurat) not only in the stark, elementary subject but also in the controlled strokes, neatly juxtaposed, of the brush. Fauvism has liberated the colour.

MONDRIAN (right)
The flowering apple-tree, 1912
Cubism has intervened. It has hastened Mondrian to break down the forms into elements reconstituted on the canvas. But there is little depth; and soon he was to discard volume altogether.

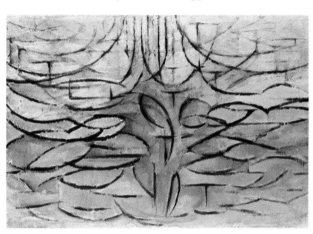

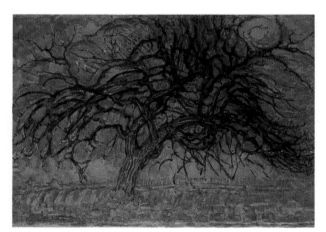

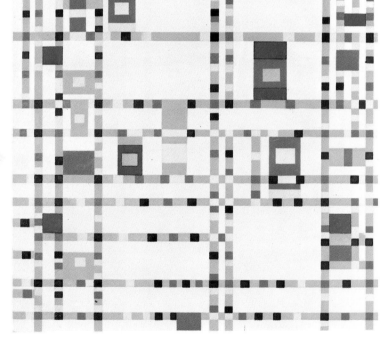

MONDRIAN (left)
Composition in yellow and blue, 1929
Mondrian's work was underpinned both by a rigorous sense of truth and by a profound belief in order. Human society was moving into a new age, in which, if there were order, there would be greater happiness. Of this art was an aspect.

MONDRIAN (above)
Fox-trot A, 1930
Mondrian observed that no loss of equilibrium was entailed in a square picture hung diagonally, although diagonals inside the picture destroyed its containment, introducing an alien commotion. He deplored other De Stijl artists' use of curves.

MONDRIAN (above)
Broadway Boogie-Woogie, 1942-43
Passionate about dancing, Mondrian was inspired by the jazzy pace of Boogie-Woogie in his last works. This painting, a delighted salute both to jazz and also to the dizzy street-grid of Manhattan, is a highly controlled explosion of colour

in a complex composition from which black has been entirely eliminated, though the other colours, red, blue and yellow, are Mondrian's usual primaries – the change does not betray principle. In 1944, only weeks before his death, he explained: "True Boogie-Woogie I conceive as homogeneous in intention with mine in

painting – destruction of melody, which is the equivalent of destruction of natural appearance; and construction through the continuous opposition of pure means . . ." to achieve dynamic rhythm. *Victory Boogie-Woogie* (not shown), his unfinished last painting, hung diagonally, has the same clean clear rhythm.

BECKMANN:
Departure

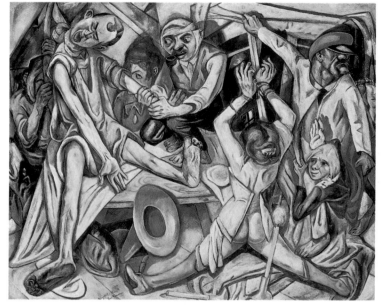

The figures are almost clamped in heavy black
outlines, and the space they occupy bears in on
them and compresses them still further – the
claustrophobic effect is overwhelming. The
subject matter is unconscionably brutal, and
worked with an appropriately coarse violence.
Yet man in the lifetime of Max Beckmann
(1884-1950) proved to be only too capable of
the imprisonment, mutilation and mental torture that ravage his first triptych, *Departure*.
The colour is generally sombre, kindling with
the glow and flush of a stained-glass window,
and the three panels read as a sort of post-
Christian altarpiece recording the events of a
modern Revelations. Triptychs soon became a
favourite form of Beckmann's, and their violent, complex themes, evoking the circus, the
stage and classical myth in a very Germanic
interpretation, have, though always personal,
a resonant twentieth-century relevance.

Max Beckmann began his career as a painter
in a relatively orthodox style. His independent
spirit, however, amounted already to high
arrogance: his reaction on his first visit to

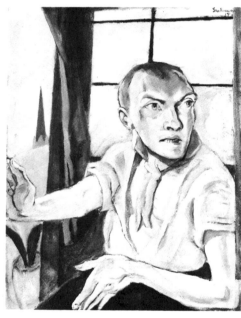

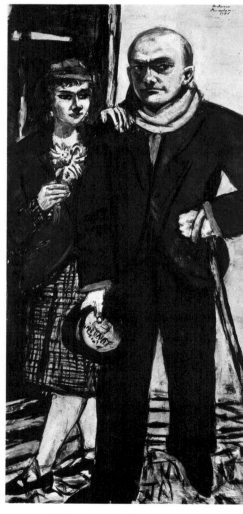

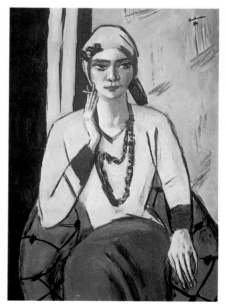

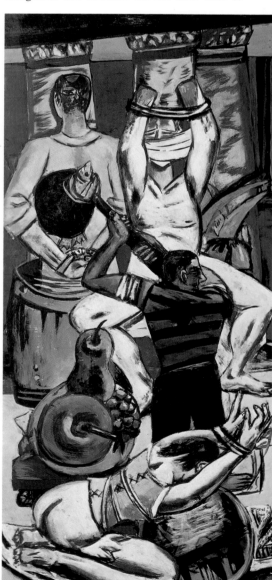

Paris, aged 19, was: "What's there, I know already." This confidence was matched by a striking ability. He had established a reputation by the time of his first one-man exhibition (in Frankfurt) in 1911, and by then he was demonstrating two qualities that would persist throughout his career – his ability to control large and complex compositions, and an obsession with horrific subject matter.

Before World War I, Beckmann had encountered in *Der Blaue Reiter* the belief of Franz Marc in an art "seeking and painting the inner spiritual side of nature", together with a demand for utter artistic objectivity towards the thing represented. In 1914, Beckmann worked as medical orderly on the front, but was released in 1915, apparently after a nervous breakdown. The experience of the horror of war proved the turning-point for his view of nature and of man. Stylistically and emotionally, his examples became Bruegel, Signorelli and the brutal assault on the emotions of Grünewald, while his stark and heavily outlined figures, massive within the frame,

directly recall the fierceness of Die Brücke artists, of Kirchner and also of Rouault. In his stubborn insistence on veristic representation he is close to some painters of the Neue Sachlichkeit, but Beckmann's intellectual stature, his ego, the thrust and concentration of his vocation, set him apart from all his German contemporaries; indeed the power of his achievement has caused some critics to compare him with Picasso (characteristically, Beckmann himself suggested that Picasso's stupendous *Guernica* was a distorted Beckmann). Undoubtedly he was a myth-maker of the order of Picasso, capable of creating a world of events rationally and even symbolically inexplicable, yet which are compelling as illustrations of hidden but eternal truths.

Beckmann seems to have absorbed what he needed from the compositional methods of the Cubists, but the structural – as it were materialist – concerns obsessing modern movements did not involve him. "Self-realization is the urge of all objective spirits. It is this Ego for which I am searching in my life and in my art

... My way of expressing my Ego is by painting ... Nothing could be more ridiculous or irrelevant than a 'philosophical conception' painted purely intellectually without the fury of the senses grasping each visible form of beauty and ugliness."

Naturally one subject to which he reverted constantly in his search for his ego was his own person – a range of *Self-portraits* in which he appears in various disguises or with strange attributes – horns, saxophones – or as a character in one of his mythologies, or, most tellingly, foursquare as a modern urban man, often in suit and bowler hat, an implacable, unplaceable presence. Leaving Germany on the eve of the Nazi exhibition of "Degenerate Art" in 1937, he established himself in obscure isolation in Paris, and then in Amsterdam. "Nothing shall disturb my composure" is a note that recurs in his diary for the catastrophic year of 1940. In America from 1947 till his death three years later, he re-emerged into critical acceptance, and his stature has since continued to grow.

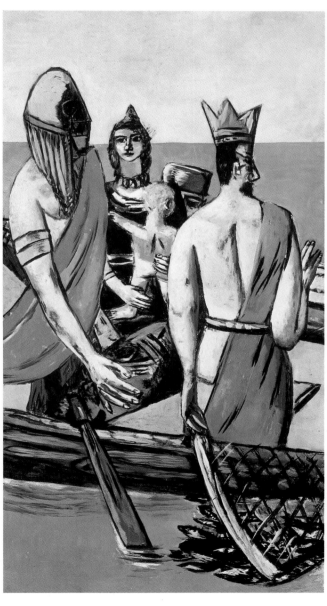
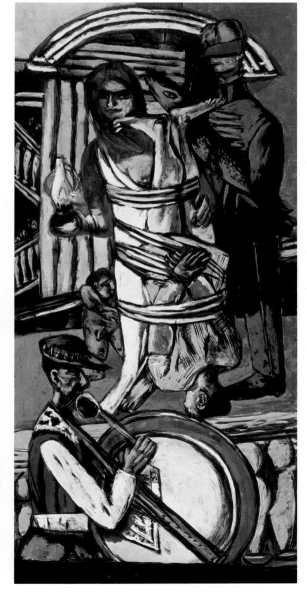

BECKMANN (left)
Departure, 1932-35
The triptych form evokes a long tradition in north European painting, from Gothic altarpieces to Hans von Marées' Symbolist art in the 19th century, and Nolde's religious triptychs in the 20th. Beckmann began to exploit the full symbolic and monumental potential of the form in 1932 with his *Departure*, the first of nine finished triptychs. The shadow of Christian imagery hangs over its mythical subject: in the left-hand panel the figure bound to a column echoes the flagellation of Christ. Beckmann's friend Perry Rathbone explained *Departure* in these words: "The side panels symbolize, on the left, man's brutality to man in the form of a callous executioner and his victims; on the right, the unbearable tragedy that Nature itself inflicts on human life as symbolized by the mad hallucinations of a woman encumbered by the lifeless form of a man. Out of this earthly night of torment and anguish, the figures of the central panel emerge into the clear light of redemption and release, embarked for eternity." Beckmann said that the centrepiece was the end of the tragedy, but could not be understood except as one part of the whole.

DE KOONING:
Woman I

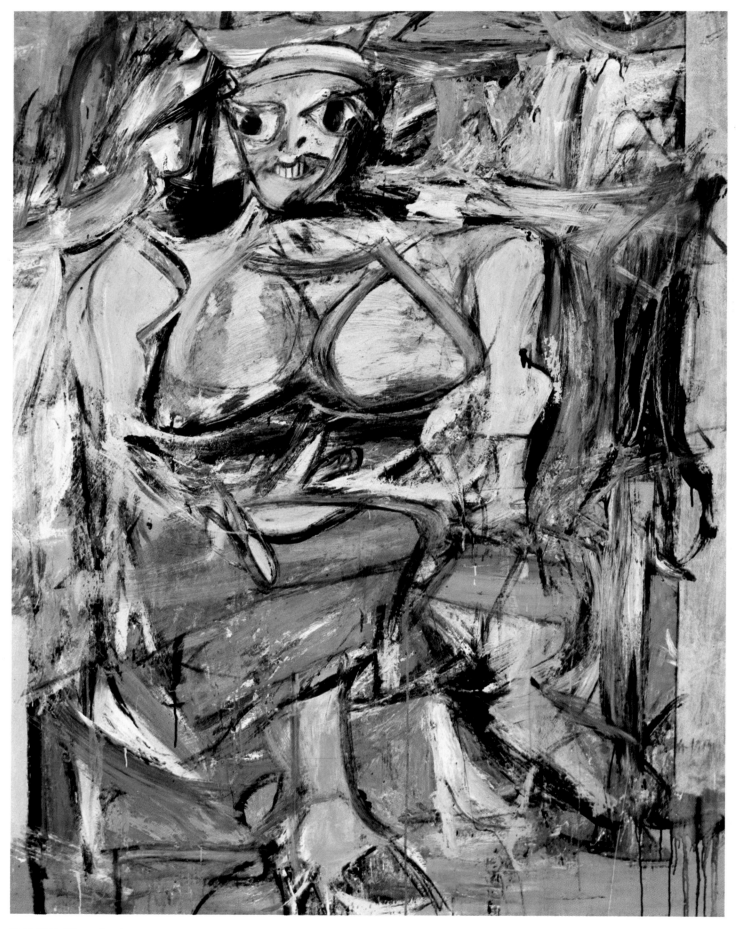

DE KOONING: *Woman I*, 1950–52

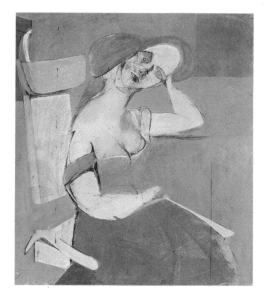

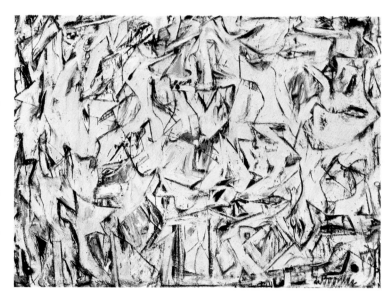

DE KOONING (right)
Excavation, 1950
Although De Kooning was at his closest to complete abstraction in *Excavation*, its shapes tend to suggest wild ghostly dancers. The painting was very heavily worked, reworked, scraped, rubbed and slashed, until its surface accumulated a solid, densely charged, intricately meshed relief.

DE KOONING (below right)
Study for *Woman*, 1949–52
Greenberg had described De Kooning's aims, before the *Women* alienated him, with sympathy – to recover "a distinct image of the human figure, yet without sacrificing anything of abstract painting's decorative and physical force".

DE KOONING (above)
Woman sitting, 1943–44
The thin washes of paint, the muted, delicate tones and graceful drawing recall some early works by Gorky, a fellow-European sharing with De Kooning a studio and an admiration for Picasso and Cubism. Gorky, however, painted very few figurative works.

DE KOONING (right)
Woman, 1943
No more than a fraction of De Kooning's 1940s work is extant. His reluctance to finish a painting was ingrained; if possibilities of further work on a canvas seemed unpromising, then often he would destroy it.

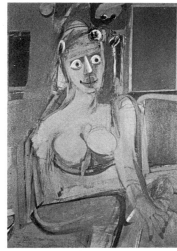

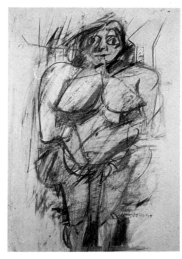

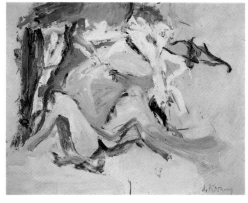

DE KOONING (below)
Woman on the dune, 1967
Splayed legs and a toothy grin are the only parts of the woman that are clearly decipherable; the rest of her is inextricably united with the riotous landscape.

The stature of Willem De Kooning (born 1904) is today clear: he was, with Pollock, the strongest and most original force amongst the painters associated with Abstract Expressionism. The intensity of dispute about the relative success or failure of his various shifts of style and subject is perhaps more telling as a witness to his importance than as criticism. While he was always committed to the physical, gestural side of Abstract Expressionism – a true, relentless Action Painter – De Kooning's work represents a figurative element in the movement: figuration seems to lurk in the tormented surface of his paint almost throughout his career: it emerges irresistibly, thrashing demonically through it.

De Kooning migrated from his native Holland to New York when aged 23. By 1939 he was a member of the group soon to be known as the New York school, and especially close to Arshile Gorky. In the 1930s he had painted, in rather delicate greyish, pinkish, greenish tones, alternately pure abstracts and what was virtually traditional figuration. By 1948, when he had his first one-man show, De Kooning's work was generally similar in effect to Pollock's – vigorous, gestural, and often in black and white, for he could not always afford to buy colour, although he was already celebrated in New York avantgarde circles. In

Excavation, an important work of 1950, he did use colour; as soon as this abstract had left the studio he was at work on *Woman I*. He continued to work on it for two years (it has been called "a noble battlefield rather than a completed painting"). Finished, or at least desisted from, in 1952, it was exhibited, with five other *Women, nos II-VI*, at his third one-man show in 1953; bought by the Museum of Modern Art, it became one of the most widely reproduced paintings of the 1950s and at the same time a focus for pugnacious controversy amongst not only public but critics: the two most influential critics of the New York avantgarde disagreed violently, Clement Greenberg attacking the rage of one betrayed, Harold Rosenberg remaining De Kooning's most loyal and articulate supporter. The believers in a rigorously abstract art were dismayed; the general public was shocked by the gross grinning ugliness of De Kooning's presentation of a classical subject, "the idol, the Venus, the nude", as he said.

On first impact, the image is indeed sinister, threatening. It has been construed as a satire on women, an ejaculation of fascinated horror at sexuality, an attempt at exorcism of the threatening Black Goddess or Earth Mother. De Kooning has insisted that it is also funny (specifically, "hilarious"), and that its banality

is deliberate ("I seem always to be wrapped in the melodrama of vulgarity") – this banality was later to be exploited, in very different techniques, by Pop artists. The ferocious leer is a sharpening of the toothpaste smile of magazine pin-ups: De Kooning liked to cut the smiles from the magazines, and in a *Woman* study of about 1950–51 the cut-out smile is pasted directly on to the oil-paint. ("I felt everything ought to have a mouth.") Portions of the anatomy of the *Women* were interchangeable: De Kooning often did drawings of details and tried them for size, pinning them here or there on the canvas.

Violence, energy and ambiguity are staple characteristics of De Kooning's work, but they are not used destructively; instead they are activated as part of the process of establishing an aesthetic order. In his later work, there is an element of landscape involved in the paint, and the female figures in the landscapes all tend to merge back into the vigorous brushwork: many of his later paintings seem closer to pure abstraction, and some find in them a falling off in power, compared to his earlier work. De Kooning is probably not worried. He once said: "Painting the *Woman* was a mistake. It could not be done . . . In the end I failed. But it didn't bother me . . . I felt it was really an accomplishment."

ALBERS:
Homage to the Square

The post-War movement in painting that shocked and dazzled the eyes of the Western world in the 1950s was the Abstract Expressionism of the New York school. The scale of their paintings, the unorthodox behaviour of the painters – the noise of it all – diverted the attention of the media and the general public from other, parallel trends in art. These did not, however, wither away. Problems of harmony and proportion in abstract painting were being explored by Josef Albers (1888-1976), who had been teaching at Black Mountain College in North Carolina since 1933, when he migrated there from the Bauhaus, closed in that year by the Nazis.

Albers was a quintessential product of the Bauhaus. He was there first as a student and then as a teacher, and was concerned as much with the applied as with the fine arts, working on the Constructivist side of Bauhaus theory, in the glass and furniture workshops. The clarity and irreducible economy of his future painting was already present in his stained or sand-blasted glass, and in his furniture designs – he was responsible for one of the first laminated wood chairs. In North Carolina, where he had a reputation primarily as a teacher, he explored the relations between geometry and colour in a series of paintings, *Variations on a Theme*, but only after he had

moved to Yale, in 1950, did he begin in earnest the sequence called *Homage to the Square*.

Homage to the Square consists of hundreds of paintings and prints all within a square format; though they vary in size, they all feature three or four squares, superimposed – a nest of squares positioned with vertical but not horizontal symmetry. Some are distinguished, within the series, by lyrical subtitles (*Distended*, *Softly spoken*, *Curious* etc.); some are only numbered. Albers used the formula to demonstrate his abiding belief in an essential dichotomy of art, "the discrepancy between physical fact and psychic effect". Thus the linear structure of his square pictures is of the most simple, unarguable clarity. The colour structure is created likewise in evenly applied paint, straight from the tube; the colour of each of the three or four squares usually has no variation of intensity, and so should be completely inexpressive of any quality other than its particular blueness, redness – its local colour. In fact, in the eyes of the onlooker, the flat picture plane becomes three-dimensional as one colour seems to advance, another to recede, according to its nature; furthermore, the pure evenness of colour within each square is affected optically by reaction to its neighbours – and all the colours shift character as the light in which they are seen changes. The colour is a mystery floating on the canvas, independent of the lines which contain it.

ALBERS (right)
Fugue, 1925
This is a good example of Albers' Bauhaus work, on opaque glass. The colour is removed through stencils to reveal the glass beneath.

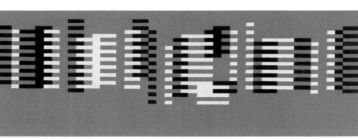

ALBERS (below)
Variation in red, 1948
Each of the *Variations on a Theme* has the same basic geometry in varied colours.

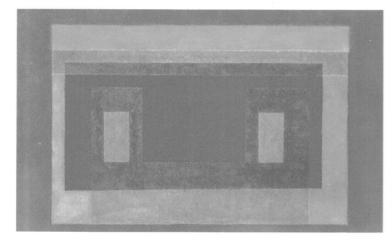

ALBERS (below)
Transformation of a scheme no. 24, 1952
The disturbing optical effect prefigures Op Art. This, too, is from a series.

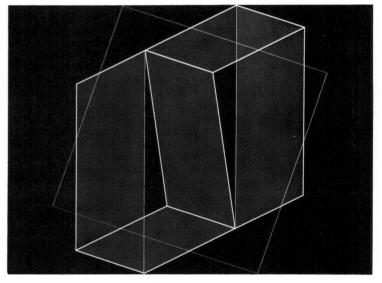

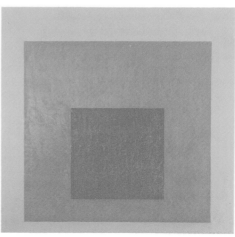

ALBERS
Studies for *Homage to the Square*:
(left) *Rain forest*, 1965;
(right) *R-NW IV*, 1966
In all the variations the largest square measures 10 units; the other squares set within it measure a varying number of units or half units. These two show a progression from base to top of $\frac{1}{2}$:1:4:3:1$\frac{1}{2}$; across the ratios are 1:2:4:2:1. *Confirming* (far right) has four squares, not three; the ratios are from base to top $\frac{1}{2}$:$\frac{1}{2}$:$\frac{1}{2}$:4:1$\frac{1}{2}$:1$\frac{1}{2}$:1$\frac{1}{2}$; across the ratios are 1:1:1:4:1:1:1.

ALBERS: Study for *Homage to the Square - Confirming*, 1971

Albers thought long and deeply on colour phenomena; his treatise *Interaction of Color* was published in 1963. He also played with another form of optical illusion in a series of linear drawings, black on white or vice versa, called *Structural Constellation* – the abstract equivalent of Escher's famous figurative nonsense drawings. Albers himself was not, however, the slave to a need to produce a closed logical system, and in *Homage to the Square* he presents the problem in an endless series of solutions, or variations, of the unreconciled yet reconciled co-existence of colour and geometrical linear structure on his canvases. He was

also a poet, and some of his poems state the paradox with equal wit and clarity.

Initial confrontation with a single Albers painting may be disappointing: they need really to be seen in a sequence, when the variation in scale, in the internal relationships of the nesting squares, but above all the play of colour over and through the invariable physical fact of the square, make their full impact.

Homage to the Square was the climax of Albers' remarkable career as a transitional figure between the European traditions and the new American. His work evolved from the European, non-objective art of the Construc-

tivists – of the early Russians, of Mondrian and De Stijl – through the aesthetic, and the moral and social commitment, of the Bauhaus. It is European in scale, best when small and intense (his large-scale murals were done by assistants from his blueprints); some have likened his *Homage* to Monet's famous series. His heirs, however, were the Americans of the late 1950s and the 1960s, who, while respecting the Abstract Expressionist achievement, found in his work a pattern and an intense colour sensation on which they could build (see over). Later again, his interest in perception became relevant for Op and even Conceptual art.

WYETH:
Christina's World

More sorts and kinds of people have responded directly to the paintings of Andrew Wyeth (born 1917) than to any other post-War American painter, yet his work remains controversial. In many accounts of post-War painting, for which the great American breakthrough of Abstract Expressionism is the springboard, he is simply omitted as an anachronistic irrelevance, yet not only is *Christina's world* (in the Museum of Modern Art, New York, since 1949) one of the best known and loved images of American art, but in 1976 Wyeth was given a major one-man retrospective exhibition in the Metropolitan Museum.

Andrew Wyeth is the son of N.C. (Newell Convers) Wyeth, a distinguished illustrator and painter. Brought up as it were breathing art, he proved a precocious virtuoso, and had his first one-man show in New York when he was only 20. In 1939 he came to know a brother and sister called Olson, on a remote farm in Maine; he spent the summers there, painting the farm, the region and a series of remarkable portraits of Christina Olson until her death in 1967. The first impact of *Christina's world* (finished in 1948) is eerie and troubling: the figure of the girl, seen from behind, twisted

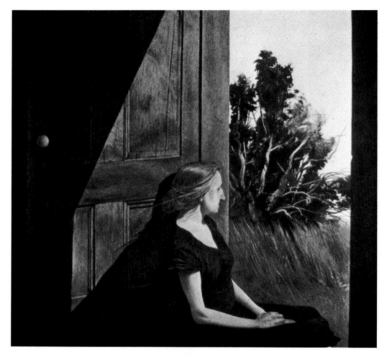

WYETH (left)
Christina Olson, 1947
Christina is sitting on the doorstep of her house. Late afternoon sun falls on the lined and wrinkled face and frail body, and it casts a strange shadow on the door behind her, which is as weathered as she is. She is looking out across the fields towards the sea: Wyeth said she reminded him of "a wounded seagull".

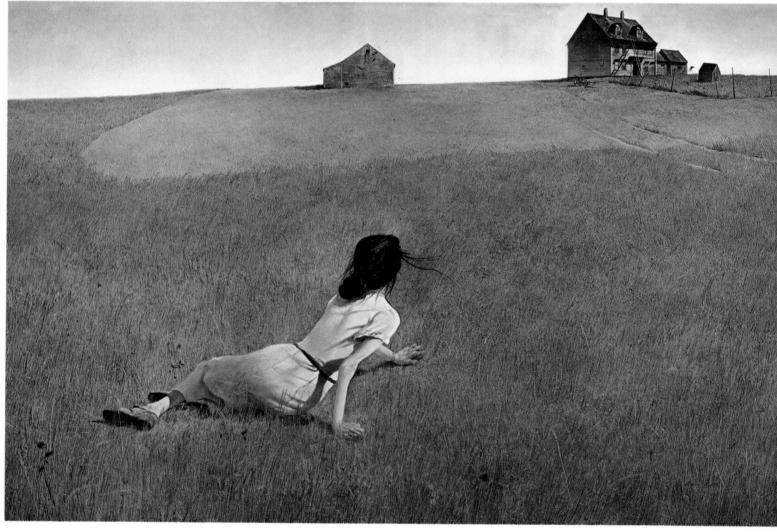

WYETH (above)
Christina's world, 1948
Wyeth was devoted to his sitter; he said: "Christina's *world* is more than just her portrait. It really was her whole life and that is what she liked in it. She loved the feeling of being out in the field, where she couldn't go, finally, at the end of her life . . . a lot of it came out of what she told me." The composition was prompted by a sight of her from a window in the house, when she had been out getting vegetables, "pulling herself slowly back towards the house".

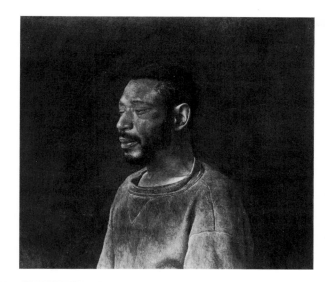

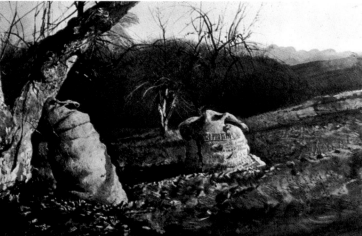

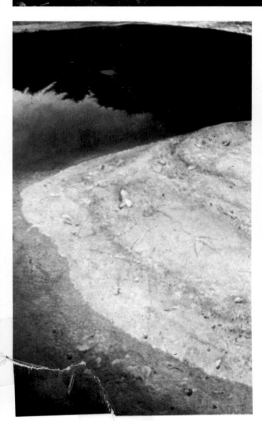

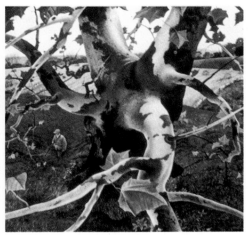

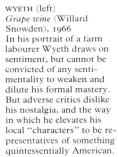

WYETH (left)
Grape wine (Willard Snowden), 1966
In his portrait of a farm labourer Wyeth draws on sentiment, but cannot be convicted of any sentimentality to weaken and dilute his formal mastery. But adverse critics dislike his nostalgia, and the way in which he elevates his local "characters" to be representatives of something quintessentially American.

WYETH (left)
Nick and Jamie, 1963
Many of Wyeth's works seem to be charged with an electric poignancy; this is particularly true of some interiors and landscapes that are portraits and yet unpeopled. Wyeth has discovered a way to invest objects and places with the presence of those no longer there; thus two sacks on a late autumn day evoke the artist's sons.

WYETH (left)
River cove, 1958
Tempera, for Wyeth, is almost a building material, and crucial to his aims: "I love the quality and the feel of it ... to me, it's like the dry mud of the Brandywine valley in certain times of the year, or like these tawny fields ... I really like tempera because it has a cocoon-like feeling of dry lostness – almost a lonely feeling."

WYETH (above)
The hunter, 1943
Apart from his holidays in Maine, on the Olsons' farm, Wyeth has spent his entire life in the small village of Chadds Ford, Pennsylvania. That is in part why his art is remote: these two regions form his world, he lives their landscapes, people and animals, while most artists, he has said, "just look at an object and there it sits".

awkwardly in the expanse of grass, is focused on the house on the crest of the slope. This house and the second house, seen directly behind Christina's head, and Christina's body are linked inexorably, pinioned on the three corners of a triangle, yet the sense of huge distance, seemingly unbridgable, physically or psychologically, between the woman and the main house on which the grey sky sits so claustrophobically is overwhelming. Many, perhaps most people assume at once that the subject is an attractive young girl, an interpretation prompted by what could be a youthful abandon in the grass, and by the slightness of the body, the adolescent fragility of the arms. In fact Christina Olson was at this time a mature woman, somewhat gaunt, and so severely crippled that she proceeded by dragging herself on her arms. Several of Wyeth's initial rough drawings (not shown) record his determination to discover the exact articulation of the maimed body, which in the finished painting seems to express both the tragedy and the joy of life with such vivid poignancy that the painting becomes a universal symbol of the human condition – and is recognized as such: the picture has had a continuing fan mail from people who have identified with it.

Wyeth has described his sequence of portraits of Christina: "I go from *Christina Olson* (1947), which is a formal one, a classic pose in the doorway, all the way through *Christina's world*, which is a magical environment, that is, it's a portrait but with a much broader symbolism, to the complete closeness of focusing in *Miss Olson* (1952; not shown). *Miss Olson* was a shock to some people who had the illusion that the person in *Christina's world* was a young, beautiful girl. And that is one reason why I did it, in order to break the image. But I didn't want to ruin the illusion really, because it's not a question of that. One has to have both sides – one, the highly poetic; the other, the close scrutiny ...."

Wyeth has denied any fundamental influence on his development from other painters, though he has acknowledged generously inspiration from artists as diverse as Winslow Homer and Albrecht Dürer. His affinities with the impassioned detail of Dürer (particularly the watercolours) are obvious, and his technique of dry brush over watercolour is close to Dürer's, and not far short of him in brilliance and virtuosity. In his large paintings, too, his techniques are resolutely traditional; he uses tempera rather than oil, with extreme sensitivity and with a range of earth colours. His practice is minute, laborious and slow, and the paintings are prefaced in great detail by preparatory drawings.

Wyeth's work at its best demonstrates that the traditional subjects, media and techniques of Renaissance painting can still result in images that have a profound significance. His work is also quintessentially American, and in a sense, though so different in technique, he offers the rural counterpart to Edward Hopper's earlier characterization of American urban townscape. A comparable sense of vastness, and of isolation and loneliness, invests the work of both, but is expressed by Wyeth in the intensity of his realization of detail.

BACON:
Figures in a Landscape

The emergence – eruption almost – of Francis Bacon's work in the 1950s was a shock to international art. Critics at first found his paintings hard to accept; his expressionist images forced attention in a context of all-conquering abstract or near-abstract art, developed in the early post-War years by Pollock and the Abstract Expressionists in America, by Ben Nicholson in England, and by Nicolas de Staël or Hans Hartung in Europe. Picasso, working in the figurative tradition, was already regarded as an Old Master.

However, the pictures of Francis Bacon (born 1909) were disturbingly relevant; and their formidable immediacy made it necessary to reconsider the assumptions made about figurative painting. Its once basic function, to achieve "a good likeness", had been undermined by photography a century earlier – portraiture especially seemed to be surviving as a social rather than as an artistic phenomenon – but this was not a return to naturalism. Bacon, abandoning the abstract decorations of his pre-War years, exploited photography for his own artistic ends. It became a springboard for a figurative art that was fundamentally unphotographic. Bacon also works from the life, but the results are not what an old-fashioned sitter would accept as portraiture. Though Bacon himself might not agree that this was his intention, he transmutes these given images into fluid, mutating visions that convey horror, violence and suffering. In his early figurative work, such as *Figure in a landscape* of 1945, he used some more or less traditional devices of Surrealism, but by 1950 he was concentrating on the theme, seemingly inexhaustible, that he has explored ever since – studies of a single figure in spotlit isolation, or two figures locked in struggle (or perhaps sometimes in love).

The origins of his images are usually clearly discernible, but always they have suffered melting, dissolving, change. Often his imagination seizes on one particular image from which a sequence of variations develops. The first and most famous of these was the *Screaming Popes* series, based on one of the most vividly sane and seemingly definitive portraits in all European painting, Velazquez's *Pope Innocent X*. This Bacon has avoided seeing in the original, but knows only from reproductions. Subsequent series included one based on van Gogh on his way to work, and one developed round the life-mask of the poet-painter William Blake. Other pictures, including *Figures in a landscape*, 1956, are inspired by the rapid-sequence photographs of the human body in action made by Eadweard Muybridge in the 1880s. In Bacon's portraits a constant theme is the confined, clinical space in which the isolated sitter is trapped.

Superficially, Bacon's compositions have a traditional structure, a perspective recession into depth; but once having entered the picture's space, the viewer's eye is puzzled and baffled. In *Figures in a landscape*, 1956, the subject seems unfocused, ambiguous – here the vertical stripes of green at the back might be a fence, or a curtain; the central landscape sprouts grass of some kind, but reads more like a pit or an arena; the two naked figures are certainly human – or used to be, or are about to be, human. Are they wrestling? If so, in hate or love? Even their sex is unclear. The subject rejects exact definition, and yet mesmerizes.

Bacon's appeal to post-War sensibility lies in the fact that while his creatures are indisputably flesh and blood and compel our unwilling identification with them, they are also convincing embodiments of mental anguish. Bacon has invented a new grammar and imagery of human expression. Its frame of reference is contemporary awareness of the horrors of the twentieth century – concentration camps, gas chambers, the continuing techniques of torture throughout the world – as well as the private mental disturbances revealed by psychoanalysis or described in Kafkaesque literature of claustrophobia and alienation. Bacon's use of a glass box (not only holding his figures in focus but trapping them) even prophesied a haunting image of post-War reality – Press photographs of the Nazi war criminal Eichmann in an armoured-glass dock at his trial in Israel.

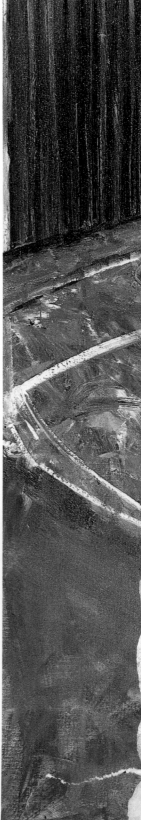

BACON (right)
Figures in a landscape, 1956
The naked human body is a main theme of Bacon's; a powerful sense of flesh as heir to pain and decay may stem from his view of man as "an accident, a completely futile being".

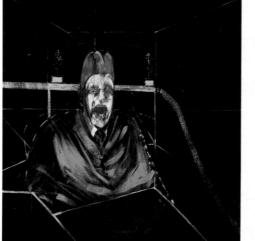

VELAZQUEZ (right)
Pope Innocent X, 1650
The very opposites of the qualities Velazquez set himself to convey – spiritual authority and temporal might – inspire Bacon: his studies of agonized beings are seemingly gripped by a horrific, negative vision of life. Feeling for colour and texture, however, is something in common.

BACON (left)
Study after Velazquez, 1953
Among the sources for this early study in the series of *Screaming Popes* are not only Velazquez's painting but a photograph of Pope Pius XII borne in a litter above the crowds and the sketch of a howling face by Poussin for his *Massacre of the Innocents* (not shown).

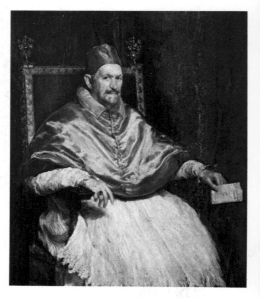

BACON (right)
Figure in a landscape,
1945
A photograph of a friend
dozing in the park becomes
an image of menace; hands
rest casually on the arm
of the chair, but the head
has melted away and at the
elbow is a machine-gun.

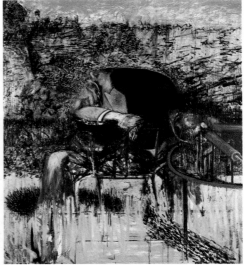

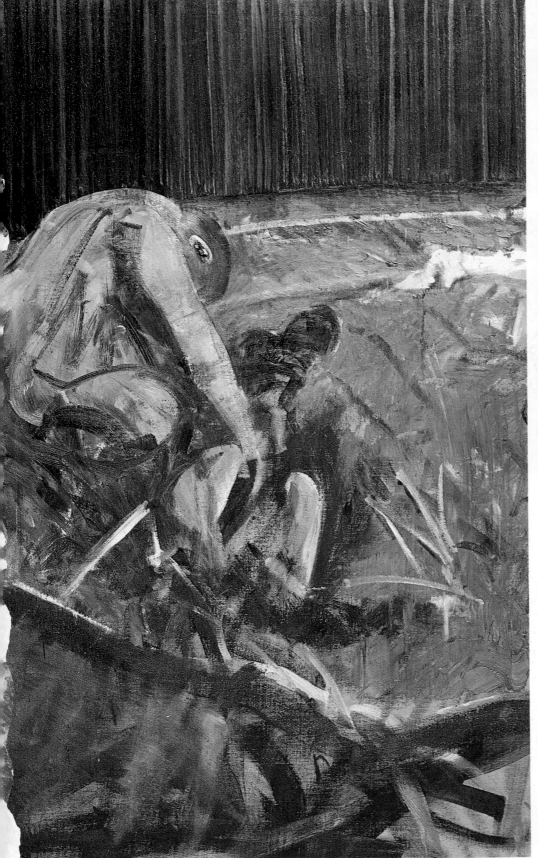

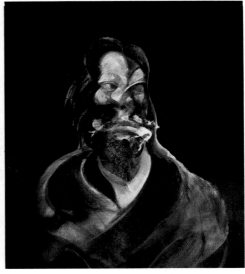

BACON (above)
Isabel Rawsthorne, 1966
Features grossly distorted
by dynamic brushwork, as if
rent by an obsessive scream,
are typical of Bacon's
expressive portraiture.

EISENSTEIN (below)
Still from the film *The
Battleship Potemkin*, 1925
The helpless individual, a
children's nurse caught in
a Revolutionary chaos, was
a potent image for Bacon.

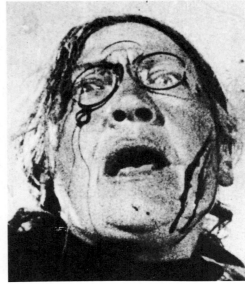

Illustrations and Acknowledgments

Works of art illustrated are listed in the order in which they appear in the book. In general, the order runs from top to bottom and left to right on each page, though works by the same artist or of the same origin are grouped together.

The name of the artist (or, if the artist is not known, the place of origin) and the title or description of each work are followed by its medium, its dimensions (metric) and its present location and ownership. Photographic credits are given in brackets (S for Scala) unless the photograph has been supplied by the owner.

Though every effort has been made to check the accuracy of these specifications, it has not always been possible to verify all of the information at source.

6–15 Introduction

RENOIR: *The theatre box* (La loge), 1874, oil on canvas, 80 × 60 cm, London, Courtauld Institute Galleries.
MASTER OF MARY OF BURGUNDY: *Maximilian and Mary of Burgundy before the Virgin*, from the Book of Hours of Charles the Bold, c. 1477, Cod. 1857, fol. 14v. Vienna, Österreichische Nationalbibliothek.

16–17 Variations on Twelve Themes

TITIAN: "*The Concert Champêtre*" (Pastoral music making), oil on canvas, 110 × 138 cm, Paris, Louvre (Scala).
LEONARDO: *A woman pointing*, after 1513, black chalk, 21 × 13.5 cm, Windsor, Royal Library (by gracious permission of Her Majesty the Queen).

18–19 The Human Face

LEONARDO: *Mona Lisa*, c. 1503–06, oil on panel, 77 × 53 cm, Paris, Louvre (Scala).

20–21 The Human Face

JOSEPH WRIGHT: *The Corinthian Maid*, 1784, oil on canvas, 106.7 × 127 cm, Upperville, Virginia, Mr and Mrs Paul Mellon Collection.
AMMAN: *Jericho skull*, c. 6000 BC, skull, shell and clay, Amman, Archaeological Museum (Scala).
RUBENS: *Susanna Lunden*, c. 1622–25, oil on panel, 79 × 54 cm, London, National Gallery.
J. S. DEVILLE: Life-mask of William Blake, c. 1825, plaster, height 29 cm, Cambridge, Fitzwilliam Museum.
POLYEUKTOS: Detail of head from the statue of *Demosthenes*, original c. 280 BC, marble, height 202 cm, Copenhagen, Ny Carlsberg Glyptotek.
DAVID: *Napoleon in his study*, 1812, oil on canvas, 202 × 124 cm, Washington, National Gallery of Art, Samuel H. Kress collection.
GILLRAY: *Maniac ravings*, 24th May 1805, lithograph, London, British Museum (John Freeman).
BRAQUE: *Man with a guitar*, 1911, oil on canvas, 116 × 81 cm, New York, Museum of Modern Art, Lillie P. Bliss Bequest.
DIX: *Sylvia von Harden*, 1926, oil on panel, 121 × 89 cm, Paris, Musée National d'Art Moderne.

22–23 The Human Face

DURER: *Self-portrait naked*, c. 1510,
pen and brush, heightened with white on green paper, 19.5 × 15.5 cm, Weimar, Kunstsammlungen (Eberhard Renno)
REMBRANDT: *Self-portrait*, 1669, oil on canvas, 86 × 70.5 cm, London, National Gallery.
HOKUSAI: *Self-portrait*, c. 1843, drawing, Leyden, Rijksmuseum voor Volkerkunde.
COURBET: *The meeting*, 1854, oil on canvas, 129 × 149 cm, Montpellier, Musée Fabre (Photo Bulloz).
VAN GOGH: *Self-portrait*, 1890, oil on canvas, 63 × 53 cm, Paris, Louvre, Musée Jeu de Paume (Scala).
CEZANNE: *Self-portrait in a hat*, 1880, oil on canvas, 65 × 51 cm, Berne, Kunstmuseum (Colorphoto Hans Hinz).
CLOSE: *Self-portrait*, 1968, acrylic on canvas, 273 × 212 cm, Minneapolis, Walker Art Center.
KOKOSCHKA: *Self-portrait*, 1913, oil on canvas, 80 × 48 cm, New York, Museum of Modern Art.

24–25 The Human Figure

TANZANIA: Rock-painting of a bushman painting a mountain, from a Neolithic site in s.w. Africa, dimensions unrecorded, *in situ* (Gerald Cubitt).
EGYPT: *Fowling in the marshes*, from the Tomb of Nebamun, 1400 BC, fresco, London, British Museum (Michael Holford).
ANAVYSOS, ATTICA: *Kouros*, c. 540–515 BC, marble, height 193 cm, Athens, National Museum (Scala).
DURER: *Nude woman*, 1493, drawing, Bayonne, Musée Bonnat (Photo Bulloz); *Eve*, c. 1506, both versions pen and bistre on wash, 26 × 16.5 cm, Vienna, Albertina.
GREECE: "*The Venus de Milo*", c. 100 BC, marble, height 180 cm, Paris, Louvre (Alinari).
KHAJURAHO, INDIA: Sculptural decoration from the Kandarya Mahadeva Temple, c. 1000 (René Roland).
RAPHAEL: *The three Graces*, 1504–05, oil on panel, 17 × 17 cm, Chantilly, Musée Condé (Giraudon).

26–27 The Human Figure

TINTORETTO: *Susannah and the Elders*, c. 1550, oil on canvas, 143.5 × 193 cm, Vienna, Kunsthistorisches Museum, (Scala).
REMBRANDT: *Bathsheba at her toilet*, 1654, oil on canvas, 142 × 142 cm, Paris, Louvre (Documentation Photographique de la Réunion des

Musées Nationaux).
RUBENS: *Bathsheba reading David's letter*, c. 1636–38, oil on panel, 167 × 125 cm, Dresden, Gemäldegalerie (Cooper-Bridgeman Library).
BOUCHER: *Miss O'Murphy*, 1732, oil on canvas, 59 × 73 cm, Munich, Alte Pinakothek (Scala).
COURBET: *The artist's studio*, 1854–55, oil on canvas, 361 × 598 cm, Paris, Louvre (Scala).
BOCCIONI: *Unique forms of continuity in space*, 1913, bronze, height 109.5 cm, New York, Museum of Modern Art, Lillie P. Bliss Bequest.
BRANCUSI: *Male torso*, after 1924, brass, height 45.5 cm, Ohio, Cleveland Museum of Art, Hinman B. Hurlbut collection.
DE KOONING: *Woman IV*, 1952–53, oil and enamel on canvas, 150 × 118.5 cm, Kansas City, Missouri, Nelson Gallery-Atkins Museum, Gift of Mr William Inge.
PICASSO: *Nude in an armchair*, 1932, oil on canvas, 130 × 97 cm, London, Tate Gallery.

28–29 Couples

DURER: *Adam and Eve*, 1507, diptych, oil on panel, *Adam* 209 × 81 cm, *Eve* 209 × 83 cm, Madrid, Prado (Scala).
VAN EYCK: "*The Arnolfini Marriage*", 1434, oil on panel, 81.5 × 59.5 cm, London, National Gallery.
EGYPT, MEIDUM: *Prince Rahotep and his wife, Nofret*, c. 2550 BC, painted limestone with inlaid eyes, height 120 cm, Cairo, Egyptian Museum (Kuhnert and Landrock); A panel of Tutankhamun's throne, before 1361 BC, wood plated with gold and silver, inlays of glass and paste, height 104 cm, Cairo, Egyptian Museum (Werner Forman Archive).
IRAN: *Salaman and Absal reach the shore of the sea*, 1556–65, manuscript fol. 194b from the *Haft Awrang* of Jami, 34 × 23 cm, Washington, DC, Freer Gallery of Art.
REMBRANDT: "*The Jewish Bride*", c. 1665, oil on canvas, 121.5 × 166.5 cm, Amsterdam, Rijksmuseum (Scala).
DOGON: *Male and female principals*, undated, wood, height 85 cm, New York, Schindler Collection (Werner Forman Archive).
MOORE: *King and Queen*, 1952–53, bronze, height 161 cm, Washington DC, Hirshhorn Museum and Sculpture Garden, Smithsonian Institution (John Tennant).
GROSZ: *A married couple*, 1930, watercolour, 66 × 47.5 cm, London Tate Gallery.
WOOD: *American Gothic*, 1930, oil on board, 76 × 63 cm, Chicago, Art Institute of Chicago.

30–31 Couples

KHAJURAHO, INDIA: The Kandarya Mahadeva Temple, c. 1000, sandstone (Werner Forman Archive).
TITIAN: *Venus and the organ player*, c. 1550, oil on canvas, 148 × 217 cm, Madrid, Prado (Scala); *Io and Jupiter*, c. 1560, charcoal, 25 × 26 cm, Cambridge, Fitzwilliam Museum.

KORYUSAI, JAPAN: *Shunga*, second half of 18th century, woodcut, London, Victoria and Albert Museum (Cooper-Bridgeman Library).
HOGARTH: *Before the Seduction* and *After*, 1731, oil on canvas, 35.5 × 44.5 cm, Malibu, J. Paul Getty Museum.
COURBET: *The sleepers*, 1862, oil on canvas, 75 × 95 cm, Paris, Petit Palais (Scala).
MUNCH: *Vampire*, 1895–1902, lithograph, 38.5 × 54.5 cm, Oslo, Munch Museet (Scala).
SCHIELE: *The embrace*, 1917, oil on canvas, 100 × 170.5 cm, Vienna, Österreiches Galerie.

32–33 Life and Work

THE LIMBOURG BROTHERS: *Les Très Riches Heures du Duc de Berri; February, October and June*, 1413–16, colour on vellum, 21.5 × 14 cm, Chantilly, Musée Condé (Giraudon).

34–35 Life and Work

DELLA QUERCIA: *Labours of Adam and Eve*, c. 1428, marble relief, height 99 cm, Bologna, S. Petronio (Giraudon).
THEBES: *Harvesting*, c. 1450 BC, wall-painting, Thebes, Tomb of Menna (Ronald Sheridan).
BRUEGEL: *August (The corn harvest)*, 1565, oil on panel, 118 × 160.5 cm, New York, Metropolitan Museum of Art, Rogers Fund.
ANTELAMI: *June* and *September*, c. 1200, stone, Parma, Baptistery (Scala).
CRETE: *The Harvesters' Vase*, c. 1550 BC, diameter 11.5 cm, London, British Museum (Ronald Sheridan).
STUBBS: *The reapers*, 1795, enamel on a Wedgwood plaque, 77 × 103 cm, Yale Center for British Art, Paul Mellon collection.
MILLET: *The reaper*, c. 1866–68, wood engraving, New York, Metropolitan Museum of Art, Harris Brisbane Dick Fund.
VAN GOGH: *The reaper*, 1889, oil on canvas, 43.5 × 33.5 cm, Amsterdam, National Museum Vincent van Gogh.

36–37 Life and Work

REMBRANDT: *The anatomy lesson of Dr Tulp*, 1632, oil on canvas, 169.5 × 216.5 cm, The Hague, Mauritshuis (Scala).
EAKINS: *The Gross Clinic*, 1875, oil on canvas, 244 × 198 cm, Philadelphia, Jefferson Medical College of Jefferson University (Cooper-Bridgeman Library).
VERMEER: *Servant girl pouring milk*, c. 1663, oil on canvas, 43.5 × 41 cm, Amsterdam, Rijksmuseum (Cooper-Bridgeman Library).
REYNOLDS: *Dr Johnson*, 1756, oil on canvas, 122 × 97 cm, London, National Portrait Gallery.
HODLER: *The woodcutter*, 1910, oil on canvas, 261 × 212 cm, Sao Paulo, Museum of Art (Giraudon).
DEGAS: *The Cotton Exchange at New Orleans*, 1873, oil on canvas, 73 × 92 cm, Pau, Musée des Beaux-Arts (Giraudon).
LEGER: *The builders*, 1950, oil on

canvas, 300 × 200 cm, Biot, Musée Fernand Leger.

38–39 Life and Leisure
RENOIR: *The luncheon of the boating party*, 1881, oil on canvas, Washington DC, Phillips Collection.

40–41 Life and Leisure
EXEKIAS: *Dionysos sailing*, c. 550 BC, black-figure *kylix*, Munich, Antikensammlung.
HARUNOBU: *Girl with a lantern on a balcony viewing plum-blossoms at night*, c. 1768, woodcut, 32.5 × 21 cm, New York, Metropolitan Museum of Art.
GIOVANNI BELLINI: *The feast of the gods*, 1514, oil on canvas, 170 × 188 cm, Washington, National Gallery, Widener collection.
BRUEGEL: *The peasant wedding*, c. 1567, oil on oak, 114 × 163 cm, Vienna, Kunsthistorisches Museum (Cooper-Bridgeman Library).
WATTEAU: *Les Champs-Elysées*, 1717, oil on canvas, 40.5 × 31.5 cm, London, Wallace Collection (John Freeman).
FRITH: *Derby Day*, 1856–58, oil on canvas, 101 × 223 cm, London, Tate Gallery.
KIENHOLZ: *Barney's Beanery*, 1965, mixed-media environment, life-size, Amsterdam, Stedelijk Museum.
MATISSE: *"La Joie de Vivre"*, 1905–06, oil on canvas, 174 × 238 cm, Merion, Pennsylvania, Barnes Foundation.

42–43 Life and Leisure
AFTER MYRON: *"Diskobolos"* (The discus thrower), original c. 450 BC, marble, height 147 cm, Rome, Museo della Terme (Scala).
DE HOOGH: *Skittle-players*, c. 1663–66, oil on canvas, 66 × 70 cm, Aylesbury, Waddesdon Manor (National Trust).
ROUSSEAU: *The ball-players*, 1908, oil on canvas, 100 × 80 cm, New York, Solomon R. Guggenheim Museum.
TERBORCH: *The concert*, shortly after 1675, oil on wood, 56 × 44 cm, West Berlin, Staatliche Museen (Bildarchiv Preussischer Kulturbesitz).
AFTER CARAVAGGIO: *The card-players*, 17th century, oil on canvas, 96.5 × 117 cm, Cambridge, Mass., Fogg Art Museum (Gift: Friends of the Fogg Art Museum).
KHNOPFF: *Memories*, 1889, pastel, 127 × 200 cm, Brussels, Musées Royaux des Beaux-Arts.
SHAHN: *Handball*, 1939, tempera on paper, mounted on board, 58 × 79.5 cm, New York, Museum of Modern Art (Scala).
CEZANNE: *The card-players*, 1890–92, oil on canvas, 45 × 57 cm, Paris, Louvre, Musée Jeu de Paume (Scala).

44–45 Narration
ALTDORFER: *The battle of Alexander and Darius on the Issus*, 1529, oil on panel, 158.5 × 120.5 cm, Munich, Alte Pinakothek (Scala).

46–47 Narration

CANTERBURY: The Bayeux Tapestry: *Construction of the fleet*, c. 1080, embroidered cotton, height 50 cm, length 69 metres, Bayeux Musée (Scala).
GIOVANNI DI PAOLO: *St John entering the wilderness*, c. 1450, tempera on panel, 31 × 39 cm, London, National Gallery.
RUBENS: *The marriage* from the Marie de' Médicis cycle, c. 1622–25, oil on canvas, 394 × 295 cm, Paris, Louvre (Scala).
LICHTENSTEIN: *Whaam!* 1963, 172.5 × 406.5 cm, acrylic on canvas, London, Tate Gallery.
HOGARTH: *The arrest* and *The prison*, from *The Rake's Progress*, c. 1733, oil on canvas, 62 × 75 cm, London, Sir John Soane's Museum (Cooper-Bridgeman Library).
GREECE: Sepulchral monument, 5th century BC, marble, Athens, National Museum (Scala).
HUGHES: *Home from the sea*, 1862, oil on panel, 51 × 65 cm, Oxford, Ashmolean Museum.
RIVERA: Mural, c. 1924–27, Chapingo, Mexico, National School of Agriculture.

48–49 Narration
POMPEII, AFTER PHILOXENES?: The *Alexander mosaic*, *Alexander meets Darius in battle*, original c. 300 BC, mosaic, height 3.7 m, Naples, Museo Nazionale (Scala).
GERMANY: *Alexander the Great in single combat*, 13th century, manuscript illumination, Hanover, Kestner Museum.
RUBENS: *The battle of the Amazons*, c. 1618, oil on canvas, 121 × 165 cm, Munich, Alte Pinakothek (Scala).
RUDE: *"La Marseillaise"* (*The departure of the volunteers*), 1833–36, stone, 12.7 × 6 metres, Paris, Arc de Triomphe (Giraudon).
PICASSO: *Guernica*, 1937, oil on canvas, 351 × 782 cm, Cason del Buen Retiro, Madrid (Museum of Modern Art, New York).
VELAZQUEZ: *The surrender of Breda*, 1634–35, oil on canvas, 307 × 370 cm, Madrid, Prado (Scala).
LEUTZE: *Washington crossing the Delaware*, 1850, oil on canvas, 387.5 × 644.5 cm, New York, Metropolitan Museum of Art, Gift of John Stuart Kennedy.
GOYA: *The same*, from *The Disasters of War*, 1810–15, etching, 16 × 22 cm (The Mansell Collection).
GROSZ: *Republican automatons*, 1920, watercolour, 60 × 50 cm, New York, Museum of Modern Art, Advisory Committee Fund.

50–51 Landscape
HOKUSAI: *Southerly wind and fine weather* from *Thirty-six views of Mt Fuji*, c. 1823–29, woodcut, 25.5 × 38 cm (Tokyo, Heibonsha Publishers Ltd).

52–53 Landscape
LI CHENG?: *Buddhist temple in the mountains after rain*, c. 1000, ink and light colour on silk, 110 × 55 cm, Kansas City, Missouri, Nelson Gallery-Atkins Museum, Nelson

Fund.
POMPEII: *Landscape with villa*, c. 50 BC, wall-painting, House of the Vettii (Scala).
GIOVANNI DI PAOLO: *Madonna and Child in a landscape*, c. 1432, tempera on panel, 56 × 43 cm, Boston, Museum of Fine Arts.
DURER: *The piece of turf*, 1503, watercolour and gouache on paper, 41 × 31.5 cm, Vienna, Albertina.
VAN EYCK: *The Madonna with Chancellor Rolin*, c. 1435, oil on panel, 66 × 62 cm, Paris, Louvre (Scala)
BRUEGEL: *The hunters in the snow (January)*, 1565, oil on oak, 117 × 162 cm, Vienna, Kunsthistorisches Museum (Cooper-Bridgeman Library).
JACOB VAN RUISDAEL: *Wheatfields*, c. 1670, oil on canvas, 100 × 130 cm, New York, Metropolitan Museum of Art.

54–55 Landscape
GAINSBOROUGH: *Mr and Mrs Andrews*, c. 1748, oil on canvas, 69 × 119 cm, London, National Gallery.
CLAUDE: *Egeria mourning over Numa*, 1669, oil on canvas, 155 × 199 cm, Naples, Museo di Capodimonte (Scala).
TURNER: *Burning of the Houses of Parliament*, 1834, oil on canvas, 92.5 × 113 cm, Cleveland Museum of Fine Art, Gift of Hanna Fund.
CONSTABLE: *Fording the river, showery weather*, 1831, oil on canvas, 136 × 188 cm, London, Guildhall (Cooper-Bridgeman Library).
COURBET: *Seaside at Palavas*, 1854, oil on canvas, 39 × 46 cm, Montpellier, Musée Gustave Courbet (Claude O'Sughrue).
MONDRIAN: *The sea*, 1914, charcoal and gouache on paper, 90 × 123 cm, New York, Solomon R. Guggenheim Museum.
HOPPER: *Highland light*, 1930, watercolour, 46 × 63.5 cm, Harvard University, Fogg Art Museum, Louise E. Bettens Fund.

56–57 Animals
LASCAUX, FRANCE: "The Hall of Bulls", in use c. 15090 BC, cave-paintings (Colorphoto Hans Hinz).

58–59 Animals
CONSTANTINOPLE: *Adam naming the beasts*, 4th/5th century AD, ivory, Florence, Bargello (Scala).
SAQQARA, EGYPT: Bronze *Cat*, after 30 BC, bronze, nose and ear-rings gold, breast inlaid with silver, height 33 cm, London, British Museum (Ronald Sheridan).
CRETE: Bull's head *rhyton*, c. 1500 BC, stone, wood, crystal and shell, height 21 cm, Heraklion, Archaeological Museum (Sonia Halliday).
COURBET: *The death of the stag*, 1867, oil on canvas, 355 × 500 cm, Besancon, Musée des Beaux-Arts (Giraudon).
CANOVA: *Theseus and the Minotaur*, c. 1781–82, marble, height 147 cm, London, Victoria and Albert Museum.

FRANCE: *To my sole desire*, from *The Lady of the Unicorn*, c. 1480–90, tapestry, Paris, Musée Cluny (Scala).
PICASSO: Vollard Suite no. 85, *Drinking Minotaur and sculptor with two models*, 1933, etching (Christie's/ A. C. Cooper).
REMBRANDT: *Three elephants*, c. 1637, black chalk, 23 × 34 cm, Vienna, Albertina.
DURER: *The young hare*, 1502, watercolour, 25 × 22.5 cm, Vienna, Albertina.

60–61 Animals
VERROCCHIO: *Bartolommeo Colleoni*, 1481–90, height about 4 metres, Venice, Campo SS. Giovanni e Paolo (Scala).
LEONARDO: *Study of a rearing horse*, c. 1498–90, red chalk, 15.5 × 14 cm, Florence, Gabinetto Nazionale dei Disegni e Stampe (Scala).
WUWEI, EASTERN CHINA: *"Flying Horse"*, 2nd century AD, bronze, length 45 cm, from tomb at Leit'ai, Gansu, China (Robert Harding Associates).
PISANELLO: *Horses*, c. 1433–38, pen on paper, height 20 × 16.5 cm Paris, Louvre (Photo Bulloz).
STUBBS: *Mares and foals*, 1762, oil on canvas, 89 × 200.5 cm, London, Earl Fitzwilliam Collection (Cooper-Bridgeman Library).
GERICAULT: *A horse frightened by lightning*, c. 1820, oil on canvas, 49 × 60.5 cm, London, National Gallery.
DEGAS: *A carriage at the races*, 1877–80, oil on canvas, 66 × 82 cm, Paris, Louvre, Musée Jeu de Paume (Scala).
MUYBRIDGE: *Sally Gardner running*, 1878, New York, International Museum of Photography.
MARINI: *Little rider*, 1946, bronze, height 49 cm, Rome, Galleria Nazionale d'Arte Moderna (Scala).
DUCHAMP-VILLON: *The horse*, 1914, bronze, height 100 cm, New York, Museum of Modern Art, Van Gogh Purchase Fund.

62–63 Still Life
VAN GOGH: *Still life with drawing board*, 1889, oil on canvas, 50 × 63 cm, Otterlo, Rijksmuseum Kröller-Müller; *Self-portrait*, January 1889, oil on canvas, 60 × 49 cm, London, Courtauld Institute Galleries (Cooper-Bridgeman Library).

64–65 Still Life
ROME: *A basket of flowers*, 2nd century AD, floor mosaic, Vatican, Museo Pio Clementino (Scala).
ZHAO JI: *Birds and flowers*, early 12th century, ink and colours on silk, London, British Museum (Cooper-Bridgeman Library).
VAN EYCK: *St Jerome*, 1442, oil on panel, 20 × 13 cm, Detroit, Detroit Institute of Arts.
CARAVAGGIO: *A basket of fruit*, 1596, oil on canvas, 46 × 64.5 cm, Milan, Pinacoteca Ambrosiana (Scala).
VAN BEYEREN: *Still life with wine ewer*, after 1655, oil on canvas, 79.5 × 63.5 cm, Ohio, Toledo Museum of Art, Gift of Edward Drummond Library.

COORTE: *A bundle of asparagus*, 1703, oil on canvas, 30 × 23 cm, Oxford, Ashmolean Museum.
BAUGIN: *Still life with a chequerboard (The five senses)*, c. 1630, oil on panel, 55 × 73 cm, Paris, Louvre (Documentation Photographique de la Réunion des Musées Nationaux).

66–67 Still Life
REMBRANDT: *The flayed ox*, 1655, oil on panel, 94 × 68 cm, Paris, Louvre (Scala).
CHARDIN: *The white tablecloth*, c. 1737, oil on canvas, 99 × 119 cm, Chicago, The Art Institute of Chicago.
REDON: *Wild flowers*, after 1912, pastel, 57 × 35 cm, Paris, Louvre (Scala).
RAPHAELLE PEALE: *After the bath*, 1823, oil on canvas, 73.5 × 61 cm, Kansas City, Missouri, Nelson Gallery-Atkins Museum, Nelson Fund.
CEZANNE: *Still life with apples and oranges*, 1895–1900, oil on canvas, 73 × 93 cm, Paris, Louvre, Musée Jeu de Paume (Scala).
GRIS: *Breakfast*, 1914, oil, pasted paper and crayon, 81 × 59.5 cm, New York, Museum of Modern Art, Lillie P. Bliss Bequest.
JOHNS: *Painted bronze II: ale cans*, 1964, painted bronze, 13.5 × 12 cm, New York, the artist's collection.

68–69 Images of Divinity
REMBRANDT: *The three crosses*, 1653 and c. 1662, etching in the 2nd and 4th states, 38.7 × 45 cm, London British Museum.
PISANELLO: *Gianfrancesco Gonzaga*, c. 1439, bronze, diameter 8.5 cm, Brescia, Museo Civico (The Mansell Collection).

70–71 Images of Divinity
ENGLAND: Crucifix, 10th/11th century, ivory, London, Victoria and Albert Museum (Cooper-Bridgeman Library).
GERMANY: Abbess Mathilde's Cross, 974–982, gold, gems, pearls, enamels and silver gilt, height 45 cm, Essen, Cathedral Treasury (Bildarchiv Foto Marburg).
GERMANY: Plague Cross, 1304, wood, Cologne, Schnutzen Museum (Rheinisches Bildarchiv).
GRUNEWALD: Isenheim altarpiece, 1515, oil on panel, 269 × 593 cm, Colmar, Unterlinden Museum (Scala).
RAPHAEL: *"The Mond Crucifixion"*, 1502–03, oil on wood, 280.5 × 165 cm, London, National Gallery.
EL GRECO: *Crucifixion with a landscape*, 1600–10, oil on canvas, 193 × 116 cm, Cleveland Museum of Art, Gift of Hanna Fund.
GAUGUIN: *"The Yellow Christ"*, 1889, oil on canvas, 92 × 73 cm, Buffalo, Albright-Knox Art Gallery (Scala).

72–73 Allegory, Myth and Fantasy
GIOVANNI BELLINI: *"The Sacred Allegory"*, c. 1490, oil and tempera on panel, 72 × 117 cm, Florence, Uffizi (Scala).

74–75 Allegory, Myth and Fantasy
RAIMONDI: *The Judgment of Paris*, c. 1516, 29 × 43 cm, engraving after Raphael, London, British Museum.
EWORTH: *Queen Elizabeth confounding the three goddesses*, 1569, oil on panel, 71 × 84.5 cm, Windsor, Royal Collection (by gracious permission of Her Majesty the Queen).
BLAKE: *The Judgment of Paris*, 1817, watercolour, 39.5 × 47 cm, London, British Museum.
RUBENS: *The Judgment of Paris*, c. 1632–35, oil on wood, 145 × 193.5 cm, London, National Gallery.
ROWLANDSON: *Englishman in Paris*, 1807, ink and watercolour over pencil, height 15 × 24 cm, London, Wellington Museum.
MANET: *"Le Déjeuner sur l'Herbe"*, 1863, oil on canvas, 208 × 264 cm, Paris, Louvre, Musée Jeu de Paume (Scala)
PICASSO: *"Le Déjeuner sur l'Herbe"*, 1962, lithograph, 25 × 32 cm, Private collection (Christie, Manson and Wood).

76–77 Allegory, Myth and Fantasy
KUNIYOSHI: From *"The Heroes of Suikoden"*, *Tameijiro dan Shogo grapples with his enemy under water*, 1828–29, woodcut, B. W. Robinson Collection (Cooper-Bridgeman Library).
GIAMBOLOGNA: *The rape of the Sabine*, 1579–83, marble, 410 cm, Florence, Loggia dei Lanzi (Scala).
TIEPOLO: *Apollo pursuing Daphne*, c. 1755–60, oil on canvas, 69 × 87 cm, Washington, National Gallery of Art, Samuel H. Kress Collection.
BOTTICELLI: *Venus and Mars*, c. 1485, tempera on panel, 69 × 173 cm, London, National Gallery.
BLAKE: *The great red dragon and the woman clothed with the sun*, c. 1800–10, watercolour, 34 × 50 cm, New York, Brooklyn Museum, Gift of William Augustus White.
BROWN: *Work*, 1852–63, oil on canvas, 134.5 × 196 cm, Manchester City Art Gallery.
DAUMIER: *The triumph of Menelaus*, 1842, lithograph, London, British Library.
MAGRITTE: *The house of glass*, 1939, gouache, 32 × 38.5 cm, Rotterdam, Museum Boymans-van Beuningen. (Edward James Foundation).
ROUSSEAU: *The dream*, 1910, oil on canvas, 204.5 × 298 cm, New York, Museum of Modern Art, Gift of Nelson A. Rockefeller.

78–79 The Inward Eye
ROTHKO: *Black on maroon*, 1958, oil on canvas, 266.5 × 366 cm, London Tate Gallery.

80–81 The Inward Eye
VAN DER WEYDEN: *The Last Judgment*, detail, c. 1450?, oil on panel, width 560 cm, Beaune, Musée de l'Hôtel-Dieu (Photo Bulloz).
BOSCH: *The Garden of Earthly Delights*, detail, c. 1505–10, oil on wood, 220 × 195 cm, Madrid, Prado (Scala).

MICHELANGELO: *The Last Judgment*, detail, 1534–41, fresco, Vatican, Sistine Chapel (Scala).
GOYA: *The colossus*, 1808–12, mezzotint, 25 × 20.5 cm, Paris, Bibliothèque Nationale (Immédiate 2).
DALI: *3 Young Surrealist women holding in their arms the skins of an orchestra*, 1936, oil on canvas, St Petersburg, Florida, Salvador Dali Foundation, Inc.
CHIRICO: *The enigma of the hour*, 1912, canvas, 55 × 71 cm, Milan, Mattioli Collection.
BACON: *Study after Velazquez*, 1953, oil on canvas, 152 × 117.5 cm, New York, Museum of Modern Art, Gift of Mr and Mrs William A. M. Burden.

82–83 The Inward Eye
BERNINI: *St Theresa*, 1646–52, marble, altarpiece figures life-size, Rome, S. Maria della Vittoria (Scala).
EL GRECO: *The Fifth Seal of the Apocalypse*, c. 1608–14, oil on canvas, 224.8 × 193 cm, New York, Metropolitan Museum of Art, Rogers Fund.
JAN AND HUBERT VAN EYCK: The Ghent altarpiece, finished 1432, oil and tempera on panel, overall height 340 cm, Ghent, St Bavo (Scala).
FRA ANGELICO: The Linaiuoli triptych, 1433, tempera on panel, 260 × 330 cm, Florence, S. Marco (Scala).
FRIEDRICH: *Moonrise over the sea*, 1822, oil on canvas, 55 × 71 cm, West Berlin, Staatliche Museen.
SPENCER: *The resurrection of the soldiers*, 1928–29, oil on canvas, 640 × 533 cm, Burghclere, Sandham Memorial Chapel (Jeremy Whitaker/National Trust).
MONDRIAN: *Composition in red, yellow and blue*, 1921, oil on canvas, 103 × 100 cm, The Hague, Gemeentemuseum.

84–85 The Language of Painting
FRA ANGELICO: *The Annunciation*, c. 1451–55, tempera on panel, 39 × 39 cm, Florence, Museo di S. Marco (Scala).
DAUMIER: *The connoisseurs*, 1860–63, oil on canvas, 23.5 × 31 cm, Rotterdam, Museum Boymans-van Beuningen.

86–87 Introduction
TITIAN: *Bacchus and Ariadne*, 1522–23, oil on canvas, 175 × 190 cm, London, National Gallery. Diagrams: (top) Alan Brown, (lower) Alan Suttie.

88–89 Scale and Space
BLAKE: *Glad day*, c. 1794, print worked up with watercolour, 27.5 × 20 cm, London, British Museum (Cooper-Bridgeman Library).
MUNCH: *Puberty*, 1895, oil on canvas, 151 × 110 cm, Oslo, National Gallery (Scala).
BECKMANN: *The trapeze*, 1923, oil on canvas, 193 × 84 cm, St Louis, Art Museum, Marton D. May collection.

MALEVICH: *Suprematist composition*, c. 1917, oil on canvas, 96.5 × 52 cm, New York, Museum of Modern Art.
COROT: *A view near Volterra*, 1838, oil on canvas, 69.5 × 95 cm, Washington, National Gallery of Art, Chester Dale collection. Diagrams: Alan Suttie.
RUBENS: *The fall of the damned*, c. 1614–18, oil on panel, 281.5 × 222 cm, Munich, Alte Pinakothek.
DELACROIX: *Librrty leading the people*, 1830, oil on canvas, 216 × 325 cm, Paris, Louvre (Scala). Diagrams: Alan Suttie.

90–91 Types of Pictorial Space
VAN DER GOES: *The Adoration of the shepherds*, from the Portinari altarpiece, c. 1474–76, panel, 245 × 297 cm, Florence, Uffizi (Scala).
NORTH AMERICA, TLINGIT TRIBE: Bear screen, c. 1840, incised wood and paint, 4.57 × 2.47 metres, Denver, Art Museum.
AUSTRIAN SCHOOL: *The Trinity with Christ crucified*, 15th century, panel, 118 × 114 cm, London, National Gallery.
HARUNOBU: *The evening bell of the clock*, c. 1766, woodcut, 29 × 22 cm, Chicago, Art Institute (Cooper-Bridgeman Library).
TINTORETTO: *Bacchus and Ariadne*, 1578, oil on canvas, 146 × 157 cm, Venice, Palazzo Ducale (Scala).
TURNER: *Norham Castle: sunrise*, c. 1835–40, oil on canvas, 89.5 × 120 cm, London, Tate Gallery (Angelo Hornak).

92–93 Projection
PERSIA: *Khosroe and his courtiers*, 1524–25, gouache miniature, New York, Metropolitan Museum of Art.
CHAGALL: *The birthday*, 1915, oil on cardboard, 79.5 × 98 cm, New York, Museum of Modern Art, Lillie P. Bliss Bequest.
THEBES: *Garden with pond*, c. 1400 BC, wall-painting, London, British Museum.
BRAQUE: *Pitcher and violin*, 1910, oil on canvas, 117 × 73.5 cm, Basel, Kunstmuseum (Colorphoto Hans Hinz).
CHINA: *Winding veranda and porches of a palace*, c. 1679, ink-drawing from *The Mustard Seed Garden Manual of Painting*. Diagrams: Alan Suttie.

94–95 Perspective
CHIRICO: *Sinister Muses*, 1917, gouache on board, 94 × 62 cm, Munich, Bayerische Staatsgemäldesammlung (Scala).
RAPHAEL: *"The School of Athens"*, in the Stanza della Segnatura, fresco, about 770 cm wide at base, Vatican (David Lees/Colorific!). Diagrams: (top) Michael McGuinness, (middle and bottom left) Alan Suttie, (right) Harry Clow.

96–97 Line, Shape, Contour, Articulation
BOTTICELLI: *Venus and Mars*, c. 1485, tempera on wood, 69 × 173 cm, London, National Gallery.

VELAZQUEZ: *Portrait of a man*, c. 1640, oil on canvas, 76 × 65 cm, London, Wellington Museum.
STABIAE, ITALY: *Maiden gathering flowers*, 1st century AD, fresco, Naples, Museo Nazionale (Scala).
MICHELANGELO: *The creation of Adam*, detail of the Sistine Chapel ceiling, 1511, fresco, Vatican, Sistine Chapel (Scala).
BUFFET: *Artist and model*, 1948, oil on canvas, Paris, Musée d'Art Moderne (Giraudon).

98–99 Movement
VASARELY: *Lomblin*, 1951–56, 65 × 60 cm, Annet-sur-Marne, the artist's collection.
MONDRIAN: *Broadway Boogie-Woogie*, 1942–43, oil on canvas, 127 × 127 cm, New York, Museum of Modern Art.
TINTORETTO: *Bacchus and Ariadne*, 1578, oil on canvas, 146 × 157 cm, Venice, Palazzo Ducale (Scala).
DUCHAMP: *Nude descending a staircase no. 2*, 1912, oil on canvas, 148 × 90 cm, Philadelphia Museum of Art, The Louise and Walter Arensberg collection.
GOYA: *The stilt-walkers*, c. 1788, oil on canvas, 268 × 320 cm, Madrid Prado (Scala).
Diagram: Dinah Lone.

100–101 Illumination and Tonality
CHARTRES, FRANCE: *"Our Lady of the Beautiful Glass"*, mid-12th century, stained glass, Chartres Cathedral (Robert Harding Associates).
VELAZQUEZ: *The water-carrier of Seville*, c. 1619, oil on canvas, 105.5 × 80 cm, London, Wellington Museum (Cooper-Bridgeman Library).
REMBRANDT: *A scholar*, c. 1630, oil on wood, 55 × 46.5 cm, London National Gallery.
CHARDIN: *Still life with a marmite*, c. 1762, oil on canvas, 30.5 × 38 cm, Oxford, Ashmolean Museum.
MONET: *Beach at Ste-Adresse*, 1867, oil on canvas, 71.5 × 103 cm, Chicago, Art Institute.
KLEE: *Painting on black background*, 1940, oil on canvas, 100 × 80.5 cm, Berne, Felix Klee Collection.
Diagrams: (top) Alan Suttie, (bottom) Keith Palmer.

102–103 Texture and Surface
GOINGS: *Airstream trailer*, 1970, acrylic on canvas, 152 × 214 cm, Aachen, Neue Galerie (Anne Gold).
TOBEY: *Barth rhythms*, 1961, mixed materials on board, Lugano, Thyssen Collection (Scala).
CONSTABLE: *The leaping horse*, 1825, oil on canvas, 142 × 187 cm, London, Royal Academy of Arts.
INGRES: *The spring*, 1856, oil on canvas, 164 × 82 cm, Paris, Louvre, (Scala).
VAN GOGH: *Chair and pipe*, 1888–89, oil on canvas, 92 × 72 cm, London, Tate Gallery.
CEZANNE: *Mont Ste-Victoire from Bibémus Quarry*, 1898, oil on canvas, 64 × 80 cm, Baltimore Museum of Art.

104–105 Edge Qualities
JAMMU, INDIA: *Mian Brij Raj Dev with attendants*, c. 1765, gouache on paper, 216 × 295 mm, London, Victoria and Albert Museum.
MANTEGNA: *The Agony in the Garden*, c. 1460, tempera on panel, 63 × 80 cm, London, National Gallery.
ROTHKO: *Red, white and brown*, 1957, oil on canvas, 252.5 × 207 cm, Basel, Kunstmuseum (Colorphoto Hans Hinz).
LEGER: *The mechanic*, 1920, oil on canvas, 155.5 × 88.5 cm, Ottawa, National Gallery of Canada.
REMBRANDT: *Self-portrait*, 1660, oil on canvas, 111 × 85 cm, Paris, Louvre (Documentation Photographique de la Réunion des Musées Nationaux).
RENOIR: *Bather drying her leg*, 1910, oil on canvas, 84 × 65 cm, São Paulo, Museum of Art.
LEONARDO: *The Virgin of the rocks* (2nd version), c. 1505, oil on panel, 189.5 × 120 cm, London, National Gallery.
Diagram: Mitchell Beazley Studio.

106–107 Pattern
HOKUSAI: *Carp leaping in a pool*, late 18th century, colour woodcut, 36 × 16.5 cm, London, Victoria and Albert Museum.
BRAQUE: *Still life on a red tablecloth*, 1936, oil on canvas, 197 × 129.5 cm, West Palm Beach, Florida, Norton Gallery and School of Art.
MATISSE: *Odalisque*, 1922, oil on canvas, 57 × 84 cm, Paris, Musée National de l'Art Moderne (Scala).
HILLIARD: *Young man in a garden*, c. 1588, watercolour on vellum, 13.5 × 7 cm, London, Victoria and Albert Museum.
WARHOL: *Marilyn Monroe*, 1962, silkscreen, Paris, René Montagu Collection (Leo Castelli).
SPENCER: *Swan-upping*, 1914–15, finished 1919, oil on canvas, 117 × 142 cm, London, Tate Gallery.
Diagram: Derek Carmichael.

108–109 The Dimensions of Colour
POUSSIN: *Lamentation over the dead Christ*, c. 1655, oil on canvas, 100 × 134 cm, Dublin, National Gallery of Ireland.
MATISSE: *The red studio*, 1911, oil on canvas, 181 × 219 cm, New York, Museum of Modern Art, Mrs Simon Guggenheim Fund.
PUVIS DE CHAVANNES: *The poor fisherman*, 1881, oil on canvas, 155 × 192.5 cm, Paris, Louvre (Documentation Photographique de la Réunion des Musées Nationaux).
BONNARD: *Self-portrait*, 1940, oil on canvas, 63 × 47 cm, New York, Private Collection (Photo: Wildenstein and Co.).
CEZANNE: *Self-portrait*, c. 1880, oil on canvas, 33.5 × 26 cm, London, National Gallery.
Diagram: Alan Suttie.

110–111 Ways of Using Colour
NOVGOROD, RUSSIA: *The Archangel Michael*, early 14th century, tempera on panel, formerly G. Hann Collection, Pennsylvania (Christie's, New York).
SEURAT: *Fishing fleet at Port-en-Bessin*, 1888, oil on canvas, 55 × 65 cm, New York, Museum of Modern Art, Lillie P. Bliss Bequest.
TIEPOLO: *The marriage of Frederick and Beatrice*, 1753, fresco from the Residenz at Würzburg (Scala).
TISSOT: *The ball on shipboard*, 1874, oil on canvas, 85.5 × 127.5 cm, London, Tate Gallery (Cooper-Bridgeman Library).
PIERO DELLA FRANCESCA: *The baptism of Christ*, c. 1440–50, tempera on wood, 167 × 116 cm, London, National Gallery.
FRIEDRICH: *Man and woman gazing at the moon*, c, 1830–35, oil on canvas, 34.5 × 45.5 cm, West Berlin, Nationalgalerie (Scala).
Diagram: Alan Suttie.

112–113 Abstraction
MONDRIAN: *Composition*, 1921, oil on canvas, 47.5 × 41.5 cm, Basel, Kunstmuseum (Colorphoto Hans Hinz).
KANDINSKY: Study for *Composition no. 7*, 1913, oil on canvas, 78 × 100 cm, Berne, Felix Klee Collection.
MIRO: *Catalonian landscape (The hunter)*, 1923–24, oil on canvas, 63 × 99 cm, New York, Museum of Modern Art.
RAJASTHAN, INDIA: *Sri Yantra*, 18th century, 33 × 33 cm, Paris, Ravi Kumar Collection (Angelo Hornak).
LOHSE: *30 vertical systematic shades with red diagonals*, 1943–70, oil on canvas, 165 × 165 cm, Zurich, the artist's collection.
FRANKENTHALER: *Madridscape*, 1959, oil on canvas, 255 × 403 cm, Baltimore Museum of Art.

114–115 Materials and Methods of Painting
CHARDIN: *The attributes of the arts*, 1766, oil on canvas, 133 × 140 cm, Minneapolis Institute of Arts, William H. Dunwoody Fund.
BRUEGEL: *The painter and the connoisseur*, 1566–68, pen and bistre, Vienna, Albertina.

116–117 Introduction
BOTTICELLI: *Venus and the Graces bringing presents to a bride*, c. 1486, detail of a fresco from the Villa Lemni, Paris, Louvre. (Documentation Photographique de la Réunion des Musées Nationaux).
Diagrams: Michael McGuinness.

118–119 Tempera and Encaustic
JOHNS: *Numbers in colour*, 1958–59, encaustic and collage on canvas, 170 × 126 cm, Buffalo, New York, Albright-Knox Art Gallery.
ORCAGNA: *The Adoration of the shepherds*, c. 1370–71, tempera on wood, 95.5 × 49.5 cm, London, National Gallery.
ANDREA PISANO: *Painting*, c. 1431, marble, 83 × 69 cm, Florence, Museo dell' Opera del Duomo (Scala).
SHAHN: *Handball*, 1939, tempera on paper over composition board, 58 × 79.5 cm, New York, Museum of Modern Art, Abby Aldrich Rockefeller Fund.
Diagrams: (centre) Byron Harvey, (right) Graham Marks.

120–121 Wall-painting
MICHELANGELO: *Adam*, detail from the Sistine Chapel ceiling, 1510–12, fresco, Vatican, Sistine Chapel (Scala).
LEONARDO: *The Last Supper*, c. 1495, 420 × 910 cm, probably oil and tempera on plaster, Milan, S. Maria delle Grazie (Scala).
Diagram: Michael McGuinness and Byron Harvey, based on Castagno's frescos of *The Crucifixion, Deposition and Resurrection of Christ*, c. 1445–50, in the Convent of S. Apollonia, Florence (Scala).

122–123 Early Oil Techniques
MASTER OF THE VIEW OF SAINT GUDULE: *A young man*, c. 1480, oil and tempera on panel, 22 × 14.5 cm, London, National Gallery.
MILLAIS: *Mariana*, 1851, oil on panel, 59 × 49.5 cm, Basingstoke, Lord Sherwood Collection (Cooper-Bridgeman Library).
MEMLINC: *The Nieuwenhove diptych*, 1487, each panel 44 × 33 cm, Bruges, Memlinc Museum (Scala).
EDDY: *Untitled*, 1971, oil on canvas 122 × 167 cm, Aachen, Neue Galerie, Ludwig collection (Ann Münchow).
ANTONELLO DA MESSINA: The S. Cassiano altarpiece, 1476, oil on panel, height of fragment 63 cm, Vienna, Kunsthistorisches Museum (Scala).
Diagrams: Byron Harvey, Michael McGuinness.

124–125 Oils on Coloured Grounds
TITIAN: *Bacchus and Ariadne*, 1522–23, oil on canvas, 175 × 190 cm, London, National Gallery; *The deal of Actaeon*, c. 1559, oil on canvas, 178.5 × 198 cm, London, National Gallery.
ZURBARAN: *A painter at the foot of the Cross*, c. 1635–40?, oil on canvas, 105 × 84 cm, Madrid, Prado (Scala).
GAINSBOROUGH: *The painter's daughters with a cat*, c. 1759, oil on canvas, 74.5 × 62 cm, London, National Gallery.
RUBENS: Sketch for *The Annunciation*, 1620–21, oil on panel, Oxford, Ashmolean Museum.

126–127 Oils: Surface Effects
CANALETTO: *The harbour of St Mark's towards the west*, c. 1760–66, oil on canvas, 51 × 66 cm, Princeton University, The Art Museum, Gift of Henry W. Cannon Jnr. in memory of his father; *The harbour of St Mark's from the east*, 1740, oil on canvas, 129 × 187 cm, London, Wallace Collection.
HALS: *A member of the Coymans family*, 1645, oil on canvas, 77 × 64 cm, Washington, National Gallery of Art, Andrew W. Mellon collection.
REMBRANDT: *Belshazzar's Feast*,

1635, oil on canvas, 167.5 × 209 cm, London, National Gallery (Angelo Hornak).

128–129 Oils: Direct Methods

WHISTLER: *Symphony in white no. 3*, 1867, oil on canvas, 52 × 76.5 cm, Birmingham, Barber Institute of Fine Arts, University of Birmingham.
CEZANNE: *Woodland scene*, 1882–85, oil on canvas, 62 × 51.5 cm, Cambridge, Fitzwilliam Museum.
PISSARRO: *The Oise near Pontoise*, 1873, oil on canvas, 45.5 × 55 cm, Williamstown, Sterling and Francine Clark Institute.
MUNCH: *Death in the room*, 1892, oil on canvas, 149.5 × 167.5 cm, Oslo, National Gallery.
JORN: *Green ballet*, 1960, oil on canvas, 144 × 199.5 cm, New York, Solomon R. Guggenheim Museum.

130–131 Twentieth-Century Developments

ERNST: *Forest*, 1929, frottage, 81 × 100 cm, Milan, Dr A. Mazzotta Collection (Scala).
DUCHAMP: *Tu m'*, 1918, oil and pencil on canvas, with collage, 70 × 31.5 cm, New Haven, Yale University Art Gallery, Bequest of Katherine S. Dreier.
TAPIES: *Ochre gris*, 1958, oil, latex and marble dust on canvas, 256 × 191.5 cm, London, Tate Gallery.
RICHARD SMITH: *Sudden country*, 1972, acrylic on canvas, 203 × 310 cm, Cardiff, National Museum of Wales.
FRANK STELLA: *Agbatana 3*, 1968, fluorescent acrylic on canvas, 305 × 457 cm, Ohio, Allen Memorial Art Museum.
HOYLAND: *Drape*, 1978, acrylic on cotton duck, 125 × 100 cm, London, Waddington Galleries Ltd.
LOUIS: *Theta*, 1960, acrylic resin on canvas, 255 × 420 cm, Boston, Museum of Fine Arts.

132–133 Mixed Media

CRIVELLI: *St Peter* from the Demidoff altarpiece, 1476, panel, 40 × 135 cm, London, National Gallery.
SCHWITTERS: *Opened by Customs*, c. 1937, collage, 33 × 25.5 cm, London, Tate Gallery (Angelo Hornak)
HAMILTON: *My Marilyn*, 1965, photographs and oil on paper, 50.5 × 61 cm, Cologne, Wallraf-Richartz Museum.
WESSELMAN: *Bath-tub collage no. 3*, 1963, 213 × 270 × 45 cm, Cologne, Wallraf-Richartz Museum.
MATISSE: *Sorrows of the king*, 1952, cut paper, 287.5 × 398.5 cm, Paris, Musée National de l'Art Moderne.
RAUSCHENBERG: *Reservoir*, 1961, oil, wood, graphite, fabric, metal and rubber on canvas, 117 × 58.5 × 37.5 cm, Washington DC, The National Collection of Fine Arts, Smithsonian Institution, Gift of S. C. Johnson & Son Inc.

134–135 Watercolour

TURNER: *Sunset on the Jura*, 1841, watercolour and pencil, 22.5 × 29.5 cm, London, British Museum (The Fotomas Index); *Tintern Abbey*, 1794, watercolour and pencil, 36 × 25.5 cm, London, British Museum. Turner's paintbox, London, Victoria and Albert Museum (Angelo Hornak).
KLEE: *Hamammet motif*, 1914, watercolour, 20 × 15.5 cm, Basel, Kunstmuseum, Kupferstichkabinett.
CEZANNE: *The black château*, c, 1895, pencil and watercolour, 36 × 52.5 cm, Rotterdam, Museum Boymans-van Beuningen.
EAKINS: *John Biglen in a single scull*, 1876, watercolour, 42 × 57.5 cm, New York, Metropolitan Museum of Art.
NOLDE: *Summer flowers*, c. 1930, watercolour, 35 × 47.5 cm, Lugano, Thyssen Collection (Scala).

136–137 Ink

TAN-AN: *Heron*, c. 1570, ink on paper, 32 × 49 cm, Tokyo, National Museum.
HAN GAN: *Night shining white*, 8th century, ink on paper, 29.5 × 35 cm, New York, Metropolitan Museum of Art.
XIA GUI: *Landscape*, c. 1200–25, ink on silk, Boston, Museum of Fine Arts.
TOSA MITSUYOSHI: *The battle of Uji river*, 16th/17th century, screen panels with colour on paper, London, Victoria and Albert Museum.
LEONARDO: *Lily*, c. 1475, pen and ink and brown wash over black chalk, heightened with white, 31.5 × 17.5 cm, Windsor, Royal Library (by gracious permission of Her Majesty The Queen).
CLAUDE LORRAINE: *Port scene*, 1649–50, pen and wash, London, British Museum.
VAN GOGH: *Washerwomen on the canal*, 1888, pen and ink, 31.5 × 24 cm, Otterlo, Rijksmuseum Kröller-Müller.

138–139 Pastel and Gouache

LIOTARD: *Self-portrait with beard*, 1749, pastel, 97 × 71 cm, Geneva, Musée de l'Art et de l'Histoire.
DEGAS: *Dancers in the wings*, c. 1900, pastel, 71 × 66 cm, St Louis, Missouri, The St Louis Art Museum.
CARRIERA: *Louis XV*, 1720, pastel, 50.5 × 38.5 cm, Dresden, Staatliche Kunstsammlung.
REDON: *Roger and Angelica*, c. 1910, pastel, 91.5 × 71 cm, New York, Museum of Modern Art, Lillie P. Bliss Bequest.
KANDINSKY: *Russian beauty in a landscape*, 1905, gouache, Munich, Staatliche Museen.
RAJASTHAN, INDIA: *Raja Umed Singh of Kotah shooting tigers*, c. 1790, gouache, 32.5 × 39.5, London, Victoria and Albert Museum.

140–141 Drawing

LEONARDO: *Head and bust of a woman*, c. 1486–88, silverpoint on pinkish prepared surface, 32 × 20 cm, Windsor, Royal Library (by gracious consent of Her Majesty The Queen).

INGRES: *The Stamaty family*, 1818, pencil on paper, 46 × 37 cm, Paris, Louvre (Documentation Photographique de la Réunion des Musées Nationaux).
SEURAT: *Place de la Concorde, winter*, c. 1882–83, Conté crayon, 23 × 30.5 cm, New York, Solomon R. Guggenheim Museum.
KLIMT: *Woman lying down*, 1904, pencil, 34.5 × 54 cm, Stuttgart, Staatsgalerie.
RUBENS: *Young woman looking down*, c. 1627–28, black, white and red chalk, 41.5 × 28.5 cm, Florence, Uffizi (Scala).
KOLLWITZ: *Woman and Death*, 1910, charcoal, 47 × 61 cm, Washington, DC, National Gallery of Art, Rosenwald collection.
HOCKNEY: *Beach umbrella, Calvi*, 1972, crayon, 42 × 35 cm, London, British Museum (copyright David Hockney 1979, courtesy Petersburg Press).

142–143 Painters and Printmaking

BLAKE: *Newton*, 1795, monotype finished in pen and watercolour, 45.5 × 59 cm, London, Tate Gallery.
GOYA: *The two old women*, c. 1808–10, oil on canvas, 181 × 125 cm, Lille, Musée des Beaux-Arts (Giraudon); *Hurry up Death*, 1799, etching on copper-plate, 21.5 × 15 cm, London, British Museum (Fotomas Index).
NOLDE: *The life of St Mary Aegyptiaca*, 1912, oil on canvas, Hamburg, Kunsthalle (Ada and Emil Nolde Foundation); *The Prophet*, 1912, woodcut, 32 × 22.5 cm, Washington, National Gallery of Art, Rosenwald collection.
HIROSHIGE: *The plum-tree garden*, 1857, woodcut, Amsterdam, National Museum Vincent van Gogh.
VAN GOGH: *The plum-tree garden*, 1886, oil on canvas, 55 × 46 cm, Amsterdam, National Museum Vincent van Gogh.

144–145 Printmaking Techniques

KUNISADA: *Making colour prints*, 1857, woodcut, London, Victoria and Albert Museum.
GAUDIER-BRZESKA: *Wrestlers*, 1914, linocut, 41.5 × 35.5 cm, London, Victoria and Albert Museum.
PICASSO: *Still life under the lamp*, 1962, coloured linocut, 52 × 64.5 cm, New York Museum, Museum of Modern Art, Gift of Mrs Donald B. Strauss.
HOLBEIN: *The Countess*, from *The Dance of Death*, 1538, woodcut, 5 × 7.5 cm, London, British Library (The Fotomas Index).
BEWICK: *Pelican*, from *History of British Birds*, 1797, wood engraving and block, Newcastle upon Tyne, Public Library.
BOYD: *Lysistrata*, from *Welcome Lampito*, 1970, etching and aquatint, 34.5 × 39.5 cm, London, Ganymed Ltd.
TOULOUSE-LAUTREC: *The passenger in cabin 54*, 1896, coloured lithograph, 61 × 40.5 cm, Paris, Cabinet des Estampes (Giraudon).
DURER: *St Jerome in his study*, 1514,

metal engraving, 24.5 × 19 cm, London, British Museum.
STUBBS: *A tiger and a sleeping leopard*, c. 1788, mezzotint, 25 × 32 cm, London, British Museum (The Fotomas Index).
CASSATT: *The letter*, 1891, etching, drypoint and aquatint, 34 × 22.5 cm, Chicago Art Institute, Mr and Mrs A. Ryerson collection.
DAUMIER: *The legislative paunch*, 1833–34, lithograph, 280 × 431 cm, Paris, Bibliothèque Nationale (Immédiate 2).
WARHOL: *Marilyn*, 1962, silk-screen, acrylic and oil on canvas, 208 × 142.5 cm, New York, Museum of Modern Art, Gift of Philip Johnson.

146–147 Looking at Paintings

GAUGUIN: *Where do we come from? What are we? Where are we going?*, 1897, oil on canvas, 139 × 374 cm, Boston, Museum of Fine Arts.
RAPHAEL: *Two apostles*, study for *The Transfiguration*, 1520, chalk on paper, 50 × 36 cm, Oxford, Ashmolean Museum.

148–149 The Virgin of Vladimir

FAYOUM: *Artemidorus*, portrait on a mummy-case, 2nd century AD, encaustic on panel, height of image 31 cm, London, British Museum.
MT SINAI: *The Madonna among saints*, 6th century, encaustic on panel, 68.5 × 50 cm, Monastery of St Catherine (Ronald Sheridan); *St Peter*, early 7th century, encaustic on panel, 93 × 53 cm, Monastery of St Catherine (Percheron/Joseph P. Ziolo).
NOVGOROD SCHOOL: *The Presentation in the Temple*, 16th century, panel, 89 × 58 cm, Moscow, Tretyakov Gallery (S).
ANDREI RUBLEV: *The Holy Trinity*, c. 1411, panel, 140 × 112 cm, Moscow, Tretyakov Gallery (G. Mandel/ Joseph P. Ziolo).
CONSTANTINOPLE: *St Michael*, c. 950–1000, silver inlaid with ivory, gold, jewels and enamel, 44 × 36 cm, Venice, Tesoro di S. Marco (S); *"The Virgin of Vladimir"*, c. 1131, panel, 78 × 55 cm, Moscow, Tretyakov Gallery (Cercle d'Art/ Joseph P. Ziolo).

150–151 Lorenzetti: The Good Commune

AMBROGIO LORENZETTI: *The effects of Good Government on town and countryside; Allegory of Good Government; Allegory of Bad Government; Grammar*, 1338, all fresco, Siena, Palazzo Pubblico (all S); *Landscape*, c. 1335, tempera on panel, 23 × 33 cm, Siena Pinacoteca (S).
SIENA: *Winged Victory*, 2nd century?, stone relief, Siena, Pinacoteca (S).
NICOLA PISANO: *The Liberal Arts*, detail of the Siena Cathedral pulpit, 1265–68, marble, height of figures 61 cm, *in situ* (S).

152–153 Jan van Eyck: The Arnolfini Marriage

JAN VAN EYCK: *"The Arnolfini Marriage"*, 1434, oil on panel, 82 ×

60 cm, London, National Gallery; *Giovanni Arnolfini, c.* 1437, oil on panel, 29 × 20 cm, West Berlin, Staatliche Museen (Archiv für Kunst und Geschichte); *A man in a turban,* 1433, oil on panel, 25.5 × 19 cm, London, National Gallery; *Cardinal Albergati, c.* 1431, silverpoint, 21 × 18 cm, Dresden, Staatliche Kunstsammlungen (Gerhard Reinhold, Leipzig-Molkau/Joseph P. Ziolo); *Cardinal Albergati, c.* 1432, oil on panel, 34 × 26 cm, Vienna, Kunsthistorisches Museum (Photo Meyer).

154–155 Masaccio: The Holy Trinity
MASACCIO: *The Holy Trinity,* 1428, fresco, 6.7 × 3.2 m, Florence, S. Maria Novella (S); detail of the Virgin (S); detail after P. Sanpaolesi by MB Studio; *The Crucifixion,* fragment of the Pisa altarpiece, 1426, tempera on panel, 76 × 63.5 cm, Naples, Museo di Capodimonte (S).
DONATELLO: *St Louis, c.* 1422–25, gilt bronze, height 266 cm, reinstated in its niche outside Orsanmichele, Florence, now in S. Croce, Florence (S).
BRUNELLESCHI?: *Crucifix, c.* 1412, wood, height about 1 m, Florence, S. Maria Novella.
LORENZO DI NICCOLO GERINI: *The Holy Trinity,* late 14th century, tempera on panel, Greenville, South Carolina, Bob Jones University.
MASOLINO: *The Crucifixion, c.* 1428, tempera on panel, 53 × 32 cm, Vatican Gallery (S).

156–157 Fra Angelico: The Annunciation
FRA ANGELICO: *The Annunciation,* at the top of the dormitory stairs in S. Marco, Florence, *c.* 1450?, fresco, 2.2 × 3.2 m (S); *The Deposition, c.* 1440?, tempera on panel, 105 × 164 cm, Florence, S. Marco; *The Annunciation,* for S. Domenico, Cortona, *c.* 1428–32, tempera on panel, 175 × 180 cm, Cortona, Museo Diocesano (S); *The Annunciation,* in Cell 3 of the dormitory of S. Marco, *c.* 1441, fresco, 1.9 × 1.6 m (S); *St Stephen preaching and addressing the Jewish council, c.* 1447–49, fresco, 3.2 × 4.1 m, Vatican, Chapel of Nicholas V (S).

158–159 Piero della Francesca: The Flagellation
BERRUGETE?: *Federigo da Montefeltro,* 1477, tempera on panel, 135 × 79 cm, Urbino, Galleria Nazionale delle Marche (S).
PIERO DELLA FRANCESCA: *Federigo da Montefeltro, c.* 1465, tempera on panel, height 47 cm, Florence, Uffizi (S); *The flagellation of Christ,* undated, tempera on panel, 59 × 81.5 cm, Urbino, Galleria Nazionale delle Marche (S); artwork by Peter Courtley.
UNKNOWN ARTIST: *Ludovico Gonzaga, c.* 1450, bronze, life-size, West Berlin, Staatliche Museen (S).
URBINO, DUCAL PALACE: The *Cappella*

del Perdono, 1468–72 (S).
ALBERTI: The Holy Sepulchre in the Rucellai Chapel, Florence, 1467, marble (S).

160–161 Michelangelo: The Sistine Chapel Ceiling
MICHELANGELO: The Sistine Chapel ceiling, 1508–12, fresco, 13 × 36 m, Vatican (S); Interior of the Sistine Chapel (S); Details of the ceiling (S).

162–163 Bellini: The S. Zaccaria Altarpiece
GIOVANNI BELLINI: The S. Zaccaria altarpiece: *The Virgin and Child with saints,* 1505, oil on panel transferred to canvas, 500 × 235 cm, Venice, S. Zaccaria (S); *The Madonna and Child, c.* 1465–70, tempera on panel, 72 × 46 cm, New York, Metropolitan Museum of Art, Bequest of Theodore H. Davis; "*The Madonna of the Meadow*", *c.* 1501, oil on panel 67 × 86 cm, London National Gallery; The S. Giobbe altarpiece, *c.* 1490, oil on panel, 471 × 258 cm, Venice, Accademia (S).
GIORGIONE: "*The Castelfranco Madonna*", *c.* 1504, oil on panel, 200 × 152 cm, Castelfranco Veneto, S. Liberale (S).

164–165 Giorgione: The Tempest
GIORGIONE: "*The Three Philosophers*", after 1505?, oil on canvas, 123 × 144.5 cm, Vienna, Kunsthistorisches Museum (Photo Meyer); "*Laura*", 1506, oil on canvas, 41 × 33.5 cm, Vienna, Kunsthistorisches Museum (Photo Meyer); *Venus, c.* 1509–10?, oil on canvas, 108 × 175 cm, Dresden, Gemäldegalerie (S); *The tempest,* 1st decade of the 16th century, oil on canvas, 83 × 73 cm, Venice, Accademia (S).

166–167 Titian: The Rape of Europa
TITIAN: *The rape of Europa,* 1562, oil on canvas, 178 × 204 cm, Boston, Isabella Stewart Gardner Museum; *Sacred and Profane Love, c.* 1514, oil on canvas, 118 × 279 cm, Rome, Galleria Borghese (S); *The Andrian Bacchanal,* 1518–23, oil on canvas, 175 × 193 cm, Madrid, Prado (S); "*The Venus of Urbino*", *c.* 1538, oil on canvas, 119.5 × 165 cm, Florence, Uffizi (S); *Diana and Actaeon,* 1558, oil on canvas, 188 × 206 cm, Edinburgh, National Gallery of Scotland (S); *The death of Actaeon,* after 1562, oil on canvas, 179 × 198 cm, London, National Gallery.

168–169 Holbein: The Ambassadors
HOLBEIN: "*The Ambassadors*", 1533, tempera on panel, 206 × 209 cm, London, National Gallery; *The dead Christ,* 1521, tempera on panel, 30.5 × 200 cm, Basel, Offentliche Kunstsammlungen (Colorphoto Hans Hinz); *The Virgin and Child with the Meyer family, c.* 1528, tempera on panel, 146.5 × 102 cm, Darmstadt, Schloss Darmstadt (S); *Sir Thomas More,* 1527, tempera on

panel, 74 × 59 cm, New York, The Frick Collection (copyright); *Jane Seymour, c.* 1535, chalk and primer on paper, 50 × 29 cm, Windsor, The Royal Library (by gracious permission of Her Majesty the Queen); *King Henry VIII,* 1542, tempera on panel, 92 × 67 cm, Castle Howard, Howard Collection.

170–171 Bruegel: August
AERTSEN: *Christ in the house of Martha and Mary,* 1559, oil on panel, 126 × 200 cm, Rotterdam, Museum Boymans-van Beuningen.
BRUEGEL: *January (The hunters in the snow),* 1565, oil on panel, 117 × 162 cm, Vienna, Kunsthistorisches Museum (S); *August (The corn harvest),* 1565, oil on panel, 118 × 161 cm, New York, Metropolitan Museum of Art, Rogers Fund; *The peasant wedding, c.* 1567, oil on panel, 114 × 163 cm, Vienna, Kunsthistorisches Museum (S); *The procession to Calvary,* 1564, oil on panel, 124 × 177 cm, Vienna, Kunsthistorisches Museum (S); *The Adoration of the Magi,* 1564, oil on panel, 111 × 83 cm, London, National Gallery.

172–173 Tintoretto: The San Rocco Crucifixion
TINTORETTO: *The Crucifixion,* 1565, oil on canvas, 536 × 1224 cm, Venice, Scuola di San Rocco (The Mansell Collection; detail S); *Self-portrait,* 1573, oil on canvas, 72 × 57 cm, Scuola di San Rocco (S); *The Flight into Egypt,* 1583–87, oil on canvas, 422 × 580 cm, Scuola di San Rocco (S); *The road to Calvary,* 1566, oil on canvas, 515 × 390 cm, Scuola di San Rocco (S); *The temptation of Christ,* 1579–81, oil on canvas, 539 × 330 cm, Scuola di San Rocco (S).

174–175 Caravaggio: The Conversion of St Paul
CARAVAGGIO: *The Crucifixion of St Peter,* 1600–01, oil on canvas, 230 × 175 cm, Rome, S. Maria del Popolo (S); *The conversion of St Paul,* 1600–01, oil on canvas, 230 × 175 cm, S. Maria del Popolo (S).
DURER: "*The Large Horse*", 1505, etching, 17 × 21 cm, London, British Museum.
MICHELANGELO: *The conversion of St Paul,* 1546–50, fresco, 6.1 × 6.5 m, Vatican, Cappella Paolina (S).
MANTEGNA: *The dead Christ, c.* 1505, tempera on canvas, 66 × 81 cm, Milan, Brera (S).
ANNIBALE CARRACCI: *The Assumption of the Virgin,* 1600–01, oil on panel, 245 × 155 cm, Rome, S. Maria del Popolo (S).

176–177 Annibale Carracci: The Farnese Gallery
AGOSTINO CARRACCI: Cartoon for *Glaucus and Scylla* on the inner wall of the Farnese Gallery, *c.* 1597–99, on paper, 203 × 410 cm, London, National Gallery.
ANNIBALE CARRACCI: The Farnese Gallery: *The loves of the gods,* 1597–1600, fresco, length of ceiling

20 m, width 6.4 m (details, *Venus and Anchises,* S; *The triumph of Bacchus and Ariadne,* S), Rome, Palazzo Farnese (S). *View of the inner wall of the Farnese Gallery,* engraving by Giovanni Volpato, London, Victoria and Albert Museum (A. C. Coopers).
RAPHAEL: The ceiling of the Villa Farnesina *loggia,* detail: *The marriage of Cupid and Psyche,* 1518, fresco, Rome (S).

178–179 Poussin: The Holy Family on the Steps
POUSSIN: *The Holy Family on the steps,* 1648, oil on canvas, 69 × 97.5 cm, Washington, National Gallery of Art, Samuel H. Kress collection (S); *Self-portrait,* 1649–50, oil on canvas, 98 × 74 cm, Paris, Louvre (S); *The poet's inspiration, c.* 1628–29, oil on canvas, 184 × 214 cm, Paris, Louvre (S); Preparatory drawing for *The Holy Family,* 1648, pen and bistre and chalk on paper, 18 × 24 cm, Paris, Louvre (Documentation Photographique de la Réunion des Musées Nationaux).
RAPHAEL: "*The Madonna of the Fish*", *c.* 1513, 215 × 158 cm, Madrid, Prado (S).
ROME, ESQUILINE: "*The Aldobrandini Marriage*", 1st century BC, fresco, 91 × 242 cm, Vatican, Museum (S).

180–181 Rubens: The Descent from the Cross
RUBENS: *The Descent from the Cross,* 1611–14, oil on panel, 240 × 310 cm, Antwerp, Cathedral (S); *The raising of the Cross,* 1610–11, oil on panel, 240 × 310 cm, Antwerp, Cathedral (A. De Belder/Joseph P. Ziolo); Drawing of the *Laocoön, c.* 1606, black chalk on paper, 43 × 25 cm, Milan, Biblioteca Ambrosiana; Copy after Caravaggio's *The Entombment, c.* 1600, reworked *c.* 1613, oil on panel, 88 × 65 cm, Ottawa, National Gallery of Canada.
DANIELE DA VOLTERRA: *The Descent from the Cross,* 1541, fresco, Rome, S. Trinita ai Monti (S).

182–183 Velazquez: Las Meninas
VELAZQUEZ: *Christ in the house of Mary and Martha,* 1618, oil on canvas, 60 × 103 cm, London, National Gallery; *The tapestry weavers, c.* 1654, oil on canvas, 220 × 289 cm, Madrid, Prado (S); *The Infanta Margarita, c.* 1656, oil on canvas, 70 × 59 cm, Paris, Louvre (S); *Philip IV,* 1634–35, oil on canvas, 191 × 126 cm, Madrid, Prado (S); "*Las Meninas*" (The maids of honour), 1656, oil on canvas, 318 × 276 cm, Madrid, Prado (S).

184–185 Hals: A Banquet of the St George Civic Guard
VERONESE: *The feast at Cana,* 1559–60, oil on canvas, 660 × 990 cm, Paris, Louvre (S).
CORNELIS VAN HAARLEM: *The banquet of Haarlem guardsmen,* 1583, 156.5 × 222 cm, Haarlem, Frans Hals Museum.
FRANS HALS: *The banquet of the St*

George Civic Guard, 1616, oil on canvas, 175 × 324 cm, Haarlem, Frans Hals Museum; *The regents of the St Elizabeth Hospital*, c. 1641, oil on canvas, 153 × 252 cm, Haarlem, Frans Hals Museum; "*The Laughing Cavalier*", 1624, oil on canvas, 86 × 89 cm, London, Wallace Collection; *The banquet of the St George Civic Guard*, c. 1627, oil on canvas, 179 × 257.5 cm, Haarlem, Frans Hals Museum; *Willem Croes*, c. 1660, oil on canvas, 47 × 34 cm, Munich, Alte Pinakothek (S).

186–187 Rembrandt: The Self-Portrait at Kenwood
REMBRANDT: *Self-portrait* in Munich, detail, c. 1629, oil on panel, 18 × 14 cm, Alte Pinakothek (S); *Self-portrait with Saskia*, c. 1635, oil on canvas, 161 × 131 cm, Dresden, Gemäldegalerie; *Self-portrait* in Berlin, 1634, 55 × 46 cm, West Berlin, Staatliche Museen; *Self-portrait after Titian's "Ariosto"*, 1640, oil on canvas, 102 × 80 cm, London, National Gallery; *Self-portrait drawing by a window*, 1648, drypoint and burin etching, 16 × 13 cm, Paris, Bibliothèque Nationale (Immédiate 2); *Self-portrait* in Kenwood, London, c. 1665, oil on canvas, 114 × 95 cm (The Greater London Council as Trustees of the Iveagh Bequest, Kenwood); *Self-portrait* in Vienna, 1652, oil on canvas, 113 × 81 cm, Kunsthistorisches Museum (Photo Meyer); *Self-portrait* in Cologne, c. 1669, oil on canvas, 82 × 63 cm, Wallraf-Richartz Museum; *Self-portrait* in London, 1669, oil on canvas, 86 × 70.5 cm, National Gallery.

188–189 Ruisdael: The Jewish Cemetery
JACOB VAN RUISDAEL: The Dresden *Jewish cemetery*, 1660s, oil on canvas, 84 × 95 cm, Dresden, Gemäldegalerie (G. Reinhold, Leipzig-Molkau/Joseph P. Ziolo); The Detroit *Jewish cemetery*, 1660s, oil on canvas, 142 × 189 cm, Detroit, Institute of Arts, Gift of Julius H. Haass in memory of his brother; *Tombs in the Jewish cemetery at Ouderkerk*, c. 1660, chalk and wash on paper, 19 × 27.5 cm, Haarlem, Teylers Museum; *Winter landscape*, c. 1670, oil on canvas, 41 × 49 cm, Amsterdam, Rijksmuseum. REMBRANDT: *The stone bridge*, c. 1637, oil on panel, 29 × 42.5 cm, Amsterdam, Rijksmuseum. EVERDINGEN: *A waterfall*, 1650, oil on canvas, 112 × 58 cm, Munich, Alte Pinakothek (S). KONINCK: *View over flat country*, 1650s or 1660s, 118 × 166 cm, Oxford, Ashmolean Museum.

190–191 Vermeer: The Artist's Studio
VERMEER: "*The Artist's Studio*" (The art of painting), c. 1665–70, oil on canvas, 120 × 100 cm, Vienna, Kunsthistorisches Museum (Photo Meyer); *The head of a girl*, c. 1666, oil on canvas, 47 × 40 cm, The

Hague, Mauritshuis (S); *A soldier and a laughing girl*, c. 1657, oil on canvas, 50.5 × 46 cm, New York, The Frick Collection (copyright); *An allegory of the New Testament*, c. 1669, oil on canvas, 113 × 88 cm, New York, Metropolitan Museum of Art, Michael Friedsam collection; *Diana and her nymphs*, c. 1654, oil on canvas, 98.5 × 105 cm, The Hague, Mauritshuis (S). REMBRANDT: *The artist in his studio*, c. 1628–29, oil on panel, 25 × 32 cm, Boston, Museum of Fine Arts, Zoe Oliver Sherman collection.

192–193 Watteau: The Embarkation for Cythera
RUBENS: *The Garden of Love*, c. 1632, oil on canvas, 198 × 283 cm, Madrid, Prado (S). WATTEAU: "*L'Enseigne de Gersaint*" (Gersaint's signboard), 1721, oil on canvas, 182 × 307 cm, West Berlin, Staatliche Museen (S); The Louvre "*Embarkation for Cythera*", properly *The pilgrimage to Cythera*, 1717, oil on canvas, 129 × 194 cm, Paris, Louvre (Documentation Photographique de la Réunion des Musées Nationaux); "*La Toilette*", c. 1720, oil on canvas, height 44 cm, London, Wallace Collection; The Berlin "*Embarkation for Cythera*", 1718, oil on canvas, 130 × 192 cm, West Berlin, Staatliche Museen (S).

194–195 Chardin: The House of Cards
CHARDIN: *Skate, cat and kitchen utensils*, 1728, oil on canvas, 114 × 145 cm, Paris, Louvre (S); *Saying grace*, c. 1740, oil on canvas, 49.5 × 38.5 cm, Paris, Louvre (Documentation Photographique de la Réunion des Musées Nationaux); *Still life with a wild duck*, 1764, oil on canvas, 133 × 97 cm, Springfield, Massachusetts, Museum of Fine Arts, James Philip Gray collection; *Self-portrait with an eyeshade*, 1775, pastel, 46 × 38 cm, Paris, Louvre (Documentation Photographique de la Réunion des Musées Nationaux); *The house of cards*, c. 1741, oil on canvas, 81 × 65 cm, Washington, National Gallery of Art, Andrew W. Mellon collection. BOUCHER: *Breakfast*, 1739, oil on canvas, 80 × 61 cm, Paris, Louvre (Documentation Photographique de la Réunion des Musées Nationaux). REMBRANDT: *The flayed ox*, 1655, oil on canvas, 94 × 69 cm, Paris, Louvre (S).

196–197 Tiepolo: The Residenz at Würzburg
TIEPOLO: *Abraham visited by the angels*, c. 1732, oil on canvas, 140 × 120 cm, Venice, Scuola di San Rocco (S); *St Thecla delivering the city of Este from the plague*, 1759, oil on canvas, 80 × 44 cm, New York, Metropolitan Museum of Art, Rogers Fund; *The banquet of Cleopatra and Anthony*, detail of the Palazzo Labia ballroom, 1745–50, fresco, Venice (S); *Olympus with the four quarters of the Earth*, detail of the ceiling of the *Treppenhaus*,

Würzburg, 1752–53, fresco (S); *America*, in the *Treppenhaus* (S); *Apollo leads Beatrice to Barbarossa*, in the *Kaisersaal*, Würzburg, fresco (S); *The marriage of Beatrice and Barbarossa*, in the *Kaisersaal* (S). NEUMANN AND TIEPOLO: The *Kaisersaal* in the Residenz, Würzburg (S).

198–199 Gainsborough: Mary, Countess Howe
GAINSBOROUGH: *Mr and Mrs Andrews*, c. 1748, oil on canvas, 70 × 119 cm, London, National Gallery; "*The Blue Boy*", c. 1770, oil on canvas, 175 × 120 cm, San Marino, California, Henry E. Huntington Library and Art Gallery; *Mrs Sarah Siddons*, 1785, oil on canvas, 126 × 100 cm, London, National Gallery; *Mrs Philip Thicknesse*, 1760, oil on canvas, 44 × 132.5 cm, Cincinnati Art Museum, Mary M. Emery Bequest; "*The Morning Walk*", 1785, oil on canvas, 236 × 179 cm, London, National Gallery; *Mary, Countess Howe*, 1763–64, oil on canvas, 240–150 cm, London, Kenwood House (Greater London Council as Trustees of the Iveagh Bequest).

200–201 Goya: The Colossus
GOYA: *The Disasters of War: This is how it is*; *This is worse*, c. 1810–15, both etchings, 16 × 22 cm (The Fotomas Index); *The straw manikin*, 1791–92, oil on canvas, 267 × 160 cm, Madrid, Prado (S); *Los Caprichos*, plate 43: *The sleep of Reason*, 1799, etching, 21 × 13 cm (The Fotomas Index); *Self-portrait with Dr Arrieta*, 1820, oil on canvas, 117 × 79 cm, Minneapolis, Institute of Arts; *Saturn*, 1820, fresco transferred to canvas, 146 × 238 cm, Madrid, Prado (S); *The colossus*, 1808–12, oil on canvas, 116 × 105 cm, Madrid, Prado (S).

202–203 Constable: The White Horse
CONSTABLE: "*The White Horse*", 1819, oil on canvas, 131 × 188 cm, New York, Frick Collection (copyright); *Oil-sketch for "The White Horse"*, c. 1819, oil on canvas, 127 × 183 cm, Washington National Gallery of Art, Widener collection; *Clouds, Sept. 5th*, 1822, oil on paper, 29 × 48 cm, London, Victoria and Albert Museum; *The haywain*, 1821, oil on canvas, 130 × 185 cm, London, National Gallery; *Stonehenge*, watercolour, 38 × 59 cm, London, Victoria and Albert Museum; *Pencil sketch*, 1814, from sketch-book no. 132, on paper, 8 × 11 cm, London, Victoria and Albert Museum.

204–205 Turner: Dawn after the Wreck
TURNER: *Dawn after the wreck*, c. 1840, watercolour on paper, 34.5 × 36 cm, London, Courtauld Institute Galleries; *Tintern Abbey*, c. 1795, watercolour over pencil with pen and ink, 33.5 × 26 cm, Oxford, Ashmolean Museum; *The slave ship*,

1840, oil on canvas, 91 × 122 cm, Boston, Museum of Fine Arts, Henry Lillie Pierce Fund; *Venice: S. Giorgio Maggiore*, 1819, watercolour on paper, 22 × 28 cm, London, British Museum (Cooper-Bridgeman Library); *Sun rising through vapour: fishermen cleaning and selling fish*, 1807, oil on canvas, 134 × 179 cm, London, National Gallery; *The Thames near Walton Bridge*, c. 1807, oil on panel, 36 × 73 cm, London, Tate Gallery; *Snowstorm: Hannibal crossing the Alps*, 1812, oil on canvas, 144 × 236 cm, London, Tate Gallery.

206–207 Friedrich: Man and Woman Gazing at the Moon
FRIEDRICH: *Abbey graveyard under snow*, 1810, oil on canvas, 121 × 170 cm, West Berlin, Schloss Charlottenburg (Bildarchiv Preussischer Kulturbesitz); *Moonrise over the sea*, 1822, oil on canvas, 55 × 71 cm, West Berlin, Staatliche Museen (S); The Tetschen altar: *The Cross on the mountains*, 1809, oil on canvas, 115 × 110 cm, Dresden, Gemäldegalerie (S); *A dolmen near Gützkow*, c. 1837, pencil and sepia, 22 × 30 cm, Copenhagen, The Library of Her Majesty Margrethe II, Queen of Denmark (Hans Peterson); *Man and woman gazing at the moon*, c. 1830–35, oil on canvas, 34 × 44 cm, West Berlin, Staatliche Museen (S); *The stages of life*, c. 1835, oil on canvas, 72 × 94 cm, Leipzig Museum der Bildende Künste (S). KERSTING: *Friedrich in his studio*, oil on canvas, 51 × 40 cm, West Berlin, Staatliche Museen (S).

208–209 Delacroix: The Death of Sardanapalus
DELACROIX: *The death of Sardanapalus*, 1827, oil on canvas, 395 × 495 cm, Paris Louvre (S); *The massacre at Chios*, 1824, oil on canvas, 422 × 352 cm, Paris, Louvre (S); *Still life with a lobster*, 1827, oil on canvas, 80 × 106 cm, Paris, Louvre (Documentation Photographique de la Réunion des Musées Nationaux); *Women of Algiers*, 1834, oil on canvas, 180 × 220 cm, Paris, Louvre (S); *Baron Schwitter*, 1826–30, oil on canvas, 218 × 143 cm, London, National Gallery, *Liberty leading the people*, 1830, oil on canvas 260 × 325 cm, Paris, Louvre (S).

210–211 Ingres: La Grande Odalisque
INGRES: "*La Grande Odalisque*" (The concubine), 1814, oil on canvas, 91 × 162 cm, Paris, Louvre (S); "*The Valpinçon Bather*", 1808, oil on canvas, 146 × 97 cm, Paris, Louvre (Documentation Photographique de la Réunion des Musées Nationaux); *The Turkish bath*, 1859–62, oil on canvas, diameter 108 cm, Paris, Louvre (S); *The apotheosis of Homer*, 1827, oil on canvas, 386 × 515 cm, Paris, Louvre (Documentation Photographique de la Réunion des Musées Nationaux); *Oedipus and the*

Sphinx, 1808, reworked 1825, oil on canvas 189 × 144 cm, Paris, Louvre (S); *Louis-François Bertin*, 1832, oil on canvas, 116 × 95 cm, Paris, Louvre (Documentation Photographique de la Réunion des Musées Nationaux); *Joseph Woodhead, his wife Harriet and her brother Henry Comber*, 1816, pencil on paper, 30 × 22 cm, Cambridge, Fitzwilliam Museum; *La Comtesse d'Haussonville*, 1845, oil on canvas, New York, Frick Collection (copyright).

212–213 Courbet: The Artist's Studio
COURBET: *The artist's studio*, 1854–55, oil on canvas, 361 × 598 cm, Paris, Louvre (Documentation Photographique de la Réunion des Musées Nationaux); *Self-portrait with black dog*, 1844, oil on canvas, 46 × 55 cm, Paris, Louvre, Petit Palais (S); *The stone-breakers*, 1849, oil on canvas, 165 × 238 cm, formerly Dresden, Gemäldegalerie, destroyed (Courtauld Institute of Art); *The bathers*, 1853, oil on canvas, 227 × 193 cm, Montpellier, Musée Fabre (Claude O'Sughrue); *A burial at Ornans*, 1849–50, oil on canvas, 314 × 663 cm, Paris, Louvre (S) *Pierre-Joseph Proudhon and his family*, 1865, oil on canvas, 147 × 198 cm, Besançon, Musée des Beaux-Arts (S).

214–215 Whistler: Falling Rocket
WHISTLER: *Falling rocket: Nocturne in black and gold*, c. 1874, oil on panel, 60 × 47 cm, Detroit, Institute of Arts, Dexter M. Ferry Jnr Fund; *At the piano*, 1858–59, oil on canvas, 66 × 90 cm, Cincinnati Art Museum, Louise Taft Semple Bequest; *Cremone lights: Nocturne in blue and silver*, 1872, oil on canvas, 49 × 74 cm, London, Tate Gallery (Angelo Hornak); *Wapping-on-Thames*, 1861–64, oil on canvas, 71 × 101 cm, New York, Collection of Mr and Mrs John Hay Whitney; *The white girl: Symphony in white no. I*, 1862, oil on canvas, 214 × 108 cm, Washington, National Gallery of Art, Harris Whittemore collection; *The artist's mother: Arrangement in grey and black no. I*, 1862, oil on canvas, 145 × 164 cm, Paris, Louvre (Documentation Photographique de la Réunion des Musées Nationaux); *Venetian palaces: Nocturne*, 1879–80, etching, 29 × 20 cm (Courtauld Institute of Art).

216–217 Monet: Rouen Cathedral
MONET: *Rouen Cathedral: morning sunlight*, 1894, oil on canvas, 91 × 63 cm, Paris, Louvre, Jeu de Paume (service de documentation photographique des Musées nationaux); *Rouen Cathedral: full sunlight*, 1894, oil on canvas, 107 × 73 cm, Paris, Louvre, Jeu de Paume (S); *Impression: Sunrise*, 1872, oil on canvas, 50 × 62 cm, Paris, Musée Marmottan (S); *Gare St Lazare*, 1877, oil on canvas, 75 × 100 cm, Paris, Louvre, Jeu de Paume (S); *Two haystacks*, 1891, oil on canvas,

64 × 99 cm, Chicago, Art Institute; *Waterlilies*, 1900–09 (*Morning III*), oil on canvas, 197 × 425 cm, Paris, Louvre, Orangerie, (Joseph P. Ziolo/ René Roland).

218–219 Seurat: La Grande Jatte
SEURAT: *La Grande Jatte*, 1884–86, oil on canvas, 205 × 305 cm, Chicago, Art Institute; "*Une Baignade, Asnières*" (A bathing scene at Asnières), 1883–84, oil on canvas, 200 × 301 cm, London, National Gallery; *The yoked cart*, 1883, oil on canvas, 33 × 40 cm, New York, Solomon R. Guggenheim Museum (Robert E. Mates); *The "Bec du Hoc" at Grandchamp*, 1885, oil on canvas, 64 × 81 cm, London Tate Gallery; *Seated boy with a straw hat*, 1883–84, Conté crayon on paper, 22 × 28 cm, New Haven, Connecticut, Yale University Art Gallery, Everett V Meeks Fund; *Study for The circus*, 1890, oil on canvas, 55 × 46 cm, Paris, Louvre, Jeu de Paume (Documentation Photographique de la Réunion des Musées Nationaux).
SIGNAC: *View of the marina at Marseilles*, 1905, oil on canvas, 86 × 114 cm, New York, Metropolitan Museum of Arts, Gift of Robert Lehman.

220–221 Cézanne: Mont Ste-Victoire
CÉZANNE: The Philadelphia *Mont Ste-Victoire*, 1904–06, oil on canvas, 53 × 91 cm, Philadelphia, Museum of Art, George W. Atkins collection; *Mont Ste-Victoire with a great pine*, 1885–87, oil on canvas, 66 × 90 cm, London, Courtauld Institute Galleries; *Still life with onions*, c. 1895–1900, oil on canvas, 63 × 78 cm, Paris, Louvre, Jeu de Paume (S); "*The Great Bathers*", 1898–1905, oil on canvas, 208 × 249 cm, Philadelphia, Museum of Art, William P. Wilstach collection (S); *Mont Ste-Victoire*, watercolour, 1906, on paper, 36 × 54 cm, London, Tate Gallery; *Self-portrait with a goatee*, c. 1906, 63 × 50 cm, Boston, Museum of Fine Arts.

222–223 Nolde: The Last Supper
NOLDE: *The Last Supper*, 1909, oil on canvas, 83 × 106 cm, Seebüll, Nolde Foundation; *A Friesland farm under red clouds*, c. 1930, watercolour on paper, 32.5 × 46.5 cm, London, Victoria and Albert Museum; *The prophet*, 1912, woodcut, 32 × 22 cm, Washington, National Gallery of Art, Rosenwald collection; *Early morning flight*, 1940, 70 × 86 cm, Seebüll, Nolde Foundation.
ENSOR: *Intrigue*, 1890, oil on canvas, 90 × 150 cm, Antwerp, Musée des Beaux-Arts.

224–225 Kandinsky: Study for Composition no. 7
KANDINSKY: Study for *Composition no. 7*, 1913, watercolour, 78 × 100 cm, Berne, Collection Felix Klee; *Improvisation no. 30 – Cannons*, 1913, oil on canvas, 110 × 110 cm, Chicago, Art Institute; *Composition no. 7, fragment no. I*, 1913, oil on

canvas, 87.5 × 100.5 cm, Milwaukee, Art Center, Gift of Mrs Harry Lynde Bradley; *The first abstract watercolour*, 1912, watercolour, 50 × 65 cm, Paris, Musée National d'Art Moderne; *Black lines*, 1913, oil on canvas, 130 × 130.5 cm, New York, Solomon R. Guggenheim Museum; *Two poplars*, 1913, Chicago, Art Institute.

226–227 Matisse: Le Luxe II
MATISSE: "*Luxe, Calme et Volupte*", 1904–05, oil on canvas, 86 × 116 cm, Paris, Mme Signac Collection (Cooper-Bridgeman Library); *The dance*, 1910, oil on canvas, 260 × 391 cm, Leningrad, Hermitage (Joseph P. Ziolo/Studio Adrion); "*La Joie de Vivre*", 1905–06, oil on canvas, 175 × 238 cm, Merion, Pennsylvania, Barnes Foundation; "*Le Luxe I*", 1907, oil on canvas, 210 × 138 cm, Paris, Musée National d'Art Moderne); "*Le Luxe II*", 1907–08, oil on canvas, 210 × 139 cm, Copenhagen, Statens Museum fur Kunst.

228–229 Modigliani: Chaim Soutine
MODIGLIANI: *Reclining nude*, c. 1919, oil on canvas, 72 × 116.5 cm, New York, Museum of Modern Art, Mrs Simon Guggenheim Fund; Study for a stone *Head*, 1909–15, coloured chalks on paper, 34 × 22 cm, London, Victoria and Albert Museum; *Head of a young woman*, 1908, 56 × 55 cm, Marvaux, Private Collection (René Roland); *Head*, 1911–12, stone, height 63 cm, London, Tate Gallery (Angelo Hornak); *Chaim Soutine*, 1917, oil on canvas, 92 × 60 cm, Washington, National Gallery of Art, Chester Dale collection.

230–231 Mondrian: Composition in Yellow and Blue
MONDRIAN: *Composition in yellow and blue*, 1929, oil on canvas, 52 × 52 cm, Rotterdam, Museum Boymans-van Beuningen; *The red tree*, 1908, oil on canvas, 70 × 99 cm, The Hague, Gemeentemuseum; *Fox-trot A*, 1930, oil on canvas, height 110 cm, New Haven, Connecticut, Yale University Art Gallery; *Broadway Boogie-Woogie*, 1942–43, oil on canvas, 127 × 127 cm, New York, Museum of Modern Art; *The flowering apple-tree*, 1912, oil on canvas, 78 × 106 cm, The Hague, Gemeentemuseum.

232–233 Beckmann: Departure
BECKMANN: *Self-portrait with a red scarf*, 1917, oil on canvas, 80 × 60 cm, Stuttgart, Staatsgalerie; *Quappi in pink*, 1932–34, oil on canvas, Lugano, Collection Thyssen (S); *Night*, 1918–19, oil on canvas, 134 × 154 cm, Düsseldorf, Kunstammlung Nordrhein-Westfalen; *Self-portrait with Quappi Beckmann*, 1941, oil on canvas, 194 × 89 cm, Amsterdam, Stedelijk Museum; *Departure*, 1932–35, oil on canvas, centre panel 215 × 115 cm, side panels 215 × 98 cm, New York, Museum of Modern

Art.

234–235 De Kooning: Woman I
DE KOONING: *Woman I*, 1950–52, oil on canvas, 192 × 148 cm, New York, Museum of Modern Art; *Woman sitting*, 1943–44, oil and charcoal, 122 × 106 cm, New York, Xavier Foucade Inc.; *Woman*, 1943, oil on canvas, 114 × 71 cm, USA, Collection of the artist (Visual Arts Library); *Excavation*, 1950, oil on canvas, 204 × 254,5 cm, Chicago, Art Institute; Study for *Woman*, 1949–52, oil and charcoal on canvas, 117 × 81 cm, Private Collection (Visual Arts Library); *Woman on the dune*, 1967, oil on paper, 137 × 122 cm, New York, Xavier Fourcade Inc.

236–237 Albers: Homage to the Square
ALBERS: *Variation in red*, 1948, oil on canvas, 51 × 77 cm, London, art market (Sotheby's); Studies for *Homage to the Square: Rain forest*, 1965, oil on board, 74 × 74 cm, London, art market (Sotheby's); *R-NW IV*, 1966, oil on masonite, 122 × 122 cm, Basel, Galerie Beyeler; *Fugue*, 1925, oil on glass, 24.5 × 66 cm, Basel, Kunstmuseum (Colorphoto Hans Hinz); *Transformation of a scheme no. 24*, 1952, engraved vinylite, 43 × 57 cm, New Haven, Connecticut, Yale University Art Gallery; Study for *Homage to the Square – Confirming*, 1971, oil on masonite, 79.5 × 79.5 cm, London, art market (Sotheby's).

238–239 Wyeth: Christina's World
WYETH: *Christina's world*, 1948, tempera on panel, 82 × 121 cm, New York, Museum of Modern Art; *Christina Olson*, 1947, New York, Private Collection (Visual Arts Library); *Grape wine* (*Willard Snowden*), 1966, tempera on panel, 66 × 74 cm, New York, Metropolitan Museum of Art, Gift of Amanda K. Berls; *Nick and Jamie*, 1963, Richmond, Virginia, Museum of Fine Arts (Visual Arts Library); *River cove*, 1958, USA, Private Collection (Visual Arts Library); *The hunter*, 1943, Toledo, Ohio, Museum of Art (Visual Arts Library).

240–241 Bacon: Figures in a Landscape
VELAZQUEZ: *Pope Innocent X*, 1650, oil on canvas, 140 × 120 cm, Rome, Galleria Doria-Pamphill (S).
BACON: *Study after Velazquez*, 1953, oil on canvas, 152 × 117.5 cm, New York, Museum of Modern Art, Gift of Mr and Mrs William A. M. Burden; *Figures in a Landscape*, 1956, oil on canvas, 152.5 × 119.5 cm, Birmingham City Art Gallery; *Figures in a landscape*, 1945, oil on canvas, 145 × 128 cm, London, Tate Gallery; *Isabel Rawsthorne*, 1966, oil on canvas, 81 × 68.5 cm, London, Tate Gallery.
EISENSTEIN: Still from the film *The Battleship Potemkin*, 1928, photograph, London, National Film Archive (Stills Library).

Index

Page numbers in **bold** refer to main entries; *italic* numbers refer to illustrations.